London in the Roman World

London in the Roman World

DOMINIC PERRING

OXFORD
UNIVERSITY PRESS

OXFORD
UNIVERSITY PRESS

Great Clarendon Street, Oxford, OX2 6DP,
United Kingdom

Oxford University Press is a department of the University of Oxford.
It furthers the University's objective of excellence in research, scholarship,
and education by publishing worldwide. Oxford is a registered trade mark of
Oxford University Press in the UK and in certain other countries

First Edition published in 2022

Impression: 3

Published in the United States of America by Oxford University Press
198 Madison Avenue, New York, NY 10016, United States of America

British Library Cataloguing in Publication Data

Data available

Library of Congress Control Number: 2021940826

ISBN 978-0-19-878900-0

Printed and bound by CPI Group (UK) Ltd,
Croydon, CR0 4YY

Preface

Acknowledgements

The writing of this book has stretched over the best part of a decade, following a very much longer period of interest in the archaeology of London. Throughout these years I have benefitted from the open generosity of numerous field archaeologists and specialists who have discussed their findings and ideas with me, and this leaves me a legion of magpie debts that I am unable to individually acknowledge: I am lucky to have been part of such an exciting research community. I am particularly grateful, however, to Gary Brown and Vicky Ridgeway for early sight of reports emerging from the investigations undertaken by Pre-Construct Archaeology, and to David Bowsher and Julian Hill for similarly keeping me abreast of work undertaken by the MoLA team. Ian Blair, Trevor Brigham, Gwladys Monteil, Rebecca Redfern, and Bruce Watson were all kind enough to give me early access to the unpublished results of their important research, whilst Damian Goodburn, Michael Marshall, and Jim Stevenson helped me to understand critical matters of detail in their replies to my questions. Andy Gardner, Martin Pitts, Louise Rayner, Jackie Keily, Sadie Watson, and Tim Williams read parts of this text in an earlier draft, and helped enormously with both thoughtful comment and encouragement. Dan Nesbitt kindly arranged access to materials and records held at the Museum of London's Archaeological Archive, an exercise that was sadly curtailed by the interruptions of Covid-19 closure. I would never have found the time to write these words without the unstinting support of my colleagues at Archaeology South-East, who have accommodated my many distractions with this work, and it would never have reached print without a generous grant from the Marc Fitch Fund to cover the costs of preparing new illustrations by Justin Russell and Fiona Griffin. Justin's diligent mapping of recent discoveries, in particular, has added enormously to my understanding of London's archaeological landscape. I am also deeply grateful to the editorial team at Oxford University Press – Charlotte Loveridge, Céline Louasli, and Juliet Gardner – for steering this work to conclusion after its lengthy gestation. Most of all, however, I thank Rui and Zi for their love and forebearing throughout.

Navigating *Londinium*

Those unfamiliar with London are likely to find the Roman town difficult to navigate. There is no agreed system for naming and locating its ancient streets and houses, and modern place-names and postal addresses have changed with confusing frequency over the years. A proliferation of catalogues has served past surveys, each sensible to a different logic. Rather than add to this number I have followed the approach adopted by Richard Hingley in his recent study *Londinium: A biography*. This involves using the unique alpha-numeric excavation codes of the Guildhall Museum and Museum of London to identify individual excavation sites. These site-codes preserve the vital link between the primary archaeological record and the different interpretations and reconstructions that have been layered onto these observations. These sites are all listed and mapped in a concluding gazetteer (Figs. A1–A4).

The maps of Roman London used to illustrate this account are necessarily highly schematic and involve a fair degree of conjecture. Those with a close interest in the urban topography may also find it useful to consult the fold-out 1:3000 scale map of Roman London published by the Museum of London. At the time of writing, this remains in print and obtainable from https://www.mola.org.uk/londinium-new-map-and-guide-roman-london. Although somewhat dated, it remains a splendid initial point of reference. A useful, if not entirely reliable, map of London's Roman environs can also be found online at https://www.arcgis.com/apps/MapSeries/index.html?appid=9a85640effc042ae91af6b0d43abbafb.

The Museum of London's Archaeological Archive remains the most valuable primary source, containing a wealth of unpublished information. This is a public archive where many of the finds and records described here can be consulted by prior arrangement. Some of the more important objects are also on public display: the British Museum draws heavily on the Roman London collection of Charles Roach Smith, and the Museum of London has long been committed to presenting the archaeological finds obtained from rescue excavations in and around London. The surviving remains of *Londinium* can also be visited, for which the City of London Archaeological Trust's online walking guide is highly recommended: https://www.cityoflondon.gov.uk/assets/roads-to-romewalk.pdf.

Contents

List of Illustrations

List of Tables

PART 1
APPROACHES TO ROMAN LONDON

1

Introduction

Points of departure

London is not only one of the world's great modern cities but also, and perhaps more unexpectedly, one of its most intensely studied archaeological sites. Today's bright and glittering City, the 'square mile' of high finance, perpetuates the site of a Roman town that commanded a strategic crossing of the river Thames. Excavations on City building sites fuel an archaeological research that continues to reveal new things about London's Roman origins, offering rare insight into the empire of which it was part. These investigations explore a complex mound of rubbish that lifts today's streets some 9 metres above the virgin soil. The core of this study area is defined by the old town's walls, whose circuit can still be traced from place names and fragmentary ruins: extending from the Old Bailey in the west, past the Barbican, London Wall and Aldgate, to the Tower of London in the east. South of the river an archaeological landscape of equal complexity and no lesser antiquity, the outwork of Southwark, stretches back from London Bridge along Borough High Street to a point a little beyond the church of St George the Martyr. A dense hinterland of cemeteries, suburbs, and satellite sites surrounded these built-up areas either side of the river.

Many hundreds of excavations have taken place across this busy landscape, generating thousands of scientific reports: each offering dense technical descriptions of disconnected fragments. Even more work remains unpublished, leaving a cumbersome archive of material awaiting analysis. An intimidating mass of part-digested detail burdens research, but is no superfluity. London emerges as a uniquely important Roman site because of the quantity and quality of its archaeological documentation: no other Roman city presents such depths of measured riches.

Many excellent books have already been written about Roman London, but new discoveries offer a constant challenge to former understanding.[1] In particular, the evidence of tree-ring dating, or dendrochronology, has radically improved our ability to set changes to London's fabric within their historical context. By way of example: dendrochronology shows that some ancient structures built no earlier than the spring of AD 60 were razed to the ground, and that post-fire rebuilding drew on timbers felled for the purpose before the autumn of AD 62. These dates are wholly the product of archaeological science, advanced independently of any historical account, but correspond with Tacitus' account of London's destruction in the revolt lead by the Icenian queen Boudica in AD 61. In this case the archaeological and written sources align so closely that scholars can confidently combine them in their studies of Neronian London. This marriage of evidence runs counter, however, to an academic hesitancy to link changes in the archaeological record with events described by history.[2] This is often a sensible caution since historical accounts aren't entirely reliable, treat only with the events that interested a distant elite society, and leave immense gaps. But London's Roman archaeology includes dozens of precisely dated activities akin to those of AD 60–62 that are equally the stuff of history. They have not usually been treated as such. Several recent studies have sought to explain local phenomena through reference to some form of environmental determinism—the cumulative weight of changing tides, erosion, and bioturbation—whilst failing to properly acknowledge the importance of the historical event as a force for change. By recognizing that alterations to London's fabric were often the consequence of political decision making, and setting such changes within their context, we open up new ways of understanding not only London but the course of Roman history.

London's greatest contribution to archaeological research stems from our understanding of how and when the city changed, which begs the more exciting question of *why* change happened. The closer our description of these changes, the greater the reward from their study. This book is consequently presented as a historically framed narrative: a biography in which each chapter explores the evidence for a closely defined period of London's history. Inevitably, the process of setting disparate fragments of archaeological evidence into a linear narrative risks giving misleading coherence to data that includes many areas of uncertainty, and some may shudder at the precision of the dating proposed here. A vital purpose, however, is to show that the city cannot be treated as a fixed destination in the past: an artefact of some coherent timeless Roman moment. London was, as it remains, a place in constant evolution experienced differently from year to year. It was recognizably Roman for at least 365 years, if not always ruled from Rome during this period. This is a longer span than stretched from the death of England's first Queen Elizabeth to the twentieth-century accession of her modern namesake. We can no more expect Constantinian London to offer an intelligible guide to its Claudian counterpart than we would treat today's London as the equal of its Tudor predecessor.

It is also necessary to recognize that at most times Roman London was nowhere near as significant a place as its modern heir. It was a provincial town on the periphery of an empire of cities. At its greatest extent Rome's empire embraced a territory of 4 million square kilometres containing at least 55 million inhabitants, possibly more.[3] Some 11–12 per cent of this population is thought to have lived in one of over 2000 cities, concentrated most densely in the eastern provinces. Most were small places, each home to fewer than 10,000 people. London grew larger than average, perhaps housing over 30,000 people at its peak.[4] This made it the biggest city in Britain but it remained relatively inconsequential when compared to the greater metropolitan centres of the Mediterranean. It is therefore no surprise that London makes only fleeting appearances in the histories written in antiquity, and was never considered a place of interest in its own right. London gained but rare mention, chiefly on occasions when it served as a theatre of war, received imperial visits, or appeared in administrative lists assembled against bureaucratic need.

Some arguments

If Londinium mattered so little to Rome's historians, why should it matter to us? The quality of its archaeological documentation captures our attention, but an abundance of data is no proof of importance. Indeed, some have questioned whether the Roman city is a useful subject of study at all.[5] Whilst there are interesting questions to be asked about the ideological nature of urbanism, cities sit within wider landscapes of political power and it is these that are more commonly studied. But cities remain curious and precious artefacts. Each was differently constituted and differently inhabited, and there is much to be learnt through an exploration of these differences. As Miko Flohr and Andrew Wilson explain in introducing their study of Roman Pompeii: 'trying to write the history of an individual town, however complicated it is, is not a cul-de-sac, but an essential part of debating the history of Roman urbanism, and of urban economies in the Roman world'.[6] This welcome advice is keenly embraced in the pages that follow.

London was unquestionably a particular place, and its examination casts a unique light on the workings of the Roman Empire. This takes us into many areas of current debate, where fashions of scholarly interest reflect on contemporary concerns. Some of these issues will be addressed in the chapters that follow, but I start from the premise that London was built by and for the exercise of imperial power. My first studies of London were framed by the work of Moses Finley, who stressed the self-governing characteristics of ancient cities drawn into the Roman Empire through the co-option of local elites.[7] I now believe that this led me to understate the importance of the provincial administration in the creation and government of London. Britain's conquest by Claudius, in AD 43, made it a late addition to Roman territories—one that remained closely associated with imperial authority because of the legions based here. It was a frontier territory at the edge of the known world and housed an exceptional concentration of Roman military power. This had an enormous impact on the trajectory of urban life in the province and on London in particular.

Archaeology shows that London was born of Roman conquest, and the stories that would give it greater antiquity are groundless. Before Roman rule, as in its aftermath, the Thames was a formidable barrier and likely frontier. The London basin was consequently something of a backwater until the Roman conquest unified southern Britain (Chapter 4). London was created as part of the apparatus of control that Rome imposed on its conquered territory, at which time the river port and crossing became vital (Fig. 1.1). The Roman settlement wasn't inspired by local need or fuelled by local desire, but was the creature of colonial ambition and underwritten by the immigration of peoples new to the British Isles. This made it a different sort of place to cities where urban living had longer ancestry, and political authority could be delegated to local aristocrats. London remained an administrative centre for as long as Rome governed Britain, housing important institutions and officials whose patronage gave London its architecture and put food and drink on its tables.

A strong case can be made for finding London's origins in a fort built to house the invasion forces of AD 43 (Chapter 5). It has become unfashionable to credit the Roman army with a significant degree of agency in the making of Britain's cities, in reaction to former exaggerations of the achievements of military engineering. There is, however, a growing body of evidence to suggest that London was built and rebuilt as a consequence of decisions made by the provincial government and this study forcefully questions the prevailing view that the forces that established London 'were driven by indigenous and immigrant groups, but very little by military or imperial administration'.[8] The army was sporadically a major presence, and some projects involved military engineering. It is important,

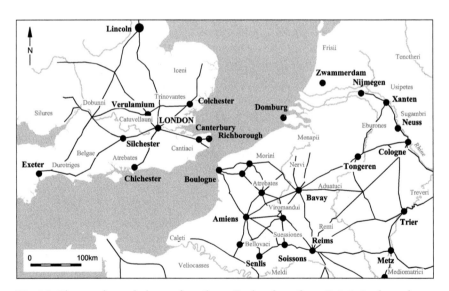

Fig. 1.1 The peoples and places of northern Gaul and southern Britain in the early Roman period (shown largely using modern place names). London's centrality to the Roman settlement pattern and road network can be contrasted with its more peripheral location in the late Iron Age as shown in Fig. 4.2. Drawn by Fiona Griffin.

however, to avoid the more simplistic binary oppositions that formerly framed debate over London's origins. Distinctions between military and civilian, administrative and mercantile, or Roman and native were not clear-cut and tend to hinder rather than aid understanding.

London presents unique Roman architectures. Its urban form was the invention of different episodes of public investment, often channelled through the governor and other senior commands. This prompts us to reassess the role of imperial politics in shaping the city. Much of what we find was invented to support the supply of the Roman forces and the movements of goods and taxes required by Rome. This mattered enormously in a province where military campaigns stretched logistical supply, much of which directed through London's port and markets. Private shippers were involved, but their services met government need. Elsewhere in the Roman world the institutionalized organization of supplies encompassed the *annona*, which was of central importance to the grain supply of Rome. The needs of Britain's administration were more modest, and we know little about the formal structures adopted to serve them. From an archaeological point of view, however, there are similarities worth exploring and an important part of the argument developed here is that London's fortunes were closely tied to some kind of directed *annona* supply.[9] If so, this would have been a procuratorial concern. The procurator was responsible for the emperor's estate and the financial aspects of provincial administration, and was apparently based in London by AD 60. He occupied a position of rival importance to that of the governor, the imperial legate, who held military and judicial command. The procurator's sphere of influence necessarily extended throughout the province, and is likely to have contributed to the management of landscapes of production in London's hinterland (Chapters 14 and 15). The Roman state needed raw materials of the sort found within the south-east, including grain, timber, leather, salt, livestock, iron, clay, wool, and stone. The availability of such materials, within reach of a well-connected port that boasted a large workforce with idle winters, made London a sensible location for seasonal industry. Local and imported produce was converted into saleable goods through busy workshops and markets.

Whilst London benefitted from the economic advantages of its privileged position within the provincial infrastructure, its dependency on Rome left it vulnerable. The history of the Roman city charts a tension between the driving forces of imperial expansion and the checks of adverse circumstance, reflecting also on the waxing and waning of Rome's interest in Britain. Since London depended on external inputs it remained especially vulnerable to exogenous influence and shock. Like all places in the Roman world it suffered at times of war, plague, and famine. The adverse effects of such events would have been amplified by London's reliance on a workforce swelled by immigration and an economy built around the needs of long-distance supply.

The narrative in brief

The story set out in the following chapters, reconstructed from the detail of archaeological discovery, can briskly be summarized as follows. After London's initial foundation, perhaps reusing a camp built at the time of the Claudian conquest, it became a supply hub at the heart of the conquered territory. Several stages in this exercise are tentatively identified. The Claudian encampment may first have been converted into an operational base *c.* AD 48, involving the construction of a network of military-engineered roads that facilitated forward supply from the river port (Chapter 6). The settlement infrastructure was transformed in a sweeping exercise of re-planning *c.* AD 52, before the city was further enlarged at the end of that decade (Chapter 7). These changes accompanied London's development into the principal centre of imperial power within Roman Britain. This busy frontier town became a principal target of the rebellion of AD 60/61, the repression of which resulted in London's military reoccupation and the re-engineering of the site (Chapters 8 and 9). Further waves of investment followed military campaigns launched by Flavian emperors (AD 69–96), whose commitment to the subjugation of the British Isles was reflected in improvements to London's port (Chapters 10–12). This was the period when London gained most of its public infrastructure, including its amphitheatre, forum, and numerous baths and temples. Some of this investment may have followed the organizing influence of a dominant procuratorial presence, meeting political goals determined by interested imperial regimes.

Growth continued into the early second century, culminating in major Hadrianic building programmes when London neared its peak (Chapter 13). In the late 120s, London was again devastated by fire, and circumstantial evidence hints that this was the consequence of renewed warfare (Chapters 19 and 20). Following this destruction a commanding new fort was built to house a garrison and the city was restored. Late Hadrianic and Antonine London retained an important role in military provisioning, although this was increasingly directed along east-coast shipping routes, thereby reducing the need to move supplies from ship to road. Despite the setbacks of the Boudican and Hadrianic fires, London's early Roman occupation was characterized by busy cycles of construction. This created a densely populated working city that also housed a wealthy community prepared to invest in architectures of private luxury and public munificence (Chapter 21). A new and more confident elite architecture emerged in the early Antonine period, following a wider fashion for the adoption of Hellenized styles of sophisticated living.

A different situation prevailed in the later second century, when growth was reversed and housing densities reduced (Chapter 22). The evidence of change is incontrovertible, but its scale and cause remain much debated. The importance of London's late second-century contraction demands emphasis: life simply didn't continue as before. There are grounds for believing that the Antonine plague, an epidemic that swept through the Roman Empire in the mid-160s, was an important contributory factor. This may have encouraged the redeployment of military and administrative staff to other centres from which *annona* supply could be better organized. Although London was diminished it continued to provide an important stopping point in the Samian trade into the late second century, perhaps with an increased reliance on market supply. At the very end of the second century, and after some decades of neglect, London's port was rebuilt and enlarged in operations that imply a significant increase in official traffic. The dating of these changes suggests that London's port may have been used to support troop movements between Britain and the continent, in events that eventually placed Severus and his heirs in command of the Roman world. As before, London benefitted from the attention and investment that attended the imperial ambitions of a new regime (Chapter 23). One of the most impressive achievements of this period was the building of London's town wall, perhaps coinciding with a wholescale reform of the administrative arrangements for ruling Britain. From this point onwards the walled city formed part of a far more complex landscape of places from which Roman power was exercised (Chapter 24).

London may have taken another downturn around the middle of the third century, when the Roman Empire came under particular stress (Chapter 25). The demolition of London's port, and changes in regional production and long-distance supply, hint at a radical change in the *annona*. The reorganization of supply in the face of exogenous shock, perhaps sparked by another episode of plague in the 250s, might account for later redundancies in London's urban fabric. This included the closure of most of London's waterfront quays, followed by the creation of temporary defences along the riverfront. London was transformed from being an open port into a defended administrative enclave. These political events were accompanied by sweeping changes to the ways in which Londoners lived and died. This was particularly evident in the rise of new belief systems and different burial customs. New approaches to the conceptualization of Roman imperial authority followed regime change, whilst some of the most profound changes to the ways in which people lived, thought, and died may have been provoked—at least in part—by the pandemics described in the historical sources.

Towards the end of the third century the city was again revived, probably involving new settlement and a thorough reconfiguration of systems of regional production and supply (Chapter 26). In this way late antique London regained its important role as a place of government, serving briefly as the capital city of the usurpers Carausius and Allectus (Chapter 27). Subsequent cycles of both decline and renewal can be read from the evidence of town houses, burials, and defences. These witness the effects of Roman imperial strategy, as when expeditions to Britain in the late 360s may have stimulated construction programmes. An ensuing political neglect of the north-west provinces was echoed in the neglect of

London (Chapter 28). Troop withdrawals to support campaigns on the continent in the 380s may also have had repercussions in London, and foreshadowed the eventual collapse of the Roman administration (Chapter 29). Whatever the direct cause, the city ceased to care for its streets and traffic diminished to a trickle before the end of the fourth century. The place that had previously flourished as home to the agencies of Rome's administration appears to have become both unnecessary and unsustainable. Some suburban estates fared better, presenting compelling evidence for continuity into the fifth century. This contrasts with the stark absence of evidence for continued use of the walled area. This suggests that whilst the town was now avoided, Rome's abdication of urban political authority within the city wasn't accompanied by a wider breakdown of order—at least, not in the short term. The post-Roman landscape that emerged in the fifth century had no need for an urban community, but elements of the late antique topography survived to reassert themselves when new political arrangements of the late Saxon period required the recreation of a port and bridge on the Thames (Chapter 30).

According to this highly compressed narrative, not only was London twice destroyed in war but it was also twice diminished by the reverberating dislocations of plague. The restoration of the town after these events owed more to the political will of the Roman government than to any innate local resilience. London thrived at times of military campaigns, such as those launched to add lustre to the political claims of new dynasts. Reconstruction also came swiftly after revolt and destruction, witnessing the decisive reaffirmation of Roman authority. The reaction to other kinds of setback was usually slower, and lengthy periods of contraction and neglect may have preceded later restoration. These exercises of urban renewal undertaken in later antiquity, coinciding with periods of relatively strong government, are likely to have relied on new waves of sponsored immigration and were marked by the building and embellishment of the city walls. These set the promise of Roman security in concrete. These promises eventually failed, but elaborated an idea of place that could be remade into the London of today.

These, then, are the perspectives and arguments brought to this study. It is essentially a work of economic and political history described from archaeological evidence. An equally important purpose, however, is to draw attention to the wealth of information obtained from fieldwork in London in the hope that this will encourage its more ambitious use. This has been the goal of antiquarian and archaeological research stretching back over many centuries. Indeed, much longer has been spent in the study of Roman London than was ever spent in its living.

2
Recovering Roman London

Antiquarian beginnings

Almost everything we know about Roman London is known through archaeo-logical research. Only fourteen ancient texts mention the city, offering a thin and unreliable framework.[1] All are secondary sources written far from the events they describe and biased towards particular themes and audiences. None treated London as its subject. The first histories of London were not written until centur-ies later, crafted from folklore to claim ancient pedigree for England's capital city. Many took inspiration from the twelfth-century writings of Geoffrey of Monmouth who credited Brutus, a descendent of Aeneas, with the foundation of a new Troy on the banks of the Thames. This appeal to Trojan ancestry set London on a par with ancient Rome, adding honour and majesty to its foundation.[2] By the end of the sixteenth century, however, these semi-mythical accounts were being ques-tioned by antiquarians whose scholarship preferred primary sources, establishing the intellectual foundations of modern study.

Late Tudor London set itself at the epicentre of the political and intellectual ferment of the late renaissance, inspired by the rediscovery of Greek and Roman antiquity.[3] It was in these changed times that brickmakers digging for clay on the outskirts of the City in AD 1576 came across a Roman cemetery. Their discovery resulted in John Stow's publication of London's first substantial archaeological report, describing burials in terms that still serve the needs of modern study.[4] Contemporary fashion involved collecting and displaying Roman antiquities: arranged to represent the world from which they were drawn in patterns that established the foundations of typological ordering.[5] One of the key Londoner's of this questioning age was the philosopher statesman Francis Bacon, who served as Lord Chancellor under King James I. Bacon directed scholars to move beyond ancient teachings to seek new understanding through the inductive processes of observation and experiment.[6] This search for empirical knowledge drew on the logic of measurement and classification, and established the tools of evidence-based inquiry. The exhortation to record first and theorize later, still common in rescue archaeology, is a prescription derived from Bacon's scientific method.

The exploration of London's Roman past ceased to command attention during the troubled early seventeenth century, but was reinvigorated by discoveries made in rebuilding after the Great Fire of 1666. Sir Christopher Wren, Surveyor General and Principal Architect, developed a close interest in antiquarian study and made detailed studies of London's Roman structures and deposits.[7] In following decades John Conyers, an apothecary from Fleet Street, recorded a Roman pottery kiln at St Paul's Cathedral and recovered objects from the Fleet ditch during construction. John Woodward of Gresham College also assembled a collection of London finds, publishing an influential paper on antiquities found at the corner of Camomile Street and Bishopsgate.[8] After a spate of discoveries the pace slowed. Sufficient was known to inform early eighteenth-century surveys of London's visible monuments, allowing William Stukeley to hazard the first known map of Roman London (Fig. 2.1).[9] Over the following century, central London saw few of the deep excavations that invited archaeological attention, although the sporadic discoveries and speculative observations of amateur collectors decorated the pages of the Gentleman's Magazine.

Victorian rebuilding

The nineteenth century was a different matter, during the course of which London's population swelled from around two-thirds of a million to over six million. This rapid growth established the conditions for accidental archaeological discovery. In the summer of 1835 a letter to the *Times* confidently claimed that 'a full description of all the Roman remains which have been brought to light in the city during the last 20 years would occupy a good sized volume'.[10] No such volume was written, but in 1826 the Guildhall Library Museum had already been established to display the antiquities found.[11]

Between 1830 and 1870, the City was transformed from being a place where people lived into the world's leading financial centre. Shops and houses were replaced by banks, and some 80 per cent of the buildings standing in 1855 were replaced by 1901. The rebuilding of the Royal Exchange in 1838 set the tone for the grand architecture of the business district, and finds from the site furnished Roman antiquities for display in the new Museum.[12] Insurance companies and banks adopted imposing Italianate offices equipped with basement strong rooms, boiler rooms and canteens dug deep into Roman archaeology. London's infrastructure was similarly overhauled. After the 'Great Stink' of 1858 the Chief Engineer of the Metropolitan Board of Works, Joseph Bazalgette, started building London's new sewer system, whilst major road improvements involved cutting new thoroughfares at Cannon Street and Queen Victoria Street.

These works involved an unprecedented amount of deep excavation and heralded London's first great period of development-led archaeology. This took place in difficult circumstances. The Corporation of London was at forefront of modernizing efforts but cared little for archaeology. This instead became the obsession of Charles Roach Smith. Smith had arrived in London as a chemist's apprentice in 1826, establishing his own business at Lothbury in 1834. Excavations for City

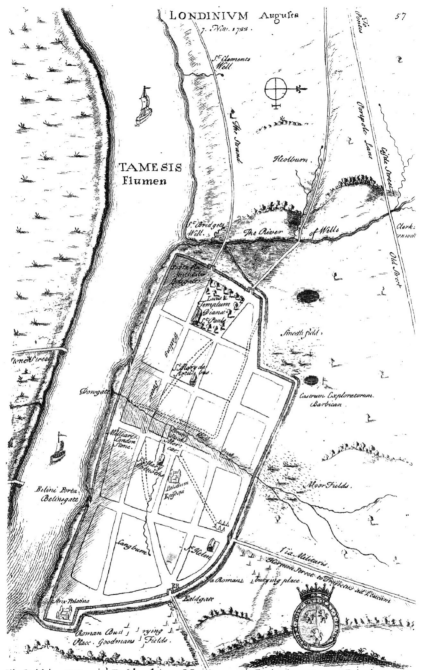

Fig. 2.1 William Stukeley's map of '*Londinium Augusta*' drawn in 1722 (Stukeley 1776, Plate 57).

improvements, including the approaches to the new London Bridge, brought Smith 'face to face with circumstances destined to give tone and character to my future life. Of course I became at once a collector; and something more; I studied what I collected'.[13] He developed an impressive network of contacts, organizing young volunteers to observe operations, and paying workmen for the antiquities that they found. This energetic interference brought him into conflict with developers, fearing distraction and delay, and eventually with the Corporation of London itself.

Smith professed three main objectives: to understand how London began and grew, to build a museum collection worthy of the city, and to preserve London's important ancient monuments. His approach to the recording and analysis of Roman finds, and evangelical approach to archaeological publication, contributed to the emerging methodological rigour of the discipline.[14] Smith did much to establish the essential practices of urban rescue archaeology, believing that the disconnected 'facts' won under accidental circumstances could be drawn on to map the Roman topography of London. His interest in using archaeological finds to study everyday life, and in the potential of zoological and botanical data, was precocious, and his embryonic Samian form and figure type series began the exercise of describing pottery typologies on which we still rely. He continued this work for nearly 30 years, forming an extensive collection that he sold to the British Museum in 1855 where it still forms the core of Romano-British displays.[15] After serving on the steering committee that established the London and Middlesex Archaeological Society, Smith retired to the country in 1855.

Smith's combative energies were irreplaceable, and the flow of discoveries slowed after his retirement. Public interest in the Roman past was, however, never greater. When a wonderfully preserved mosaic pavement was uncovered in Bucklersbury in 1869, more than 50,000 visitors came to see it *in situ* during a three-day temporary display (Fig. 2.2). It was subsequently lifted for permanent exhibition in the new home of the Guildhall Museum in Basinghall Street.[16] Other important investigations took place in the Walbrook valley where Colonel Lane-Fox, better known to archaeology as General Pitt-Rivers, recorded wooden piles during the construction of the Gooch and Cousins warehouse in 1866, and in John Price's excavation of a bastion of London Wall in Camomile Street in 1876.[17] In 1880–2, the rebuilding of Leadenhall Market exposed the walls of what was later recognized to be the Roman forum basilica. The recording of these features by Henry Hodge working as an artist for John Price, included remarkable water-colour illustrations of the archaeological stratigraphy and careful scale plans of the basilica.[18]

Roman studies come of age

The early twentieth century was a formative period in Romano-British studies. With the British Empire ascendant, ancient Rome became a treasury from which imperial lessons were sought.[19] Britain's provincial finds were an educational part

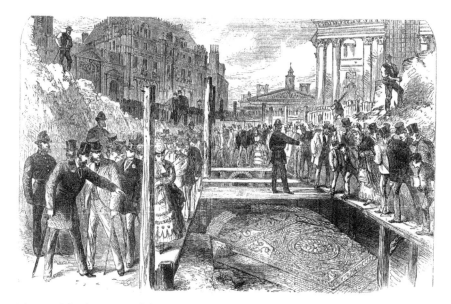

Fig. 2.2   The discovery of the mosaic pavement in Bucklersbury in 1869 as shown in the *Illustrated London News* (reproduced by kind permission of the Illustrated London News Ltd/Mary Evans Picture Library).

of this legacy, illustrating a narrative of imperial accomplishment. The doyen of such studies was Francis Haverfield, generally regarded as the founder of Romano-British archaeology as an academic discipline. Taking inspiration from the German scholar Theodor Mommsen, Haverfield wanted to know how Britons came to adopt Roman ways.[20] This study of the 'Romanization' of Britain, backed by public interest in Roman history and archaeology, gave impetus to academic work. In 1909, this resulted in the publication of the first detailed study of the Roman city and its surroundings, at which time there were about 300 discoveries to report.[21] Shortly afterwards, in February 1910, the hulk of a Roman ship was found during the construction of County Hall near the present site of the London Eye. Once again public interest was awakened, and in grand showmanship the ship's remains were carried to the new London Museum at Kensington Palace in a procession lead by the museum director riding on horseback.[22] Despite their popular appeal, public funds for rescue investigations remained scarce, encouraging Philip Norman to apply to the Goldsmiths' Company and Corporation of London in 1914 for a grant to work on their construction site opposite Goldsmiths' Hall, in one of the earliest known instances of developer funded investigation.[23] Despite these sporadic successes, Walter Godfrey of the Society of Antiquaries wrote in 1926 that 'it is common knowledge that...no reliable expert has been available to watch the excavations that proceed daily in the City in the various building reconstructions...the whole strata recording Roman and Medieval London are destroyed and the absence of detailed observations is a calamity'.[24]

These words were written to support Mortimer Wheeler's appointment as Director of the London Museum. As soon as he was in post, Wheeler applied his whirlwind energies to the problems of Roman London. This resulted in a major new history and a catalogue of Romano-British objects held by the Museum.[25] These works established lines of argument that flow through all more recent studies, and remain vital sources for our understanding of London. They were unashamedly products of their imperial age, presenting the Roman army as pioneers of civilization and Roman merchants as conveyors of 'trade before the flag'. Wheeler's grand ambitions for the London Museum conflicted with the Corporation of London's backing of the Guildhall Museum, complicating arrangements for field research.[26] The Society of Antiquaries, responding in part to pressure from Wheeler, provided funds for an Investigator of Building Excavations in London to watch city development sites from 1928 until 1937. This post was first held by Eric Birley, followed by Gerald Dunning and then Frank Cottrill. Their discoveries included the funerary monument of the procurator Classicianus (Fig. 9.7, p. 107), the identification of the Boudican and Hadrianic fire horizons, and the reconstruction of the plan of London's forum basilica.[27] By 1937, however, responsibility for observing city building sites reverted to a single officer at the Guildhall Museum, a post held by Adrian Oswald at the outbreak of the Second World War.

The 'blitz' of 1940–1 destroyed swathes of the City, prompting extensive postwar reconstruction. Sensitive to earlier failures, and in the progressive spirit of the age, the Roman and Mediaeval London Excavation Council was formed, funded largely by the Ministry of Works. A small permanent archaeological team commenced operations in earnest in 1947 under the direction of Peter Grimes, Wheeler's successor at the London Museum.[28] This was an exceptional research opportunity, since extensive bomb-site clearance made it possible to treat London as an open archaeological site rather than a living city, allowing for more purposive sampling strategies. The fieldwork was led by Audrey Williams and concentrated on areas that had not yet come under development pressure, leaving the monitoring of building sites to the continuing attentions of the Guildhall Museum in the person of Ivor Noel-Hume. A judicious programme of trial trenching, followed by large open-area excavations where results showed promise, brought reward. Grimes was proudest of his work on London's urban defences, where he explored topographic peculiarities to identify a fort at Cripplegate pre-dating the city wall (below p. 240). His most famous discovery was the temple of Mithras, accidentally located during the excavation of a transect across the Walbrook valley at Bucklersbury House (Fig. 24.4, p. 318). The discovery of a marble head of Mithras on the last day of excavations, Sunday 18 September 1954, captured the attention of austerity Britain and drew an avalanche of press and public interest. A halt to the building programme was hastily agreed to let investigations continue, and a fortnight of public viewings arranged. On one day alone an estimated

35,000 visitors joined a mile-long queue to see the site. The campaign to preserve the temple resulted in an editorial in the Sunday Times and discussions within Prime Minister Churchill's cabinet.

This public enthusiasm fostered the popularization of archaeology on television, whilst alerting developers to the perils of unexpected archaeological discovery. Studies of Roman London continue to benefit from both developments, even if they were slow to affect practice. The campaign to preserve the temple of Mithras resulted in a promise to lift and rebuild its remains. But the project was only completed in 1962, with scant regard to the archaeological detail and attracting limited public interest. A happier use of the temple remains waited on a later cycle of redevelopment, when they were reassembled to form a dynamic new display beneath the Bloomberg building in 2017. Whilst the City continued to receive the lion's share of attention, Southwark to the south of the river was the subject of an important post-war programme of archaeological excavations under the direction of Kathleen Kenyon.

The post-war period saw several important changes in the conduct of archaeological research, in both London and other war-damaged cities. Field archaeological techniques were introduced to establish the correct stratigraphic context for all of the finds recovered, and this required closer oversight of excavation labour than had been possible on Victorian building sites. The recording exercise came to rely on the participation of a skilled workforce, drawing on the enthusiasms of students and volunteers whose involvement created a new route into archaeology.[29] In 1963, however, the Roman and Mediaeval London Excavation Council ceased fieldwork, leaving Peter Marsden who had replaced Noel-Hume at the Guildhall Museum as the lone professional archaeologist working within the City. Marsden has described the following decade as a bad dream in which busy rebuilding caused untold damage to buried remains.[30] In trying circumstances major discoveries were made at Huggin Hill (p. 141), Cannon Street (p. 137), and around the forum (p. 133). These investigations relied on teams of volunteers rushed onto site when building works could be interrupted at weekends and holidays, organized into local archaeology groups through the energies of Harvey Sheldon, Brian Philp, and Nick Fuentes.

Professional archaeology

Britain's building boom of the 1960s, layered onto the destructions of the Second World War, damaged the historic fabric of many English cities. A strong political reaction, allied to the slowing pace of economic growth in the 1970s, brought conservation policies to the fore. Archaeology was a major beneficiary of these changes in attitude. Encouraged by the lobbying of the pressure group 'Rescue', public funds were directed towards the establishment of a series of full-time archaeological teams ready to intervene on building sites ahead of the bulldozer.[31] In London this resulted in the Corporation of London forming a dedicated Department of Urban Archaeology (DUA) within the Guildhall Museum (which merged with the London Museum to form the Museum of London). In its study 'The future of London's past', 'Rescue' concluded that there would be little of Roman London left to study within 15–20 years, and recommended the creation of a seventy-four-strong team of staff.[32] Initially funded by the Department of the Environment, the DUA started work in December 1973, sending field archaeologists onto the vast majority of sites where remains were endangered. Most of the full-time excavators were graduates, but their main qualification for employment was fieldwork experience, usually gained through earlier voluntary involvement. This influx of diggers meant that archaeological research was increasingly treated as a technical skill, in which the practice of archaeology became its purpose. This professional attention arrived in time to address the consequences of the wholescale rebuilding of the Thames waterfront. The advent of containerization had rendered London's port and warehouses obsolete, opening space for the expansion of the financial centre and prompting waterside works that exposed London's buried Roman port.[33] By 1978, staffing levels had risen to the levels originally recommended by 'Rescue'. Although the City remained the main focus of attention, this network of professional coverage was extended throughout the Greater London area.

Despite these successes, public funds remained insufficient to meet the escalating demands of the work. The increased density of trained archaeologists digging in the City resulted in ever greater volumes of finds being recovered, generating an ever more complex body of documentation. The expectation grew that the most important findings might only emerge during post-excavation analysis, since there was too little time on site for notes to be compared or conclusions drawn, and finds were removed from site long before specialist study could be undertaken. The immediate consequence was to discourage selectivity of what to recover and record, for want of sufficient knowledge or courage to make the judgements required. A post-excavation backlog of unprocessed information grew, placing ever greater demands on the over-stretched resources of the DUA. These resource were, in any case, diminishing as pressure was brought to bear on public sector finances.

In London, there was a ready solution to hand. City developers had become accustomed to making time in their building programmes for archaeological attendances, and the planners of the Corporation of London and neighbouring Boroughs worked closely with their archaeological colleagues in the Museum of London to ensure that this was a near universal requirement. These delays were a significant cost and became difficult to contain. Memories of construction being halted by unexpected archaeological discovery, as at the temple of Mithras, haunted planners, architects and builders alike. Faced with many competing commitments publicly funded archaeologists can be slow to mobilize, and it made sense for developers to invest in speeding the progress of their works. The high value of city property, and the need to create space by digging deep—since it wasn't possible to build upwards and obscure views of St Paul's Cathedral—brought developer funding headlong into City archaeology at the close of the 1970s.

During the heady 1980s, London's big-bang of deregulation and the needs of new technology resulted in the widespread replacement of London's Victorian building stock with new offices and trading floors. The team of archaeologists working to clear the ground for these projects grew fast, and by 1990 the DUA employed nearly 350 professional staff, including around 200 fieldworkers working on City sites.[34] This resulted in the recording of hundreds of archaeological sites threatened by destruction: fifty-four new excavations started in the City of London in 1988 alone. Distracted by the demands of this busy fieldwork schedule the programme of analysis and publication continued to lag behind. A small post-excavation team was set to work on the archives of excavations conducted before the advent of developer funding, aided by grants from the Department of the Environment (subsequently English Heritage). This work became a learning ground for better managing the complex flows of ill-digested information generated by the stratigraphic recording of the post-war years. These new skills also matched the expectations of commercial sponsors, anxious to secure a return on their expenditure on archaeology. As a consequence, the advances in archaeological field methodology were belatedly matched in areas of project management and analytical reporting.

The speculative building rush of the late 1980s resulted in a massive oversupply of new offices. City construction work juddered to a halt in 1991, leading to widespread redundancies amongst archaeologists working on building sites. This contraction also concentrated attention on structural problems in how resources were managed. Several programmes of post-excavation study were left incomplete as budgets were sucked into the vortex of organizational implosion, with the consequence that many important discoveries of the late 1980s and early 1990s remain unpublished to this day. The relationship between developers and archaeologists was also put under pressure by high-profile disputes over the conservation of the remains exposed. A case in point was the 1989 investigation of the Roman baths at Huggin Hill. The redevelopment of this site was planned on the assumption that the funding of professional archaeological attendances would allow the site to be cleared, creating space for new basements where plant rooms could be housed. Inconveniently, if not unexpectedly, the excavations exposed a wonderfully preserved Roman bathhouse whose walls survived up to 3 metres high. Since these formed part of a scheduled ancient monument their preservation could be insisted on, leaving the developer, Hammersons, with an obligation to bury the remains and redesign their building. The outcome satisfied no one: the bathhouse was reburied, remaining wholly inaccessible, massive costs were incurred in the redesign of the new offices, and the results were never properly published.[35] Similar problems emerged in the wake of the developer-funded investigations of The Rose, an Elizabethan theatre on the south-bank. Here the public outcry matched the excitement of the discovery of the Temple of Mithras. The weight of these episodes of conflict contributed to an overdue reform of how archaeological remains were addressed in the planning process. New guidance published in November 1990 established a framework of dialogue between developer, archaeologist and planner aimed at better identifying problems through fact-finding and avoiding conflict through informed consultation.[36] Conservation goals were set at the heart of the investigative process, although it was recognized that the professional recovery of finds and records might sometimes mitigate destruction if it advanced understanding. In London, English Heritage was identified as a source of planning advice on these archaeological matters. At the same time, the Museum of London reformed its fieldwork teams, in the wake of the 1990 slump, and new commercial procurement practices resulted in other archaeological teams being recruited by developers to work in London.

The opening-up of competitive tendering for fieldwork commissions relied on the establishment of a regulatory regime to manage conflicts of interest and counter the perceived risk of a cost-cutting decline in quality. This involved giving emphasis to the quality of the research design and to standardizing practice. This has helped to ensure that a growing proportion of the work results in the publication of comprehensive specialist reports. Over the last quarter of a century all proposed building programmes have been assessed for their impact on buried archaeology, resulting in either the conservation or investigation of the Roman remains. This has been underpinned by carefully programmed research-orientated sampling strategies, implemented by professional teams drawing on budgets sufficient to result in publications that add to our understanding of Roman London.

More than 500 separate investigations of Roman remains were undertaken in London in the quarter-century following the publication of the planning policy guidance on archaeology in 1990.[37] It is not easy to make sense of the Roman city from this body of work. These studies explored small fragments of the archaeological landscape and published output is dominated by site-specific accounts. The Museum of London alone has published nearly 100 reports on its excavation of Roman sites since 1997. The chief object of this reporting is to present sufficiently comprehensive scientific descriptions to compensate for the destruction of the physical evidence: an exercise misleadingly known as 'preservation by record'. These are consequently works of dense descriptive detail written for narrow specialist audiences. Even more information sits in unpublished archives, and nearly two-thirds of the important excavations of Roman London undertaken in the last quarter-century have yet to be published. Much of this material can be consulted at the Museum of London's Archaeological Archive, but its complexity and inaccessibility makes it an under-utilized resource.

The pace of new development within the City slowed significantly after the financial crisis of 2008, offset in part by railway schemes such as Thameslink and Crossrail, and ground to a halt with the uncertainties of Brexit and the Covid-19 pandemic. At the time of writing, there are few prospects of large-scale investigations within the Roman town. Several programmes of post-excavation analysis remain ongoing but we are witnessing the end of an era of exploration, making it an appropriate moment to take stock. The intensity of archaeological research makes London one of the best-studied Roman cities, but its potential to contribute to our understanding of the ancient world remains incompletely realized. There is an enormous amount of new information to explore, but before doing so we need to give thought to its nature and the avenues of research that it serves.

3

Understanding Roman London

Questioning fieldwork

The archaeological study of London is propelled by discovery, where the urgency of collection dominates research practices that remain true to the inductive and empirical values that first inspired antiquarian survey. Busy excavators tend to assume that we can afford to postpone interpretation until some happy future of greater leisure and more comprehensive knowledge. As a consequence, the occasional advance of understanding can seem the fortuitous consequence of accidental encounters with the past rather than the product of purposive research. The fieldworker's dependency on the serendipity of discovery is sometimes seen as intellectually sterile by an academic community that renounced inductive approaches in favour of more theoretically aware exercises in hypothesis building and testing. The Roman archaeologist and philosopher R.G. Collingwood was an early critic of 'blind digging' undertaken in the hope of discovery rather than to study problems, recommending a theory-informed 'question and answer' approach.[1] This is the object of Karl Popper's refutationist form of scientific inquiry: where theories are advanced as stepping stones towards better theories, in which new understanding is won by testing ideas to destruction, refinement or acceptance.[2] Popper's critical concept of 'falsification', or the ability to disprove, makes the primary hypothesis a vital part of research, since arguments that are not vulnerable to error cannot be tested. If we accept this position unreservedly, then data-driven or 'inductive' philosophies self-evidently lack validity.[3]

This puts rescue archaeology at a disadvantage. It is unavoidably the case that opportunities to excavate in the City of London are the product of development decisions made with scant regard to the needs of archaeological sampling. Even where the response to such opportunity is guided by research questions these tend to be concerned with finding things rather than understanding them. The continuing expectation is that knowledge is won by gathering facts, from which generalizing explanations might later be drawn. This remains an inductive process.

Matters are further complicated by the way in which the post-war growth of urban rescue archaeology inspired the development of new techniques designed to improve the accuracy of stratigraphic recording on open-area excavations. The recruitment of a burgeoning army of dedicated field archaeologists stimulated the emergence of what Richard Bradley has described as a craft tradition, where the goal of methodological consistency within an increasingly technical profession was served by an architecture of codified recording systems that separated interpretation from description.[4] Ideas explored in field projects of the early 1970s, most notably by Philip Barker at Wroxeter, were drawn together by the Museum of London's Department of Urban Archaeology (DUA) in landmark excavations of Roman sites in Milk Street and Newgate Street, where the contribution of Steve Roskams was particularly influential.[5] The DUA system codified on these sites requires each digging archaeologist to separately identify, record and excavate every unique 'stratigraphic unit' or 'context' encountered. These contexts include the physical remains of past buildings, cut features such as ditches, pits and wells, as well as erosional and other sedimentary layers. All descriptions of these contexts—their attributes, components and spatial coordinates—are recorded on standardized pro-forma sheets cross-referenced to scale plans, and located in stratigraphic order as components of a sequence diagram (or 'Harris matrix'). A complex archaeological site contains tens of thousands of these stratigraphic units, generating an equivalent number of written descriptions, drawings, and catalogued finds assemblages. The order of stratigraphic deposition presents a relative chronology, from which the wider reconstruction of phases of change can be attempted. These activities combine to witness changing uses of urban space, whilst the stratified rubbish describes changing patterns of consumption and discard.

When a large workforce is engaged in recording archaeological stratigraphy in this fashion the process of description risks becoming unwieldy. Engineering considerations can reduce a single archaeological site into dozens of different areas, each dug to a separate timetable. Sites are consequently explored as a host of disconnected fragments, not viewed as coherent archaeological horizons. Large projects will involve fifty or more professional archaeologists recording islands of isolated stratigraphy, working at different speeds in different areas. The traces of a single past event, such as the demolition of a wall, might be encountered in numerous places recorded by different people at different times. Each record might reach different conclusions as to what the evidence meant within its local context. This complicates the task of reassembling the records into a single account, which exercise invariably awaits 'post-excavation' study when specialist scientific reports on the finds recovered are also available. The problem with a system that assumes that post-excavation data will improve understanding, as it so often does, is that it encourages an over-worked field team to marginalize the role of interpretation, replacing strategic reasoning with routine collection.

We therefore find that at the very time that university-based research turned against earlier positivist and empiricist traditions, fieldworkers on development-led projects became more entrenched in such practices. The tendency to privilege the documentation and recovery of material evidence as an end in itself was reinforced by the urgency of rescue archaeology and the emphasis placed on the chimerical concept of 'preservation by record'.[6] The planning regime put in place to protect buried archaeological remains was aimed at their conservation, but accepted that development needs sometimes made it necessary for archaeological deposits to be removed. The system therefore established mechanisms for a 'second best' solution that involved recording remains in such detail that the archive of records and finds became a surrogate for that part of the archaeological heritage being lost. The principle goal of 'preservation by record' can sometimes involve the creation and maintenance of a record, rather than achieve advances in understanding.

The consequence is a disciplinary fracture between problem-oriented research and data-led cultural resource management.[7] Frustration has understandably crept into academic debate over the direction taken: especially with the proposition that excavation is an objective exercise of gathering empirical data best kept free of interpretive presuppositions.[8] A problem with this critique, however, is that it risks devaluing the potential of the information obtained from rescue excavations. In his studies of the formative periods of Romano-British studies Richard Hingley has shown how it was this gradual accumulation of knowledge that gave impetus to new ways of thinking about the Roman past, amongst other things inspiring Haverfield's work on Romanization.[9] Such reasoning continues to play an important role.[10] The philosopher James A. Bell has described the intellectual space left to inductive research, acknowledging that it remains a useful method when individualistic elements are drawn on in proposing archaeological explanation.[11] The very presence of unique components makes it difficult to develop models that yield testable explanations. This is the situation that applies in the study of Roman London: where separately observed sequences of unique events allow the reconstruction of an explanatory narrative history. What matters is that these explanations are consistent with the wealth of available data, and don't selectively ignore or disqualify findings that fail to fit preconceptions brought to the research. Much has been achieved in the excavation of Roman London: achievements made because of, and not in spite of, the research practices of urban rescue archaeology and a centuries-old concern with the scientific description of London's Roman finds.

Studying change

The main goal of this book is to use this wealth of descriptive documentation to understand how and why London changed through time. The reconstruction of historical narrative was once a principal goal of Romano-British studies, best realized by Sheppard Frere in his confidence that 'it is folly not to use the material to construct a history, however provisional'.[12] More recent scholarship has preferred the different challenges of thematic and theoretical exploration, exploiting the contribution that material culture can make to our understanding of the past.[13] But it remains the case that most archaeological writing starts as narrative, setting disparate activities into a sequential order to aid explanation. As Ian Morris has observed, archaeological data allows us to write chronologically tight, sequential stories that draw on the centrality of the event as an analytical category.[14] The tighter the chronology the greater the opportunity to shift from elusive grand theory onto the microanalysis of events that illuminate aspects of the past. Our goal is to understand the factors and forces that link events one to the other, exposing possible causes of change.[15] Our point of departure, therefore, is a site specific sequence of events, from which we can ask how and why London differed to other Roman cities and what this tells us that cannot be learnt elsewhere.

London's exceptionally tight chronologies are the product of deep stratigraphies that establish relative sequences, the exceptional potential of absolute scientific dating, and an abundance of typologically distinct classes of finds. The opportunity to compare and contrast relative and absolute dates across hundreds of different excavation sites refines and enhances these frameworks. Some of the most valuable information comes from tree-ring studies, or dendrochronology, since this introduces calendar dates to the narrative. Dendrochronology emerged as a significant archaeological tool at the end of the 1920s, and was successfully applied to waterlogged oak in London from the mid-1970s. Oak was widely used in London: in waterfront revetments, piled foundations, and lining wells and drains, where anaerobic and water-logged conditions aid survival. Over 1,000 structural timbers from Roman London have been dated by measuring tree-ring growth.[16] In many constructions, timbers were used in large numbers without trimming away sapwood and bark. Usually these show none of the 'shakes' that occur when timbers are allowed to dry out before use, the tool marks show no sign of the grain tearing that happens when seasoned timbers are reworked, and there is no evidence of woodworm or decay in the vulnerable sapwood.[17] These features show that the oak was used 'green', most probably in the season after it was felled. Where several fresh timbers were used in a single construction, the weight of corroborating evidence means that we can be reasonably certain of the exact year in which the works took place. Even where timbers are divorced from their original context by later reuse they still date an earlier procurement exercise. It is difficult to over-state the research potential of knowing exactly when so many different building programmes began.

London's pottery assemblages also allow us to reconstruct surprisingly tight chronologies. Vast quantities of tablewares, cooking vessels, storage containers, and specialist products were used and broken. Many tonnes of sherds have been recovered and classified by form and fabric using consistently applied typologies.[18] More than 230 Roman fabric types are represented within the Museum of London's pottery recording systems. These reflect on the different sources and circumstances of manufacture, and include elements of design introduced by potters to distinguish different wares. At a rough estimate, about one million separate Roman assemblages have been studied since the Museum of London started archaeological explorations in 1973, with over 440,000 different 'spot-dating' records entered into the Museum's database since 1995. In addition to identifying the forms and fabrics present, these records usually describe the weight, sherd count, estimated number of vessels (ENVs), and estimated vessel equivalents (EVEs) allowing for advanced statistical analysis.

Changing networks of production and supply create differences between assemblages of different dates. Pottery forms change through time, as sources of manufacture change, as products are added to and dropped from the repertoire, and as new kilns come into use. Date ranges for different periods of pottery currency are established from excavations that also draw on scientific and epigraphic dating, and are refined through the comparative review of hundreds upon thousands of different relative sequences. Although deposits can be reworked and rubbish recycled, the sheer volume of these stratified assemblages allows us to establish confidently when certain classes of material first appeared in London. What this means is that the absence of the more ubiquitous types of pottery from a large assemblage signals that it was formed before such pottery came into widespread use.

The study of so many sites, some containing tens of thousands of sequenced stratigraphic activities, has allowed the identification of a series of ceramic phases. Five major phases of ceramic supply have been recognized within the first 120 years of Roman London's history (to c. AD 165), and five more from the subsequent 250 years.[19] Pottery does not offer the absolute dating of dendrochronology, but its ubiquity makes it the most useful of all dating tools. Whilst the individual potsherd carries little weight, there is a security in numbers. The horizons of change represented by London's different ceramic phases are therefore key to the narrative presented here. Further opportunities for close dating are provided by a select number of dated inscriptions and writing tablets. Coins also provide absolute dates, although these are less useful than might be expected since most issues remained in circulation long after they were minted. When viewed within stratified sequences these absolutely dated finds only suggest a date after which the layers were deposited, but how much after is not always clear. Although reworking and residuality can result in deposits being formed from misleadingly old rubbish, these anomalous deposits can be identified from their stratigraphic context. In the vast majority of cases finds dating fixes building events to within a decade or so although there were some periods of poorer supply, particularly during the later years of Roman London, where our dating frameworks are more uncertain.

This precision of archaeological dating presents an exciting challenge. Since we know exactly when parts of London's fabric changed we can treat these as historical events, setting local episodes of re-planning and redirection within their broader context. The narrative that emerges hints at London's vulnerability to 'acts of god'—such as war, famine, pestilence, and natural disaster—which checked growth and interrupted archaeological sequences. This too is an important challenge. Koenraad Verboven has encouraged historians to study the role of such stochastic shocks on institutional change, and the reading of particularities in London's archaeological record allows for exactly such study.[20]

Objectscapes and landscapes

The description of London's ceramic phases is, of course, far more than a dating tool. This artefactual evidence charts changing patterns of supply and consumption that were a product of the social and economic developments we seek to understand. Each major change in the range of goods deployed in London begs questions as to how and why it occurred. Explanation cannot assume that this evidence was uniquely the outcome of market forces, where suppliers changed the direction and nature of trade in adapting to consumer demand. Political considerations also shaped London's access to the different forms of goods that have become archaeological finds.

The study of material culture is central to archaeological study. People surround themselves with possessions to sustain status, both materially and symbolically, and patterns of consumption can be interrogated against their implications for questions of identity and belief. The complexity of power relations and the sheer density of social networks in Rome's expanding empire created space for many different forms of belonging. New combinations of objects—dress accessories, tablewares, and burial goods—reveal the spread of new customs. This has generated a significant body of research relevant to the study of Roman London that can only be touched on here.[21] Much of this has involved explorations of human agency in social practice, drawing on the theories of Pierre Bourdieu and Anthony Giddens to explore how individual actors contribute creatively to processes of change.[22]

Identities were also expressed and shaped through urban design, and studies of how space was constructed and experienced forms an important strand of contemporary research into the ancient city.[23] The first attempts to reconstruct London's Roman town plan emerged from the late sixteenth-century interest in cartography to map knowledge, and subsequent research has focused on reconstructing the urban layout as a means to understanding the origins and functions of the city. Studies of London's urban form also build from an interest in town-planning as social engineering, where modern planners took inspiration from the ideals of orthogonally planned Greek and Roman cities.[24] Analysis now addresses issues of movement and connectivity, whilst recognizing the importance of urban design in the reproduction and manifestation of imperial power.[25]

The design of Roman London was the product of many distinct phases. Its environment was the ordered creation of considered interventions, accommodating major changes in population scale and density, but designed with close regard for the topography of the site. The hundreds of excavations undertaken allow a detailed understanding of when and how London's architecture evolved, although the fragmentary nature of archaeological survival and the limitations of access leave many gaps. Some four-fifths of the reconstructed plan of the Roman city depends on an informed exercise in joining the dots. There is sufficient, however to show how profoundly and frequently the landscape was transformed, and this allows new readings of the ideological meaning of the city.

A good example of the potential and pitfalls of such study is found in John Creighton's comparative study of Romano-British town planning.[26] He suggests that irregularities in London's plan came about because its architecture was determined by acts of individual patronage, mirroring elite practice elsewhere. This would suggest that there was no grand design for the city. In Creighton's view, London developed as the product of social competition rather than externally imposed Roman ideals. The argument is elegant, but lacks supporting evidence. On the contrary, most of London's irregularities seem likely to have been the product of different episodes of planned urban growth. It is consequently possible to describe a form of architectural rhetoric, in which individual monuments introduced new arguments and practices to city living but were shaped in response to earlier arguments already written into the landscape. Place-making framed the new within the old, naturalizing the artificiality of construction through corporeal anchors that respected inherited and sacred landscapes. In trying to understand these architectural arguments, we find scant evidence for the creative agency of most Londoners in the process of design. London's public architecture and urban shape can be credited to the patronage of senior officials in the administration, perhaps acting on imperial instruction. Investment in London was born of Imperial attention not the product of local competition, and London's architecture reveals a history of Roman intervention.

The relevance of 'Romanization'

A principle concern of Romano-British studies involves the study of how ideas drawn from the Graeco-Roman world came into currency in Britain, inspiring a provincial culture that was visibly and materially Roman but locally conceived and elaborated. Martin Millett's 1990 book the *Romanisation of Britain* involved an explicit shift away from the event-based narrative approach that previously prevailed, and has framed debate for a generation. In Millett's view, the process of acculturation, or Romanization, depended on the involvement of Britain's landowning elite society, who benefitted through their active and creative engagement with the ideas that supported the political authority of imperial Rome.

The emphasis on Romanization as process helped scholars move beyond earlier top-down descriptions of how Rome was supposed to have brought civilization to its provinces. As Ray Laurence has observed, Millett's model was closely influenced by Moses Finley's earlier work on the ancient economy.[27] In this model, Roman territorial annexation introduced a monopoly of force and imposed taxes, but otherwise relied on a federation of diverse self-governing communities. These communities were governed through cities, where local propertied aristocrats controlled economic and political activity. Cities were nodes through which Rome raised taxes and administered justice, where political careers were forged, and where rituals and ceremonies gave temporal power divine mandate. These activities were entrusted to a local elite, co-opted as magistrates and public officials. Rome relied on institutionalized competitive office-holding within such communities, and on the attendant networks of patronage that embedded local communities within wider imperial landscapes. Land was the principal source of wealth, whether in the form of rents, taxes, or agricultural surplus. Power consequently resided with those who owned land, and this also served as a qualification for participation in civic life. Drawing on these political and economic understandings Millett was able to describe an exercise of Roman imperial rule that remained largely decentralized, at least in territories outside of military control.[28] In his minimalist vision, Millett describes Britain as a place that held relatively little interest to those who governed the empire, except as a place where political prestige might be won, and who preferred to leave administration in local hands. Rome is argued to have gained and held onto its empire with remarkably little in the way of centralized imperial administrative bureaucracy. Government was achieved by co-opting local, provincial elites who ruled as agents of Rome. This empowered local aristocrats, who governed and raised taxes on Rome's behalf.

A generation of scholarship has explored this 'Romanization' model to the point of exhaustion. It isn't possible to do justice here to the many competing and complementary perspectives developed by way of critical approaches to 'Romanization', including those rooted in post-colonial theory, world-systems theory, globalization, and other explorations of relationships of power and social identity.[29] This study is taken in a somewhat different direction by the nature of London's archaeology. London was a new foundation, planted beside the Thames early in the history of the Roman administration (Chapter 5). There is little to suggest the presence of local aristocrats ready to be drawn into government and the city relied on an immigrant community of officials, soldiers, and merchants. The evidence marshalled here suggests that the provincial administration was more actively involved in London's affairs than usually assumed. This makes it a place where we can trace the consequences of Rome's imperial rule. Far from witnessing the light touch of a distant governing power, the study of London describes twists and turns in the direct exercise of Roman authority. The decisions of emperors and their representatives had consequences. This gave agency to the powerful few, where London's experiences and manifestations of Rome were imported and imposed. The government may have sometimes been creative, adding value and generating surplus, but at times—perhaps most of them—was brutal and exploitative.

The Romanization debate is concerned with the ways in which locally based elite society found it advantageous to work within Roman cultural norms, themselves of Hellenistic inspiration, whilst elaborating new ways of being Roman. This shifted the focus of attention away from Roman rule as a purportedly civilizing force and onto the creative role of provincial society, but it has also moved the issue of military and political command to the margins of debate. This study offers a different take on the relationship between colonial forces and the colonized, one sympathetic to David Mattingly's description of an oppressive imperial presence.[30] The 'trickle down' and 'upward mobility' issues addressed in discussions about Romanization don't really apply. This was a place dominated by the political establishment, enjoying lifestyles that were radically different to those of subject populations within the urban hinterland.[31] London was, it is argued, a creature of Roman political purpose. As in more recent times, it can be described as a city unmoored from the territories it governed, identified with the rule of interconnected 'elites' of commercial, political and social classes who served their own interests ahead of all others.[32]

An alien city

Visions of London's origins have variously lauded its mythical antiquity, the civilizing glories of Roman imperial expansion, the proud mercantilism of its thriving port, and the exotic diversities of an open and multi-cultural city. Shadows of these arguments can be found in the chapters that follow, but they say more about the presumptions of the present than they do about the constitution of the past.

London was the largest and arguably the most Roman city of Britain. Throughout much of our period it was a principal point of entry into the province, and London's fortunes were to ebb and flow with the tide of imperial interest. London is important, therefore, not just as the principal town of Roman Britain but also as a part of the Roman Empire. The city was founded on the borders of existing polities, exploiting a previously marginal location to stand free of pre-existing political structures. It served Roman colonial needs: a city mediating between Rome and a conquered territory; the product of imperial patronage and an instrument of imperial control. London was consequently its own place with its own identity, unfamiliar to both Rome and to Britain.

Britain was a frontier province with an unusually large garrison, and remained an active sphere of military operations long after the Claudian conquest.

Campaigns were intermittently underway throughout the first century, and well into the second. They were a recurring feature of many periods thereafter. Since London lay within southern Britain, it is usually considered as part of a self-governing 'civil' zone behind areas under direct military occupation. It needs to be remembered, however, that London fell within the command structure responsible for military operations. Politically and strategically, it was a frontier city and its port continued to play an important role in official supply well into the third century. This meant that power was exercised by senior government officials, military commanders, and the extended household of the emperor and his servants. There was space within these structures for competition and political diversity, but they marginalized civic institutions and local magnates. London was dominated by immigrant officials and their agents, with no evident role for local land-owning aristocracies, and witnessed an imposed colonial power. Because of its particular role to the colonial government, London became a hub for the introduction and elaboration of cultural practices of Mediterranean and continental inspiration. These differed in important detail from more exclusively military styles of living found in the camps, giving Roman London a discrete and individual cultural identity. As a consequence, it remained an exotic ephemera: neither Roman nor British, military nor civilian, mercantile nor administered. These are false distinctions to draw. What it was, however, was a place apart with its own story. To this our attention can now turn.

4

Before London

Landscapes of origin

There is a persistent literary fancy that would make London a more ancient and venerable place than the evidence allows.[1] Such wishful thinking, however poetic, has no basis in fact. There is no archaeological trace of Brutus and his fabled fleet, no Celtic fortress to explore on the banks of the Thames. Our problem, as John Kent so perceptively observed, is that 'we are so used to thinking of the site of London as destined by nature to be the focal point of England's political and economic entity that it requires a considerable effort to envisage those times when it was otherwise'.[2] We need to remember that the gently flooding Thames was a formidable frontier. In their description of the medieval river, John Baker and Stuart Brookes show how it both defined and divided territories, carving a boundary that forced overland routes towards rare crossing points.[3] This medieval landscape owed a considerable inheritance to the pre-Roman geography. London only became a commanding site when the competing kingdoms of southern Britain were brought under unified government by the force of Roman conquest. Because of this the story of London starts, inevitably, with Rome.

The fact that there was no pre-Roman city does not, however, leave us contemplating a prehistoric wilderness. The political revolutions of the late Iron Age reconfigured a landscape that was already ancient.[4] Stone tools show that people arrived in Britain during the early Stone Age, or Lower Palaeolithic, with anatomically modern humans entering the scene some 38,000 years ago. Some of the first people to glimpse the Thames were transient hunter-gathers whose Mesolithic sites have been identified close to London in Bermondsey. Farming communities were slow to establish themselves, but there is patchy evidence for their presence from c. 4500 BC. These pioneers left trace in north Southwark in the late Neolithic and early Bronze Age, where buried land surfaces preserve marks left by the wooden ards they used to till the land. A network of wooden trackways eventually crossed the estuary wetlands, and the Thames became a focus of ritual activity.[5] Bronze Age swords and weapons recovered from its waters are the likely legacy of votive ceremony, as may also be the case for the prehistoric human crania occasionally found on the river bed.

Pollen indicates that fields were cleared for small-scale arable farming in a lightly wooded pastoral landscape around the turn of the first millennium BC, a full 1,000 years before the Roman invasion of Britain.[6] Late Bronze Age ring-forts at Carshalton and near Heathrow became regional centres of power.[7] Some pottery of this period has been found on sites within the City where it is associated with pits and occupation surfaces. These discoveries were mapped by Nick Holder and David Jamieson, who identified three clusters that might mark the sites of farmsteads buried beneath the Roman town.[8] The fact that sufficient has been recovered to identify these Bronze Age sites, but nothing so tangible to attribute to the following centuries, shows that settlement densities reduced after a Late Bronze Age peak. There was no continuity of occupation, and the City of London and its environs were sparsely populated throughout the Iron Age.

Metropolitan London was born of the Thames: raised into being by a topography that made this the lowest point where a fixed river crossing was readily engineered. The dark river, the Roman *Tamesis*, rises west in the Cotswolds whence it flows east to the sea. London itself sits some 80 kilometres (50 miles) inland, close to the river's tidal head. The Thames, navigable deep inland, afforded ready access to England's coast, facing the European Continent where the busy Rhine emptied into the North Sea. Its estuarine reaches benefit from twice-daily tides that draw rivercraft inland and, by turn, flush them seawards on the ebb. The earliest Roman foreshore at London Bridge is rich in species of diatom that only thrive in brackish water, indicating that the river was tidal to this point.[9] Similar evidence shows that it had also been tidal a little further upstream at Westminster in the Bronze Age, although this may no longer have been the case by the early Roman period since water snails on the Roman foreshore belong to freshwater species. Low tide at London Bridge must have been below OD in the first century AD, since quarry pits were dug into the foreshore at this level, whilst waterfront structures suggest that land above 1 metre OD was expected to escape flooding.[10] The tidal range was therefore between about 1 metre below OD and 0.5 metres above OD, although spring tides would have extended this by an extra 0.5 metres in both directions.

The meandering river settled to its present position well before the Roman conquest, but occupying a much broader channel than it does today. At low tide the Roman Thames was 275 metres wide at its narrowest, compared to the modern embanked river which is only 200 metres across. At flood tide it spread a kilometre wide, drowning mudflats on the south bank. Critically a few sandy gravel eyots stood proud of the tide, separated by braided river channels that carved inlets and creeks. Two areas of firmer ground, now buried deep beneath Borough High Street in Southwark, formed a pinch-point in the river channel, above and below which the river widened considerably (Fig. 4.1). These precious islands became stepping stones to London Bridge: the lowest fixed crossing of the Thames in Roman and Medieval times.

Opposite, the Thames cut directly against two brickearth capped gravel hills. Geologically these are known as part of the Taplow terrace, with the brickearth belonging to the Langley Silt complex. David Bentley's interpretation of an 1841

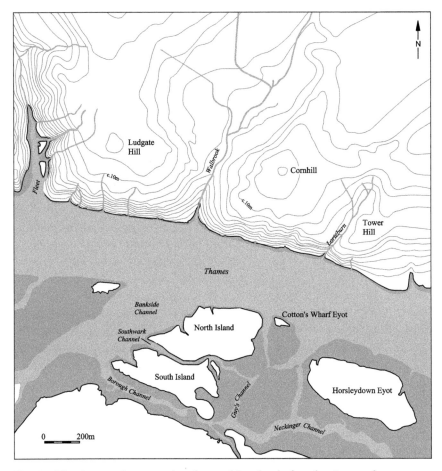

Fig. 4.1 The rivers and topography of central London before the city was first established (based in part on work by David Bentley, amended to take account of research by Myers 2016 and Ridgeway *et al.* 2019). Drawn by Justin Russell.

survey of surface relief, supplemented by modelling from archaeological and engineering investigations, allows a detailed reconstruction of the pre-settlement topography. First published as the Ordnance Survey map of Roman London, this is a vital starting point in understanding the Roman settlement.[11] The City was contoured by three watercourses which dissected the drift geology to form two steeply sloped hills overlooking the river. The western hill, Ludgate Hill, now crested by St Paul's Cathedral, had a summit at *c.* 13 metres OD. This was flanked by the River Fleet to its west and the Walbrook stream to its east. The eastern hill, rising to about 12 metres OD, lay between the Walbrook and a smaller stream known as the Lorteburn.[12] This area, aptly known as Cornhill, is now home to Leadenhall market.

The Fleet, with its headwaters on Hampstead Heath, was the largest of these rivers flowing into the Thames, occupying a substantial valley that is still easy to follow on the ground. The lost Walbrook, which bisected the Roman city, has been the subject of several recent studies.[13] Stephen Myers describes two principal branches of the river that came together north-east of Finsbury Circus. A substantial western stream, 3.4 kilometres long, originated in springs at Barnsbury and Highbury Fields on the Islington ridge. A slower-flowing eastern tributary was fed by springs at Hoxton and Holywell Priory in Shoreditch. The combined river then flowed through the city for a distance of approximately 0.9 kilometres, receiving additional water from springs rising near the Barbican and around Gresham Street, before entering the tidal Thames at Dowgate, just west of Cannon Street Station. This lower stream was originally up to 7 metres wide, although later reclamations pressed it into a 3-metre-wide channel. Insects and plant materials show that the upper Walbrook was a slow moving watercourse before London was built. Areas of rough pasture with scattered trees flanked the river, where the presence of dung beetles suggests that herbivores grazed. Pollen shows that alder grew along the valley floor, where the marshy banks included bracken, rush and sedges. The wider landscape included woods of oak with some hazel on the higher and drier slopes, but was dominated by long grass pasture. Some local cereal cultivation was also in evidence. South of the river, in Southwark, was a low lying marshy fen-type environment with little woodland cover, but areas of oak dominated woodlands, with some alder carr, lay further to the south.[14] This was the landscape that awaited Rome, at a time when the climate was probably a little warmer and drier than it is today.[15]

Southern Britain before Rome

Although London wasn't established until after the Roman conquest, southern Britain's pre-conquest political geography is a proper starting point in seeking to understand how and why it came into being. The late second and early first centuries BC witnessed busy contact between south-eastern Britain and north-eastern Gaul, at least at the level of aristocratic society.[16] New funerary practices involving urned cremations were adopted in some regions, alongside the use of wheel thrown and grog-tempered pottery that imitated Gallo-Belgic types and may have been introduced by immigrant potters.[17] Italian wine and Italic-type bronzes were imported, and new fashions of dress from the near continent involved a distinctive use of brooches (*fibulae*) as dress-fasteners. Collectively these features are known as the Aylesford–Swarling tradition, itself part of the wider late La Tène cultural package, which came to characterize elite sites in Kent, Essex, and Hertfordshire: territories later identified as Trinovantian and

Catuvellaunian. Goods connected with feasting were given emphasis, highlighting the importance of hospitality in building networks of clientship. Whilst we cannot rely on Roman sources to have understood or accurately described the societies that they encountered, Caesar's description of patron–client relationships in Gaul seems credible.[18] Politics involved factional rivalries and alliances within and between ruling dynasts supported by armed retinues. Payments of gold and precious metal, in the form of high-value coinage, was used to reward loyalty or rendered as tribute. These transactions account for the presence of continental coins in Britain from c. 200 BC, and for the British copying of Gaulish prototypes from the middle of the second century BC onwards.[19]

Julius Caesar's description of the settlement of Belgae in coastal Britain before the Gallic wars has been seen as a possible stimulus for the introduction of aspects of Gallic social practice represented by the Aylesford–Swarling package.[20] The concept of a single, large-scale, Belgic invasion has, however, long fallen from favour. The changes in southern Britain took place over a longer time-frame, involving an extended history of cross-Channel interaction.[21] The fact that we have no convincing evidence for pre-Caesarian mass migration should not, however, blind us to the fact that there is abundant evidence of people moving between Britain and Gaul before, during and after the Roman invasions. Alliances and affiliations, as well as rivalries and hostilities, extended across the English Channel with ease. These connections involved immigration from Gaul to Britain c. 25–15 BC, and a network of clientage and kinship relations between Britain and Gallia Belgica. This made the aristocrats of northern Gaul important intermediaries in the spread of Mediterranean influences into Britain, both before and after the Roman conquest. The subsequent reception of Roman social practices in southern Britain, and adaptation to Roman political rule, were influenced by these established links with Gallo-Belgic society.

Caesar's campaigns in Gaul brought Roman armies to the English Channel, resulting in his invasions of 55 BC and 54 BC.[22] Until recently no certain trace of these expeditions had been identified, but excavations by the University of Leicester at Ebbsfleet in Kent between 2015 and 2017 found a large defended enclosure similar to Caesarian fortifications in Gaul and associated with military equipment of the right date.[23] Caesar's expeditions enhanced his reputation in Rome, as was their purpose, and created a model for the subsequent use of British conquest to burnish the credentials of imperial rule. They also established the principle of Roman authority in Britain, giving local rulers reason to value Roman protection.[24] Caesar described the political groups he encountered in southern England using the term *civitates*. Tacitus' subsequent descriptions of Germanicus' campaigns in Germany mentions Roman contact with the *regules* (little kings) of Southern Britain who ruled over *gentes* (peoples) such as the Iceni or the Silures.[25] These pre-Roman polities are sometimes referred to as 'tribes' in modern accounts, although the appropriateness of this term is questionable.[26] The sources suggest that these peoples were sometimes ruled by kings whose power could be inherited within a lineage, and who were able to enter into alliances, raise armies and conduct wars.

Caesarian arrangements laid the foundations for the emergence of two major powers in southern Britain, sometimes termed the Eastern and Southern kingdoms, which came to prominence in the Augustan period.[27] Distributions of coins issued by the pre-Roman rulers of southern Britain have been used to reconstruct changing areas of territorial influence and suggest lines of dynastic succession, although might be better viewed as illustrating fragmented sets of social networks rather than territorially coherent entities. Their design showed a close awareness of Roman political and religious symbolism, and John Creighton has suggested that British kings were recognized as clients of Rome where members of the ruling dynasties had spent time as guests or hostages.[28] Some rulers adopted the Latin title *rex*, and used Latin to claim descent from earlier rulers in apparent confirmation of political arrangements described by Roman sources. Coins were minted at sites of political authority that the Romans knew as *oppida*. These were usually multi-focal sites where banks, or dykes, enclosed relatively large open areas and including sites of elite burial, ritual activity and craft production.

Coin distributions and Roman texts shows that the 'Eastern kingdom' was associated with the House of Cunobelin, with important *oppida* at St Albans (known to the Romans as Verulamium of the *Trinovantes*), and Colchester (Camulodunum of the *Catuvellauni*). Patterns of elite consumption and burial within this region were remarkably similar to those of Reims and Trier in northern Gaul.[29] Suetonius described Cunobelin as king of the Britons (*Rex Britannorum*), implying that he ruled various peoples.[30] Colchester may have been the principal centre of his royal power, but important ritual functions also took place at high-status secondary centres, such as Heybridge near Maldon in Essex.[31] These were perhaps the seats of aristocrats and lesser kings on whom Cunobelin depended. The Southern kingdom, with its main seat of power at Chichester is generally associated with the Atrebates, ruled by the house of Verica before the Claudian conquest. A city was established at Silchester (Roman *Calleva*) in the last quarter of the first century BC.[32] The material and biological evidence suggests that this was a planned and colonial settlement, involving immigrants from the northern parts of Gallia Belgica, probably Amiens or its environs.

Late Iron Age London

Coins naming Tincomarus and Verica are distributed across a coherent territory south of the Thames, representing the Southern (Atrebatic) Kingdom, whilst the gold coinage of Cunobelin occupies an area largely north of the Thames but which included northern Kent.[33] There was little overlap between these distributions, and London was peripheral to both (Fig. 4.2). There is a genuine scarcity of coins of the post Caesarian Iron Age in the London region, where the absence of the coinage of Cunobelin is notable. This is not simply the consequence of low levels of metal-detectorist finds in a built-up area, since other metalwork doesn't show the same pattern.[34]

The Iron Age coins found nearer to London are more usually the cast 'tin' potins that pre-date the middle of the first century B C. Their distribution has been used to suggest that a political centre was established near the Thames west of London, perhaps in the vicinity of Brentford or Kew. Occupation in Putney close to the confluence of the rivers Beverley and Thames, represented by Iron Age pits and ditches, is the most recently identified candidate for this hypothetical site.[35] There is no evidence, however, that any such place retained importance beyond the *c.* 60/50 B C date suggested by the coinage. Some hoards of potin coins found west of London, including one from St James' Park, are also thought to date

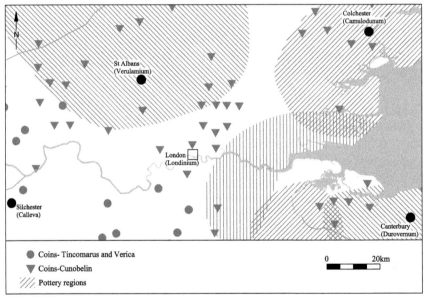

Fig. 4.2 The political geography around the place where London was founded, as suggested by the evidence of material culture. The distribution of the coins of Tincomarus and Verica marks the extent of influence of the 'Southern Kingdom' (*Atrebates*), whilst the presence of the gold coins of Cunobelin reflects a dependency on the 'Eastern Kingdom' (*Catuvellauni/Trinovantes*) ruled from Colchester (information drawn from Fulford and Timby 2000 Fig. 238). The late Iron Age ceramic zones, shaded, are those identified by Thompson (2015) and suggest the extent of discrete territories within Cunobelin's 'Eastern Kingdom'. Drawn by Fiona Griffin.

from the approximate period of the Caesarian invasions of 55/54 B C.[36] Similarly, whilst there are other defended Iron Age sites along the Thames, including the Middle Iron Age fort at Uphall Camp beside the Roding and a late Iron Age site at Woolwich Power station enclosed by massive V-shaped ditches, these appear to have lost importance by the time of Caesar's expedition.[37]

Despite the difficulties of seeing the Iron Age landscape through the confusion of later metropolitan clutter, we have sufficient evidence to be confident that the dearth of evidence in Greater London reflects on a real scarcity and is not the product of later disturbance or a reduced intensity of research. Grog-tempered pottery, showing Gallo-Belgic influence, has a similar pattern of distribution to Trinovantian/Catuvellaunian coinage, with London on the fringe of its area of use.[38] Aylesford-Swarling style wheel-thrown pottery, of the type abundant in Kent, Essex and Hertfordshire, is largely absent in Greater London, which area has few cremation burials and none with rich grave goods.[39] We can conclude that the London basin was peripheral to the 'kingdoms' associated with the Houses of Cunobelin and Verica.[40] This in turn suggests that the Thames may have been a contested frontier zone between the emerging polities. Substantial earthworks known as Grim's Dyke that lie close to Brockley Hill might have originated as a late Iron Age territorial boundary, possibly the southern frontier of polity based on the pre-Roman oppida at St Albans (*Verulamion*), but the dating evidence is inconsistent and an early medieval date is perhaps more likely (below p. 396).[41]

London may have been a backwater before the Claudian invasion but it was no wilderness. Palaeoenvironmental evidence, especially from Southwark, describes a pre-Roman agricultural environment involving some cereal cultivation. There is a growing body of evidence for the rural settlements from which the area was farmed, some of which were occupied at the time of the conquest. Our reading of this landscape is complicated by the fact that pottery assemblages following Iron Age traditions are found in contexts associated with the first Roman presence in London (pp. 41–2 and 53). These include rare examples of grog-tempered jars and other forms normally associated with the late pre-Roman Iron Age.[42] Precise dating is difficult because these kinds of pottery continued in use until the Flavian period, and in many cases a post-conquest origin can be surmised from the contexts in which they were found. It is consequently difficult to use the distribution of these finds to map the distribution of pre-Roman settlement.

There are sites on the south bank of the river, however, where people were living around the time of the conquest (Fig. 4.3). Excavations near Bermondsey Abbey have located the likely site of a small Iron Age farmstead represented by pits containing Iron Age pottery and loom-weights.[43] Bermondsey eyot, perhaps an island at high tide, lay about 1 kilometre south-east of the later site of London Bridge and appears to have been occupied at most periods from the Middle Iron Age onwards. Louise Rayner's study of the pottery identified several vessels of Gallo-Belgic type, along with wheel-made vessels copied from imported Gaulish

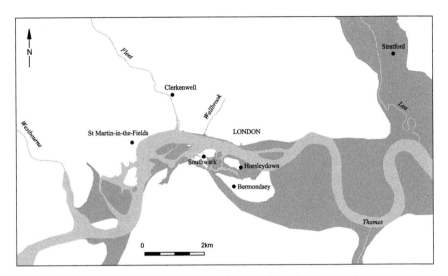

Fig. 4.3 Late Iron Age settlements around the site where the Roman city was founded. It is not certain that all were occupied at the time of the Roman conquest. The shaded areas flanking the principal rivers include both an inter-tidal zone and water-meadows subject to rarer flooding. Drawn by Justin Russell.

beakers.[44] Sherds in greensand-tempered fabrics are thought to be products of the Medway valley of a type that had gone out of use by the conquest. The range of types, and the absence of the Romanized products normally found in London assemblages after *c.* AD 50, suggests that these features date within the first half of the first century AD. Evidence of contemporary occupation has been found on the neighbouring Horsleydown eyot.[45] Two parallels ditches that defined a track-way leading towards the river contained late Iron Age pottery likely to date to the early first century along with cereal remains suggestive of local arable farming. The presence of a couple of pits, one of which contained a large storage jar in late Iron Age or early Roman North Kent shell-tempered ware, and an oven are indicative of a small settlement occupied around the time of the conquest.

Finds of this approximate date have also been found in Southwark, chiefly on its northern island.[46] Most come from Roman deposits and may have been introduced after the conquest, as is the case for the seven Iron Age coins found here. One of the more recent discoveries is a potin coin of the Cantii, likely to have been issued in the first century BC.[47] More certain evidence of pre-Roman occupation was identified at 15–23 Southwark Street.[48] This site lay on the southern side of the north island beside a small tidal creek that later housed a Roman wharf. It attracted settlement as early as the Bronze Age, generating a rare and important group of Beaker period pottery. Later pre-Roman activity was represented by a ditch, gullies, and timber constructions that included a circular structure. The gullies contained late Iron Age grog- and sand-tempered pottery, whilst pottery reworked in Roman deposits included coarse fabrics likely to date to the Middle Iron Age. The stratigraphic complexity of the earliest features allows the identification of several different phases of pre-Roman settlement and a bronze coin of Greek Massalia came from one of these features.[49] The bronze fittings from the leather sheath for a Roman *dolabra*, or military pickaxe, were found in the upper fills of one of the Iron Age gullies.[50] John Creighton has drawn our attention to the possibility that it reached Southwark before the conquest after the adoption of Roman-style military dress by the upper echelons of pre-conquest society.[51] Such items could have accompanied British or Gallic veterans returning from participation in the Gallic wars as mercenaries and kinsmen. The site at 15–23 Southwark Street is about 1.5 kilometres distant from Bermondsey Abbey so these two Iron Age sites were separate but neighbouring settlements. Southwark was more evidently linked to waterfront activity but cannot be mistaken for a significant port. We simply do not have the range or volume of imported goods, from either the site or its surrounds, to stand comparison with the known trading sites of the period.

Richard Hingley suggests that activities in Iron Age Southwark included the exposure of corpses to the water, in rituals that drew on a history of depositing metalwork and human crania in and around the Thames, which practices could have survived to influence choices made in the creation of the city.[52] The sacred properties of watery places, at the interface between material and spiritual worlds, were widely appreciated (below pp. 110 and 254). The river's tidal head, where fresh and salt water co-mingled under the pull of the moon, was undoubtedly a singular and suggestive place. It is harder, however, to demonstrate any continuity of practice. Most evidence for the manipulation of disarticulated human remains took place on the margins of the Roman city after its establishment, and there is no evidence for late Iron Age corpse exposure in Southwark. The prehistoric votive deposits of metalwork were considerably earlier and concentrate further upstream. Different stretches of the river attracted votive practices before and after the conquest, but there is no evidence to suggest a continuing tradition where London was built.

Some pottery from the north bank might also derive from late Iron Age occupation, but it is difficult to distinguish between material that pre-dates and post-dates the Roman conquest. A pit containing late Iron Age flint-tempered pottery was found at 14–18 Gresham Street, and another, containing a single sherd of possibly Iron Age pottery, was found at Plantation Place.[53] In both cases a cautious reading would see these as early Roman features backfilled before post-conquest production and importation introduced significant quantities of more closely dateable material. This is the likely explanation for the Iron Age character of pottery found in Roman-style ditches at Walbrook House discussed in the next chapter.[54] Redeposited and residual finds of similar material have been noted in stream channels in the upper Walbrook valley.[55] These suggest early occupation nearby, but not necessarily of pre-conquest date. Abraded sherds of flint-tempered pottery, probably of Iron Age date, were also recovered from river-silts on the foreshore at the Tower of London, with similar material in a large pit dug into the foreshore.[56] These finds might illustrate the nearby presence of a pre-Roman settlement, perhaps a farmstead on the south-facing slopes of Tower Hill, but we cannot rule out the possibility that the material arrived here after the conquest. A burial cut into these deposits has also been argued to be a late Iron Age find, although a post conquest date may be more likely (below p. 68). In all cases the quantities involved are miniscule and the dating imprecise, leaving no certain evidence of Iron Age building activity.

An important group of unusually early first-century pottery was found at Pinners' Hall, at the corner of Great Winchester Street and Old Broad Street.[57] Here a shallow ditch, perhaps a field or enclosure boundary, was dug across a plateau of higher ground east of the Walbrook and north of the first Roman settlement. These finds remain unpublished, but according to notes by Barbara Davies the ditch contained a simple shell-tempered bead-rim jar, sherds of friable briquetage and an early product of the Highgate Wood kilns. The presence of hand-made forms, and the use of grog, shell, and flint to temper the clay, are characteristic of late Iron Age assemblages, whilst the Romanized products ubiquitous in London by c. AD 50 were absent. A feature thought to be a contemporary well was found south of the ditch. This might mark the site of pre-Roman settlement, but could equally date shortly after the Roman conquest. This latter option seems marginally more likely.

There is more certain evidence of late Iron Age settlement in further-flung areas. One was found where the church of St James Clerkenwell stands on a hill above the east bank of the river Fleet and a little over 1 kilometre north-west of the urban site.[58] Pits and ditches with Iron Age pottery contained fragments of daub from timber buildings. The absence of Early Iron Age forms indicate that the site wasn't occupied prior to c. 200 BC, and the presence of glauconite-rich or greensand-tempered sherds shows similarities to the Bermondsey eyot material, suggesting that these sites were in contemporary occupation prior to the conquest.[59] Building material from later features indicates that occupation continued into the Roman period. This was probably another small Iron Age farmstead that survived the invasion, continuing to exploit the advantages of a well-watered site on a south-facing slope.

Another place with Iron Age origins was probably located some 2 kilometres west of the Roman city at St Martin-in-the-Fields, next to Trafalgar Square, on the slopes of a low hill beside a stream and overlooking a bend in the Thames.[60] This site is better known for its late Roman and early medieval finds, but a small pottery assemblage suggests that it may have been settled prior to the conquest. This included a large shell-tempered storage jar and a bead-rimmed chaff-tempered jar, similar to the Southwark and Clerkenwell finds. A timber beam-slot may have been part of a pre-conquest building, although an early Roman date cannot be excluded. These were probably the traces of a pre-Roman farmstead that survived through the Roman period, growing in importance in late antiquity. No other late Iron Age sites are known from London's immediate environs, with the next nearest some 10 kilometres away in the Lea Valley.

Other farms probably await discovery, but the intensity of fieldwork in Greater London makes it likely that we have a reasonably complete picture of the settlement landscape encountered by Rome. This shows that a few high-status rural sites were established on the south bank of the Thames. These places in Southwark and Bermondsey shared in the material culture of other north Kentish sites fringing Cunobelin's Eastern kingdom. Both may have been occupied at the time of the Roman conquest and remained important thereafter. Finds from 15–23 Southwark Street might witness the involvement of a local leader in military campaigns in Gaul, where service in the *auxilia* would have resulted in the adoption of aspects of Roman military dress although these could have reached Southwark in other ways. The evidence from the City, north of the river, is less conclusive. Although a few pottery assemblages with late Iron Age characteristics have been identified, these could derive from satellite activities around the initial Roman presence (Fig. 5.2). A couple of small rural settlements were found a little further away, at Clerkenwell and St Martin-in-the-Fields. These were naturally advantaged sites, on south-facing slopes with sources of fresh water, which accounts for continuities of occupation into the Roman period and beyond (below p. 393). These late Iron Age sites give no hint of the imminent foundation of a great city. They were not places of wealth and power with far-reaching trading connections. In his review of the pottery used around the time of the conquest, Paul Tyers concludes that 'we have assemblages that echo more than one of the surrounding areas, but without any one of them predominating. Pre-Roman London's status as an area without a strong indigenous material culture seems to be confirmed'.[61] The Thames remained a borderland until the arrival of Rome.

There is one last piece of evidence to draw on in our consideration of pre-Roman London: its name. Rome first knew the place as *Londinium*. The earliest historical citation is found in Tacitus' description of the revolt of AD 60/61, and a writing tablet addressed to *Londinium* internally dated to AD 62 was found at the Bloomberg headquarters.[62] The etymology of the name leaves little doubt that it was a Latinization of *Londonion*, which belonged to the British Celtic language that the Romans would have heard at the time of the conquest.[63] The fact that London has a Celtic place name doesn't make it a Celtic settlement or require the name to have been used before the conquest. According to Theodora Bynon it incorporated a collective-forming suffix and a lexical base which names an object or feature of the local environment.[64] Its exact meaning is unknown, and suggestions that it might derive from a British compound of *Llyn-don* 'the fort by the lake' or from a Celtic personal name have not withstood scrutiny. Bynon cautiously proposes a derivation from the Celtic *landa*, or 'low-lying open land'. This would, of course, be a name better suited to the mud-flats south of the river than the hills to its north.

Ptolemy, a Greek geographer writing in the second century AD but drawing on sources likely to date to the first century, mentions *Londinion* as a *poleis* of the Kantioi, along with Richborough (*Rutupiae*) and Canterbury (*Durouernum*).[65] Until recently most scholars were reluctant to consider London a Kentish town, since it was built north of the river.[66] Martin Millett has, however, been more sympathetic to the idea and opinion has turned in favour of accepting Ptolemy's identification.[67] If communities on the south-bank were friendly to Rome this offers a route for converting a British place name for Southwark into the name of a Roman town on the other side of the river. An honorary arch erected in AD 54 recorded the surrender to Claudius of eleven kings of barbarian *gentes*, presumably local leaders hastening to preserve their estates from the confiscations imposed on those defeated in war.[68] We can imagine that small kingdoms in Kent were fairly easily detached from their loyalties to Cunobelin's heirs and quick to side with Rome.

Why London was Roman

The reason that London is seen as a Roman foundation is because it lacks the archaeological footprint of other pre-conquest sites. There was no *oppidum* here to compare with the late Iron Age sites at Colchester, St Albans, Chichester, or Silchester, all of which became important Roman towns. We have no comparable high-status burials or elite-consumption assemblages, and no surrounding distribution of high-value coins describing a sphere of political influence exercised from the site. Reports on pre-conquest imports of arretine ware to London have been shown baseless, the product of spurious attributions made by dealers of antiquities.[69] Not only does London compare poorly with the territorial oppida, but it lacks the artefactual signatures and settlement densities of secondary sites within the region such as Heybridge in Essex. In any case, there was no need for a political centre at this location. Prior to the Roman conquest the lowlands of south-east Britain were politically fragmented and the Thames estuary a backwater.

The train of events that lead to the Claudian annexation of Britain had origins in the political settlements that followed Caesar's earlier invasion, and Rome's recognition of friendly kings in Britain.[70] The ostensible reason for invasion, according to Cassius Dio, was the flight across the Channel of Berikos, usually identified as Verica the king of the Atrebates. This was a pretext for military intervention aimed at restoring Verica to his throne and forcing the submission of the Catuvellauni whose political capital was at Colchester. Claudius' decision to prosecute this war was also influenced by the fact that military success was the best way for an emperor to establish his credentials as commander in chief and head of state. Rome's militarized systems, and the need for new emperors to win personal and dynastic legitimacy, made it expedient to follow in Caesar's illustrious footsteps. Such were the circumstances that brought Roman troops back to Britain, and established the conditions for the foundation of London.

PART 2

MAKING LONDON

5

The Roman invasion (*c.* A D 43)

Debating London's Roman origins

There may be no more contentious issue to be tackled in this book than the story of London's origin. The site enters written history in descriptions of the Icenian revolt of A D 60/61 and Tacitus, our main source, goes out of his way to inform us that London wasn't a Roman colony at this time.[1] This emphasis on what London was not begs the question of what it was: if it was neither a pre-Roman town nor an early Roman colony, how then did it come into being?

Many studies, especially those written after the Second World War, argued that London started life as a fort built during the Roman invasion.[2] A detailed account of this invasion is found in the second-century writings of the historian Cassius Dio, drawn from earlier sources.[3] Forces commanded by Aulus Plautius landed on the south-coast of Britain in the summer of A D 43 in a moment that has generated a considerable literature, lately dominated by a lively dispute over whether the landings took place at Richborough in Kent or on the Solent.[4] Wherever the army started its British campaign it soon advanced to the Thames, which is where our interest quickens. After forcing its way across the river, the army halted for a few weeks to await the Emperor Claudius who wished to take personal command of the capture of the enemy capital at Colchester.

This pause in the campaign gave scholars reason to seek evidence for a Claudian fort or marching camp controlling the Thames. The idea of a military forerunner to Roman London also seemed consistent with the example of Colchester, where the first town reused the shell of a disused legionary fortress.[5] Lands expropriated by the army would have remained imperial property, facilitating their gift to colonists or civic authorities, leaving a legacy of infrastructure fit for re-purposing. The supposition that London had military origins aligned with contemporary interest in the Roman army as a driving force in the pacification and administration of Britain. It was assumed that civilian communities struggled to find the architects, engineers, and craftsmen needed to build new towns, which deficiencies were made good through the military support and patronage of the provincial government. The impetus for the foundation of towns in Britain was therefore seen as a Roman affair: state-driven, top-down and interventionist. Drawing on such expectations, discoveries at London of V-shaped ditches of a style sometimes associated with Roman fortifications were taken as proof of London's military origins.[6] Building on these assumptions, the idea that London came into existence as the site of a military establishment commanded widespread support into the 1970s.[7]

At this point, however, a combination of new data and new thinking prompted a radical reassessment. Despite the increased intensity of archaeological investigations following the creation of the DUA in 1973, this work failed to isolate features early enough to belong to a conquest phase establishment.[8] London's earliest coin assemblages were dominated by issues known as Claudian copies. These are more typical of places established towards the end of Claudius' reign, rather than those of conquest date.[9] A relative scarcity of finds of military equipment also weighed against a military origin. The information fitted better with a foundation date c. AD 50 and this made it impossible to argue for direct military involvement, since Roman forces were deployed further inland by this time. Since it was also possible to argue that the original Claudian encampment might be found elsewhere in the Thames basin, perhaps south of the river or in Westminster, opinion shifted towards seeing London as a civilian foundation brought into being after the initial military campaigns.

London was, however, in the wrong place to have been founded at the behest of a local civilian community with urban ambitions. As we have seen, there is no evidence that any such community existed. It consequently seemed likely that credit for London's creation should fall to the merchants and shippers who followed the advancing forces, and whose needs were served by a strategically located port. This argument was first advanced by Francis Haverfield who concluded 'that London began, not at the nod of a ruler, but through the shrewdness of merchants'.[10] Peter Marsden, writing in 1980, returned to this hypothesis, suggesting that London 'did not have a military beginning as a camp built during the Roman invasion of AD 43, but was founded about AD 50 as a carefully planned civil trading settlement of Roman merchants'. This reinforced the view, gaining ground following Moses Finley's seminal study of the ancient economy, that earlier studies had over-stated the importance of the Roman state as an actor in urban affairs.[11] Towns were instead seen as largely self-governing entities, directed by local elites who self-identified with Roman power and ideology. This removed the need to ascribe any great importance to the Roman military in the creation of towns. Martin Millett's work, in particular, emphasized how little evidence there was for a significant official intervention.[12] The idea that Romano-British cities relied on an inheritance of military engineering became difficult to sustain, and could be dismissed as guilty of ignoring the creative capabilities and political interests of other communities. By 1994, Millett could write of 'a consensus emerging about the development of the city. Uniquely in Britain, the town seems to have grown up as a planned trading settlement of citizens from other provinces within a decade or so of the invasion'.[13] As the busy programme of investigations continued, an absence of evidence seemed evidence of absence, leading to the conclusion that excavation had been 'sufficiently widespread for us to be sure that had a major fort existed we would know about it'.[14] Thus, a new generation of scholarship found agreement over the combination of events that brought London into being. The city was seen as the creation of mercantile endeavour, inspired and underwritten by the trading opportunities that attended the making of *Britannia*. Speculation continued over where the invasion period fort might be found. But since this would have been a temporary establishment, perhaps located to control a pre-existing crossing of the Thames, there was no need to look for it beneath a city built at a post-conquest river crossing.[15]

London's Claudian defences

The argument seemed settled. But against all expectation it was reopened as a consequence of chance discoveries made in 2007. A team led by Ian Blair, working on a construction site at the junction of Cannon Street and Walbrook known as The Walbrook, found ditches that they identified as having formed the west side of a large fortified enclosure built immediately after the conquest (Fig. 5.1).[16] This surprising conclusion was not the outcome of a purpose-designed exercise in exploratory research, but the product of the routine investigation of a threatened site. Since the idea that London had originated in a conquest phase fort had long been dismissed the study of its early defences did not figure in any research agenda. This was despite the fact that in 1974, Ralph Merrifield and Harvey Sheldon had drawn on topographic evidence to suggest a likely location for the Claudian encampment, predicting that the only evidence likely to survive would be the buried fort ditch. They concluded that Claudian defences would be found at exactly the spot where Blair and his team were later to make their discovery.[17] What came as a complete surprise in 2007, had been accurately predicted in 1974. A neglected hypothesis had been put to accidental test and supporting proof obtained.

The discoveries at The Walbrook reopen the issue of how and why London was built where it was, reminding us that our models need constant questioning in the face of new data. This return to a long-rejected argument has understandably met with scepticism. Lacey Wallace has strongly re-asserted the reasons why the fort-into-town model is suspect, and questioned the reliability of the evidence used to identify Claudian fortifications.[18] Her arguments, and a continuing hesitancy to challenge received wisdom on this topic, require us to give close attention to the evidence now before us.

The earliest features at The Walbrook were two parallel V-shaped ditches set on the upper slopes of the east bank of the stream. The ditches were about 4 metres apart: that closest to the river survived for a depth of 0.8 metres and was distinctly smaller than the eastern ditch, which survived to a depth of 1.8 metres. Both contained a square-cut cleaning trench or 'ankle breaker' at the base, and were

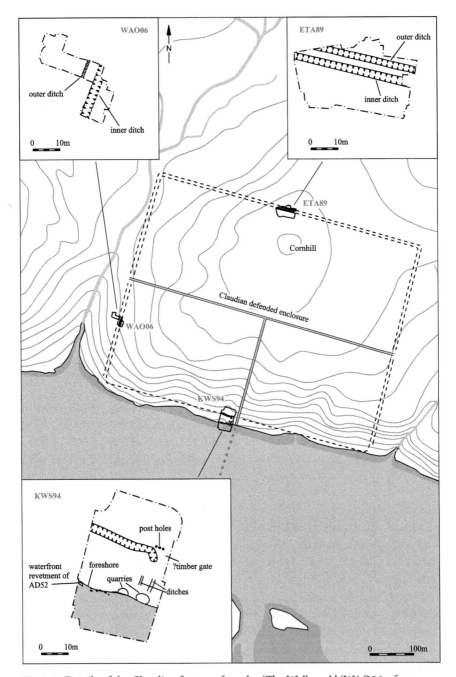

Fig. 5.1 Details of the Claudian features found at 'The Walbrook' (WAO06: after Blair 2010), 7–11 Bishopsgate (ETA89: after Sankey 2002) and Regis House (KWS94: after Brigham and Watson in prep.). Drawn by Justin Russell.

comprehensively backfilled shortly after being dug. The crisply defined and un-weathered profile of the ditches, and the absence of any hill-wash sedimentation, makes it unlikely that they were left open throughout an entire winter. The lower fill of the inner, eastern, ditch included the remains of a storage jar in a late Iron Age 'Romanizing' grog-tempered ware: a transitional fabric of unusually early date for a London assemblage. Both ditches also contained late Iron Age flint-tempered pottery.[19] Since these types of pottery remained in use after the Roman conquest their presence is not proof of an early date. The complete absence of the 'Romanized' products ubiquitous in all London assemblages after *c.* AD 50 pro-vides a more compelling reason to believe that the ditches were early. Only in unusual, and improbable, circumstances would a collection of broken pottery assembled after *c.* AD 50 remain wholly free of examples of post-conquest imports and local Roman products. An early Claudian date is also implied by the extended sequence of pre-Flavian activities that took place after the ditches were filled. These activities included quarrying on the banks of the Walbrook, followed by the dumping of rubbish from a nearby bone-working industry, and then the digging of a new pair of ditches that reasserted the line of the earlier boundary (below p. 67). After these later ditches had in turn been backfilled a late Neronian or early Flavian road was built over their line (below p. 122). We can be reasonably confident that the earliest ditches were Claudian, and they are more likely to have been backfilled before *c.* AD 50 than after.

Two similar ditches had previously been recorded at 7–11 Bishopsgate in 1995, and it now became clear that they may have formed the northern boundary of the same enclosure. These large parallel V-shaped ditches, set 2 metres apart, were found at the base of the archaeological sequence and only incompletely investi-gated. They were aligned east-west, some 150 metres to the north of the site of the early forum. The excavator, Dave Sankey, described both as originally about 2.5 metres wide and 1.4 metres deep, with a square-cut 'ankle-breaker' at the base, but accompanying plans show that the 'inner' southern ditch was nearly 0.5 metres wider than the northern one.[20] They were also quickly backfilled. The site produced little dating evidence, but the ditches were clearly part of the pre-Flavian topography. Parallels have since been drawn with the fortifications established after the Boudican revolt of AD 60/61, leading to the suggestion that they formed part of a short-lived military post set on Cornhill after the rebellion.[21] An earlier date is equally consistent with the evidence. Interestingly, in the light of the parallel it provides with the sequence at The Walbrook, an early Flavian road was subse-quently built over the line of the outer ditch. If the ditches at Bishopsgate were contemporary with those found at The Walbrook then these observations com-bine to identify two sides of a large Claudian enclosure on Cornhill.

Why then should these ditches be identified as defensive? Ditches serve many purposes. Although V-shaped ditches with square 'ankle-breaker' cleaning trenches at the base were introduced to many parts of Britain by the Roman army, they were neither exclusively Roman nor exclusively military. The *dolabra* sheath found in Southwark (p. 41), is a reminder of how the paraphernalia and practices of Roman military engineering might advance independently of the Roman army, and similar V-shaped ditches at Silchester may have been dug prior to the Roman conquest.[22] Lacey Wallace has also drawn our attention to instances where V-shaped ditches were dug alongside later roads into London.[23] She consequently suggests that rather than being defensive, the ditches might have been roadside features, dug in anticipation of a planned extension to the street grid that was interrupted by the Boudican revolt. This argument doesn't withstand closer scrutiny. In the first places it assumes that the ditches were designed to flank roads, but they were too close together for this to have been physically possible. Roads important enough to have been marked by major ditches were usually set within an easement 10–15 metres wide. Even the small drains flanking minor roads were usually placed more than 5 metres apart, but the ditches at Bishopsgate were no more than 2 metres apart. Wallace's suggestion also assumes an interrupted construction exercise, but this does not square with the evidence that the ditches were comprehensively backfilled soon after they were dug. The backfilling was a major exercise, consistent with the deliberate slighting of associated earthworks rather than a suspended building programme. When roads were eventually built at these sites, they were set over the line of the earlier ditches, not between them. No attempt was made in these later phases of roadbuilding to reinstate or replace the Claudian ditches. Not only were the ditches dug without regard to road construction, it is also difficult to identify any need to drain the land in the places they were found. Those investigated by Ian Blair's team were on well-drained slopes of the river Walbrook, set parallel to the line of the river in such a way that they neither directed water towards or away from it. Most importantly of all, Wallace's suggestion fails to account for the fact that the paired ditches were of different sizes. This is a characteristic feature of defended enclosures, in which ramparts were protected by a larger inner ditch and a smaller outer ditch. There are no parallels for such a configuration from a roadside context, where it would serve no purpose.

The double-ditch configuration was, however, common in the forts of this period.[24] London's arrangement was identical to Claudian ditches found at Richborough that some think protected the site of Aulus Plautius' landing in AD 43.[25] The Richborough defences consisted of an inner ditch 3 metres wide and 1.8 metres deep and an outer one 2.13 metres wide and 1.2 metres deep, with an interval of 1.8 metres between them. This arrangement finds parallel in other temporary Claudian military defences, as at Longthorpe near Peterborough.[26] The ditch systems of these temporary camps, like those of London, were smaller in scale than those of permanent legionary fortresses.[27] No trace of the original ramparts was found at any of these sites, suggesting the application of a consistent policy of slighting the defences of temporary forts on their evacuation.

The two sightings of a double-ditch enclosure at London combine with other topographic evidence to permit the tentative reconstruction of a defensive circuit. The ditches were at the western and northern boundaries of London's inner core, as marked by the extent of the orthogonal Claudio-Neronian street grid. This grid was symmetrically laid out around the approach road from London Bridge and a central T-shaped junction at the site of the forum. Although this urban topography was the product of later Claudian development, its essentials were dictated by the earlier topography. If so, and assuming the original enclosure to have been both rectangular and symmetrical, we can take a mirror to the evidence to locate the southern and eastern sides of the enclosure.

On this basis the southern boundary of the site, overlooking the Thames, should lie between Cannon Street and Thames Street. A ditch of appropriate form and date has, indeed, been found at exactly this location: at Regis House.[28] This was a substantial east-west aligned feature, 2.8 metres wide and 0.9 metres deep, with an 'ankle-breaker' cleaning slot at its base. The east end of the ditch turned slightly south-eastward, where it terminated a little short of the line of the main road to London Bridge. A timber structure, represented by a row of three post-pits set 1.2–1.3 metres apart, stood between the ditch terminal and the road. The posts were on a line parallel to that of the ditch, slightly to its north. They could have supported a timber palisade closing the gap between ditch and road but are more likely to have been the forward side of a flanking tower to a gateway. The configuration is identical to the post-built gateway of the Claudian fort at Wigston Parva in Leicestershire.[29] This would have been the main gate into London, set at the northern end of London Bridge. The natural defences provided by the Thames might account for the presence of only a single ditch along this side of the enclosure. Two timber pales found reused in a nearby waterfront revetment built c. AD 52 may originally have been part of the gateway or a palisade set over the rampart. These pales were made from oak poles, halved by cleaving, and carved at one end to form spear-shaped 'hastate' terminals. This was a common military design and the timbers were significantly larger than needed for domestic construction. The sapwood showed no signs of borer damage indicating that they had not been exposed to the elements for long, almost certainly less than 2 years. Whilst we cannot be certain that these southern defences were contemporary with those found to north and west, this is a reasonable supposition given the early date and brief working life of the palisade. These observations and reconstructions identify three sides of a Claudian enclosure, and Merrifield and Sheldon's original topographic argument suggests the location of the fourth side. This combines to define an area about 610 by 450 metres, with an internal area of nearly 27.5 hectares (Fig. 5.2).

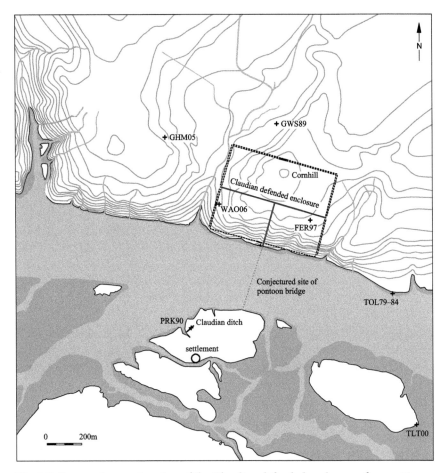

Fig. 5.2 Proposed reconstruction of the Claudian defended enclosure of *c.* AD 43, illustrating also the locations of discrete finds assemblages with conquest period characteristics (marked + and identified by site-codes). These small groups of pottery came from ditches and pits likely to have been dug early in the Roman occupation, although a pre-Roman origin for some of the material cannot be discounted. Individual finds are not plotted. Drawn by Justin Russell.

The evidence indicates that London was provided with a defensive enclosure of likely Claudian date and military execution. There are three possible reasons for its construction. One is that the army built the defences on behalf of a civilian community, following the example suggested for the Augustan site of Waldgirmes in Germany.[30] If so, the ditches might date from *c.* AD 48 when London's street system was engineered (below p. 64). This would suggest that London's foundation was part of a programme of urbanization promoted by the provincial government in an area where there was no native community to coax into taking this initiative. On balance, however, this seems improbable. A military involvement in

Table 5.1 A suggested timeline of events affecting London in the period AD 43–70

Suggested date	Building activities in London	Salient events possibly relevant to London
43+	A temporary defended enclosure built on Cornhill, perhaps to accommodate the army of conquest.	Invasion of Britain by troops commanded by Aulus Plautius who halts his advance on the Thames to await the arrival of the emperor Claudius.
48	Engineering of roads into London, and establishment of a settlement within the site of the former defended enclosure.	Arrival of a new governor Ostorius Scapula, and campaigns into Wales.
		Veteran colony established at Colchester AD 49.
52	Settlement rebuilt with a grid of streets and houses laid out on a more ambitious scale.	Ostorius Scapula replaced as governor by Didius Gallus.
52–4	Facilities established for beaching ships on the foreshore by London Bridge. Offices and stores built around the forum site. First baths erected and supplied with piped water.	Nero succeeds Claudius as emperor AD 54.
55–9	Lull in the pace of building works.	
60	Settlement expands onto land west of the Walbrook where new streets and houses laid out.	Procurator Catus Decianus perhaps based in London by this date.
60–1	London destroyed by fire.	Revolt of the Iceni lead by Boudica.
62–3	Military reoccupation involving the building of a fort, new road(s), massive waterfront quays, and waterworks.	Army of occupation reinforced by auxiliary cohorts from Germany.
	Tomb of the procurator Classicianus erected on Tower Hill.	
65–70	Lull in the pace of building works.	Vespasian assumes power at conclusion of civil war in AD 69.

building a new town seems unlikely given the other demands on the army at this date (Table 5.1). A town of sufficient importance to warrant urban defences should also have housed civic buildings of the sort not seen in London until the Flavian period. The second possibility is that the ditches enclosed an army-engineered supply-base established soon after the conquest. This too would suggest a date *c.* AD 48 and might be consistent with other evidence for the establishment of a supply-base at London (Chapter 6 below). Although this remains a distinct possibility, it doesn't explain why the ditches were backfilled so promptly and failed to include the types of Roman pottery found in assemblages associated with other constructions of this period. The third possibility is that this was the site of a temporary fort. If so, its scale only makes sense within the context of troop deployments at the time of the conquest. We cannot securely date the defences from archaeological finds, but there was no need for a large military post here once the Claudian army had advanced on Colchester. If the defences protected a military garrison, then the history of Claudian military deployment presents no credible alternative to AD 43.

The problem with this hypothesis is that although many sites have been excavated within the fortified area, none has produced evidence securely dated before AD 50.[31] The trouble is that a campaigning army leaves little trace and the evidence of proof that we need may be highly elusive.[32] Historical accounts suggest that Aulus Plautius' army only waited on Claudius' arrival for a few weeks during the summer of AD 43. Since the site was occupied at a critical point in the Roman campaign, it would have warranted more imposing defences than normal for a marching camp. These building operations would also have kept troops busy during the pause in campaign. But despite the scale of the defences it would have remained the temporary station of an army bivouacked in tents. Not only do tents leave no foundations, but the use of mess kits limited the use of pottery. No buildings are to be expected and the camp would only be traceable by its defences, which is why temporary Roman camps are notoriously difficult to date. The fleeting nature of this occupation would explain why London presents a lower density of military finds than the Claudian fortress at Colchester, and proportionately few of the early south Gaulish Samian pottery types found at permanently occupied conquest sites.[33] The temporary installations would also have been highly vulnerable to truncation in the subsequent engineering of the Roman town, which in places reduced the pre-urban land surface by more than a metre.[34]

London's Claudian enclosure was about the right size to have housed the bulk of the invading Claudian army. Philip Crummy's speculative reconstruction of the successor Claudian encampment at Colchester comes up with something of similar size.[35] London's 27.5 hectare site was certainly larger than normal for a legionary fort. It has been estimated that tents might have made it possible to accommodate some 1,174 men per hectare, in which case the enclosure presented space for over 32,000 men.[36] A lower density of occupation is more likely but it is entirely credible that the enclosure quartered 15,000–20,000 men. This would have been around half of Aulus Plautius' total force, which is generally reckoned to have included around 40,000 troops, although a lower figure is possible.[37] This seems about right, since a significant part of the army would have been deployed to secure the supply route from the channel forming garrisons at key locations between the south coast landing site and bridgehead of the Thames crossing.

If troops had also been stationed to secure the south bank of the river, this might help explain the discovery of an early Roman V-shaped ditch with an 'ankle breaker' at Park Street in Southwark in 1990.[38] The lower fills of this feature included an important assemblage of late Iron Age pottery, also notable for the absence of products of London's 'Romanized' industries, and a single sherd of a fine-ware beaker likely to have been imported from northern Gaul. The final silting of the ditch contained glauconite-rich or greensand-tempered sherds similar to those found in late Iron Age assemblages at Bermondsey and Clerkenwell, as well as two early or middle first-century brooches. The ditch was located some 180 metres to the north of the line of the Roman approaches to London Bridge, close to the western end of the island. The character, date, and context of this feature are consistent with it having been associated with the Claudian settlement of London. A small fortification here would have controlled access to the important pre-conquest and Roman waterfront site at 15–23 Southwark Street (above p. 40). Another early Roman V-shaped ditch was identified at Winchester Palace, parallel to the south-bank of the Thames. This might also have been associated with a Claudian military presence, although it is described as a drainage ditch in the excavation report and its fills included Verulamium region ware that first occurs in archaeological assemblages at the end of the 40s.[39]

The Thames crossing

If Aulus Plautius waited on Claudius at London in the summer of AD 43, having taken command of the river crossing, then this might also be the place where his army had first crossed the Thames in pursuit of British forces. Dio described how the Britons fell back on the river at a point near where it enters the sea and at high tide forms a pool.[40] He explained that the British crossed easily because they knew where to find firm ground and an easy passage, but the Romans in trying to follow them were not so successful. However, Celtic auxiliaries (*Keltoi* in the original Greek) swam the river, and other troops crossed by a bridge a little way upstream, after which they attacked the barbarians from several sides and killed many of their number. The Roman army then sustained losses of its own when pursuing the retreating Britons into marshes.

This description fits the site of London, where the islands at Southwark created a pinch-point, above and below which high tides would have pooled before ebbing. There has been speculation that Plautius' crossing might alternatively have been achieved further downstream. This claim has been most strongly advanced for a crossing from Higham to East Tilbury, where the river might have split into several meandering channels making them individually easier to cross.[41] There is, however, no credible evidence that the river was ever fordable at this point. The expanse of exposed inter-tidal marshland along the lower Thames has usually been a barrier to all but waterborne traffic along this reach. Early medieval sources and place names indicate that the Thames was then impassable except by ferry all the way upstream to Shepperton, with the lowest all-season ford found further up-river at Wallingford.[42] A campaigning army would, of course, have been prepared to risk crossing at places not routinely fordable, and the gentler tidal regime of the early Roman period may have made the river less formidable than it later became. Nonetheless, Dio's description of troops crossing by a bridge close enough to military action to determine the outcome, along with the need to avoid intractable marshlands on either side of a contested crossing, eliminates most sites in the lower estuary from serious consideration. If his account is to be believed, it is more likely that the Roman forces crossed the river closer to its tidal head, leaving London and Westminster as the preferred candidates.

The idea that the Romans might have crossed the river at Westminster was first advanced to make sense of alignments of Roman roads, specifically elements of Watling Street, which appeared to have been directed towards Westminster rather than the City.[43] It was consequently suggested that Watling Street followed the line of a pre-Roman route that used an Iron Age river-crossing at Westminster. Although this idea was promptly dismissed as improbable by Francis Haverfield it has remained curiously persistent.[44] As matters stand, the physical remains of Watling Street south of the Thames have been traced from Deptford to Southwark, but are not found further to the west. The topography shows that the road followed the best line achievable if the purpose was to keep to higher ground (Fig. 14.2). It did not head in a straight line for London Bridge because it skirted tidal inlets and marshes on the south bank, not because it was aiming for Westminster. The line of Watling Street north of the Thames is found beneath Edgware Road, but never further south than Oxford Street where it joined the great west road that exited London through Newgate. The decision to route Watling Street along the line of Edgware Road is likely to have been dictated by a preference to hold to higher ground west of the river Fleet, whose valley made a more direct line to London impractical. The road system does not, therefore, bypass or otherwise ignore the Roman city. Nor did it direct traffic through Westminster.

Whilst there is no need to identify a river crossing at Westminster to make sense of the Roman street pattern, this is not proof that no such crossing existed. There are other grounds, however, for considering Westminster an unlikely place for a ford. There was an important late medieval crossing from Lambeth to Westminster, but this was achieved by means of a horse-ferry. Archaeological investigations on both sides of the river have failed to find any evidence to suggest that the river was regularly crossed here before the ferry was established, and the point where the line of Watling Street is projected to have met the river is too close to its bend to have been suitable for a ford. Excavations on Thorney Island, beneath the Palace of Westminster, indicate the presence of a high-status building and elite burial from the second century, but this is likely to have been associated with a later villa.[45] Evidence for an approach road to the supposed crossing has also been sought south of the river, in the gardens of Lambeth Palace. Investigations undertaken for the 'Time Team' television series in 1994 drew a blank, and contour mapping showed that most of the land lay below the probable water level in Roman times. Despite the positive gloss provided by a programme editor reluctant to trumpet failure, the archaeologists involved concluded that 'the case for any river crossing at Westminster appears to be...without any real substance at all'.[46] This wasn't a sensible place to approach the river, and there was no attempt to engineer causeways and roads to bring Roman troops to its banks.

If we return to Dio's description, this makes it clear that whilst some soldiers swam the river, which is feasible at numerous locations along the river, the main force crossed by bridge. This was the only sensible option for moving an entire army and its supplies over the river. The Greek text described this as a γέφυρας, a term which could embrace a variety of fixed crossings including pontoon bridges formed from ships lashed together.[47] This would have suited the needs of the time. In the absence of any archaeological or topographic evidence for a fixed pre-Roman crossing, or evident need for one to have existed prior to the conquest, Dio may have described a bridge built as part of the Roman campaign. It is consequently worth drawing attention to observations at Regis House in 1929–31, where two crossed timber beams were found on the riverbank in the only appropriate location for the landward abutment of a conquest-period pontoon bridge.[48] This crossing point exploited gravel islands projecting into the Thames at Southwark to reach a natural gravel promontory beneath modern Fish Street Hill. On topographic grounds, London is the only sensible site for a fixed-river crossing down-river from Staines, where the Roman place name *Pontibus* shows that a bridge also existed. The configuration of islands in Southwark, facing Cornhill where the river flowed through a narrow channel, uniquely eliminated the need to traverse areas of intertidal marsh. The advantages of the site, and the impracticality of the alternatives, meant that London remained the lowest bridging point of the Thames into modern times.

The need to bridge the Thames is certain to have figured in campaign planning, drawing on intelligence obtained from Caesar's earlier expedition and Rome's allies in Britain. Aulus Plautius had a large transport fleet and it would have been logistically and strategically necessary to develop seaborne supply lines along the north coast of Kent and into the Thames estuary. This adds gentle weight to arguments in favour of seeing Richborough as the principal point of entry into Britain. In any case, some ships of the invasion fleet could easily have been lashed together to form a pontoon bridge, the need for which was foreseen.

Once Aulus Plautius had occupied his position on the Thames, he halted his advance and waited on the arrival of the Imperial party. It seems inconceivable that he would have withdrawn south of the river after securing the necessary bridgehead. Dio's account explains that Claudius joined the troops who were awaiting him near the Thames when he crossed into Britain.[49] It also specifies that Claudius was only in Britain for 16 days. This was too short a period to have involved a landing on the south coast: the distances involved were too great to permit the return trip to Colchester within the available time.[50] His timetable was, instead, consistent with a sailing that made directly to the welcome of the army waiting on the Thames. The waterfront site at 15–23 Southwark Street, presently a car-park near Borough Market, was an established landing place of exactly the sort where Claudius might have disembarked. A landing in Southwark would have allowed Claudius to lead his forces across the Thames, as described by Dio, to join troops already camped on Cornhill. The timeline is uncertain, but Claudius probably arrived in Britain in late July or early August.[51] The Claudian party was a large one, including soldiers of the Praetorian Guard, elephants and siege engines, and an extended court of senators and members of the imperial household. It may even have included an additional Roman legion. His triumphal march to Colchester, navigating marshlands flanking the river Lea, would have started immediately. The departing troops would have evacuated their temporary site beside the Thames, leaving it redundant.

6

A supply-base (*c.* A D 43–52)

After the conquest

The discovery of a large defended enclosure of likely Claudian date beneath the Roman city has revived the proposition that London was built in the summer of A D 43 to house the invasion forces. This hypothesis accommodates new-won evidence and is consistent with both historical sources and topographic context. The Roman army set up a camp somewhere on the banks of the Thames and nowhere was better suited for their purpose then the Cornhill site.

Whilst it is of more than passing interest to fix the point and purpose of London's first creation, the argument in favour of a military origin doesn't require us to abandon the idea that other processes helped make London a town. Far from it. The evidence of London's earliest Roman stratigraphy shows this to have been a complicated process: involving at least two phases of major investment that gave London its essential shape. There were significant differences in the scale of ambition of these two exercises, but both involved planned components suggestive of central direction. The argument developed here, presented as a model for future testing, is that an initial foundation of *c.* A D 48 made London an important supply-base before it was remodelled into a fully fledged town *c.* A D 52.

The disuse of the defensive enclosure on Cornhill is our starting place. If we are correct in identifying this as a military site, it makes sense to see the slighting of London's defences as an act of decommissioning when the army departed (p. 53). It is also likely that any pontoon bridge over the Thames would have been dismantled, allowing the redeployment of the boats involved in forward campaigns. It is hard to believe, however, that London simply ceased to exist. The strategic value of the Thames crossing was increased, not diminished, by Rome's advance, and the bridge could have been replaced by a ferry pending more permanent arrangements.

We have no certain archaeological evidence of London in the 5 years after the conquest, but continuity of occupation is likely at late Iron Age sites in Southwark and Bermondsey. There is a suggestive concentration of early Roman military finds at 15–23 Southwark Street, and London could easily have been controlled from the south-bank in these years.[1] This would account for a higher representation of Claudian coinage in Southwark's assemblages, as compared to sites north of the river, finding parallel in conquest-period supply ports at Fishbourne, Fingringhoe, Sea Mills, and Richborough.[2] The creeks around Southwark remained a sensible destination for shipping coming up the Thames, at a secure point for organizing the inland movement of goods and supplies. There may, however, have been a hiatus in the occupation of the Cornhill site on the north side of the river. Some temporary structures might belong to this period, such as a timber building found at the base of the archaeological sequence at 5–12 Fenchurch Street and ditches pre-dating the earliest streets at Plantation Place, but the evidence is inconclusive.[3]

The streets of London

In contrast we have a more substantial body of evidence for what came next. Lacey Wallace has made a close study of the evidence for the earliest permanent settlement on the north bank. Using conservative criteria, she identified nearly 3,000 archaeological assemblages pre-dating the Boudican fire from fifty-six different sites.[4] The earliest activities were associated with clearing and draining the land, and quarrying gravel for building the first streets. These quarries were dug without regard to the needs of later users, creating a pockmarked landscape that needed landscaping and consolidation before house-building could proceed. This was a lazy choice, since it would not have been difficult to relocate quarries into areas destined for back-plots. We can conclude that the road engineers were largely indifferent to the needs of the eventual owners of properties established along these streets, suggesting that engineering took place before property interests were fixed or by powers remote from the concerns of those who settled here.

The best dating evidence for these first streets comes not from the core of the settlement, but from one of the main approach roads. Excavations at One Poultry, 50 metres west of a Walbrook crossing, found metalled surfaces of the main west road.[5] The earliest surface was laid over timber culverts that diverted water from springs rising in the Gresham Street area. These culverts were part of the primary road engineering and incorporated at least one timber felled in the winter of AD 47/48. Others felled the following spring or summer were reused in later repairs. These timbers were procured for road-building in the AD 48 construction season, presenting a credible date for the creation of London's first permanent street system.

According to Wallace the culvert cut into a deposit that contained products of the first Romano-British pottery kilns, including locally manufactured Verulamium region wares.[6] This might imply that these kilns started production immediately after the conquest. But the excavation report is less definitive, describing sherds of a Verulamium whiteware mortarium from adjacent landscaping. This landscaping might have followed the insertion of the culvert, allowing pottery production to have commenced c. AD 48 in time for a new-made mortarium to be introduced in a foundation ritual. Rubbish beneath this first road included leather panels likely to have come from tents, perhaps those of the army of conquest.[7] The likeliest source of this material is the defended site east of the Walbrook, reaching Poultry by means of a crossing established before the metalled road surfaces were laid.

At this date most roads were army-built, but since the focus of military attention lay elsewhere, engineering capacity would have been stretched. By c. AD 48, however, Rome had invested in the construction of a road system that consolidated London's position at the heart of the transportation network. Streets converging on the Thames linked ports in the south-east with areas of military deployment to north and west. The road from Richborough to the Thames formed the trunk of this communication system which branched once the river was crossed, heading to pre-Roman centres at Colchester and *Verulamium* (St. Albans), and areas of military operations in the Midlands and Wales. The road to London Bridge has been investigated in Southwark, where it was laid over log causeways across lower areas and buildings erected alongside are dated c. AD 50.[8] Pottery assemblages from roadside sites at Brentford and Old Ford show similarities with those associated with the initial Roman presence in London, including grog-tempered fabrics following Iron Age traditions.[9] These finds may shadow conquest phase activities, as Rome secured important river crossings along routes where metalled roads were later built.

The need to cross the Thames and bring supplies inland gave London abiding strategic importance. The point where the roads came together to cross the river was the hub.[10] The main streets within the settlement formed a central T-junction, taking the road that climbed Cornhill from the site of London Bridge as its trunk (Fig. 6.1). This was London's main north-south axis throughout its Roman history: identifiable as a *cardo maximus* if we follow modern misuse of the term imported from Roman surveying.[11] It rose to meet an equally important east-west axial route, similarly described as the *decumanus maximus*. When first laid out this road was no more than 4 metres wide which was barely sufficient for two-way traffic.[12] The roads were primarily designed for waggon travel, facilitating the overland movement of goods. River transport along the Thames would have been equally important, allowing ships to reach deep into southern Britain. There was, however, no contemporary investment in waterfront facilities: Roman harbours could be simple affairs, where larger ships anchored mid-stream off-loading their cargoes into smaller vessels that beached on the foreshore.[13]

The vast quantities of grain transported by the army required marshalling yards and storage-facilities where hauliers could congregate. In the absence of waterfront facilities, this may have taken place more centrally. An area about half the size of a football pitch (at least 25 metres across and 37 metres deep) north of the central T-junction, had been de-turfed and levelled in preparation for a hard-wearing gravel surface.[14] Lacey Wallace has estimated that its construction involved between 180 and 380 person days' work.[15] This was the heart of London, where a monumental forum was later built. The central hardscape was integral to

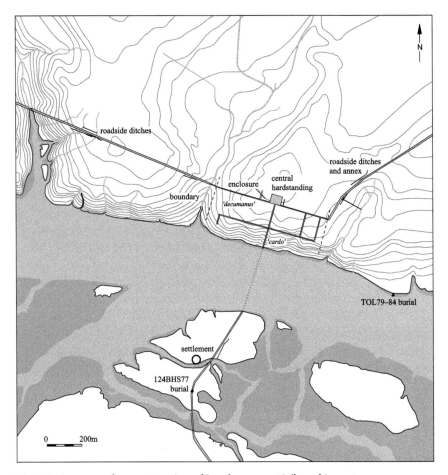

Fig. 6.1 A proposed reconstruction of London *c*. AD 48 (based in part on Wallace 2016). Drawn by Justin Russell.

London's original design, establishing a place where people, goods, livestock and vehicles could assemble.[16] Early London had no evident need of the grand public buildings usually associated with city centres: the open space mattered more than the buildings around it. Excavations at 168–70 Fenchurch Street, east of the metalled area, showed that the first buildings were modest timber-framed and earth-floored structures, separated by narrow north-south alleys barely wide enough for a single cart to pass.[17] These were probably built before *c*. AD 52. An early U-shaped ditch, up to 1.8 metres deep, found west of the gravelled area at Lombard Street might have formed a sacred boundary (*temenos*) to a ritual or administrative enclosure west of the forum hardstanding.[18] A parallel can tentatively be drawn with the larger late Iron Age or early Roman enclosure beneath the forum at Verulamium, the purpose of which is also unknown.[19]

In addition to the narrow backstreet found east of the central hardstanding, a 3- to 4-metre-wide north-south road dating to the first phase of settlement was found at Plantation Place.[20] This lay close to the eastern boundary of the settlement and was perhaps a perimeter road similar to the intervallum road of a Roman fort. A row of narrow timber buildings, each 25 metres long and 3.5 metres wide, was erected alongside. Almost all of the early buildings and property boundaries within this Cornhill settlement shared the strictly orthogonal orientation established by the principal streets. London was laid out on a regular grid from the outset.

At the gates

Shallow ditches dug along the line of the slighted defences at The Walbrook suggest that the settlement boundary was reasserted before AD 60, although no longer as a defensive feature.[21] This perimeter, perhaps defining something akin to a city *pomerium* (the space beyond the walls), would have held functional and symbolic significance: the ritual marking of boundaries gave cities a sacred identity from which threatening impurities could be expelled.[22] The establishment of a formal boundary might account for the way in which roads into London narrowed on entering the orthogonal core. Whilst the roads approaching London were 6–14 metres wide, those inside the initial settlement were generally only 4 metres wide.[23] A bottle-neck occurred where traffic congregated at entrances, suggesting the presence of gates. If so, London's main west-gate was near the site of St Stephen Walbrook and its east-gate beneath Minster Court. These locations, equidistant from the central T-junction, marked the limits of the orthogonal settlement.[24] Traffic was notoriously difficult to manage in Roman towns, and gates created checkpoints to restrict access.[25] The wider approaches allowed waggons to halt beside the road during tax inspections or to transfer cargoes onto pack animals better suited to narrow streets.[26]

The broadways into London were flanked by large V-shaped ditches with a characteristic square 'ankle-breaker', or cleaning-trench, at the base.[27] The ditch on the north side of the Colchester road was set nearly 20 metres back from the metalled street surface. It had a brief life and was backfilled before being covered by buildings destroyed in AD 60. Finds from its fills are consistent with a Claudian date and include the bone handle-grip of a legionary sword. Claudian ditches also chased the road west from London over Ludgate Hill. These too were set back from the metalled surfaces, leaving a gap of at least 6 metres. At one point the ditch was preceded by a fence or hedge that similarly separated the street from its surrounds.[28] The ditches improved local drainage and provided quarried materials for the raised streets, but were over-engineered for this alone. They also protected traffic within a wider corridor that may have included livestock droveways flanking the metalled highway. Other ditches may have defined temporary annexes on the borders of the settlement, similar to those outside the early fortress at Exeter.[29] The areas outside the orthogonally planned core were sensible locations for compounds where livestock could be corralled. This was perhaps the motive for the excavation of V-shaped ditch set perpendicular to the Colchester road, some 60 metres to its south, at Northumberland Alley.[30] A row of pits along the east side of this ditch might have supported a palisade for added security.

Two unusually early burials on the borders are sometimes treated as evidence of late Iron Age occupation. If so, they might have been associated with the pre-Roman farmsteads described in the Chapter 4. It is more likely, however, that they belonged to the first phase of Roman settlement. One occupied a shallow grave on the southern island next to Borough High Street.[31] The body of a man, perhaps between 26 and 35 years old based on the evidence of tooth wear, had been placed in a flexed position with his head at the north end of the grave raised to face south. The grave contained no funerary goods, but was sealed by a layer containing early Roman pottery. According to interim reports this was cut by three parallel rows of post-pits then buried during the construction of the main road to London Bridge no later than c. AD 55. Finds from the site included a bone wrist-guard of late Iron Age type.[32] The burial was placed beneath the main road into London at a point where it deviated as it passed a river inlet and took a new heading towards London Bridge. The post-pits may therefore define an important structure, perhaps a gate. It is consequently possible that the burial was an early Roman foundation deposit facing those approaching London from Kent.

The other early burial was found at the Tower of London. The body of a youth, perhaps aged 13–16, was placed with his legs flexed in a shallow grave cut into foreshore deposits containing abraded Iron Age pottery.[33] A Carbon-14 date of AD 70+/-70 leaves it uncertain if this was a late Iron Age or early Roman burial but the presence of a copper alloy finger-ring of Roman type hints at a post-conquest date. It is notable that both of these unusually early inhumations were buried in a flexed position. It is also worth drawing attention to the importance of the Thames as the main route into London. Might the foreshore burial have also been a foundation deposit placed to face those arriving into London?

Who built London and why?

The decision to build a hardstanding at the site of the forum and to set out carefully protected broadways and compounds beyond the gates was integral to the design of the post-conquest settlement. This emphasis on traffic management and security betrays something of the thinking behind London's establishment. Preparations for road-building appear to have been put in hand shortly after the arrival of a new provincial governor, Ostorius Scapula. Scapula is thought to have reached southern Britain late in AD 47 and is credited with shaping the new territories into a Roman province.[34] His objectives were tied-up with plans for further military action in the Midlands and Wales. Scapula's frontier wars relied on supply routes along Watling Street, and this gave London considerable strategic importance. This was the place where coastal traffic intersected with roads that headed inland. The decision to invest in London's facilities, perhaps made in the winter of AD 47–8, anticipated the needs of following campaigns. It may also have been part of a wider programme of investment in the development of the infrastructure of the pacified parts of the province following the suppression of an Icenian revolt described as having occurred in AD 47. According to Tacitus, Scapula also established a veteran colony to replace the fortress at Colchester, following the redeployment of *Legio*XX in AD 49. This is also a likely date for the foundation of a chartered town at Verulamium and the establishment of London may have been part of a concerted programme of urban foundation at this time.[35]

It is open to question, however, whether the London of *c.* AD 48 was intended as a town. It lacked the civic and elite architecture that normally formed part of the urban package, although this may have been intended to follow. The early site had more in common with the settlement at Richborough, which is usually identified as a supply-base. This too was a place where a Claudian defensive enclosure was slighted, probably in the early 50s, before a regular grid of metalled roads was laid out. Timber warehouses and granaries that flanked these streets were used for the storage and distribution of supplies needed by the Roman army.[36] Ptolemy was later to describe Richborough and London in identical terms and there is no evidence to suggest that the two sites were differently conceived or held different status at this date.[37] It is only because of their divergent later histories that they are understood so differently. In the early 50s, both places primarily served the needs of Roman military supply.

Roman military campaigns commonly involved establishing operational bases behind the frontier, where equipment and provisions could be stockpiled for onward movement. River ports were inevitably favoured, and the practice of converting abandoned fortifications for this use was well established.[38] As Jonathon Roth has shown, these bases served a variety of ancillary functions. They contributed to the manufacture and repair of armour, were places where cavalry remounts were stabled, housed the army's money and documents with the personal baggage of commanders and officials, and were holding sites for hostages and captives. This made them into secure locations where forces could be gathered before campaigns were launched. These functions required an investment in the settlement infrastructure and gave such bases a distinct urban character, regardless of their formal standing.

It is likely that London's main roads were built by the army. Absent any pre-existing self-governing community, it is difficult to recognize any alternative authority with the need or means to take oversight over the exercise, and the engineering skills employed were those learnt in military service. Objects found beneath the metalled surfaces of the first roads into London may have held symbolic and votive significance, perhaps placed as foundation deposits rather than casually lost or discarded.[39] These included a fist-and-phallus amulet, a symbol of masculine virility used to ward off the evil eye and popular with Roman soldiers, found beneath the surface of the main road through Southwark. A young sheep or goat buried under the earliest buildings at Fenchurch Street, east of the central hardstanding, may also have been a sacrificial offering of this period.

The decision to build London required the support of the provincial government, perhaps facilitated by the fact any redundant military site would have been owned by the emperor. The initial programme betrays signs of haste, both in the distribution of gravel quarries and in the way that the town centre needed extensive re-planning soon after. This is consistent with the unsettled circumstances that faced Scapula on his arrival. The likely involvement of army engineers in setting out London's first streets, and the use of the site as an operational base, does not make London a military site and the distinction between military and civilian is not straightforward. Private contractors (*publicani* and *negotiatores*) were closely involved in the supply of the army, particularly in providing sea transport. Roman commanders benefitted from the support of private parties, including those attracted to the lucrative opportunities of public contracts, whose involvement reduced demands on a short-handed colonial administration.[40] For example, Caesar placed a private citizen, C. Fufius Cita, whom he described as a businessman (*negotiator*) in charge of logistics (*res frumentariiae*) during his Gallic campaigns.[41] Many recent studies of Roman London have emphasized the importance of merchants and civilian traders to its early history.[42] This argument has been championed by Martin Millett, in his reluctance to ascribe agency to the military in the Romanization of Britain (p. 29). In Millett's view the principal dynamic for the growth of London came from a community of opportunistic Gallic traders, although he recognizes that London must have housed many soldiers.[43] These issues will be explored further below, but an important distinction needs to be drawn between understanding how London came into being and how it was populated. As Mike Fulford has observed, whilst the majority of London's inhabitants might have been civilians their reason for being there was dictated by imperial policy.[44] The argument developed here is that London was designed to meet the needs of army supply rather than for the convenience of traders, although these interests were so closely aligned that the distinction is largely academic.

London in the geography of Roman Britain

The Roman conquest changed Britain's political geography to London's advantage. London was placed on borderlands between pre-Roman polities, where the absence of a pre-Roman seat of power gave the new colonial authorities consider-able operational freedom. The infrastructure of the new province converged on the optimal site for the economic and political domination of southern Britain. There were few powerful landowners and no population centres whose interests needed accommodating. Officials and merchants could operate with greater lati-tude than elsewhere. Land could be annexed and impositions made without dis-rupting the existing social order. These freedoms reduced the risk of conflict, and increased the rewards available to new settlers.

Rome had long recognized the value of borderland riverside sites. This finds ancestry in the origin stories of Rome itself, founded on the Tiber frontier between Etruscan and Latin peoples.[45] The choice of the site of London finds closer parallel in the colonial foundation at Lyon (*Lugdunum*). Here an earlier Gallic settlement at the confluence of the Rhône and Saône gained political cen-trality through the conquest of Gaul, resulting in the foundation of a Roman col-ony by the governor Plancus to house a community of citizens expelled from Vienne.[46] The city was subsequently developed into the main base from which the Roman forces on the Rhine were supplied, and transformed into an *emporium* by Agrippa and Augustus in preparation for campaigns in Germany.[47] This involved the construction of new facilities on the navigable rivers and a network of roads, largely for military purposes. The main difference is that at Lyon these functions accrued to a formally constituted city, designed to accommodate resettled citi-zens. There was no need to give London an equivalent political identity. Other Roman riverside cities at politically liminal locations included Cologne (*Colonia Claudia Ara Agrippinensium*) and Mainz (*Moguntiacum*) on the Rhine, and York (*Eboracum*) on the boundary of the Brigantes and Parisi at the confluence of the rivers Ouse and Foss.[48] Nicholas Purcell has described how these rivers were neu-tral spaces between debatable terrains, but also arteries in the inter-regional negotiation of trade, supply and government.[49] In all cases the cities were used as instruments of imperial domination, but drew authority and legitimacy from the potency of their river locations.

London was in many regards an unusual case. Most Roman cities drew either on the urbanizing ambitions of pre-existing communities, or came into being as organized settlements of colonists supported by land grants within a surrounding territorium. Some sites, Lyon and Colchester amongst them, could be both: where a new colony was settled onto an earlier centre. London appears to have been neither. As a consequence, we can imagine a more tenuous link between land-ownership and social power than was normal. If London came into being without the involvement of a resident, land-owning elite society this helps to explain the later vulnerability of the site to cyclical growth and contraction. Government offices and business interests enjoyed fewer ties to the land, and were naturally transient.

7

Shaping the city (*c.* AD 52–60)

New streets for old

Within a decade of the Roman conquest, London was Britain's largest settlement: a creation that owed little to anything previously seen in Britain and everything to Roman ideas of town planning. Its growth appears to have been charged by a phase of rebuilding in the early 50s. Evidence for extensive cadastral reform of this date has been found throughout the settlement's south-eastern quarter. At Plantation Place the '*decumanus*' was widened by 1.5 metres creating space for pedestrians and pack-animals, adjacent houses were demolished to clear a path for the construction of a new north-south road, and the earlier intervallum street was made redundant as new buildings were set over its line.[1] Sweeping pre-Boudican changes were also recorded at 20 Fenchurch Street, the site of the skyscraper known as the 'walkie-talkie', where a north-south road was replaced by a new street a few metres to its west. Works east of the forum also involved new planning: an east-west street was inserted, cutting across an earlier north-south alleyway and adjacent buildings.[2] A room in one of the buildings erected at this time was repainted four times before its destruction in AD 60/61, placing these alterations no later than the early 50s.

By the end of the 50s a regularly surveyed street grid extended across the urban area. Lacey Wallace has identified six north-south aligned roads either side of the '*cardo*' rising from London Bridge, creating evenly sized blocks of housing about 300 ft. wide by 450 ft. long (using the Roman *pes monetalis*).[3] She suggests that this orthogonal layout was confined to an area south of the forum, although findings at Whittington Avenue imply that it extended further north.[4] The reconstruction proposed here identifies a chequerboard settlement served by three streets aligned east-west and seven north-south, covering a somewhat smaller area than the Claudian defensive enclosure (Fig. 7.1). In several areas the new engineering showed little respect for earlier land division, introducing new property rights and responsibilities. The invention of this street grid was an important statement, incorporating changed expectations of how London was to be ordered. It carried ideological force. In becoming a place of order, London established a community of rights whilst affirming a sacred identity. It is from this point that it appears convincingly urban.

Investigations in the town centre show that the new streets were laid out in the early 50s, but a more exact date is suggested by evidence from the town borders.

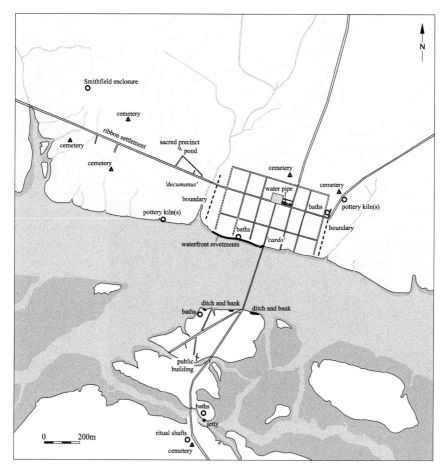

Fig. 7.1 A proposed reconstruction of London *c.* AD 52. The sites of bathhouses are those suggested by concentrations of redeposited building materials but their locations have not been confirmed by discoveries of *in-situ* structural remains. Drawn by Justin Russell.

Major repairs to the '*decumanus*' at One Poultry, west of the Walbrook, involved the insertion of a new culvert using timbers felled in the winter of AD 51/52, whilst adjacent building plots were prepared for development with timbers felled AD 52/53.[5] If these roadworks were contemporary with those in the town centre, which seems likely since they addressed different ends of the same street, then the re-planning of London took place *c.* AD 52. Rebuilding at this date also embraced the Thames waterfront, where beaching facilities were established on the fore-shore. Hardstandings of mortared gravel, and sloping flint and chalk surfaces, were laid near the low water mark upriver and downriver of London Bridge, cre-ating areas where shallow flat bottomed boats could beach and vehicles might meet them at the water's edge.[6] Associated waterfront revetments incorporated timbers felled in the spring of AD 52, drawing on both Roman and insular styles of woodworking.[7] Timber jetties and landing stages were subsequently built into the river a little further upstream, where post-and-plank revetments employed piles felled in the winter of AD 54/55 and the riverbank behind was terraced for development.[8]

More structural timbers are dated AD 52–5 than from any equivalent period in the history of Roman London.[9] These witness a major programme of rebuilding that started in the year that Didius Gallus replaced Ostorius Scapula as provincial governor.[10] Gallus' appointment has been argued to have involved a suspension of Claudian aspirations for further conquest in Britain. If so, the rebuilding of London might be deemed an exercise in consolidation within pacified territories. It seems more likely, however, that Gallus' intentions were more ambitious than the sources allow, and investment in London's transport infrastructure antici-pated campaigns of conquest that came to be postponed. The accession of Nero in AD 54 may have imposed delay, consistent with Suetonius' observation that he had considered withdrawing from Britain.[11]

Around the forum

London's importance to the business of the new province is described in letters and contracts inscribed in Latin on wax-coated wooden tablets found at the Bloomberg headquarters. One, from a context dated no later than *c.* AD 53, advised its recipient to be more discrete in money-lending activities since 'throughout the entire marketplace (*per forum totum*), [your debtors] are boast-ing that you have lent them money'.[12] London's forum was already a place for banking. Money-lending lubricated the transactions that turned conquest to profit, and business credit secured the flow of supplies needed by the Roman administration. In another document, dated 8 January AD 57, Tibullus promised to repay Gratus 105 denarii for goods delivered.[13] This, the earliest legal contract known from Britain, was made between two men described as freedmen and concerned a sum equivalent to half a year's pay for a Roman legionary.

Some supplies were kept in a large building south-east of the forum hardstanding.[14] This was a massive structure, some 55.3 metres long, built along-side the '*decumanus*'. Its walls of air-dried bricks were set over concreted flint foundations in a distinctive architecture previously found in Lyon and barrack blocks at Colchester (Fig. 7.2).[15] The building housed a row of stores, offices and workshops, broadly similar to those arranged around the later forum courtyard and identifiable as *tabernae*. A broad veranda or portico added to the façade pro-vided a covered area suitable for goods handling.[16] Bread wheat was kept in one of the rooms at the time of the Boudican revolt.[17] Weeds within the crop of

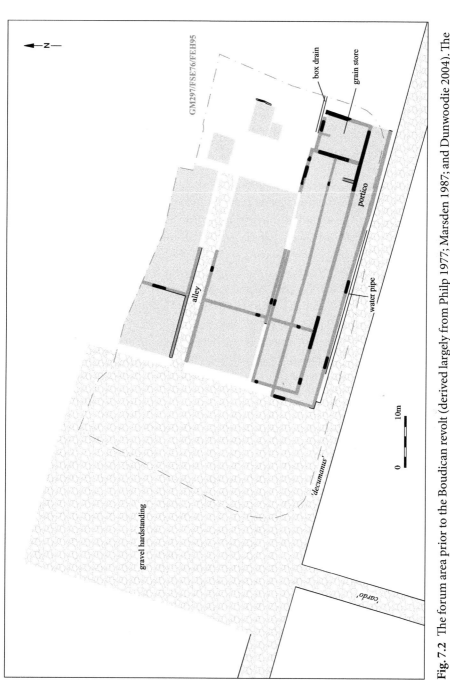

Fig. 7.2 The forum area prior to the Boudican revolt (derived largely from Philp 1977; Marsden 1987; and Dunwoodie 2004). The northern and western limits of the central gravel hardstanding have yet to be located. Drawn by Justin Russell.

de-husked spelt wheat included alien elements such as bitter vetch that suggest it to have been imported from the Mediterranean or Near East. Sacks would have been shipped up the Thames, unloaded onto the foreshore, and carried to the forum by cart or pack-animal. We don't know if this grain was waiting to be moved along Watling Street to feed the army or was imported for London's use, but long-distance shipments were a feature of military supply and reserves of this sort would have anticipated the needs of the AD 60 campaign season. These imports contrasted with contemporary crop-processing waste from the outskirts of town that included a mix of grain, seeds, and chaff indicative of the small-scale hand-cleaning of cereals, perhaps obtained locally for sale from roadside premises.[18]

London's granaries created an environment where new species of pest thrived. Remains of black rat have been found near to the forum in pre-Boudican contexts.[19] Several sites preserve grain burnt and buried after being spoiled by flour beetle infestation.[20] Quantities of such material were incorporated into stable waste and domestic rubbish dumped on the banks of the Walbrook at One Poultry during construction in AD 53, probably brought here from the town centre as land-fill.[21] The presence of red flour beetle (*Tribolium castaneum*) suggest that some of the grain spoiled by AD 53 was also imported from the Mediterranean or Near East, where this species can over-winter in unheated stores.[22]

The forum didn't yet incorporate monumental civic architecture, but a fragment of coloured marble from the Greek island of Skyros reused in a later repair hints at the high-status decor of parts of the Fenchurch Street building.[23] Elite architecture is also indicated by fragments of marble veneer and mosaic pavement from a pre-Boudican pit at Leadenhall Court.[24] The official nature of the Cornhill settlement is implied by an unusual concentration of pre-Flavian Samian inkwells and seal boxes at Plantation Place.[25] The area also housed armourer's workshops where military fittings could be repaired or recycled, as indicated by items of Roman body armour (*lorica segmentata*).[26] Similar activities might account for small-scale iron and bronze working opposite the forum, and metal working waste on the Thames foreshore.[27] A pre-Flavian pit within the town centre, at Eastcheap, contained four unfinished intaglios that may have been a gem-workers stock.[28] These gems, destined to be set within seal-rings, were part of the executive paraphernalia required by senior officers and administrators. These finds reflect on London's role as an operational base for Britain's colonial government, and the expansion under Gallus' administration is likely to have been planned for this purpose.

Baths and temples

The new town was provided with the facilities essential for Roman social life, and these included heated bathhouses.[29] These are only known from scatters of demolition debris and were probably small establishments catering for select communities, with larger public baths not built before the Flavian period. One of the earliest was probably situated just inside the east gate, which would have been a sensible location for a bathhouse following an arrangement familiar from Roman forts.[30] Gateway sites were easy to supply with fuel and made focal points suited for public architecture. Box-flue and voussoir tiles from heating systems and vaulted roofs were found in debris beneath the ramparts of the Neronian fort at Plantation Place. Some of this material was scorched, presumably from destruction in AD 60/61. It also included a Carrara marble moulding from the architrave of an entablature that possibly adorned the façade of a bathhouse, an oolitic limestone Attic column from a colonnade, and fragments of marble wall veneers, opus sectile and mosaic floors from decorated interiors.[31] This material was tipped onto site without sorting for reuse and is unlikely to have travelled far.[32] The presence of this bathhouse is also implied by a water-pipe along the northern side of the 'decumanus', drawing water from springs or wells north-west of the forum to supply a site near the town's eastern entrance.[33] Valuable bathhouse equipment, consisting of a strigil for cleansing oiled skin and a splendid six nozzled bronze lamp for illuminating a hot-room, was buried nearby at 116–20 Fenchurch Street.[34] These discoveries combine to suggest that the baths stood somewhere between Mincing Lane and Mark Lane. Excavations here in 1923 revealed the foundations of a brick-walled building with heated rooms that may have housed the warm rooms (tepidaria) of a small bathhouse, and a curved foundation that might have supported the apsidal end of a hot room (caldaria).[35] These features are, however, undated and may belong to later rebuilding. Another bathhouse may have been established on a terrace overlooking the Thames at Arthur Street, upstream of London Bridge. This was the site of a precociously early masonry building with an apsidal chamber and building debris that included roofing tiles, bricks, and painted wall plaster.[36] The later Neronian addition of water-lifting machinery suggests a bathing establishment, perhaps serving an important town house.

In another sign of the gathering complexity of social life within the new community, a religious precinct may have been established around springs on the hillside north-west of the urban settlement. This site was later marked by a series of Romano-Celtic temples, but the earlier importance of the precinct is suggested by its primacy within the urban topography. A road leading here, on a diagonal to the later street grid, was planned as early as AD 48.[37] A large pond, 20 metres long and 10 metres across, was dug where roads converged, and parts of a bronze statue in its fills hint at votive deposition (p. 112).[38] The area presents similarities with the ceremonial enclosure at Folly Lane which overlooked Verulamium across the river Ver.[39] Both sites attracted unusual Claudio-Neronian practices that generated scatters of stray human bone, and were later subsumed within religious complexes containing temples and baths (p. 153). At Folly Lane, these activities developed around the site of a mortuary shaft with exceptionally rich pyre offerings. Nothing similar has been found in London where the ceremonial focus may have been provided by holy springs rather than a princely burial. Springs formed points of contact with other worlds and religious sites commonly began as open-air sanctuaries.[40] Prominent hilltop locations were also widely favoured, complying with Vitruvian prescription that gods associated with city protection should be housed on the highest ground.[41] Border sanctuaries mediated the fraught relationship between urban order and the wild beyond, and the anchors provided by these hilltop springs would have been particularly meaningful in a city of new invention.[42]

South of the river

The south-bank settlement retained its earlier importance. Attempts to order the site may be represented by ditch-and-bank arrangements along the foreshore at Winchester Palace and Toppings Wharf, perhaps intended as river-defences in areas susceptible to flooding.[43] No orthogonal street grid was imposed: the topography simply did not allow, with development constrained by the need to follow higher ground between tidal channels and marsh. The main roads converged on the London Bridge crossing. The Kent road (Watling Street) is roughly beneath modern Borough High Street, reaching the mainland around the site of St George the Martyr where it swung east to form Watling Street (to Canterbury). A gravel-surfaced road also converged on the bridgehead across Southwark's north island. Remains beneath Southwark Cathedral suggest that it was built in the late 50s, although the route may have been used before it was metalled. At 8 metres wide, this was unusually substantial for a secondary street, marking the importance of this settlement.[44]

Southwark's first masonry structures are known only through stray building materials, but these hint at the presence of at least three important Claudio-Neronian buildings. One had been demolished before the revolt. Fragments of moulded stone imported from quarries near Reigate and Merstham in Surrey had been reused in the construction of a building at Borough High Street that was destroyed in AD 60/61.[45] These must have been salvaged for reuse no later than c. AD 55. The source may have been the building complex at 15–23 Southwark Street. This site, first occupied prior to the conquest, remained an important part of the landscape.[46] The Claudio-Neronian features included trenches tentatively identified as the foundations of a substantial earth-walled building. Two oolitic limestone column shafts found on the site indicate that this building included colonnades. Wall tile, box-flue tile, tufa voussoirs and fragments of limestone columns found at Borough Market, Stoney Street and Park Street may have derived from this or associated buildings.[47] Items of military equipment and irregular Claudian coins, mostly struck c. AD 50–5, were also concentrated at Southwark

Street.[48] Some of these irregular issues were probably made in London to rectify shortages of official supply: a hoard buried at corner of St Swithin's Lane and King William Street included silver plated copies of denarii made from the same small group of dies which hints at local manufacture.[49] High concentrations of these coins were a characteristic of early supply-bases.

Another high-status building occupied a commanding riverfront location 200 metres upstream of London Bridge, at Winchester Palace, where Flavian buildings replaced an important Claudian or Neronian complex.[50] Demolition debris included quantities of box-flue tiles in the same early fabrics found at Plantation Place, along with ceramic water pipe fragments. These imply the presence of a bathhouse built in tandem with the amenities at Plantation Place. Roads radiating from the site gave it unusual primacy within the urban topography, and later finds suggest an association with the Roman administration (below p. 260). The prominent riverside location would have suited the 'palatial' residence of a senior official, and David Mattingly has suggested that this may have been the residence of the imperial procurator whose leading role would have warranted unusual domestic luxury.[51]

A bathhouse may also have stood close to the southern margins of the settlement. Kevin Hayward's study of building material found at Tabard Square suggests the presence of a Claudio-Neronian building similar to the baths of legionary fortresses.[52] Finds included quantities of flue tiles from vaulted ceilings, Purbeck marble fragments similar to mouldings that decorated legionary bathhouses at Exeter and Caerleon, and column fragments and a Bath-stone Tuscan capital similar to stonework in the baths at Silchester. The water-supply for these baths may have relied on wells and water-tanks close to where Watling Street crossed onto the southern island. Excavations at Long Lane found the remains of a 9-metre-long timber landing-stage, incorporating a timber pile felled no later than AD 53, which may have been built for ships delivering building materials and fuel.[53] A bathhouse at this location might have been associated with a religious precinct at the approaches to London, close to the junction of Stane Street and Watling Street. The later temples at Tabard Square (p. 267) may have been attracted to an earlier sacred site defined by votive shafts found at Swan Street.[54] Items buried here between the mid-first and mid-second century included human and animal body parts and largely complete pots. These may have been offerings to propitiate spirits in ritual acts of closure following Iron Age and Roman tradition and the faunal assemblages included a high proportion of sheep/goat, which sometimes characterize sites of animal sacrifice.[55] This crossroads site on London's southern boundary was ideally suited for offerings to propitiate the gods from departing travellers or in payment of vows against journeys safely completed.

Southwark's other early buildings shared much in common with those north of the river, with building activity drawn along the main roads. Excavations along Borough High Street revealed a building with raised plank floors likely to have housed a granary and bakery, indicated by brick-and-tile ovens and quantities of clean grain charred in the destruction of AD 60/61.[56] A nearby building may have been a blacksmith's, indicated by finds of hammerscale generated from working hot iron. Roman Southwark bears comparison with cross-river sites found associated with other Roman cities such as Lyon, Trier, Cologne, Lincoln, and York. Parallels can also be drawn with the pre-Flavian industrial and commercial site at Sheepen, outside the fort and colony at Colchester.[57]

Other suburbs

A contemporary suburb stretched alongside the '*decumanus*' as it crossed Ludgate Hill to the west. Pre-fabricated timber-framed and thatch roofed buildings were built over terraces at One Poultry c. AD 54, drawing on a wide repertoire of advanced woodworking techniques, involving base-plates, stud and post walls, wattle-and-daub infill and boarded coverings (Fig. 7.3).[58] One housed a stock of Samian, spoons and spices when razed in the revolt of AD 60/61, offering a selection of fine-dining exotica that mirrored contemporary shop assemblages from Colchester and Verulamium.[59] This specialized retail of luxuries for the table met a common demand within Britain's new cities unmet by other forms of supply. The presence of a tavern was indicated by a concentration of amphorae and Samian drinking vessels alongside high-status food waste, including olives, grapes, and almonds, with traces of grape pollen probably derived from wine. Adjacent Neronian buildings contained decorated reception rooms, using imported marble and hypocaust floors. Wells were dug into the yards, and open drains between house plots carried surface run-off and foul-water into the Walbrook. Environmental data shows that pigs and chickens were kept in the yards, whilst house mice and black rats scavenged amidst household waste. The excavators noted a scarcity of evidence for industrial activity. Shops at this privileged location, London's original west-end, concentrated on upmarket retail and hospitality instead. Manufacturing sites were found further downstream on the banks of the Walbrook. At the Bloomberg site, banks and ditches defined rectangular enclosures where metalworking workshops recycled and repaired armour and cavalry equipment.[60] Miscast and unfinished items show that the craftsmen were working on enamelled mounts, a military belt buckle, and armour including *lorica segmentata* fittings. A massive assemblage of highly fragmented ox bone in Neronian contexts nearby at The Walbrook may have been waste from boiling down carcasses for grease to treat harnesses and other leather goods.[61]

Developments at One Poultry were soon matched by building activities further along the west road. Timbers felled in AD 53 were found in quarries backfilled for house construction at 72–5 Cheapside, and occupation soon extended to 76–80 Newgate Street, 1 kilometre west of the town centre, where three phases of

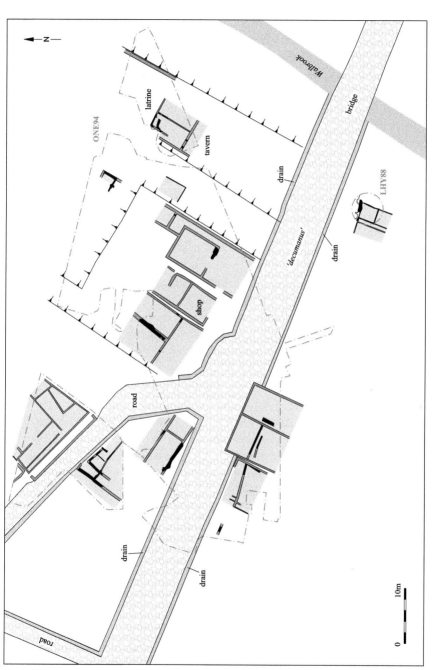

Fig. 7.3 Neronian shops and houses, at the approximate time of their destruction in the Boudican revolt, found at One Poultry (chiefly from ONE94, after Hill and Rowsome 2011 Fig. 57). Drawn by Justin Russell.

building preceded the destructions of AD 60/61.[62] These may have formed a secondary settlement cluster, possibly established before the expansion of c. AD 53. There is evidence of a pre-Boudican military presence nearby: finds from the opposite side of the road, at Paternoster Square, included military equipment and high-status kitchen waste of the sort produced by army supply trains.[63] These included a copper-alloy name-tag that labelled the property of Vitalis, son of Similis, an auxiliary solider with a family name common around Cologne and the lower Rhineland. This roadside settlement served busy traffic along Watling Street, likely to have included convoys of military supplies and troops. As a consequence of this suburban growth the roads into town were no longer cut off from adjacent land by large roadside ditches, but flanked by shops and workshops in a more permeable settlement landscape. A much smaller suburb of houses and workshops flanked the Colchester road leaving the town's east gate.[64] The north road, Ermine Street, destined to connect London with the Legionary fortress at Lincoln, attracted even fewer buildings although gravel surfaces and banked enclosures at Bishopsgate may have formed roadside paddocks outside the Neronian town.[65]

Whilst most roadside properties were built using techniques familiar from Roman Gaul and Germany, some roundhouses were built following insular traditions. At 76–80 Newgate Street, three wattle-and-daub roundhouses, up to 6.5 metres wide, were built in a backyard behind roadside buildings where they were burnt AD 60/61.[66] A similar building, about 5 metres wide, temporarily occupied a site along the 'decumanus' at Cheapside.[67] Others were found in a later Neronian enclosure at Gresham Street (Fig. 9.5), outside the east gate, and on the Southwark waterfront.[68] Some of these buildings housed small-scale industrial production following pre-Roman technologies. It has been suggested that they housed Britons drawn to London by opportunities for trade and social advancement, but who used indigenous styles of housing and pottery to set themselves apart.[69] Adam Rogers argues that it would be over simplistic to assume that circular buildings were inferior to rectangular ones because of their form.[70] It must be noted, however, that London's circular structures were smaller than most Iron Age roundhouses, better resembling the lesser outbuildings of the period.[71] They were placed within the curtilage of larger rectangular buildings in undistinguished suburbs, built from slight wattle-and-daub walls, and housed noxious industrial practices in cramped quarters. Whether through choice or circumstance their occupation generated finds assemblages that appear impoverished.[72] It therefore seems likely that London's roundhouses were the workshop-dwellings of an under-class with limited access to the technologies and resources that allowed alternative forms of self-representation. It is even possible that they had quartered British slaves, using 'native' architectures to set them apart from the dominant community.[73]

Craft technologies drawing on pre-Roman technologies were housed in other street-side buildings on the outskirts of town. A bowl furnace was associated with metalworking involving bronze and brass alloys at Arcadia Buildings, some 1.4 kilometres south of London Bridge, using crucibles made following pre-Roman Iron Age traditions.[74] These insular craft traditions were only evident on London's outer margins, and despite London's increased permeability some communities may have been excluded from the town centre. There is little evidence for post-Neronian continuities in the techniques that drew on pre-Roman traditions, although a late first-century timber roundhouse used for metalworking at Toppings Wharf in Southwark may be an exception.[75]

Other forms of industrial production also gravitated to the borderlands. A pottery kiln manufacturing flagons and tablewares of types previously made in southern Burgundy was established at Sugar Loaf Court on the Thames riverfront to the west the Walbrook, where misfired wasters were found near Neronian timber buildings.[76] An amphora made here carried a stamp that identified the potter Gaius Albucius. His wares are unevenly distributed through London, appearing commonly on sites with a military connection from AD 50/55. They account for almost half of all oxidized wares in pre-Boudican London, but disappeared soon after the revolt. The highest concentrations of these products were on Cornhill, along Fenchurch Street, and at One Poultry, perhaps reaching these sites by way of the forum. Early pottery production also took place at kilns on the eastern borders of town, where two hearths or clamp kilns were associated with wasters from oxidized ware manufactured in local clay. The products made here included a range of flagons.[77] A tile kiln was located near to Paternoster Row, south of the 'decumanus', where over-fired and misshapen wasters from the manufacture of bricks and roof-tiles were reused in pre-Boudican road foundations and associated buildings.[78]

Early Roman finds have also been made at Smithfield near St Bartholomew's church, 600 metres north-west of the Roman town. We know little about this area since opportunities for excavation have been limited, but the south-east corner of a large ditched enclosure was identified in 2016.[79] This consisted of a V-shaped ditch, 1.5 metres deep and 3.3 metres wide with an 'ankle breaker' slot at the base. This was perhaps a camp for troops in transit on the outskirts of town, although too little information is presently available to know when it was in operation. Whatever its purpose it appears to have attracted satellite occupation, including at least one house with a cement (opus signinum) floor.[80]

The new west-end

By c. AD 70, new residential districts had been laid out over the backlands behind the ribbon development west of the Walbrook, perhaps in planned urban expansion (Fig. 7.4). Two areas of housing can be identified: one to the north of the 'decumanus' (beneath Cheapside) and another to its south. These were laid out on slightly different orientations, resulting in a herringbone configuration against

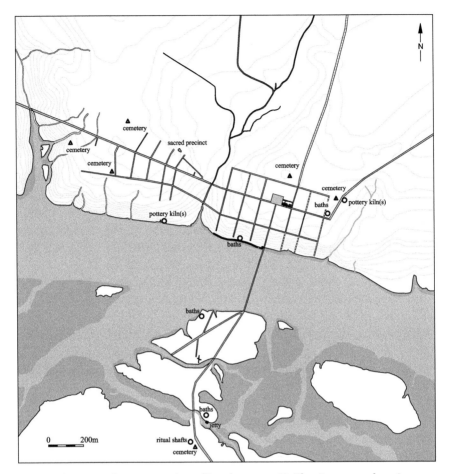

Fig. 7.4 A proposed reconstruction of London *c.* AD 60. The city was undergoing a busy phase of expansion in the year prior to the revolt. Drawn by Justin Russell.

the Cheapside spine. It is possible that the addition of these areas was decided on shortly prior to the Boudican revolt, although they were not fully developed until the following decade. The planned nature of this expansion is suggested by the topography between Cheapside and the Thames. This area was opened for development by a road along the line of modern Cannon Street. There has been some uncertainty over whether this was built before the Boudican revolt or in early Flavian renewal, but since it gave access to a pre-Flavian timber bridge over the Walbrook the earlier date is more likely.[81] Remains of this lower Walbrook crossing were found at the Bloomberg headquarters, where its 6.3-metre-wide foundations employed timbers felled after AD 48 but before AD 60.[82] The road eventually headed west towards a bridge over the Fleet, from which it gave access to Westminster.[83] Although most development on Ludgate Hill post-dated the revolt, some structures were destroyed in a fire tentatively dated AD 60/61.[84] These included a building at Watling Court with a raised plank-and-joist floor of a type associated with granaries. These developments established property boundaries followed in subsequent phases. The area covered by this new quarter extended westwards towards the site of St Paul's where excavations at 25 Cannon Street revealed timber buildings apparently built during the 50s.[85]

Development north of the '*decumanus*', between Cheapside and springs to the north, introduced a series of parallel north-south roads that defined new street blocks. Pottery suggests that the street closest to the Walbrook was laid out after *c.* AD 55, giving access to buildings destroyed in the Boudican revolt, and excavations at Milk Street gave a pre-Flavian date for the roadside ditch associated with another of these north-south streets.[86] The westernmost element of the new district was formed by a gravelled road at Foster Lane, tentatively identified as pre-Flavian and flanked by buildings destroyed in a fire thought to have been Boudican.[87]

Altogether these areas of settlement added about 12–16 hectares to London's extent. The low density of housing, and absence of phases of alteration before AD 60/61, suggests that this district was in its infancy when it burnt. This is consistent with a wider pattern of investment in London's infrastructure *c.* AD 60. Large oak baulks felled in the winter of AD 59/60 were deployed to create terraced platforms for new buildings at One Poultry, and contemporary timbers formed post-and-plank revetments along the waterfront.[88] A massive worked stone block abandoned on the Thames foreshore at the time of the revolt was perhaps destined to be an engaged pilaster section for use in a major public building, such as a ceremonial arch.[89] These strands of evidence show that London's infrastructure was undergoing improvement *c.* AD 60, probably following expansionary policies introduced by Suetonius Paullinus on his arrival as governor in AD 58.[90]

The London that emerged from this urban expansion comprised three distinct neighbourhoods: one either side of the Walbrook (Ludgate Hill and Cornhill) and another south of the Thames (Southwark). London's three areas of settlement had somewhat different origins and topographies, and it is tempting to see them as having housed differently organized communities. There is, however, little evidence—in either the architecture or patterns of consumption—of significant difference. Greater contrasts are found between sites within the urban core and those on its margins. For example, rubbish found on the borders of town contains fewer of the finds that mark high-status activities, such as tablewares, lamps, coins and writing implements.[91] A contrast has been drawn between pottery discarded at 76–80 Newgate Street, on the outskirts, and contemporary refuse behind the site later occupied by the forum at Leadenhall Court.[92] A higher proportion of storage jars at Newgate Street might reflect on a preference for serving food from jars brought to the meal, rather than using tablewares of dishes, bowls, and cups as preferred in the town centre.

This reconstruction of London's Claudio-Neronian geography shows how the orthogonally planned town sat at the core of a wider landscape. A regularly ordered city of streets and houses around the central hardstanding stood in contrast with different worlds beyond the city boundary. Here the presence of springs and rivers where gods were found and burial sites where ancestors could be commemorated dictated patterns of development and provided nodal points for an architectural armature that emerged with greater clarity in later building programmes. This later architecture offers proof that the ritual and political topographies shaped in the first years of London's existence remained fundamental to the developing townscape, establishing a framework that was manipulated and enhanced by later generations.

8

The Boudican revolt (*c.* AD 60–1)

On the eve of rebellion

London's destruction in AD 60–1 forms one of the more certain points in this narrative thanks to the attention given to the event by Roman historians. Archaeology shows that London was enjoying vigorous growth before disaster struck. It is argued here that London started life as a temporary encampment where the army of conquest waited on the emperor Claudius in the summer of AD 43, but that a more sustained use of this site waited until *c.* AD 48 when roads radiating from London Bridge were built. This first permanent bridgehead settlement may have been little more than an operational base, before town planning of *c.* AD 52 gave it a more urban character. New areas of housing were subsequently laid out west of the Walbrook as the settlement expanded. As a consequence London was Britain's most important town in AD 60, eclipsing earlier seats of regal power in Colchester, Chichester and Silchester. Estimates of London's extent vary from 39 to 45 hectares.[1] These assume, however, that areas west of the Walbrook and on Southwark's southern island were not settled until after the revolt. Since these districts were probably established a little earlier, the Neronian town may have spread over 60 hectares, making it twice the size of the contemporary Roman colony at Colchester. Hedley Swain and Tim Williams have reviewed a range of models to estimate population density, and concluded that the city was probably inhabited by around 10,000 people at the time of the revolt. If the city was more extensive than they assume, as argued here, then this total might sensibly be increased by a couple of thousand. If we think of London as a place of 10,000–15,000 souls, about the size of the modern Yorkshire town of Whitby, we are probably not far wrong.

The city was home to an immigrant community of soldiers and officials working for the provincial administration. Martin Pitts' analysis of patterns of consumption shows that Londoners shared tastes with people from Rome's German frontier, which differed from those of wealthy Britons and civilians of Gaul west of the Rhine.[2] The dress accessories and dinner services used in London mirrored those preferred in contemporary forts and supply-bases, indicating that elite fashion took inspiration from people whose careers were forged at Trier and in the Rhineland. This is where the legions involved in the conquest of Britain were formerly stationed and many auxiliary troops deployed in Britain were recruited. The emerging Romano-British towns at Silchester, Canterbury, and Chichester drew, instead, on a Gallo-Belgic repertoire that incorporated cultural preferences inherited from the kingdoms that preceded the Claudian invasion.

A feature of the new urban foundations was the adoption of 'Romanized' grey wares, produced at kilns operated by immigrant potters, to the exclusion of grog-tempered wares common elsewhere. Pottery assemblages show that London enjoyed more elaborate forms of food preparation and consumption than other places in Britain, receiving greater quantities of imports and Romano-British regional wares through its superior connections.[3] Many items—writing equipment, glass vessels, coins, lamps, toilet equipment, and continental-style adornment—witness preferences likely to have formed on the Rhine frontier. It would be misleading, however, to see these as marking a military identity distinct from a mercantile or civilian one. Business affairs were dominated by military supply and official contracts, and the mercantile community drew its members from veterans and the *familia* of government officials, blurring distinctions between soldiers, administrators, businessmen, and merchants. As a result Londoners dressed, ate, and drank in ways that mirrored behaviour in contemporary military establishments, and differently from the self-governing communities of Gaul and Britain.

London destroyed

London's bustling growth was halted when the city fell to Boudica's rebels. The razing of the town's earth-walled and thatch-roofed structures is marked by a distinctive black smear of charcoal beneath a band of bright-red burnt clay. The reading of this horizon is not without problems, since debris is often redeposited and other local fires can confuse the picture.[4] On many sites, however, the evidence is clear and the burning of *c.* AD 60/61 adds archaeological testimony to the history of the uprising.

According to Tacitus, writing some 50 years after the event, the death of the client king Prasutagus resulted in the Roman annexation of his Icenian territories in East Anglia.[5] His account describes how abuses directed at Icenian nobles, in which the widow Boudica was flogged and her daughters raped, accompanied the confiscation of estates and foreclosing of loans. These excesses, undertaken at the behest of the procurator Decianus Catus, sparked an armed uprising. Colchester was the first city assaulted by the rebels. Since the governor and his forces were away in north Wales, the colonists appealed to the procurator for help but he could only send 200 troops to their aid. Since these soldiers were within reach of Colchester they may well have been stationed with the procurator in London.[6] Whilst Colchester was sacked the governor, Gaius Suetonius Paullinus, moved his cavalry to London. This testifies to London's strategic importance, but Paullinus lacked sufficient strength to mount a defence and withdrew, reportedly 'taking those who would follow as part of his column; and those whom the weakness of sex, frailty of age, or reluctance to leave their homes remained within the town were overwhelmed by the enemy…massacred, hanged, burned and crucified with a headlong fury'.[7]

Excavations in the City show that few buildings escaped the flames. Southwark was also damaged, and fire debris has been traced from London Bridge along Borough High Street.[8] This destruction is largely restricted to the northern island, and Neronian buildings to the south may have survived unscathed, but shows that the Thames failed to halt the rebels. Either there was no attempt to defend the river crossing, or the rebellion raised support on the south bank. Burnt deposits of this approximate date have also been found in Putney, Brentford, and Staines, possibly marking a path of destruction towards, but not necessarily reaching, the town at Silchester.[9]

London's fire horizon helps to date the revolt. Tacitus placed its outbreak in AD 61 but the events he described took place over 2 years, and political appointments made in the rebellion's aftermath are more consistent with an uprising starting in AD 60. This is the chronology preferred by most scholars, although doubts remain.[10] Tacitus provides sufficient contextual information for us to know that the revolt started around March, after the start of the campaign season but before the planting of crops.[11] If we allow time for news to reach Paullinus in north Wales, and for him to reach London, the evacuation of London can hardly have occurred before May. This establishes an historical context for dendrochronological dates obtained from London's timber structures. As already noted, the period c. AD 60 witnessed considerable investment in London's urban infrastructure, possibly including the setting out of a new district west of the Walbrook. Dendrochronological evidence establishes that some new buildings were not built before AD 60, and would have been only a few months old if destroyed that summer. It is tempting to suggest that this investment was made in preparation for Paullinus' campaigns in Wales, perhaps contributing to the financial squeeze that provoked the revolt.

We can also draw on dendrochronological dating to show that post-war rebuilding was in progress by the summer of AD 62. One of the earliest post-revolt constructions was a sump cut into fire debris at One Poultry using wood felled in the winter of AD 61–2, whilst timbers felled in AD 62 were used in road construction at Drapers' Gardens.[12] These imply that materials were being procured for re-building in the winter of AD 61/62. This is consistent with a chronology in which Paullinus defeated the main rebel army in the summer of AD 60 before engaging in punitive actions later that season. Subsequent to this a new procurator, Classicianus, replaced Decianus Catus and a new governor, Petronius Turpilianus, replaced Paullinus.[13] These political changes were finalized in the spring or summer of AD 61 and the woods around London were busy with loggers the following winter. The rebuilding of London can therefore be seen as an early action of the new regime, started soon after the crisis passed. The effectiveness of this restoration is demonstrated by a contract drawn up for provisions to be transported to London from Verulamium dated 21 October AD 62, found at the Bloomberg headquarters.[14]

The status of London in AD 60

In AD 60, London was evidently a town. Most Roman communities had their status defined by charter, describing a legal relationship with Rome and establishing civil administrations with rights and responsibilities.[15] The principal chartered towns were *coloniae* and *municipia*, of which the former offered greater legal advantage. Lesser self-governing communities were recognized as *civitates*, or peoples, who retained 'native' administrative structures. In Romano-British scholarship the centres of these communities are generally referred to as civitas capitals.[16] These political instruments made it possible to appoint officials, raise taxes, enforce laws, and implement decisions. Places that lacked formal recognition were usually ruled from other places that held it.

We do not know how early Roman London was governed. Important questions are raised by Tacitus' description of the Boudican revolt where we are told that London wasn't distinguished by the name of colony (*cognomento quidem coloniae non insigne*), but famed for an abundance of dealers and supplies (*sed copia negotiatorum et commeatuum maxime celebre*).[17] This last phrase can be translated as 'large numbers of merchants and great quantities of merchandise', but this misleadingly evokes an image of retail trade. Merchants were more usually termed *mercator*, whilst the noun *negotiator* described civilians concerned with organizing and financing long distance shipments. Furthermore, the term *commeatus* was associated with food supplies, and regularly used of military provisions.[18] The implication of the passage is that London was a hub for supplies needed by the Roman administration and housed the many businessmen involved. It was sufficiently unusual in this regard to warrant the description provided by Tacitus, which implies that local land-owning classes who usually controlled civic affairs were either absent or unimportant.

Although Tacitus describes the sacking of Colchester, London, and Verulamium, other sources mention only two cities as having been destroyed in the revolt.[19] This offers indirect confirmation that London lacked civic status, distinguishing it from the *municipium* at *Verulamium* and the colony at Colchester. London also differed by virtue of the fact that it had not been a seat of pre-Roman power. The establishment of a colony at Colchester was, in part, a strategic response to the need to control newly conquered peoples. It had been an important centre of pre-Roman political authority, and the governor, Scapula, needed to maintain control of this Catuvellaunian capital whilst releasing troops for redeployment elsewhere.[20] The settlement of a veteran colony was therefore politically expedient, putting former soldiers where they were most useful. This foundation might have drawn fully on the available pool of veterans. Similarly, the existence of a powerful pre-Roman community at Verulamium may have encouraged the formalization of a relationship with Rome through the grant of a city charter. The arrangements made for these other cities were less necessary at London.

As Martin Millett has explained, London was an anomalous site: not a formal colonial or chartered settlement, but nor a self-governing civitas capital of the sort developed elsewhere in Roman Britain.[21] This may be explained by London's status as a foundation populated without recourse to pre-existing communities or colonial settlers. The provincial authorities may have found advantage in arrangements that did not require surrender of political control. As Guy de la Bédoyère has observed the absence of legal status does not mean that there was no formal intent behind the foundation.[22] The archaeological evidence identifies a series of enhancements of transport infrastructure at times when forward campaigns were planned by incoming administrations. In recognizing that London was unlikely to have built on the initiative of local elites, Millett has suggested that it was deliberately created to function as an entrepôt for the developing province. Since he finds no evidence that Roman state had a policy of creating such towns, in line with the minimalist view on the role of the Roman state advanced by Moses Finley (above p. 29), he prefers to see London as the creation of enterprising traders from other provinces. This leaves us to speculate as to how and why such an association might have come together, how coordinated programmes of investment in London's infrastructure would have been achieved by such agents, and how successful their venture might have been without the patronage and protection of the Roman provincial administration. Christopher Fuhrmann has usefully challenged the scholarly consensus that imperial government was essentially passive, and depended on the contribution of local elite society because it lacked the bureaucratic instruments and institutions that allowed direct control.[23] Drawing on the evidence of Roman policing he describes a powerful, organized, and avaricious state. David Mattingly has similarly emphasized the exploitative nature of Roman imperial power and the large-scale impact of the state.[24] In the light of these arguments, and since minimalist views of the Roman state have been called into question, it is timely to reassess the role of the provincial government in making and ruling London.

The government of London

Two key officials ruled Neronian Britain: the governor and the procurator. Britons are supposed, in Tacitus' account, to have complained of this arrangement because 'we used to have our kings one at a time, but now two are imposed, with a governor to savage our lives, a procurator for our goods. Whether the two are in concord or discord with one another, it's equally deadly for their subjects, as both add insult to injury—the governor with his bands of centurions, the procurator with his slaves'.[25] The governor (*legatus Augusti pro praetore*) held supreme military and juridical authority on behalf of the emperor, serving terms that usually lasted 3 or 4 years. He commanded the armies stationed in Britain and often campaigned from spring to autumn. Soldiers detached from active forces served clerical, administrative, and policing duties within the governor's office (*officium*). Troops also sometimes worked on construction and engineering projects where these served the interests of the provincial government, as described in the letters of Pliny, although cities were expected to draw on their own resources for civic building programmes.[26]

The procurator (*procurator Augusti*) was a salaried official employed by the emperor to manage his wide-ranging interests and provincial finances. Many rose to this position after service as equestrian officers in command of auxiliary regiments. The procurator's duties involved raising revenue through taxes and tolls, and profitably managing the imperial property acquired as spoils of war and in confiscations and inheritances. The procurator drew on these resources to supply and pay imperial forces, and deliver imperial building programmes.[27] He was supported by a bureaucracy of freedmen and slaves from the imperial household, known collectively as *Caesariani*, and small contingents of troops detached from the governor's command. The events of the Boudican rebellion suggest that the procurator was already based in London at this time. This would explain how Decianus Catus was near enough at hand to be able to send a small contingent of men to the aid of the colonists in Colchester.[28] This finds confirmation in the fact that Catus' successor in post, Classicianus, was buried in London where his tombstone has been found (p. 105). We have already noted that if London occupied the redundant site of a military encampment it would have been built on captured lands, and as such been imperial property managed by the procurator. Since London was not recognized as a self-governing chartered city it may have remained imperial property, a situation which would have facilitated the implementation of sweeping changes such as those described in Chapter 7.

From at least AD 52, and perhaps as early as AD 48, London was a major port and financial centre. This made it the most convenient place for the procurator to establish his place of business, and hence David Mattingly's suggestion that he was housed in the high-status building complex at Winchester Palace (p. 79). The procurator had a clear incentive to develop infrastructure to speed the passage of goods through London's port. His responsibility for military supply would have brought him into a close working relationship with the private shippers and businessmen acting as middlemen in this exercise, as well as with those who won contracts to manage taxes, mines and estates under his jurisdiction. This business community may have been prevailed upon to take responsibility for some of the actions needed to run the city.

Whilst there is a strong case for placing the procurator in London before the revolt, there is greater uncertainty over whether the governor was also seated here. These two commands overlapped but could operate from different cities.[29] Elements of the provincial administration, most notably the provincial council and imperial cult, were initially established in the pre-Roman capital of the defeated kingdom at Colchester, but we don't know if this caused the governor to take up an official residence there.[30] London was the more convenient site, and officers serving with the governor were based here before the end of the century.[31] London was destined to house the governor's main palace (*praetorium*), and it may have sometimes been the seat of both procurator and governor before the revolt.

The governor and procurator held distinct and competing commands, and the geography of early London might have been engineered to accommodate their different spheres of influence. We have noted that the elite residence at Winchester Palace might have housed the imperial procurator, and it has long been speculated that a high-status building found near Cannon Street station on the north bank was the governor's palace.[32] Both identifications are highly speculative, but there is an attractive symmetry to the idea that these rival commands occupied riverside palaces on opposite banks of the Thames, foreshadowing the fraught relationship between County Hall and the Palace of Westminster in the 1970s. Differences in the character of the Roman settlements north and south of the river might have followed from such an arrangement. It is also the case that the relocation of different offices of the provincial administration might have been a spur to London's urban expansion and account for the addition of new areas of planned settlement *c.* AD 52 and *c.* AD 60.

In the first century, London became the site from which Britain was ruled. It is not certain that this was the case *c.* AD 60, and most scholars are more comfortable seeing it as a later promotion.[33] Whatever the political geography, this doesn't tell us how affairs within London were governed. Most Roman cities depended on a town council (*ordo decurionum*) to appoint magistrates needed to supervise markets, raise taxes, maintain civic buildings, and supervise religious matters. Where did London find its magistrates? It is widely assumed that it must have had a town council, but there is no evidence for the existence of such a body.[34] John Mann suggested that London might instead have remained a *vicus*, a subsidiary administrative district perhaps nominally within the territory of the Cantiaci.[35] We know that a vicus in London was later able to take responsibility for building activities: an inscription found in Budge Row in 1854 commemorated the restoration of a shrine to the mother Goddesses by the district (*vicinia*) at its own expense.[36] A lead sheet found at Billingsgate Lorry Park in 1984 also mentions a 'Vico Iovio' (vicus of Jupiter), although this need not have been a place in

London.[37] It is possible to imagine a city divided between separate vici: perhaps providing separate district administrations for Southwark, the Cornhill settlement, and Ludgate Hill. Mann's suggestion has been criticized, however, for underestimating the legal complexities of the Roman world.[38] Those exercising political authority in a place as important as London are unlikely to have been left within the jurisdiction of a native *civitates*, such as the *Cantiaci* whose administrative centre was found at Canterbury. London is more likely to have been an autonomous community, even if it drew on territory carved from Kentish lands.

London's immigrant community may have included a sufficient body of resident Roman citizens to form a responsible authority (a *conventus civium Romanorum*). It has long been argued that such an arrangement would explain the absence of a chartered settlement.[39] Roger Wilson has questioned this conclusion on the basis that we only know the arrangement to have been adopted in places where the Roman population needed separate juridical status from a non-citizen community, which was unlikely to have been the case at London.[40] Harvey Sheldon has alternatively proposed that London may have been excused the legal instruments normally deployed for the governance of urban communities, leaving the emperor's representatives to rule directly through appointed subordinates.[41] Roman political systems were designed to serve aristocratic interests, but these were not a natural or necessary fit for Roman London where the military administration was probably paramount. The absence of a local aristocracy of consequence meant that there was no pressing need to use civic office as a vehicle for the promotion of political careers and social status. More politically convenient options were available. We have no evidence for the existence of a town council in early Roman London, and it is possible to question if one had ever existed. Governors were able to appoint an official (*praefectus civitatis*) to take charge of local government, and could place areas under the military command of a 'centurion of the region' (*centurio regionalius*).[42] The physical presence of governor or procurator in London might have made it unnecessary, however, to delegate powers in this fashion. The governor's intervention in managing London's affairs is indicated by the record of a legal judgement made on 22 October AD 76, preserved amongst the writing tablets found at the Bloomberg headquarters.[43] The judge opened his decision by declaring that he had been given this responsibility by the emperor. As Roger Tomlin has explained, the appointment would have been made by the governor or his representative. In chartered towns, judges were appointed by the annually elected city magistrates, but the intervention of the governor in this case suggests that London lacked these instruments of self-government in AD 76.

London may have remained imperial property, where the governor ruled using his authority, office, and patronage to have others undertake duties that elsewhere fell to city magistrates and officials. Londoners might therefore have found themselves in a similar legal situation to peasants who farmed imperial estates, who lacked access to traditional organs of municipal organization but relied instead on a direct right of appeal to the emperor.[44] This may have given rise to a situation in which parallel forms of political association would flourish (below p. 151). The truth is that we don't have enough evidence to know how London was governed, and in any case the arrangements would have changed through time. Notwithstanding such uncertainty, power ultimately resided with the emperor's representatives: the governor and procurator. These officials probably took the decisions that resulted in the foundation of London. They would have been equally important in post-war reconstruction, to which attention now turns.

9

Post-war reconstruction (*c.* AD 61–70)

Military reoccupation

The city destroyed by British rebels was swiftly restored in a military reoccupation (Fig. 9.1). Excavations at Plantation Place revealed the north-east corner of a small fort built over the town's ruins between the forum and east gate (Figs. 9.2

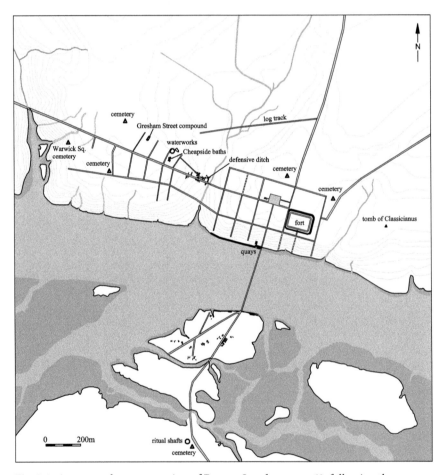

Fig. 9.1 A proposed reconstruction of Roman London *c.* AD 63, following the military reoccupation of the city after the revolt. Drawn by Justin Russell.

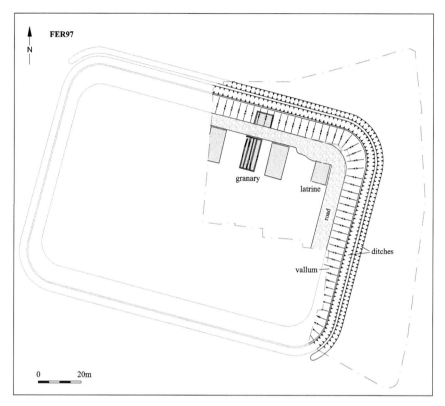

Fig. 9.2 The Neronian fort at Plantation Place (FER97: after Dunwoodie *et al.* 2017). Drawn by Justin Russell.

and 9.3). A 7-metre-wide, turf-fronted, mudbrick rampart was raised over a lattice of reused burnt timbers set behind a pair of 3-metre-wide ditches.[1] An *intervallum* road followed the inside of the defences, giving access to timber buildings that may have included a cookhouse, latrine and granary. No barracks were found, implying that the soldiers lived in tents. A reconstruction based on local topography suggests that the fort occupied an area of about one hectare, making it large enough for a 480-strong cohort.

Texts from the Bloomberg headquarters mention personnel drawn from cohorts of Nervians, Vangiones, and Lingones that included part-mounted units (*equitatae*), which are likely to have been amongst the auxiliary reinforcements that Tacitus tells us came to Britain from Germany in AD 61.[2] One document was addressed to Classicus, prefect of the Sixth Cohort of Nervii, who is almost certainly the Treveran noble who commanded a cavalry unit in the Batavian revolt of AD 70.[3] Classicus was a kinsman of Britain's new imperial procurator, Julius Classicianus, whose patronage may have helped him secure his commission. The presence of these troops accounts for the fact that items of military equipment are

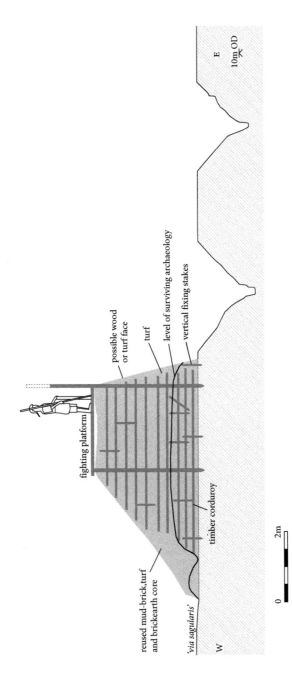

Fig. 9.3 Section through the Neronian fort defences (adapted from Dunwoodie *et al.* 2017 and reproduced by kind permission of Museum of London Archaeology).

more common in assemblages formed after the revolt, and include armour, military dress and cavalry harness fittings from sites within the fort and on the banks of the Walbrook.[4]

Post-revolt engineering also involved the construction of a timber corduroy across the upper Walbrook valley using massive close-set cleft oak logs felled in the spring and winter of AD 62.[5] This was built following British, not Roman, woodworking traditions, suggesting the involvement of a contingent of allies or captive labour. It may have enabled troops and supplies to move between Watling Street and Ermine Street without entering town. In contrast, Watling Street was restored by Roman-trained engineers who re-laid roadside drains using timbers felled in the winter of AD 61/62, and a timber boardwalk was built besides the southern Walbrook crossing using timber felled the following year.[6] A V-shaped ditch dug at One Poultry was perhaps a defensive outwork protecting the bridge. Facilities around the forum were also replaced after the revolt. Excavations in Lombard Street revealed the tile-capped masonry foundations of a substantial earth-walled building that preceded the construction of the Flavian forum.[7] Masonry foundations were unusual in town houses at this time, and this was probably a public building replacing earlier storage and office facilities.

Building the port

The most significant restoration project took place along the waterfront, where massive Neronian quays were built in sections upriver from London Bridge to the mouth of the Walbrook.[8] The earliest section was found at Regis House where enormous squared oak beams, up to 8.2 metres long, were stacked 2 metres high to form boxes extending onto the foreshore that were filled with rubbish and earth to create a riverside terrace (Fig. 9.4). Several of the timbers were felled in the winter of AD 63-4, presumably for building in the spring of AD 64. The need to set base timbers over the submerged foreshore makes it likely that the lowest tier was laid during the low spring tides of March AD 64.

The builders used a standardized range of thin bladed tools to prepare the timbers, leaving marks consistent with the use of military *dolabra* axe-picks. A stamp branded onto the end of the longest quay timber probably reads TRAECAVG, suggesting the involvement of a Thracian *cohors* or *ala*.[9] These works drew on skills and resources usually only available to military engineers, perhaps provided by units brought to London after the revolt. According to Gustav Milne some may have been attached to the Roman fleet, the *Classis Britannica*, thought responsible for building similar facilities at Dover.[10] Finds from the infill of the quay included fragments of scale armour (*lorica squamata*) and leather tents from earlier military activity. Several tent panels were discarded whole without cutting and

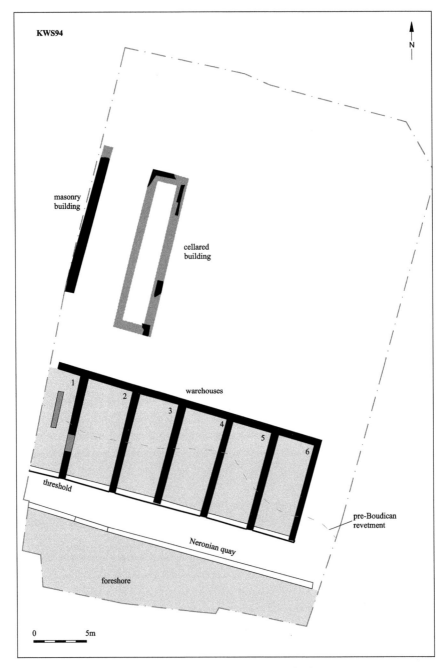

Fig. 9.4 The Neronian waterfront quays and warehouses built *c.* AD 63 at Regis House (KWS 94: after Brigham 1998). Drawn by Justin Russell.

recycling, despite areas of good leather surviving.[11] This profligacy is characteristic of assemblages formed during garrison redeployment.

The new quays changed the way in which the port operated. Goods had previously been manhandled across temporary jetties and gangways onto waggons and beasts of burden, but the new quays brought transports within reach of fixed cranes capable of managing enormous loads.[12] Larger ocean-going vessels would still have anchored in mid-stream for unloading by flat-bottomed lighters that beached on the foreshore. Stevedores gained dry access over multiple gangways uninterrupted by the changing tide. In addition to speeding goods handling, warehouses reduced the risk of theft, spoilage, and loss. Their presence made it easier to keep the harbour busy between sailings, and road traffic could be staggered to reduce congestion. This transformed the ability of the port authorities to manage shipments, ensuring that consignments could be properly processed and port dues paid.

This begs the question of why such facilities were not built earlier. The likely explanation is that London lacked access to sufficient resources—skilled engineers, construction manpower, and supplies of timber—for the undertaking. London may have been strategically important before the revolt, but troops and military engineers were deployed elsewhere. The soldiers brought to London in the post-revolt reassertion of Roman authority could, however, be assigned to such tasks when not engaged in policing operations. There are many reasons to suspect a direct military involvement in the construction of London's Neronian port, and the scale and timing of the building exercise makes it difficult to see this as the product of private or civic enterprise.[13]

Warehouses were built behind the quays. A large Neronian masonry building, built of ragstone with brick string-courses, at Regis House contained at least four, later six, rectangular bays 4.5 metres wide and 10 metres long. These opened onto the wharf through shuttered openings or wide folding doors.[14] This row of open-fronted units provided similar facilities to those around Roman marketplaces and *fora*. The use of stone as a building material, still rare in London, created secure storage for high value goods. One bay contained a succession of small furnaces where a glassworker made luxury items that included faience melon beads, twisted stirring rods, free-blown bottles, and drinking vessels. Large masonry buildings behind the quays included warehouses and granaries, one dendrochronology dated AD 66–8.[15] Although we suspect that the army built London's port infrastructure, these buildings might have served private shippers and guilds. The principal Neronian quays were built upriver of London Bridge, an area favoured for supplies directed west along Watling Street. The arrangement meant that tall-masted ships arriving up the Thames would have had to cross the line of the bridge, perhaps by way of a central drawbridge. It is not certain that a fixed crossing was maintained, but a bridge would have better served the needs of cross-river traffic and timber structures antedating AD 63 have tentatively been identified as a bridge abutment.[16]

The town restored

Large wells equipped with sophisticated water-lifting machines were installed on the hillside west of the Walbrook (Fig. 12.3, p. 154).[17] The earliest was 2.6 metres square and 5 metres deep, lined with oak and cross-braced timbers felled in AD 63. Machinery found at its base consisted of boxes of hollowed-out oak joined in a continuous chain by iron links that had been attached to a gear system, that would have been driven by a human or animal powered treadmill to raise water to a point from which it could gravity feed a piped water supply. The technological ambition of this advanced engineering and the entailment of operational labour show that these waterworks met an important need, perhaps supplying the bath-house found at Cheapside in 1952.[18] Although this bathhouse is poorly dated its flint foundations are of an early type, and tiles from a heating system were found in a Neronian assemblage nearby at Bow Bells House. In its primary phase these baths contained three principal rooms arranged in a 21.6-metre-long row. Entrance was through a cold room (*frigidarium*) which had red-painted walls and a herringbone tile pavement and was furnished with a small cold-water plunge bath. The succeeding warm room (*tepidarium*) was heated by a hypocaust, as was the apsidal-ended hot room (*caldarium*) at the end of the range. This had a hot-water bath to one side. A fragment of volcanic pumice used in the baths was found nearby.[19] The facility may have served soldiers quartered in the district west of the Walbrook, perhaps offering thermal healing for visitors to the adjacent sacred precinct.[20]

Post-fire redevelopment generally respected property boundaries established in the 50s, indicating that land interests were registered and respected. The build-ings followed earlier preferences for rapidly built timber-framed construction and timbers reused in later constructions at the Bloomberg headquarters show that some had walls only 2 metres high but included cramped loft accommoda-tion under a wooden shingle roof.[21] Not all of London was restored. Only three out of thirteen properties were quickly replaced at One Poultry, and the presence of Flavian wares in post-Boudican dumps suggests that rebuilding was sometimes delayed by a decade.[22] A reduced population pressure may account for the con-version of a building plot into a market garden at Whittington Avenue.[23] Some of those who had lived in London before AD 60 never returned, and the civilian community may have shrunk. The potter responsible for making finewares near Sugar Loaf Court may have been amongst the missing, since his production wasn't resumed.[24] Elsewhere new potters set up in business: a kiln dated *c.* AD 60–70 was found in a yard behind buildings within the suburb along the Silchester

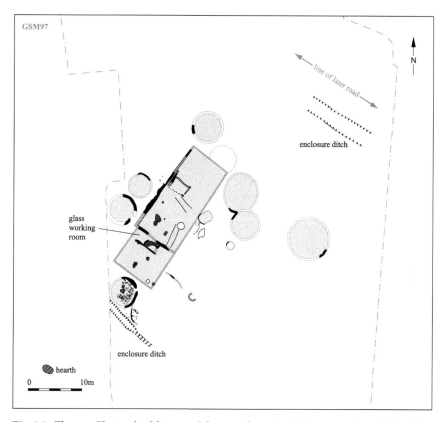

Fig. 9.5 The pre-Flavian buildings and features found at 10 Gresham Street (GSM97). The evidence presented here may belong to more than one phase of construction, but appears to illustrate a rectangular structure surrounded by roundhouses and pens within an enclosure delimited by boundary ditches. Hearths within the main building were associated with debris from glass-bead manufacture following pre-conquest tradition (after Casson *et al.* 2015). Drawn by Justin Russell.

road at 1 New Change.[25] Luxury imports were in shorter supply for a while, suggesting that the new harbour was not used to bring such goods for local consumption.[26]

An unusual ditched compound, some 50 metres across, was established on the north-west margins of town at 10 Gresham Street (Fig. 9.5).[27] A rectangular timber building set in the middle of the enclosure was surrounded by short-lived roundhouses, sheds and animal-pens. Up to fourteen circular buildings were identified, some with south-east facing entrances and central hearths. The architecture was consistent with British rather than Roman building traditions, similar to that found on the fringes of the settlement before the revolt (above p. 82). A narrow room inside the rectangular building was used as a workshop for the manufacture of glass beads in a late Iron Age British tradition, as indicated by the presence of hearths and waste materials. The site contained less pottery than typical for the time, with assemblages dominated by jars and storage vessels. Unlike other suburban developments, these buildings were not placed alongside a main road, but along a route not metalled until the Flavian period. This was a satellite site, tucked beyond the urban margins, occupied by a community that represented itself differently to people within town. The precinct and its houses were cleared away within a decade of its construction, adding to the impression that insular traditions of housing were restricted to marginal and transient communities. It is possible to imagine a situation in which some of the 'native' workforce involved in laying the log causeway across the Walbrook in AD 62 was housed in this discretely located compound.

The construction of new roads, quays and waterworks was compressed into the years when London was occupied by a military garrison. The forces stationed in Britain were subsequently reduced by redeployments to quell an uprising in Gaul in AD 66/67, and others left the province to participate in the civil wars following Nero's deposition.[28] As a consequence the number of soldiers serving in Britain almost halved between AD 65 and AD 69, probably involving the evacuation of the auxiliary forces stationed in London.

The first cemeteries

Several small burial grounds were placed on the outskirts of the Claudio-Neronian city, following Roman custom in removing the dead beyond the city limits.[29] Roman funerals at this time usually involved a ceremonial procession to the site of a pyre, where orations and offerings were made. The act of burning was the primary rite, using fire to counteract the polluting effects of death. The collection and burial of cremated remains and pyre debris was a secondary activity, resulting in the interment of ashes within containers such as pottery vessels and wooden caskets. London's principal early cemeteries were in small suburban plots set back from main roads on prominent sites. Two unurned cremation graves containing redeposited pyre debris were found outside the likely site of the town's east gate on the road to Colchester at 60–3 Fenchurch Street.[30] A cemetery on the other side of this road was found at the corner of Fenchurch Street and Billiter Street where cremations were buried in timber cists, one with a Purbeck marble cover and one in a Spanish amphora.[31] Another small cremation cemetery was located at Leadenhall Court, beneath the later basilica. Five vessels, dated no earlier than the late 50s, one of which contained cremated bone, were set into the fills of a disused quarry.[32] A single urned cremation of similar date found north of the 'decumanus' at Lime Street was thought to have been a foundation deposit.[33] These burials were surprisingly close to the town centre and inside the limits of the presumed Claudian defensive enclosure. This may indicate that the town's northern boundary had moved inside its earlier line in post-Boudican contraction, or that interments were tolerated within the settlement because of London's ambiguous status.

Three more cemeteries have been identified west of the town on Ludgate Hill: at St Martin's le Grand, St Paul's Cathedral, and Warwick Square.[34] The most important was discovered in 1880 during building works at Warwick Square, near the Old Bailey (Fig. 9.6).[35] It occupied an area little more than 12 metres across, overlooking the river Fleet about 75 metres south of the 'decumanus'. The standout discovery was a two-handled urn, some 385 millimetres high, carved from Egyptian porphyry into a shape like a soup tureen, following the perfect proportions of Pythagorean geometry. Simona Perna has shown how this exclusive type of urn, the only one of its kind ever found in Britain, had connections to the Julio-Claudian imperial family and household.[36] It contained the cremated remains of an adult male, around 30 years old, and a single Claudian coin. It was placed near the centre of the graveyard and may have been the burial around which the cemetery formed. A lead cinerary canister containing a two-handled glass jar full of calcined bones was buried nearby.[37] The canister was stamped with the repeated relief of a charioteer racing his quadriga, identified with Helios/Sol. Borrowing from Platonic philosophy, the image of this celestial charioteer may have served as a metaphor for the ever-moving eternal soul.[38] In the light of the Egyptian origins of the adjacent porphyry urn, it might be significant that Helios was held in special veneration in Hellenistic Egypt.[39] The cemetery contained two other important lead ossuaria. One was decorated with an eight-rayed star, cast on the base, which is likely to have been a solar symbol, whilst the other had four pairs of concentric circles that might denote Plato's divine soul circling the cosmos. This group of burials incorporated cultural and philosophical references drawn from the Hellenistic east, at a time when such ideas were highly influential in imperial ideology. They would have carried meaning to the educated elite amongst the highest officials and businessmen in Britain. Since the porphyry urn contained the ashes a person of the very highest rank it is worth passing mention that the governor Ostorius Scapula died in Britain in AD 52, and inherited a connection with Egypt from the time of his father's prefecture there.[40] The cemetery also contained several ceramic cinerary urns, glass vessels, and a tile lined grave or cist. In 1966 a re-examination of the site by Peter Marsden found ashes from the double burial of an adult and child in an amphora with two lamps to provide light for the soul.[41]

London's most famous Roman tomb stood on the other side of town, on Tower Hill (Fig. 9.7). This was the monument to the imperial procurator Julius Alpinus Classicianus, the stonework from which was reused in the foundations of a late Roman tower added to the town wall at Trinity Square.[42] Classicianus succeeded Decianus Catus and died in office c. AD 65 after playing an important part in London's restoration.[43] His funerary monument was an imposing free-standing

Fig 1. Glass.

Fig. 3. Cast Lead.

Fig 2. Cast Lead.

Fig 4.

Stone.

Fig 5.

C.F.Kell Lith

OBJECTS FOUND NEAR WARWICK SQUARE LONDON, 1881.

Fig. 9.6 Claudio-Neronian cinerary urns found in excavations at Warwick Square in 1881. These included a rare Egyptian porphyry vessel (bottom right), decorated lead canisters, and glass jars of which one is illustrated (© The Society of Antiquaries of London, and reproduced from Tylor 1884 by kind permission of Cambridge University Press).

DIS
MANIBVS
CIVLGFFABALPINICLASSICIANI
....
....
PROCPROVINCBRITANN
IVLIAINDIFILIAPACATAINDVTA
VXOR

Fig. 9.7 A reconstruction of the tomb of the imperial procurator C. Julius Classicianus (drawn by Richard Grasby and reproduced by kind permission of the Centre for the Study of Ancient Documents, Oxford).

altar-shaped structure on a high plinth, of a type known around Trier. The stone was set up by his wife, Julia Pacata, the daughter of Indus a Treveran aristocrat with pro-Roman sympathies. From the evidence of his name it seems likely that Classicianus came from the same region.

A grave found at Harper Road in Southwark during a training excavation in 1979 presents a contrasting example of Neronian burial practice (Fig. 9.8).[44] The body was interred in a wooden coffin at a time when cremation was preferred. It may have been located within an enclosure on slightly higher ground beside Watling Street, about 300 metres beyond the possible sanctuary site on the Southwark borders. Study of the skeletal remains indicates that the deceased was a dark haired and brown eyed woman, physically female but with male

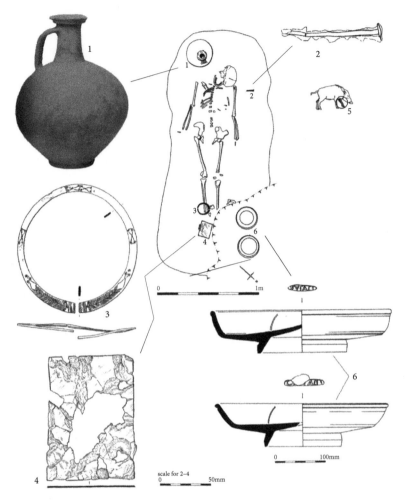

Fig. 9.8 The Neronian burial found at Harper Road, Southwark in 1979 containing the body of a woman with grave goods that included a mirror and unusual torc (HR77/HR79: adapted from Cotton 2000 and reproduced by kind permission of Museum of London Archaeology).

chromosomes. She was of northern European ancestry, grew up in Britain and died in her twenties or thirties. She was buried with vessels typical of Roman-style dining manufactured *c.* AD 50–65: a flagon was set by her head and Samian dishes at her feet. The grave also contained a rectangular bronze mirror, perhaps imported from Italy, and a broken bronze penannular neck ring, or torc. These were precious items. Mirrors are occasionally found in late Iron Age burials in Britain, alluding to other realms, appearance and fertility.[45] The torc was an even more curious item. It was decorated with motifs that schematized peacock feathers: widely deployed as a symbol of immortality. Similar decorations were used on torcs found at Baldock in Hertfordshire, and aspects of the design find parallel in a regionally distributed type of *armillae* that Nina Crummy suggests were used as battle honours gained from service in the Roman army in Britain.[46] The design of this torc might, therefore, have contained references to military honour won at the time of the Roman conquest. Since the deceased had been born in Britain prior to the conquest, and was buried with high-status goods that drew on both British and Roman forms of social display, she may have belonged to a pre-Roman aristocracy. Her burial describes an accommodation with Roman power whilst retaining aspects of an identity formed prior to the invasion. This would have made her an unusual figure in an immigrant community where native identities were not widely evident. It has already been argued that pre-Roman farmsteads in Bermondsey and Southwark may have survived the conquest to become part of the Roman topography south of the river, and a case can be made for seeing the *dolabra* sheath found at 15–23 Southwark Street as a pre-conquest import obtained from service in the Roman army. The evidence of the Harper Road burial can be read in similar fashion. The location, character, and date of this grave are in keeping with what might be expected for the burial of someone native to one of these local settlements.

London's first burials show remarkable diversity. East of the city lay the imposing tomb of the Gallic nobleman who had served as imperial procurator. Another elevated cemetery west of town contained the cinerary urns of people from the highest ranks of the administration vaunting philosophical and cultural attachments to the Hellenistic east. The southern approaches to town were instead dominated by the resting place of someone connected to the pre-Roman aristocracy, drawing on the Gallo-Roman culture that prevailed prior to the conquest perhaps coloured by military service within the Roman army. These different burials commanded the main routes into London, embedding it within a landscape of Roman power.

Irregular burials

These important individuals, celebrated in death through the attention paid to their burial, can be contrasted with other communities of dead. Several irregular and disturbed inhumations have been found on the borders of early Roman London. These include corpses placed in unusual positions, usually prone or flexed, dispersed skeletal material, and burials of immature individuals. Some inhumations have also been found in unusual contexts, such as ditches and pits, rather than graves. These tend to be found close to the main roads into town. Excavations at Paternoster Square revealed two pre-Flavian skeletons in a ditch perpendicular to the '*decumanus*' on Ludgate Hill.[47] One was laid prone and the other on its side, along with a dead dog and rubbish. On the other side of town, a man buried in the ditch flanking the Colchester road before A D 60–1 had a girl's cranium placed over his pelvis.[48]

At Regis House, on the waterfront beside London Bridge, disturbed human remains were incorporated into harbour construction in A D 64.[49] Excavations by Gerald Dunning recovered part of the skull of a middle-aged man and the right arm and left humerus of another individual. These bones hadn't moved far, since the arm retained its articulation. Other body-parts found in 1995–6 included three crania, and a femur with cut marks suggestive of tool or weapon injury. Bruce Watson and Trevor Brigham suggest that these were victims of the Boudican revolt whose unburied remains were incorporated in waste material. Human remains of similar date, including an intact cranium, were found in waterside dumps at the Bloomberg site.[50] Here too the body parts were found amidst rubbish next to a river, close to a bridge approaching the site of a town gate. Concentrations of irregular burials have also been identified on the boundaries of sacred precincts (p. 255). Disturbed remains were found in ponds, streams and rubbish dumps dated *c.* A D 50–70 at Blossom's Inn.[51] A disused well contained part of the skull of an adult male, who had suffered a blunt force injury to the head which had healed before death. Two burials were also identified on this site: one a perinate and the other a young adult male buried prone in a shallow grave before being scavenged by animals. At Swan Street on the southern borders of Southwark, at a site of supposed animal sacrifice and votive deposition, two disarticulated human femurs were found in pre-Flavian ditches.[52] Human crania have been found in several other late Neronian and early Flavian watery places.[53]

These disturbed remains occupied important liminal locations, placed in or near water at entrances to town or on boundaries of sacred precincts and cemeteries. These were recognizably in-between places, where souls might win passage to the underworld. Some bodies were accompanied by dogs: a creature known to guide souls to other realms. Although irregular burials occur at various sites in Rome's north-west provinces, it is important to stress that this was an unusual treatment.[54] Most Roman communities believed that departed souls would suffer if mortal remains were not treated with care. Burial was a moral duty, demonstrating respect for ancestors and kin.[55] Dismemberment, whether in corpse abuse or Dionysian *sparagmos*, was considered a terrible thing. Why then, were some bodies in early London treated in ways considered horrific to Roman society? Richard Hingley has suggested that this was because of ideas borrowed from Iron Age rites of passage involving corpse exposure and the deposition of body parts in rivers and wetlands.[56] Rituals involving excarnation are attested in pre-Roman Britain and neighbouring provinces, and placed a particular emphasis on the manipulation of elements of the skull.[57] Such practices were of long tradition, witnessed by the prehistoric crania recovered from the Thames. The places where these crania were found had also been used for deposits of metalwork, suggesting a common origin in votive activity. Whilst London may have drawn on ideas that predated the Roman conquest, there is insufficient evidence to suggest a continuity of practice at the site itself. The earliest human remains found in the City and Southwark are likely to be early Roman, whilst the prehistoric votive deposits come from much further upriver. It is, in any case, more likely that London would have adopted customs preferred by those who settled here after the conquest, most of whom appear to have arrived from the continent.

Practices of corpse abuse described in classical sources might account for the evidence found in London. Denial of burial was an extreme punishment directed at those who challenged public order through treason and betrayal.[58] Punishment could involve the removal of body parts, exposure to birds and beasts, and the display and dispersal of remains. Eusebius' description of the AD 177 execution of Christian martyrs from Lyon and Vienne provides an illustrative example. After being beheaded in the amphitheatre, the victims' bodies were mutilated by beasts, exposed for six days under guard to prevent their burial, then burnt and swept into the Rhône.[59] Roman histories also describe how the corpses of traitors were dragged to the Tiber, leaving the river and sewers of Rome filled with bodies.[60] The purifying waters of the Tiber and Cloaca Maxima removed these polluting elements and cleansed the city of hostile spirits, where the need for ritualized river disposal was a consequence of practices of corpse abuse that included denial of burial.

London's Roman evidence also bears comparison with early medieval execution sites.[61] Attributes that identify these execution cemeteries include decapitation, bodies with hands or feet tied, prone and cramped burials, shallow and intercutting graves, mutilation around the time of death, and a demographic profile skewed towards younger males. Ethnographic parallels suggest that backward (prone) burial may have been adopted to prevent the spirits of those who died badly from returning to avenge themselves on the living.[62]

Decapitation was a favoured form of capital punishment in the ancient world, also used in the mutilation of corpses and to prepare trophy heads for display.[63] The head was singled out for separate treatment by virtue of its relationship to the human soul, and the distancing of the head from the body meant that funerary rituals could not be properly enacted nor the remains properly interred. Such practices might account for instances of decapitation followed by the reburial of the skull or cranium.[64] The exposure of heads and body parts, thought to derive from victims of Roman judicial and military violence, witnesses excarnation rituals that share characteristics with late Iron Age practice.[65] Some of these concepts applied to the treatment of war-dead: studies in both Denmark and Holland suggest that body parts and weapons were collected from late Iron Age and early Roman battlefields for ritual deposition in rivers and lakes.[66]

Rome's use of body fragmentation in the annihilation of its enemies, followed by the ritual deposition of selected remains in rivers and wet-places, presents a model that accounts for the evidence from London. Fragmented and irregular burials shrouded the settlement borders, concentrating alongside the main roads amidst a landscape of discard. They occupied the urban *pomerium*, a zone recognized by Roman law and practice to lie beyond the sacred borders of the city and dedicated to the punishment of criminals and burial of the poor.[67] Irregular burials on the borders of Neronian London seem likely to include the mortal remains of those killed by the Roman authorities. In other cases, body fragmentation may have been the consequence of post-mortem corpse abuse or the tidying away of the remains of people unworthy of proper burial. Evidence of this type can be traced down to the third century (p. 266). The late Neronian material was found in contexts associated with post-revolt rebuilding in the early 60s, lending credibility to the suggestion that it included victims of Roman retribution after Boudica's uprising. There is no need, however, to place too much emphasis on this particular event. Roman authority was underpinned by force, and it would be surprising if London didn't routinely witness this sort of violence.

There is no need to explain all irregular burial in this fashion. Other troubling deaths warranted unusual ritual. In excavations at Drapers' Gardens, a short distance north of the earliest town, small oak caskets containing infant burials were carefully buried alongside a tributary of the Walbrook in the pre-Flavian period.[68] As Maureen Carroll has pointed out, Roman textual sources express reservations about cremating the very young and those robbed of their future by premature death were also at risk of becoming restless souls.[69]

Ritual dismemberment and votive deposition were also visited upon statues and effigies.[70] The left hand and forearm of a gilded bronze statue found in a pond at Gresham Street may have been associated with a sacred area (p. 77). It had been hacked from a slightly over life-sized statue, perhaps an imperial figure such as Nero himself.[71] Associated ceramics suggest that the arm was buried *c.* AD 60–70. The destruction of a powerful and valuable symbol was a significant undertaking, as was the decision to bury rather than recycle the valuable metal. This suggests a votive act, possibly following an act of iconoclasm during the Boudican revolt or on Nero's overthrow in AD 69. The decision to send this hand of authority into the pond reminds us of the sacred importance of watery places. A marble head detached from a life-size statue found in Islington, probably also of Nero, might similarly evidence trophy hunting by Boudica's rebels or a *damnatio memoriae* following his death.[72]

Late Neronian London

London's restoration, enabled by military engineering, was in hand by the summer of AD 62. Neighbouring cities didn't benefit from an equivalent level of attention: post-war reconstruction may have been delayed for 15 years in parts of Verulamium, and there is little evidence of late Neronian investment in Colchester.[73]

London was singled out for attention because of its particular value to the administration rather than because of any more broadly based revival of Romano-British cities. As Mike Fulford has proposed, territories north of the Thames may have been placed under direct military control.[74] This followed the arrival of a new provincial governor and procurator, as described in the previous chapter.[75] The rebuilding of AD 62–3 directed by this new administration was concerned with roadworks, harbour facilities, storage capacity, and new bath-houses. The priorities were the same as those that gave London shape a decade earlier, in AD 52–3, reinforcing the impression that the earlier programme was also undertaken at the behest of an incoming administration. The resources of the auxiliary forces stationed in London after the revolt allowed, however, for more ambitious engineering.

Coins witness a massive injection of bronze coinage into Britain in the years AD 64–7.[76] This served the needs of numerous business transactions, but is likely to have been organized by the procurator's office following the rehabilitation of London's port. The London that emerged from Neronian reconstruction remained the principal administrative hub of the province, with a busy port engaged in military supply. Merchants and businessmen connected to the political and military authorities were an important part of this community, but not necessarily as its driving force.

During the decade following the Boudican revolt the distinctive Gallo-Roman styles of consumption and dress that characterized elite society at the time of the Roman conquest fell from use as tastes were realigned around the lifestyles enjoyed by the new regime.[77] This was of relatively minor consequence in London, which had already adopted tastes imported to Britain from the Rhineland, but insular traditions of building design and craftsmanship became progressively rare. Whilst the army played an important part in rebuilding London in the early 60s, its presence was reduced towards the end of the decade. The closing years of Nero's reign left little trace in London. This may in part be a failure of archaeological recognition, but it is not unreasonable to assume that the wars that accompanied Nero's overthrow checked investment. If so, matters changed following Vespasian's assumption of power at the conclusion of the civil war in AD 69 as we will explore in the next chapter.

PART 3
MONUMENTS OF ROME

10

Bread and circuses (*c.* AD 70–80)

The amphitheatre

The years following Vespasian's accession witnessed a remarkable urban flores-cence (Table 10.1). This was set in motion by a series of building projects designed to deliver an architecture of 'bread and circuses', bringing to mind Juvenal's famous critique of Rome's dependency on such imperial handouts.[1] London's first great public building was its amphitheatre (Fig. 10.1). Archaeologists identified this structure when its eastern entrance was uncovered at Guildhall Yard in 1988, giving coherence to earlier discoveries in the area.[2] The arena was sunk into a hollow formed by a tributary of the Walbrook that had been landscaped to form an elliptical gravel-floored stage. This was enclosed by a timber wall, possibly with a main entrance on its southern side. The east gate was about 3.4 metres wide, closed by a pair of doors with a small wicket gate to one side and a wooden tank fed by water-pipes inside the gateway that may have housed a fountain. An earthen bank enclosing the arena formed a *cavea* for tiers of timber seating rising to the line of an outer timber wall. It has been estimated that there was enough space to seat around 6900 spectators, little short of London's likely adult male population of the time. The ambition of the project makes one wonder if it were not also designed for audiences swelled by troops in transit.

The passage through the *cavea* was formed by timbers felled in AD 70 and AD 71, and a pile beneath the main threshold was felled AD 74. The building programme might, therefore, have stretched over several years. The distribution of dated timbers is consistent with groundworks starting *c.* AD 71, using wood procured the preceding winter, with the final fit-out delayed until after *c.* AD 74. Works may have been suspended for a couple of years between raising the *cavea* and installing the seating and fittings. Alternatively, the entire construction pro-gramme may have been compressed within the period *c.* AD 74–5, but drawing on timbers procured a few years earlier. Some timbers were marked by stamps, including 'ICLV' and 'MIBL', likely to have tracked an official procurement exer-cise. We don't know whether these identified civic, procuratorial, or military sup-pliers, although the decision to build would have relied on the authority of the provincial government.

This early Flavian construction, perhaps Britain's first amphitheatre, confirms London's importance to Vespasian's project.[3] The building was a symbol of the new regime, presenting an architecture typical of military and veteran

Table 10.1 A suggested timeline of events affecting London in the period AD 70–125

Suggested date	Building activities in London	Salient events possibly relevant to London
71–2	Building materials assembled for the construction of an amphitheatre and a possible *mansio* beside a canalized channel in Southwark.	A new governor, Cerialis, arrives in Britain. Annexation of Brigantian kingdom.
	Waterworks extended or restored, perhaps in preparation for new baths at Huggin Hill.	
73–4	Work on the amphitheatre and *mansio* completed.	Frontinus replaces Cerialis as governor.
70–5	New landing stages and revetments built downstream of London Bridge. Settlement enlarged with planned extension to the street grid. Road network extended to reach suburban villas along the north bank of the Thames.	
76–9	Water-mills, granaries, and bakeries built besides bridges over Walbrook and Fleet, particularly *c.* AD 78. A bank and ditch defines London's northern boundary. Temporary fort(s) perhaps built north-west of town. Neronian fort cleared and 'decumanus' restored.	An imperially appointed judge makes a record of a legal decision in London on 22 October AD 76. Agricola assumes post of governor AD 77.
79	Jetty/boardwalk built alongside the Thames on the Southwark mainland.	Vespasian dies and Domitian becomes emperor.
	Forum and basilica built, with adjacent temple.	
83–4	Riverside terrace built to house imperial baths (or 'governor's palace') at mouth of Walbrook. Extensive hydraulic engineering east of the Walbrook. New luxury town houses on town borders.	Agricola's victory at Mons Graupius 'completes' the conquest of Britain.
85–90	Alterations to forum courtyard.	Troops redeployed from Britain to Danube frontier AD 87.
91	East gate of amphitheatre repaired.	
	New bridge built over the Thames.	
94–8	Port improved, with new quays and warehouses established downstream of London Bridge.	Nerva becomes emperor after Domitian's assassination AD 96.
		Colonies founded at Gloucester and Lincoln.
		Trajan succeeds Nerva AD 98.
102	Further waterfront revetments built.	First Dacian war concluded.
	Work starts on a massive new forum complex.	

104	Blossom's Inn waterworks improved. Huggin
108–9	Hill baths enlarged (but soon disused).

	Approximate date of London's first masonry-built Romano-Celtic temples.	Hadrian succeeds Trajan as emperor AD 117.
119–22	Building of the great forum completed.	Hadrian visits Britain AD 122.
		Hadrian's wall built and east-coast supply routes developed.

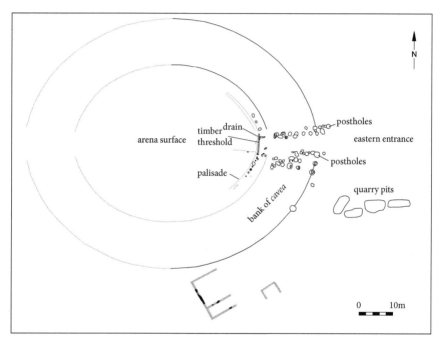

Fig. 10.1 The Flavian amphitheatre (chiefly GAG87: after Bateman *et al.* 2008). Drawn by Justin Russell.

communities.[4] Notwithstanding vast differences of scale and sophistication, London's amphitheatre shared ideological and political purpose with Rome's Colosseum: itself a gift from the emperor Vespasian to his capital city. Both were the product of the reconfiguration of urban performative ritual that followed Vespasian's ascent to power. Festivals associated with the Imperial cult were placed at the centre of religious and civic life throughout the cities of the western empire, in which arena audiences were entertained by games (*munera*) involving gladiatorial combat.[5] This theme was popular in the decorative arts of Roman

Britain showing that such performances were a significant part of provincial culture.[6] Roman games normally started with a ceremonial procession that collected the gods from temples and carried them proudly to the arena.[7] This made the amphitheatre the principal destination for religious pageants, and a setting for theatrical events.[8]

The amphitheatre was also the chief venue for public execution, where Roman authority was affirmed in violent spectacle. Killings supervised by Roman soldiers could involve beheading, burning, crucifixion or being thrown to wild beasts.[9] London's amphitheatre was therefore a direct manifestation of Vespasian's assumption of control, marking an end to the chaos that attended Nero's fall. This public building, the largest in London at the time of its construction, was placed on the town's northern limit. Here it defined a ceremonial area where ritualized civic violence could be accommodated without polluting the urban *templum*, perhaps giving monumental shape to an earlier execution ground (above p. 110).

At the same time as the amphitheatre was planned, unusual building activity took place on the banks of a tributary of the Walbrook some 300 metres to its east. Excavations at Drapers' Gardens found two palisade fences using timbers felled in the winter-spring of AD 70/71. The fences were more than 2 metres high, formed from upright radially cleft pales with spear-shaped (*hastate*) upper ends and fastened together by horizontal rails nailed into place. These were the product of military-style engineering, forming one or more irregular enclosures on the northern boundary of the settlement.[10] We have no direct evidence for their purpose, but it is tempting to suggest an association with the amphitheatre. One might imagine captives and wild beasts destined for the arena being held in pens and stockades here on the town borders.

An administrative complex in Southwark

Southwark also warranted early Flavian attention (Fig. 10.2). The channel between the north and south islands was canalized by post-and-plank revetments that reduced its width to about 15–20 metres, creating quays and moorings for rivercraft.[11] A small jetty on the south side of this channel used timbers felled in AD 72, and the revetments that formed the north bank of the channel are dated as early Flavian by pottery within the land reclamations. The canal served a major building complex on its northern bank. Excavations by Carrie Cowan at 15–23 Southwark Street revealed parts of a massive early Flavian courtyard building, measuring at least 50 by 30 metres, laid out with unusual symmetry over three main wings.[12] This was one of London's earliest and largest masonry buildings, commanding the southern borders of the settlement. The principal rooms were set behind a 3.2-metre-wide ambulatory around an east-facing courtyard. The flint and ragstone foundations rested on closely packed timber piles that had been

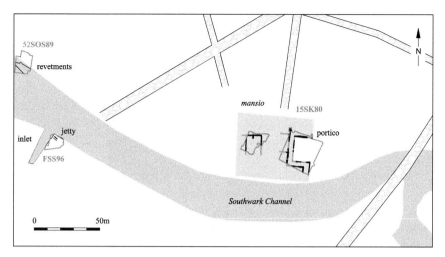

Fig. 10.2 The Southwark Channel and '*mansio*' (15SK80: based in part on Cowan 1992, adapted to include more recent information on the revetments associated with the Flavian canalization of the watercourse). Drawn by Justin Russell.

felled in AD 72 and AD 74. It replaced one of London's more significant Claudio-Neronian buildings, itself on the site of a pre-Roman settlement, and the occupation here generated a concentration of objects associated with the army (pp. 63 and 78).

The location, date and character of this complex mark it out as unusually important. Cowan suggests that it may have been a *mansio*, or *praetoria*, offering facilities for high-ranking imperial officials travelling through London on public business. These administrative compounds were also places for marshalling goods obtained through taxation and rent, typically laid out around large courtyards with ambulatories providing covered space for the loading and unloading of waggons. Richard Hingley has questioned this identification, pointing out that it might have been the house of a wealthy Londoner.[13] This is not beyond the bounds of possibility, but it would have been an exceptional residence, unparalleled in the domestic architecture of the period. The building's layout, with its symmetrical projecting wings, finds closer parallel in an early second-century building at Chelmsford that is also thought to have been used as a *mansio*.[14] These establishments were distinguished from contemporary townhouses by their scale, symmetry, location, masonry architecture and courtyard layout. They were also provided with richly decorated interiors and bathhouses, all of which were eventually provided at 15–23 Southwark Street (p. 263).

Praetoria were found not only at roadside locations but at entrances to cities where large official entourages could avoid the congested city streets.[15] The borders of Southwark were an eminently sensible place for such a facility, meeting the needs of those arriving at London from the south, commanding river traffic and the approaches to London Bridge, and as base for the administration of the south bank settlement. Vespasian's administration promoted centralization, transferring responsibilities for collecting indirect taxes from agents (*publicani*) to government officials, and is credited with a policy of improving communications.[16] A new transportation network was developed around London in the 70s, when new roads were built alongside the Thames and penetrating into the ironworking districts of the Sussex Weald (p. 174). This may have contributed to the development of an industrial area, possibly associated with ship-building, between the *mansio* and Thames (p. 212).[17]

The canalization of the Southwark channel and building of the supposed *mansio* were contemporary with the construction of the amphitheatre. Materials for both projects were procured as early as the winter of AD 70/71, and work was still ongoing at both sites in AD 74 perhaps after interruption. There are also intriguing similarities in the later histories of the two complexes. Both witnessed several phases of alteration and improvement before becoming the sites of small late antique cemeteries (p. 382). These might hint at common institutional links between these buildings controlling the opposite borders of town.

Improvements to port and city

London's Neronian port remained busy throughout the Flavian period.[18] Landing stages built onto the Thames foreshore immediately downstream of London Bridge added to handling capacity. These were investigated at Pudding Lane where an open framework structure with a front wall of horizontally stacked timber baulks extended 57 metres along the waterfront.[19] This supported timber decking reached by gangways from the quays behind, and was built with timbers procured after AD 69 but probably before AD 77.[20] Simple post and plank revetments of this date stretched further downstream at Three Quays House and Sugar Quay, combining to suggest that quays now extended 620 metres along the riverfront.[21] Behind them, the glassworker's shop (above p. 101) may have been converted into a mosaicist's workshop. In the neighbouring unit three lead ingots stamped as property of the emperor Vespasian from British lead-silver mines, each weighing about seven kilos, were buried upside-down beneath the floor.[22] They are likely to have come from mines in the Mendips, obtained on behalf of the procurator and shipped to London for use in construction works or industrial production. We can only guess as to why they were never recovered from their place of safekeeping.

Several streets were added around London's borders in early Flavian expansion (Fig. 10.3). These included roads built over the long-redundant ditches along the northern and western perimeters of the Claudian enclosure.[23] If this land had been part of the defensive circuit it may have remained part of the emperor's

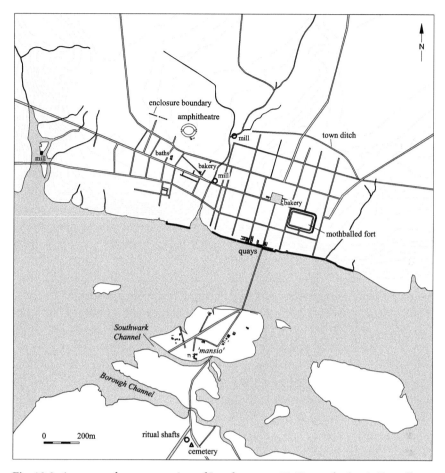

Fig. 10.3 A proposed reconstruction of London *c.* AD 74. Drawn by Justin Russell.

patrimonium, in which case the procurator would have been responsible for releasing it for development. The northern road carried eastwards beyond the former city limits to a junction with the road to Colchester.[24] It then continued into the countryside, where ceramics found at St Clare Street suggest that road surfaces were laid between AD 70 and 80, heading towards a riverside establishment near Shadwell (p. 176).

Another east-west street was inserted mid-way between the amphitheatre and the '*decumanus*', extending the line of a Neronian street on Cornhill by bridging the Walbrook near the Bank of England. Primary street surfaces along this route, at Old Jewry and Ironmonger Lane, were pottery dated to the late first century.[25] This road joined onto an earlier, unmetalled, route which skirted the sacred area at Blossom's Inn: the first metalled surfaces of this stretch of road are dated by the presence of a locally produced (VRW) mortarium with a counterstamp of

Matugenus, dated *c.* AD 80–90, at 120–2 Cheapside.[26] It then veered north-west into the countryside, becoming the 2-metre-wide cambered track recorded at 7–12 Aldersgate Street.[27] This probably carried wheeled traffic past the farm at Clerkenwell towards a crossing of the Fleet, offering a short-cut onto the road to St Albans (*Verulamium*). Another important route out of town headed towards Westminster along the line of Fleet Street. This crossed the Fleet over a bridge built no later than the early Flavian period: facilities built alongside this crossing incorporated a plank cut from a tree felled AD 67–73.[28]

Later in the 70s the west bank of the Walbrook was reorganized following the introduction of two new north-south aligned streets meeting at the street junction at One Poultry.[29] Drains built in contemporary engineering employed freshly carpentered planks felled in the winter of AD 77/78. These streets gave access to properties along the west bank of the Walbrook, where land was prepared for housing by massive terraces formed by timber box-revetments. This was a major landscaping exercise, dendrochronologically dated AD 73–81. The scale of these works finds parallel in the construction of the Neronian waterfront quays, suggesting a public venture drawing on advanced engineering capabilities. One of the buildings, possibly a two-storied granary, incorporated several timbers felled AD 78 and one felled AD 79.[30] It appears that the main landscaping works along the banks of the Walbrook took place AD 78, and building plots were filled out with new structures the following year. Further engineering took place south of the Thames a year later. Excavations near where Watling Street crossed from the mainland onto the south island exposed a zone of timber posts felled in the winter of AD 79 or spring of AD 80.[31] The timbers were arranged in rows radiating back from the waterside and perhaps supported a raised riverside boardwalk.

The roads built in the 70s opened up new areas for property development. Income from these developments might have contributed to revenues managed by the procurator, possibly underwriting the costs of celebrating the *munera*. The commissioning of London's amphitheatre entailed a commitment to forward expenditure, and it was common practice to secure resources for public festivals by consecrating landed property in a foundation bequest.[32] It is also possible that some properties rewarded veterans and others who supported the Flavian cause. Early Flavian investment also involved building roads to reach satellite sites within London's hinterland, including riverside sites at Westminster and Shadwell, and the construction of quays at the base of the river Fleet and in Southwark.

Mills and bakeries

Food security must have been an acute concern during London's uncertain infancy. The larger charred grain assemblages found in London consisted chiefly of cleaned (de-husked) spelt wheat brought into town in bulk after processing and cleaning.[33] In the early city this grain was ground into flour in rotary hand-mills made of lava from the Eifel Hills in Germany, imported via the Rhine. These querns are rare on domestic sites and milling is likely to have been associated with bakeries. Exceptionally large numbers have been found in the Cheapside area, where bakeries and granaries stood alongside the '*decumanus*' before the revolt of AD 60–1.[34] More than 1,000 fragments of broken quern stones were used to form cobbled surfaces around a water-tank dated *c.* AD 75–80. This assemblage also included three fragments from animal-powered millstones, supplementing the evidence of an hour-glass donkey-mill found nearby in Princes Street.[35]

Grain would have been unloaded at quays along the lower Walbrook and granaries have tentatively been identified on the opposite side of the road to the quernstone pavement (Fig. 10.4). The first, built *c.* AD 78, was replaced by a structure with a raised wooden floor using timbers felled AD 79–92/4. Cleaned freethreshing wheat, with some spelt and a little barley, was found here in a 'grain bin' and large quantities of carbonized grain were found at the National Safe Deposit Company site in Bucklersbury.[36] A bakery was tentatively identified at One Poultry, 50 metres west of the cobbled surfaces with discarded quernstones.[37] This unusual Flavian structure housed several ovens, along with debris suggestive of food-processing. It occupied a prominent corner location formed by the amalgamation of several earlier properties. The core of the building was built of brick or masonry set over coursed flint and mortar foundations, and a narrow portico was set along both street frontages. It was located on the midway point of the route from the forum to the amphitheatre, making it a suitable point for selling or distributing food to processions on feast days. Other bakeries have been identified around London's central forum. Three circular tile-lined ovens suitable for baking were found in a late first-century timber building opposite the south-east corner of the forum at Fenchurch Street, and two others in a contemporary building at Birchin Lane.[38]

In an important initiative a series of water-powered mills were introduced to London before the end of the first century. Andrew Wilson describes seven large millstones from London, including three from Bucklersbury House where the Walbrook channel appeared to narrow and a mill may have stood.[39] Excavations at the Bloomberg site found two rare survivals of oak machinery that may have derived from this mill. One may have been part of the mill wheel, consisting of a paddle blade sculpted from a sawn oak plank. The other was part of the lantern gear used to drive the rotating shaft set through the millstones, represented by an oak disk pierced by six round holes for gear bars and a square axle hole for the drive shaft. Vertical mills require right-angled gearing to convert the waterwheel's rotation into the horizontal rotation of a spindle to turn the lower millstone. Another complete millstone from a water-powered mill was found at Pinners' Hall in Great Winchester Street suggesting that a second mill was located higher up the Walbrook valley.[40] Stephen Myers' doctoral dissertation shows that the Walbrook provided sufficient head to power watermills at both locations.[41] The river arrived at London's northern boundary some 7.50 to 8.00 metres above

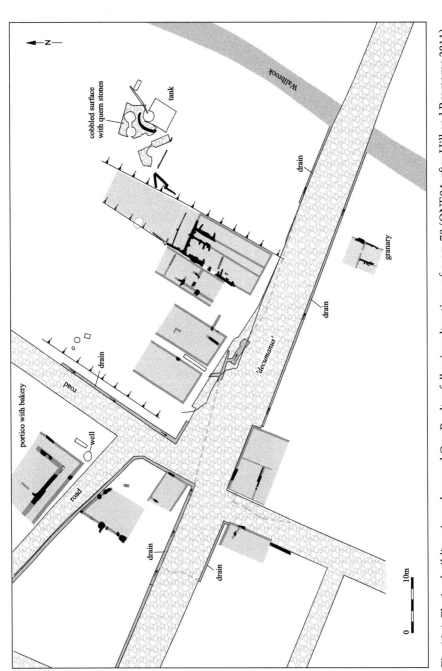

N

cobbled surface
with quern stones

tank

Walbrook

drain

granary

drain

'decumanus'

drain

road

drain

portico with bakery

well

road

drain

drain

0   10m

Fig. 10.4 Flavian buildings in and around One Poultry following alterations of c. AD 78 (ONE94: after Hill and Rowsome 2011). A water-mill may also have stood on the north side of the bridge over the Walbrook. Drawn by Justin Russell.

OD, but reached the Thames between 0.50 and 1.50 metres OD: a drop of 6–7 metres. A typical late first-century overshot waterwheel had a diameter of 2 metres, requiring a fall from water offtake to riverbed of less than 3 metres. On this basis, the head of the Walbrook was sufficient to drive two overshot wheels in series.

A water-mill may also have stood where the Fleet flowed into the tidal Thames. Excavations between 1988 and 1992 identified two small eyots on the east bank of the Fleet, just north of Ludgate Circus (Fig. 10.5).[42] Reports prepared by Bill McCann describe a substantial jetty and timber-framed warehouse on the downstream eyot associated with pottery dated *c.* AD 100–120 and crop-processing waste from the parching and threshing of spelt wheat. Features believed to have been associated with a substantial tidal mill were found on the upstream, northern, eyot. Here a 2-metre-deep channel, perhaps a mill race, may have fed a mill pond. The channel also contained charred spelt wheat and chaff, showing that threshing took place nearby. Dendrochonological analysis shows that the waterside revetments used timbers felled AD 76–99.

It is not clear if London's water-mills were built in a single programme although this is distinctly possible. The mill near the Walbrook bridge was probably built *c.* AD 78, since this is when the banks of the Walbrook were re-engineered in ways consistent with the insertion of a mill leat. The arrival of this new technology helps to explain the mass discard of hand-mills *c.* AD 75/80. Whilst the watermills may have been operated by private contractors, their construction was integrated with other aspects of hydraulic engineering and relied on advanced engineering associated with military and public contracts. The introduction of water-powered mills would have radically transformed the feeding of the city. They were more than five times as productive as animal-powered mills but cheaper to operate, and Myers estimates that two mills on the Walbrook could have produced flour for up to 5000 civilian consumers. With those on the Fleet, London's water-mills could have met a third of the needs of the entire city. Their construction would have eased the problems of keeping London's population fed, supporting distributions of bread from adjacent bakeries.[43]

City limits and defences

A massive late first-century ditch found at Baltic House during the construction of the 'Gherkin' skyscraper was of a suitable scale and character to have formed the northern boundary of the enlarged city.[44] This V-shaped ditch was originally about 6 metres wide and 2.45 metres deep, almost twice the size of contemporary city ditches, with a square-cut 'ankle-breaker' slot at the base. It was open long enough for weathering to occur, and contained pottery dated AD 70–100. No trace of a rampart survived, but upcast from the ditch allowed the construction of

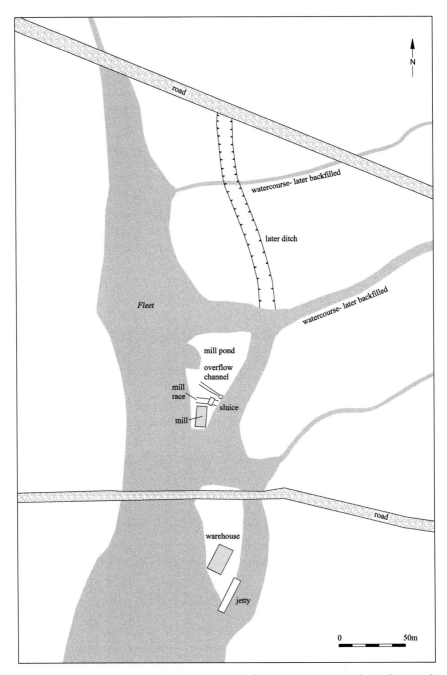

Fig. 10.5 A proposed reconstruction of the late first-century topography at the mouth of the river Fleet (VAL88: after McCann 1993). Drawn by Justin Russell.

a substantial bank about 125 metres forward of the line taken by the Claudian defences. The ditch hasn't been found anywhere else, largely for want of investigations in appropriate areas, making it difficult to know whether it was part of a town boundary or a more local feature. Guy Hunt has suggested that ditches at Cooper's Row, on the eastern side of town, might also have defined a late first-century urban boundary.[45] These were, however, smaller and of uncertain date. Despite the failure to identify other stretches of the ditch-system, its character and location is consistent with its interpretation as an early Flavian defensive earthwork.

Other towns in south-east Britain were provided with formal boundaries at this time. A V-shaped ditch of similar dimensions was dug to enclose parts of Verulamium, perhaps *c.* AD 75–80, before being backfilled by the middle of the second century.[46] Late first- or early second-century ditches also drew boundaries to the town at Silchester (*Calleva Atrebatum*).[47] In all three towns the earthworks appear to have been discontinuous, suggesting that their symbolic role was more important than their defensive one. The provision of defences implies an elevation in status, and it has been argued that the bank was built when London was granted a formal urban charter.[48] It is also possible, however, that London was important enough to warrant urban defences because of its association with the provincial government regardless of its formal status.

London's new Flavian streets also included an unusually important metalled road that cut a swathe through housing at 10 Gresham Street.[49] The late Neronian enclosure here (Fig. 9.5) was cleared to make way for a 7.5 metres wide road flanked by substantial drains. This was significantly wider than normal for contemporary city streets and later subsidence shows that the aggregate for its metalled surface was quarried from adjacent gravel pits without regard to the needs of subsequent house-builders. Since a perfectly viable Claudio-Neronian street lay only 25 metres to the west the new road was probably inserted to take traffic towards an important destination rather than service local houses.[50] This important destination was later the site of the second-century Cripplegate fort (Fig. 19.2). Although excavations have yet to find certain trace of an earlier fort, the site was comprehensively cleared of vegetation before dumps of imported brickearth containing Flavian pottery established a level building platform over an area of at least 18,000 square metres. These works took place long before the Hadrianic fort was built. This area was also bounded by a V-shaped perimeter ditch, up to 2.4 metres wide and 1.6 metres deep with an 'ankle breaker' that was found at Barrington House where it may have enclosed an early Flavian encampment preceding the Hadrianic fort.[51] Pottery suggests that it was backfilled before the end of the first century. It has not been possible to identify features associated with a fort interior, but a similar absence of evidence characterized the Neronian fort in the south-east quarter.[52] The presence of a temporary camp to the north-west of the settlement might explain why a principal road was built to give access to an extensively landscaped site bounded by a ditch of a type associated with military engineering. The large V-shaped ditch found at St Bartholomew's Hospital, discussed in Chapter 7, might have defined a similar enclosure. We can surmise that the area of higher ground north-west of the city housed passing military units at various points in London's early Roman history.[53] Whether or not Vespasian's forces used temporary camps on the north-west outskirts of town, they had continuing access to the Neronian fort in its south-east corner. This was an increasingly neglected feature, but wasn't levelled until c. AD 85.[54] The failure to convert the redundant fort into housing in the mid-70s may have been no more than institutional inertia, but it is more likely that the site was kept vacant for the sporadic needs of troops and goods transiting London. These forces could have brought engineering skills and physical labour to aid the construction of the amphitheatre, *mansio*, river channels, quays, terraces, water-mills, new roads, and town defences that were built in the busy 70s.

Vespasian and London

These early Flavian changes have implications for our understanding of imperial policy in Britain. Vespasian was proclaimed emperor in the summer of AD 69 but didn't arrive in Rome until the autumn of AD 70. According to Josephus this was the year that he appointed Petillius Cerialis, probably his son-in-law, to govern Britain.[55] Cerialis was dealing with the aftermath of the Batavian revolt in Germany when appointed, and this probably delayed his departure to Britain until the spring of AD 71. This coincides with the date that work started on assembling materials for the construction of London's amphitheatre and the supposed *mansio/principia* in Southwark, and perhaps also the renewal of water-lifting devices at Blossom's Inn.[56]

Britain was important to the new regime. Both the emperor and his legate had previously served here, the former at the time of the Claudian conquest and the latter during the Boudican revolt.[57] Vespasian was the first Roman emperor to rule without the benefit of dynastic legitimacy, and success in Britain offered a way of grafting Flavian achievement onto earlier Julio-Claudian victory.[58] Britain was the place where the divine Caesar and Claudius had consolidated their authority as guardians of Roman destiny, and where Vespasian gained early military glory. These factors help to explain why London, the symbol of Roman power in Britain, was the precocious beneficiary of Flavian patronage. It is difficult to see how resources for the changes described here could have emerged from private or civic munificence within London's diminished late Neronian community. The scale of the engineering and political character of the monuments suggest the involvement of the administration. The likely patrons were senior officials, acting to consolidate Flavian political authority.

Many scholars are reluctant to credit the Roman army with works undertaken on behalf of Britain's civilian communities, offering corrective balance to earlier studies that were unduly dismissive of civilian capabilities. The army was, however, a versatile tool in the implementation of imperial policy, and easily deployed onto construction projects when not on active campaign.[59] The particular circumstances of London's Flavian reconstruction might have warranted such help. A parallel can be found in the actions of Vitellius, Vespasian's principal rival for power in the year of the three emperors, who sent a legion to help build amphitheatres at Cremona and Bononia.[60] This precedent may have encouraged the Flavian commitment to provide *munera*, as Vespasian adopted this aspect of Vitellius' political strategy. This is not to say that other agencies were not involved in the construction works undertaken in London, where the administration could enlist the support of a range of public and private contractors.

Although elements of London's urban renewal may have been planned on Cerialis' appointment in AD 70, dendrochronology describes subsequent peaks of activity *c.* AD 74 and *c.* AD 77/78. Political and military considerations may have contributed to a cyclical pattern of investment in London's infrastructure at these dates.[61] Flavian preparations aimed at the completion of the conquest of Britain involved exaggerated movements of labour and capital. Julius Frontinus replaced Cerialis late in AD 73, a few months before supplies of timber were obtained to complete the fit-out of the amphitheatre and supposed *mansio*.[62] Similarly, Frontinus was succeeded by Agricola in the summer of AD 77, which arrival was promptly followed by the procurement of timbers for the landscaping of the lower Walbrook valley and related urban improvements.[63] These works included the construction of water-powered mills and new arrangements for feeding the city. Comparable, if not entirely synchronous, investment cycles can be reconstructed from the evidence of major injections of fresh supplies of imported coin in the periods AD 64–7; AD 71–3; AD 77–8 and AD 86–7.[64] There is the hint of a correlation between the arrival of new governors commanded with expansionary goals, exercises of procuring timber for major construction projects in London, and injections of new coin. Political impetus for the improvement of London may have stemmed from the arrival of new provincial governors, each ambitious to leave a stamp on the leading provincial city.

11

Britain's capital? (*c.* AD 80–90)

The Flavian forum

At the time of Vespasian's death in AD 79, London was the most important seat of Roman power in Britain, but it remained architecturally impoverished when compared to leading cities elsewhere in the empire. Many ancient cities were richly endowed by wealthy patrons following the practices of civic euergetism described by Arjan Zuiderhoek.[1] Britain lacked an equivalent tradition of using monumental architecture to frame political life, and social competition in London may also have been stunted by the arrangements made for the government of a city of uncertain legal status.

London's urban status was perhaps acknowledged in a writing-tablet found in a context dated AD 65/70–80 at the Bloomberg site. This registered a financial agreement affecting one Atigniomarus who came to the city, termed *civitatem*, on the eighth day before the Kalends of January (25 December) of an unknown year.[2] The reference implies that London was a place with autonomous urban status. London's identity as a *civitatem* did not, however, require it to have the political institutions normal to peregrine cities. Military officials and imperial legates sometimes retained the powers elsewhere invested in city magistrates, perhaps routinely so during the transition from military to civilian rule in conquered territories.[3] Another writing tablet found at the Bloomberg site suggests that this may have been the state of affairs in London AD 76. It preserved the preamble to a preliminary judgement, dated 22 October AD 76, made by a judge appointed by the emperor.[4] The appointment would have been made on the emperor's behalf by the governor, Julius Frontinus, and implies that the city lacked its own elected magistrates. Whilst it was ultimately in Rome's interests to empower the political institutions of local self-rule, these came slow to London and were apparently still absent in the autumn of AD 76. London's public architecture has been used to suggest that it gained the instruments of a self-governing community soon afterwards, perhaps during the term in office of the governor Agricola *c.* AD 77–85, although we have no certain evidence that this was the case.

London's first public works had been utilitarian engineering projects associated with moving goods through the port and forum, followed by the construction of heated baths similar to those favoured by military communities on the town's borders. The projects put in hand during Vespasian's reign introduced new concepts of urban order around the city, as represented by the formal ceremonies of the amphitheatre and a controlled network of roads and quays administered from sites such as the Southwark *mansio*. This early Flavian architecture enveloped the Neronian city and attracted new areas of elite housing around its borders. Initially the town centre was little changed, but this area was transformed by ambitious building projects later in the Flavian period starting with the construction of a new forum.

In most Roman cities political and social life revolved around the forum, where a principal basilica housed the offices of the civic administration. The decision to build London's first forum and basilica was consequently an important matter. Our knowledge of this complex, built opposite the T-junction at the city centre, rests on Peter Marsden's synthesis of the results of excavations along Gracechurch Street (Fig. 11.1).[5] The forum was twice as long as wide, at 104.5 by 52.7 metres, and dominated by a basilica at its further (northern) end. Its walls were built of concreted ragstone blocks separated by horizontal string-courses of red tiles, raised over flint foundations. External buttresses probably supported engaged columns for architectural emphasis. The basilica was a large aisled building, some 44 metres long by 22.7 metres wide, raised on a 1-metre-high platform, with a central nave some 8.38 metres wide flanked by aisles of unequal width. Cross-walls at the east end of the nave might have supported a raised dais to seat magistrates, and a sunken room at the west end of the north aisle could have provided a secure treasury.[6]

The other sides of the forum were enclosed by narrow ranges of rooms suitable for use as offices, stores, workshops, and shops, replacing the earlier *tabernae* around the forum hardstanding. Those in the southern range were set behind a portico facing the street, while the east and west ranges probably looked inwards. The southern façade incorporated a portico of columns supporting a tiled roof, with a main entrance at the junction of Gracechurch Street and Lombard Street. The enclosure of the forum adds to the sense that this was a closely managed space.[7]

The forum was probably built in the late 70s or early 80s. Excavations at 83–7 Gracechurch Street in 1934 found that the basilica's south wall cut through a pit containing Flavian pottery and a coin of AD 71, and rubbish beneath the street east of the forum contained Southern Gaulish Samian no earlier than AD 75.[8] This probably pre-dated the forum's construction, although this is not certain. These finds suggest that London's forum was roughly contemporary with the basilica at Verulamium, dated to AD 79 or AD 81 by a dedicatory inscription, and Silchester's timber basilica which has a *terminus post quem* provided by a coin of AD 77–8.[9] These buildings must all have been erected with official sanction but were differently designed, indicating that different architects and builders were involved. A political context for the works is found in Tacitus' description of how the governor Agricola gave private encouragement and public aid to building temples, fora and houses during his second winter in post (i.e. AD 78/79).[10]

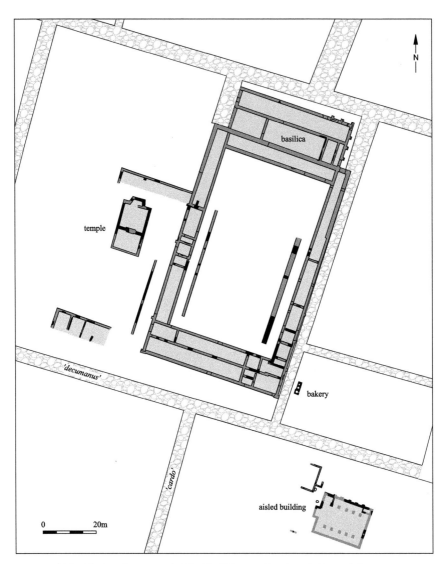

Fig. 11.1 The Flavian forum and aisled building at Fenchurch Street (after Marsden 1987 and Hammer 1987). Drawn by Justin Russell.

London's Flavian forum may have been a product of this Agricolan policy, and if so is likely to have been commissioned *c.* AD 79 onwards.

Scholars have long been attracted to the idea that the building of London's forum accompanied the grant of an urban charter, perhaps elevating the city to the status of a *municipium*.[11] The argument is consistent with wider evidence for political reform during Agricola's administration, but there is no certain relationship between the construction of a basilica and the award of chartered status.[12] Although Flavian London was the largest city in Britain its forum was unusually small. Verulamium's extended over three times the area, with a basilica almost three times as long.[13] There are several possible explanations for this. Peter Marsden has suggested that London's forum was the first to be built, establishing a prototype improved-on by neighbouring cities.[14] London's forum was planned after *tabernae* had already been set along London's waterfront, reducing the scale of storage facilities required. We can also question whether it shared equal status to the buildings in neighbouring cities. John Wacher argued that it might be better identified as the seat of the procurator or a market building.[15] Although usually considered a civilian administrative building, it could have been dedicated to the management of official supplies. In this case the courtyard and surrounding rooms might have been modelled on the offices of trading associations found in port cities. The Piazzale delle Corporazioni at Ostia presents a similar layout to the London forum, although lacking the dominating basilica, where the large rectangular courtyard was enclosed by a colonnade concealing rows of small rooms which housed the offices of guilds, merchants and shippers. On balance it seems likely that London's basilica was built to house administrative facilities, and the forum to accommodate business interests around the open piazza.

Public architecture in the forum district

In 1934, Frank Cottrill found the foundations of a building likely to have been a small classical temple, 20.7 metres long, set within its own precinct west of the forum.[16] Its walls were formed of roof tiles laid with the flange outward to resemble brick, perhaps for a stucco render, set over flint foundations similar to those used in the forum. Peter Marsden has suggested that the building was approached by a low flight of steps, leading to a south-facing façade of two substantial columns forming a porch (*pronaos*) into the chamber (*cella*) at the back of which a polygonal apse could have housed a cult statue. These are the characteristics of the *distyle in antis* façade used in temple architecture. Gravelled surfaces around the building were enclosed by a precinct wall.[17] This enclosure was clearly separated from the adjacent forum, in a layout that faintly echoed arrangements in *fora* in Gaul and Spain, although on more modest scale.[18] This provided a setting for bargaining with the gods through vows and sacrifices made at altars on the temple steps.[19]

We don't know who was worshipped here, but a temple to the imperial cult was probably established hereabouts. An incomplete monumental inscription found at Nicholas Lane in 1850, half way between the forum and Thames, appears to have included a dedication to the divinity (*numen*) of the Emperor by the province of Britain.[20] The formula used in this inscription is an unusual one, and its expansion uncertain, but it implies a Flavian date. Flavian patronage emphasized the imperial cult, and collective practices organized around the figure of the emperor would have reinforced London's identification with the colonial project, solidifying the hegemony of the Roman state.[21] Loyalty to the imperial person and symbol offset the risks of fragmentation posed by the power of Rome's frontier armies. The temple dedicated to Claudius at Colchester has been identified as a meeting place of the provincial assembly (*concilium provinciae*), where leading members of Britain's different communities could celebrate the sacred games associated with the imperial cult.[22] But by the 80s it was possible for more than one city in a province to perform such a role. We have already noted the importance of the imperial cult to the celebration of games in the amphitheatre. The forum would similarly have been dominated by the imperial presence, reinforced by sacrifices on days set aside for the veneration of the imperial house in front of statues and images of the imperial household. Prayers would have been organized for the guardian spirit of the emperor (the *genius Augusti*) and his divine essence (*numen*). The religious processions organized on these occasions are likely to have started by collecting the images of the emperor from the temple where his divine spirit resided, and culminated in the games held at the amphitheatre.[23]

The construction of London's forum and temple prompted improvements to the surrounding streets. In addition to a new road built against the east side of the forum, the '*decumanus*' was re-established *c.* AD 85 after the vestiges of the Neronian fort were finally cleared.[24] The line of this road was eventually extended eastwards, with traces of gravel metalling observed in Pepys Street.[25] New properties were also established alongside a north-south street set over the site of the fort. Several important buildings were built south of the forum. Excavations in Fenchurch Street uncovered the corner of an unusual aisled building with internal pier bases and external buttresses (Fig. 11.1). The timber and brickearth walls were built over distinctive foundations formed of bands of gravel and crushed mortar laid horizontally in a deep trench.[26] Partitions subsequently divided the narrow aisles into smaller rooms, one of which contained a latrine set over a brick-built drain flushed by running water. Friederike Hammer's interim report suggests that the building was Flavian, although an earlier date has also been proposed.[27] The unusual features of the building have resulted in suggestions that it might have been a meeting place for a guild (*collegium*), or a market hall (*macellum*) involving booths set within the aisles. Traces of another important building were found a short distance to the south, at 55–8 Gracechurch Street. We know little about this large south-facing winged building, but it was supposedly a late first-century construction containing a hypocaust of tile pilae set between parallel ragstone foundations.[28]

An even more imposing public building was built over terraces overlooking the Thames on the east side of the Walbrook (Fig. 11.2). Peter Marsden's report on excavations at Bush Lane between 1961 and 1972 argued that these were the remains of a Flavian palace, possibly that of the provincial governor.[29] Its

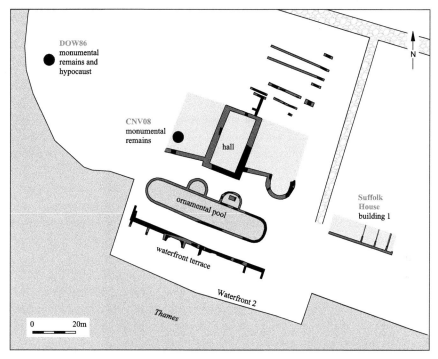

Fig. 11.2 The monumental building complex in the area of Cannon Street station (the 'governor's palace') at around the time of its construction *c.* AD 84/85 (after Marsden 1978, Spence and Grew 1990, Milne 1996, and Brigham 2001a). The difficult circumstances of excavation leave several areas of uncertainty over the location and date of individual features. Drawn by Justin Russell.

foundations employed such strong cement that explosives were needed to clear the site when Cannon Street Station was built in 1868.[30] A distinctive feature was an enormous apsidal-ended pool, over 10 metres wide and up to 55 metres long, which could have held 900,000 litres of water. Its base was set over concrete foundations over 1.8 metres thick, and a small apse on its northern side contained a rectangular masonry base where a statue may have stood. This pool occupied an open terrace in front of a monumental building dominated by a massive central hall with 3-metre-wide walls and a concrete floor. East of this hall was another massive room with a projecting apse, north of which hypocaust floors were found. Foundations found beneath Cannon Street Station in 2008 may derive from a similar apsidal chamber to the west.[31] The complex may have extended 140 metres along the river terrace towards the Walbrook, as implied by the presence of a hypocaust floor and monumental wall faced with thin slabs of Purbeck marble at 3–7 Dowgate Hill.[32]

A separate range of masonry rooms occupied a lower terrace south of the pool. Marsden suggested that these were the palace's residential wing, but subsequent work shows that they belonged to a later and probably unrelated development. Excavations beneath Cannon Street station in 1988–9 found that the tile-built terrace wall included curved and squared buttresses forming a decorative river façade.[33] The terrace below this wall was originally an open quayside. Excavations to the east, at Suffolk House, found that these quays were built using timbers felled spring AD 84.[34] Since the river façade was an integral part of the original design these timbers may date the entire monumental complex. Further high-status rooms lay east of the monumental pool, where Marsden suggested that the administrative offices of the palace were located. These too are likely to have been part of an unrelated development.

The argument that this public architecture was part of the Governor's palace rested on the assumption that the building contained high-status residential quarters as well as monumental state reception rooms. This no longer appears to have been the case, and Gustav Milne's review of the evidence found little to recommend the palace hypothesis.[35] Several alternative interpretations have been advanced, but the most convincing is that this was a bathhouse.[36] If so, the ornamental pool would have been the focal point of a *palaestra*, or exercise court.[37] The massive Cannon Street 'hall' might have been a large cold or changing room (*apodyterium*), giving access to separate suites of heated rooms either side. These would have been laid out in the monumental 'imperial' style involving cross-axial symmetry that came into fashion at this time. Altogether the complex occupied an area in excess of 10,000 square metres, not much smaller than the Baths of Titus built in Rome a few years earlier.

The vast quantities of fuel required to heat the baths would have arrived by river, landing at the new riverside quays. Water was piped to the site from the north and a sunken masonry structure found at 119–21 Cannon Street may have been a reservoir built for this purpose.[38] A supply-pipe, represented by a row of iron connecting collars, was set into the western roadside ditch of the Flavian road at The Walbrook and Cannon Place.[39] These supplies were probably arranged in the mid-80s drawing from the upper Walbrook where an oak water-pipe was recorded at the Bank of England in 1933–4.[40] Excavations at 6–8 Tokenhouse Yard, just north of the Bank of England, found a narrow gravel-surfaced alleyway built to gain access to the Walbrook outside the northern boundary of the Flavian town. This was flanked by fences built with timbers dated to AD 83 onwards and contained a drain built with a timber felled in the spring of AD 85.[41] These alterations may have been associated with the hydraulic engineering that supplied the baths and other buildings between the forum and Thames. Water engineering of a broadly contemporary date is evidenced by the presence of a wooden water-pipe set alongside the '*decumanus*' re-established over the site of the Neronian fort, recorded at Plantation Place where it was dated AD 70–80 from associated ceramics.[42] This supply was aimed in the direction of the town's east gate, perhaps supplying a replacement of the Neronian bathhouse (above p. 77).

Although it is difficult to sustain the argument that the monumental remains at Cannon Street were those of the governor's palace, it is plausible that palatial residences occupied the river terraces either side of London Bridge where buildings included luxurious mosaics, hypocausts and wall-paintings. Some houses saw significant Flavian investment, such as a masonry structure with flint foundations found at Suffolk House decorated with white marble inlay.[43] This was a busy period for rebuilding around Cannon Street, indicated by the use of construction timbers felled in AD 83 in buildings east of the bridge across the Walbrook.[44] Moulded stones reused in early second-century foundations next to the bridge, at Regis House, included part of a stone conduit that may have come from a nearby public fountain or bathhouse.[45]

The procurator as patron

Trevor Brigham has drawn attention to the fact that although London's earliest masonry buildings were usually built over flint foundations, the monumental northern range of the 'governor's palace' used ragstone and tile.[46] The early use of these materials may have been associated with the opening up of new supplies of brick and tile to meet the elevated needs of building programme in the mid-80s. At about this date local kilns also started producing brick and tile stamped by the office of the procurator of the province of Britain at London.[47] Discards of over-fired and underfired tiles carrying this stamp have been found near Gresham Street on the western margins of the Flavian town, indicating that the kilns lay nearby.[48] Similarly stamped material was manufactured near the roadside settlement at Brockley Hill, north-west of London (below p. 183). None of these distinctive tiles has been found in pre-Flavian contexts. The earliest stratified example was found at Newgate Street, in a context thought likely to be early Flavian but where a later Flavian date cannot be discounted.[49] They were used in several important buildings from the mid-Flavian period into the second century, but there is no record of their presence in the first phase of the Flavian forum and other building programmes dated to the 70s. This might indicate that they were first produced to supply construction programmes in the mid-80s, possibly commencing with the construction of the monumental complex at Cannon Street c. AD 84. Tile kilns could be built to supply particular construction projects where capacity was lacking, and bathhouses had a particular need for specialized building materials.

Procuratorial involvement in this tile production may have made particular sense at this time. Whilst army engineers were involved in some earlier phases of building, particularly after the Boudican revolt, this would no longer have been feasible. The forces commanded by the governor Agricola were heavily engaged in campaigns aimed at completing the conquest of Britain.[50] Agricola's crowning victory, the battle of Mons Graupius, was won in the Scottish Highlands in the summer of AD 83. Any support the Roman army might have lent to earlier programmes of building would have been diminished by these competing needs. The absence of the governor would, however, have left the procurator in a commanding role.

The fact that the procurator's office was involved in local tile manufacture, using official stamps to manage production and supply, doesn't mean that it was responsible for the buildings where the tiles were employed. The tileries could have been commercial enterprises, exploiting imperially owned assets to meet market opportunity and generate income for the imperial treasury.[51] London's civic administration, perhaps newly installed in the Flavian forum, could have taken on increased responsibility for public works funded from local resources and employing architects and engineers brought in for the purpose. The patronage of London's leading merchants and aristocrats, now competing for social status using the time-honoured tools of civic euergetism, might also have contributed resources for the building of the baths and other public monuments of Britain's premier city. On the other hand, the Roman emperors are known to have endowed various cities with public baths.[52] If Domitian had wished to make a gift of a new bathhouse, drawing on the spoils of northern conquest, then the procurator would have been tasked with bringing this about. In the absence of any building dedication claiming credit for the works, we cannot know whether this was a private, civic, or imperial project. But the involvement of the procurator's office in supplying building materials, as well as the style and date of the building, weigh in favour of seeing this as the product of imperial patronage.

London's Flavian growth started in the public sector, anticipating rather than reflecting on the town's success. Whichever agencies or individuals were responsible, these projects required the approval of the provincial government.[53] It has consequently been suggested that London's public works were enabled by imperial patronage and aimed at the creation of a suitably impressive provincial capital.[54] The completion of the conquest of Britain in AD 83 warranted official celebration, and was the likely inspiration for the construction of a monumental marble-clad arch at Richborough.[55] London, the most important city of the province, might also have merited commemorative architecture. The programme of Flavian advance may have been initiated in London after Vespasian's accession to power, perhaps marked by festivities that accompanied the building of the amphitheatre. A decade later, Domitian's general finished the task and London ruled all of Britain: a status soon to be lost and only regained 1600 years later with the 1707 Acts of Union. This was an appropriate moment for the erection of an imperial bathhouse, a symbol of the rewards that Flavian patronage brought to the people of London.

The Huggin Hill baths and town houses

The monumental building at Cannon Street was one of a series of late first-century building projects. Ian Betts has noted similarities in the building materials used in Roman monuments at Cannon Street station, Huggin Hill, and Winchester Palace in Southwark, suggesting a coordinated programme both sides of the river.[56] At its conclusion, large public bathhouses probably stood in all three of London's main districts.

London's best-preserved bathhouse occupied a terrace overlooking the Thames west of the Walbrook, where natural springs emerged from the junction of gravel and impervious clay (Fig. 11.3). It was first identified at Huggin Hill in 1964 and investigations in 1987–9 found that its walls survived 3 metres high, culminating in the reburial exercise described above p. 19.[57] The tile-walled building was set over a thick ragstone and concrete raft supported by timber piles. The baths initially followed the row layout favoured in Romano-British forts and towns, similar to Silchester's late Neronian baths. The entrance was at the east where changing and cold rooms were located. These gave access to a warm room (*tepidarium*), about 11 metres square, from which the hot room (*caldarium*) was reached. This apsidal-ended vaulted space measured 13 by 5.5 metres with a bath set within a

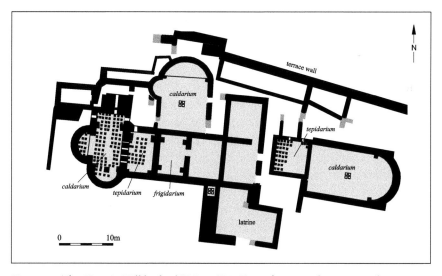

Fig. 11.3 The Huggin Hill baths (GM240/DMT88: after Marsden 1976 and Rowsome 1999). Several phases of construction are illustrated. The caldaria on the north side and at the east end of the complex were both later additions, as was the latrine block to the south. The changing line of the waterfront to the south of the baths is not shown. Drawn by Justin Russell.

smaller apse to one side. These rooms were decorated with polychrome mosaics, only fragments of which survived. Pottery suggests an early Flavian date for their construction. It is an open question as to which of the two monumental buildings that flanked the Walbrook was the first to be built, but the differences in layout and context suggest that different communities were catered for.

The Huggin Hill baths served the district west of the Walbrook. Although this residential area was probably planned before the Boudican revolt (p. 84), it wasn't densely populated until the Flavian period (Fig. 11.4). The character of the occupation hints at the arrival of settlers with a background in military service. Town houses at Watling Court were strikingly similar to contemporary centurion's quarters in the fortress at Gloucester (Fig. 11.5).[58] One of these building's earth walls were built over masonry foundations formed of ragstone rather than flint, favouring a construction date after c. AD 80/85 which is consistent with the sparse pottery dating evidence. At the time of its destruction in the Hadrianic fire the building housed a bronze diploma recording a grant of citizenship and marriage rights of a type issued to members of the Roman auxiliary army on completion of 25 years' service.[59] The names of witnesses to the document indicate that it was issued between AD 98 and 108, which means that its recipient probably started his military career between AD 73 and AD 83. He might have been in service when the diploma was issued, since it was only after AD 110 that such documents were restricted to veterans. We don't know why this individual chose to settle in London, but he may have served here in an administrative role.[60] Auxiliary centurions included personnel recruited from provincial aristocracies commanding the status and wealth implied by the design of this house.[61] It contained an important series of late first-century mosaic pavements with black-and-white designs showing close stylistic parallels to pavements at Reims in Gaul. The floor in one room, decorated with small mosaic crosslets inset into a highly polished crushed brick terrazzo (opus signinum) floor, slumped into an unconsolidated quarry and required replacement with an entirely new floor of the same kind. These repairs showed that client and contractor retained a continuing commitment to the project over some years. Although the design of this house may have drawn on skills drawn to London for unrelated reasons, perhaps to work on public contracts, the client's tastes and contacts may also have been a factor. If so, this may have been the house of someone recruited to the army from northern Gaul, who had commanded auxiliary troops under Agricola and was employed on imperial service in London.

A comparable town house was found at Gresham Street, west of the Cheapside baths, next to a road built c. AD 80. Debris from the structure included Purbeck marble wall veneers, hypocaust flooring and tesserae from a disturbed mosaic.[62] A copper pipe suggests that it was supplied with running water. A carnelian intaglio depicting Mars found on the opposite side of the street hints that someone associated with the military lived hereabouts. Nearby, at Gutter Lane, a black

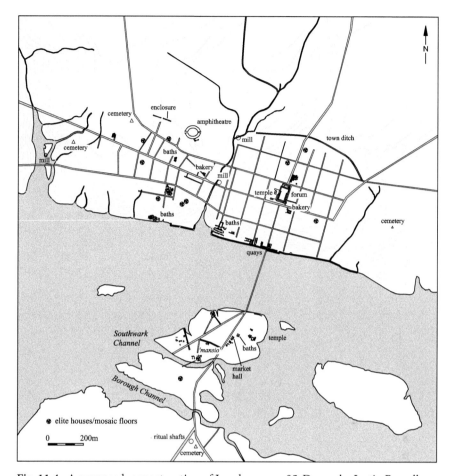

Fig. 11.4 A proposed reconstruction of London *c.* AD 85. Drawn by Justin Russell.

and white mosaic panel set within a red border was found inside an apsidal-ended reception room in a clay-walled building beside the road to the south gate of the Cripplegate fort.[63] These formed part of a cluster of at least six houses flanking Cheapside that contained impressive late first- and early second-century mosaics.[64]

High-status town houses were also introduced to other districts in the late first century, if in smaller numbers. Houses containing mosaics were built either side of Bishopsgate (Ermine Street), on the north side of town. This investment in luxurious display was reflected by a stone inlay (*opus sectile*) floor at 28–32 Bishopsgate and a large terrazzo-floored cellar reached by a flight of stairs at 7–11 Bishopsgate.[65] The presence of mosaic pavements indicate that another high-status property was found over the site of the Neronian fort at Plantation Place.[66] These houses were probably built soon after AD 85, when the materials that they

Fig. 11.5 The Flavian town houses at Watling Court (WAT78: after Perring and Roskams 1991). Drawn by Justin Russell.

employed came into common use in London's domestic architecture. Most were built of timber and unfired clay, and the best had solid walls of rammed earth, mud brick, or clay slab set over masonry footings. Only monumental public buildings were wholly stone-built at this time, although brick was increasingly used for string coursing, and for quoining around doors and corners. Most pavements survive only as small fragments with geometric designs, the best of which were of a quality only surpassed in Britain at a handful of palatial villas on the Sussex coast. Terrazzo floors (*opus signinum*) of cement and crushed tile were also a late first-century innovation following the increasing availability of brick. The houses were commonly decorated with painted walls, where red panels with decoration on a black background were particularly popular. The distribution of these higher-quality town houses witnesses an influx of wealthy settlers into districts on the fringes of earlier housing, concentrated west of the Walbrook. They afforded space for sophisticated city living. Morning attendance to business in the forum could be followed by an afternoon with comrades at the baths, before closing the day with supper-parties in rooms fitted out with mosaics and wall-paintings. Some of the new residents were connected to the military adminis-tration, likely to have been brought here by the opportunities arising from the Flavian advance.

On the south-bank

Contemporary improvements south of the river involved the redevelopment of the riverfront site at Winchester Palace *c.* AD 80 (Fig. 11.6).[67] Reclamation dumps behind piled revetments incorporated a range of expensive building materials, suggesting that an earlier building had been refurbished or replaced. The earlier Flavian building included wall paintings of unparalleled quality in Roman Britain, incorporating cupids, dolphins, sea-monsters and a head of Medusa.[68] The new development included two unusual buildings associated with early Flavian pot-tery that encroached onto a metalled road. A large masonry building fitted out with a raised floor over parallel masonry sleeper walls, about 1.2 metres apart may have been a granary, as the excavator Brian Yule proposed, or perhaps a hypocaust floor of unusual design. An adjacent curved wall of massive posts, with tile noggin infill, formed a circular structure about 7 metres across. This tower-like structure may also have provided storage space. It consequently seems likely that the mid-Flavian development involved the addition of new monumental facilities, including bulk storage, to an establishment that included luxurious resi-dential quarters and heated rooms. Associated food waste included high propor-tions of game, poultry, and pig, indicative of wealthier households.[69] This was an appropriate site for an official residence, facing the urban community across the Thames, and the suggestion that it was the residence of the procurator has already been noted (above p. 79).

The building tentatively identified as a *mansio* at 15–23 Southwark Street was also rebuilt in the late first or early second century, perhaps after brief abandonment. It is not clear if it retained its earlier function, although the presence of a hypocaust floor demonstrates its high status.[70] This floor was unusual both for being set within a clay walled building and for the use of circular tiles made in kilns at Radlett on the Verulamium road.[71] Finds of metal junction collars used to join wooden water-pipes found nearby suggest that the reconstruction involved the addition of a small bathhouse.[72] Another public building may have been built or restored on Southwark's southern island. Demolition debris from a high-status structure was found over Flavian reclamation dumps at 33 Union Street.[73] The material included imported marble and coloured stone from floors and wall

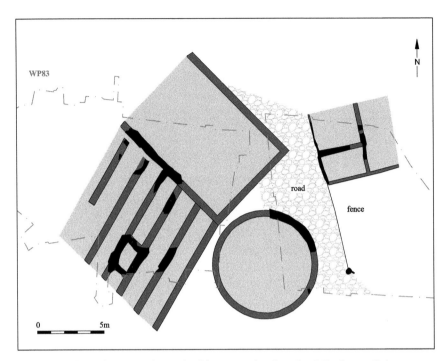

Fig. 11.6 The high-status Flavian building complex found at Winchester Palace, Southwark (WP83: after Yule 2005). Drawn by Justin Russell.

veneers. Loose tesserae included unusual examples made in glass, forming the largest group of such tesserae from Roman London. Associated ceramic building material included fragments of ceramic water pipe. Some of the earlier tile fabrics support a first-century date, although the coloured marbles probably reached London in the early second century, perhaps in a phase of refurbishment. These construction materials were different to those associated with the high-status buildings at Winchester Palace and 15–23 Southwark Street, and derived from a different building.

In addition to these higher-status buildings, the road to London Bridge was crowded with Flavian shops and workshops (Fig. 11.7). One had walls of roughly worked ragstone and tile when such materials were rarely employed in London's domestic buildings.[74] It consisted of three ranges set around an inner courtyard, occupying a street frontage at least 14 metres long. The building lacked the expensive interior decoration and high status finds one would expect to find in a town house. The excavators suggest it to have been a market building or *macellum*, drawing parallels with a similar structure found in Cirencester.[75] This is a type of building better known from the cities of Roman Italy, where small units for retailing meat and fish were arranged around central courtyards.[76] Although the Southwark building lacks the architectural complexity of these Mediterranean

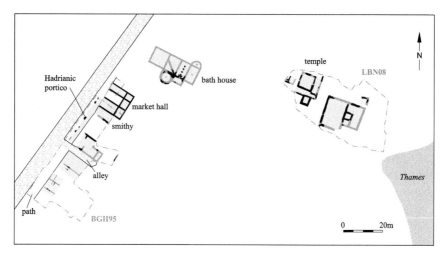

Fig. 11.7 Late first-century street-side buildings and possible market-hall (*macellum*) found at Borough High Street in Southwark, with nearby baths and a building that might possibly have been a temple (in large part from BGH95, LBN08 and BVK11: after Drummond-Murray and Thompson 2002 and Ridgeway *et al.* 2019). Drawn by Justin Russell.

examples it was a likely place for the distribution of foodstuffs. It was built next to a butcher's shop, indicated by cattle bone waste, and a bakery containing brick-and-tile ovens associated with burnt cereal grain was built nearby.[77] The building next door may have been a smithy. Other works of this period include the construction of a road leading to new housing between Watling Street and the river at Tabard Square.[78] Rubbish associated with this development, notably animal bone and glass, suggests a high-status character to the occupation. The earliest architectural embellishment of the ritual landscape beyond London's southern border may also date to the late first century, when a timber colonnade was built around an open area that may have housed a shrine at Trinity Street.[79]

This was one of the busiest periods of building activity on both sides of the river. The variety of this architecture suggests the operation of a developed housing market, drawing on supplies of imported materials and the skills of specialist craftsmen. Some of the most important building works may have been commissioned by the procurator, but the entire urban community appears to have enjoyed a confident and busy prosperity.

12

Episodes of renewal (*c.* A D 90–110)

Later Flavian London

The pace of change slowed somewhat after London's rapid early Flavian growth. No new roads are known to have been created between *c.* A D 90 and A D 120. Those that existed were sufficiently busy to warrant repair, but at longer intervals than previously, such that the '*decumanus*' beneath Cheapside was only resurfaced once between its reinstatement after the Boudican revolt and the Hadrianic period.[1] This may reflect on changed circumstances. In A D 87, shortly after Agricola's victory at Mons Graupius, some troops were withdrawn from the province to strengthen the Danube frontier against Dacian invasion.[2] Britain is thought to have received new supplies of low-denomination coins of Domitian at about this time.[3] Guy de la Bédoyère identified a concentration of these coins along the Thames foreshore at Billingsgate, which he identified as losses from supplies of coin shipped to London for provincial dispersal.[4] Since troops facing redeployment would have needed small-change to arrange transport, lodgings, and local purchases, London may have been one of the places where this coin was most needed.

Some buildings were damaged by fire towards the close of the first century. Properties at One Poultry, beside the Walbrook crossing, were burnt around the 90s, as were houses at opposite ends of the settlement at 14–18 Gresham Street and 60 Fenchurch Street.[5] A building behind the forum, at Leadenhall Court, was also incinerated in the late Flavian period.[6] South of the river buildings along the Watling Street were destroyed in a late Flavian fire and a coin of Domitian (A D 81–96) was recovered from pre-fire deposits at 22 Borough High Street.[7] These traces of destruction are unlikely to have been the product of a single conflagration, since they were widely separated and many houses were unscathed. It is likely that they evidence a series of isolated house fires, largely restricted to single properties, but we cannot dismiss the possibility that some damage was caused by incendiary unrest along London's principal streets.

What is more certain is that there was a pronounced decline in the volumes of Samian pottery reaching London at the end of the first century.[8] Since these imports serve as a proxy for other goods it seems likely that there was a hiatus in port activity. There are also instances of properties left undeveloped around this date and a decrease in building density at Bow Bells House on the west side of town is dated *c.* A D 100 from associated pottery.[9] If there were problems in

London towards the end of Domitian's reign they were neither persistent nor universal. A new portico was built around the forum's central courtyard using ragstone foundations that hint at a date after *c.* AD 85, and brick piers witness a later phase of alteration to its south wing.[10] The addition of covered areas in front of the *tabernae*-style units around the forum would have benefitted shippers moving goods around the complex. The east gate of the amphitheatre was also rebuilt, using timbers that suggest that work was underway *c.* AD 91 perhaps involving repairs to the timber superstructure and *cavea* seating.[11] A new bridge may have been built across the Thames: a timber box-structure, about 5 by 7 metres across, found on the Thames foreshore at Pudding Lane in 1981 was probably a pier-base for a temporary replacement of the fixed crossing.[12] The timbers used in its construction were dated AD 78–123, but it was in certainly place before adjacent quays were built by *c.* AD 98.[13] The Neronian warehouses and workshops immediately up-river of the bridge, investigated at Regis House, were also restored and enlarged.[14]

Waterfront renewal under Nerva and Trajan

Towards the close of the century, work began on a major overhaul of the port.[15] Construction started down-stream from London Bridge where a new timber-fronted embankment subsumed the Flavian landing stage (Fig. 12.1). Two tile-roofed masonry warehouses separated by a narrow passage were built facing the river. Each measured about 25 metres long by 6 metres deep, and was divided into five timber-floored open-fronted bays secured by removable wooden shutters. Their design was similar to the warehouses built upriver of London Bridge some 30 years before (p. 101). Gustav Milne suggests that this new quay was built *c.* AD 90, since it employed construction timbers felled AD 86–98. Timbers used to build associated warehouses had, however, been felled no earlier than AD 94. Since these were an integral part of the new waterfront it is likely that the improvements were all undertaken AD 94–8.[16] Wider urban renewal at this date is hinted at by excavations at the Bloomberg headquarters, where buildings fronting onto the main road were all replaced during the 90s.[17] The Neronian waterfront up-river from London bridge wasn't replaced until a few years later, but a vulnerable section was buttressed with timber felled no earlier than AD 95.

The decision to rebuild may have been influenced by a reduction in the Thames' tidal range, evidenced by the fact that later Roman waterside structures were built at levels previously inundated at high-tide.[18] Waterfront advance would have placed the quays into deeper water. On the other hand, the main effects of tidal regression may not yet have been in evidence. Tides are thought to have powered a mill built at the mouth of the river Fleet within the period AD 76–99, and a colony of acorn barnacles (*Balanus improvisus*) attached to early second-century

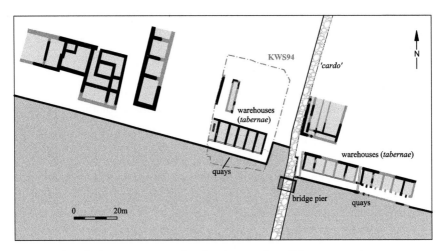

Fig. 12.1 London's port *c.* AD 95 after the construction of the new warehouses downstream of the bridge (ILA79, PEN79, PDN81, FM085: after Milne 1985, Brigham 2001b, and Brigham and Watson 1996). The bridge itself is shown in the short-lived arrangement represented by the timber pier-base found at Pudding Lane. Earlier and later iterations of the fixed crossing may have been located immediately upstream of this location. Drawn by Justin Russell.

revetments at Regis House show that the river remained brackish.[19] What is certain, however, is that the enlarged waterfront terrace added space for handling cargoes and vehicular access, and new warehouses increased secure storage capacity. The constructions downstream of London Bridge suggest that this capacity was targeted on shipping arriving upriver, seeking to dock close to London's forum.

These building activities merit considering within their historical context. We have no reliable sources for events in Britain in the decades after Agricola was recalled, but an inscription in Rome indicates that a veteran colony was established at Gloucester during Nerva's short reign AD 96–8.[20] Archaeological evidence suggests that the colony at Lincoln was also established around this time.[21] These new foundations on the sites of redundant legionary fortresses were the gift of imperial patronage. Nerva's involvement is an interesting one. Like Vespasian before him, he had no dynastic right to succession and relied heavily on the support of the army. Investment in Britain's garrison was a prudent strategy, and would account for land-grants to veteran colonists and spending on the infrastructure of supply through London's port. It might also account for the presence in Britain of unusually high numbers of a rare coin-type issued by Nerva showing Neptune holding a trident and a ship's prow.[22] One of these was found by Charles Roach Smith near London Bridge where a shrine to Neptune may have stood (below p. 230).[23] Other coins of Nerva, issued *c.* AD 97, employed the legend *annona August(i)* and showed *annona* as the personification of Rome's grain supply.[24] These rare types followed a model set by coins minted under Nero AD 63–7 and Domitian AD 85–6. All three *annona* issues were minted at dates when new quays were built along London's waterfront. There is no suggestion that these coins were minted to celebrate building works in London, but there may have been an underlying connection between the imperial intervention in *annona* supply celebrated on the coins and the commissioning of new harbour works in London. In a similar vein, it can be observed that the warehouses in London were contemporaries of Nerva's warehouses in Rome (the *Horrea Nervae*), one of only two public works in Rome known to have been the product of his benefaction.[25] London's new waterfront may well have been built as part of a considered programme of investment in *annona* supplies under Nerva's administration.

This programme of waterfront renewal wasn't completed until somewhat later, when the Neronian quay at Regis House was eventually replaced. The new revetments, built 4.5 metres further onto the foreshore, employed a pile foundation with a final sapwood ring dated to AD 101, matching a date of *c.* AD 102 obtained from alterations to waterfront buildings a short distance down-river.[26] This suggests that the works were undertaken under Nerva's heir Trajan after his triumphant conclusion of the first Dacian war. Projects initiated at this time included harbour works in Rome, dated AD 101–3, and improvements to the harbour infrastructure at Ostia and Portus to provide safe anchorage for transports associated with the grain dole.[27] London may have similarly benefitted from investment in the *annona*. Changes in the scale and direction of supply at this time were marked by the arrival of new imports of Samian from the central Gaulish kilns of Les Martres-de-Veyre following a decline in imports from the southern Gaulish kilns at La Graufesenque.[28] Work is also likely to have started on the construction of London's massive new forum complex, as described in the next chapter.

Other public works

The aisled building opposite the forum, at 5–12 Fenchurch Street, was also refurbished early in the second century. One room was painted with an architectural illusion featuring a standing woman with arms aloft: a pose typically used in prayer.[29] An adjacent room furnished with amphorae and flagons may have been a kitchen. The suggestion that this building was the meeting place of a *collegia* or guild has its attractions. Roman cities relied heavily on such guilds to function from the early second century onward.[30] In Chichester a collegium of *fabri* (builders) was sufficiently important to have dedicated a temple to Minerva and Neptune and we can assume the existence of similar institutions in London (see p. 269).[31] Collegia functioned as 'brotherhoods', establishing an institutional framework for members to further shared business interests. This was important at port cities where transient communities had need of such patronage networks. They also compensated for any under-development of other civic institutions, mediating between the provincial authorities and local community. Collegia scheduled regular feasts and banquets, and were cult associations figuring prominently in public ceremonies and processions. This would have included devotions to the imperial cult. The praying lady painted on the wall of the building at Fenchurch Street would have been at home in such a context.

A few years after the rebuilding of London's port the Blossom's Inn waterworks were improved.[32] A new timber-lined well was built using timbers felled AD 104, and another *c.* AD 108–9. This was a larger feature, some 3.6 metres square, and its fills contained the remains of a water lifting device formed from two heavy wrought iron chains linked to a series of open-topped, oak-board box-buckets that carried water (Fig. 12.2). The bucket-chain was discarded in the well after the destruction of the well-house in the Hadrianic fire alongside several complete box-flue tiles and roofing-tiles, three bearing procuratorial stamps, that may have come from the nearby Cheapside baths. This was a different device to the one found in the Neronian well. The earlier mechanism relied on tread-wheel-powered box-chains with side-ports, but the new one involved bucket chains using capstan and gears. This improved water-lifting technology reached London at the start of the second century. The chain would have held at least thirty box-buckets, each containing approximately six litres of water when full, capable of lifting over 72,000 litres (16,000 gallons) of water over a ten-hour operating day. It is probable that the main demand for this water came from London's thirsty bathhouses, including those at Cheapside and a proliferating number of private establishments.[33] The Flavian baths at Huggin Hill also saw several major alterations in the Trajanic period, possibly drawing on the same improved water-supply. Works included the insertion of a large timber drain around the building, the addition of second double-apsed hot room (*caldarium*) onto the northern side of the complex, and a further eastern suite of rooms built over the probable site of an earlier *palaestra* which included another large new caldarium (Fig. 11.3, p. 141).[34] The interior was decorated with a range of imported marbles. The new rooms increased the capacity of the building, perhaps allowing for social and gender segregation. Curiously, however, the baths fell out of use soon after these improvements. Interim reports describe a rapid abandonment, involving stripping reusable fixtures and fittings from the furnace rooms and service areas. Trajanic pottery was associated with the subsequent closure of the larger *caldarium* on the western side of the building. Earth-walled buildings were eventually set within the disused buildings, whilst the main vaulted sections of baths may not have been demolished until the late second century. One can only imagine that the building developed a structural fault that left it unfit for use, or was associated with a community that had departed London.

Fig. 12.2 A reconstruction of the water lifting device from Gresham Street (GHT00), showing the operation of the tread-wheel-driven Type-A bucket-chain (drawing by Bob Spain and reproduced by kind permission of Museum of London Archaeology).

At some point in the late first century, a Romano-Celtic temple was built between the amphitheatre and the Blossom's Inn pool (Fig. 12.3). It had long been recognized that masonry walls in this area were not orientated on the local street-grid, but not known why.[35] It can now be suggested that this unusual alignment prevailed because these structures were built within a temple precinct established around the hillside springs (above p. 77). The corners of Romano-Celtic temples were commonly aligned on the cardinal points of the compass, disregarding the orientation of neighbouring streets.[36] Although the springs here may have been the focus of earlier attention, the earliest temple was built in the late first century.[37]

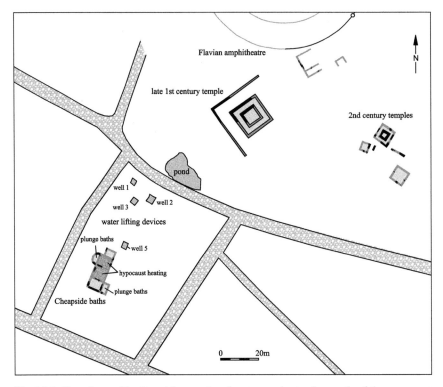

Fig. 12.3 Temples and baths, with associated waterworks, to the south of the amphitheatre. The northern part of this figure involves a considerable amount of conjecture and is based on incompletely published interim plans (after Blair *et al.* 2006). Drawn by Justin Russell.

This consisted of a square central *cella* surrounded by a colonnade with pier-bases clad in Purbeck marble.[38] Most temples in southern Britain were built to this Romano-Celtic design, and precincts containing clusters of such buildings have been found on the borders of several towns.[39] As has already been noted, the Cheapside baths may have been associated with this temple complex.

A bathhouse was also built in Southwark close to the road to London Bridge, near the market hall and bakery at Borough High Street (above p. 80). Four rooms of this masonry structure were discovered in excavations for the Thameslink railway.[40] A coin of Domitian of AD 86 was recovered from construction deposits, and the building materials are consistent with a late first- or early second-century date. The structure contained a circular room, about 5 metres across, that may have been a sweat room (*sudatoria*), dry heat room (*laconicum*) or sunken plunge bath.[41] Too little of the building was found to establish its scale, but it is unlikely to have rivalled the larger bathing complexes north of the river. These baths may also have been associated with a temple precinct, mirroring arrangements at

Cheapside. A roughly square masonry walled building, found 50 metres east of the baths at 25 London Bridge Street, may have been a Romano-Celtic temple.[42] Little information on this building is presently available, and its identification is far from certain, but a statue-base dedicated to Silvanus by Publius Fabius confirms the presence of a shrine in the area.[43] Silvanus was a pastoral deity whose cult appealed to men from the lower economic classes within Roman cities.[44] A late first-century flagon found nearby in Tooley Street in 1912 carried a scratched graffiti '*Londini ad fanvm Isidis*' identifying it as vessel that belonged to a shrine of Isis.[45] The cult of this Egyptian goddess was popular with administrators and officials along Rome's frontiers.[46] The survival of the vessel suggests that it was buried intact, probably as a structured deposit within a well or ritual shaft, and that a nearby Iseum shared the ritual landscape with the worship of Silvanus. A sacred site at this location would have faced the incoming tides, where cult practices could have used the rising water to replicate the Nile floods. The topography of this area finds parallel in a shrine to Silvanus at Ostia that was reached through a bakery, and which included images of the deified Augustus, Isis, Harpocrates, Fortuna, and Annona amongst others.[47] The Ostian bakers negotiated with these gods to secure the harvests and supplies of *annona* grain. Similar concerns may have contributed to the development of a religious complex behind the market-hall and bakery on the road to London Bridge.

London may now have had five or more bathhouses, including two public baths flanking the mouth of the Walbrook (at Huggin Hill and Cannon Street), and three smaller roadside establishments alongside routes into town (at Cheapside, Borough High Street, and Fenchurch Street). This was not excessive. London was larger than Pompeii, which had at least four public bathhouses at the time of Vesuvius' eruption.[48]

Extending the city

London is likely to have been defined by a formal boundary, separating and sanctifying political life within the settlement and expelling polluting activities. These limits were redrawn as the city expanded. London's first boundary probably reproduced the slighted defences of the Claudian army encampment, and early Flavian expansion may have resulted in the construction of earthworks to define a northern perimeter (above p. 127). At some point in the early second century, the ditch that marked the Flavian limits was levelled.[49] The western limits of the city are not so easily recognized. It is likely that London was undefended for much of the time, and boundary markers are difficult to trace on the ground. The topography suggest that an early boundary existed close to the east end of St Paul's Cathedral since burials are not found east of this line and the street grid did not extend to its west.[50]

By the end of the first century, London's western boundary might have followed canalized stream channels between St Paul's Cathedral and the river Fleet. Much remains uncertain about the history and purpose of these features, which diverted small streams that flowed into the Fleet south to the Thames.[51] Two large channels near the source of these streams were recorded north of Newgate Street in 1907–9.[52] They appeared to predate the masonry city wall, suggesting that they were here before c. AD 200. This finds confirmation in the presence of late first- and second-century pottery in the fills of a ditch at Paternoster Square into which they were directed.[53] The eastern channel was described as a boundary ditch, with artificially cut sides 12.2 metres wide and 5.3 metres deep. A 2.45-metre-thick monumental ragstone wall was inserted along its east side. There is little doubt that ditch and wall were Roman, and a late first- or early second-century date is likely. The scale of these features suggest the presence of an important public construction close to the settlement boundary. Despite its location, the structure doesn't appear to have been a town wall, and it remains one of Roman London's more enigmatic features. The engineering involved in redirecting the streams towards the Thames must have been born of some significant need, resulting in the excavation of channels that were both larger but more irregular than the other boundary ditches known from Roman London. One possibility is that the water was being channelled towards mills by the Thames.

A large ditch may have marked the northern boundary of the settlement west of the Walbrook. In excavations at St Bartholomew's Hospital, some 25–33 metres to the north of the later town wall, a 6-metre-wide U-shaped ditch a little over 1 metre deep, was traced east-west for a length of c. 100 metres.[54] This was apparently dug after trees had been cleared in the early Flavian period, and contained Hadrianic and Antonine pottery within its fills, before being recut as a smaller feature, probably in the late second century. This differed from the large V-shaped ditches that defined major boundaries in London prior to AD 85, possibly indicating that these earthworks were later and differently engineered.

Cemeteries and tombs

Most Claudio-Neronian cemeteries remained in use throughout the Flavian period. New cemeteries were also established further into the countryside flanking roads radiating from the city. Several of the main graveyards of the later city started in use at this time. Four areas of burial can be described, each the result of later expansion agglomerating smaller Flavian plots.[55] The cemetery east of town developed around the Flavian road to Shadwell (p. 123), especially after c. AD 120. These graveyards eventually extended over some 12 hectares, from which more than 140 cremations have been recovered.[56] The western cemetery expanded to cover an area of 24 hectares, in an arc from Holborn to Aldersgate. Roadside burials also flanked Roman Watling Street, extending more than 1.5 kilometres west of the city to Endell Street where a cylindrical leaden cist containing cremated bones and coins of Vespasian was found.[57] Smaller burial plots included a group of cremations found west of Fleet Street in Shoe Lane in 1927.[58] Roman Ermine Street (modern Bishopsgate) also attracted cemeteries, although perhaps not until later. Several other cemeteries were located on the mainland to the south of Southwark.

Cremation was initially the preferred burial rite. Ashes were placed in vessels, cists and casks similar to those used in earlier cemeteries, sometimes accompanied by other vessels with food to sustain the deceased on their journey.[59] A couple of pits within which bodies were cremated (*bustum*) have been found, as well as spreads of redeposited pyre material.[60] The pyre, rather than the grave, was the main focus of funeral rites. The debris suggests that corpses were often clothed, wearing dress accessories, and had sometimes been cremated on nailed wooden biers.[61] Finds from these and other cemetery assemblages indicate that meals took place at the funeral and visits to the grave. Offerings, mainly pig and chicken, are present within half of the cremations: both as cremated materials from the pyre and unburnt.[62] Handfuls of lentils, a token of mourning, were thrown onto some pyres.[63] A preponderance of drinking vessels, rather than cooking or serving dishes, suggests that libations were more widespread than feasts.[64] These funerals were important occasions, leaving burial grounds well-tended.[65]

A few tombs were set within imposing masonry mausolea. A sculpture of Cotswold limestone buried in a late first- or early second-century roadside ditch at 24–6 Minories portrayed a half life-sized eagle with spreading wings that held a writhing serpent in its beak.[66] This personification of Jupiter was a fitting subject for a funerary monument. It declared the victory of celestial power over the chthonic forces of death represented by the serpent, whilst alluding to the supremacy of Roman imperial power. The piece was shaped to fit into an alcove or niche within a tomb and its style suggests a Flavian or Trajanic date, indicating that the monument only survived for a generation or two before demolition. It would have been removed from a tomb in London's eastern cemetery where the foundations of several mausolea have been found.[67] Fragments of wall veneers, including Purbeck and Carrara marble, dispersed amongst later burials in this area would have decorated these structures. Other fragments of architectural stonework from monumental tombs were reused in fourth-century towers added to the town walls and include the effigy of a Flavian soldier and a lion-and stag sculpture found at Camomile Street.[68] The female head of a small sphinx, also carved in Cotswold limestone, was found in a second-century pit at Drapers' Gardens.[69] Blocks of rusticated purple sandstone reused in the footings of the west gate of the Cripplegate fort are likely to have derived from a monumental Flavian tomb that stood in the western cemetery area.[70] A female figure pouring water from an urn, probably Venus or a nymph, found at Skipton Street in

Southwark may have derived from a Hadrianic funerary statue on the southern approaches to the settlement.[71]

These funerary monuments along the roads that converged on London proclaimed the status and Roman identity of successful individuals whose achievements mattered after death.[72] Those who merited extravagant commemoration tended to be outsiders, particularly with a background in military service. It is also notable that some tombs were conspicuously more monumental than contemporary houses. This suggests that we are looking at the graves of a few persons of rank, whose heirs were anxious to retain a status that could not be taken for granted and whose marginal status limited other options for political participation. This uncertain inheritance might explain why some tombs were demolished relatively soon after their construction.

13

The great forum (*c.* AD 110–25)

Hadrian and the forum

In the summer of AD 122, the emperor Hadrian visited Britain on his extended travels through the empire.[1] London is likely to have been his first port of call, and his arrival a splendid occasion marked by sacrifices, processions and games. The emperor was attended by a large entourage that included his new provincial governor, Platorius Nepos, and a detachment of the Praetorian Guard. The imperial party also included the empress Sabina and historian Suetonius, and would have been entertained in the London residences of the governor and procurator.

Roger Tomlin has cautiously suggested that this may have been the occasion when London was awarded the honorary status of *colonia*.[2] He bases this on a reconstruction of an inscription on a Purbeck marble slab found at the Huggin Hill baths in 1989. Only a few letters survived and various readings are possible, but one word appears to have ended with the letters NIA, for which *colonia* is a credible reconstruction. The style of lettering suggest an imperial dedication under Trajan, Hadrian, or Antoninus Pius. Hadrian might well have elevated London, tidying-up an anomalous institutional arrangement, but the evidence is too slight for certainty. Since the inscription was found at a site where the main phases of architectural renovation are Trajanic, it may well date from this earlier time.

Whatever London's formal status, it gained a grand new civic centre in the early second century (Fig. 13.1). The monumental walls of London's vast forum were carefully recorded in the late nineteenth-century rebuilding of Leadenhall Market, supplemented by more recent discoveries around Gracechurch Street and during the construction of Richard Rogers' Lloyd's building.[3] These studies suggest that work started on the new complex whilst its smaller Flavian predecessor remained standing. Massive new ranges were set around the earlier structure, which was later demolished to make space for a new central courtyard. When complete the new complex extended over an area of 2.75 hectares, making it five times the size of its predecessor. It extended to the line of pre-existing streets to south, west, and east, filling a double-width block equivalent to 600 Roman feet. The earlier streets were re-laid and a new one built along the north side. In the process, the street to the east was widened from around 5 metres to 9 metres across, sufficient to allow waggons to pass in both directions and leave space for others to halt for loading and unloading.[4] The main entrance remained at the south, where the road rising from London Bridge crested Cornhill.

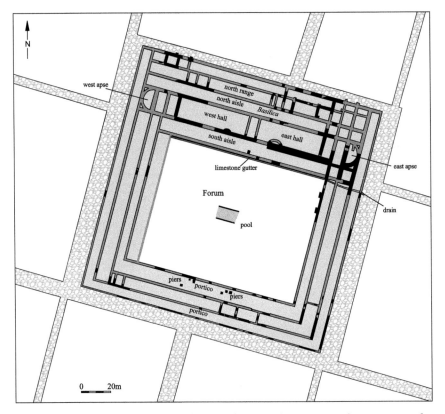

Fig. 13.1 The early second-century forum (after Marsden 1987, Brigham 1991a, and Dunwoodie 2004). Although Trajanic in original conception, the ranges of rooms to the north of the basilica were not completed until the Hadrianic period. Drawn by Justin Russell.

The principal basilica lay to the rear of the complex, and its remains have been traced from St Michael's Alley in the west to Lime Street in the east. Brick and ragstone walls, up to 1.5 metres thick, were set over 2.5-metre-deep foundations of concreted ragstone, and the ground level was raised by 1 metre. When complete this block measured 167 metres long by 52.5 metres across, making it longer than St Paul's Cathedral and the largest building of its type in the north-west provinces. The central range is often described as a nave running the length of the building, as one might expect to find in a basilica. This would, however, have resulted in a peculiarly elongated space. Foundations recorded in 1881 by Henry Hodge at 3 Gracechurch Street suggest that it might instead have been divided into two separate halls, each about 13.7 metres wide and 43.3 metres long, facing each other across a 6-metre-wide entry chamber. Although unusual, this arrangement finds parallel in the Flavian forum at Silchester.[5]

Drawing on the evidence of the building's proportions Trevor Brigham has suggested that the central range may have been 25 metres high and lit from clerestory windows. Aisles were built to either side. The north aisle was added in a secondary phase of construction, after which the nave's north wall was replaced by an arcade of brick piers. This was mirrored by another arcaded opening onto the southern aisle. A further range of rooms was then added along the outside of the northern aisle. Painted walls and cemented floors in the middle of this range are presumed to have decorated high-status offices. A final range to the north included a portico along most of the length of the basilica, with smaller shops and stores (*tabernae*) reached independently from the road beyond. Large external buttresses added strength and emphasis to the building, recalling the smaller buttresses around the Flavian forum. The building carried a red tile roof. Some of the imbrices and tegulae in the most common fabric were stamped PPBRLON, as were some wall bricks, suggesting that these were obtained from brickworks controlled by the procurator. Mortar surfaces throughout the principal parts of the building may have supported timber floors.

An apse at the east end of the central range was separated from the nave by a double antechamber. The walls of the eastern antechamber, next to the apse, were painted in red panels with floral designs and included at least one robed figure. It is possible that the apse was clad with marble veneer, a panel of which was found at Whittington Avenue.[6] The importance of this part of the building is suggested by the fact that it was left standing when the rest of the basilica was demolished in late antiquity (below p. 356). The antechamber and apse may have provided a setting for a tribunal, the raised platform where magistrates sat in judgement, in an arrangement consistent with Vitruvian prescriptions.[7] It is alternatively possible that the apse housed a cult shrine. The demolition of London's Flavian forum involved the destruction of the small classical temple to its west, but it is improbable that the gods who had inhabited this space would have been forcibly removed. Since there was no separate temple, they are likely to have been rehoused in shrines and cult spaces within the new basilica. These may have included Rome's traditional Capitoline gods, the imperial *numen* and cult, the deified ancestors and predecessors from whom the emperor claimed power and other divine patrons linked to the imperial family and Roman state.

A second apse may have been located at the west end of the basilica, beneath the church of St Michael Cornhill, mirroring arrangements to the east and finding parallel in the design of the Hadrianic forum at Silchester.[8] The room at the centre of the northern range, now beneath the church of St Peter Cornhill, might also have housed a shrine since this was the location favoured for the shrines of military principia.[9] In sum and assuming some symmetry to the building layout, we can speculatively identify three parts of the basilica as having special importance: apses at the eastern and western ends of the 'naves', and an axially central room to their north. The building may also have housed a council chamber, or curia, where magistrates and governing officials could meet. Council chambers were an important part of earlier Roman fora, and according to Vitruvius their design had to match the importance of the community.[10] In London, however, real power lay within the offices commanded by governor and procurator.

Basilicas were assembly halls for legal, political, and business affairs.[11] It is likely that government departments were housed within offices on the north side of the central range: perhaps including libraries, archives and counting rooms associated with the census and treasury. These were places where taxes could be assessed and bullion banked within the secure masonry walls. Scribes, notaries and legal clerks may have occupied adjacent spaces, from which they could attend public courts within the basilica. The most important proceedings would have been presided over by the governor, and his court would have filled the larger halls within the nave. A prison, and places for attendant officers, may have been found nearby. Despite our assumptions about the uses to which the building was put, we are unable to positively identify any of these activities from archaeological evidence, and it may be misleading to expect to find clear functional demarcation. Chambers may have been used flexibly depending on the needs of the government of the day: changing seasonally and from one administration to the next. Some parts of the basilica were little used, as illustrated by the fact that a badly damaged floor in one room was left unrepaired.[12]

Whilst the basilica dominated the new forum, two-thirds of its space was given over to the central courtyard and enclosing ranges. This courtyard measured about 116 by 84.4 metres, making it almost as large as Trafalgar Square. The principal gateway would have been to the south, facing the road to London Bridge, and there may have been side entrances through the western and eastern ranges. These were easily secured, allowing close traffic control for the purposes of security and taxation. The imperial fora offered a different kind of space to the open city centres of the Roman republic: controlled, exclusive and segregated.[13]

The ranges that enclosed the forum courtyard were set behind a vast 9-metre-wide portico, with a further portico attached to the outside of the complex facing out to the surrounding streets. These ranges probably included secure storage and workshop facilities for renting-out to business, with activities spilling out from shops into the covered portico. Parallels can be drawn with the roofed markets known as *qaysariyya* in Islamic cities.[14] Vitruvian description also placed bankers' shops (*argentariae tabernae*) within such places, where the money-lenders described in the Bloomberg writing-tablets are likely to have conducted business.[15] An instructive parallel can be drawn with the *tabernae* set around Trajan's forum in Rome. Drawing on a reference in the *Fragmenta Vaticana* these are thought to have included ground floor offices for the treasury supervised by imperial officials (*Caesariani*), with upper rooms occupied by officials associated with the grain dole (*annona*).[16] At Ostia the prefect of the *annona* commanded an office surrounded by the offices of private merchants.[17] Other parts of the forum might have included facilities for public distributions made on state occasions: according to a later source the future emperor Commodus enjoyed sitting in Trajan's basilica to dispense food and cash subsidies (*congiarium*) in person.[18]

The forum was the public focus of an imperial ideology built around the unifying figure of the emperor, whose power was sanctioned and favoured by the gods. Statues reinforced this message, converting an abstract concept of imperial rule into a direct relationship between ruler and ruled.[19] As a bishop in Galatia was later to observe, 'the emperor's image has to be put up in every place in which the governor governs, in order that his acts have authority'.[20] Statues were probably set over the piers and bases in the southern wing of the forum, some reusing stumps from walls and column bases of the Flavian forum, and in the portico on the south side of the basilica.[21] These were busy locations close to the main entrance, creating focal spots for those meeting here. Fifteen fragments of bronze statues have been recovered from Roman London, representing at least five large figures, and many more will have been melted down over the ages.[22] Their distribution suggests that some stood within temple complexes on the borders of the city, at Gresham Street and Tabard Square. Two of these pieces, however, seem likely to have come from the forum. The most important is the life-size bronze head of the emperor Hadrian recovered from the Thames below London Bridge in 1834, and now in the British Museum. This had been hacked from the body of the imperial statue, and may have been thrown into the river in an act of ritual abuse and expurgation similar to those vested in mortal remains (p. 110). The emperor is portrayed at the age of about 30, clearly recognizable from his incipient beard and distinctive features. The statue was intended to be viewed from in front and probably stood within an apsidal niche in the new forum. It was perhaps commissioned from a London workshop to coincide with the imperial visit of AD 122. The other bronze likely to derive from a statue in the forum was a life-size left hand found at 83–7 Gracechurch Street in 1867.

The open square provided a setting for both markets and ceremonial activities, such as the annual swearing of oaths of loyalty to the emperor.[23] Altars may have been placed here, and the piazza appears to have been dominated by a large ornamental pool. This was provisionally identified from observations made in a telecommunications tunnel dug along Gracechurch Street in 1977, where the side walls of a sunken mortar and clay lined feature 7.43 metres wide was recorded.[24] The length of this feature wasn't established, but it would have been at least 14 metres long if set centrally and symmetrically within the courtyard. Although some reconstructions present this as a covered wing bisecting the forum courtyard, Peter Marsden remains convinced that the features he observed formed a pool. The new forum was undoubtedly supplied with running water. A wooden supply-pipe, identified by a row of iron interconnecting collars, was built alongside a new road built along the north side of the forum. A large drain on the north-east side of the courtyard relied on a running water to be flushed, and indicates the likely presence of a public latrine. The water supply might also have allowed for one or more fountains, providing drinking water at the entrance to the basilica where a limestone gutter was observed. Whilst popular reconstructions imagine the forum as crowded with market-day stalls, it is equally possible that it was sometimes laid out as a garden. A grey soil intervened between phases of hard-surfacing, and the space presents similarities with Rome's forum of Vespasian (*Templum Pacis*) with its decorative water features and plantings.[25]

Dating the forum

Sufficient Flavian material has been found beneath the main body of the forum to show that it couldn't have been built much before AD 100, although parts of the building site could have been cleared in the 90s.[26] A coin of Domitian (*c.* AD 85) left in one of the buildings demolished to make way for the new basilica provides a *terminus post quem*.[27] Work is likely to have started during Trajan's reign, although a slightly earlier date remains possible. It is tempting to suggest that the harbour improvements of *c.* AD 102 onwards, described in the previous chapter, anticipated the need to deliver vast quantities of building materials by river. It is also worth noting that the construction of water features in and around the forum required the services of hydraulic engineers, and the evidence from Gresham Street shows that such engineers were busy in London *c.* AD 104 (p. 152). There are also similarities in the ceramic building materials supplied to the forum and those used in the supposedly Trajanic baths at Huggin Hill, including the use of Procuratorial tiles stamped with the same die types.[28] This suggests that work had started on building the baths and forum at about the same time, drawing on the same procurement chain. These various points of reference allow it to be suggested that work started on building the new forum soon after AD 102, perhaps in a programme of public investment planned after Trajan's Dacian victory that year. This would make London's forum a close contemporary of Trajan's forum in Rome, where building work began in earnest in AD 106/107.[29] Trajan's forum was dominated by the massive *Basilica Ulpia*, measuring 176 by 59 metres, which presents superficial similarities of scale and form with London's early second-century basilica.

Despite the ambitious plans made around the beginning of the century, the northern ranges of London's basilica were not finished until sometime later. The layout leaves no doubt that these rooms formed part of the original plan, but structural details indicate that the builders had curtailed their ambition. These parts of the complex were no earlier than Hadrianic, as demonstrated by the presence of black-burnished pottery in construction deposits. These building ranges were subsequently damaged by fire in the second century: in Chapter 19, it is argued that this was the Hadrianic fire of the mid-120s. This places the completion of the basilica within the same decade as Hadrian's visit to Britain in AD 122. It would be consistent with Hadrian's role as a benefactor of cities for his visit to have been the spur for a programme of public construction, involving the completion of a forum started almost 20 years earlier under his adoptive father Trajan.[30] Hadrian had, after all, played a similar role in the completion of Trajan's forum and temple in Rome. Although the scale of London's new forum seems excessive for the needs of the city, it is a mistake to think of its architecture in purely functional terms. The building carried ideological and political symbolism, serving as a simulacra of the fora of imperial Rome and built to commensurate scale.[31]

The completion of London's forum may have encouraged competitive improvements to other Romano-British civic centres, with the masonry fora at Silchester, Caerwent, and Leicester, all likely to be Hadrianic in date.[32] Tom Blagg has shown that the decorative stonework used in these second-century buildings finds no parallel in military architecture, implying that the stonemasons were recruited from civilian projects.[33] Although the Roman army provided labour for some projects financed by Hadrian, it seems more likely that London's forum was a civilian construction, perhaps subsidised by the procurator whose office managed the tileries that supplied the building works.[34]

Before the Hadrianic fire

The quays built upriver from London Bridge at Regis House after AD 102 were replaced shortly prior to the destructions of the Hadrianic fire.[35] This new waterfront, recorded by Gerald Dunning near Regis House, was more substantial than the Trajanic waterfront, using crossed beams similar to those of the Neronian quays rather than a simpler timber revetment. Here, and along most of the waterfront, the embankment was advanced into the river beneath the line now taken by Thames Street where it remains largely inaccessible to archaeological study.[36] We lack close dendrochronological dating, but at Miles Lane a group of timbers felled between AD 114 and AD 142 were associated with a revetment of this phase.[37] Pottery from reclamation dumps suggests an early Hadrianic date. The working surfaces associated with the new quays were lower than before suggesting a significant fall in the levels reached by the high tide, and it has been suggested that the quays were extended further into the river to find deeper water.[38] The monumental nature of the new waterfront might suggest an official involvement in the exercise, perhaps prompted by the need to import large quantities of building material to complete the construction of the forum and contemporary building projects.

Before the fire, London was a busy and crowded city, benefitting from investment in the port and public facilities inspired by the policies of particular regimes
seeking to secure allegiances, underwrite dynastic claims and further military
campaigns (Fig. 13.2). This is likely to have applied whether or not the building
works were funded by the administration or drew on other sources of patronage.
Whilst early investment was chiefly directed towards developing London's port
and infrastructure of supply, the interests of the urban population were addressed
in the construction of Neronian baths. From the Flavian period, this also included
an architecture of games and public festivities following the promotion of the
imperial cult, and might have involved subsidized grain supply and distributions
of bread.

These facilities supported the presence of a large urban population within the
80-year-old city. Several town houses destroyed in the Hadrianic fire were

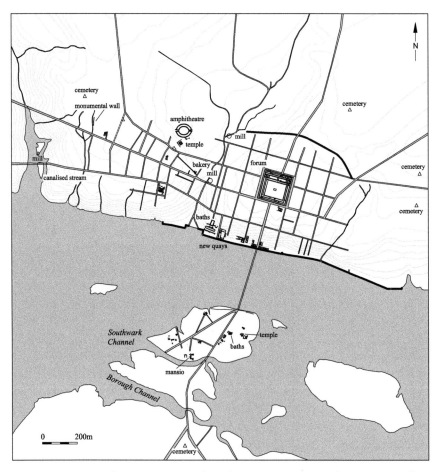

Fig. 13.2 A proposed reconstruction of London *c.* AD 120. Drawn by Justin Russell.

expensively decorated in a confident display of social status. Examples include a large early second-century courtyard building with masonry footings at Clements Lane, and an earth-walled building at 10 Gresham Street where a mosaic-floored reception-room was set behind a corridor, perhaps a peristyle veranda, overlooking a yard or garden.[39] This was an unusually crowded city, with remarkably little open space. At Watling Court, for instance, half a dozen high status buildings were divided by narrow alleyways but contained no gardens or yards.[40] In one of these buildings a mosaic appeared to have collapsed from an upper room: only in densely populated towns was space at such a premium that reception rooms were placed in upper floors. Despite the city crowds, open space wasn't far distant. An owl pellet, containing the bones of a mole and three voles, was incorporated within early second-century repairs of a floor within the forum basilica. The bird had roosted in the roof, indicating both the presence of nearby open country and the underuse of the forum facilities.[41]

PART 4

THE WORKING CITY

14

The urban hinterland

Roads and roadside settlements

The foundation of London transformed the landscape of south-east Britain, inspiring a network of roads and secondary sites radiating from the city (Fig. 14.1). The roads that issued from the river crossing connected London to other strategically important places in southern Britain. This street system may have incorporated pre-Roman components, but was largely the product of post-conquest engineering. The first cambered metalled surfaces and flanking droving ditches were almost certainly army-built. Rome required a public infrastructure of roads, bridges, and quays to move vital goods, and collect the taxes in kind and tribute on which it relied. The hard-wearing surfaces were designed for convoys of waggons carrying heavy goods, rather than soldiers on the march. This road traffic was served by a series of overnight staging points. Many are listed in the Antonine Itinerary, housing facilities used in the imperial communication and transportation network later administered as the *cursus publicus*.[1]

Four main roads approached Claudian London: one from each cardinal direction. To the south, the Kent road followed the Thames inland, bringing traffic from Richborough and Canterbury across the Medway at Rochester before heading towards Greenwich Park and thence into London along the Old Kent road via Southwark. Most goods arriving from the European continent reached London by river, but travellers would have taken the shorter Channel crossing and made their way by road. Soldiers arriving or departing Britain would have marched or ridden along Watling Street, crossing the Thames at London Bridge with caravans of pack-animals and camp-followers. Before reaching London Watling Street made an important stop at the sacred springs and wells of Springhead.[2] This was already a place of votive offering before the conquest, but saw significant expansion in the Roman period. Several masonry Romano-Celtic temples were built here in the second century, accompanied by ritual shafts containing dogs' skeletons and a human cranium. These features find close parallel in the sanctuaries that guarded London's borders at Blossom's Inn and Tabard Square (pp. 266–7). Roadside settlements were also established at crossings of the rivers Darent and Cray, serving as focal points for settlements along these fertile river valleys.[3] Another was at Welling where timber buildings and burials of the first and second centuries have been identified.[4] Closer to London a substantial masonry building with tessellated floors was found on the hillside overlooking the Thames

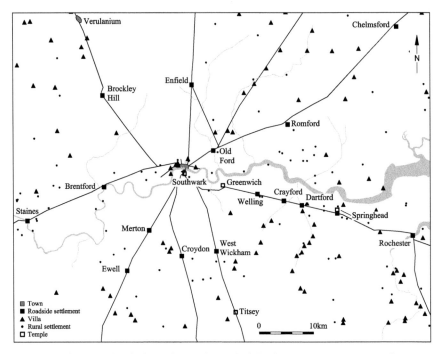

Fig. 14.1 The hinterland of London at the end of the first century A D. Drawn by Fiona Griffin.

at Greenwich Park.[5] This was probably a small Romano Celtic temple. Occupation started by *c.* A D 100, although most finds derive from later restoration. These include fragmentary marble inscriptions that might have included a dedication to the imperial divinities, although the reading is uncertain, and an arm derived from the two-thirds life-size statue of a female figure that Martin Henig fancies as *Diana Venetrix.* The building was supplied with roof-tiles bearing the distinctive stamp of the Procurator's London tilery.

The Colchester road, described as routes 5 and 9 in the Antonine Itinerary, headed east from London to meet the marshes of the Lea valley at Old Ford in Bow, about 4.6 kilometres distant, before reaching the site of *Durolito* (possibly Romford) *en route* to the crossing of the River Chelmer at Chelmsford.[6] Excavations at Lefevre Walk Estate in Old Ford show that the road occupied a 25.5-metre-wide easement between boundary ditches, with an 11-metre-wide gravel carriageway flanked by side-tracks up to 5.5 metres across.[7] Old Ford was an important site because it commanded the crossing of the river Lea and its fertile water-meadows. A 7.5-metre-wide Roman road along the eastern side of the valley, between Leyton and Walthamstow, helped manage this landscape.[8]

The line of the main road west from London, Watling Street, can be traced from Newgate along Oxford Street to Marble Arch, where it divides. The north-west route to St Albans (*Verulamium*) is followed by the Edgware Road to the summit of Brockley Hill, a distance of about 16.5 kilometres. This was the location of early Roman pottery kilns and tile works, and perhaps the site of *Sulloniacis* mentioned in the Antonine Itinerary although its core may have lain further south at Burnt Oak.[9] Finds associated with the earliest metalled surfaces of Watling Street outside *Verulamium* are late Neronian, suggesting that the northerly section of the road wasn't provided with its metalled agger until some 10–15 years after work started outside the gates of London.[10] The west road continued along what is now the northern side of Hyde Park, making its way towards the crossing of the river Brent at Brentford, and thence to Staines (*Pontibus*), before reaching Silchester (*Calleva Atrebatum*). Excavations at Brentford have shown that the earliest road, about 4–6 metres wide, was established soon after the Roman conquest.[11] This was then doubled in width during the Flavian period. Timber houses flanked the road in sufficient numbers for it to be estimated that some 300–500 people lived here.

The other main road leaving London, Ermine Street, may also have been completed sometime after the conquest. A roadside ditch found at 201 Bishopsgate, 520 metres north of the line of the later city wall, contained late first- or early second-century pottery, although arrangements within the settlement suggest that the southern end of Ermine Street was planned before the revolt of AD 60/61 (above p. 82).[12] This road headed north from Bishopsgate, following the line now taken by Tottenham High Road, eventually destined for Lincoln and York. A slight deviation in its line at Holywell in Shoreditch might mark a landmark along its course, such as a shrine at a source of the Walbrook. Isolated Roman inhumations have been found some 5–6 kilometres north of the city, between Stamford Hill and Hackney, but the main roadside settlements along Ermine Street were at Bush Hill Park near Enfield, nearly 15 kilometres from London, and Cheshunt Park 8 kilometres further to the north.[13] Flue tiles from Bush Hill Park suggests that one of the buildings contained a heated hypocaust. Ermine Street itself was recorded at Snell's Park in 1956 where the roadway was some 7 metres wide.[14]

Roads also reached London from the Sussex Weald, converging on Watling Street south of Southwark. The most important of these was Stane Street, which connected London to Chichester (*Noviomagus*) by way of a roadside station at Ewell.[15] This may have had a ritual focus, including a temple with ritual shafts established around a sacred spring. A roadside hamlet may also have existed at Mitcham.[16] A section of the metalled surfaces of Stane Street, flanked by roadside ditches, was uncovered at Harper Road in 2017.[17] The gravel had been quarried from the sides of the route, and backfilled with material dated AD 55–70. Ritual shafts or wells, similar to those from Swan Street (above p. 79) were dug nearby. The road may have been built *c.* AD 70, making it contemporary with other Flavian additions to the road system around London (pp. 122–3).

Two other routes reached London across the Sussex Weald. Neither served other urban centres or known theatres of Roman military action, and their construction highlights the importance of goods-traffic between London and iron-working sites in the High Weald. The road from the Brighton area joined onto Stane Street near the Oval and was flanked by a roadside settlement at Croydon. That from the Lewes area aimed for a junction with Watling Street at Peckham, after passing the ridgetop site of a masonry Romano-Celtic temple in Titsey Park near Biggin Hill. The road appears to have been orientated on this temple close to the source of the river Eden.[18] First- and second-century pottery has been recovered from the site, although much of the architecture is likely to have been later. A settlement also developed alongside this road at West Wickham.[19]

These observations show that the main roads into Roman London were planned within a decade of the conquest, although some sections were not surfaced until the Neronian period. This street system was significantly enhanced in the early Flavian period (c. AD 70–80/85), when several secondary routes were established and cambered metalled street surfaces became universal. Several roadside settlements around London may have come into being in the Flavian period. We lack sufficient archaeological detail to describe their early histories but only a few were certainly in existence before AD 70. The earlier foundations include Springhead and Staines, both established as waterside settlements prior to the conquest. Brentford was also early, and pottery production at Brockley Hill may have begun c. AD 55, before expanding massively c. AD 70.[20] The roads respected the sacred properties of the landscapes they traversed. Temples built on hilltops—as at Greenwich and Titsey Park—may have been useful sighting points for Roman engineers, and places for hauliers to marshal transport before and after the steepest ascents. Others at springs and river crossings, such as Springhead and Ewell, formed sensible watering points and attracted larger satellite communities. Votive offerings made at these places are likely to have purchased or rewarded safe passage, reminding us of the vulnerability of people and goods in movement.

One of the gods addressed was Mercury. Altars and statues to Mercury have been found close to the entrances to London. These include a small limestone altar from Smithfield, just beyond London's north-western boundary, a limestone statue of the god wearing his characteristic long cloak found on the northern borders of town at Moorgate and a votive altar found at St Bartholomew's Hospital in 1907.[21] Another statue of the god was found in the roadside settlement at Usher Road in Bow.[22] According to Caesar the Gauls were particularly attached to his worship, claiming him as the guide for all roads and journeys, and holding special power over money-making and trade.[23] Intriguingly some of these statues were mutilated and discarded within roadside ditches during the second or third centuries.

Most roadside settlements comprised a cluster of timber buildings strung out either side of the streets, typically covering some 5–6 hectares. Riverside locations were favoured: they made natural stopping points where animals could be watered and grazed, and connected with longer-established routes along the valleys. The inhabitants of these sites commonly engaged in small-scale craft production and industry, along with crop-processing and domestic activities. There was a ring of these settlements, about 15–20 kilometres out from London. These are likely to have been official stations (*mutationes* and *mansiones*) in the *cursus* (or *vehiculatio*), where couriers on imperial service could exchange post-horses and take rest.[24]

It is important to remember that the roads were built to cater for slow-moving wheeled traffic. The pattern of roadside settlement around Roman London coincided with the distances that hauliers and drovers could expect to cover in a day. A parallel can be drawn with arrangements in later Roman North Africa, where *annona* grain was brought to port in heavy four-wheeled ox-drawn waggons that travelled the roads at an average speed of about 3.2 kilometres per hour.[25] Drovers herding livestock to meet military and urban demand were no faster, perhaps covering 15–20 kilometres a day. Most would have been private operators, but the supporting infrastructure required government investment and control.[26] Posting stations would have incorporated official residences, grazing lands and storage facilities, alongside the publicly owned land corridor formed by the roads themselves. The presence of these facilities made them suitable places for the collection, storage, and onward dispatch of the taxes and rents from the surrounding countryside. Much will have arrived in the form of grain and agricultural surplus.[27] Some roadside settlements may also have held periodic markets (*nundinae*) attended by pedlars operating from nearby towns, where seasonal labour might be hired.[28] Markets were closely regulated, and usually kept at least 10 kilometres away from the nearest town to avoid competition. Roman posting stations could be run by licensees who had successfully bid for a 5-year contract (*manceps*), but were increasingly entrusted to low-ranking officials or military appointees.[29] These outposted *frumentarii* could be placed at stopping points along important transport and communication routes to manage and requisition necessary transport. In addition to opportunities to profit from tax-collection and market dues, rents would also have been taken from roadside commercial properties. The presence of an administrative apparatus supported by these sources of income might account for the occasional evidence of higher-status architecture and burials.

In addition to these new roadside settlements, riverside communities were established at Putney, Charlton and Thamesmead.[30] These too may have facilitated the collection and transport of local agricultural surplus commanded by London, but may also have become sites of villa estates, accounting for the masonry structures identified at Charlton and Thamesmead. Despite Rome's invention of a new geography of control, the Iron Age settlements closest to London remained remarkably little changed. Farmsteads at Bermondsey Abbey,

Clerkenwell, and St Martin-in-the-Fields may have carried on much as before, and there are no signs of significant new building at these places until considerably later.[31]

Suburban sites

A few new settlements of entirely Roman character were established along the north bank of the Thames within easy reach of London (Fig. 14.2). The early Flavian road laid out across open land east of London, later the axial focus of the eastern cemeteries, headed towards Shadwell and perhaps Ratcliffe.[32] The settlement at Shadwell was located 1 kilometre east of London, overlooking a channel of the Thames about 100 metres south of the line of the road, and subsequently became the site of an important late antique complex. These later buildings replaced timber-framed structures associated with late first- and second-century pottery, one with a raised floor that may have been a granary.[33] The road may have continued east towards Ratcliffe, 1 kilometre further downriver, where lead and stone coffins found in 1858 imply the presence of an important late Roman settlement.[34] Although the site at Ratcliffe awaits archaeological investigation, and the early structures at Shadwell are of uncertain significance, at least one of these sites was sufficiently important c. AD 70 to warrant building a road to London.

Similar developments took place upriver. A bridge over the river Fleet, probably built in the early 70s, served a Roman road beneath Fleet Street that reached suburban sites along the Strand.[35] The church of St Bride's occupies the site of a

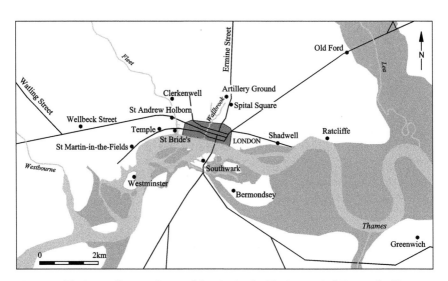

Fig. 14.2 The immediate environs of the city in the Flavian period. Drawn by Fiona Griffin.

late Roman building on the west bank of the Fleet, where unstratified pottery includes sufficient early material to suggest settlement before the end of the first century.[36] Another important early site was established at The Temple, 0.5 kilometres west of the Roman city. Excavations at 11–23 New Fetter Lane, near Dr Johnson's house, found the iron connecting collars of a piped-water supply, a masonry wall, and a scatter of late first- and early second-century material including flue-tiles.[37] These mark the presence of buildings, probably including a bath-house, close to where the Knights Templar built Temple Church in the twelfth century. The Roman precursor of Fleet Street continued westwards towards Thorney Island in Westminster, 2 kilometres upriver from London, passing close to the site of the farmstead and villa at St Martin-in-the-Fields. We don't know when this area was first occupied, but scattered finds around Westminster Abbey mark the presence of a high-status settlement from the second century.[38]

In sum, suburban sites were established at Shadwell and the Temple by the end of the first century, whilst later sites at Westminster Abbey, St Bride's, and Ratcliffe may have had early origins. These commanding locations on the north-bank of the Thames were reached by new roads built during the AD 70s. The high status architecture might indicate that these sites were the suburban villas of wealthy Londoners, although they might alternatively have started life as estate centres. Whilst Claudian and Neronian engineering had concentrated on London's port, the early Flavian investment widened to embrace other locations where goods moved between road and river, as illustrated by the improvements to the Southwark Channel and at the mouth of the Fleet (above pp. 120 and 127). The suburban sites may have been the product of investment in the infrastructure of communication and control after Vespasian's accession. The river and its navigable tributaries were essential to the movement and management of resources, establishing a network of connectivity around which the Roman infrastructure of quays and roads was developed.[39]

High-status architecture and finds have also been identified at a handful of sites on the immediate borders of the Roman town, at St Andrew Holborn, the Artillery Ground, and Spital Square, and it is likely that these were suburban villas (p. 124). Finds including Roman building material and a well containing a second-century flagon hints at the presence of another villa or farmstead next to the river Tyburn where it was crossed by the main west road some 2.5 kilometres west of the Roman town.[40]

Villas and elite settlement

With the important exception of these suburban sites, the landscape around London contained remarkably few villas. Successful towns in the western provinces were usually surrounded by country estates managed from expensively decorated villas. Villas were enjoyed as symbols of an aristocratic status that relied on urban institutions, defining a clear relationship between land ownership, wealth, and political power. Villas in southern Britain tend to cluster within 10–20 kilometres of major towns.[41] London, however, was different and few were built within 20 kilometres of the town.[42] The absence of villas north of London and towards the Weald may in part be explained by the unfavourable character of the wooded clay soils found here, but this doesn't account for their infrequency on the farmed gravel terraces to east and west. Nor can gaps in distribution be dismissed as the consequence of a failure to recognize sites beneath the modern urban sprawl, since low-status settlements and Roman burials have been found in areas where villas are under-represented. If we exclude suburban and riverside sites, only two rural Roman masonry buildings have been certainly identified in Greater London north of the Thames and west of the Lea: at Wembley and Ruislip.[43] A few more appear to have been built east of the Lea, especially along the Roding valley. The closest of these to London was found at Leyton Grange in 1718, with others likely at Wanstead Park, Chigwell, and Abridge.[44] Although the high-status architecture on these sites is unlikely to date before the second century, their occupation may have had earlier origin. All were located on the south-western margins of the late Iron Age 'Eastern kingdom' ruled from Colchester, and their distribution is consistent with a pattern of elite settlement established prior to the conquest. This suggests that these villas were located within Catuvellaunian territories and remained politically independent of London.

Similar arguments apply south of the Thames. Several luxuriously appointed villas were built along the fertile Darent and Cray valleys and in the chalk downlands above their headwaters. The earlier high-status architecture found at these sites dates *c.* AD 80–90 and involved masonry foundations supporting clay and timber walls like the best town houses of the period. Examples include the villas at Lullingstone, Orpington Station, and Keston, with slightly later establishments at Farningham and Darenth.[45] Several of these villas replaced high-status Iron Age farmsteads. At Keston, for example, an enclosed late Iron Age farmstead was occupied into the Roman period and *c.* AD 60–85 included a kiln that manufactured local Gallo-Belgic fine wares.[46] These sites were culturally and geographically part of Kent, drawing on Gallo-Belgic aristocratic traditions introduced prior to the Roman conquest. If Ptolemy was correct in describing London as a city of Kent, then these villas west of the Medway might have been home to wealthy landowners qualified to participate in London's governing council (*curia*).[47] In this case the Flavian investment in the villas of west Kent might have been prompted by the changes in political arrangements implied by the building of London's forum (above p. 133). This may, however, give too much credit to London. Flavian reform was felt throughout the province, and these Kentish villas may have remained outside of London's political jurisdiction looking instead to Canterbury or Rochester.

A connection between London and Kentish property is established by the text of a writing tablet found in Walbrook reclamation dumps at Throgmorton Avenue in 1986.[48] The scratched text, dated to the Ides of March AD 118, described a two-hectare (15 *arepennia*) wood located in a parish (*pagus*) in the territory of the people of Kent (*ciuitas Cantiacorum*), that Lucius Julius Bellicus claimed to have bought from Titus Valerius Silvinus for 40 denarii. Roger Tomlin has observed that the name of the wood, *Verlucionium*, derives from the Celtic for 'shining grove' hinting that it might have been a sacred grove. Since the Imperial Procurator would have kept records of provincial landholding for taxation purposes we don't know if the Roman citizens who had bought and sold this wood lived in London, but this is a possibility. It is easy to imagine this document to have described woodlands belonging to one of the villa estates along the Darent and Cray valleys. Although the estates of west Kent may not have lain within London's political territory, they enjoyed a close economic relationship with the city.[49] Their arable lands are a likely source of grain that supplied the city. Ernest Black has noted that the villas of west Kent had larger granaries than elsewhere in region, and this may have been influenced by the opportunities presented by the London market.[50] Beer may also have been brewed for export to London: with malting and milling attested at the Northfleet villa.[51]

Villa architecture was the product of an urban social order that relied on wealth and status displayed on rural estates, and the flourishing of villa economies was closely linked to the development of political careers.[52] London's failure to attract a penumbra of villas suggests that it enjoyed a different relationship with its surrounding territory to other self-governing cities. This lends support to the argument that it was a creation of the Roman authorities, governed by imperially appointed administrators and their servants in an arrangement that limited opportunities for the emergence of a land-owning aristocracy. It seems likely that much of the countryside around London was instead governed directly from the city, or from the network of roadside and riverside sites developed in the Flavian period. This placed considerable power in the hands of the lessees and officials based at such sites, but leaves open the question of who owned the lands around London and ultimately controlled the wealth they produced.

15

The region and its resources

The estuary

London made significant demands on regional resources: both for its own needs and for onward supply. The establishment of the city spurred an expansion of extraction industries (Fig. 15.1). The most archaeologically visible include the stone quarries of northern Kent, salterns along the Thames estuary, iron working in the Weald, and woodlands that supplied London's fuel and building timber. These existed alongside the agricultural exploitation of arable lands, principally for grain, and pastures for livestock providing traction, meat and secondary products such as leather. Cattle bones form a larger part of assemblages from the London basin compared to the rest of south-east Britain where sheep/goat are more common.[1] This may be because of the importance of plough animals in an area where grain was an important crop, and the use of oxen for haulage in and around London. Horse bones are also found in greater abundance on rural sites in the Thames estuary and London basin, reflecting on the development of cattle-droving and horse-breeding for the Roman cavalry.

London has no building stone and the Roman city imported Kentish ragstone for most of its concrete constructions. This sandy grey limestone was quarried from the banks of the river Medway around Maidstone and came to be used in Roman constructions within a decade of the conquest.[2] Its export may have contributed to the precocious development of a villa economy in this part of Kent.[3] This in turn suggests that local land-owning aristocrats profited from their ownership of these mineral resources.[4] Whilst the stone may have been acquired from private estates, quarrying and transport are more likely to have been undertaken by licensees managing the exceptional demands of large public building projects. Ragstone only came into widespread use as a building material in London from *c.* AD 80, involving regular shipments into the Thames and up-river to London's quays (below p. 308).

The estuary wetlands provided a wealth of resources.[5] Watermeadows in the Thames and Lea valleys were used for pasture: supporting oxen needed for traction, animals destined to be slaughtered for their meat and hides, equids for official use, and haymaking for winter fodder (below p. 193). Cattle were herded to town for slaughter, passing through roadside sites such as Old Ford, Staines and Enfield. Some livestock was butchered at these places, but most reached London on the hoof, illustrated by carcass processing waste from the city.[6] Roman

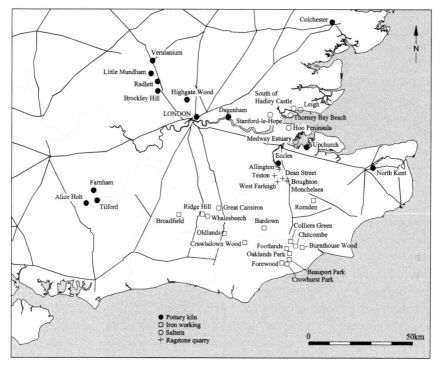

Fig. 15.1 Some of the key resources exploited by London and the Roman administration in south-east Britain, chiefly in the late first and early second centuries. Drawn by Fiona Griffin.

intervention in cattle management is suggested by stock improvements evident in animal bone assemblages, as larger breeds of cattle were introduced to the south-east.[7] Investment on this scale might have been easier to achieve on larger managed estates, and allowed for the breeding of the stockier and more muscular cattle useful for traction. Sheep would also have been pastured on down heathlands and estuarine saltmarshes.

The river offered opportunities for fishing and fouling, and oyster beds were exploited on the Essex and Kent coasts.[8] Products reached London by river, and dumps of oyster shells around the late first-century landing stage at Peninsular House suggest that this was where they arrived.[9] The value of many wetland resources was realized through the use of salt to transform perishable seasonal produce into commodities transported to towns and forts for over-winter consumption.[10] Salt enabled taxation. James Gerrard has estimated that if the entire meat ration of the Roman army needed curing, this alone would have required some 113 tons of salt annually.[11] The potential to extract salt from evaporating tidal pools was enhanced by digging brining channels, followed by boiling the product over hearths in briquetage vessels. This was a seasonal activity, best undertaken in the early autumn or later spring. Red hills, formed of waste from burning marsh plants to produce salt ash to strengthen the saline content of the brine, are found on both sides of the Thames estuary, as at Canvey Island, on the Upchurch marshes and the Hoo Peninsula. Following rapid early Roman expansion this production peaked in the first and second centuries AD.[12]

Salt production was accompanied by pottery production. Containers were needed to store salt and salted goods, and a shared dependency on fuel and river transport added to the utility of establishing winter potteries at the sites of salterns. James Gerrard has suggested that the manufacture of Black Burnished ware (BB1) in Poole Harbour in the first century AD was associated with local salt production for military supply.[13] This seems likely to have involved the military control of production, perhaps involving requisitioning of salt and salted goods as a form of taxation. Similar arguments can be advanced for the pottery industries established within the Thames estuary, including early Roman lid-seated shell-tempered jars and later production of black burnished pottery.[14] The army was probably the most important market for these goods, but London is likely to have managed their procurement. The estuary wetlands attracted relatively few villas and high-status settlements, with a material culture that was poorly integrated with areas to north and south.[15] Some of these territories may have comprised estates administered from London, possibly including imperially owned land.

Woodlands

London relied on woodlands for its fuel and building materials. We have already described the importance of timber in developing the urban infrastructure, especially along the waterfront. A further supply of structural timber went into the walls, roofs and floors of London's houses, with more destined for shipyards. The heated public baths had massive fuel requirements, alongside industrial and domestic use. It was prohibitively expensive to transport wood by road, and most would have reached London by water. Oak was favoured for most uses. The timbers used in London present similar tree-ring profiles, suggesting that they were sourced sufficiently close to the city to have grown in like conditions. Extensive areas of coppiced woodland were found on the London claylands where soils are ill-suited for agriculture. The relative scarcity of settlement sites and field ditches suggests that such areas retained a significant degree of tree cover. Woodlands upriver of London would always have been preferred for ease of transport. As in the medieval period, London probably drew on woods in Surrey, Hampshire, Berkshire and Hertfordshire.[16] We do not know on whose land the trees were grown, although woods could be privately, publicly and imperially owned.[17] It is probable, however, that most procurement was undertaken against specific project needs. Timber was generally only felled when required, and supervising carpenters probably visited the woods to select the trees.[18]

Damian Goodburn's studies of structural timbers give detailed insight into for-estry management around London.[19] Coppiced timber and underwood was har-vested from managed woodland, on anything from 3- to 40-year rotations, with an emphasis on producing small, fast-grown timbers for house-building. For example, the timbers used in a warehouse dated AD 152–3 found at the Courage Brewery site in Southwark were obtained from oak coppice cut on a long rotation, witnessing extensive woodland management that started no later than the late first century.[20] These managed woods existed alongside areas of wildwood, where larger slow-grown and straight-grained timbers were found, pockets of which were still available for exploitation into the third century. Additional supplies were obtained from field and hedgerow oak, and alder from the riverbanks.

The felling and transport of London's timber was a labour intensive process, best undertaken in the autumn and winter when lower moisture content reduced the weight of timber needing transportation.[21] It was also easier for carpenters to select the trees suited for their needs when leaves had fallen. After felling, unwanted side branches were removed and the main stems cross-cut or 'bucked' as necessary. This was accomplished using thin-bladed axes similar to the Roman army *dolabra*. The large oak baulks used in the waterfront quays were probably dragged by oxen to collection points on the banks of the Thames and its tributaries to be loaded into barges. These timbers could be over 6 metres long and weigh up to two tonnes, making them too heavy to float unaided. Conversion into beams, planks, and boards is likely to have taken place in town, but trimmed branches and other logging debris would have been converted into charcoal.

The ready availability of such fuel supported industrial uses bordering forested areas. This, combined with the availability of clay and excellent transportation contributed to the development of pottery kilns along Watling Street, between Brockley Hill and Verulamium.[22] These made a standardized series of specialist forms not found in the repertoire of native potters, including flagons and mortaria in oxidized fabrics. Verulamium region wares are found in archaeological contexts at One Poultry predating AD 53–5 and production probably commenced before AD 50.[23] By *c.* AD 60 this industry provided nearly a quarter of all oxidized wares used in London, and more than three quarters of such wares by the end of the century. The rapid emergence of this industry relied on immigrant potters who set up in business to supply urban and military consumers. The kilns located close to the posting station at *Sulloniacis* might have suited the interests of a lessee supplying public and military contracts before urban markets were established. An opportunity of this sort might account for the early date of settlement at Brockley Hill, and explain the distribution of these products along army supply routes.[24] Mortaria and flagons in Verulamium region white-ware were widely used along the northern frontier in the Flavian-Trajanic period.[25] Intriguingly the early products of these kilns included amphorae of a type (Dressel 2–4) that usually contained wine, suggesting that vineyards were established near London by *c.* AD 60.[26]

Most of the utilitarian coarse wares used in early Roman London were made in potteries at Highgate Wood, between Watling Street and Ermine Street, some 10 kilometres north-west of town. Ten kilns and associated features were excavated here in the late 1960s and early 1970s.[27] From c. AD 50/55 onward jars and bowls were made in the pre-Roman 'Belgic' style using grog-tempered fabrics. Early in the Flavian period, however, new and more efficient kilns started producing wheel made Romanized sand-tempered wares. By the end of the century, native pottery traditions had all but disappeared.[28] The kilns were located near to the woods that fuelled them, and it is likely that they took advantage of the transport links and seasonal labour brought here by woodsmen and charcoal burners. This relationship might help explain the success not only of the Highgate Wood pottery industry, but also of London's import of Alice Holt pottery from near Farnham in Surrey.[29] These potteries on the borders of woodlands produced grey-ware jars, dishes and bowls soon after the Roman conquest, that were abundant in London down to c. AD 90 (and again after c. AD 270). They probably reached London along supply routes that followed the navigable rivers Slea and Wey down to the Thames. The Farnham area may have been an important source of London's building timber, as it was in 1395 when it supplied timber for the roof of Westminster Hall.[30]

The forested claylands around London also supported brickworks that supplied London with tiles for hypocaust systems, roofs, and floors. Around 90 per cent of the tile used in London in the late first and early second centuries came from kilns within 30 kilometres of the city.[31] These were usually near sites involved in supplying London with other bulk materials, exploiting the same transportation infrastructure. Some tile was imported from parts of Kent involved in the supply of Kentish ragstone along the Medway and Thames. Another tilery supplying London was located on the south coast of Sussex: products are likely to have reached London overland following routes established to transport Wealden iron, and from the area of potteries at Ashtead (Surrey) and Brockley Hill.[32] London also imported pottery from North Kent, joining the carriage of grain and ragstone down the Medway and up the Thames.

Wealden iron

The metalled roads that penetrated the Sussex Weald were the likely product of military engineering during the early Flavian reorganization of the transport infrastructure around London.[33] We have already noted that Stane Street's entrance to London was laid out in the early Flavian period. A similar date obtains from roadside ditches at the southern end of the London–Lewes road, at Bridge Farm.[34] Two of these roads traversed the High Weald, a notoriously intractable and sparsely occupied wooded terrain, opening up the area for the export of iron.

Over 100 Roman iron-smelting sites are known from the Weald, with many clustered against the roads to London.[35] Although the earliest iron working pre-dated the conquest, the industry expanded rapidly after the invasion, contributing to a fourfold increase in the number of sites and even larger increases in volumes of production. Some witnessed exceptionally high levels of industrial activity, although much production remained small-scale, probably integrated into the annual farming cycle and drawing on a skilled local workforce. In addition to producing the iron needed for nails, chains, and fittings, the Weald may have provided ship-building timber.[36]

Iron blooms would have been brought into London by ox-drawn cart, supplying smiths working in Southwark.[37] The growth of this industry was stimulated by the value placed on iron. Texts found at Vindolanda on Hadrian's Wall show that refined iron commanded a high price, perhaps about 1.1 *denarii* per kilogram in the early second century.[38] A massive slagheap associated with a major production site at Beauport Park, just north of Hastings, suggests that production here averaged 50–65 tons of iron a year, with an estimated value of up to 71,500 *denarii*. At the close of the first century, this was equivalent to the annual salary of 317 legionary soldiers, fully covering the costs of extraction and transportation. The iron produced at Beauport Park is unlikely, however, to have supplied London. Output from the south-eastern Weald was more sensibly taken to the coast for the Roman fleet, *Classis Britannica*, through ports on the English Channel. Tile kilns operating alongside the iron smelting manufactured tegulae carrying the CLBR stamp of the *Classis*. Massive numbers were used in the construction of the bathhouse at Beauport Park, where a fragmentary inscription recorded repairs possibly undertaken by a *vilicus* named Bassus or Bassianus.[39] Henry Cleere has argued that the distribution of CLBR stamped tiles defines a maritime area controlled by the fleet deep into High Weald.[40] He proposed that iron-production was under direct procuratorial control, with operations handled by civilian workers supervised by the Imperial *vilicus* and integrated into the supply-chain controlled by the fleet.[41]

During the reign of Antoninus Pius, the post of procurator was, on at least one occasion, combined with command of the British fleet.[42] This united control of key raw materials, including the iron and timber extracted from the eastern Weald, with the enhancement of the naval capacity that relied on these materials. In the absence of evidence for a significant distribution of villas or other elite settlements, Cleere proposed that the Weald remained part an Imperial estate managed by the procurator. A medallion dating to the reign of the emperor Antoninus Pius found at Bardown had probably been given to a very high-ranking official, reflecting on the importance of this command.[43]

Production in the western high Weald may have been differently organized.[44] Sites in this area were not supplied with tiles produced by the *Classis*, and relied on the road links to London for their export. One possibility is that the iron smelting operated through concessions leased to middlemen (*coloni*), who paid a share of production to the Imperial fiscus.[45] It is important to note that these differences in approach to managing surplus exaction don't imply differences of tenurial arrangements or in the state's interest over the iron produced.[46] It is perfectly possible that some parcels of land, imperially owned or not, were managed by leaseholders supplying London, whilst others were farmed by public officials to secure supplies for Channel ports operated by the fleet. In both arrangements the ironworkers might have been found locally, whether paid for their services, organized as share-croppers, or as forced labour. It is similarly possible that in both areas the main end-user of the iron was the Roman state, exploiting the metal resources in its newly reorganized territories.[47] London's role in the administration of mines is evidenced by an iron punch, marked M.P.BR for stamping ingots of soft metal, such as gold, as property of the mines of the province of Britain (*metalla provinciae Britanniae*).[48] There is some evidence for the further intensification of iron extraction in the High Weald into the early second century, coinciding with Hadrianic reform.[49]

Were there imperial estates?

The issue of whether or not the Weald and its ironworking sites formed part of an imperial estate has divided opinion. Martin Millett correctly argues that we cannot identify such estates from the evidence of settlement archaeology.[50] Imperial estates look pretty much like land owned by others, and the absence of villas from any given landscape indicates only that the wealth obtained from the land wasn't being invested in this type of social display. This increases the odds that those who profited from the land resided elsewhere, but even this is not certain: architectural display is only one way in which the rich might represent social rank. On the other hand, Cleere's argument remains a plausible speculation. The Roman state had a direct interest in controlling the mineral resources on which it relied, and important quarries and mines were often publicly owned or brought within the imperial *patrimonium*.[51] In principle, imperial land was no different from the estates of other private individuals. It was the Emperor's personal property run by his slaves and freedmen, the *familia Caesaris*, or rented by them to private contractors (*conductors*). Any such agents and middlemen would ultimately have served the London-based procurator. Imperially owned quarries might also draw on the support of the provincial administration for the supply of provisions and animals, and on military specialists and aid for their management.[52] It can be argued that the building of metalled roads across the western Weald, and the involvement of the *Classis Britannica* in estate production in the south-eastern Weald, witness support of this nature.

There has been much speculation about the extent of imperial holdings else-where in southern Britain, notably in discussion about landscapes in the Fens and Thames estuary.[53] Like the Weald, these marginal territories saw intensified exploitation in the Roman period, but little evidence of having been managed from villa estates within the orbit of self-governing *civitates*. Here too, there is no way of establishing who owned the land at any given point in time. The fact that we cannot securely identify specific imperial estates doesn't mean that they weren't ubiquitously present. The imperial government controlled a considerable part of productive land throughout the empire, such that by the fifth century the emperor is thought to have owned up to 18 per cent of the total area of two North African provinces involved in the *annona* supply of grain to Rome.[54] The conquest of Britain, which was very much the emperor's project, created golden opportunities for the expansion of his patrimonium. The property of those who fought against Rome fell forfeit as spoils of conquest, bringing extensive tracts of land under procuratorial control.[55] Pre-conquest royal holdings may well have concentrated in strategically important borderlands flanking the Thames, where territorial annexation may have disproportionately rewarded victorious kings such as Cunobelin. Further confiscations took place when Rome assimilated allied kingdoms, as when Icenian nobles were stripped of family estates on the death of their king Prasutagus.[56] Even more would have taken place in the suppression of the Boudican revolt, whilst the imperial patrimonium routinely incorporated property seized from convicted criminals, the intestate and tax defaulters. The conquest of Britain and disproportionate presence of the forces of imperial power are certain to have brought many lands under the Procurator's control. As Mike Fulford and Jane Timby have asked: how much of the pre-Flavian province would *not* have fallen into the emperor's estate?[57]

Much of the territory seized by Rome would have been given away. Land rewarded veterans and supported colonial settlement, and could be given to powerful allies. It could also be donated to cities as public land, and endowed to underwrite the costs of supporting temples, baths, and games. Other estates would have been sold for profit where buyers could be found. Much, however, is likely to have been retained for administration by the procurator from his offices in London. Imperial property provided income to support imperial expenditure. The procurator was responsible not only for raising taxes and revenues from imperial lands, but also for the payment and supply of the troops.[58] The army needed grain, livestock, leather, salted goods, timber, and iron. Since the procurator was responsible for ensuring that these goods reached the army, it made sense to retain control of the estates that produced them.[59] The acquisition and development of imperial estates are bound to have featured importantly in an economy aimed at finding local sources of goods to reduce dependency on long, exposed and costly supply lines. Flavian investment in the extraction industries and regional infrastructure can be seen as a strategic response to such needs.

The role of London

In a sense it matters not so much who owned the land where resources were found, so long as the procurator in London commanded the materials he needed. There were different ways in which this might have been achieved. The ragstone quarries and granaries of western Kent were situated within a landscape dominated by villas, and those who owned these villas are the likely owners of these natural resources in like fashion to the ownership of the wood at *Verlucionium*. They would have been at liberty to seek the best market and sell for cash or credit, even if some portion was diverted to settle tax and other obligations. Produce may have been sold at the 'farm gate' to agents with the established business contacts for its onward sale and equipped for its transport and storage. In this scenario, the procurator would simply have been the most highly valued city-based customer, securing privileged access to goods through the favoured trading relationship with middlemen that came with his powerful office.

Different arrangements would have applied on imperially owned estates. Epigraphic sources describe sharecropping on such land in North Africa during the early empire.[60] Tenant farmers (*coloni*) paid rent in kind, normally set at a third of their crop, to middlemen (*conductores*) who held 5-year leases awarded by the imperial administration. The treasury took its rent from these *conductores*, probably also in kind. Similar leaseholding arrangements extended to other spheres of economic activity, including tax collection.[61] This is an attractive model to apply to the countryside around London. Sharecropping would have been an effective way of raising rent from farmers poorly integrated with a cash economy, in a countryside that was never fully monetized.[62] It made no demands of cash liquidity whilst reducing the administration's vulnerability to fluctuations in supply. The emperor wasn't the only landowner to take sharecropping rent from tenant farmers. Pliny did the same, as described in his letters, although cash rents are more widely attested.[63]

It was also open to the procurator to control estates within his authority using officials drawn from the imperial household or other branches of the military administration. The presence of such agents is implied by military-style buildings found at the ironworking site in the Weald at Bardown, and in the administrative compound at Mucking in the Thames estuary.[64] In considering evidence for the grain supply of Rome, Geoffrey Rickman suggested that the late first century AD may have been a moment of transition, involving a shift from drawing supply from pubic land farmed by *publicani*, to a greater reliance on imperial estates run by imperial officials.[65] Might the early Flavian changes to the landscape of control in and around London witness such a transition?

In Britain, a managed system of rent and taxes is likely to have replaced earlier reliance on unsustainable requisitioning by the occupying forces, underwritten by extended supply lines from the continent. The weight of these initial exactions is described in a statement attributed to the Briton Calgacus by Tacitus, which translates as 'our goods and chattels go for tribute; our lands and harvests in requisitions for grain'.[66] Tacitus describes Agricolan reforms aimed at alleviating the burdens of corn levies and taxes (*frumenti et tributorum*) by distributing the burden more fairly and cutting out abuses introduced by tax collectors.[67]

Throughout much of the empire local taxes were raised by members of the *civitates* town council or *ordo*, using mechanisms similar to those they employed as landowners in calling in their rents.[68] It is open to question how extensively this model applied around London, given our doubts over the extent to which political power in London rested with local elite society. It is instead possible that direct taxes (*tributum soli* and *tributum capitis*) were collected by tax-farmers and imperial fiscal officials.[69] It would have made sense to raise taxes in kind in newly acquired territories lacking monetized economies.[70] There are documented instances of grain from imperial estates being supplied to soldiers, but as Keith Hopkins observed, we don't know how much of the grain that fed soldiers had been raised as tax in kind, and how much had been purchased at fixed prices or on the open market.[71] Imperial policy tolerated taxation in kind in grain-producing provinces as a means of underwriting food supplies, but coin revenues were more valuable. Tax collectors were under pressure to convert rural produce into bullion—the stores of wealth that could underwrite wages and pay for capital projects—by selling surplus for money.[72] The businesses of the middlemen handling these agricultural surpluses—whether obtained through purchase, tax, or rent—were necessarily structured through town.[73] This process of converting local perishable surplus into bullion/gold relied heavily on urban markets and manufacture, stimulating industrial growth in cities such as London.

The roadside and riverside settlements found around London established places where rents and taxes could be assessed and collected, serving as points of contact between London's cash-based economy and subsistence farming communities in its hinterland. Produce could have been brought to these places by tax-paying communities, leaving the state responsible for onward transport using private contractors or soldiers.[74] Such supplies may have made an important contribution to the grain supplies needed by the army and state. Paul Erdkamp has argued that taxation in kind, supervised by provincial administrations, was more important than market supply.[75] The army was sometimes directly involved: an exchange of letters between Pliny when serving as governor of Bithynia and the emperor Trajan described the use of detachment of soldiers to assist the procurator in grain collection.[76] The assertion that most grain was moved by the state rather than private trade can, however, be questioned.[77]

The complex and varied systems of rent and tax collection used in the Roman world could thoroughly distance landowners from those who farmed their land, involving a hierarchy of intermediary agents such as administrators, leaseholders, and bailiffs.[78] This may have acted as a break on the development of rural markets amongst producer communities, whilst stimulating their development within towns. This may go some way towards explaining why many of the farming settlements near London remained comparatively unaffected, at least in terms of the material culture on display, by the presence of the city. Since our main concern is with London, in its role as a hub for the exploitation of regional resources, this chapter doesn't explore the full range of evidence for farming in the Thames basin. It is possible that some communities retained traditional rights over the land that they farmed, little touched by the need to render tax and rent to London. It is evident, however, that the Roman conquest lead to the reorganization and intensification of regional production and that surpluses were obtained through the settlement and transportation network that focused on London. The early Flavian enhancement of this infrastructure of control is the likely product of official policy, perhaps connected to military supply and the *annona*.

16

Economy and supply

Roman economies

We have seen how London was brought into existence to support the Roman conquest of Britain, and that the logistical supply of Rome's armed forces remained a critical concern during a succession of campaigns aimed at the pacification of Britain. Even when imperial attention was distracted by the Dacian wars at the end of this period of advance, and the British garrison reduced, the loyalty of the remaining troops was retained through investment in their welfare and supply.

Despite the opportunities for wealth creation carried by the flow of resources through London, the early Roman city boasted few monuments of elite patronage. This suggests that the civic euergetism of a land-owning aristocracy remained unimportant to political life. London was unusual in this regard, making it a poor fit for interpretative models based on Mediterranean city politics where the exercise of Roman power was mediated by local elite society. In Chapter 3 we noted how Moses Finley's studies of the ancient economy encouraged a minimalist view of the role of the Roman state in civic affairs, contributing to a scholarly reluctance to credit Roman authorities with a determining role in the foundation of London. This was the outcome of a long-standing debate over the nature of the ancient economy, where opinion divided over whether development can be understood as the consequence of the working of market forces, or whether such forces were fundamentally constrained by social and political factors.[1] A key concept within this debate is that of the 'consumer city': an ideal type that characterizes cities as places where aristocrats enjoyed a political life sustained by rents and taxes drawn from rural estates, and where trade and industry remained subordinate to their interests.[2] Although still enormously influential, it is now recognized that Finley's model underestimated the scale and complexity of ancient trade, overstated the uniformity of the ancient world across time and space, and failed to acknowledge the extent to which imperial expansion promoted economic growth.[3] More recent studies have turned to ideas developed in the field of New Institutional Economics in order to explore the impact of different institutions of the Roman state on economic performance.[4] These new avenues of research have stimulated a concerted attempt to characterize and quantify economic growth in the Roman Empire.[5] The implications of this work for the study of Roman London are considerable, offering analytical tools that encourage us to treat London's early urban development as a product of imperial strategy.

Military demand

Rome's military success stemmed from its ability to support large concentrations of professional troops, establishing supply arrangements that also underwrote the needs of large cities. Whilst the importance of military demand to the economic development of Rome's frontier provinces is easily recognized, it is harder to pin down the detail of the mechanisms employed.[6] The respective contributions of market provisioning and directed supply are much discussed: were goods moved because traders found profit in meeting the needs of cash-rich army communities, or as official rations secured from tax and rents raised in kind that could be supplied to troops without consumer purchase?[7] Both forms of supply are attested in our fragmentary sources, and since the logistical needs of the armed forces were met on an ad hoc basis involving much improvisation, different situations would have encouraged different solutions. In a sense it is not critical to our understanding of London's economy to know how much supply was the consequence of the directed 'push' of rations issued by the state, and how much the aggregate 'pull' of purchasing decisions made by army units and individual soldiers. In either case, London's port was the critical pumping mechanism, speeding supplies along a network of arterial haulage routes.

In order to assess the importance of London's role in military supply, it helps to briefly review what is known about the scale and character of military demand. A campaigning army had immediate call on a baggage-train of supplies known as *impedimenta*, with longer-term needs met by the organized shipments known as *commeatus*.[8] Soldiers and their mounts required equipment, food, fodder, and firewood. Whilst local supplies were requisitioned and foraged, major campaigns relied on amassing significant reserves in advance of troop deployment. The staple was grain, delivered to troops as unground wheat, bread, or biscuit. This was accompanied by a meat ration that might consist of salted, smoked, or fresh veal, mutton or pork.[9] Soldiers additionally consumed copious quantities of wine (usually as sour wine or vinegar), olive oil and salt. There was considerable variation over which of these foodstuffs formed part of the regular dole, the costs of which were deducted from pay, and which the soldiers had to purchase on their own behalf. At one point the daily ration issued to soldiers in Egypt was described as consisting of two pounds of bread, a pound and a half of meat, a quart of wine, and half a cup of oil.[10] Late second-century ostraka from the same province recorded cash payments received by soldiers in lieu of the wine that was their due from official rations.[11] In addition to routine supplies, soldiers and officials also benefitted from special distributions of free meat and wine made at religious festivals and sacrifices.[12] The scale and frequency of such distributions should not be underestimated.

Writing tablets found at Vindolanda on Hadrian's Wall describe various cash-based transactions that secured supplies for the military community there between *c.* AD 85 and *c.* AD 130.[13] Threshed grain and hides were purchased locally by middlemen, reducing reliance on long-distance supply.[14] At least one of the dealings involved *Caesariani*, the imperial freedmen and slaves who managed imperial assets and had command of goods raised as tax and rent in kind.[15] These documents were written to formalize business agreements, and perhaps biased towards recording market transactions, but leave no doubt that civilian traders played an important part in the fort's supply. These traders were not serving soldiers but remained part of a wider military community. Commanding officers were responsible for the wellbeing of the troops under their command, and may have used payroll budgets to purchase goods from contractors who may, in turn, have acquired some supplies from imperial sources.

Drawing on what we know of military diet, James Jones calculated that the earlier campaigns in Wales, involving about 20,000 men, needed the equivalent of 900 shiploads a year of grain, fodder, wine, and oil.[16] Prudent planning involved building sufficient reserves to cover the needs of the campaign season. Some provisions may have been found locally, and coastal supply was developed to avoid trekking goods through the Midlands, but in the early stages of advance much of this material is likely to have arrived via London since this was the hub where coastal routes intersected with the inland road network. The stores of imported grain in the Neronian city (above p. 74), may been destined for overland carriage along Watling Street.

These supplies were an important concern of the provincial governor, but the direct responsibility of the procurator. Their issue anticipated the later Roman institutions of the *annona militaris*, used to organize the delivery of the soldier's rations and drawing on goods raised as tax in kind. We don't know the extent to which these later arrangements developed from solutions instituted to guarantee supplies to active forces in earlier phases of Roman imperial expansion. What we do know is that Rome developed a bureaucracy to police the contracts that kept its forces fed and equipped.[17] The institutional frameworks and physical infrastructure that this engendered were available for the supply of other goods and other consumers within the orbit of the provincial government, such that official rations were sometimes issued to civilians and slaves including those working on major construction projects.[18]

The first concern of the Roman state was to satisfy the needs of its legions, guaranteeing food security and sealing their loyalty to the emperor. Military campaigns placed an enormous burden on supply mechanisms at times when manpower was in greatest demand. The higher command relied on contracted middlemen (*navicularii*, *negotiatores*, and *mercatores*) to move goods to their destination.[19] These merchants and shippers added capacity without depleting the forces at the governor's disposal. The entrepreneurial activities of this business community were underwritten by the contracts and facilities afforded by the patronage of military commanders and administrators. Long distance trade was shaped by these official supply routes and patronage networks, even when it involved privately owned cargoes destined to be sold for profit on the open market.

Wherever the army went, merchants and contractors followed. Tombstones and inscriptions suggests that in the north-west provinces businessmen (*negotiatores*) formed a powerful community. Lyon was an earlier hub for their activities which stretched through Gaul, Germany, and into Britain along the Rhone-Rhine axis. Votive inscriptions witness the presence of *Negotiatores Britanniciani* and specialist traders in particular products along this route. Koenraad Verboven has described the emergence of a business class of merchants, producers and traders that relied on the market represented by the military garrisons of the north-west frontier.[20] These private operators were part of a community in which distinctions between military and civilian could be highly blurred.[21] Veterans and freedmen were perfectly placed to benefit from military contracts and some soldiers were involved in private business ventures whilst in military service.[22] Shippers (*navicularii*) could be hired to carry state-owned *annona* cargoes. *Navicularii* can be distinguished from *negotiatores* or *mercatores* in that their duties did not require them to take ownership of the goods they carried. They could work individually or within consortia, using their own or chartered vessels.[23] Shippers were able to take advantage of capacity developed around the needs of particular campaigns or building programmes, as well as for the seasonal haulage of agricultural surplus raised as tax or rent in kind. The logistical infrastructure on which they relied was in large part army engineered. Additional goods could be carried piggyback with bulk shipments and as makeweights to fill empty space on transports returning from officially commissioned deliveries.[24] These circumstances, allied to the considerable purchasing power of soldiers and officials, contributed to unprecedented levels of trade.

The preparations for the campaigns in Wales described by Jones would have involved docking and unloading an average of 7.5 ships every day during the 120 sailing days of the season (below p. 204). The routine provisioning of London would have been an equal task, with the urban population rising to as many as 30,000 by the middle of the second century.[25] Supplies of building materials for public construction projects and fuel for the public baths added significantly to river traffic. On busy days, dozens of ships were carried into London by the tides, with balancing numbers making their exit. Most cargoes served official needs, but the attendant infrastructure and institutions opened the way for a host of other trades.

Elsewhere, the most significant example of official intervention in underwriting food security were the yearly imports of grain to Rome known as the *annona*.[26] This scheme shows how Rome approached the issue of administered supply. Although originally used as a reserve to protect Rome from shortages, the *annona* came to involve free monthly distributions of grain to the heads of urban households through the *frumentationes*. There was a tendency to centralize and extend the *annona* through time.[27] At some point large quantities of olive oil were imported into Rome in similar fashion, eventually being added to the dole under Septimius Severus. Imports of Spanish olive oil contributed to a massive dump of broken amphorae at Monte Testaccio in Rome, where control marks suggest that the imperial authorities purchased olive oil from producers in order to guarantee its supply to Rome.[28] Until distributed free under Severus, this oil may have been sold at a fixed or subsidized price or simply released onto the market at times of shortage.

Rome's *annona* was administered on the emperor's behalf by a dedicated public official (the *praefectus annonae*), combining produce taken as rent or tax in kind with market purchases.[29] Shipments were made by private merchants, who gained tax privileges in return for their involvement.[30] Massive harbour facilities were built at Portus to accommodate the *annona*, and we have seen that similar arrangements might account for some phases of building activity at London's port (p. 101). Although not a commonplace measure, cities other than Rome stockpiled grain with the support of the imperial government, giving the authorities the means to stabilize prices by releasing reserves onto the market at times of scarcity.[31] London's vital role in administered military supply, frontier vulnerabilities, and close association with the provincial government, may have combined to occasion such intervention. This might also provide a context for late first-century investment in buildings associated with food supply and distribution within the city (p. 151). Changing patterns of supply in later Roman Britain are also best explained in the context of third-century reforms to a provincial *annona* designed around the needs of the army and government (p. 327).

Long-distance supply

London was a hub for the trans-shipment of products imported to Britain across the English Channel. This is seen in London's pottery assemblages, where imported goods included amphorae, Samian, other Gallic and Rhenish fine wares, and mortaria. This pottery is our main source of evidence for long-distance supply, but a poor proxy for the larger volumes of perishable materials that must have been transported. Nearly a quarter of the pottery found in first-century deposits in London was imported across the Channel, compared to 10 per cent or less in most other Romano-British towns.[32] Amphorae used to carry wine and oil produced in Gaul, Italy, and the Mediterranean, as wells as concentrated grape syrup (*defrutum*) and fermented fish sauces (*garum* and *liquamen*), make up about 40 per cent (by weight) of all Neronian pottery in London. They are not evenly distributed across the city, but concentrate in the port and forum where they are almost twice as abundant.[33] Fewer amphorae reached the outer parts of the early town, suggesting that their importation wasn't primarily aimed at supplying these urban communities.

The commonest type of amphorae found in London, the Dressel 20, contained olive oil imported from Baetica in southern Spain. Studies of its distribution show that this reached Britain following military supply routes along the rivers Rhone and Rhine.[34] José Remesal Rodriguez has argued that the oil was acquired through tax and rent in kind, transported by shippers employed by the state and supplied to troops in exchange for sums docked from pay. He supposes the involvement of the *praefectura annonae*, responsible for the grain supply of Rome, in managing the exercise. This has been questioned in more recent studies where the importance of market-based supply has been reasserted.[35] These arguments over the mechanisms involved, important as they are, don't change the fact that the bulk transportation of olive oil was directed to places where the legions were deployed, shadowing other officially sanctioned supplies.

A significant volume of wine also reached London in large wooden barrels sealed with pine resin. Examples made of silver fir, probably imported from the Rhineland, were reused to line wells and others were broken up and trimmed to make writing tablets.[36] Many were stamped with the names of shipper, producer, or retailer and an example from One Poultry was stamped across a bung to prevent tampering.[37] Army-influenced tastes are likely to account for other particularities in imports to London, and involved extending supply routes from the Rhine to the Thames. Examples include the clay lamps that are more common in early Roman London and Colchester than elsewhere in Britain and the quern- and millstones imported from Germany. Various other luxuries were imported against the needs of wealthy residents, perhaps sometimes as private property accompanying high-status immigrants and otherwise as merchandise. These included textiles, ivory bracelets, amber beads from the Baltic, and gold and emerald necklaces. A variety of new and exotic foods were also imported.[38] A shop destroyed in the Boudican revolt sold imported spices, herbs and fruits (above p. 80). Elsewhere black pepper, an import from across the Indian Ocean, pomegranate, peaches, olives, figs, grapes, cucumber, edible stone pine kernels, and walnuts have been identified.

Ragstone, flint, and chalk were imported from Kent for use in concrete foundations but were unsuited for most stoneworking. Kevin Hayward has reported on the wide variety of building stone imported to London.[39] This included Reigate stone and Hassock greensand, and the dark brown-black 'Purbeck Marble' from Dorset. High-quality oolitic limestone from the Cotswolds, Cambridgeshire, Lincolnshire, and Northamptonshire provided the detailed carvings on major monuments. London also imported stone from quarries on the French coast. Clay roofing tiles and bricks came mainly from Hertfordshire and local brick-fields, and some Yorkshire roofing slates have also been found.

Relatively large quantities of tablewares were imported into Britain through London. Martin Pitts describes a series of such finds commonly associated with military and colonial establishments including Lyon ware beakers and cups, decorated *terra sigillata*, Gallo-Belgic bowls, glass vessels, and mortaria.[40] The most ubiquitous of these was the glossy red Gallo-Roman *sigillata*, or Samian. London's late first-century pottery assemblages contain unusually high percentages of Samian, sometimes forming over 10 per cent by weight.[41] Lyon ware and *terra sigillata* were particularly popular with communities associated with the military and colonial infrastructure along the Rhine, and which reached into Britain after the conquest. Distribution patterns explored by Nico Roymans suggest that the soldiers stationed at the earliest Rhine military bases probably owned a cup and platter of *terra sigillata* for individual use, with larger sets used by officers when throwing banquets.[42]

At various points in time, London was the major port of entry for Samian. During the second century large quantities of these glossy red platters, cups and bowls were stored in warehouses next to the quays where they had been landed. London may have been the most important single destination for products of the Central Gaulish workshops of Les Martres-de-Veyre, with only small quantities 'leaking' out from supply route along the Rhine. Mike Fulford has considered how Samian could reach Britain without any tail-off in volumes of supply.[43] Where market supply prevails, the costs of transportation are added to the price charged to consumers and will depress sales at more distant locations. Fulford suggests that transport costs may have been subsidized or met in full by the state when the vessels were included with equipment issued to senior soldiers and government officials, the costs of which were deducted from pay. He also suggests that the Samian that travelled beyond London may have been transported along official supply networks set up through the posting stations of the *cursus publicus*, which offered points from which these goods reached more remote consumers. Allard Mees suggests that the aggregate buying power of regular soldier's pay offers a less complicated explanation for the bulk movements of Samian, questioning Fulford's 'subsidized distribution' argument.[44] He is heavily influenced, however, by the idea that London's import of Samian witnesses the importance of civilian markets. He suggests that onward supply from London was the consequence of city merchants selling goods to customers who came to the city. This is not the conclusion drawn here. The dendrochronological evidence shows that investment in London's port and transportation infrastructure coincided with preparations for military campaigns and phases of *annona* reform aimed at retaining the loyalty of the Roman forces in Britain. Some of these episodes of official investment related to changes in the pattern of long-distance supply routed through London, which impacted on the source and volume of the Samian brought to the city.

This doesn't require us to believe that administered supply was the dominant mechanism. It is possible to imagine circumstances in which new colonial and administrative settlements, major public building programmes and particular festivities and celebrations were accompanied by subsidized supplies arranged by the administrative authorities. These could have been sponsored by the governor or procurator, involving the use of public slaves and troops, and perhaps state-transportation at times of surplus capacity. At other times, particularly those of scarcity or untoward need, public authorities may have commissioned private contractors to arrange additional supplies, sometimes moving imperially owned goods (as shippers) and sometimes bringing to market the goods that they had acquired for this purpose (as merchants). Between these officially subsidized distributions, local arrangements and market supply is likely to have prevailed. This diversity of approach absolves us of the need to fully endorse or reject the models that have been brought to bear on the tortured issue of how state control intersected with market forces.

Monetary transactions

As noted in Chapter 7, Neronian Samian appears to have been sold from a shop at One Poultry alongside other exotica used at dinner parties, including spoons and spices. The demand for these table luxuries stemmed from patterns of consumption that also relied on imported oil and wine. Martin Pitts has described how these elite tastes had derived from military communities along the Rhine.[45] They don't necessarily identify military consumers, but were found in the wider patronage networks attracted to command sites in general and London in particular. City shopkeepers met some of this demand, presumably through the offer of fairly priced goods. Shops and the emergence of a monetary economy, supported by state intervention to facilitate the movement of vital supplies, all contributed to the expansion of market activities and stimulated growth.[46]

London's commercial transactions relied on coin. It has been estimated that some 6.5 million *denarii* needed to be imported to Britain each year to pay the soldiers and officials in imperial service.[47] These were followed into currency by smaller bronze denominations that facilitated low value transactions within the military and administrative community. The cumulative spending power of employees of the Roman state was the gateway through which currency entered the economy.[48] Coin use and coin loss was consequently higher in towns and at military sites, where it seems reasonably certain that the economy was fully monetized. Urban growth depended on the transactions facilitated by the pervasive use of coin, set in train by the presence of troops and officials with cash to spend and commissions to meet. Elsewhere the spread of coinage was limited, and supplies of small change were insufficient to have supported their routine use. In any case the face-value of the available coin was skewed way above levels useful for the rural poor.[49] Early Roman Britain can consequently be described as presenting a landscape of 'coin using islands...in an overwhelming sea of virtually coinless peasants'.[50]

We are reminded of the importance of small change to London's daily life by a record of the payments due to a haulier described on one of the writing tablets found at the Bloomberg site.[51] This text, dated 21 October AD 62, which we have already considered in the context of post-Boudican rebuilding (p. 90), recorded a contract made between Marcus Rennius Venustus and Gaius Valerius Proculus to bring twenty loads of provisions to London from Verulamium by 13 November. Roger Tomlin suggests that this timetable might represent the operation of a single waggon going to and fro between the cities on a daily basis, but this could not have been achieved within the allotted time using ox-drawn transport given the slow speed of such transport. It seems more likely that two waggons were employed, one travelling in each direction: the distance of about 30 kilometres could just about be covered in the ten hours of daylight available at that time of year. The contract agreed a transport charge of one quarter denarius, or four asses, for each shipment. This would result in a day-rate of two asses: a modest sum, given that a soldier's rate of pay amounted to ten asses a day, indicating that the haulage contractor had access to low-cost labour. Roger Tomlin suggests, from his reconstruction of conditions attached to the contract, that three asses were paid on receipt of each transport, with the remainder held as a retention against completion. It is difficult to see how this arrangement could have worked without coin changing hands on the safe receipt of each consignment, presumably at the forum or city gates. This reliance on small-change to pay contracted hauliers, and lubricate a host of similar routine transaction, might explain why it was sometimes necessary to manufacture low-value irregular coin (pp. 79 and 330). The value of this small-change was amplified by the access it provided to the carriage goods.

The use of coin also simplified the collection of the port duties levied on imported goods.[52] Tax income from the transportation of routine goods was considerable, as shown by customs-house registers from Egypt.[53] It is therefore possible that investment in transport infrastructure in London was not only aimed at easing bulk haulage associated with the *annona*, but at improving tax collection on goods entering the city. The riverside quays controlled access to and from the river. A parallel can be drawn with restrictions on river traffic imposed under Queen Elizabeth I, who limited the unloading of goods to a number of legal quays where customs duties could be collected.[54] Public investment in the construction of docks could become profitable where this gave control over lucrative port duties, just as the adjacent warehousing was a source of rental income. Various transactions were taxed, generating income for the state. Inscriptions from neighbouring provinces suggest that efforts to improve on tax collection were underway in the late second and early third centuries. We know that such taxes were levied at London late in the Roman period, since lead seals used to identify tax exempt imperial property have been found on the Thames foreshore (below p. 301).[55] Merchants carrying state goods did not have to pay these customs (*portoria*), and goods belonging to veterans and military personnel could also be exempt.[56] Shippers are likely to have taken advantage of these tax waivers to import products alongside official supply cargoes.[57]

London and the Roman economy

Gustav Milne has suggested that many of the luxuries imported into early Roman London were brought to meet the needs of the town's richer inhabitants, and that the town itself was the magnet that attracted exotic materials.[58] It is difficult to believe, however, that London's thriving economy was sustained by internal demand alone. It is more likely to have prospered because of opportunities to profit from military contracts and subsidized links with Germany and Gaul. As a map of Roman roads clearly illustrates, London was the principal nodal point in the network of control that Rome established over southern Britain. The needs of long-distance supply justified building and maintaining an infrastructure of quays and warehouses at this hub. Rome's earlier experiences of territorial expansion meant that such needs were well understood and could be addressed through strategic planning. London's growth was the product of this determined state involvement in establishing the physical infrastructure and institutional frameworks conducive to trade, and which included the engineering of transport infrastructure, creation of storage capacity, and market intervention to secure the flows of staples and luxuries on which Roman communities relied.[59] London would have been modelled on the earlier example of places such as Lyons (above p. 71), which played a pivotal role in military supply and civilian commerce where facilities were developed to support the Roman forces.[60]

Capital expenditure on public building projects added to the flow of resources into London. Urban markets helped to convert local surplus— obtained as tax, rent, or tribute—into army supplies, defraying their cost and underwriting security. London's shops and workshops made it possible for contractors to transform other produce into goods for sale, for conversion into coin and thence into the bullion on which the state ultimately relied. The cash-using consumers found amongst this urban population created additional opportunities for economic growth. Many of the activities now focused in London's port and town were highly labour intensive, as the next chapter describes, and stimulated population growth. The procurator stood at the heart of this rapidly expanding economy. The contractors that his patronage drew to London would have claimed a major role in collecting, storing, and shipping both annonary goods and the ancillary luxuries that facilitated competitive social display amongst the ruling elite. The *annona* supplies, and a complex range of attendant institutional arrangements, would have both powered and distorted London's Roman economy.[61]

David Mattingly has described how Rome's market economy operated along-side socially constrained and politically dominated systems of exchange.[62] The military supply of the frontier provinces formed part of the political economy, which also relied on exploiting mineral and resources obtained from extensive imperial and public estates. The logistical demands of exploiting and transporting these resources required the state's involvement in a redistributive exchange system that defied normal economic logic. On the margins of this directed economy, lay a separate world of subsistence and peasant farming that made limited use of the cash economy or of the goods available through urban markets.

London changed as Roman power became established, and it is possible to explain phases in the evolution of the port as a product of the institutionalization of *annona* supply. The conquest phase was characterized by a relatively low investment in port infrastructure, despite the importance of London in the business of supply. The military reoccupation of London after the Boudican revolt prompted the construction of new harbour facilities that were then episodically extended and improved down to the middle of the third century. Some phases of port construction may have involved direct military support, drawing on the engineering capacity of auxiliary forces commanded by the governor.

Reforms of the early Flavian period appear to have been aimed at improving government control over the extraction, movement and management of resources obtained regionally, reducing dependency on long distance supply and establishing an infrastructure aimed at a making the rule of Britain more sustainable. Such reforms are likely to have involved tightening-up the administrative apparatus used to raise tax and rent, and ensure its speedy delivery to military consumers through the transport infrastructure. The development of London in this period may, in part, have been at the expense of the supply-base established at Richborough on the south coast. It has been suggested that the military use of this site was reduced from as early as *c.* AD 70 before ending *c.* AD 85.[63] These Flavian reforms penetrated deep into the countryside in south-east Britain, which witnessed a significant change in the character and range of ceramic use at this period as Gallo-Belgic patterns of elite consumption gave way to styles of consumption and display imported to Britain from the German frontier.[64] This may also have put in place the essentials of a market-based economy, albeit one that was largely restricted to a money-using elite community soldiers, officials, landowners, and middlemen.

London's early development, down to *c.* AD 85, can best be explained through reference to military campaigns planned in Britain. After that date sporadic attention may have been given towards the infrastructure of *annona* supply, as implied by the waterfront building programmes of *c.* AD 94–8 (arguably AD 97) and *c.* AD 101–4. These works were undertaken at times of wider reform of Rome's supply infrastructure, under Nerva and then Trajan. These later phases of investment in London's harbour might be considered a form of path dependency, in which the existence of institutions aimed at supplying goods imported from the Mediterranean became an essential part of the relationship between emperor and the military forces, resulting in continued investment in port infrastructure beyond the point where there was clear economic or strategic benefit to these arrangements. The concept of path-dependency may also help explain the radical nature of third-century changes to London's economy, when the inherited ineffi-ciencies of an unnecessarily burdensome supply system became unsustainable in the face of exogenous stochastic shock.[65]

17

London at work

At the port

London was an exceptionally busy city in the late first century, thriving on opportunities brought to the banks of the Thames by its port. This made it home to an important financial and business community attending the needs of imperial expansion, whose activities are documented in writing tablets recovered from waterlogged contexts along the Walbrook valley. These preserve numerous business contracts and declarations formalized by literate lawyers and scribes, introducing us to people such as the merchant Optatus (*optato neg.*) to whom one such letter was addressed.[1] About half of the texts whose subject matter is known referred to loans or debts.[2] This credit lubricated commerce, and was critical to the operations of the army and administration. Property management was another topic of concern: in A D 64 the slave Florentinus wrote on his master's instruction that he had received payments, probably rent, in respect of a farm.[3] In another letter Rufus, son of Callisunus, sent greetings to Epillicus and all his messmates asking him to 'turn that girl into cash'.[4] This seems to be an instruction to a business or estate: was a debtor to be pressed or a slave girl sold?

Others communications were concerned with issues of transport and haulage.[5] London's main business was shipping. Boats arriving on the rising tide would have been assessed for customs duties before being assigned a berth, whence cargoes could be disembarked into warehouses and waiting transports.[6] Many shipments required multiple handling. Larger boats would have moored in the river channel and been serviced by smaller rivercraft shuttling back and forth to riverside quays. Barges and smaller vessels beached on the foreshore, crowding the quayside. At their greatest extent the quays extended for more than 1 kilometres along the north bank of the river, providing space for at last two dozen berths for broadside-on mooring.[7] Jetties and Mediterranean style perpendicular mooring might have added significant capacity. Facilities on the south-bank probably catered for a similar scale of use if more irregularly organized. Heavy loads of amphorae, barrels, crates, bales, and sacks were manhandled from the waterside into stores, aided by cranes and pulleys such as one set over an early third-century base at Billingsgate.[8] Some goods were moved directly to the forum, where the enclosed piazza and surrounding offices formed a controlled handling point suitable for dividing shipments into new consignments for onward transport by ox-drawn cart and pack animals. We can picture an administrative and transportation hub, involving a community of public officials, *negotiatores*, bankers, warehouse agents, porters, and hauliers. Other handling points flanked the city gates, where goods arriving by road could be taxed, drovers could find paddocks for their livestock, and waggons might load and unload without entering the narrow city streets.

London's harbour needed manpower. The city is estimated to have grown to be home to some 19,000–32,000 people by the second century, making it considerably larger than Pompeii and a match for Rome's port at Ostia.[9] At its busiest the great harbour of Rome might have employed some 3,000 labourers. London had only a fraction of the urban population to provide for, but was the principal port of supply for a large provincial garrison. Dozens of boats needed offloading and reloading daily in busy summers, commanding the services of hundreds of labourers. Sailing schedules generated peaks and troughs of employment for bargemen, stevedores, porters, and hauliers.[10] A close season was probably observed by most shippers. According to Vegetius, writing in late antiquity, safe sailing was only possible between 27 May and 14 September, with outside limits from 10 March to 10 November.[11] London's port must have hibernated through the winter, when road haulage also became increasingly difficult. Even in fair weather, shorter days reduced the distances that could be covered and fodder became scarce. Since the oxen that transported heavy loads were tilling fields from late March into May, most traffic travelled in the height of summer with an autumn rush after harvest. The November deadline for the haulage contract of AD 62 on the short route from Verulamium to London was just such a late season transaction. Similar difficulties in transporting supplies and finding fodder interrupted military campaigns, and the army normally retired to winter quarters from November to February.[12] These seasonal considerations combined to present high levels of labour demand from spring to autumn, interrupted by slack winters of underemployment.

The construction industry

Building sites were also busiest in summer. Again the availability of traction and daylight were important considerations, and earth-built and concrete walls set best in summertime.[13] Janet DeLaine has estimated that between 3 and 6 per cent of the population of Rome and Ostia worked in the building industry, keeping thousands of workers employed.[14] A similar proportion seems credible for London during its expansion, implying the existence of a construction workforce several hundred strong.

Most of London's first houses were timber-framed structures, employing wattle-and-daub and air-dried mudbrick infill between timber uprights, set beneath thatch, plank and shingle roofs.[15] Many buildings lasted only 5–10 years before replacement. This involved levelling-off redundant brickearth components to make building platforms for new construction, the repeated frequency of which contributed to the build-up of London's Roman stratigraphy. Brickearth and gravel were quarried locally, leaving a pockmarked landscape of redundant quarries backfilled with rubbish and earth. Access to suitable quarries diminished as the built-up area expanded, and by end of the first century AD earth walls were often built with material recovered from earlier constructions.

Timber was imported from coppiced woodlands around the city. Trees would have been selected for felling in the autumn, cut down and converted into logs in the bare winter, before river transport to London in the spring. This established a stock for summer building. The demands of larger engineering works required a dedicated procurement chain, with timber felled to order and transported direct to construction sites, but routine house-building probably relied on recycled timber supplemented by purchases from lumber-yards. Timber merchants would have gravitated to waterfront sites, but avoided the crowded harbour. This suggests that sites in Southwark, and perhaps at the mouth of the Fleet, would have been preferred.

Town-based carpentry involved the use of regular oak timbers, squared with axes and planks or sawn on trestles to standard sizes. Cross-cut and rip-saws were widely used, as were elaborate joints and iron nails.[16] Many early houses were built from pre-fabricated timber-frames with vertical studs rising from horizontal ground sills to wall plates. A distinctive type of wattle and daub was commonly used as infill between studs and posts, formed from horizontal cross-staves that dropped into slots cut into the uprights, through which vertical roundwood elements were woven. This was then covered with clay daub, sometimes sheathed in timber or keyed for plaster by roller-stamping. This technique had been employed on sites along the Rhine frontier before it came to London. More substantial structures employed solid earth-walls, also following construction technologies introduced to Britain by the conquest.[17] Their design drew on a range of specialist trades: plasterers and painters to decorate the walls, mosaicists and stonemasons to lay marble floors and wall veneers, and heating engineers to design and install hypocausts.

The labour market

London relied on seasonal labour. There was a reduced need for dock-workers, hauliers, and construction workers in winter, and the cyclical nature of these activities made it impractical to maintain a permanent workforce for such purposes alone. It has been suggested that peaks in demand for unskilled menial labour in ancient Rome were met by a combination of urban poor and seasonal immigration from the countryside.[18] Slaves were better suited to activities offering steady employment since it was uneconomical for their owners to hire them out for part of the year only.[19] London's urban poor would have struggled to make ends meet if left idle in the depths of winter, unless supported by a corn dole. Seasonal immigration from the countryside offered greater flexibility and required less in the way of state intervention, but is unlikely to have been viable during London's earlier decades since the countryside around London wasn't densely populated. One would also expect to see greater evidence for economic integration between town and country if rural labourers had regularly spent part of the year in town as hired hands.

London's major construction projects, and the haulage needs of important supply campaigns, might instead have depended on directed labour. There were several ways in which the provincial administration could command manpower at times of need. The army was sometimes used for civilian construction, as attested on inscriptions from various corners of the Roman world. At Vindolanda, soldiers were detailed to a range of building and craft activities including shoemaking, bathhouse construction, and fetching wood and water.[20] At times when London was garrisoned soldiers would have been available for such tasks, but this wasn't routinely sustainable. Larger numbers of soldiers were more likely to appear on the streets of London at the end of summer campaigns, swelling the city's population just as the sailing and construction seasons were ending.

Corvée labour might have been mobilized to assist in building public infrastructure. Roman municipal authorities were able to draw on some days' compulsory labour each year along with draught animals for public building projects.[21] Such impositions could have been placed on London's urban populace and surrounding communities. Labour could also be obtained from those condemned to public work, and military campaigns would have generated a ready supply of forced labour through London's slave markets. The contribution that slave labour made to road haulage is hinted at by an ink-leaf tablet found discarded in a first-century well at Temple House in Queen Victoria Street in 1959.[22] This was sent to London (*Londinii*) from someone probably in Rochester (*Durobrivae*) about a boy, perhaps a slave, who had run away with a waggon. London's circumstances were such that conscripted and slave labour may have contributed more of the necessary manpower than was feasible in cities further from the frontier.

The working year

London needed oxen for haulage, whose availability would have followed the agricultural cycle. In medieval England, spring ploughing started around 25 March (Lady Day), continuing through April into early May. June was occupied by haymaking, and London's enormous demand for fodder would have drawn on extensive pastures in its environs. July and August were quieter months, making this the best time of year for beasts of burden to be redeployed onto the city streets. Tile and pottery kilns were also most productive in drier weather.[23] Summer kilns drew on fuel generated by forestry operations, taking advantage of surplus transport capacity when logging was complete. Salt working in the estuary was also best undertaken in the summer. Plant remains associated with the Roman salterns at Stanford Wharf in Essex are consistent with summer and early autumn gathering of saltmarsh plants to provide fuel and create brine.[24] Harvesting occupied rural labour from August into September, following which the grain was threshed and the share due in rent and tax could be collected and transported before autumn sowing.[25] Once the harvest was gathered, processed, and moved to winter storage, the pace of life could slow. Old and surplus livestock could be slaughtered and salted in November, along with the products of autumn fishing and hunting. This was also the season for marking out trees for felling in managed woodlands. Between late November and early March there was little outdoor work, and this became a time for making and mending. In London, this would have entailed a massive redirection of effort from outdoor labour into workshop production.

The winter months would have seen a significant change in the social composition of the city as the army returned to the comfort of winter quarters, and the governor and his entourage to their administrative base. Whilst the governor would have toured the cities and forts under his authority, London was the most important theatre for political activity. Documents from Vindolanda and London suggest that many soldiers attached to the governor's administration were based in London by the end of the first century.[26] It was here that representatives of provincial communities could petition the governor, where important trials took place, and business affairs were best organized. Cameron Hawkins has drawn a telling parallel with the winter 'season' of seventeenth-century London, when court and parliament took residence.[27] The rich and powerful brought large retinues in their wake, and town houses reopened after summer closure. One of the largest sectors of employment would have been domestic service. A seasonal influx of staff attending the wealthy officer classes joined the more permanently established households of the procurator and his *Caesariani* responsible for managing the *annona*, taxation, and imperial property. Places of entertainment and trade were busied by increased demand.

Craft production concentrated into the winter months when patrons commissioned specialist and luxury items. Much industrial production, manufacture and repair, worked to spring deadlines as stock was readied for construction, shipping and campaigning seasons. This heightened seasonal demand coincided with the easier availability of labour between November and March. Whilst skilled artisan proprietors could have staggered work through the year, using slack periods to build inventories, seasonal product markets would have limited the demand for permanent labour and encouraged manufacturers to recruit assistance on a short-term basis only. Here too we lack evidence on the relative importance of free and servile labour within London's workshops, although the common use of the Roman *tria nomina* in manufacturers' stamps indicates that proprietors were often citizens.[28] London relied on skills unknown in Britain before the conquest, and many craftsmen are identifiably immigrants. Some may have arrived speculatively but it is likely that most drew on existing contacts, following powerful patrons to ready commissions. If so, many of London's first professional craftsmen would have already been known to the contractors and officials that served the Roman provincial government, sharing in a common background. Slaves would have formed a significant proportion of the workforce, given their ready availability and the low status of wage employment. Slaves could develop skills in winter employment within their owner's shops and workshops, and be hired out to help in summer porterage. Skilled slaves also ran and managed the imperial household and other private estates, occupying some of the most senior positions in the administration (below p. 222).

Shops and workshops

Urban industry and city marketplaces converted perishable rural surplus obtained in rent and tax into coin and thence bullion. London's internal economy developed around transactions which established the conditions for market specialization. Private shops and workshops were a necessary part of this economic landscape, serving both urban consumers and military demand (Fig. 17.1). Craftsmen and shopkeepers consequently formed a significant presence within the city, and there is sufficient evidence of specialization to suggest that London easily matched the 85 different occupations attested at Pompeii.[29]

London's markets used the standard weights and measures promoted by Rome as part of the apparatus of regulatory control. Unsurprisingly, more weighing instruments have been found in London than any other Romano-British site.[30] These included equal balances, steelyards and dual balances. Many of the weights can be related to specific Roman units of measurement, such as the *uncia* (ounce) and *libra* (pound). This instrumentation indicates that the weighing out of small amounts mattered more in London than elsewhere in Britain, in a marketplace where high-value commodities were commonly exchanged. Rulers, marked using the standard Roman foot or *pes monetalis*, have also been found.[31] There is evidence for regulation of property divisions, and detailed records allowed the recreation of property boundaries after fires.[32]

Most production took place in small workshops from which finished goods were sold, each probably only employing a small number of people.[33] Two main types can be identified. Buildings around the forum and behind the waterfront

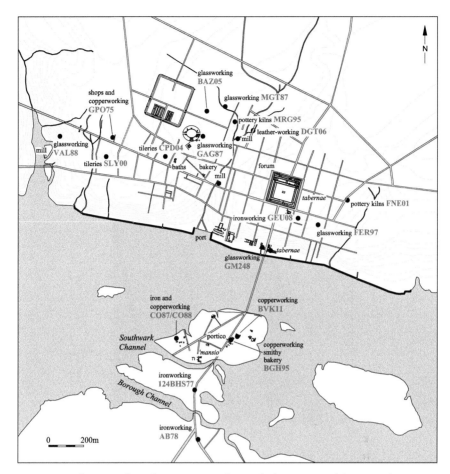

Fig. 17.1 Industry and production in London at the beginning of the second century: the urban layout is that of the later Hadrianic period, but some of the industrial activities belong to slightly earlier and later phases. Drawn by Justin Russell.

presented rows of small-scale open-fronted units used as stores, factories, and shops, but which may have included living space in mezzanine or upper floors. These were similar to the premises described as *tabernae* in other Roman cities, and likely to have been designed as rental units.[34] Other workshops were located within large rectangular buildings known as strip-buildings built alongside the main roads into town with their gable-end against the street.[35] The best preserved examples were excavated at Newgate Street in 1977–8 (Fig. 17.2).[36] These earth and timber walled buildings were some 8–9 metres wide by 20–8 metres long, largely given over to workshops and stores, with smaller residential quarters to the rear. By the end of the first century, the living quarters in some of these buildings were decorated with painted walls and concrete floors. Later the reception

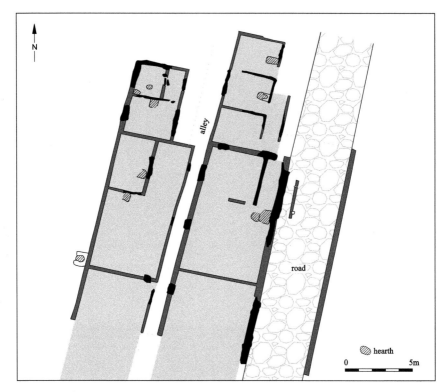

Fig. 17.2 The early second-century 'strip buildings' at Newgate Street (GPO75: after Perring and Roskams 1991). Drawn by Justin Russell.

rooms set to the rear of strip buildings at One Poultry were furnished with costly mosaic pavements and hypocaust floors suggesting that patrons who lived behind their shops accumulated sufficient wealth to invest in conspicuous social display.[37] London's prosperous workshop owners saw no need to distance themselves from the source of their wealth: there was no shame to business success.

Retailing commanded the better locations at One Poultry, where a Neronian shop sold luxuries for fine dining and another may have been a tavern (above p. 80).[38] The urban retailing of ceramics may have been largely restricted to fine wares, using a similar distribution network to other imported luxuries.[39] London's shops and workshops addressed the needs of the urban community, but also served a passing trade who used the big city to find things difficult to obtain elsewhere. One of the accounts found at Vindolanda lists purchases made in London and brought to Hadrian's Wall by one Adiutor.[40] This included a set of kitchen bowls along with mustard-seed, anise, caraway and thyme. This order would have been filled in a shop of the sort found at One Poultry. There is little to suggest, however, that the urban marketplace attracted many customers from the surrounding countryside: few of the goods made and sold here found their way onto the rural sites excavated within the region.[41]

A row of narrow single storey buildings, separated by narrow alleyways, was squeezed behind the early forum (Fig. 17.3).[42] Some contained rows of near-identical rooms, each about 4 metres square, containing a small fixed fireplace. Similar rooms were set behind a workshop at Newgate Street consisting of a row of three slightly smaller near square rooms, each with a fireplace against one wall.[43] These were possibly one-roomed lodgings or perhaps brothels.[44]

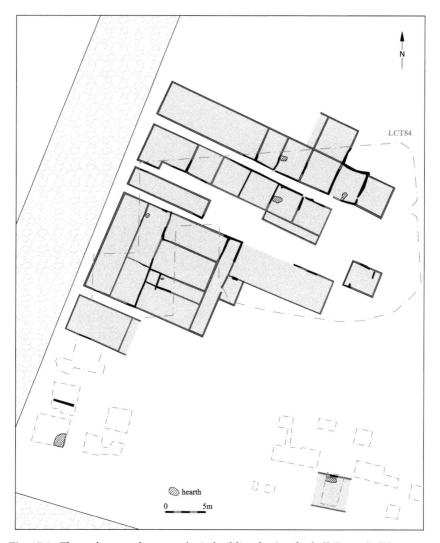

Fig. 17.3 The early second-century 'strip buildings' at Leadenhall Court (LCT94: after Milne and Wardle 1993). Drawn by Justin Russell.

Shipbuilding

London's port was served by a merchant fleet, attracting communities of sailors and fishermen, and contributing to the development of a local ship-building industry. The Roman fleet (*Classis Britannica*) might also have played a role in London's supply during some campaigns. Ships were built in large numbers on such occasions, as when Germanicus' ordered the construction of a fleet of 1000 ships on the Rhine, but most were privately built and owned.[45] The hulks of Roman ships found along the Thames show that some were locally made. A large flat-bottomed lighter submerged in a channel near Guy's hospital must have been built on the river since it would not have survived a sea voyage, whilst timbers used in a barge found near Blackfriars bridge present a dendrochronological profile showing them to have grown nearby.[46] A distinct Romano-Celtic ship-building tradition can be recognized from this evidence, borrowing from coastal regions of Belgic Gaul where skills and capacity were long established.[47]

The Thames was flanked by tidal creeks where shipyards could be established, and the city provided the necessary concentration of skilled craftsmen. Timber and iron were locally available, and the Roman reintroduction of flax cultivation to the Thames valley may have been encouraged by a demand for linen to make sails.[48] The ship-building industry was the subject of a text preserved on a writing tablet found close to the Walbrook at Lothbury in 1927.[49] This included references to sales from a shop or workshop (*vendidisse ex taberna sua*), shipbuilding (*navem faciendam*), and the making of a tiller or rudder (*clavi faciendi*), although gaps in the document leave us uncertain as to the nature of the transaction.

The hulls of local ships were made from overlapping planking secured to frames by nails. Peter Marsden has calculated that the Blackfriars barge, built with timbers felled in the early or middle part of the second century, used 1,500 massive nails containing over half a tonne of iron. Iron was also needed for ship's anchors and chains. These uses explain why the Roman fleet was involved in Wealden iron production (p. 185). The Flavian expansion of ironworking was a likely consequence of escalating military and naval demand, allied to the emphasis on local procurement. We have already noted that Wealden ironworking areas were connected to London by roads converging on Southwark. Iron transported along these roads had various uses, but the strategic importance of ship-building may have encouraged the military investment in the transport infrastructure. There are topographic grounds for believing that London's important shipyards lay south of the river. The north-bank was largely taken up by the harbour and too cramped for boatyards.[50] Low-lying Southwark was better suited, and the point of entry for both Wealden iron and timber rafted down-river from Surrey and Hampshire. Most of the wrought iron arrived in a semi-forced condition in need of further working. Much of this took place beside the river at the western end of Southwark's northern island where evidence of iron-working and copper-alloy working has been recovered from over 60 separate production sites across a four-hectare area.[51] Some small scale iron-working started soon after the conquest, indicated by hammerscale in the upper fills of the Claudian ditch at Park Street. Activity increased massively in the early Flavian period, following the construction of the roads that brought Wealden iron to London. Initially the iron working was an open-air activity, but sites were subsequently protected by timber shelters. Many dozens of clay-lined hearths were used for smithing iron, casting copper alloy, and smelting ore fuelled chiefly with oak charcoal.[52] The products of this industry are thought to include nails, tools and other fittings. This production would have been stimulated by London's shipyards but London's road hauliers would have created a parallel demand for wheelwrights and wainwrights working in timber and iron at similar locations.

Other industry

Several of London's early workshops made and repaired military equipment and armour (above p. 76). Some items were destined for military consumers elsewhere in Britain, such as the purchases described in letters at Vindolanda.[53] Evidence for casting and working small copper alloy items comes in the form of crucibles, moulds and slag in workshops along the roads into town at Newgate Street and Borough High Street.[54] Many of the things made here were dress accessories, such as brooches, used to define social and official standing.[55] The finds at Borough High Street also included the remains of an investment mould likely to have been used to make a larger vessel or statue.[56]

Blacksmiths occupied roadside locations on the edges of town.[57] These are recognized from concentrations of hammerscale: the iron flakes generated by beating hot metal on an anvil. The slightly built and well-ventilated buildings where forges were located also contained hearths, rake-out debris, and iron slag. One stood alongside the main approach road to London Bridge in Southwark before the Boudican revolt.[58] Blacksmithing resumed nearby after the revolt and continued into the early second century in a trade sustained over several generations. Blacksmiths made and maintained road vehicles, armour and cavalry gear, and tools for London's craftsmen.[59] The fashioning of iron is magical, and small shrines and votive deposits are commonly associated with metalworking.[60] A timber-lined well behind the workshop contained a 'smith urn' depicting a smith's hammer, anvil and tongs, perhaps placed here as a ritual closure deposit propitiating the smith god Vulcan.[61] The remains of about twenty dogs found in this well and adjacent pits contributed to protective ritual: Carrie Cowan and Angela Wardle have drawn attention to the chthonic symbolism attributed to dogs and their association with the 'mallet god' *Sucellus*, identified with Dis Pater the patron of coopers and other craftsmen. At Bucklersbury House, in the Walbrook valley, the charred remains of an arcaded wooden screen that may have formed a small domestic shrine associated with early second-century ironworking debris.[62]

London has produced an impressive range of iron tools, especially along the Walbrook where they probably entered the ground as votive items alongside rubbish dumped in land reclamation.[63] They witness a range of new crafts and industries, including woodworking (chisels, gouges, awls), metalworking (tongs, punches, hammers, an anvil, a furnace bar), timber and masonry construction (plasterers' tools, trowels), garden horticulture, tanning, and leatherworking. Some served the needs of distinct professional trades such as coopers, sawyers, joiners, metalworkers, vessel manufacturers, tanners, and shoemakers. Specialist tools simplified repetitive tasks: including the planes and rip saws used in woodwork, dies used in metalwork, and hole punches used in leatherwork.[64] This made it easier for craftsmen to standardize the manufacture of decorative items and achieve a degree of mass production. Dies and stamps suggest that most were controlled by private citizens, invariably men.

Several iron knives were locally made, including a group stamped by the cutler Basilius.[65] Lead and tin were used both separately and in combination (as pewter) for making small implements such as knives, spoons, toilet implements, tablewares, cooking vessels, furniture fittings, horse fittings, armour, and statuettes.[66] A group of seventeen decorated spoons cast in lead-tin alloy found along the London waterfront were probably of London manufacture.[67] These probably date to the early second century and were decorated with Bacchic motifs of canthari, parrots or doves, and fish. Stone moulds used for making lead-alloy bowls have been found at Dominant House in Queen Victoria Street and Cannon Street station.[68] The working of precious metals is represented by the discovery of parts of crucibles used for refining gold, sealed by clay stamps showing lions and boars, in late Flavian contexts at Suffolk Lane.[69] The processes included gold melting, cupellation and parting: possibly from melting down late Iron Age coin or jewellery for refashioning into new wrought-gold objects. Crucibles used in gold and silver working have been found in St Thomas Street in Southwark and the upper Walbrook valley, and another containing liquid mercury from 62–4 Cornhill was perhaps used in soldering decorative metalwork.[70]

Leather goods included tents, body-armour, jackets, breeches, sacks, protective covers, saddles, shield coverings, harnesses, and shoes.[71] At the time of the conquest these were imported, but discarded waste shows that production started in London by the end of the first century. Rome introduced sophisticated new leatherworking practices based on vegetable-based tanning.[72] Hides were steeped in water with large quantities of oak bark, abundantly available as a by-product of construction and ship-building. The need for a ready water supply drew London's tanners into the upper Walbrook valley and parts of Southwark, and numerous large wood-lined tanks and channels were associated with the Hadrianic redevelopment of the upper Walbrook valley.[73] Although no tanning pits have been identified, waste known as crust leather from Drapers' Gardens shows that post-tanning processing took place nearby. Hundreds of leather fragments have been found on adjacent sites, along with a pegged-out skin. Fragments of tent panels found in earlier Roman contexts in London show that these were predominantly made from goat-skin, although waste from New Fresh Wharf witness the third-century use of calf-skin.[74] Some leather waste carried identifying letters and numerals incised into the borders of the hides before tanning. Where names are found these are generally in the *tria nomina* form, and it is likely that tanning was undertaken by private contractors. Leather-working, as opposed to tanning, is represented by both waste materials and specialist punches and awls used in the workshops.[75] Incomplete shoes, leather pieces, and cobblers' tools have been found at 60 London Wall and a second-century building at Drapers' Gardens is thought to have been used by a shoemaker.[76] Some shoes may have been marked with size indicators, with a size 'X' found at Billingsgate Buildings, a size 'VIII' from Angel Court, and a size 'XII' from the Bank of England.

Some of London's workshops were involved in textile manufacture. Wooden and bone spindles and spindle-whorls are common finds, but it is difficult to distinguish between household and factory production. The two-beam vertical loom favoured by weavers leaves little archaeological trace, leaving us unable to identify centres of production.[77] A bone-working assemblage found at Cross Keys Court included cattle scapulae cut to remove flat plates in order to make triangular weaving tablets and cutting shears have been recovered from Walbrook deposits.[78] London is likely to have housed professional weavers, dyers, fullers, woolcombers, and sellers of dyed and washed wool and hackled flax.[79] The army required large quantities of cloth and there were advantages to developing a textile industry at this supply hub, drawing on wool procured from sheep-farming within the region.

One of the writing tablets found at the Bloomberg headquarters was addressed to Junius the Cooper (*Iunio cupario*) opposite the house of Catullus.[80] Another may have been addressed to Tertius the brewer, whom Roger Tomlin identifies as the same individual known from a writing tablet found at Carlisle. The name Tertius was also scored on a wooden barrel-head found in a well dated AD 63–4 at Blossom's Inn.[81] Barrel-making involved a high level of professional specialization, and examples of a specialist cooper's saw, the croze, have also been found in London.[82] This expertise allowed Tertius to establish a successful business supplying barrels of beer the length of Britain.

London's waterfront workshops housed another highly specialized type of woodworking: the manufacture of writing tablets used to document business transactions. Wooden shavings found at Pudding Lane, in contexts dated *c.* AD 80, came from the recycling of the silver fir wine barrels used to import wine.[83] The refashioning of these barrel staves involved paring them down to form facing rectangular leaves, each recessed and filled with blackened bees-wax (a by-product of local apiculture) to take the incised text.

Massive dumps of oyster shells near London Bridge suggests that a pickling or salting industry was located on the waterfront.[84] This might account for a concentration of north Kent shelly-ware storage vessels in this area, bringing salt or salted goods from Kentish salterns. A late Roman drain near the waterfront contained thousands of small bones from young herring and sprat, representing a catch of 'whitebait' from the estuary perhaps being converted into fish sauce nearby.[85] Livestock entering town was directed towards specialist butchers and markets, identified by waste involving head and foot parts and secondary products.[86] The carcasses left after hides and meat had been removed supported several craft industries. Bone, antler and horn were used to craft items such as hairpins, combs, dice, handles, drinking vessels and knife handles.[87] Assemblages of smashed bone fragments may have been boiled to extract grease for treating horse harness and equipment (above p. 80). These may be a characteristic of sites with military connections, and have been noted on the borders of the second-century district in the upper Walbrook valley where leatherworking was common.[88]

The productive periphery

Noxious industries, particularly those with fuel-hungry kilns, were generally located on the borders of town. At least twenty-one different glass-making sites have been identified from manufacturing waste. Their products included blown-glass wide-mouthed cups and containers (for water, wine, oil, and ointments), window-glass (used in bathhouses), glass tesserae, and stirring rods. London's earliest known glass-blower set up business in the 60s or 70s in a waterfront unit at Regis House (p. 101). By the end of the century these operations had ceased, but new kilns were found on the western boundary of the city at Gateway House and Bow Bells House.[89] Others were located on the town's eastern borders, represented by glass-working waste and fragments of a glass furnace in late first- or early second-century rubbish pits at Plantation Place and Colchester House.[90] Parts of furnace lining, pot metal, droplets, cuttings and waste were found beneath the rampart of the city wall at the Tower, suggesting the establishment of another second-century glass-blowing workshop in this area.[91]

Glass-makers subsequently established kilns in the upper Walbrook valley on the northern margins of town, following Hadrianic marsh reclamation. Parts of a tank furnace were found near Moorgate, and a 50 kilogramme dump of glass cullet was recovered at Guildhall Yard.[92] Finds at 35 Basinghall Street, south east of the amphitheatre, derived from two phases of second-century glass-working that ended with the catastrophic failure of an ageing furnace.[93] The glassmakers concentrated on basic tablewares and containers including bottles. Finds included 70 kilos of broken vessel glass and production waste, including tank metal and the moils left over from glass blowing, and droplets and threads used to test viscosity. As with London's other glass making, this was 'secondary' production using glass imported in raw blocks, and broken glass collected for re-cycling (cullet). Compositional analysis shows that the raw glass had been imported from the eastern Mediterranean in three separate batches. It seems that the glass-blowers were seasonal craftsmen, returning to the site and starting production afresh, hence drawing on fresh imports of raw-materials when setting-up rather than using cullet accumulated from earlier operations.

Eight glass-making kilns, one much repaired, were also located on the banks of the Fleet south of the road to Newgate.[94] These operated from the Hadrianic period until the early third century. This evidence combines to suggest that skilled glass-blowers with access to imported technologies and materials had established short-term furnaces in under-developed areas on London's margins. This was a seasonal activity, with the returning glass-blowers often relocating in the face of competition from other forms of land-use. The scale of production increased considerably in the second century, especially in the Hadrianic period when London's industrial production was at its height.

Pottery and tile kilns were also established on the western boundaries of the city, largely meeting local demand. The first were established before the Boudican revolt producing flagons and table wares. After the revolt several were set behind ribbon development along the main road approaching London from the west. These included updraught kilns with perforated floors uncovered in rebuilding St Paul's Cathedral after the Great Fire. Another was found in the Paternoster development south-east of the Cathedral in 1961; this was also of the updraught design with pottery dated to the late first to the early second century.[95] This pottery production may also have been largely seasonal. Early second-century kilns producing wheel-thrown whitewares were found at Northgate House in the upper Walbrook valley.[96] Two large circular kilns were set within clay-lined pits given solid floors of sun-dried bricks pierced by circular vents. They were fuelled by oak from tree-tops, perhaps the by-product of converting trees to timber. The potters used locally sourced London clay and clay imported from the Reading beds to make oxidized wares, reduced London ware, and mica dusted, marbled and eggshell finewares identical to Verulamium region products. Specialist products included mortaria (mixing bowls), lamps, small amphorae, lids, bowls, and dishes.[97] The evidence suggests that potters from workshops at Brockley Hill, close to Verulamium, had also opened kilns in London in the early second century. Stamps identify the potters Lucius, Valentinus, and Maximus. A timber structure next to the kilns is thought to be the workshop, where a stock of unused Gaulish Samian suggest that pottery was sold.

Market gardens bordered the town, supplying perishable produce to urban consumers and perhaps pioneering the cultivation of exotic species. The inventory of tools recovered from London includes a wider range of gardening implements than anywhere else in Roman Britain, and London's pottery assemblages include planting pots with drainage holes made in Kentish Eccles ware suggesting that that saplings were sourced from nurseries in this area.[98] Cultivation soils and bedding trenches occupied a roadside plot left vacant after the Boudican revolt at 1–7 Whittington Avenue, and field systems, stock enclosures, and animal byres have been identified on the borders of town.[99]

18

People and society

Written Londoners

We know the names of more than 400 residents of Roman London. A few reach us from historical sources: chiefly emperors, governors, and procurators. Other important Londoners were named on inscriptions, and many more mentioned in transactions on writing tablets. Tombstones, altars, and building dedications talked to a literate minority, communicating a particular relationship between temporal and sacred. In Britain, epigraphic commemoration was closely associated with the military administration and high-status immigrants.[1] Those commemorated were usually identified as agents of imperial authority, but unlike many other parts of the Roman Empire civil magistrates rarely featured. It is open to question whether this was because these office-holders were less politically relevant, or chose to participate in public life in different ways.

In his survey of the evidence then available, Nick Holder considered the names of about 235 Londoners recorded on inscriptions, including 175 men and twenty-three women.[2] Over half were scratched onto pottery vessels, marking personal items kept at communal venues such as taverns and clubs. Wooden stylus tablets present an alternative cast of individuals. These letters and agreements were scratched into the blackened beeswax of the paired tablets by a sharp stylus, penetrating the wood behind. Some 745 have been found in London, over half from excavations at the Bloomberg headquarters building.[3] From these Roger Tomlin has deciphered the names of another ninety-two individuals most of whom had business in London between *c.* AD 50 and 90.

This sample is inescapably unrepresentative in an empire where less than 10 per cent of the population is likely to have been literate.[4] Writing probably mattered somewhat more in London, since record-keeping was critical to business conducted across distance: as instruments of taxation and government, and to establish legal rights and responsibilities. In addition to the objects that were written upon—wood, stone, bone, metal, and ceramic—we can trace the spread of literate behaviour through the distribution of inkwells, seal boxes and the styli used as writing implements. London's collections include over 630 styli, mostly recovered from Walbrook deposits, and more than 134 Samian inkwells.[5] These were commonly found in commercial areas, around port and forum, where activities associated with the regulation of administered supply concentrated.[6] At least seventy-five seal boxes have been found in London. It is not certain how these small boxes containing wax seals were used: whether on official communications, on military documents, on goods and bags, or on personal vows deposited at shrines.[7] Carved intaglios set into rings were also used as seals, and several designs, such as the eagle and standards shown on gems from Southwark and Drapers' Gardens testify to the military status of their owners.[8]

Soldiers and officials

Memorials erected to soldiers from three different Roman legions have been found in London, with *Legio* II Augusta the best represented. The broken funerary monument of a legionary soldier or junior officer buried face down in the foundations of a late Roman tower at Camomile Street is particularly evocative (Fig. 18.1).[9] The 1.32-metre-high effigy showed the deceased wearing a military cloak, fastened by buttons and toggles, over a military tunic and leather apron. He wore a short sword and scarf, and a scroll and a block of six writing tablets held in his left hand show him to have been a clerical officer. His missing right hand would have held the staff that identified him as a standard-bearer or *optio*, or the lance that identified him as a junior officer seconded to the governor's staff (*beneficiarius consularis*). His Julio-Claudian hairstyle might be as late as Trajanic, but not later.

The permanent offices of the governor's staff (*officium*) were based in London before the end of the first century. The administration relied on *beneficiarii consularis* to manage the supply and logistical support for the army, and each legion provided sixty men for these duties, creating a centralized bureaucracy of 200 or so soldiers.[10] Soldiers could also have been tasked with other low-level administrative duties: governing out-stations, collecting tax and rent, and maintaining security.[11] Members of the governor's office responsible for policing operations were known as *speculators*, whom the sources describe as executioners: the second-century tombstone of Celsus, a *speculator* from *Legio* II Augusta that had been set up by three of his fellow colleagues was found near Blackfriars.[12] Each legion would have seconded about ten such officers to work with the governor, giving London a forty-strong contingent whose responsibilities included arranging public executions in London's amphitheatre.

The governor was also supported by a guard picked from the auxiliary cavalry and infantry cohorts (*singulares consularis*), perhaps numbering around 1200 men.[13] These forces were not legionaries and most weren't Roman citizens.[14] Although many followed the governor on campaign and in his administrative tours, most were likely to have had winter quarters in London and some were permanently based here. A list found at Vindolanda on the northern frontier, dated *c.* AD 90, enumerates soldiers from the Cohort of Tungrians absent on secondment. Eleven soldiers and a centurion were at London, sixteen others were

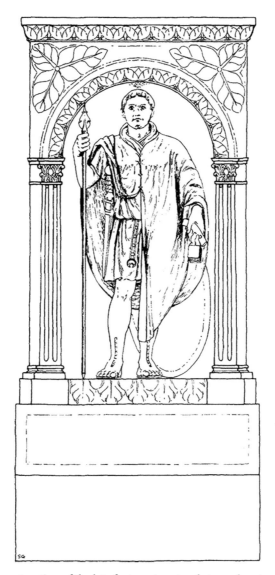

Fig. 18.1 A reconstruction of the late first-century tombstone showing a soldier engaged in clerical duties that was found reused in the foundations of a fourth-century bastion at Camomile Street (drawn by Mike Bishop and reproduced with his kind permission).

with the governor and a few were with someone named as Ferox, who may have been the procurator.[15] If this was typical of the auxiliary cohorts deployed in Britain, then 800 men from these forces would have been with the governor and 600 seconded directly to London. One of the writing-tablets found at the Bloomberg site, in a context dated no later than *c*. AD 80, refers to Rusticus, a member of governor's guard (*singularis*), adding weight to the proposition that the governor was based in London at this date.[16] A tablet from a similarly dated context was addressed to a former member of a Roman emperor's bodyguard (*emerito Aug*), who was perhaps also in London in the governor's service.[17] Altogether some 10 per cent of the individuals named in the Bloomberg texts were part of the military community, including several members of the auxiliary forces probably stationed in London in the aftermath of the Boudican revolt (above p. 97). Altogether nine officers and men can be identified from three cohorts.

Other serving men in London included the grooms responsible for procuring and managing cavalry mounts.[18] An early second-century letter found at Vindolanda was addressed to Veldedeius, a groom (*equisio consularis*) serving in London and probably attached to the governor. London would also have housed a records office requiring the services of census-officials. Other military commands may have had officers stationed in London, including the fleet (*Classis Britannica*).[19] All told, London must have routinely been home to hundreds of soldiers regardless of where the governor was to be found, perhaps rising to 1,800 or more when the legate was in winter residence. There are times when London's military community would have constituted more than 10 per cent of the entire population. These soldiers were easily identified in the streets by their dress.[20] Soldiers normally wore cloaks over belted tunics, and carried armour. This not only marked them as military men, but signalled differences between legionary and auxiliary unit as well as of rank. A growing corpus of objects associated with this military presence has been found in London.[21] These soldiers would have been accompanied by slaves and servants, sometimes forming large households.[22] Soldiers were ever-present in London, but as part of a decidedly mixed community.[23]

Elite society

The procurator's office may have been of even greater consequence to the life of the city. The emperor drew on an immense private household (*familia*), to manage his affairs. Business relationships were conducted through a network of friends and dependants, relying on imperial slaves and freedmen. These were the emperor's people, the *Caesariani*, under the command of the imperial procurator. As we have already noted the procurator may have had staff in London prior to the Boudican revolt. From Vespasian's time the office is thought to have gained in administrative importance, taking closer control of economic management.[24] It was staffed by imperial slaves whose responsibility for managing large estates and raising taxes involved them in diverse credit arrangements, and placed them close to the pinnacle of power.[25] Their presence in London is marked by the discovery of a writing tablet branded with the stamp of the Procurators of the Emperor in the Province of Britain, indicating that this was an official record from the procurators record office or *tabularium* (Fig. 18.2).[26] Another writing tablet, found at One Poultry, described the sale of a Gallic slave-girl called Fortunata to Vegetus, who was himself an assistant slave of Montanus a slave of the Emperor (Fig. 18.3).[27] Fortunata was expensive, costing 600 denarii equal to 2 years' pay for a soldier. Montanus and Vegetus were representatives of an imperial bureaucracy that was every bit as important to London as the army but civilian in character. The date of the context where the tablet was found suggests that they served towards the close of the first century, probably under Domitian, Nerva, or Trajan.

A second-century hexagonal tombstone found at Ludgate Hill was set up to Claudia Martina, a Roman citizen who died when she was nineteen, by her widower Anencletus, a slave of the province.[28] Anencletus probably served the provincial assembly which was chiefly concerned with the important ceremonies of the imperial cult (p. 136). By contrast, as we have noted, no inscriptions testify to the activities of London's magistrates or *curia*. If London had gained self-governing status, then it would have been ruled by magistrates drawn from its resident land-owning citizens. This group commissioned few commemorative inscriptions anywhere within the province, and remains wholly invisible within London.[29] At the very least this reticence suggests a degree of disengagement with imperial politics, as also implied by the fact that no Briton is known to have reached senatorial rank in Rome.

Many of those who lived in Roman London would not have been recognized as citizens of the city: a status normally inherited by descent from a male citizen, or by manumission or adoption by someone who held such status. Residents who were not citizens were identified as aliens, known as *incolae*.[30] This was usually an inferior standing, and *incolae* along with freedmen were barred from civic office. Most of the more important Roman Londoner's whom we know about, and who were not themselves soldiers and government officials, are likely to have been *incolae*. The shippers, merchants, and money-lenders who took up business in London remained citizens of other cities, as illustrated by the dedicatory inscription of Tiberinius Celerianus discussed in Chapter 21. Tombstones from London's eastern cemetery include funerary inscriptions to *incolae* such as Lucius Pompeius Licetus from Arretium in Italy, and A. Alfidius Olussa who was born at Athens and buried in London in the first century AD.[31] These inscriptions celebrate a community of important foreigners.[32] It is also evident that many of London's first craftsmen and shopkeepers arrived in London from the continent, perhaps as camp-followers, boasting skills that simply did not exist in Britain before the conquest.[33] At some point successful entrepreneurs amongst this immigrant community may have moved wealth into local property, establishing residential credentials that would have carried their heirs into the local curial

0   5cm

Fig. 18.2 Writing tablet branded by the Proc(uratores) Aug(usti) Dederunt Brit(anniae) Prov(inciae) probably found in the Walbrook (reproduced by kind permission of the Trustees of the British Museum).

Fig. 18.3 Writing tablet found in excavations at One Poultry describing the sale of Fortunata, a Gallic slave-girl, to Montanus who was himself a slave employed in the imperial bureaucracy (ONE94: reproduced by kind permission of Museum of London Archaeology).

class. There is, however, little evidence to illustrate this process at work and alien identities continued to dominate the archaeological record. If we return to the evidence of the ninety-two names found on the writing tablets recovered from the Bloomberg site, thirteen were identifiable as Roman citizens, one of whom held equestrian rank, whilst ten more could be identified as non-Romans (*peregrine*) identifiable by their patronymics. Another ten had Celtic names, although this should not be mistaken for evidence of British birth since these names are found in Gaul and other Celtic-speaking provinces.[34]

As far as we can tell from the written record, officials, freedmen, and *incolae* occupied the heights of society in early Roman London. Since such people were normally excluded from participation in local self-government this may explain a lack of urgency in granting London such status. Rather than being seen as a reward to a native community, the normal institutions of civic self-government might have formed a competing vehicle for social progression from which those most central to the affairs of the city were excluded. Executive power lay in the hands of public officials who typically served no more than 4 years in post, with longer-term political cohesion likely to have been provided by the more powerful bureaucrats and contractors who remained in residence from one administration to the next. This would have privileged the contributions made by imperial slaves and freedmen, by the officer class, and the business community of contractors. The importance of such functionaries may have robbed oxygen from alternative patronage networks, contributing to a lack of civic euergetism.

Immigration

Whilst we can identify a significant number of incomers from other Roman provinces amongst the biased sample of written and epigraphic sources, it is often assumed that London must have attracted a significant working population from the surrounding countryside, making the city a major meeting place for Briton and Roman.[35] Jenny Hall has described how London's rapid urban expansion required a large workforce and concludes that most were probably native Britons.[36] This is a doubtful proposition. We can be reasonably certain that many of the first people to settle in Roman London were immigrants from the continent, since they drew on a host of new skills and techniques. There were, in any case, no neighbouring population centres from which London could recruit.[37] These immigrant skills could, of course, be learnt and their practice soon ceases to be a reliable guide to a craftsman's place of origin. What is more telling is that we have negligible evidence of knowledge exchange between London and the surrounding countryside. This suggests that there was no substantial return-flow of workers and families returning to villages of origin. We can identify a few places in pre-Flavian London where insular building and craft traditions were practised (see pp. 82–3 and 103), but only in small and marginal communities. If London was home to a large influx of locally born people, it is hard to believe that these traditions would not have been more widely distributed.

London, like most port cities, was a cosmopolitan place that relied on immigration.[38] This remained the case throughout its history. DNA and oxygen isotope evidence indicate that a significant proportion of the people buried in London in late antiquity had spent their childhoods elsewhere.[39] We know less about London's earlier populations but it seems likely that the same applied (see p. 348). The Roman conquest moved over 100,000 people across the channel, and many of those discharged from the army would have settled close to their place of service, perhaps including the recipient of the diploma found at Watling Court.[40]

Many who came here would have been accompanied by large households including a significant number of slaves. Slaves and freedmen are identified at least six times in the texts found at the Bloomberg site, sometimes as agents of their owners.[41] This is what we should expect, since census returns in Roman Egypt indicate that almost 15 per cent of urban residents could be slaves.[42] A significant population of male immigrants from overseas may help to explain why males outnumber females, to a ratio of 3:2, in the later cemeteries of Roman London.[43] The skeletal remains of the people buried in London also show abnormally high numbers of stress indicators formed during childhood (*cribra orbitalia* and *enamel hypoplasias*) when compared to other Romano-British populations. Since these lesions tend to be higher in Mediterranean populations, Gowland and Redfern suggest this might reflect on childhoods spent outside Britain. As an aside we can note that although ancient towns could be unhealthy places the osteological data from Roman Britain indicates that townsfolk generally enjoyed better physical and oral health than rural populations.[44]

Fashion and identity

We have already noted that the lifestyles of the first Londoners owed much to fashions developed along the Rhine. Early Roman London was more closely aligned on the cultural world of Trier and Belgica than its British hinterland. Many factors contributed to the continued importance of social and cultural links between London and these areas. This included direct immigration, although the connectivity established by commerce and supply directed through the Rhineland was probably equally important. The new city was a place where hybrid identities could be forged around new opportunities.[45] Neville Morley described Roman cities as integrating landscapes, where people were drawn into new patterns of behaviour and social customs that fostered the development of a distinct social identity.[46] One area where this might be in evidence was in the use of jewellery and personal ornament. Hairpins help trace changing fashions in women's hairstyles, following the example of imperial fashions represented on Roman coins. Bone pins were scare in London during the first century AD, conspicuously so in assemblages recovered from excavations at One Poultry where all types of artefact associated with women were rare in the pre-Flavian period.[47] This may reflect a scarcity of women amongst the town's population. Some losses of metal hairpins in the late first century might mark the presence of a small community of wealthy women, but cheaper bone pins only started being lost in significant numbers in the second century. By this date, more women in London were wearing hairstyles that needed hairpins, perhaps marking a time when earlier high-status fashions were more widely adopted.

Brooches also illustrate changing fashion. By the beginning of the second century, London began to diverge from its earlier wholesale adoption of continental dress accessories. This was a period when fewer brooches were being made and used, which has been described by Hilary Cool and Mike Baxter as the fibula abandonment horizon. Some Londoner's used a type of brooch of local manufacture that included a loop at the head that allowed them to be worn in pairs with a chain strung between.[48] In adopting this custom, women in London followed Romano-British fashions that differed from those on the continent. This social dialogue with neighbouring Romano-British cities may also have contributed to the way in which metal cosmetic and toilet sets came to be used in personal grooming within London.[49] These small sets of implements, including tweezers and scoops, had been adopted by the Catuvellaunian elite prior to the conquest before coming into wider use in Roman Britain in the later first century.

For the most part, however, finds assemblages recovered from the City indicate that London remained a place apart into the second century. It was not only provisioned differently to neighbouring settlements but it made use of different combinations of pots, witnessing different preferences in preparing and serving food and drink. Far more Samian was used in London than anywhere else in Britain. Although some came to London in transit, much was destined for use within town.[50] These tastes account for uncommonly high numbers of ceramic flagons used to serve wine and drink. London's appetites are also illustrated by an elevated presence of amphorae that contained imported olive oil, wine and fish-sauce. One of those found on the Thames foreshore in Southwark was marked with a Latin text that translates as 'Lucius Tettius Africanus' excellent fish sauce from Antipolis', showing it to have been an import from Antibes in southern France.[51] It still contained mackerel heads. Mortaria were sufficiently important to consumers in London to warrant local manufacture, with some products stamped by the Procurator's office using the same dies as for the tiles.[52] These gritted bowls were probably used for grinding and pulverizing leafy plants and meat or fat following a continental taste in food preparation that arrived with the Roman conquest and became particularly popular in London.[53] Excavations in London have also recovered palaeobotanical evidence of an exceptionally wide range of exotic and imported plants, most of which supported high-status dining.[54]

Cereals, chiefly wheat and barley, necessarily formed the staple part of the diet. In addition to being made into bread it provided cakes, porridge, and gruel.[55] Barley may also have been used in brewing beer, supplementing imported beer from sites along the river (p. 179). Charred plant remains from London include peas, beans, and lentils, whilst pollen evidence and seeds identify cabbage, carrots, and cucumbers.[56] Fruit was also well represented in the diet and appears to have included grape, fig, plum, sloe, cherry, apple/pear, and strawberry. Hazelnut and some walnut were also consumed.

Adult cattle provided most of London's meat.[57] The predominance of mature animals indicates that most beef derived from redundant working animals, used in dairy and traction, butchered at the end of their working lives. Dairy farming is also implied by the local use of ceramic strainers probably used to convert milk into cheese. Younger animals are present in sufficient quantities, however, to show that some consumers could command more tender meat. Sheep and goat were also consumed, but in smaller numbers. Sheep may sometimes have been preferred for sacrifice, perhaps contributing to their higher representation in individual contexts. Pigs, instead, were bred largely for their meat which made them more of a luxury item. Their greater abundance in animal bone assemblages from riverside sites in Southwark as at Winchester Palace and Tabard's Square, especially in the Flavian period, adds weight to the suggestion that these were high-status sites. Poultry and fowl also made a contribution to the diet. Chickens are the most commonly identified species, and a relatively high-status food at this time. Wild game made only a small contribution, with low quantities of deer, hares, and woodcocks relative to other settlements in Roman Britain. Fish bone shows that London made good use of local river and estuarine resources. The main species consumed included eel and flounder/flatfish, but cod, mackerel, herring, pike, chub, and trout are all found in London, as were some species more expensive to bring to table such as turbot and sturgeon.[58]

This brisk summary risks understating the significant variety in patterns of consumption and display across London. On the other hand, it is clear that city living permitted extravagancies that were harder to support elsewhere. London consumed a higher proportion of luxury goods than any other civilian settlement in the province. These patterns of conspicuous consumption, housed within well-appointed reception rooms, were evident prior to the revolt of AD 60/61 but became both more widespread and more uniform after Flavian investment in London's growth. This was when London society gained confidence in elaborating a culture of its own: still drawing heavily on northern Gaul and the German frontier, but including elements of more insular tradition. This cultural hybridization did not necessarily involve any significant levels of immigration from elsewhere in Britain, at least not in ways that are easily identified. One suspects, however, that British slaves and wives were found in many households: a likely outcome if the immigrant population was predominantly male.

Pervasive ritual

The fortunes of London's urban community were shaped by its identity as a sacred place. The invention of new cities gained legitimacy from being seen as ordained, where destiny was guided by the gods and spirits who dwelt there. London also relied on the good fortune of its imperial patrons and of the Roman state. Londoners consequently bargained with myriad supernatural forces in religious observances and public ritual, particularly in acts of purification and propitiation that followed the seasons and shaped the year.[59] This gave life to institutions and ceremonies that helped cement local identities, and shaped architectures that articulated a relationship between the living, their ancestors, gods, and emperors. The gods of Rome held supreme authority in a place built by Rome, but not to the exclusion of local powers. The text of an oath found on a writing tablet found in Lothbury, near the Walbrook, neatly covered these different bases by swearing to Jupiter, the genius of the emperor Domitian, and the native gods (*deos patrios*).[60]

Gods were thought to inhabit specific locations, which is where they were best approached. These were gateway locations, recognized as portals between different realms. The Thames was recognizably a river deity, and the comingling of fresh and salt water at the tidal head must have added to potency to the point where the river was bridged.[61] The very building of the bridge risked offending the river, engendering prophylactic placation through ritual performance, whilst simultaneously witnessing the Roman ordering of space and signalling the supremacy of an imperial authority sanctioned by the gods.[62] The stray finds from the Thames foreshore that referenced Neptune, described on pp. 150 and 244, may have derived from a shrine to this god on London Bridge. The splendid marble torso of a bearded male found in the Walbrook near the temple of Mithras where it was probably displayed presents the likeness a river deity, perhaps conflating the characteristics of *Oceanus, Neptune* and *Tamesis*. The second-century sculpted head of a river god found at 165 Great Dover Street in Southwark had probably decorated a tomb in the adjacent cemetery.[63]

Representations of the gods were commonplace. Sculptures and reliefs in stone and bronze include most of the more popular deities.[64] These were also well represented amongst the small bronze and pipeclay figurines found in excavations.[65] London has a larger collection of such material than anywhere else in Britain, with Hercules, Mars, Minerva, Mercury and Venus particularly well represented. Altars and dedications establish the certain presence in London of places dedicated to the worship of Jupiter, Isis, Faunus, Mithras, and Mars Camulus. The presence of a shrine to Diana Nemesis at the amphitheatre seems fairly certain. The decorative arts witness the widespread diffusion of ideas drawn from Bacchic mysteries, and other mystery cults are well represented amongst London's finds assemblages. The city was crowded with gods.

A key function of civic government was to appoint magistrates to attend to sacred sites, make sacrifices, and celebrate the games.[66] Some of the most important religious celebrations were introduced as part of the imperial cult (above p. 136). Participation was a mark of status, and a vehicle for the social advancement of freedmen and *incolae*.[67] Foreigners were legally obliged to perform liturgies in the cities where they resided, in addition to their place of origin. These rituals were performative, contributing towards a shared Roman and civic identity that accommodated the particular nature of social power within the city.[68] The focal point of public ritual was the sacrifice or offering, commonly presented on altars and shrines in events that marked the importance of the ritual vows made to the gods.[69] Examples from London include the small stone altar found behind the buildings along the main road through Southwark at Borough High Street, and the burnt remains of a wooden structure with an arcaded timber panel thought to have been part of a shrine established on the banks of the Walbrook.[70] A strip of lead decorated with two standing female figures, perhaps goddesses or muses, found at Trinity Square had decorated the sides of cupboard-like shrine.[71] The sacrifice itself involved offerings, sometimes involving the slaughter of livestock, in the form of a meal where food was shared.[72] Many of the more unusual finds assemblages recovered from Roman London are likely to have derived from such feasts.[73] In order to be effective these ritual activities were anchored in both time and space. Sacred spaces were enclosed and protected by ritually defined boundaries, from which the word *templum* derives.[74] Monumental temple architecture was often a later addition to these landscapes. In London this gave rise to a significant phase of Antonine temple building, below p. 265, that respected religious topographies inherited from the earlier Roman settlement.

The need to propitiate the gods, whether seeking favour or averting danger, attached to particular actions and rites of passage. Rivers, springs, hilltops, bridges, gates, ditches, wells, and shafts were all places where offerings were made to spirits of place. Deposition of metalwork and other objects within natural watery settings, in particular rivers, were commonplace.[75] It has consequently been argued that finds from the rivers Thames and Walbrook included such votive objects, although it can be difficult to distinguish these from domestic rubbish contained within reclamation dumps.[76] The ritual 'killing' of objects, by bending or mutilation, can help identify offerings sacrificed to the river. Communication with supernatural powers depended on the proper conduct of prescribed rites, commonly involving written vows and curses.[77] Temple and votive offerings were deposited as an element in the ritual of such vows as part of a pact made with the god. This involved promising a gift in return for divine service and a payment on fulfilment. Several lead curse tablets from London record the private arrangements made with the gods by those seeking help in redressing a wrong.[78] An example is the rectangular lead tablet found at One Poultry that listed the names of those to be cursed: Plautius Nobilianus, Aurelius Saturninus, Antiola, daughter of Domitius, and another. The tablet had been folded into four concealing the writing in such a way that the text could be read by the gods alone.[79]

Unusual and structured finds assemblages are a particular feature of foundation and closure deposits (also p. 385). New houses sometimes included a foundation offering buried beneath a threshold or wall. These included animal burials, especially dogs who were presumably favoured because of their association with household protection and the supernatural.[80] Small jars at such locations contained offerings.[81] The use of mortaria in foundation deposits suggests the food that they produced was particularly appropriate to these ritual occasions.[82] At Walbrook House a small unguent jar placed as votive offering within one of the late first-century walls contained seven objects: a textile, carbonized fruit, a bone die, a fragment of amber, a piece of an iron key, part of a bone buckle and an uncut chalcedony gemstone.[83] Each material added magically to the offering. Votive offerings also reused prehistoric objects as amulets, such as a Neolithic axe found at the Bloomberg headquarters.[84]

Unusual finds assemblages recovered from shafts, pits, and wells can be identified as closure deposits: votive offerings made at ceremonies that marked endings.[85] Similar deposits were a feature of pre-Roman ritual in Britain, and occur on urban and rural domestic sites as well as temple precincts throughout the Roman period.[86] The assemblages placed in these shafts also included dogs, famed for their connection with the underworld, as in the late second-century well at St Thomas Street (above p. 213) and a contemporary feature at Lant Street.[87] The chronology, distribution and composition of these assemblages needs further attention, but they seem to have been more common on the town borders, particularly in Southwark. Roman London was a restless city, peopled by immigrant and temporary residents many of whom would have been classed as *incolae*. This transience, with its risks and uncertainties, must have added to the enduring importance of rituals that closed pacts between people and place.

PART 5
DESTRUCTION AND RECOVERY

19

The Hadrianic fire (*c.* AD 125–35)

The burning of London

Soon after Hadrian's visit to Britain in AD 122, London was overwhelmed by a catastrophic fire. This left a distinctive horizon of fire-reddened daub and destruction debris that can be traced across most of the settlement (Fig. 19.1).[1] It may have been an entirely accidental event like the Great Fire of 1666, but it is also possible that London had been razed in a largely forgotten British war. Evidence of fire damage is particularly intense around London Bridge, coincidentally close to the Pudding Lane bakery where the Great Fire began.[2] To the west the Walbrook had failed to act as a fire-break, and burnt debris can be traced either side of the river's lower reaches.[3] The horizon is not evident further upriver along the Thames waterfront, perhaps because the area was under-developed after the Huggin Hill baths were closed.[4] Otherwise destruction engulfed roadside buildings to the westernmost fringes of town, if not to the banks of the Fleet where the quays and mill at the river mouth escaped damage.[5]

On the northern side of town the fire skirted the amphitheatre, but left no trace within the arena itself.[6] This may have been because the timber superstructure had already been dismantled awaiting rebuilding. More probably, the Hadrianic rebuilding here was necessitated by partial fire-damage, and much of the superstructure could have been burnt without leaving archaeological trace. In either case, the amphitheatre marked the boundary of the built-up area and the northern limit of fire damage. Further to the east fire debris can be traced as far north as the settlement then extended, including areas of suburban development along Bishopsgate.[7] Buildings flanking the forum were also burnt although it is not certain that the basilica was destroyed.[8] This was damaged by an early second-century fire, but it has been suggested that this was a later event.[9] Eastwards the destruction reached Plantation Place and Mark Lane, but not as far as the Tower where there is no certain evidence of occupation before the late 120s.[10] It also extended north-east along Fenchurch Street as far as Lloyd's Register and St Katherine Coleman, possibly to 3–4 Jewry Street.[11] A few buildings on the eastern margins of the settlement, set back from street frontages, show no direct evidence of fire damage.[12] Fire debris is also generally absent from the upper Walbrook valley and Cripplegate fort, which areas may not have seen significant development until after the fire.[13] Only a few buildings within the area of destruction show no clear trace of fire damage, but these are isolated examples where the

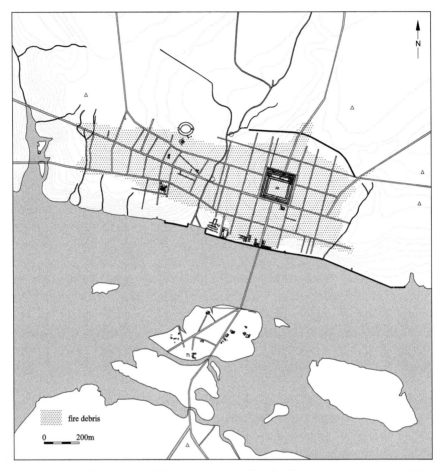

Fig. 19.1 The likely extent of destruction caused by the Hadrianic fire of *c.* AD 125/6 based on observations of *in-situ* fire debris. Drawn by Justin Russell.

subsequent rehabilitation of partly ruined buildings may have cleared away destruction debris.[14] Taken collectively, the evidence indicates that little of London north of the Thames survived, leaving a smouldering wasteland over some 64.5 hectares.

The situation in Southwark was different. There is no evidence of a general conflagration, although a couple of buildings may have seen fire damage at about this time.[15] The high-status building complex at Winchester Palace was comprehensively rebuilt *c.* AD 120/130 and the floor of one of the structures replaced at this time, a possible granary, was covered by an unusual charcoal layer.[16] In the absence of a more substantial destruction horizon, Brian Yule suggested that this was a deposit of soot. On the other hand, the horizon included window glass distorted by fire, and subsequent levelling dumps included burnt material. It is possible that the charcoal was a residue from burnt roof timbers, generating a distinctive destruction horizon in the absence of burnt mudbrick and daub.

London's Hadrianic fire is conventionally dated *c.* AD 125 by a massive warehouse assemblage of fire-damaged Samian found at Regis House.[17] Destruction at One Poultry also included numerous potter's stamps from Samian made at Les Martres-de-Veyre dated *c.* AD 105-25, and a Pulborough Samian vessel made from a Lezoux mould dated *c.* AD 125-50.[18] Dendrochronological evidence from timber structures damaged by the fire confirms, but doesn't refine, the dating suggested by the pottery.[19] Archaeomagnetic samples from Regis House have also provided dates of AD 110-30 and 130-80 for the fire.[20] These sources combine to confirm the dating of the fire to the period AD 125/130. A very slightly earlier date is not wholly impossible, but can be considered highly improbable.

Post-fire reconstruction appears to have been underway by *c.* AD 128. Dumps associated with the replacement of short-lived Hadrianic quays investigated at Suffolk House included scorched and fire-sooted pottery dated AD 120-60, with *in-situ* fire debris nearby.[21] The waterfront had probably been rebuilt following the fire and timbers used to line a box-drain within the new harbour facilities were felled AD 128. Although we cannot discount the possibility that these timbers were reused, this is improbable. Most of the timber used in rebuilding London's harbour would have been procured for the exercise, and since felled after the fire should provide a *terminus ante quem* for the event. A substantial jetty was also built over the Thames foreshore at the Tower of London using timbers felled in the winter of AD 126-7.[22] This was an unusual location for waterfront activity, since the site lay some distance downstream from the settlement, in an area that was only built-up later in the second century. It is tempting to suggest that the jetty was a temporary facility for ships coming up-river whilst the port was in ruin.

In sum, the fire is dated *c.* AD 125/130, and post-fire rebuilding was almost certainly underway in AD 128 if not by the spring of AD 127. This establishes a strong case for dating the fire to AD 125-6. This is also the earliest date that easily accommodates the evidence of fire damage in the north range of the forum basilica. This structure wasn't built before the Hadrianic period, and was perhaps completed in time for the imperial visit of AD 122 (above p. 165).[23] The building was subsequently modified, involving the replacement of the nave wall with brick piers, before it was destroyed in a fire of Hadrianic date. The road built alongside the basilica's north range had been resurfaced twice before this fire. If the basilica was completed AD 119/122, and a minimum of 2 or 3 years elapsed between each road repair, it is hard to date the fire much earlier than *c.* AD 125.

This review of dating evidence is complicated by the fact that we cannot be certain that London only suffered one Hadrianic fire. A report on excavations at 10 Gresham Street proposed two successive periods of activity ending in Hadrianic conflagration, both dated *c.* AD 130 by assemblages with diagnostic forms in Verulamium region white-ware.[24] The presence of successive fire horizons is not, however, securely demonstrated by the published evidence. Clearance operations may have resulted in fire debris being redeposited, converting a single event into several archaeological horizons. Elsewhere in London there is overwhelming evidence for a massively devastating conflagration that was capable of leaping 8-metre-wide fire-breaks presented by the Walbrook and wider streets, and there is good reason to see this as a single event dated *c.* A D 125/126.

Accident or arson?

Cautious scholarship has generally preferred to treat the Hadrianic fire as a terrible accident.[25] In such a fire, however, one would expect to find buildings upwind of the fire's starting point that escaped destruction. This doesn't appear to have been the case, and the comprehensive nature of destruction along areas of ribbon development leading into the city hints at deliberate action. London's Hadrianic destruction also gave rise to unusual post-fire interventions which mirrored those which took place after the rebellion of A D 60/61. Activities after the Boudican revolt included the construction of a fort, the building of a track across the Walbrook valley to bypass the town centre, a scatter of fragmentary human remains on the city borders suggestive of retributive corpse abuse, and the heavily engineered enhancement of the port infrastructure (pp. 99 and 110). An identical pattern of activity can be described from London's Hadrianic archaeology. This embraced the building of a fort, the engineering of a road to bypass the town centre, a spike in the volume of human remains scattered on the city borders, and the rebuilding of the port and public buildings. The details of this archaeological 'signature' are considered in the following chapters, but these similarities suggest a common context for both Neronian and Hadrianic rebuilding.

This encourages us to explore the possibility that London was destroyed by war *c.* A D 125/126. The very idea of a war at this time runs counter to the view, drawn from Edward Gibbon's confident opinion, that 'the empire flourished in peace and prosperity' during Hadrian's reign.[26] History may, however, have been over-kind to Hadrian. Although we have no detailed sources for political developments in Britain during the second century there is the clear testimony of a letter written to the emperor Marcus Aurelius by his tutor Cornelius Fronto in A D 162, which refers to a British slaughter of Roman soldiers during Hadrian's reign that stood comparison with the disastrous war in Judea.[27] This was a serious matter: according to Cassius Dio, 580,000 men were slain during the Judean revolt.[28] A late fourth-century life of Hadrian also refers to the difficulties he met in keeping Britons under Roman control.[29] These sparse references are sufficient to suggest the historical reality of a British revolt during Hadrian's reign, but tell us nothing about where, when or why it happened. Until recently most scholars were inclined to see this as an event preceding Hadrian's visit to the province and confined to the northern frontier.[30] Inscriptions describing the military careers of Maenius Agrippa and Pontius Sabinus encourage a slightly different reading of events. These officers participated in an expedition to Britain likely to have been mounted to quell the revolt. Other details in Sabinus' career path make it difficult for this expedition to have taken place before AD 124.[31] Events along Hadrian's Wall also suggest some form of crisis c. AD 123/4. A tombstone from Vindolanda commemorated a war casualty of the period, and the building of the wall was interrupted and modified.[32] John Casey has drawn attention to successive coin issues from the mint at Alexandria that appeared to celebrate Roman victories obtained in AD 124/125 and AD 125/126, which he argued were won in the British campaign.[33] The celebration of victories in successive years suggests a prolonged war, involving a setback or different theatres of action. The second victory, obtained in the months prior to September AD 126, is appropriately dated to have been won in a war that encompassed London's burning in AD 125 or 126.[34]

There is no direct proof that other parts of southern Britain was affected, although Hadrianic fire debris found in Staines and Brentford might chart a route of destruction west of London.[35] It should come as no surprise, however, that London would have been sacked if Rome lost control of the province. The city's role in raising tax and rent, as the seat of government, and as the wealthiest place in Britain, made it a prime target.

London was in the midst of change at the time of the fire, perhaps following reforms made on Hadrian's visit. Change was also evident in the surrounding landscape which was extensively farmed into the second century AD.[36] Zoological and palaeo-botanical remains suggest a greater emphasis on cultivating spelt wheat and cattle farming, accompanied by improvements in cattle livestock.[37] Farmers appear to have been maximizing agricultural production, perhaps in response to more elevated demands of tax and rent. Wheel-thrown black-burnished vessels produced on both sides of the Thames estuary started arriving in London early in the Hadrianic period, probably by AD 120, contributing to the archaeological definition of a new period of ceramic supply.[38] These vessels also appear in quantities on Britain's northern frontier in the following decades, witnessing a marked increase in traffic along the east coast.[39] It has been suggested that some of this was carried by the *Classis Britannica*, since the fleet was directly involved in building work on the wall and must have been an important presence along the coast. These pots were probably moved such distances because they contained valued commodities, probably including salt and salted produce. The use of black burnished pots to package such goods imitated earlier production in Dorset, which packaged salt or salted goods from an area likely to have been under military control. The east coast trade drew on a significant increase in production within the Thames estuary. New kilns either side of the river, in south-east Essex and northern Kent, ramped up their seasonal production of black-burnished vessels.[40] Excavations at Dagenham Farmstead illustrate the introduction of new pottery kilns, involving radical new technologies and production techniques, c. AD 125.[41] These changes within the Thames estuary are likely to relate to new lines of supply associated with the building of Hadrian's Wall, the garrisoning of which relied on taxes and rents raised elsewhere.[42] Production responded promptly to new military demand in the north, perhaps managed by the procurator's London office. We can speculate that the increased exactions implied by this evidence might have provoked tax rebellions similar to those of the revolt of AD 60/61.[43] Unrest may also have followed the example of the rebellions in Judea, coming to a head after Hadrian's tour of the western empire was broken off in AD 123 when an emergency is believed to have summoned him east.[44]

The Cripplegate fort

If London had been sacked in a British revolt this might explain why a new military garrison was subsequently stationed at the north-west corner of town. Excavations by Peter Grimes after the Second World War traced the plan of an imposing early second-century stone-walled fort (Fig 19.2).[45] The defensive perimeter was formed by a high stone wall backed by an earthen rampart, fronted by a V-shaped ditch about 3 metres wide and 1.5 metres deep. A second, outer, ditch may have been dug along its western side.[46] Peter Marsden's excavations next to the Guildhall extension found evidence of two phases of fort construction since the original ditch was comprehensively backfilled soon after it was dug, presumably because the associated earthworks had been slighted. A new ditch of identical profile was then dug along the same line to restore the defensive circuit, before this ditch was in turn silted up c. AD 140–80.[47] In sum it appears that plans for the construction of the fort were cancelled before being swiftly revived.

The corners of the fort were reinforced by internal towers and smaller rectangular turrets set along the line of the perimeter wall.[48] The west gate, now preserved within the London Wall car-park, consisted of a double portal flanked by square towers, with each carriageway about 2.75 metres wide.[49] Some of the stones used in its construction were salvaged from an earlier monument, probably a tomb.[50] Other gates would have been placed at each of the fort's cardinal points. The fort measured 220 by 215 metres, covering an area of c. 4.7 hectares, which was less than a quarter of the size of contemporary legionary fortresses. A recent survey of contemporary garrisons suggests a mean density of about 260 men per hectare making the Cripplegate fort the right size for a force of about 1,200 men.[51] The fort's interior is incompletely studied, but was laid out around a T-junction, with a principal entrance at the south. A 5-metre-wide intervallum road followed the inside of the fort's wall and a grid of lesser streets (via vicinaria)

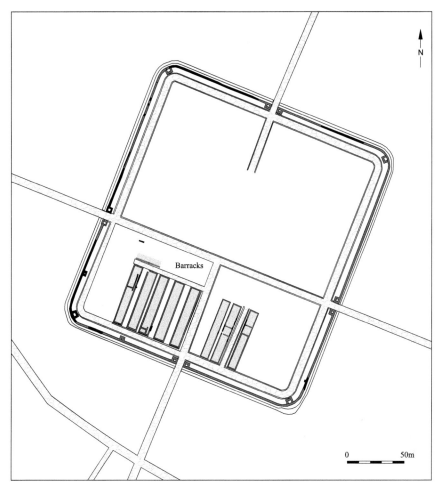

Fig. 19.2 The second-century Cripplegate fort (after Shepherd 2012). Some detail of ill-preserved buildings immediately to the north of those shown is omitted. Drawn by Justin Russell.

separated barrack blocks and other internal buildings. Parts of eight timber-framed buildings set over masonry dwarf-walls have been identified within the southern part of the fort (*praetentura*). Assuming that the internal layout was essentially symmetrical, this allows us to extrapolate the presence of eighteen or twenty-two buildings in this southern area.[52] Most were rectangular, around 52 metres long and up to 10 metres wide, containing rows of rooms fronted by a corridor. Separate mess-groups are assumed to have inhabited each room, combining to provide housing sufficient for an infantry century of about 80 men within each block. Other, perhaps shorter, buildings were aligned east west. The different design suggests a different purpose, and these may have housed smaller cavalry units (*turmae*). Neither style of building appears to have included officers' quarters. Objects associated with the buildings include armour fittings from *lorica segmentata*, of the sort principally used by legionaries. The range of finds also suggests the presence of auxiliary cavalry and the fort is likely to have been garrisoned by a mixed unit. The rear of the fort is largely unexplored but likely to have included further barracks with working and storage facilities.

A Hadrianic date is indicated by Samian from within the fort's earthen ramparts. Hadrianic fire debris hasn't been identified inside the fort, although layers of charcoal and burnt daub were recorded beneath its bank.[53] It is therefore likely that the fort was built after the fire, although an earlier date cannot be discounted. The fort was both larger and more substantial than that built after the Boudican revolt, following the fashion for stone building that characterized second-century public architecture. It presented an argument of permanence and control that must have carried particular resonance in the aftermath of the fire. It was also an unusual feature, since urban garrisons were exceptionally rare. A cohort had been stationed at Lyon to protect the mint, and Vespasian based another at Carthage to secure *annona* supplies.[54] These stations protected Rome's interests at places of exceptional strategic importance. London's stone-built fort might indicate that it too belonged to this select group of imperial cities.[55]

It has alternatively been argued that the Cripplegate fort housed soldiers serving on the governor's staff and bodyguard.[56] These functions might have employed some 1,000 men, divided between infantry and cavalry. The fort was slightly over-large for such a force, but the additional space might have accommodated other military personnel serving in London. This requires us to assume, however, that soldiers previously garrisoned elsewhere in London were relocated into the fort when it was built. If this was the case, we ought to find new centurions' quarters to match the town houses where these officers previously lived (p. 142). There is no such evidence, and senior personnel serving with the Governor are unlikely to have moved into the fort. The soldiers stationed within the fort were regular troops rather than senior officers and quartermasters. It is also reasonably certain that the fort was abandoned at a time when the governor and his entourage continued to be London based, showing that the fort wasn't necessary to this arrangement.[57] There must have been an important strategic or political reason for building the fort at this point in time, and the Neronian fort built after London's destruction in AD 60/61 offers a clear precedent. The Cripplegate fort could have been built in similar response to political circumstance, involving the settlement of a new garrison after revolt rather than in anomalous administrative display.

The only other fort known to have been built in southern Britain during Hadrian's reign was attached to the base of the fleet, the *Classis Britannica*, at Dover.[58] There are important similarities between the Cripplegate fort and the Dover fort. The construction of both appears to have been interrupted, perhaps in changing strategies similar to those noted on Hadrian's Wall. The likelihood that

Dover's fort was built by the fleet deserves particular attention, given the contemporary use in London of rare examples of tiles carrying the CL.BR stamp produced in the fleet's Sussex tileries. These bases would not only have helped secure and police the supply routes, responding to vulnerabilities exposed in earlier conflict, but brought new manpower and capacity to the operations. Seen in this light the Cripplegate fort should not be seen as simply a defensive feature, but as a hub for marshalling troops and supplies.[59]

Post-fire rebuilding

London's public buildings were rebuilt promptly after the Hadrianic fire. This is the likely context for the construction of a splendid new masonry amphitheatre: the largest such building in Britain and able to accommodate over 10,000 spectators (Fig. 19.3).[60] A new oval arena was enclosed by a masonry wall surmounted by an iron railing, which retained an earthen bank supporting rising tiers of wooden seats. The eastern entrance was rebuilt as a 7-metre-wide tunnel, flanked

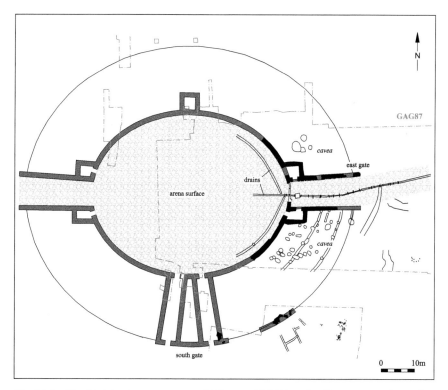

Fig. 19.3 The Hadrianic masonry amphitheatre (GAG87: after Bateman *et al.* 2008). Drawn by Justin Russell.

by two small chambers with sliding doors to release wild beasts into the arena.[61] This ambitious rebuild followed the installation of the new garrison in the Cripplegate fort and may have been necessitated by fire damage to its Flavian precursor. Like the fort, it proclaimed a restoration of Roman order in the wake of London's destruction. One of three small inscribed lead tablets found in later destruction addressed a curse to the hunter goddess Diana, often associated with the Roman amphitheatre in the guise of Nemesis, who is likely to have had a shrine here.[62] The cult was linked to both city protection and retributive justice exercised killing of criminals and beasts, celebrating the supremacy of Roman authority. The forum basilica may also have been restored, reusing its pre-fire walls, and a portico paved with a herringbone-patterned tile floor added along the east side of the complex.[63]

The Thames waterfront was also rehabilitated. Substantial quays, formed by tiers of large squared timber baulks retained by dovetail jointed tiebacks, were built between London Bridge and the Walbrook. As already noted, the earliest may have been under construction from *c.* AD 128, although pottery dating suggests that others may not have been completed for the best part of a decade.[64] As in the Neronian period the more substantial facilities were built upriver of the bridge. Simpler post-and-plank revetments of late Hadrianic or Antonine date occupied other locations along the north bank, reaching as far upstream as the mouth of the Fleet and perhaps as far downstream as the Tower.[65] These may have been the product of various local initiatives. At some point in the early second century, new quays subsumed the temporary pier-base associated with the bridge over the Thames, suggesting its replacement. A new bridge may have been built in masonry, accounting for broken Roman tile found when piles for London Bridge were dug in 1832.[66] A curse inscribed on lead and addressed to *Metunus*, a Vulgar Latin spelling of Neptune influenced by its spoken Celtic pronunciation, was found on the adjacent foreshore, giving rise to the suggestion that the bridge housed a shrine to the ocean god.[67] Clusters of Roman finds recovered from river dredging might represent votive offerings made to the Thames.[68]

The streets leading to the bridge were given monumental aspect by masonry porticoes. Arcades flanking the street from London Bridge to the forum were built of walls and pier-bases set over chalk footings cut into Hadrianic fire debris.[69] South of the river, along the stretch of Watling Street beneath Borough High Street, pier-bases were built for a similar purpose using bricks in a fabric dated AD 120–60.[70] These covered porticoes can be seen as part of an empire-wide fashion of Hellenistic inspiration that took-off in the Hadrianic and Antonine periods.[71] The street architecture drew activities out of the forum and along London's axial streets. Rather than the geometric uniformity of the street grid, second-century urban design emphasized the importance of colonnaded streets encouraging movement between public spaces, forming an architectural armature suited for street festivals and processions.[72]

Differences in structural detail suggest that London's porticoes were commissioned piecemeal from different builders, perhaps in private investment. For the most part, however, reconstruction after the Hadrianic fire is likely to have relied on official support and engineering, perhaps benefitting from imperial patronage following the example of Hadrian's contribution to the restoration of other war-damaged cities.[73] Water supply was presumably restored, and this may have been the date for the insertion of a water supply-pipe along the southern side of the Colchester road at 60-3 Fenchurch Street.[74]

Most areas of housing were restored after the fire, although some plots remained vacant.[75] At Watling Court rainwater puddles formed over the destruction debris, but needn't have marked the passage of more than one wet winter.[76] The slightly built timber houses that subsequently occupied the site failed to reproduce the architectural sophistication of the earlier town houses. Builders reverted to types of construction favoured in the Neronian city, perhaps husbanding resources whilst capacity was stretched. Elsewhere post-fire rebuilding involved some amalgamation of earlier properties, although earlier boundaries were generally maintained.[77] The impression is of a city rebuilt in haste, but along former lines. Some areas near the waterfront may have been treated more ambitiously. At Regis House the opportunity was taken to redesign the arrangement of warehouses, and the scale of clearance and rebuilding hints at the involvement of a central authority operating on a grand scale.[78]

The upper Walbrook 'vicus'

Although some areas were not as densely populated as previously, the establishment of a new district in the upper Walbrook valley suggests a new influx of settlers (Fig. 19.4). The northern margins of the Flavian city reached to the borderlands of the upper Walbrook valley, a basin of open land dissected by small streams that had attracted sporadic activities from the close of the first century.[79] At 10-12 Copthall Avenue a drainage channel feeding into the Walbrook employed a timber felled in AD 107, whilst a timber building at 55-61 Moorgate housed a wooden tank associated with industrial production.[80] Nearby were the robbed foundations of a large masonry building that fell into disuse c. AD 120, and from about AD 110/120 pottery kilns at 20-8 Moorgate made vessels of types associated with the Roman military.[81] But the main phase of expansion into the upper Walbrook valley was Hadrianic. An ambitious engineering programme introduced new streets between the Cripplegate fort and Walbrook, including at least three aligned north-south and perhaps two east-west. Marshy areas were drained and reclaimed before gravelled road-surfaces were laid over timber and turf causeways flanked by timber drains.[82] Pottery from these construction levels establishes their Hadrianic date and a terminus *ante quem* for the layout of the

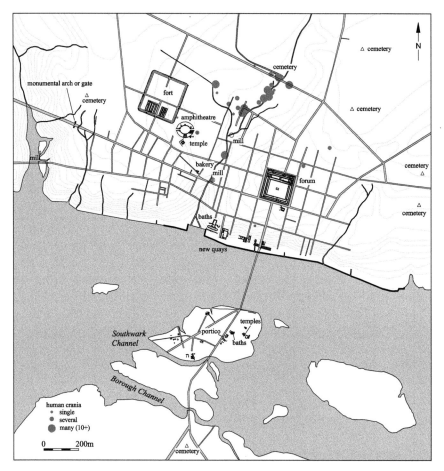

Fig. 19.4   A proposed reconstruction of London *c.* AD 130, also showing the distribution of 'Walbrook skulls' and other detached crania found in Hadrianic contexts. Drawn by Justin Russell.

new district is provided by timbers felled AD 129 used in roadside buildings at Drapers' Gardens.[83]

The new streets, between 5 and 8 metres wide, were set on a slightly different alignment to the earlier street grid, perhaps orientated on the Cripplegate fort instead. The scale of the engineering suggests military involvement.[84] The district presented characteristics similar to those of a fort vicus, housing industrial production likely to have been stimulated by the demands of the fort garrison.[85] These included facilities for preparing leather goods and glassworks: which industries were relocated into this part of town and production was increased. The district also contained its own taverns, indicated by pottery assemblages dominated by flagons at 12–18 Moorgate.[86] It was probably developed in tandem

Table 19.1 A suggested timeline of events affecting London in the period AD 125-65

Suggested date	Building activities in London	Salient events possibly relevant to London
125-6	London destroyed by fire	Possible conclusion of a British war.
127-8	Rebuilding of waterfront quays. Forum repaired. Amphitheatre rebuilt in stone. Cripplegate fort built. Streets restored. New urban district laid out in the upper Walbrook valley. New suburban road built, perhaps to shorten route to Verulamium via a ford at Battle Bridge.	
138		Antoninus Pius succeeds Hadrian as emperor
140-60	Significant investment in new domestic architecture. Luxurious riverside complex on south bank (Winchester Palace) perhaps home to an important government official. 'Mansio' rebuilt and perhaps changed in function. New waterfronts built near the Tower after c. AD 133.	M. Maenius Agrippa combines the office of procurator with the command of the British fleet.
153	Warehouses built beside the Southwark waterfront (Courage Brewery). Amphitheatre refurbished.	Influx of new coin. Major fire in Verulamium c. 155.
161	Timber revetments built to canalize the tidal channel along eastern side of Southwark (Guy's Channel)	Antoninus Pius dies and is replaced as emperor by Marcus Aurelius.
165	New temple precinct built along the riverfront in the south-west quarter. Approximate date of temple building in religious precincts next to the amphitheatre and at the entrance to Southwark.	Tiberius Celerianus, moritix, dedicates temple to Mars Camulus in Southwark.

with the creation of the fort early in post-fire recovery (Table 19.1). Parallels can be drawn with the situation after the Great Fire of 1666, when London's displaced population was resettled in camps north of the ruined city, although the Hadrianic expansion had more to do with servicing the military-run administration than looking after homeless Londoners.[87]

20

The Walbrook skulls

The new north road

North of the Roman town, beyond its streets and houses, lay a backland of meadows prone to flooding. A brand new metalled road was driven across this area around the time that London's new fort was built.[1] The road surfaces cambered over a clay and brushwood causeway that was carried over the Walbrook tributaries by a series of timber bridges, and at 9.7 metres across was much wider than the city streets. The western stream was redirected into a large ditch flanking the north side of the road, before being diverted beneath. Finds associated with road building included a Trajanic coin (AD 96–117), central Gaulish Samian and black-burnished ware, which date its construction c. AD 130. Burials anticipating the line of the earliest roadworks suggest that the route was established a little ahead of its physical engineering.

The scale of works suggests that the road served an important purpose. Road construction is frequently linked to the needs of the army, and a connection with official supply is implied by the presence of lost or discarded hipposandals along the route. These iron shoes were tied to hooves to improve traction on slippery roads, and are associated with military haulage.[2] Other roadside finds included brooches, spearheads and belt fittings of types associated with the army. The faunal remains were dominated by horses that had reached the end of their working lives before death or slaughter, drawing on stock that was distinctly taller than usual and likely to have included cavalry mounts. These features suggest a road traffic including cavalry and heavily laden supply waggons. Timber platforms built where the road crossed the Walbrook may have been stations for watering animals and making offerings to the river. One was built reusing two doors made from timbers felled AD 110–34. Traffic may also have included prisoners and slaves, as suggested by the presence of a Roman shackle in later marsh deposits.

The road's north-west heading aimed towards a known crossing-point of the river Fleet at Battle Bridge, near King's Cross. This was where the medieval river was most easily crossed, and the likely site of a Roman ford. First- or second-century building material found near King's Cross might derive from associated settlement and a legionary tombstone was found at Battle Bridge.[3] Two phases of road surface associated with Roman coins were observed during sewer excavations at Old Street in 1867 and are appropriately located to have been part of the route.[4] A road over the Battle Bridge crossing would have carried traffic north-west from Bishopsgate, continuing to join Watling Street just short of its crossing over the river Brent. This route from London to Verulamium navigated difficult terrain requiring substantial engineering, but was significantly shorter than the main road along Oxford Street and the Edgware Road.

Wayside human remains

Human remains were scattered alongside the road, filling adjacent ditches and channels. The unusual burial practices that generated this evidence started before the first road surface was laid. Excavations beneath Liverpool Street found the partially articulated right arm of a young adult or youth, left lying on open ground before it was buried in the road construction.[5] It has been suggested that the arm was washed-out of a nearby grave, but since it was found 0.3 metres above the floodplain floor this requires us to assume a major flood. This is unlikely since no river-lain sedimentation was identified, and fact that the arm retained connective tissue suggests that it hadn't spent significant time in water. The limb is more likely to have reached its location through animal or human intervention, with the absence of scavenging pathologies more suggestive of the latter. Semi-articulated remains from at least three other people were found on the other side of the river channel at Finsbury Circus.[6] These too were found beneath the road, where the partly fleshed remains would have been visible to road engineers. At least one other body was buried in a grave here before the road was built. A concern with stray body parts was subsequently evidenced by the excavation of a charnel pit containing parts of seven individuals buried with pottery dated *c.* AD 140–60.[7] These remains were treated in a similar fashion to the disturbed Neronian bodies suggested to have been victims of retributive abuse after the Boudican revolt (above p. 110). The pre-road scatter of semi-articulated body-parts in the upper Walbrook took place within a few years of the Hadrianic fire, suggesting that these too might witness abuse vested on enemies slain in the course of a revolt or its suppression. The landscape reminds us of the sight that Tacitus describes as having greeted Vitellius after the first battle of Bedriacum in the civil war of AD 69: the body of the imperial legate was cremated in customary fashion and a few bodies were buried by friends, but otherwise the battlefield was strewn with mangled corpses, severed limbs, and the putrefying forms of men and horses.[8]

A burial ground was subsequently established alongside the road west of the Walbrook, where it occupied a strip little more than 20 metres wide. Excavations in Finsbury Circus and Eldon Street between 1987 and 2007 recovered ten cremations and over 100 inhumations, most dated between the early second and early third centuries.[9] The graves included an unusually high male:female ratio (at 4:1), and older adults are under-represented. This was a sorry place for a graveyard, the low status of which was suggested by a low incidence of coffins and containers, an absence of animal bones associated with funerary meals, and a range of irregular burial practices including prone and crouched body positions. It is also unusual to find such a high proportion of inhumations at a time when cremation was widely preferred, reminding us that a quickly dug grave was the cheaper way of disposing of a corpse. Several shallow graves belonging to this cemetery were placed within the ditch that channelled the tributary of the Walbrook, following the earlier tradition of ditch burial. These graves were soon eroded by watercourse migration and flooding, carrying away parts of the body and adding to post-mortem body fragmentation. Some unstratified bones from the site also carried de-fleshing cut-marks, from the butchery of corpses.

The unusual practices also included a decapitation burial, and two instances where iron rings had been forged around the lower legs. One adult male, aged about 18–25, had iron rings welded around both ankles. In another case a corpse appears to have been buried with its hands tied behind its back. Other burials were treated with respect: the handful of cremations found here necessarily involved funeral pyres with attendant ceremony and offerings, and a fifth of the inhumations were accompanied by grave goods. These more 'ordinary' burials involved a fairly representative group of deceased, including adults, teenagers, children and babies. Six roadside inhumations were also found east of the Walbrook crossing, dated *c.* A D 140–60 by associated finds.[10] Three of these bodies, all of individuals 18–35 years old, had been decapitated from the rear or right side in violent blows made by short-bladed instruments, probably swords. The angles of the wounds are consistent with execution from behind to victims kneeling with head bowed.[11] One of those decapitated was a woman with an isotopic signature suggestive of a childhood in chalklands like those surrounding the London basin, with a high presence of lead in tooth enamel indicative of early life spent in a city. Another roadside burial contained a male aged 26–35, with an iron ring forged tightly around his right wrist. The hot metal had been beaten into shape around the outstretched arm, either in brutal torture or to disfigure the corpse. We can conclude that these burials included victims of military punishment and execution. The northern marshland, on the banks of the Walbrook, within sight of fort and amphitheatre, was an appropriate place for the marginalized dead: including some who were allowed a poor burial but others who were not.

Heads of the dead

Many human crania have also been found around the upper Walbrook valley (Fig. 19.4, p. 246), and early discoveries of these Walbrook 'skulls' may have inspired Geoffrey of Monmouth's twelfth-century story of a massacre of Roman soldiers besides a brook. Immense numbers were found in nineteenth-century sewer digging and construction around Finsbury Circus.[12] No count was made of these early finds, but subsequent discoveries result in over 300 crania being listed in published accounts.[13] Some antiquarian discoveries came from the stream-bed, and many were marked and stained from submersion with organic material in stagnant or slow moving water. Few can be dated, but they generally derived from contexts likely to pre-date the Roman town wall built *c.* AD 200. Drawing on our understanding of the urban topography, it is difficult to identify a source for large numbers of skulls in the upper Walbrook valley prior to *c.* AD 120 and most of the more recent discoveries were deposited between *c.* AD 120 and AD 160. Those that have been examined are disproportionately from young males, and some show evidence of violent treatment.[14] The exceptional nature of this concentration of crania merits emphasis. Altogether these finds represent nearly a tenth of all recorded human 'burials' from Roman London.[15] Since only a small fraction of the relevant landscape has been archaeologically investigated, perhaps no more than 5 per cent, we can confidently conclude that the river's environs contained many hundreds of crania and probably several thousands.

Many crania had spent time in the river before burial, but we don't know how they had first found their way into the water. It has long been thought likely that some were washed out from upstream burial grounds.[16] Skulls can be river-rolled further than other human remains, carrying them to river bends where they are deposited in slower water. Such remains are also easier to identify than other skeletal parts, encouraging their selective recovery for later reburial. Ease of identification is also likely to have resulted in their disproportionate retention by workmen digging on Victorian sewers and construction sites. This idea seemed to find confirmation in the fact that several graves in the roadside cemetery at Eldon Street were damaged by river erosion. Altogether fifteen burials in this cemetery missing their heads were identified as having been disturbed by flowing water. These missing crania are likely to have been carried downstream, adding to the material within the Walbrook. The cemetery was much too small, however, to have generated hundreds of Walbrook skulls. Although fifteen heads had washed from their graves, nineteen isolated crania were recovered nearby. There was no net loss of crania from this cemetery into the wider river system. The dating evidence is also somewhat contradictory, since some of the fragmentary material predates the known phases of inhumation burial. Nor can we find any trace of a larger upriver burial ground from which thousands of crania might derive. Extensive investigation between Moorgate and Bishopsgate shows that the river catchment area was dominated by pasture and marsh, not cemeteries.[17] Although cemeteries have been found either side of Bishopsgate these lay on the margins of the Walbrook headwaters. The burials found here are also later than the dated Walbrook skulls and show no sign of water damage.[18] It is not possible to reconstruct any pattern of flooding that would have carried numerous crania from this area into the main channels of the river. The argument that several hundred skulls were washed into the Walbrook from ill-positioned graves is simply not tenable. It is instead likely that most entered the water by human agency, as was demonstrably the case for the non-fluvial finds. There was a deliberate pattern of disposing of fragmentary human remains, disproportionately the heads of young men, in wet places. This involved the massive intensification of ritual practices previously witnessed on the borders of the Neronian city.

These remains are scattered over a wide area. Second-century drainage ditches investigated at Moor House, half way between the Walbrook and the Cripplegate fort, contained parts of human skulls and long-bones that showed evidence of dog gnawing and post mortem knife cuts, which Jon Butler suggested might derive from the manipulation of skulls and long bones in excarnation rites.[19] Previous studies of the Walbrook skulls have given particular weight to the possibility that Celtic ideas concerning the veneration of the human head may have contributed to such practices.[20] But the emphasis on the manipulation of select body parts finds parallel throughout north-west Europe, and cannot be characterized as a particularly Celtic practice.

Several more recent excavations have added significantly to our understanding of the Walbrook 'skulls'. In 2013, the cranial remains of thirty-seven individuals were recovered from reworked gravel deposits on the river bank during tunnelling for the Elizabeth Line ticket-hall at Liverpool Street. Many showed signs of damage consistent with being rolled along the river bed, and the deposits in which they were found may have been dredged from the river c. AD 140/160. All of the deceased were adult, none more than about 45 years old, and four-fifths were male. One presented evidence of a blunt force injury.[21] Radiocarbon dating shows that although most of these remains come from people who might have died in the Hadrianic period, two were certainly earlier, dated cal AD 55–80. This confirms the reworked nature of the assemblage, and shows that the practices that resulted in crania entering the river had longer ancestry.

Other crania were subsequently found in the fills of the roadside ditches that flanked the Hadrianic road east of the Walbrook. Elements from the skulls of at least twenty-one individuals were placed in clusters at roughly 5 metre intervals along the southern side of the road, with others along its north side.[22] Other body parts were also present, but in smaller numbers. Radiocarbon dating indicates that the crania came from individuals who died after c. AD 90, and all were buried in contexts dated no later than c. AD 160. All were adults, with about twice as many men as women. One had a depression typical of healed blunt force trauma. Several were polished and scratched, suggesting that they had been exposed to running water, whilst others were brown-stained from lengthy submersion in stagnant water or bog. Whilst the roadside ditches were sometimes water-filled, this doesn't account for the extent of water discolouration and wear. It is probable that the crania had been recovered from some other wet-place, such as the adjacent river, before being placed in the ditch. None was intact at the time of burial, and the mandibles had probably become detached as a consequence of natural decomposition or river damage before being collected for reburial. A fragment of woven textile indicates that at least one cranium was wrapped in a bag or cloth when buried.

One of the most curious discoveries made during this study was that two individuals had teeth with highly unusual isotopic profiles.[23] Both were males, aged 26–35, whose limited childhood exposure to lead is a sign of a rural upbringing and who had grown up in an area of granitic geology. These geological conditions cannot be found in England, but occur in the Scottish Highlands. Sources in Scandinavia or Ireland are also possible, along with a handful of other remote locations.[24] These two men might have been Scottish highlanders, or perhaps seafarers from Ireland or Scandinavia. Since only four crania from the ditch were analysed the fact that two shared such an exotic origin is wholly remarkable. It leads us to imagine a circumstance in which a British rebellion included highlanders from beyond the wall amongst a host that met its end on the banks of the Walbrook: an imagining prompted in part by the fact that this was the path incompletely trod by the Stuart pretender's Jacobite army in the 1745 uprising.

Another of the studied crania was from an immigrant to the province, having grown up enjoying a diet found around the Mediterranean. The presence of foreigners from different parts of the Roman world is consistent with the cosmopolitan nature of London, but reminds us of the dangers of assuming a simple fault-line between Roman and Briton. The working hypothesis adopted here is that the unusual concentration of fragmented human remains in the upper Walbrook valley was in part the consequence of corpse abuse vested on British rebels. There are many reasons, however, why some may have come from people who were not British by birth. The disaffected communities drawn to revolt against Rome often included the urban poor, slaves, brigands, and deserters. We are reminded that when Goths descended on Rome in AD 409 they were met by crowds of slaves streaming out of the city to join them and that many of Rome's most successful enemies were deserters from its own armies.[25]

Further valuable information derives from thirty-nine skulls found in waterlogged pits further downstream, on the west bank of the Walbrook close to another bridge over the river.[26] These were also deposited c. AD 120–60. Dog gnawing and puncture marks shows that some had been scavenged when soft-tissue was still present. Almost all came from young men, 28–35 years old, and most carried injuries inflicted around the time of death, including one individual whose cheek was horribly shattered by a violent blow. At least one of these heads had been decapitated with a sword, and many had healed earlier wounds. The aDNA analysis of one suggests that the deceased, a black haired and brown eyed male, was an immigrant whose mother's family came from eastern Europe or the Near East.[27] Rebecca Redfern and Heather Bonney suggest that some of these crania were trophy heads, perhaps deriving from contests and executions in the nearby amphitheatre or brought to London from wars elsewhere.[28] Whilst it is unlikely that large numbers of expensively trained gladiators died in the amphitheatre, the arena was also a place of legal execution.[29] The governor's judicial duties included condemning criminals and enemies to death, and hence the presence in London of *speculatores* such as Celsus who were responsible for beheadings.[30] The unwanted corpses of such *noxii* risked being denied burial and disposed of in the river.[31] In Rome, the decapitation and display of severed heads was closely associated with the punishment of treason, and histories describe how the heads of defeated emperors and usurpers were paraded in proof that they no longer threatened public order. These heads were sometimes brought to Rome for display in the forum, before being disposed of in rivers and sewers (see p. 111).[32] By the end of the first century A D headhunting was also associated with auxiliary troops, illustrated by scenes on Trajan's column that show Gallic troops presenting the severed heads of slain Dacian warriors.[33] The tombstones of two auxiliary cavalrymen buried in Britain in the late first or early second century also showed severed heads being presented, celebrating the importance of such trophies to the status and identify of soldiers stationed here.[34]

We don't know if any Walbrook crania were discarded trophies, but Hadrianic wars offered opportunity for the practice. Whether they had been displayed or not, the unwanted remains needed expurgation. At Rome such remains were flushed away by the Cloaca Maxima and Tiber, and in London the Walbrook and Thames were ideally suited for the same purpose (above pp. 163 and 231). The comparison would not have escaped the attention of commanding officers some of whose careers had embraced responsibility for Rome's sacred rivers before service in Britain.[35] Each and every Walbrook skull boasts an individual history of post-mortem treatment, but collectively they show that the upper Walbrook was an appropriate location for the disposal of disturbed human remains. At the end of the first century the river may have helped define a city *pomerium*, an area favoured for the execution and burial of criminals. This marshy area lay northwest of the city, reinforcing an association with deathly endings at the setting of the sun.[36] The looming presence of the amphitheatre added to the mortal aspect of an almost Stygian landscape. Crania littered the ditches and pits dug close to the river, concentrated in greatest numbers near places where roads bordered or bridged its tributary channels. Such places provided practical and meaningful platforms from which river-offerings could be made. In some cases, the crania had rolled along the river, before being dredged from its bed or banks for reburial nearby. It is possible that this dredging became necessary because the river was too slow-moving to flush the remains away, leaving them banked at bridges and bends. Might the river have been choked by hundreds of skulls?

The process of reburial shows that heads were accorded special treatment—not necessarily as trophies, but because these elements were more easily identified and recovered, and privileged for treatment as the seat of the soul. The other elements of the dismembered corpse were perhaps more widely dispersed, and it is possible that in some cases, bodies were burnt on collective pyres and only the heads retained.

The fort and its associated landscape suggest that London witnessed an increased military presence after the Hadrianic fire, coinciding with a significant increase in the ritual deposition of human crania in the upper Walbrook. Auxiliary cavalry would have been at the forefront in policing exercises, and London may have been influenced by headhunting practices normalized within the early second-century Roman army. Whilst the Walbrook skulls may have been obtained in reprisals that continued over several decades, and drew on practices that continued for the better part of two centuries, the exceptional scale of second-century evidence hints at a major Hadrianic slaughter.

Other irregular burials

Smaller numbers of irregular burials were found along London's other borders, including three crania in the second-century fills of the ditch thought to form the Flavian town boundary.[37] Excavations at Duke's Place, beside the road to Colchester, uncovered two skeletons 'unceremoniously dumped' in a drainage ditch with pottery of c. AD 120. Skeletal fragments from at least three people were found in the infilling of the waterfront revetment on the Thames foreshore along with finds dated AD 80–130.[38] At Paternoster Square, on the western borders of town, a small pit dug after the Hadrianic fire contained an upturned cranium with two mortaria.[39] Disarticulated remains were also found in quarries at 16–17 Old Bailey near a small inhumation cemetery of c. AD 70–120 beside the Fleet.[40] Others have been identified at sites with religious and ritual connotations In Southwark, including crania from two people of possible African origin from a second-century ditch beneath the cemetery at Lant Street.[41]

The skulls placed in boundary ditches may have drawn on the Janus-like association of heads with gateways.[42] The circumstances of their deposition are consistent with the earlier disposal of the fragmentary remains of uncremated corpses in wet-places on the settlement margins. These practices favoured sites where intact bodies were subsequently buried, and some cemeteries may have come into existence at places known to receive the dead. There are grounds for supposing that the disarticulated bones came from bodies denied normal burial, which had provoked a necrophobic response. It is alternatively possible, however, that some bones were carried to site with soil removed from places where human remains were exposed, or that rites involving recycled body parts removed from earlier burials were involved. Richard Hingley has suggested that rituals of this kind might be linked to the acculturation of land through the selective use of anthropogenic material.[43] This would not sit well with the idea that unburied human remains required expurgation, although we should not assume that all dead were equally threatening.

The rituals associated with trophy heads may have a bearing on finds of head-pots made in the upper Walbrook. There is a marked concentration of these vessels, shaped like human heads, in contexts dating from the late first century to *c.* AD 160.[44] Gillian Braithwaite has shown that they were often linked with the presence of auxiliary troops recruited from the Rhine delta and northern Belgium, and potentially used as ritual offerings influenced by Bacchic ideas. Some resembled death masks, where the eyes were shown closed, accentuating links between natural and supernatural realms. This would suit rites of transition where the lifeless head represented the dead trapped in the world of the living. The process of violent exorcism once practised on skeletal remains may have transferred to these surrogates.

Some statues may also have been ritually decapitated and their heads cast into watery places, accounting for the presence of the bronze head of Hadrian in the Thames (see pp. 112, 163 and 306–7). We don't know when this statue was dismembered and this is sometimes attributed to iconoclasts of late antiquity, but the desecration might equally have been associated with the events of the mid-120s. The imperial image was a target for attack during riot and revolt, and their heads thrown into rivers in violent desecration analogous to the abuse vested on enemies of flesh-and-blood.[45] The decapitation of the imperial image could have symbolized a rejection of Hadrian's authority.

These diverse strands of evidence buttress the argument that London's destruction *c.* AD 125/6 was the consequence of hostile action. This was followed by swift and emphatic restoration, including the construction of a new fort, the building of roads to aid supply and communication, and a spike in the number of irregular burials involving features suggestive of military retribution. These details mirror those associated with London's military re-occupation after the Boudican revolt.

21

Antonine sophistication (*c.* A D 135–65)

Ostentatious town houses

London continued to command a wholly disproportionate measure of Britain's wealth after Hadrianic restoration, but this was now more evident in private than public architecture. The Procurator's office may have been less directly involved in supporting public works, and probably ceased to produce stamped tiles after the Hadrianic fire.[1] Powerful Londoner's spent on large town houses furnished with expensively decorated dining rooms, peristyles and heated baths in establishments built with masonry walls, mosaics, marble veneers and glazed windows.[2] Houses displaying such features first appeared in London shortly prior to the Hadrianic fire but were only commonplace from *c.* A D 140 (Fig. 21.1).[3] An early example was found down a ventilation shaft excavated for the Dockland Light Railway in Lothbury, where a masonry walled building heated by a hypocaust and furnished with tessellated floors was dated *c.* A D 140 by associated pottery.[4] Grand Antonine houses were found throughout town, clustered around the forum and approach roads to its north and east. They were generally larger than their predecessors and laid out over several ranges. Few have been studied in their entirety, but an almost complete ground plan can be reconstructed from foundations at Plantation Place. This house was built shortly after *c.* A D 150, as indicated by colour-coated Gallic wares associated with its construction, and contained at least seventeen rooms at ground-floor level arranged over three principal wings enclosing a courtyard or garden (Fig. 21.2).

Carefully worked mosaic floors decorated reception rooms in several Antonine houses.[5] These followed an imaginative range of designs including nine-panelled schemes of a type fashionable in contemporary homes in Colchester and Verulamium. One showed a peacock facing a cantharus, alluding to the Bacchic philosophies popular at this time. A few of the best houses also boasted private bathhouses. At Pudding Lane, a masonry building erected after the Hadrianic fire contained a small bath-block with a mosaic-lined apsidal plunge-bath and a latrine set over a tile-lined drain; a similar plunge-bath was found at Crosby Square.[6]

Despite the popularity of concrete architecture, some houses continued to rely on earlier traditions of timber-framing and earth walling. This should not be mistaken for an architecture of poverty. A timber-framed building at Drapers' Gardens, of the mid-150s, incorporated ranges of rooms set behind a peristyle or

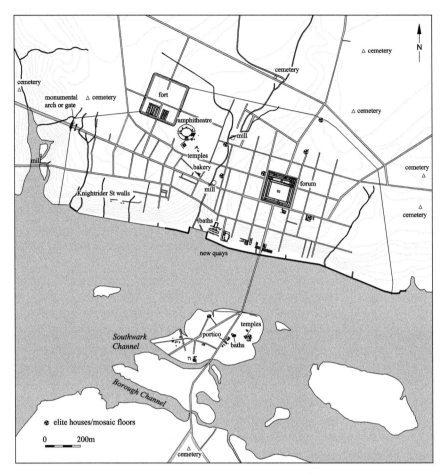

Fig. 21.1   A proposed reconstruction of London *c.* AD 160, illustrating also the locations of the best-appointed Antonine town houses as marked chiefly by the use of mosaic pavements. Drawn by Justin Russell.

corridor overlooking a courtyard and benefitted from the unusual luxury of a piped water-supply (Fig. 21.3).[7] At Milk Street an earth-walled reception room at the back of an Antonine building contained a handsome polychrome mosaic decorated with the two-handled mixing vessel, or cantharus, that symbolized the mixing of wine and water at dinner parties and in Bacchic ritual.[8]

London's elite residences shared features with town houses in contemporary Romano-British cities. At Verulamium the earliest private hypocaust and mosaic floors also date from the early second century, where larger houses extended over 12 rooms or more.[9] This period witnessed the elaboration of a distinct provincial domestic architecture, creatively drawing on empire-wide fashion to use peristyles and porticoes to direct guests towards grand dining rooms. London may

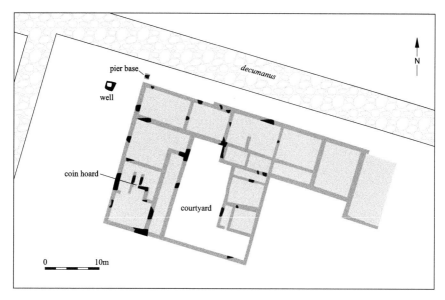

Fig. 21.2   A reconstructed plan of the mid-second-century town house with masonry wall foundations found in excavations at Plantation Place (FER97: after Dunwoodie *et al.* 2015). Drawn by Justin Russell.

have been where some of these ideas first gained currency in Britain. The introduction of new building technologies possibly benefitted from an influx of craftsmen brought to work on Hadrianic public buildings, spurred by a community of wealthy patrons keen to use private houses to vaunt sophisticated taste. These changes might witness the emergence of a local curial class, as suggested for other Romano-British towns.[10] But this confident expression of propertied wealth might equally have followed the social elevation of people 'in trade': the merchants and middlemen on whom the Roman administration of London had long relied.

Whatever their origin, London was home to a community willing to invest in fashionable town houses. They did so by adopting ideas of Hellenistic origin: evident in the Bacchic iconography of the mosaics, and in lifestyles served by private heated rooms and peristyles.[11] These manifested a new cultural outlook, consciously or otherwise taking inspiration from the Greek world by way of the philosophical fashion known as the Second Sophistic. This movement had a fundamental influence on the art and architecture of late Hadrianic and Antonine aristocratic society.[12] Sheltered colonnades and ambulatories enclosing gardens were valued as places for discussing literary and philosophical concerns, borrowing from the Greek *gymnasium* to demonstrate an educated and performative *paideia*.[13] These houses alluded to a Platonic spatial dialectic inspired by the Greek *symposion*, contrasting the rational discourse of the *ambulatio* with the

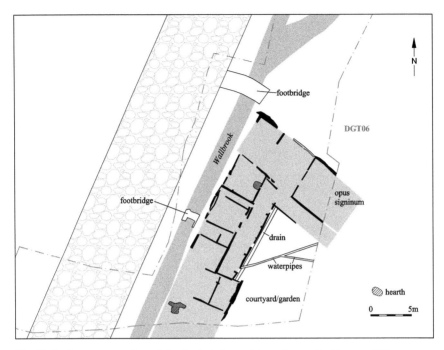

Fig. 21.3 A reconstruction of the timber-framed town house, built *c.* AD 128, excavated at Drapers' Gardens (DGT06: after Ridgeway 2009 and Hawkins forthcoming). The *opus signinum* (cement) floor may mark the main reception room set towards the rear of a separate wing of the property. Drawn by Justin Russell.

more irrational arguments of the wine-lubricated dinner party.[14] London followed wider imperial fashion in adopting architectures influenced by such conceits, perhaps ultimately inspired by Hadrian's palace at Tivoli.[15]

Southwark was also dominated by high-status houses and palaces. The luxurious riverside complex at Winchester Palace on the south bank was extensively rebuilt (Fig. 21.4).[16] New rooms were decorated with polychrome mosaics and exotic marble veneers from Tunisia, Asia Minor, Phrygia and the Aegean. In one, a richly painted lunette showed a winged Cupid within an elaborate architectural fantasy. The workmanship was equal to the finest paintings of Italy and Gaul, employing precious pigments such as red cinnabar and gold leaf.[17] The complex included a bathhouse built using types of tiles normally associated with military sites.[18] Some bearing the stamp of the *Classis Britannica* and others with the stamp of the procurator were reused in later rebuilding (below p. 317). *Classis* tiles have occasionally been found elsewhere in Southwark and in the Cripplegate fort, and were probably imported to London from the Weald for use in select Antonine building projects. Fragments of rectangular marble panels inscribed with the names of a detachment of soldiers were later reused in the furnace pit of the baths *caldarium* (Fig. 21.5).[19] They listed seven or eight members from at least four

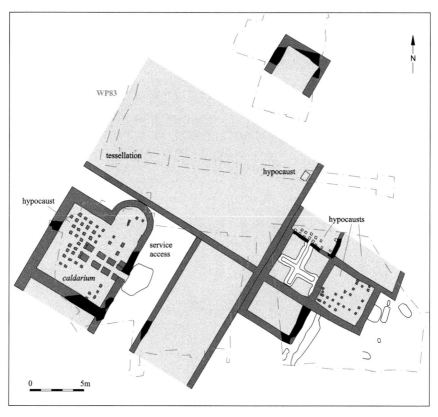

Fig. 21.4 The bathhouse and high-status building excavated at Winchester palace (WP83, Buildings 12–14) towards the end of the second century (after Yule 2005). Drawn by Justin Russell.

cohorts of a legionary detachment. If all ten cohorts had been represented the dedication would have acknowledged some seventy to eighty men. Many carried the *nomen* Aur(elius), indicating that the inscription was not earlier than the reign of Antoninus Pius, and the style of lettering probably excludes a Severan or later date. It is therefore likely that the inscription was erected when the complex was rebuilt *c.* AD 150. We don't know if the men formed a vexillation involved in the building works or were *beneficiarii* assembled into a guild. In either case, their association with this building suggests it to have been an important locus in the exercise of imperial and military authority. The structural remains present the aspect of a palatial suburban villa, consistent with the suggestion that it may have been an official residence.[20] The combination of building materials stamped by the offices of both the procurator and the fleet echoes the fact that M. Maenius Agrippa held both commands. We can speculate that this equestrian procurator based his command here, taking control over the Roman fleet to manage coastal traffic and maintain the infrastructure on which it relied.[21]

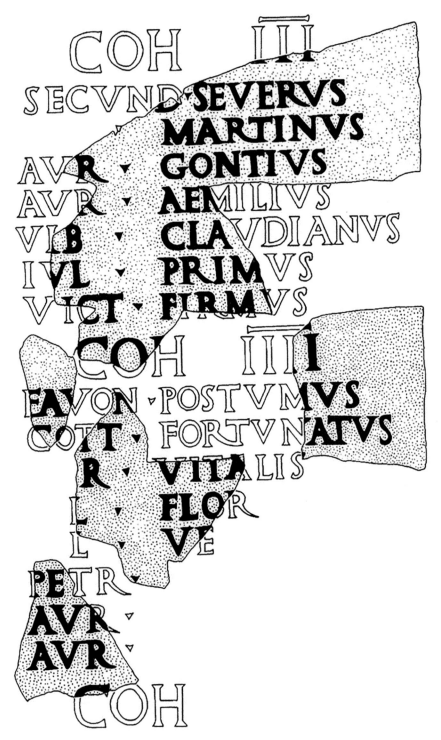

Fig. 21.5 Reconstruction of the marble inscription found in excavations at Winchester Palace listing soldiers (drawn by Sue Hurman and reproduced by kind permission of Museum of London Archaeology).

The supposed *mansio* at 15–23 Southwark Street was also refurbished with a new bath suite, mosaics, Purbeck and Aegean marble wall veneers, and an inlay of igneous gabbro-diorite imported from Egypt.[22] A masonry hexagonal apse was added to the rear of this building in the late second century, whilst the addition of rooms over the earlier courtyard and portico suggests change in the way the building was used.[23] It offered high-status reception facilities, but no longer needed covered porticoes.

New styles of domestic architecture reached beyond London into the surrounding countryside. Sites along the north-bank of the river, including Thorney Island in Westminster and perhaps St Bride's, were rebuilt in stone as luxurious suburban villas.[24] At Beddington in Surrey a late second-century winged-corridor masonry villa with heated rooms was built over the site of an Iron Age enclosure, and at Keston in Kent new timber buildings incorporating painted walls were built in the mid- to late second century.[25] Contemporary building works were in progress at other villas bordering the London basin in north-west Kent and Surrey.[26] The preferences that had marked London out as culturally distinct to the self-governing urban communities of southern Britain are increasingly difficult to identify, and the town became more socially and economically integrated with its rural hinterland. This is evident in the supply and use of pottery, where the repertoire of vessels used within London's hinterland showed a convergence of tastes with those of the city.[27] There are different reasons why this may have been the case. It is possible that the demands of taxation encouraged engagement with the cash-economy, promoting the integration of regional markets. It is also possible that more land around London came to be owned by wealthy Londoners, transferring wealth obtained from trade into country estates, and exporting urban tastes and patterns of consumption. This might in turn have created new opportunities for local landed interests to engage with their urban counterparts, both socially and economically.

Changing traffic

Whatever the spur to these building activities, London remained an important port. Parts of unwanted cargoes of Gaulish and German Samian, broken in transit or from redundant stock, were dumped on the Thames foreshore between London Bridge and the Tower.[28] Gwladys Monteil has identified several discrete groups amongst this material, dating from the late Hadrianic to late Severan periods. One was dominated by fire-damaged vessels, perhaps from a warehouse fire of *c.* AD 155 or slightly later. Shippers of these imported tablewares continued their operations in a dedicated part of the port for the best part of a century. A 40-metre-long quay built at Sugar Quay in the caisson style, with oak timbers laid in regular courses forming a series of twin boxes, incorporated a timber pile felled after AD 133 in its foundations. Timber baulks in this construction carried circular lettered stamps suggestive of administered supply. The quays were poorly located for shipments destined for the forum or carriage along Watling Street, and more convenient for estuarine and coastal traffic. This shift in London's centre of gravity is reflected in the distribution of the wealthier town houses, many of which are found east of the forum. This area may have become more fashionable as merchants and administrators established residences near their place of business.

Luxurious living sustained a local demand for imported goods, and London remained an important hub in the onward supply of continental imports and regional produce for the army. Hadrianic changes had, however, reconfigured this traffic. The development of east coast supply routes diminished the volumes of goods that needed to be transferred from ship to road, with consequences for traffic flows through London. London had formerly served as the principal entrepôt for traffic between Britain and the continent, but the rise of alternative centres gave it a less central role in such traffic.[29] This may have influenced the decision to reduce the width of the main road to Colchester. Formerly a three-lane highway this was reduced to a dual carriageway in the mid- to late second century.[30] The forum, in particular, became less important in handling operations. This may explain subsequent phases of neglect in parts of the complex and account for declining volumes of broken amphorae noted within London's pottery assemblages.[31] In Neronian levels, amphoras make up about 40 per cent (by weight) of all pottery found, but by the middle of the second century this had fallen to 20 per cent.

Goods continued to flow through Southwark. A wonderfully preserved half-cellared warehouse was found at Courage Brewery on the western side of the main island.[32] It was built with pre-fabricated wooden frames formed from timbers felled in the winter of AD 152/3. A ramped entrance and solid oak floor suggest that it was designed to store barrels arriving down-river. In following years an extensive inter-tidal area on the east side of Southwark was reclaimed from the river using rubbish and gravel dumps. These were taken out to the line of a deeper river channel, the Guy's channel, which was canalized by revetments of horizontal oak planks retained by uprights felled AD 161.[33] Timber-lined vats provided wet storage in the open areas behind this new waterfront, but much of the newly reclaimed area remained under-developed. The main purpose of the engineering was perhaps to improve navigation along the river channel rather than win new land.

The amphitheatre was also refurbished around this time. New floors to its eastern entrance are dendrochronologically dated after c. AD 145, and alterations to the arena floor and drainage used timbers felled after AD 149 with one dated no later than AD 158.[34] The troops stationed in the Cripplegate fort may have kept the arena busy. This garrison may also account for the presence of a group of unusual coin issues, dated AD 154, found in river spoil at Billingsgate. Guy de la Bédoyère has suggested that this was a consignment of coinage shipped from Rome for official disbursement in London.[35] These findings indicate that London remained busy in the 150s, perhaps providing logistical support for campaigns resulting in the victories implied by coins showing a 'dejected Britannia' AD 154–5.[36]

Housing the gods

The new elite architectures established a landscape of masonry town houses studded across the city. This was soon mirrored by developments in temple design, as the gods were rehoused in masonry monuments.[37] In much the same way that the architects of town houses exploited construction skills brought to London for the Hadrianic public works, so the patrons of London's temples may have benefitted from the availability of artisans formerly engaged in house-building. Some of London's grandest new buildings occupied a terrace overlooking the Thames in the south-west of the city. Two successive public building complexes have been identified west of the redundant bathhouse at Huggin Hill. Dumps of marble veneers at Peter's Hill included richer materials than were associated with the baths and probably came from a different monumental building.[38] This is likely to have been built in the first or second centuries since it included material, such as Italian Carrara, that was rarely used afterwards. Parts of a monumental complex were explored in excavations at the Salvation Army Headquarters, near the approaches to the Millenium Bridge.[39] Although most of the remains date to later rebuilding, the complex included a masonry apse facing onto the river built using a foundation pile felled AD 165.[40] The structures are likely to have formed the river façade of an important temple precinct, later extended to include ambulatories and exedra housing statues and altars (below p. 302). Unpublished research by David Bentley, drawing on the alignments of various finds of monumental masonry, speculatively concluded that the precinct could have housed a large classical temple similar in size and layout to the temple of Sulis Minerva at Bath.[41] Altars erected in third-century restoration indicate the presence of temples dedicated to both Jupiter and Isis (below p. 303). Jupiter was the supreme protector of Rome and frequently named on votive altars.[42] By the second century the deity was synonymous with Roman imperial law and political order, and London's temple to Jupiter would have been an important point of reference within the urban landscape.

Two parallel walls, a little under 10 metres apart, along Knightrider Street have long puzzled archaeologists but might have formed the boundary of a monumental precinct.[43] The northern wall was at least 115 metres long and enclosed an open-space. It was cut into a pit with late first-century pottery and pottery of the third-fourth centuries was dumped to its side. Extensive gravel surfaces and several quarry pits have been noted on sites to the north, and a 21-metre-long masonry wall set perpendicular to Knightrider Street was seen at Sermon Lane. It has been suggested that this was a circus where chariot races were held, although the evidence is uncertain. A circus was, however, built at Colchester in the second century and it is not unlikely that London followed suit.[44]

Another temple may have been built on the western bank of the river Fleet in the late second or third centuries, overlooking the bridge towards Newgate. Nothing of the superstructure survived, and its identification relies on fragmentary traces of the wall-robbing trenches found at Old Bailey. These might describe a central octagonal *cella*, 16 metres in diameter, surrounded by a 3.75-metre-wide portico or ambulatory with concrete (*opus signinum*) floors.[45] Building debris indicates that the roof was tiled and some walls painted red with a border of white and green. A pit next to the outer wall contained a human skull. The interpretation of the building as a Romano-Celtic temple remains uncertain, although Ralph Merrifield drew attention to parallels with an octagonal temple of Apollo Cunomaglus built at Nettleton in Wiltshire.[46] With a total area of 520 square metres this would be the largest Romano-Celtic temple found in Britain.

Masonry temples were added to the religious sanctuary south of the amphitheatre, filling out the area east of the temple described in Chapter 12. One was found at 54–66 Gresham Street in 2007, where the distinctive features of a Romano-Celtic temple followed the same cardinal orientation as the other temples south-east of the amphitheatre.[47] It consisted of a small rectangular *cella*, 4.5 metres square, rising above a 1.4-metre-wide surrounding portico. A solid foundation of mortared flint cobbles in the southern half of the building may have supported a cult statue or altar. Interim reports suggest that this was built in the late second or early third century. A similarly aligned rectangular masonry building was found at Ironmonger Lane by Adrian Oswald in 1949.[48] The near-square chamber was about 6.5 metres across internally, and its construction dated by a large dump of finds dated 140–60 found in the 1995 reinvestigation of the site.[49] The room's mosaic floor was decorated with flowers and eight-lozenge stars arranged within a hexagonal compartments in a design that finds parallel in late second-century Silchester.[50] The south-east corner of another masonry building on the 'temple orientation' was found at 13–14 King Street in 1955.[51] No dating evidence was recovered, but a tessellated floor laid nearby after the Hadrianic fire may have been part of the same building.[52] The large Neronian pool to the south may have been backfilled in the expansion of the temple precinct, with fills dated by *c.* AD 120–60 ceramics.[53] A further temple may also have been located 150 metres west of the Gresham Street pond, indicated by monumental foundations and an altar found at Goldsmiths' Hall in 1830.[54]

Tiberinius Celerianus

Excavations at Tabard Square in 2002 and 2003 revealed another large temple precinct on the southern margins of town, between Watling Street and the southernmost channel of the Thames, and built over buildings whose demolition is pottery dated *c.* AD 125–65.[55] A small shrine might have been located amongst these earlier buildings, but the main focus of votive deposition had lain on the other side of Watling Street.[56] This activity declined significantly *c.* AD 140–250, coinciding with the establishment of the Tabard Square precinct.

The temple temenos consisted of near-square trapezoidal gravel-surfaced enclosure, about 92 metres across at its widest point, defined by open ditches (Fig. 21.6). A small square masonry building was placed outside a riverside entrance, perhaps marking a station for worshipers entering the sacred area.[57] The precinct was dominated by two square Romano-Celtic temples about 40 metres apart. The northern temple consisted of a small square *cella*, 4.85 metres square, with a surrounding portico or ambulatory. Its interior was decorated with painted red panels enhanced by a candelabra motif, and the lower portions of the external walls were painted dark red. The southern temple was of similar design but perhaps slightly larger. Each temple may have been flanked by a column, represented by a robbed-out masonry foundation. Ephemeral timber structures towards the centre of the precinct were associated with ovens and hearths, perhaps used in

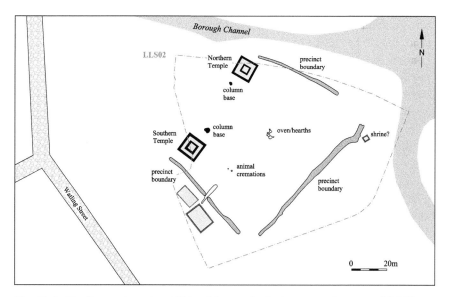

Fig. 21.6 The Roman temples at Tabard Square in the late second century (LLS02: after Killock *et al.* 2015). Drawn by Justin Russell.

banqueting ceremonies. The buried remains of a few cremated sheep were per-haps the residue of foundation rituals rather than more routine sacrifice. The enclosure ditch contained votive deposits and ritually sacrificed vessels amongst finds assemblages dated AD 140–60. These included a tin-alloy canister contain-ing a greasy white preparation, still showing finger marks left from its last use.[58] This might have been a medicinal preparation used at a place of healing, or a cosmetic treatment for lightening skin tone in religious processions where whitened faces identified men performing female roles.

The most important find from the Tabard Square excavations was a dedication inscribed onto a small marble slab buried in a fourth-century shaft at the heart of the complex.[59] The lettering, which retained red pigment, followed second-century style. The circumstances of burial suggest that the inscription held par-ticular importance to the sanctuary, and may have been an original temple dedication. The bottom lines of the inscription have been lost but the rest is clearly legible and translated by Roger Tomlin as reading: 'To the Divinities (Numina) of the Emperors (and) to the god Mars Camulus. Tiberinius Celerianus, citizen of the Bellovaci, moritix, of Londoners. The first...' (Fig. 21.7). The formu-laic reference to the Divinities of the Emperors (NVM.AVGG) indicates that the dedication was made during a joint reign, as when Marcus Aurelius was co-emperor with Julius Verus (AD 161–9) or Commodus (AD 177–80). The earlier of these dates is a better match for the finds from the *temenos* ditch.

Tiberinius Celerianus is likely to have been the patron responsible for the endowment. He was a Roman citizen, as evidenced by his *duo nomina*, who iden-tified himself as a citizen of the *Bellovaci*. This was a territory in Belgic Gaul centred on the modern city of Beauvais. He was also described as a *Moritix* 'of the Londoners' (*Londiniensi*). Moritix was a Celtic compound word formed from *mori*, meaning sea, and *(s)teigh*, to stride or mount, that must have meant 'seafarer'.[60] It is attested in two other inscriptions: an altar was dedicated to Apollo at Cologne by a *negotiator Britannicianus moritex*, and a sarcophagus from York com-memorated an individual responsible for the imperial cult from Bourges in northern Gaul.[61] Both individuals were probably freedmen. Moritix appears to have been a term applied to Gauls engaged in seaborne trade between Britain and the Continent, but we do not know if it described a profession or was an official title. These are not mutually exclusive, and Tiberinius Celerianus may have been the foremost member of a guild (*collegium*) of shippers from coastal Gaul operat-ing in London.[62] If a ship-owner, he would have ranked amongst the wealthiest members of society, and been closely tied to the administration if not directly employed as a state official. This gave him sufficient status to rank amongst London's most important patrons.[63] A series of altars and shrines found at Domburg and Colijnsplaat, in the Rhine delta, testify to the activities of a kindred merchant community. These dedications were made by *negotiatores* who special-ized in trade with Britain, and in products from the coastal regions where they

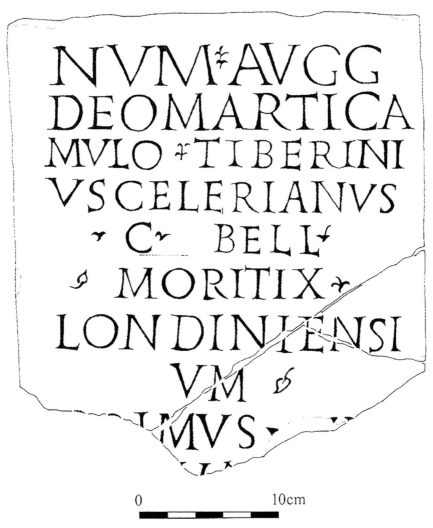

Fig. 21.7 The dedication to the god Mars Camulus (*DEOMARTICAMVLO*) made by Tiberinius Celerianus (TIBERINIVSCELERIANVS) found buried face-down in a shaft dug within the temple precinct at Tabard Square (drawn by Dr Roger Tomlin and reproduced with his kind permission).

operated.[64] Although London is not mentioned in these inscriptions, it was the principal British port within this network. *Collegia* were vital social institutions in cities where power resided with a diaspora community. On occasion these guilds were agents of the administration, collecting taxes and distributing liturgies. They established networks of patronage directed through organized worship: building temples and sponsoring festivals.[65] It has consequently been suggested that the Tabard Square temples belonged to a private guild.[66]

This begs the question of whether London's conspicuous Antonine investment in houses and temples should be credited to wealthy merchants, or to land-owning aristocrats setting-up in town and importing architectural tastes from country villas.[67] We have already seen that few amongst London's high society arrived from the immediate countryside, where few villas were to be found, although a case can be made for seeing the hand of immigrants from other Romano-British communities in the architecture. Some details are similar to those found in neighbouring cities at Silchester, Colchester, Verulamium, and Canterbury. The needs of political representation at the provincial council, embassy to the governor, and financial and legal engagement with London-based businessmen may have attracted a community of Romano-British aristocrats to the city. London remained under the political sway of the institutions developed by the provincial administration, but others may have been drawn to invest in city property.

Camulus, to whom Tiberinius Celerianus made his dedication, was a god of the Remi from northern Gaul (around Reims) identified with Mars. Mars was not just a god of war but also a guardian of place, and his Tabard Square temple was ideally located to protect London.[68] It would have been an important landmark for those approaching London from the south, by river or road, and visible from the temple on Greenwich hill. These routes connected Southwark with the important sanctuary at Springhead, where the area around the sacred spring was transformed into a larger complex in the mid- to late second century.[69] Travellers looked to the gods for good fortune when setting forth or when giving thanks for safe arrival, giving life to these roadside and gateway sanctuaries. Parallels can be drawn with temples at the south-eastern approaches to Silchester, where the masonry architecture is also likely to date to the second century, and in the temple enclosure at Balkerne Lane in Colchester.[70] These precincts, home to several gods in inter-related worship, commanded gateways into town in an architecture of contrast that set extra-mural sanctuaries in opposition to a central forum.[71] A dialogue between suburban sanctuary and urban core is likely to have been recognized in religious processions that traversed the city. These are likely to have been regular events. In Ephesos the parade from the extra-mural sanctuary to the theatre and back, took place fortnightly.[72] A papyrus found at Duro-Europus dated AD 225–7, lists the frequent festivals, sacrifices and parades conducted by an auxiliary garrison stationed on the eastern frontier for the imperial cult, military celebrations, and in the worship of the gods of Rome. Most of these religious holidays involved public distributions of free meat and wine after the sacrifices.[73]

In order to attend games at the amphitheatre, the priests and worshippers of Mars Camulus would have paraded through town accompanied by pipes, cymbals, bells and rattles.[74] The life-size moulded pipeclay theatre-masks, such as the Bacchic mask depicting Silenus found at Green Dragon Court and others from the Bank of England, were made for these religious processions.[75] The porticoes, temples and baths of Antonine London formed a ceremonial backdrop for the festivities. Celebrants leaving the Tabard square temples would have made their way along Watling Street through Southwark, perhaps pausing at a precinct on the north island where Faunus and Isis were worshipped.[76] A shrine to Neptune on London Bridge might have been the next station before reaching the forum and a shrine to the imperial cult. The onward route to the amphitheatre crossed the Walbrook, from which offerings to the river could be made.[77] From here the road headed up to the temples of the northern precinct and the amphitheatre itself. Processions following this route would have united London's different districts in shared celebration. The entire journey could be made on foot in under an hour, but would have taken much of the day if sacrifices and offerings were made at each shrine along the way.

Funerary architecture

Funeral processions headed in the opposite direction, leaving the city to attend burials in roadside cemeteries. Here too, a monumental landscape emerged in the middle of the second century, drawing on the masonry construction techniques introduced to public and domestic architecture. Some of the better tombs were set alongside the southern approach to London. Mausolea within walled cemeteries were found flanking Roman Watling Street at Great Dover Street, nearly 0.5 kilometres south of the Tabard Square temples (Fig. 21.8).[78] These combined to form a monumental street of tombs (*Gräberstrasse*).[79] Associated ceramics indicate that this cemetery was established no later than the middle of the second century. A square masonry building, some 8 metres across, may have been a temple or mausoleum. It included a well or soakaway, and the base of a possible altar between the inner and outer walls of the building. A cremation pit, or *bustum*, was found 30 metres away. This contained a woman's cremated remains along with exotic foods, including figs, almonds, dates and the remains of chickens and other birds. The organic remains included Mediterranean stone pine: a symbol of immortal life and source of aromatic smoke. Molten glass within the incinerated remains may have derived from an ungentuaria. These testify to the feasts and funerary rituals undertaken once the body reached the graveyard. Offerings made after the pyre debris had been gathered together included at least nine pottery tazze and eight pottery lamps. Three of these lamps showed the Egyptian jackal-headed Anubis who controlled entry to the underworld and was sometimes associated with oriental cults such as that of Isis. The lamps also included the depiction of a fallen gladiator, which encouraged speculation that this might have been the burial of a female gladiator. Lamps and tazze were commonly used in funerary ritual, giving light and hope to the dead on their perilous journey to the underworld, and since gladiatorial combat originated in the celebration of funerary

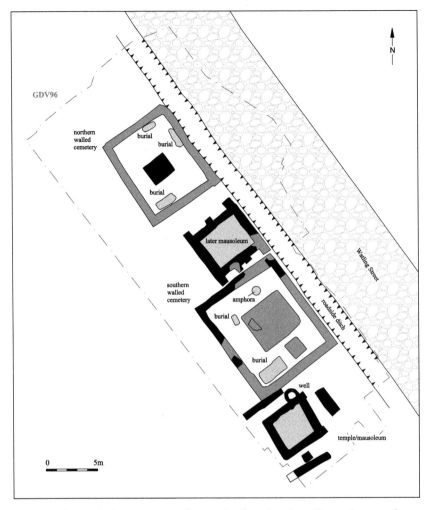

Fig. 21.8 The roadside cemetery and mausolea found at Great Dover Street to the south of the Southwark settlement (GDV96: after Mackinder 2000). Drawn by Justin Russell.

games this was an entirely appropriate topic for a burial assemblage. Other structures were added north of the temple or mausoleum over the following decades. These included two walled cemeteries, each built around a centrally located base for a tomb or statue and flanked by a buttressed mausoleum. An upright amphora in the southern walled cemetery was perhaps a receptacle for libations. Rubble within the cemetery included a carved stone pine and moulded cornice, likely to have derived from a funerary monument, and the carved head of a river god likely to have come from a funerary sculpture. Further burials took place outside these walled graveyards.

Funerary monuments lined Watling Street for at least 1 kilometre out of town, reaching at least as far as 82–96 Old Kent Road where the foundations of a second-century mausoleum have been recorded.[80] Carved stone fragments derived from these monuments, including elements found at Tabard square, include pine-cone finials of a type used to symbolize immortality and usually confined to military sites. These might have marked the burials of officers serving in London or imperial officials with similar tastes.[81]

The presence of important Neronian funerary monuments on the east side of town, such as the tomb of Classicianus (above p. 105) which probably remained standing until fourth-century demolition, attracted other tombs. A masonry structure with a marble veneer at Tenter Street is likely to have been a mausoleum, and at least four masonry monuments were recorded in the Mansell Street cemetery.[82] A stone mausoleum and a round or octagonal building have also been found at Prescot Street near Aldgate.[83]

Marking boundaries

Processional routes through London may have attracted other types of monumental architecture. A substantial concrete foundation 6 metres square and 1.1 metres high, perhaps the base for a column or statue or alternatively some form of ceremonial gateway, was set next to the main west road inside the line of the later town wall.[84] Roadside buildings were demolished to make way for this monument, c. AD 160. On the north side of the road a smaller contemporary foundation could have supported columns, perhaps a portico. Another massive roadside foundation, at least 2.7 metres across, of uncertain purpose was found c. 8 metres west of the later city wall outside Ludgate.[85]

City gates may have been built as ceremonial arches before the early third-century town wall was built, to mark the sacred and political borders of the city.[86] The gate at Newgate was set on a higher plinth than the town wall, suggesting that it started life as a freestanding structure (Fig. 21.9).[87] It comprised a double portal, each carriageway about 5 metres wide, flanked by two square towers housing 'guardrooms' from which customs and tolls might be managed. A flint and brick-earth foundation seen during tunnelling next to Bishopsgate might have supported a similar monument on the northern boundary of the Roman city.[88] Parallels can perhaps be drawn with Trier's Porta Nigra, built in AD 170.

The presence of these ceremonial gateways suggests that the later city wall followed an established boundary. This was probably marked by a small ditch: excavations at Dukes Place found traces of a shallow feature with second-century fills that anticipated the line of the city wall, with other pre-wall ditches identified at Aldersgate and London Wall.[89] The earlier town boundary, perhaps represented by the ditch at Baltic Exchange, may have continued to mark London's formal

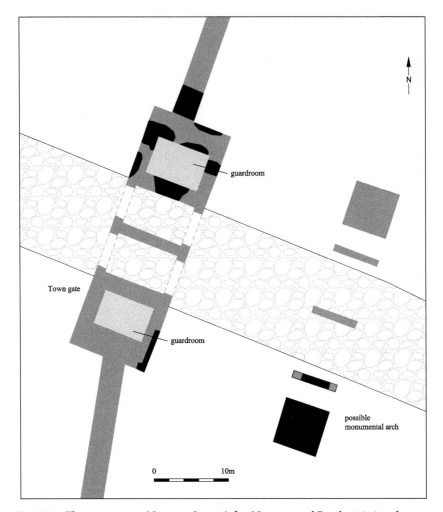

Fig. 21.9 The town gate at Newgate Street (after Norman and Reader 1912 and Pitt 2006b). This illustrates three separate phases of monumental construction: a possible ceremonial archway or roadside monument, the Roman town gate at Newgate, and the third-century masonry town wall that was added to either side. Drawn by Fiona Griffin.

limits into the Hadrianic period.[90] The abiding significance of this feature is indicated by the fact that crania were deposited within its upper fills in the early second century. An Antonine coin is also supposed to have been found with the remains of a cremation cemetery inside the line of the later wall at Camomile Street, near Bishopsgate, in 1707.[91] These finds imply that the town boundary had not advanced to its later line before the Antonine period. A parallel can be drawn with the situation at Verulamium, where the Flavian town boundary was marked by an earthwork feature known as the '1955 ditch' which was allowed to silt up by *c.* 140. Verulamium's city boundary was subsequently marked by an earth-work known as the 'Fosse', which appears to have been raised before a fire dated *c.* AD 155.⁹² A similar chronology of urban expansion would fit the evidence from London. Hadrianic expansion might have encouraged an Antonine redrawing of the city limits when the legal boundary was probably marked by little more than a low bank and ditch. This was followed by the construction of ceremonial arches at the entrances into the city later in the century. It was at this time that the city reached its greatest extent, covering an area of *c.* 168 hectares (133 hectares north of the river and 35 hectares in Southwark), and may have been home to a population of around 30,000 if not slightly more.⁹³

After a century of near-continuous growth London was a city of visible consequence, vastly larger than any other Romano-British town and boasting numerous temples, baths and palaces. The Roman city may never have been more populous than it was when Tiberinius Celerianus prepared to dedicate his new temple to Mars Camulus on the borders of Southwark. Indeed, it was more than a thousand years before London outgrew the limits reached at this time.

PART 6
LONDON DIMINISHED

22
Antonine contraction (*c.* A D 165–80)

The puzzle of London's missing late Roman stratigraphy

Archaeologists working in London have long puzzled over a surprising change in the character of the evidence for its later Roman occupation. Whilst the deeply stratified remains of first and early second-century buildings are ubiquitous, later Roman sequences are scarce. In some cases this is easily explained: modern basements have removed all but the deepest, and earliest, stratigraphy. The puzzle lies in the fact that late Roman stratigraphy is also missing in areas that escaped such truncation. This was noticed as long ago as 1927 when Gordon Home observed a 1.2 metre depth of stratigraphy deriving from the first century of Roman occupation at a site in King Street, but a complete lack of deposits from the following two and a half centuries.[1] Drawing on this work, Quintin Waddington concluded that 'Londinium, a very flourishing town at the beginning of the 2nd century, may have afterwards dwindled very markedly in size'.[2]

These observations left little mark on wider scholarship. It wasn't until nearly half-a-century later that Harvey Sheldon renewed debate by using the evidence of interrupted sequences in Southwark to propose a rapid urban decline *c.* A D 160.[3] Sheldon's dating evidence was promptly questioned by John Morris, who was more comfortable with the idea that London's decline was a later event, but has proved robust.[4] Rescue excavations added other examples of occupation terminating in the Antonine period, and Sheldon's argument gained wide acceptance amongst London's fieldworkers.[5] A note of caution was raised by Brian Yule in 1990, who recognized that late Roman horizontal strata were sometimes eroded during the formation of a distinctive type of archaeological horizon known as 'dark earth'.[6] In some cases this dark earth was not dumped over Roman stratigraphy, as previously thought likely, but the product of root and worm action that had eaten into underlying floors and deposits. Because of such bioturbation the remains of some late Roman buildings may have been disturbed beyond recognition.

The idea that London witnessed a catastrophic abandonment was further challenged by discoveries at One Poultry and Lloyd's Register where masonry and timber buildings were rebuilt and repaired from the second century into the fourth.[7] These instances of renewal suggested that the case for late second-century desertion may have been over-stated.[8] For most scholars the question is one of degree, with contraction in some districts but not others. As Sadie Watson has observed, 'although some argue that the evidence for later Roman buildings at many sites may have been destroyed in antiquity by subsequent soil formation processes, the abrupt disappearance of buildings from so many areas is still generally accepted as providing evidence for a marked decline in settlement'.[9] Richard Hingley has taken a more extreme view, arguing that although some areas may have been abandoned there is no definitive evidence of decline or a radical reduction in population.[10] He thinks that later Roman London contained more ephemeral timber structures than hitherto assumed, and these have eluded identification within disturbed later Roman horizons. These changes in the character of the architecture would have contributed to a slower build-up of stratigraphy, making it harder to find evidence. The earth-walls and floors of the earlier city had needed frequent repair and replacement, generating a rapid stratigraphic accretion of elements that couldn't be recycled, but the later use of concrete walls and floors reduced the frequency of rebuilding and the volume of material discarded. Similarly, a move towards using timber in place of earth, in both floors and walls, may have reduced the volumes of debris generated by rebuilding. These changes are real, and diminish the body of evidence (see pp. 377–8). It remains the case, however, that excavators have successfully identified the slight traces of late antique timber buildings on numerous sites. Since later Roman sequences can be described, even where the evidence is ephemeral, instances where they appear wholly missing demand closer explanation.

The problem of dark earth

This requires us to give attention to the dark earth. This horizon, generally between 0.4 and 1.2 metres thick, commonly buries London's latest Roman remains. Micromorphological analysis by Richard Macphail shows that it was often composed of finely mixed material from the decay and disturbance of earth and timber buildings, heavily augmented by human coprolites, ash, cereal waste, decayed organic matter and other detritus from the surface middening of domestic waste.[11] In some cases two distinct horizons are evident: a lower layer representing the initial formation of biologically reworked Roman strata mixed with dumped material, and an upper, more uniform, horizon resulting from soil formation, dumping and reworking. The biological reworking often disturbed underlying deposits, in a zone that rose as soils accreted and new waste was introduced. These processes continued into the middle Ages, involving extensive digging-over where night-soil was buried.[12]

Where dark earth covers ruined buildings this unequivocally demonstrates that built-up areas reverted to open land. It is not, however, evidence of wholescale desertion since the middening waste derived from proximate human settlement. Pits and wells containing later Roman finds were also dug into affected areas, serving nearby houses or for watering livestock and irrigation.[13] The presence of pollen and phytoliths (the silica spicules of plant cells) from wasteland grasses suggests that the open areas were not routinely cultivated, but were grazed or cleared with sufficient frequency to prevent the spontaneous growth of woodland. These areas where houses had formerly stood became parcels of open land within a shrunken but not desolate city.

The crux of the issue is to establish when the areas covered by dark-earth became open land. Many studies assume that dark-earth was the product of de-urbanization at the close of the Roman period, but since the deposit is sometimes sandwiched between early Roman stratigraphy and remains of third and fourth century re-occupation we know that it sometimes started formation in the second century.[14] The assumption that dark earth subsumed all evidence of entire centuries of building activity must also be questioned. Even where bioturbation caused damage, better preserved sequences are sometimes slumped into earlier quarries and pits. This was the case at 76–80 Newgate Street where the floors of Antonine buildings had sunk into the fills of a poorly consolidated Flavian quarry.[15] Tellingly, the latest floors were covered by an unusual demolition horizon formed from broken-up plaster-faced earth walls. Previous architectural practice had involved the comprehensive recovery of upstanding clay walls for reuse, but this uppermost horizon marked an unusual and profligate levelling-off of building remains at the close of the occupation sequence. In all earlier phases numerous structural elements had been dug into the ground: particularly wall foundations, drainage channels and sumps. The absence of such features penetrating into the Antonine stratigraphy from higher levels also represents a radical change in the site's architectural history. A similar story can be told from the evidence of hearths and ovens. These tile-built structures were too solid to be erased by bioturbation, and their presence in late Hadrianic and Antonine build-ings contributed to the survival of higher areas of stratigraphy, supplementing the evidence from areas of subsidence. In sum: whilst bioturbation had disturbed the Antonine demolition horizon and eroded parts of the underlying floors, it left hearths intact along with wall foundations and drainage features. From this we conclude that the Antonine timber buildings were the latest to have been present, and had been demolished before dark-earth formation commenced. The better-preserved sequences suggest that the biological processes that accompanied early dark-earth formation penetrated little more than 10–20 centimetres into underlying stratigraphy. This reduced density of occupation would also explain why the dark earth did not contain rich reworked assemblages of late second-century pottery to match those from earlier second-century occupation.

Similar sequences were noted south of the Cripplegate fort, at Foster Lane and Wood Street, where Antonine floors survived bioturbation slumped into earlier pits.[16] There are other instances where the walls of Antonine buildings were spread out rather than salvaged for reuse, suggesting that demolition preceded abandonment, as at 88 Borough High Street in Southwark where a clay-walled structure was demolished *c.* AD 150–70.[17] Pits dug into this demolition debris contained assemblages dated *c.* AD 175–225 and were covered by dark earth. Elsewhere second-century buildings stood in ruin before demolition, as shown by weather damage to wall-plaster in a building within the Cripplegate fort.[18]

This landscape of dereliction invokes comparison with modern Detroit. Pam Crabtree has used the decline of Michigan's Motor City as a model for understanding urban decline in fourth-century Britain.[19] Although we are interested in an earlier period of change, the analogy remains useful. Detroit's population declined by 25 per cent between 2000 and 2010, leaving functioning public buildings and a working urban infrastructure but numerous abandoned houses. This generated a mix of open and built space that stands comparison with the landscape of later Roman London. Some mid-second-century assemblages from London's western and southern margins also include an abnormally high proportion of dog bones, which are thought to have witnessed culls of feral animals that roamed these areas.[20] A picture emerges in which vacant plots became wastelands, but could be reinvented as urban commons entertaining a range of adventitious uses. The creation of urban commons for animal grazing might explain a particular feature of the archaeological interface between dark-earth and underlying stratigraphy.[21] At several sites the demolished houses were pock-marked by numerous small stake-holes cut from within the dark-earth. There was no evident pattern to their distribution, and the posts were too slight to have been load-bearing. It is possible that some were tethering posts for goats and sheep, moved day to day, and others might have supported livestock pens or drying racks. The presence of grazing animals is implied by an increase in the presence of caprids in bone assemblages from the middle of the second century in areas where settlement contraction seems most pronounced.[22]

Peter Marsden and Barbara West drew on different sources to describe later second-century change.[23] They attempted to quantify changing approaches to waste disposal from the dates of rubbish pits recorded by the Guildhall Museum. From a sample of 134 pits, 62 were dated AD 50–150 (0.6 pits per year), and 16 were dated AD 150–400 (0.06 pits per year). It is evident that patterns of rubbish disposal changed around the middle of the second century. Perhaps there was less rubbish to bury, or waste was redirected towards surface middens. Marsden and West also reviewed 114,624 spot date records (each a dated assemblage from a discrete stratigraphic context) from over 350 different excavations, finding that 41,878 were dated AD 50–150 (418 *per annum*), 3052 were assigned AD 150–270 (25 *pa*), and 6920 were from AD 270–400 (53 *pa*). More recent studies have confirmed a drastic reduction in the numbers of archaeological assemblages after *c.* AD 160 (Fig. 22.1).[24] The contrast between earlier and later periods is exaggerated by later truncation and disturbance, and influenced by changes in construction techniques and patterns of refuse disposal. Attention must,

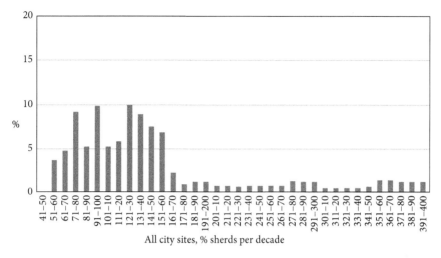

All city sites, % sherds per decade

Fig. 22.1 Profile of all the Roman pottery from Museum of London excavations in the City of London down to 2005, in percentage of sherds by decade, where the dates are those of the context in which the pottery was found (after Symmonds 2006, fig. 80). This not only shows the dramatic fall-off in the numbers of later Roman deposits known from the City (with a modest revival in the late third century), but also peaks of activity in the early Flavian (71–80) and Hadrianic (121–30) periods.

however, be drawn to the evidence for an increase in the number of assemblages after the late third century. This evidence of later recovery confirms that the late second century was a period of exceptionally reduced activity. Various classes of archaeological confirm this pattern. For example, there was a pronounced decline in the numbers of seal-boxes, signet rings and intaglios dated from the late second century onwards, even though these items came into wider use at exactly this time.[25] Since these objects survive reworking and are readily recovered from post-Roman levels their scarcity cannot be accounted for by processes of bioturbation, changed architectural traditions, or the surface middening of waste. In sum: all available sources of archaeological evidence witness a significant reduction in levels of activity.

Continuities and discontinuities

In order to assess the scale of change we are now able to draw on a large sample of residential and commercial sites where we can reconstruct patterns of land-use from the second century into the third.[26] These are mapped on Fig. 22.2, distinguishing between sites with evidence for structural continuity and those where building densities appear significantly reduced before AD 200. These suggest late second-century contraction on 57 per cent of sites. In contrast many

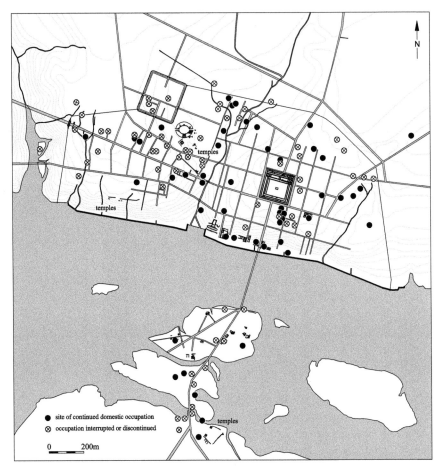

Fig. 22.2 A proposed reconstruction of London *c.* AD 170, illustrating the distribution of sites presenting evidence for continuity of domestic occupation at this time (in black) and of sites where occupation appears to have been interrupted or discontinued (crossed open circle). Drawn by Justin Russell.

substantial town houses built around the middle of the second century were altered and improved in the third century, suggesting continuity of occupation. A building investigated during the excavation of a ventilation shaft for the Dockland Light Railway in Lothbury is representative.[27] A hypocaust floor and furnace was built *c.* AD 140, and the heavily sooted channels of the underfloor heating witness a lengthy period of use before the building was altered in works that introduced pottery with a likely *terminus post quem* of *c.* AD 230.

These assumptions of continuity are tested, however, by the evidence of a town house at 60–3 Fenchurch Street.[28] This large Antonine residential compound, dated by Colchester colour coated ware pottery in its foundations, saw various third-century alterations. But a fire that took place before these alterations were made left a carbonized debris of stems and branches from saplings and brambles cut with a slashing implement. This burnt material wasn't from a structural fire, but was consistent with a bonfire of overgrowth. One of the burnt oak stems included five growth rings, suggesting that the house had been overgrown for at least 5 years before being cleared. The implication is that the third-century restoration took place after a period of dereliction.

Buildings found at the Lloyd's Register site on Fenchurch Street have also been presented as evidence for continued urban vitality.[29] The redevelopment of this site after late first and early second-century occupation involved the construction of at least four masonry buildings set over piled foundations alongside ancillary clay and timber structures. The architecture included a semi-basemented aisled building with brick piers, similar in layout to the Flavian aisled building at Fenchurch Street. The dating evidence leaves it uncertain, however, as to whether this redevelopment took place before c. AD 200.[30] Intriguingly a large quarry pit on the site was filled with rubbish dated c. AD 160–200 that included waste from the production of bone hairpins and needles along with finished objects. Jackie Keily identified this as rubbish from the clearance of a workshop that ceased production at this time, and perhaps as a casualty of late second-century contraction.[31]

What these examples show is that we cannot be confident that places occupied around the middle of the second century, and which witnessed new building in the third century, had prospered in the intervening period. Some instances of restoration may have been necessitated by earlier ruin. To take another example, the second-century town house at Plantation Place was maintained and improved throughout much of late antiquity.[32] A hoard of forty-three gold coins (*aurei*), was concealed in a sunken chamber, presumably a strong-room, beneath the main reception room. The latest coins were dated AD 173–4, and the hoard may have been buried soon after this date. Another hoard, of at least twelve silver coins with the latest minted in AD 166, was found on the opposite side of the road at 146 Fenchurch Street in 1922.[33] We do not know why these late second-century treasuries were buried, but the fact that they were never recovered hints at dislocation.

The scale of change

At One Poultry buildings continued to occupy plots flanking the main street into the later second century, although density reduced and the pace of building slowed.[34] Empty plots appeared throughout town, but contraction was most evident around the Cripplegate fort and west of the Walbrook, as well as along the line of Watling Street as it crossed Southwark towards London Bridge. It is likely that the fort itself was evacuated, and pottery later than c. AD 165 is conspicuously absent from sites within its interior.[35] The fort's northern and western walls survived for reuse in the early third-century town wall, but its east wall was reduced to its foundations.[36] The south ditch was filled with late second-century rubbish, including a jar made in the Highgate Wood kilns that ceased production c. AD 165.[37] Some surrounding streets also became redundant. The suburban north road, laid out around the time the fort was built, was resurfaced at least once during the second century, coin dated after AD 154, but was soon in disrepair following flood damage.[38] Although the road was eventually restored, late second-century burials encroached onto its line and rubbish spread over its surface. Parts of the east-west road midway between the Cripplegate fort and Cheapside also appears to have fallen into disuse, with pits dug into its surface to quarry gravels.[39] A stretch of the road along the western bank of the Walbrook valley also became redundant at some point, with the latest floors in adjacent buildings dated c. AD 140, before it was built over in the late third or fourth century.[40] These redundancies are telling. Up until this point London's road system had only seen expansion, but in the late second century some streets were no longer used by wheeled traffic.

Other aspects of the urban infrastructure failed. The mill at the foot of the Fleet was abandoned towards the end of the second century never to be replaced.[41] Some Walbrook revetments collapsed c. AD 150–70, reducing the energy reaching mills on this stretch of river, and the fact that wooden fittings were removed from the mill near the Bloomberg site suggests that it ceased to function.[42] These mills were nearly a century old, and may have become difficult to maintain, but their loss must have drastically reduced milling capacity. If less flour meant less bread, then appetites changed. It can also be noted that the later city used fewer timber-lined wells than before, despite the failure to fully restore water-lifting devices after the Hadrianic fire.[43] The management of some market gardens and stock enclosures on the town borders also changed. At Rangoon Street, in an area that remained peri-urban throughout the Roman period, Flavian ditch systems were routinely maintained into the second century but fell into disuse c. AD 140–160/70, to be sealed by dark earth containing late third- and fourth-century finds.[44]

The stretch of Watling Street leading from Kent to Southwark may also have been in disrepair in the late second century, along with the supposed market hall and shops on the approaches to London Bridge.[45] River lain sediments dated c. AD 170–90 found next to the Guy's Channel suggest that these newly reclaimed lands were surrendered to intermittent flooding.[46] In contrast, nearby public buildings were maintained through this period. New *opus signinum* surfaces and internal structures were added to the baths at 11–15 Borough High Street, although there may also have been a phase of partial collapse.[47] Continued attendances at the Tabard Square temple precinct generated rubbish dated AD 170-200.[48]

Some industrial production around London ceased. Until the middle of the second century, London was amply supplied with pottery from kilns between Brockley Hill and Verulamium, and Highgate Wood. These potteries ended production *c.* AD 160/80.[49] Brick supply was also reorganized, and local kilns stopped making tile for use in the city.[50] Glass-making furnaces near the amphitheatre, at 35 Basinghall Street, also failed *c.* 160/70-80.[51] Here the formation of a peaty organic layer, dated from *c.* AD 180 onwards, shows that the area reverted to open land following the closure of the glassworks. Reduced demand, perhaps following the departure of the troops stationed in the Cripplegate fort, may have contributed to de-industrialization. Clusters of stake-holes driven into the ground following the abandonment of the glass kilns suggest the occasional presence of tethered or penned livestock following the pattern seen at Newgate Street. The metalworking workshops of Southwark showed greater resilience.[52] The presence of hearths, hammerscale and slag shows that production continued through the later second century without evident interruption. Interestingly, however, an open area between two of the workshops was also covered by the dense pattern of stake-holes possibly indicative of livestock management.

Dating these changes is key. It is consequently worth summarizing what we know of the chronology of development leading into the period of contraction. At the close of Hadrian's reign London was a larger and more populous place than ever before. The period AD 140-160 witnessed confident investment in domestic architecture, up to and including the construction of a courtyard building at Drapers' Gardens *c.* AD 160. Engineering works in the 150s improved the amphitheatre, and road-repairs north of town took place after AD 154. Programmes of waterfront improvement included the construction of a carefully built timber-framed warehouse in Southwark AD 152-3 and the canalization of Guy's channel AD 161-2. There is no sign of hesitancy in any sphere of building activity before the AD 160s. The following years witnessed investment in new temple precincts, one of which was probably under construction AD 165 and Tiberinius Celerianus may have dedicated the temple to Mars Camulus in this decade. This spate of temple building might have continued whilst other parts of town were already in decline, but a date of *c.* AD 165 is a good fit for the closing phase of second-century building activity on many sites.

The two unclaimed coin hoards found on the eastern side of town, one formed *c.* AD 166 and the other after *c.* AD 174, were buried soon after this turning point in London's fortunes. Whatever weight we place on these individual strands of evidence, they combine to show that London shrank in the decade after AD 165. Heading into later periods there is less evidence to work with. A timber felled AD

174 was associated with a timber-framed building at St Mary at Hill and a well in the rear-yard of a roadside property at One Poultry was built using timbers felled in the summer of AD 181.[53] These rare signs of late second-century activity witness a continued or revived supply of timber from managed woodlands, albeit at much reduced levels, a decade or so after the supposed interruption to building activity within town.

Despite the evidence of settlement contraction, there is no question that London remained a place of importance. Overall, somewhere between a third and two-thirds of the building plots occupied at the middle of the century are thought to have become vacant entering into the last third of the century. If the population of London exceeded 30,000 in its early second-century heyday, as suggested above (p. 275), then contraction of this scale would have reduced the population to somewhere between 10,000 and 20,000. A city of this size would have remained the largest in Britain and still more populous than at the time of the Boudican revolt. Continuity of occupation was most evident in areas along the Walbrook valley and along the Thames riverbank below the forum, in areas where natural sources of running water were more easily obtained. Despite reduced building density, the city spread out over a much larger area than in Neronian times. The fact that London was no longer a high-density settlement has no direct implication for its status, or indeed for the continuing prosperity of those who remained here.

London's population decline wasn't offset by growth in the surrounding countryside. On the contrary, many nearby sites also witnessed contraction. A break in occupation from *c.* AD 150–70 until the middle of the third century has been identified at roadside settlements including Enfield, Ewell, Brentford, and Staines.[54] The evidence is similar to that recorded within London. At Brentford, for example, dark earth deposits were found over early to mid-second-century buildings, but buried beneath timber structures dating after the middle of the third century. Since these sites served London bound traffic, it is understandable that they shared in its decline. The changes of this period were, however, more widespread. Rural settlements in south-eastern England probably doubled in number between the late Iron Age and early second century, which is when the landscape was most densely occupied. After this early Roman expansion the number of rural settlements in Essex, Kent and East Sussex declined steeply, especially in the Weald (Fig. 22.3).[55] Settlement contraction is also evident within the Thames estuary, with a particularly sharp reduction in the number of salt production sites in operation, whilst field systems ceased to be maintained on farmsteads within London's immediate urban hinterland.[56] The sharp decline in settlement numbers suggests rural depopulation, and farmers may have retreated from marginal sites at a time of reduced demand. London's mid-second-century contraction may also have been echoed at other places in southern Britain linked to military supply and commerce, as at Richborough.[57]

What happened?

So what happened *c.* A D 165 to reverse the trajectory of London's earlier growth? For all that we can question aspects of detail, the evidence reveals a population haemorrhage. London's economy was labour intensive and the town's expansion had relied on immigration and population growth. Any reversal of this process had repercussions for the way in which the city could function. Several explanations of London's late second-century contraction have been advanced. Much research has focused on the economic impact of changes to patterns of supply, as the later Roman provincial economy became increasingly efficient at meeting the needs of urban and military consumers through local production rather than imports.[58] In particular, *annona* provisioning, arguably the motor to London's economy, may have become over-cumbersome resulting in radical reform (below p. 328). Other factors might include the vagaries of imperial patronage and administrative interference, resulting in the promotion of competing centres of power such as York. Within London itself, much has been made of practical problems caused by tidal regression making it harder to bring ships to harbour (pp. 149 and 299).

London's contraction was probably the product of myriad factors, some reinforcing others in a feedback loop that exaggerated outcomes. It is consequently difficult to distinguish between causes and consequences. The key question to ask, however, is: did London shrink because manpower was no longer needed at a failing port and could be relocated elsewhere, or was population decline the prompt for this economic rebalancing? It is therefore significant that it wasn't just London's port that went into decline, but the productive capacity of the entire region. This is inconsistent with the idea that London's reversal was a consequence of an increase in provincial capacity to substitute for earlier imports. Without wishing to dismiss the importance of economic factors, to which our attention will return, we need to explore the possibility that population decline was triggered by a more direct form of shock. This brings us to consider the impact of those perennial harbingers of flight: war and plague.

Although urban populations flee warfare, London generally benefitted from campaign traffic and was emphatically restored after violent destruction.[59] The indirect consequences of more distant wars were perhaps of greater consequence. London's contraction coincided with the Marcommanic wars prosecuted by Antoninus Pius's successor Marcus Aurelius.[60] A gruelling series of campaigns were launched in response to frontier invasions into Pannonia and Dacia *c.* A D 166, and continued intermittently until A D 175. These actions distracted attention from Britain and could have had recessionary consequences, but a similar situation had applied during the Dacian wars some 80 years earlier and had only slowed the pace of London's growth. It did not put it into reverse.

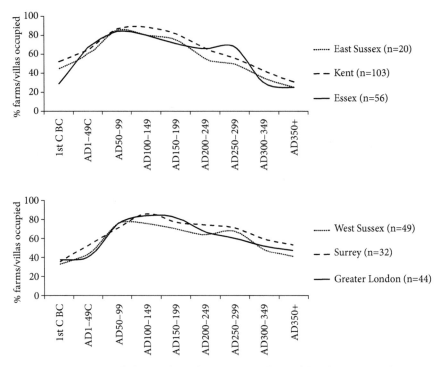

Fig. 22.3 Proportional change through time in numbers of dated Roman settlements identified in the course of development-led excavation projects in Greater London and surrounding counties (Essex, Sussex, Kent, and Surrey), from the first century BC until the fourth century AD. This suggests declining settlement densities within the region from the mid- to late second century onwards, with partial revival towards the end of the third century. The pattern is more marked to the east of London than to its west (after Smith *et al.* 2016).

This was also a time of plague. Historical accounts describe a pestilential death carried into the Roman world by soldiers returning from campaigns against the Parthians.[61] Plague was probably present in western Asia Minor by the summer of AD 165 before it reached Rome. The Greek physician Galen described soldiers over-wintering in Aquileia dying in their masses in AD 168, and later chronicles claim that the Roman army was reduced almost to extinction by AD 172. Outbreaks may have continued down to *c.* AD 189 when Dio describes 2,000 people dying daily in Rome. These accounts may exaggerate and there is an appreciable risk that modern scholarship has conflated accounts of unrelated episodes of more commonplace urban disease, which leaves scope for wildly different views over the scale and character of the Antonine plague. Modern estimates of mortality range from as little as 2 per cent, equivalent to the death rate from 'Spanish flu', to a third of the empire's entire population. Galen's descriptions might be consistent with smallpox (*variola*), which is the diagnosis most widely accepted by modern scholars.[62] If this was Europe's first full exposure to smallpox then epidemiological models suggest that 22–4 per cent of those living at its outbreak might have died. The economic consequences would have been considerable. Richard Duncan-Jones has noted that a sharp doubling of prices and wages in the late second century, implied by epigraphic and archaeological data, might witness economic dislocations and labour scarcities following the epidemic. Since other factors may have been at work, and the absence of mortality statistics hinders research, scholarly opinion remains divided over the plague's impact on the Roman economy.[63]

The purpose of this study is not, however, to measure the scale of the Antonine plague, but to seek explanation for London's depopulation. Plague was first advanced as a possible cause of London's second-century contraction by Harvey Sheldon in 1981.[64] Archaeologists have found it difficult to build on this suggestion since the consequences of plague are so hard to trace in the material record. We know for certain, however, that the Antonine plague was feared in London. In 1989, metal-detecting on the Thames foreshore at Vintry turned up an amulet made of lead pewter that contained a thirty-line metrical phylactery written in Greek, the language of magic and medicine (Fig. 22.4).[65] Using various incantations it called upon deities including Apollo (in the guise of Phoebus) to protect one Demetrios from plague, imploring: 'Phoebus of the unshorn hair, archer, drive away the cloud of plague'. The words quoted from a spell circulated by Alexander of Abonoteichos, a prophet of the snake-god Glycon who sent his clients to shrines of Apollo.[66] Instructions issued by the oracle of Claros c. AD 165 elicited the erection of a series of dedications using this spell as a prophylactic measure against the plague.[67] The amulet found by the Thames was prepared to protect Demetrios from plague soon after AD 165. Prior to its discovery, Ralph Merrifield had already proposed the presence of an important second-century London cult of Apollo the archer.[68] In 1830 an altar was found at the site of Goldsmiths' Hall in Foster Lane alongside a mass of stonework so hard that it had to be blasted away with gunpowder.[69] This foundation suggests the presence of a public building, perhaps a temple added to the western borders of the religious precinct beside the amphitheatre (above p. 266). The altar portrayed a long-haired hunter god best identified as Apollo. The same deity was present amongst sculptures found under Southwark Cathedral and again on an altar found at Bevis Marks. Merrifield suggested that the Antonine plague was a likely stimulus for the development of the cult served by these altars. According to the *Historia Augusta*, one of the actions taken against the plague by Marcus Aurelius was to restore the cults of the gods.[70] This raises the possibility that the temples built in London c. AD 165 might have been inspired by heightened attention to prophylactic observances as the outbreak spread. Although news of the disease may have prompted the dedication of temples, altars and magic spells, we have no proof that anyone in London actually died of plague. There are no first-hand accounts,

α	⊼	⊼	⊓
β	Β	Β	
γ	Γ	Γ	
δ	Δ	Δ	
ε	Ε	Ε	Ε
ζ	Ζ	Ζ	
η	Η	Η	
θ	Θ	Θ	
ι	Ι	Ι	
κ	Κ	Κ	Κ
λ	Λ	Λ	
μ	Μ	Μ	
ν	Ν	Ν	
ξ	Ζ	Ζ	
ο	ϙ	ϙ	
π	Τ	Τ	
ρ	Ρ	Ρ	Ρ	Ρ
σ	C	C	
τ	Τ	Τ	
υ	Υ	Υ	
φ	Φ	Φ	Φ
χ	Χ	Χ	
ψ			
ω	ⱳ	ⱳ	ⱳ

αβραι β[α]ρβασω
βαρβασωχ
βαρβασωθ, ευλιωρ
αθεμορφι, λάβρου
5 λυμοῦ παράπεμ-
πε δυσκέλαδον
ρύζημα, διῆρι-
ον, τανυχιζον,
νυδρολεες, ὀ-
10 δύμης δια-
μηχόμαιμον, βα-
ρύθοιμον, εαρκο-
τακές, διατηκόμε-
νον, φλεβίων ἀ-
15 πὸ κόλπων. μέ-
γας Ἰάω, μέ-
γας Σαβαώθ,
διαφύλαξον τὸν
φοροῦντα. Φοῖβε
20 ἀκερσικόμα, το-
ξότα, λοιμοῦ νε-
φέλησι ἀπέλαυ-
νε. Ἰάω, Ἀβρ(α)ς-
αξ θεέ, βοη(θ)εῖ.
25 Φοῖβος ἅπαξ ἐ-
κέλευσεν βρο-
τοῖς χιλεων ἀ-
πέχεσθαι. κύρι
θεὲ, τηρῆσον
30 Δημήτριν

—————————————— 50 mm

Fig. 22.4 The prophylactic inscription on pewter written to protect Demetrios from plague and recovered from the Thames foreshore at Vintry (drawn by Dr Roger Tomlin and reproduced with his kind permission).

no plague pits or mass burials.[71] This proves little, however, since cremation remained the more popular burial rite and we cannot count the ashes of the dead.

Plague and its consequences

The effects of plague may, however, be echoed in other ways. Evidence suggests that the army struggled to retain manpower in these critical years. Most notably there was a complete hiatus in the issuing of military diplomas to grant citizenship rights to auxiliary soldiers from AD 167/8 to AD 177, suggesting that soldiers were not being released from service.[72] The practice of marking lead ingots from the Mendips with imperial stamps also ended abruptly AD 164–9, whilst a private contractor replaced army tile production for the fortress at Chester in AD 167.[73] These disruptions to army managed supply might hint at labour shortages. Losses within the British garrison may also have contributed to Marcus Aurelius' decision to settle 5,500 Sarmatian cavalry in Britain in AD 175.[74]

A sense of alarm may have sufficed to evacuate the Cripplegate fort, given that this garrison may no longer have been needed for policing duties. Epidemics put people to flight, provoking labour shortages within military and urban communities. Daniel Defoe's account of the plague of 1665 highlights the disastrous consequences of a year when ships refused to dock at London's port, when tradesmen closed shop and dismissed staff, and when city construction abruptly halted.[75] A busy city cannot easily accommodate such change, and pre-Modern London was particularly vulnerable to food shortages as farms and docks fell idle. Famine follows disease. London's consequent depopulation may have spurred wider reforms to military and administrative supply, and some activities may have moved to York whose third-century ascendancy may have been laid on foundations established by London's decline.[76]

Major epidemics have a devastating effect on social fabric and belief systems, influencing burial practice, art and architecture.[77] London changed radically in the Antonine period: not only in the built environment but also in social practices embracing both burial and dress. Women ceased to use the types of brooches that previously fastened their garments, perhaps following the introduction of a kind of top-garment known as the Gallic coat, whilst sandals with elaborately hobnailed soles became fashionable amongst men.[78] These changing fashions may have been a consequence of both demographic change and social disruption. This was nowhere more evident than in the adoption of new burial practices and the spread of soteriological beliefs (below p. 322).

There are many other reasons why the arguments of late antiquity differed to those of the early empire, and there is a risk of over-stating the contribution that the Antonine plague made to changed mentalities. But the advent of plague must be taken seriously in seeking explanation for changes in London *c*. AD 165. Some of London's religious architecture may have been inspired by prophylactic measures of the sort encouraged by Marcus Aurelius and described on the magical charm found on the Thames foreshore. The departure of the garrison from the Cripplegate fort might have been decided mindful of the fate of Aquileia. Consequent reforms may have involved some reconfiguration of London's *annona*, shrinking the corn-supply that kept water-mills busy and reducing traffic into London's port. The circumstances of the plague years might account for both the chronology and trajectory of London's contraction after AD 165. This has enormously important implications for how we approach and understand other aspects of second-century change (Table 22.1).

Table 22.1 A suggested timeline of events affecting London in the period
AD 165–270

Date	Building activities in London	Salient events relevant to London
165–80	Housing densities reduced. Vacant plots converted to urban commons or left waste. Water-mills on Walbrook and Fleet cease to be maintained. Pottery kilns near London end production. Likely evacuation of Cripplegate fort.	Disruptions of Marcommanic wars and 'plague of Galen'.
185–6		Pertinax governor of Britain.
191–3	Quays either side of London Bridge extended using unsophisticated engineering.	Clodius Albinus, governor of Britain, becomes claimant for imperial throne
196		Albinus withdraws troops from Britain to support his bid to become emperor.
197	Work begins on more substantial extension to waterfront quays.	Albinus defeated by forces of Septimius Severus and Britain regained by Virius Lupus.
208		Severus, accompanied by Caracalla and Geta, leads campaigns in Caledonia.
211		Death of Severus in York. Peace settled by Caracalla who returns to Rome.
		Constitutio Antoniniana extends citizenship to most free inhabitants of empire
213–14		Britain divided into provinces of Britannia Inferior, ruled from York, and Britannia Superior, ruled from London. York granted colonial status.
209–24	Extensive waterfront redevelopment, adornment of temple precinct in south-west quarter, other monumental buildings erected along the waterside.	
190–230 (215/25)	Construction of the masonry town wall.	
228	Baths built at the suburban villa at Shadwell	
225–32	Busy house-building on both sides of the river.	
235–45	Samian imports continue to reach London's port. Temple of Mithras built beside the Walbrook.	

Continued

Table 22.1 Continued

Date	Building activities in London	Salient events relevant to London
241	Repairs to Guy's Channel on east side of Southwark	
243+	Amphitheatre restored. Road to Battle Bridge repaired.	
253	Repairs to roadside drains along the '*decumanus*'.	
250–60	London's port ceases to handle significant levels of imports amidst wider failure of long-distance supply. Contraction of extraction industries within region. Forum basilica burns down.	Wars and frontier raids. 'Plague of Cyprian'. Troops redeployed from Britain to continent. Last known references to *Classis Britannica*.
260–70	Waterfront quays cut back, perhaps to form defensive bank along waterfront.	Gallic Empire established by Postumus.

23

Severan revival (*c.* AD 180–225)

London in the late second century

We know little about London in the 170s and 180s. The diminished city built less and consumed less, and a consequent dearth of evidence leaves us hanging on a patchy historical record.[1] Dio described a military setback of the early 180s when Britain was invaded from the north, and subsequent operations may have inspired an issue of victory coins in AD 184 and justified Commodus' adoption of the title *Britannicus Maximus*. In following years the British legions were twice charged with backing usurpers, implying episodic unrest. Some of these actions may have echoed on London's streets, although not in ways we should expect to trace from archaeological evidence. There is passing intrigue, however, in the fact that some houses were destroyed by fire in the closing decades of the second century.[2] But we have no certain way of distinguishing between accident and arson, and these are more likely to have been local house-fires than anything of wider consequence.

One of these fires, identified in excavations at 7–11 Bishopsgate, destroyed a kitchen that contained a Samian table service assembled *c.* AD 175. This shows that London continued to receive fresh cargoes of Samian in the years after the Antonine contraction, as more amply illustrated by broken warehouse assemblages heaped on the Thames foreshore at Three Quays House and New Fresh Wharf.[3] At least one of these had been put together *c.* AD 170. This Samian trade filled ships crossing from Gaul, and hundreds of Samian tableware sets of the 180s have been dredged from the sea at Pudding Pan Rock, off Whitstable in Kent, probably from cargoes carried by vessels lost *en route* to London.[4] London evidently remained a staging point on an east-coast supply-route, as traced by distributions of north Gaulish fine wares extending from the continent to York. The prayers of shippers involved in such commerce are commemorated on altars dedicated at sanctuaries in the Scheldt estuary (above p. 268).[5] These record the concerns of a merchant community similar to that present in London earlier in the century, although there is little to suggest that the city remained a particularly important centre for their activities. London's quays were no longer dispatching bulk supplies onto the roads radiating from the city, and the town had no need of a workforce equal to that of its busier infancy. As a consequence there was no significant rebuilding on plots vacated earlier in the century.

Despite its diminished state, London's role in coastal trade gave it access to a variety of luxury imports. It remained Britain's principal ruling city and an important market where wealth and power concentrated. Martin Henig has suggested that the nearby villa at Lullingstone in Kent was the rural retreat of the provincial governor Publius Helvius Pertinax.[6] Pertinax governed Britain in AD 185–6, before rising briefly to the imperial throne following Commodus' assassination AD 193. Henig's argument draws on the evidence of two marble busts found in the villa's cellar thought to show Pertinax and his father. The villa's aristocratic credentials are further demonstrated by an exceptional cornelian intaglio of victory, once set in a gold signet ring held by a man of equestrian or higher rank. The bust identified as Pertinax had been decapitated, probably with an axe. This could have taken place during disturbances in Britain whilst he was governor, or in an act of *damnatio* following his deposition and murder in Rome. The exaggerated overthrow of the images of deposed emperors was a useful act of political theatre when regime-change precipitated a public realignment of loyalties.

The chaos that followed the murder of Pertinax carried another governor of Britain, Clodius Albinus, towards the imperial throne.[7] Albinus had probably taken office in Britain by AD 191, where he was one of three provincial governors' to be acclaimed emperor in AD 193. Albinus' claim to power derived from the legions under his command—in Caerleon, Chester, and York—but he is likely to have ruled from London. After Severus secured Rome, Albinus tactfully accepted the more junior position of Caesar before later reasserting his rival claim. In AD 196, he crossed to Gaul with his armies, only to be defeated by Severan forces near Lyon in February AD 197. According to the authors of the Historia Augusta, Albinus' head was cut off and paraded on a pike before being sent to Rome, whilst his decomposing body was mangled by dogs before being thrown into running water. The victorious Severus is reported to have acted to make sure that affairs in Britain were settled, before turning his attentions east.[8] A decade later, however, Severus came to Britain to complete its conquest, arriving here with new forces and accompanied by his sons Caracalla and Geta.[9] This ambitious military venture was cut short by his death in York in February 211, leaving Caracalla to agree a British peace and return to Rome with the imperial party.

These various events were of enormous consequence for London. For the first time since Hadrian's visit the city had hosted emperors and their retinues. The campaigns launched by Albinus and Severus, although headed in opposite directions, involved a massive traffic between Britain and the continent. These, it can be suggested, provided the likely spur for a new era of waterfront building along the Thames.

The late second-century waterfront

Excavations at various riverside sites along the north-bank of the river have exposed a complex series of late second- and early third-century waterfront revetments. Their presence shows that after many decades of neglect London's port was revived and enlarged, implying a significant increase in traffic (Fig. 23.1). Several discrete phases of improvement have been identified from this evidence, some of which are better understood than others. In the first of these, the substantial Hadrianic quays between the mouth of the Walbrook and London Bridge were replaced by slightly built revetments of superimposed horizontal boards retained by timber uprights. These advanced the embanked area some 4–6 metres onto the foreshore.[10] Frustratingly, none of the timbers preserved sapwood from which an exact felling date can be calculated, and some are likely to have been reused from nearby Antonine constructions. One of the timbers used at New Fresh Wharf was dated AD 188–223, and had probably been felled by

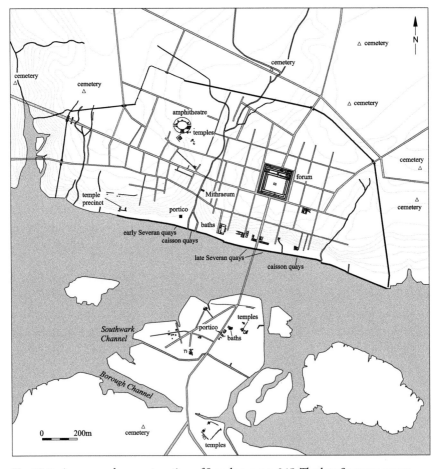

Fig. 23.1 A proposed reconstruction of London *c.* AD 245. The late Severan quays replaced more temporary constructions likely to date to the 190s. Drawn by Justin Russell.

AD 204, whilst late second-century pottery was associated with the revetments at Swan Lane.[11] Since these works are likely to have preceded the more heavily engineered programme of *c.* AD 197, discussed below, we can suggest that the slightly built waterfront was probably assembled after AD 188 but before AD 197. Other parts of London's infrastructure were repaired in these years, as indicated by a felling date of AD 191 on timbers used in a Walbrook channel at Angel Court.[12] These works signalled the end of a long interruption to investment in London's public infrastructure.

Why then, did the Hadrianic facilities need replacing at this particular point in time? And why were the new quays built with inferior engineering? It is entirely credible that the earlier port was no longer fit for purpose following its neglect. Tidal regression may also have handicapped ships coming upriver towards London, making it harder to moor alongside the quays and encouraging shippers to build further into the river (below p. 327). Despite this the late second-century Samian trade was accommodated in unimproved parts of the waterfront during the 170s and 180s, when boats could still sail upriver and beach on the foreshore. The decision to build new facilities is likely to have been provoked by a more pressing need than this routine trade. It is tempting, therefore, to suggest that it stemmed from Albinus' plans for a naval expedition to Gaul. This campaign almost certainly involved the largest movement of people and goods between Britain and the continent since the Claudian invasion. The need to assemble and dispatch campaign supplies at short notice would account for a hurried programme of engineering along this prime stretch of London's riverfront.[13]

Other phases of waterfront improvement were soon to follow. The north bank was eventually transformed by a series of more substantial quays, stretching from Queenhithe in the west to Tower Hill in the east.[14] An early component was built at Queenhithe, upstream from the mouth of the Walbrook. Large squared oak timbers were laid in horizontal courses to form an embankment at the westernmost end of the port, using timbers felled in AD 197.[15] This is a date of enormous resonance, being the year of Albinus' defeat in Gaul. These quays must have been built following the arrival of Severus' newly appointed provincial governor, Virius Lupus, in the aftermath of the battle of Lyon.[16] Albinus had withdrawn all campaign-ready troops from Britain, leaving Lupus under considerable pressure to establish Severan authority in this formerly restless province. The location of the Queenhithe quays further upriver than earlier facilities, suggests a renewed interest in using London as a springboard for moving goods inland along Watling Street. Incoming traffic is likely to have included troops and materials aimed at reinforcing the forts at Chester and Caerleon, perhaps directed through London since overland routes were safer outside the normal sailing season. Traffic through the Queenhithe quays may have hastened a revival of the surrounding district. Timber and clay-walled workshops built over the disused bathhouse at Huggin Hill in the third century housed glass and iron working.[17] The site of the baths was now given over to craft production that may have helped equip troops in transit.

Carefully constructed quays of a different type were built around the mouth of the Walbrook and Lorteburn near the Tower of London. At both locations, new waterfronts were built of large timber baulks laid in tiers to form two parallels rows of boxes. This form of caisson construction may have been preferred where larger areas of low-lying ground needed reclamation. It is not possible to date these quays closely, although it seems likely that they belonged to a slightly later phase of improvement than the works at Queenhithe. The double-box quay along the east side of the Walbrook was investigated at Cannon Street Station, where it reclaimed some 25 metres of the former river channel at the foot of the 'governor's palace' complex. It incorporated reused timbers felled AD 169–89 and another felled no earlier than AD 185.[18] Further box constructions at Dowgate Hill House may have lain between two separate channels forming the mouth of the Walbrook.[19] The quays built near the mouth of the Lorteburn, investigated at Custom House and Three Quays House, were formed from 1.5 metres square openwork boxes that must have supported plank decking.[20] The quay at Custom House was pottery dated to the end of the second century, predating the more substantial extension of c. AD 209–24 described below. The latest structure at Three Quays house included timbers felled AD 197–224 and incorporated early third-century East Gaulish Samian. These late second- and early third-century building works combined to considerably enlarge the working port. New quays were inserted in previously under-developed areas at the port's western and eastern ends, and in deep-water areas at the confluence of the Walbrook and Lorteburn, significantly increasing London's ability to handle large volumes of shipping.

The later Severan waterfront

Initially the central section, either side of London Bridge, was left in a more primitive state. Here the late second-century post-and-plank revetments, suggested to have been installed during Albinus' government of the city, were retained for several years. They were eventually replaced by the construction of a more uniform and durable embankment in the early third century. This consisted of a new terrace of massive oak beams trimmed to standard sizes, set in five superimposed tiers, and held in place by a framework of tie-back braces. This was set 4.4–5.2 metres in front of the earlier post-and-plank revetments either side of London Bridge.[21] Underpinning piles were driven into the foreshore and mortised to the underside of the base timber in an innovation that characterized this particular construction programme. Clay and gravel dumps infilled areas behind the riverfront, although some may have been left as openwork structures. Similar construction techniques were used to infill a gap in the waterfront between the Queenhithe quays built *c.* AD 197 and the mouth of the Walbrook, and to extend the waterfront eastwards towards the Tower.[22] These quays were constructed in the first quarter of the third century, with timbers from New Fresh Wharf and Billingsgate Lorry Park suggesting a date within the period AD 209–24.[23] Although the engineers made more economical use of timber than in first and early second-century building, the extended length of the waterfront meant that unprecedented quantities of timber were required, necessarily resulting in extensive woodland clearances around London. Damian Goodburn has noted that the bulk of trees felled for a massive construction project in AD 293/294 (below p. 350) had started growth between AD 217 and AD 234, concluding that the parent trees had grown in woodlands cleared by heavy felling for a large London project at this time.[24] Although this is a somewhat indirect source of evidence, it seems credible that the busiest period of port rebuilding took place in the later Severan period starting *c.* AD 215/220.

The waterfront expansion created new land in front of the old quays, allowing the authorities to regain control of access to the river and over goods passing through the city. Early third-century timber-framed buildings behind the quays at Seal House and Swan Lane added warehousing capacity. An important group of lead seals was found on the Thames foreshore in front of the quays at Billingsgate.[25] These included imperial seals of Septimius Severus with Caracalla and Geta, a provincial seal of *Britannia Superior*, one of the Arles customs station and a wine importer's private seal. These seals had marked cargoes exempt from port duties and their distribution follows official supply. London accounts for 14 of the 32 imperial seals found in Britain, and Billingsgate was evidently an important port of entry for official cargoes. The facilities here were also equipped to receive unusually heavy goods, using lifting equipment set over wooden crane bases.[26] These would have helped in the landing of massive wooden barrels used to import wine from the Rhineland, which were generally too heavy for normal handling. Parts of these barrels were reused to line wells, and one found at Drapers' Gardens had batch and volume marks which show that it had contained 935.45 litres of wine (105 *modii* and 11.5 *sextarri*) from a place called *Capriacum*.[27]

A dozen barrels this size would have filled the hold of a river barge such as that found in the mouth of the Fleet during building works near Blackfriars in 1962.[28] Peter Marsden's studies show this to have been a flat-bottomed vessel designed to sit on the river bed at low water. It was about 18.5 metres long, with a beam of about 6.12 metres and a gunwale height amidships of about 2.86 metres. It had been made from sawn oak planks nailed to a frame, caulked with hazel shavings and pine resin, following Romano-Gallic ship-building traditions and probably using trees grown in south-east England. The deck presented a large hatchway for goods to be lowered into the hold, with the mast step set forward in the hull and rudders and living quarters at the stern. A worn coin of Domitian showing the goddess Fortuna holding a ships rudder was set into a recess at the base of the mast-step socket for luck. The ship's timbers were felled AD 130–75, probably before AD 156, whilst the absence of repair suggests that the boat was unlikely to have been much over 20 years old when it sank. It was well suited for river work, but its woodwork was riddled by the saltwater teredo worm showing that it travelled the estuary to the coast. Since the wreck was found upstream of London Bridge this suggests the presence of a drawbridge to let it pass. The barge contained 26 tonnes of Kentish ragstone within its half-filled hold, and had perhaps sunk in a collision whilst supplying stone for an Antonine or Severan building project.

Parts of another boat were found at Guy's Hospital in 1958 and re-examined in 2010.[29] This broad barge-like vessel was at least 16 metres long, clinker-built with oak planks nailed to a skeleton formed of keel and frame with the joints also caulked with hazel shavings and pine resin. It had been designed to rest on the foreshore at low tide, with a low freeboard that would have left it totally unsafe for the sea. The hulk had been abandoned in a channel of the Thames where it was preserved by an accumulation of river mud containing pottery dated c. AD 190–225, suggesting that it also served London's port in the late second or early third century.

Riverside buildings

Several buildings were built or restored behind the working waterfront, combining to present an impressive panorama to those approaching by river. It is not clear whether this was intentionally achieved, or the incidental product of different projects attracted to the waterside. It is notable, however, that the new buildings hugged the river. The westernmost constructions were perhaps the most important. The riverfront terrace here may have housed a temple precinct here from c. AD 165 (above p. 265), which was extensively rebuilt in the early third century.[30] Alterations included the addition of new colonnades enclosing one or more courtyards, and a river-facing apsidal *exedra* giving architectural emphasis to the river vista, using timber piles felled AD 205–32 (Fig. 23.2).

Sculptured blocks reused nearby in the later riverside wall at Baynard's Castle may have derived from monuments within this precinct.[31] Some limestone carvings had formed a small free-standing arch about 7.5 metres wide, 1.15 metres deep and little over 8 metres high (Fig. 23.3). This was too narrow to have stood over a road and probably marked a ceremonial gateway. The sides of the arch were flanked by standing divinities: parts of Minerva and Hercules are recognizable. A frieze above the arch included busts of gods, perhaps including Saturn, Sol, Luna, Mars, Mercury, Jupiter, and Venus, representing the days of the week. The spandrels contained sea monsters and busts of the seasons. These classical features find parallel in the design of the temple façade at Bath, with

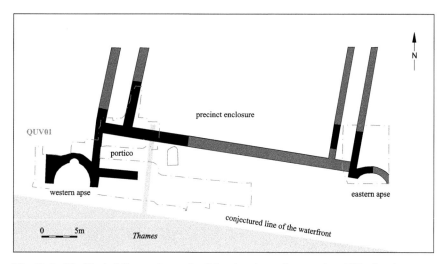

Fig. 23.2 The 'Period I' complex at the Salvation Army International Headquarters, a possible sacred precinct of the early third century (QUV01: after Bradley and Butler 2008). Drawn by Justin Russell.

stylistic links to works in Gaul and the Rhineland. Tom Blagg's careful study concluded that the ornament was no earlier than late Antonine and was probably Severan. This is consistent with dating evidence obtained from the nearby foundations. Other carved stones derived from a decorative screen, 6.2 metres long, 1.4 metres high and c. 0.55 metres wide, decorated back and front with three pairs of niches containing standing figures of gods. Vulcan and Minerva, Diana and possibly Mercury, and Mars can be identified, with features that suggest the presence of Hercules, Summer or Autumn, and Luna. It is not clear if this screen, dated to the second or third centuries, stood in the open or within a building. The figure of Minerva on both arch and screen had her spear turned down which is best read as symbolizing a province at peace. This would be consistent with the situation that applied in Britain after Caracalla's peace of AD 211, but anomalous at dates earlier in the century.[32]

Two inscribed altars of Lincolnshire limestone were also recovered from the riverside wall (Fig. 23.4).[33] According to Mark Hassall's translation one read 'Aquilinus the emperor's freedman and Mercator and Audax and Graecus restored this temple which had fallen down through old age for (or to) Jupiter best and greatest', although the dedication to Jupiter is not certain. The other announced that 'In honour of the divine house, Marcus Martiannius Pulcher, deputy imperial propraetorian legate of two emperors ordered the temple of Isis…which had fallen down through old age, to be restored'. These inscriptions commemorated the rebuilding of temples likely to have been located within the religious precinct. The governor Pulcher is otherwise unknown, but the reference to two emperors

Fig. 23.3 A ceremonial arch reconstructed from sculptures found reused in the riverside wall at Baynard's Castle and probably deriving from the religious precinct in the south-west quarter (BC74: drawn by Sheila Gibson and reproduced kind permission of Museum of London Archaeology). The figure shown to the left of the arch is Minerva, shown with her spear turned down.

suggests that he held office at some point between AD 221 and AD 259, since the style of lettering seems late for the joint-rule of Caracalla and Geta. Hassall suggests that these altars were likely to have been erected under Trebonianus Gallus and Valerian in AD 251–3 or Valerian and Gallienus in 253–9. An earlier date is, however, possible and Anthony Birley considers the joint reign of Elagabalus and

Fig. 23.4 Altar to the restoration of a temple of Isis that had fallen down made by the governor Marcus Pulcher (MMARTIANVSPULCHER) (BC74: drawn by Sue Hurman and reproduced by kind permission of Museum of London Archaeology).

Severus Alexander in AD 221–2 a possibility along with other episodes of joint-rule. The dedications show that the temple restorations relied on the patronage of government officials. Another sculpture reused within the later riverside wall showed four seated mother goddesses (*matronae*), of a type who featured prominently in the cults of Cisalpine Gaul and the Rhineland. Their worship in Britain reflects on the imported origins of both dedicators and deities.[34]

A different type of building, also dated to the third century from associated pottery, was set on a terrace some 40 metres to the west of the Walbrook's confluence with the Thames.[35] A large terrace wall, was fronted by brick piers which responded with a second line of piers to form an aisled building. The reuse of tiles stamped by the procuratorial office hints at a public involvement in its construction. The presence of tesserae, painted wall-plaster and hypocaust box-flue tile amongst demolition debris implies the presence of high-status reception facilities within the building. One possibility is that this was a portico or guild building associated with the nearby quays.

On the other side of the Walbrook the monumental building complex known as the 'Governor's palace' was extended and rebuilt in the late second or early third centuries, perhaps following the construction of the new quays alongside the Walbrook. It was perhaps at this time that the pool was filled-in, and the large 'hall' on its north side replaced by smaller rooms with hypocaust floors.[36] This phase of rebuilding might provide a context for many of the hypocausts and mosaics found nearby. If this had been a bathhouse, as suggested above p. 138, it may have been largely rebuilt during London's Severan renewal.

Another monumental building was set over a terrace further downstream of London Bridge. Excavations in Botolph Lane found a splendidly preserved stretch of a roofed masonry culvert, large enough for a person to crawl along, which drained towards the Thames.[37] A silt trap beneath a manhole shaft was made from timbers felled AD 176–221. The culvert was an integral part of a monumental structure overlooking the river. Its masonry construction testifies to the importance of running water to the architecture, and associated pottery includes types of vessels commonly associated with ritual use. The new structure may have incorporated running water, perhaps forming a nymphaeum: a monument type favoured in Severan patronage.[38]

A short distance further downstream Peter Marsden recorded a small east-facing rectangular masonry structure behind the waterfront at St Dunstan's Hill.[39] This was possibly a small shrine. We don't know when it was built, but it might belong to early third-century restoration. An inscribed slate panel found in Walbrook Street in 1954 came from another monument of this period, although the incomplete text leaves its exact date and significance uncertain. It commemorated a victory, and may have been set up by the Province of Britain. It has sometimes been reconstructed as a reference to Trajan's Dacian victory, although the style of the lettering makes a later date more probable. Anthony Birley suggests a reconstruction that would allow it to refer to Caracalla's German victory of AD 213.[40]

Two marble statue heads found in London appear to portray members of the Severan ruling family, and perhaps graced the public architecture of the revived city.[41] The head of a young boy carved in Italian marble, found at an unknown location in London, has provisionally been identified as a portrayal of the young Caracalla. Another, found in the Thames, probably showed his younger brother and co-emperor Geta after AD 205 when he was first elected consul. This image had been mutilated in antiquity, involving the 'amputation' of the shoulders and sides of the chest with a chisel and a horizontal decapitation gash at the back of the neck. This is the sort of thing that might have happened following his *damnatio memoriae* after murder by Caracalla in December AD 211.

The town wall

London's town wall was the grandest and most enduring of its Roman monuments, following an ambitious urban circuit that may have been first defined in the early Antonine period. It stretched over 3 kilometres from Blackfriars in the west to the Tower in the east, enclosing an area of 133 hectares, but leaving the riverfront open.[42] This made for a walled city larger than any other in Roman Britain, exceeded by only four in Gaul. The wall stood over trench-built foundations of puddled clay and flint capped by a layer of ragstone rubble (Fig. 23.5). The ground level on the outer face was marked by a plinth of large chamfered red sandstone blocks from Kent, with a triple facing-course of tiles at the corresponding level inside. Above this, squared blocks of ragstone were laid in regular courses to form the sides of a concrete wall some 2.0–2.7 metres wide. A double or triple course of bonding tiles was laid through the wall at intervals of five or six courses, at which points there was usually an offset on the inner face to reduce the thickness of the wall. The greatest height of surviving wall is 4.4 metres but it is estimated to have originally stood 6.4 metres high. The tile course at this point is likely to have supported a parapet protected by a crenelated breastwork formed from round-topped coping stones. A V-shaped ditch, 3–5 metres wide and up to 2 metres deep, was dug 2.7–5.2 metres outside the wall. The earth from this was piled in a bank against the inner face of the wall to make a 2-metre-high rampart. A gravel road surface found beneath this rampart at both America Square and Cooper's Row preserved cart ruts from the construction traffic that had carried building materials from ships docked along the waterfront.[43]

Culverts were placed where the wall crossed streams and a channel of the Walbrook was carried through a 1-metre-wide arched opening at Blomfield Street protected by a rail of five iron bars.[44] The north-west angle of the town wall reused the corner of the Cripplegate fort, whose walls were thickened to bring them into line with those of the city. Rectangular chambers, no more than 1.83 metres wide and 3.35 metres long, built onto the inside of the wall probably housed timber stairs giving access to the parapet walk.[45] There were four principal gates into town probably with double portals: the Colchester road passed through Aldgate; Ermine Street through Bishopsgate; Watling Street through Newgate; and the road to Westminster through Ludgate.[46] Some may have been built as free-standing structures before the construction of the wall (above p. 273). Additionally,

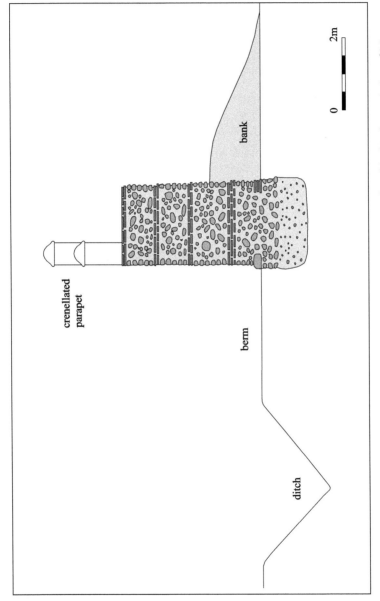

Fig. 23.5 Profile of the masonry town wall (adapted from Maloney 1983, reproduced by kind permission of Museum of London Archaeology).

the northern and western gateways of the Cripplegate fort remained in use, and posterns are conjectured to have existed at Aldersgate, Aldermanbury, Moorgate, and Tower Hill, combining to provide access at intervals of 250–350 metres.[47] A tile-coursed ragstone structure north of Ludgate Circus formed a contemporary masonry bridge across the Fleet.[48]

Material associated with the construction of the town wall is consistently dated AD 190–230.[49] Substantial pottery assemblages of this date came from the ramparts and construction road at America Square.[50] A worn coin of AD 183–4 found beneath the thickening of the external wall around the Cripplegate fort at Falcon Square could not have been lost much before *c.* AD 190, and provides a *terminus post quem* for the wall's construction.[51] The wall may, however, have been built some decades later. This can be inferred from what we know of the chronology of waterfront development. Tens of hundreds of boatloads of building material needed landing on the riverbank for loading onto the carts that trundled their way along haulage roads to supply the masons. It is likely that the Roman engineers followed the sensible expedient of improving the riverfront handling facilities before building the wall. The quays at the easternmost end of London's port were best placed to serve the haulage road found at America Square, and formed a later addition to the early Severan waterfront. Elsewhere these later Severan waterfront developments are dated AD 209–24 (above p. 300). The evidence is indirect, but weighs in favour of a construction date in the first quarter of the third century.

Debris from the reproduction of Roman coins found in a wall-turret at Warwick Square confirms that the wall was in place by *c.* AD 225/230 (p. 331).[52] This manufacture involved taking impressions from official issues onto clay moulds that were broken up when the replicas were extracted. The coins that were copied had been minted AD 201–15 and the absence of later types suggests that the 'forger' was at work in the following decade. An early third-century date would also account for finds recovered from the associated ditch at London Wall.[53] These included several unbroken funerary pots made of black burnished ware fabrics dated AD 160–230 which held offerings of chickens and coins. The archaeological evidence combines to indicate that London's town wall was built after AD 190 but was standing by AD 225/230. It is also more likely to have been built after the waterfront improvements of AD 209 onwards than before.

It is estimated that somewhere between 82,000 and 86,000 tonnes of material were used to build the wall, chiefly ragstone quarried from near the River Medway in Kent.[54] If the Blackfriars barge was representative of the river vessels of the time, then the wall required 1720 barge-loads of 50 tonnes apiece. Each delivery required a week-long round-trip, involving two days for each leg of the river journey and one day each loading and loading. A fleet of a dozen barges would have taken the best part of 3 years to deliver the stone, although a more compressed timetable involving a larger fleet is equally likely. Most bricks used within the wall were made in local fabrics, probably from kilns set up for the purpose. The hemispherical coping stones used in the wall crenellations were made from limestone that matches sources near Boulogne, perhaps supplied by the *Classis Britannica* from its base there. An exercise of this scale required imperial sanction, and might have been managed by the *procurator* drawing on vessels within the command of the *Classis*. Even if the work was undertaken by civic authorities employing private shippers and local resources, it is difficult to imagine that a commitment of this scale would have been permitted whilst Severus was campaigning in Caledonia AD 208–11. Severus' need to retain capacity for the supply and transport of his forces must surely have taken priority.[55]

We can therefore conclude that London's wall was probably built after Caracalla's peace of AD 211 had ended forward operations. Surplus capacity could then have been redeployed into peacetime engineering projects. Severus and Caracalla were committed to a high level of public expenditure to secure dynastic legitimacy and new masonry walls were built around the main legionary fortresses and forts and supply-bases on the northern frontier at around this date.[56] The design of London's defensive circuit drew inspiration from this military architecture, notably in the use of the distinctive chamfered plinth at the base of the wall.[57]

London renewed

London's town wall wasn't built in hurried response to political crisis, but confidently enclosed a larger area than necessary and left the riverfront undefended. It was a carefully planned monument that secured the city's revival, making an assertive statement that anticipated the late antique conceptualization of the *urbs* as a place encircled by walls. In a sense, the town wall took on the argument of the Hadrianic fort built a century previously, but amplified and extended to embrace the city entire. From this point forward there was a military aspect to the way in which London presented itself to the world.

For all of its ideological force, the wall wasn't only an argument of stone but a device that framed patterns of life. It channelled travellers to supervised entry-places, policing those drawn to the city. Rome's Aurelianic wall, built later in the century, were allegedly used to exclude people wearing barbarian dress and long hair, and we can similarly imagine London's privileged community seeking to separate themselves from outside folk.[58] Rome's walls also facilitated controls over goods in transit, enabling tax collection at city gates.[59] These were an important source of urban income, and the lead seals found at Billingsgate testify to their importance. These tolls and taxes would have offset the costs of policing the walls and gates.

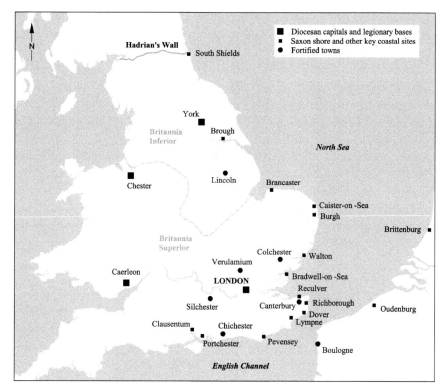

Fig. 23.6 Britain in the early third century showing the likely extent of the separate administrations formed for *Britannia Superior* and *Britannia Inferior* (governed from London and York respectively), along with the emerging network of defended coastal sites some of which later formed the command of the Saxon shore and some other late Roman walled towns. Drawn by Fiona Griffin.

Town walls marked privileged status, and their building required the emperor's consent.[60] Whilst there is no certain relationship between political status and the right to build a city wall, walled towns were more likely to have been *coloniae*. It is possible that London now gained this honorific status as part of a wider package of reforms made when Britain was divided into two separate administrations (Fig. 23.6). According to Herodian, the province was split into *Britannia Inferior* and *Britannia Superior* by Severus *c.* AD 197/198.[61] Since inscriptions show that Britain was undivided in AD 212, this reform was probably not implemented until after Severus' death, probably under Caracalla *c.* AD 213/214.[62] *Britannia Inferior* came to be ruled from York, which was described as a *municipium* in events of AD 211 but as a *colonia* in an inscription of AD 237.[63] The implication is that York was promoted at around the time of the reform of the provincial administration. A similar arrangement may have applied to London on the creation of *Britannia Superior*. The presence of the tombstone to the *speculator* Celsus (p. 220), dated to this period because his affiliation to *Legio II Augusta* included the title *Antoniana* which was not bestowed before AD 213, has been seen as proof that London was recognized as a capital city of equal prominence. London's promotion would have been most easily affected after AD 212, when Caracalla extended Roman citizenship to free inhabitants of the empire in his *Constitutio Antoniniana*.[64] This served to blur distinctions between resident *incolae*, who were citizens of other cities, and those whose status relied on their ownership of estates in and around *Londinium*.

The building of the city walls and adornment of waterfront temples and public buildings revitalized London at around the time of these reforms. We do not know how much of this architecture was the work of a newly empowered civic administration, borrowing ideas from military engineers, and how much the product of a direct imperial patronage, but the scale of operations hints at the involvement of military engineers and transports. Severus' confiscation of estates from Albinus and his supporters may have won funds that could be lent to such building projects, and may have secured access to grain, oil and wine that could then form part of the *annona*.[65] Severus was supposedly the first emperor to establish regular distributions of oil at Rome, increasing state control over processes that previously relied on market arrangements. Similarly conceived policies may have inspired London's restoration, in particular at the port. This investment in improving the flow of goods, whether through imperial estates or other private domains, may have prompted changes within London's hinterland, accounting for sporadic evidence of early third-century building works within the estuary and Weald.[66]

24

Britannia Superior (c. AD 225–50)

Shadwell and suburban villas

London's revival continued in the decades following the building of the city wall. One of the most significant construction projects of this time took place 1.2 kilometres east of town, at Shadwell. This had been the site of an important Flavian settlement, perhaps a villa, that was extensively redeveloped in the early third century when a substantial bathhouse was built.[1] This was a larger and more formal structure than one might expect to find on a villa estate, containing at least eleven rooms, six heated, laid out over two suites reached independently from a shared central entrance (Fig. 24.1). Parts of the baths were built *c.* AD 228, which is the felling date of timbers used in the foundations of a water tank associated with the original hydraulic engineering. A monumental tower was built nearby, perhaps a little later in the century.[2] This 8-metre-square structure was built with chalk and mortar walls faced by knapped flint set over 2-metre-wide foundations. It has sometimes been described as a watchtower but the suggestion that it was a mausoleum seems more convincing. It later became the focus of a small burial ground whilst other high-status burials have been found nearby, including a lead coffin from the churchyard of St Paul's, Shadwell.[3]

Joanna Bird's study shows that a large shipment of East Gaulish Samian reached Shadwell in the middle of the third century.[4] This unusual import of high-status tableware, contemporary with the building of a new bathhouse, implies the arrival of new owners with imported tastes in bathing and dining.[5] Shadwell was perhaps rebuilt to house an important government official and his retinue, who moved here shortly after the building of the city wall. A suburban villa outside the jurisdiction of the civic authorities might have afforded greater political autonomy than obtained within the newly walled city. Shadwell's riverside location made it particularly suitable for an official involved in supply and communication, such as the imperial procurator or a commander of the fleet. The site may have been the product of a coordinated programme of investment along the coastal supply route. Stone built forts were established along the coast at Brancaster, Caister-on-Sea, and Reculver in the early third century, with an inscription at Reculver suggesting that the fort here was completed by AD 230.[6] These sites later formed part of the military command of the Saxon Shore (below p. 341). The reorganization of the coastal supply and communications network may have impacted on the *Classis Britannica*.[7] The important *Classis* fort at Dover was demolished

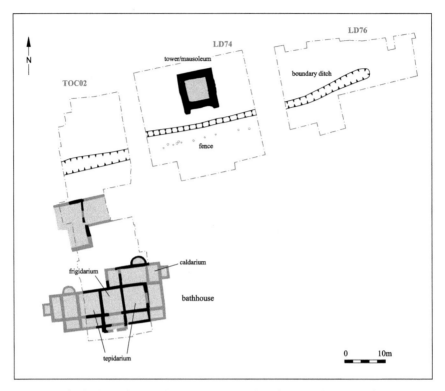

Fig. 24.1 The baths and tower (probably a mausoleum) overlooking the Thames at Shadwell (LD74 and TOC02: after Douglas *et al.* 2011 and Johnson 1975). Drawn by Fiona Griffin.

c. AD 215, when its garrison must have been redeployed. The site at Shadwell is unlikely, however, to have housed a garrison since few items of military equipment were lost here.

Another unusual pottery assemblage dominated by East Gaulish Samian, dated *c.* AD 235–45, was found beneath waterfront quays at New Fresh Wharf.[8] Vivien Swan has drawn attention to the presence of North Gaulish grey wares amongst this material. She suggests that this pottery was also linked to the activities of the *Classis*. Although rarely found at inland sites it is present at sites along the east coast, including Shadwell, and at Wealden iron-working sites in Sussex where tiles stamped by the *Classis* were used in building operations. Most of these imported wares could have been shipped to Britain through the Rhine mouth, serving cooking practices popular within the auxiliary forces that formed the fleet command. The implication is that both London and Shadwell, although not significant as military garrisons, were closely integrated with coastal supply routes involving the *Classis*.

Shadwell wasn't the only suburban settlement to benefit from new investment. A mosaic found during the construction of Armoury House at the Artillery Ground suggests the presence of an early third-century villa some 0.5 kilometres north of the city walls.[9] There is a suspicion that another stood near Spitalfields Market, on the other side of Ermine Street, since quantities of painted wall plaster, pottery and glass crucible waste were associated with a late Roman ditched enclosure at Spital Square.[10] Another high-status building stood west of the river Fleet at St Andrew Holborn, just south of Watling Street. This is identified from the antiquarian record of a mosaic pavement, supplemented by evidence of early third-century pottery found in the church crypt in 2001.[11] Slightly further afield, the site at St Martin-in-the-Fields by Trafalgar Square grew in the early or mid-third century, where finds assemblages included East Gaulish Samian and late Cologne colour-coated beakers.[12] Another villa may have been built overlooking river Lea, east of London, where the presence of a high-status settlement is indicated by a late second- or third-century sarcophagus from Lower Clapton in Hackney.[13] The decorative vertical fluting indicates that this sarcophagus, which also carried a dedication to Atia by Gaius Etruscus, was designed for placement against a wall or within a niche in a mausoleum.

Renewed domestic luxury

Several Antonine town houses were refurbished in the early third century.[14] Much of this building-work is dated around AD 230, perhaps stimulated by the presence of the Severan imperial bureaucracy. These houses were built in a conservative style that owed much to the traditions of the previous century (Fig. 24.2). They were, if anything, slightly grander in scale, drawing on a range of imported building materials. Some third-century building projects used new sources of roofing tile, arriving from kilns in Surrey and on the south coast.[15] They also provided work for a school of mosaicists who favoured designs with elaborate plant forms, particularly a stylized acanthus, that David Johnson identified as a Londonian Acanthus *officina*.[16] These craftsmen didn't work much, if at all, elsewhere in southern England and their pavements may all date within a fairly brief period. One was laid as part of the original decorative scheme of a reception room added to the back of a strip building at One Poultry using piles felled AD 223–36.[17] Large buildings containing mosaics of this type have been found at Lothbury, Bucklersbury, beneath the Bank of England and at the corner of Leadenhall Street and Lime Street.[18] The third-century mosaic found here in 1803 is one of the finest from Roman Britain. The central roundel, now displayed at the British Museum, shows the divine Bacchus astride a tigress (Fig. 24.3). David Neal and Stephen Cosh have noted that the extensive use of glass tesserae

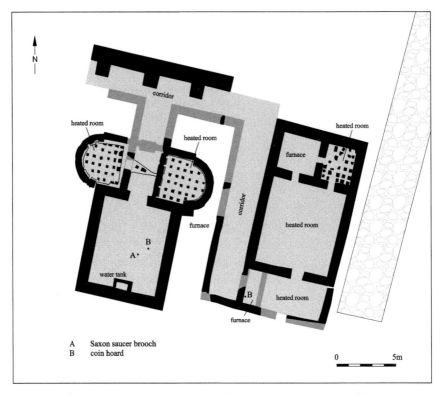

Fig. 24.2 The eastern and northern wings of a third-century house and baths at Billingsgate (GM111, BBH87: after Rowsome 1996 and Marsden 1980). Drawn by Justin Russell.

is unparalleled in Britain a feature of the best mosaics in Trier and Cologne, where the mosaicist may have learnt his skills.

The distribution of these handsome town houses followed a similar pattern to that established in the second century. There was a distinct eastern bias, with wealthy houses clustered along the Walbrook valley and flanking the road through Bishopsgate. Others occupied slopes overlooking the Thames downriver of London Bridge. The best known is the Billingsgate house, the remains of which can be seen beneath offices in Lower Thames Street.[19] This was set over a terrace overlooking the river, probably early in the third century. It was arranged over two or three wings, with rooms heated by hypocaust floors, linked by a flanking portico with a tessellated floor. A small bathhouse on the southern side of the property was entered from a vestibule, either side of which were apsidal-ended heated rooms. Beyond the vestibule was a square *frigidarium* with a red tessellated floor and a small stone-lined water-tank against one wall. Although some districts were dominated by larger establishments, the town also contained several more

Fig. 24.3 Reconstruction of the third-century mosaic pavement found in 1803 at the East India Company site in Leadenhall Street showing Bacchus reclining on a tigress (drawn by J. Basire and reproduced from a digital copy held by the Wellcome collection under a Creative Commons licence).

modest timber buildings, especially in peripheral areas, including those dedicated to industrial production in the upper Walbrook valley.[20]

Southwark also saw renewal towards the middle of the third century. Building improvements have been identified within at least eight domestic compounds, as well as the site of the supposed *mansio* and palatial complex at Winchester Palace.[21] Although some of this building work is only loosely dated, precise dating was obtained from a well at London Bridge Hospital that used timbers felled AD 231, and a waterfront revetment on the western edge of Horsleydown eyot used timber felled AD 232.[22]

Mithras and other cults

London's most famous archaeological discovery, the temple of Mithras, was built in this time of relative prosperity. This small temple, 17.83 metres long by 7.84 metres wide with walls of mortared ragstone and tile quoins, was placed on a terrace on the east bank of the Walbrook (Fig. 24.4).[23] John Shepherd's careful analysis of the pottery indicates that it was erected in the late 230s or 240s.[24] It was entered from the east, where rooms may have included an area for ritual ablutions and a narthex. A double door opened onto a flight of three steps. These were worn from prolonged use and descended into a lowered nave floored with planks laid over joists. Raised aisles either side were defined by low sleeper walls that supported seven pairs of red-painted limestone columns, perhaps symbolizing the seven grades of cult indoctrination. The cavern-like Mithraeum would have been illuminated by lamps and torches.[25] The focal point of the building was a semi-circular apse with painted walls, raised two steps above the nave floor, where the altar was placed. A square timber-lined well in the south-west corner may have provided water for ceremonial use. The design of the building and sculptures discovered nearby show that it was used for the worship of the Persian god Mithras.

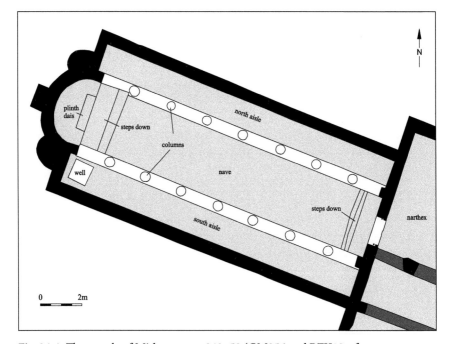

Fig. 24.4 The temple of Mithras *c.* AD 240–50 (GM256 and BZY10: after Shepherd 1998 and MoLA 2017). Drawn by Justin Russell.

A rectangular marble panel with a relief carving of Mithras slaying the sacred bull may have stood on a dais behind the altars. The bull-slaying scene forms a central medallion within this panel, where Mithras is flanked by two small figures carrying torches symbolizing life and death known as Cautes and Cautopates. A dog, snake, and crab rise to the sacrifice. The signs of the zodiac are circled around the scene, with Sol driving his four-horse chariot in one corner, and Luna driving down with her oxen in the other. The lower corners are filled by busts probably representing winds. This was a cosmic map placing Mithras, associated with *Sol Invictus* and representing the triumph over darkness, at its centre. The stone carried a dedication that translates as: 'Ulpius Silvanus, veteran of the second Augustan Legion, paid his vow: he was initiated (or enrolled) at Orange'.[26] Silvanus was perhaps the *Pater*, or father, of the London temple at the most senior of the seven grades of initiate.

The stone head of Mithras found in 1954 probably completed a plaster statue of the bull-slaying group. It portrayed a beardless youth with curly hair and a characteristic Phrygian cap, and Martin Henig suggests that it was most likely sculpted *c.* AD 180–220. A monumental hand, clutching the hilt of a knife-handle, was perhaps attached to the wall. Several other religious sculptures were buried in and around the temple.[27] Some pieces in Carrara marble were probably manufactured in Italy during the second century, making them at least 50 years old when the temple was built and they were presumably moved here from an earlier shrine. These included a small statue of Mercury, heads of Minerva and Serapis and statuette of a bearded water deity that possibly personified London or the Thames.[28] Their quality illustrates the exceptional wealth of the religious community. Mithraic rituals involved imprisonment and release, baptism and meals with offerings, and the animal bones found on the site included several chickens consumed at gatherings.

Other finds from London witness the presence of a wide range of mystery and salvation cults.[29] One of the most striking finds is an impressive decorated bronze clamp decorated with small busts of the goddess Cybele and her consort Attis, found in the Thames by London Bridge in 1840. It is thought to have been used in the ritual castrations of the eunuch priests of this eastern cult.[30] Many other small items recovered from London—including stone sculptures, decorative hairpins, bronze and terracotta figurines—show familiarity with this and other exotic systems of belief. In addition to the mysteries associated with Isis, Cybele and Mithras objects found in London suggest familiarity with the cult practices of Hercules, Bacchus, Orpheus and the sky-father god Sabazius.[31] Bacchus was the most widely celebrated of these figures and the symbols and images of his cult permeated the decorative arts.[32] A wide repertoire of Bacchic motifs was employed in mosaic pavements and are likely to have been equally prevalent amongst wall-paintings.[33] These are normally too poorly preserved to allow their reconstruction, but Bacchus' garlanded head and the tip of his knobbed stick, or *thyrsus*, can be identified on a collapsed wall-painting found at 30 Gresham Street in 2002.[34] Amongst numerous portable items found in recent excavations, attention can be drawn to a figurine of the god with a basket of grapes and a mount in the shape of a panther found at Poultry and a Bacchic *balsamarium* from Bishopsgate. As we have already noted (p. 214) a London workshop was responsible for the manufacture of a series of spoons that carried images of canthari, peacocks, and parrots, suitable for use in the Bacchic symposion.[35]

These initiatory cults sought to make sense of the universe, addressing themes of life and death and the immortality of the soul. They did so by combining ideas from eastern cults and astrologers with those of Greek philosophy, gleaning allegorical significance from mythology and cosmological phenomena. As a consequence, most forms of representation carried layered meanings, and understandings could migrate between belief systems that were both holistic and particular. A recurrent theme involved finding unity with the divine to save the individual spark of life from extinction. Cults were concerned with the heavenly soul, and the journey to salvation that could be achieved through correct philosophical understanding and religious observance. The growth in their popularity followed what Edward Bispham has described as a religious 'turn' in philosophical schools such as those of the Neoplatonists, who sought mystical identification with the divine.[36] These beliefs tended towards a monotheistic world-views in seeking one originating deity cloaked behind the many gods known to man.[37] It is no surprise that these ideas found currency in cosmopolitan London. Belief that individuals could address the divine, climbing paths to salvation through religious revelation and philosophical study, responded to late second-century preoccupations.

Public infrastructure

London's Severan restoration was qualitatively different to earlier periods of renewal under Vespasian and Hadrian. This was shown in a relative neglect of the civic architecture that symbolized imperial authority. These ideas were now embedded in the city whole, with its walled circuit, rather than in individual buildings. The forum basilica was, however, refurbished in the early third century when new tessellated and *opus signinum* floors were laid in some rooms. The building remained in use, but there is no record of later alteration.[38] The road flanking its northern side was resurfaced nine times after its Hadrianic creation down to *c.* AD 270, suggesting renewal every decade or so but at a slowing pace.[39] Similarly, there is no certain evidence of any repair or alteration to the amphitheatre after *c.* AD 150 until the drainage system was repaired some 90 years later. Four timbers felled in the winter AD 242–3 were used beneath the

eastern gate, perhaps in restoration for an important programme of games celebrated *c.* AD 243.[40]

Intriguingly the Hadrianic road built outside town across the upper Walbrook
valley was also restored. This may have served as a military short-cut for traffic
heading towards Verulamium when the Cripplegate fort was garrisoned, but saw
little use in the later second century apart from occasional funerals in the small
roadside cemetery. The surrounding area had become increasingly marshy after
blockages to the culverts that carried the Walbrook through the city wall.[41] It was,
however, improved by a new metalled surface some 10.2 metres wide, that is
dated to the middle of the third century by a coin of AD 235/6 within the road
metalling.[42] An iron spearhead buried within this road surface had been bent out
of shape, perhaps as a ritually damaged votive deposit. A row of elder trees was
planted at even intervals along the south side of the restored road, following the
line of the roadside ditch where crania had been placed a century or so before.
Their small diameter of growth shows that they could not have stood for more
than 15 years before being felled. There is something unusual about this regular
planting. It might may have been part of a screening hedgerow to hide the road
from the city wall, or perhaps part of a more formally laid-out approach to some
destination to the west. In either case the choice of elder for the planting may
have carried meaning.[43]

We do not know what specific sequence of events resulted in these new
roadworks, but they facilitated army-directed traffic between London and the
north-west. We know of no military campaign involving London in this period,
although legionary vexillations and auxiliary cohorts heading towards the
German frontier may have passed through London at various points in the third
century. On the other side of town a line of piles was driven into the channel bed
in front of the Antonine revetments found at Guy's Hospital.[44] These timbers
were felled AD 241, and are likely to have improved the Guy's channel for ships
navigating the eastern reaches of Southwark. This rebuilding of the early 240s
brings to mind the description given by the authors of the *Historiae Augusta*
to the activities of Timesitheus, the Praetorian Prefect under the emperor Gordian
III in AD 241–3. Timesitheus was a key figure in the management of imperial
interests and property. According to the source, 'so excellent was this man's management of public affairs that there was nowhere a border city of major size, such
as could contain an army and emperor of the Roman people, that did not have
supplies of cheap wine, grain, bacon, barley, and straw for a year'.[45] This presumes
an elevated level of investment in annonary supply. Whatever the political and
economic context of these building activities, London was home to an important
community of high-ranking military and government officials, alongside well-
connected veterans such as Ulpius Silvanus. One was the recipient of a rare and
prestigious commemorative medallion awarded by the emperor Philip I on 1

January AD 245, found near Liverpool Street station beside the restored north-road.[46]

In death

Several military tombstones were erected in the third century. One commemorated Vivius Marcianus, a centurion of Legio II, set up by his widow Januaria Martina. The deceased, his face now obliterated by time, was shown holding a centurion's staff in his right hand and a scroll in his left, wearing a short tunic held in place by a low-slung belt (*cingulum*) with a circular clasp and a cloak (*sagum*) gathered at his right shoulder.[47] Another stone, inscribed to Flavius Agricola of Legio VI by his wife Albia Faustina, was found in Goodman's Fields east of the city in 1787.[48] Funerary inscriptions commemorating soldiers and important immigrants were more common in London and York than elsewhere in Britain, if rare in comparison to those in the cities of Gaul.[49] As in previous centuries, there is little evidence that local elites invested in such monuments.[50]

London's later Roman cemeteries expanded from earlier burial grounds, extending along the roads heading out from the city. To the west the main graveyards lay north of Watling Street, between Newgate and Smithfield, as well as on the further side of the river Fleet towards Holborn.[51] The eastern cemetery, served by the Shadwell road, extended over an area of at least 12 hectares south of Aldgate High Street.[52] The burial grounds north of the city flanked Ermine Street around Spitalfields and Bishopsgate, covering over 16 hectares.[53] South of the river burials covered more than 30 hectares between Stane and Watling Street and encroaching onto the southern eyot.[54]

Whilst cremation had been favoured in earlier periods, inhumation became the dominant burial rite accounting for the expansion and greater archaeological visibility of the later cemeteries. This followed a significant, empire-wide, shift in ideas about how the dead should be treated that gained traction in the mid- to late second century.[55] Inhumation had been a more marginal practice and cremation the burial rite of preference for wealthy Londoner's until the Antonine period. By the middle of the third century, however, most people were buried in graves, usually in wooden coffins. Cremation wasn't entirely abandoned, continuing well into the fourth century, but funerals pyres became a rarity: reflecting on old-fashioned ways, unusual beliefs, or culturally distinct minority communities.

It is difficult to establish how quickly fashion changed since burials can be difficult to date. Graveyards contain few of the stratified rubbish assemblages that help establish chronologies, and there is a risk that grave goods were already old when buried. It seems likely, however, that the larger inhumation cemeteries surrounding London were established in the mid- to late second century.

Cemeteries on the northern side of town developed in plots that had been open fields into the second century, extending over 1 kilometre north of the city and up to 300 metres back from Ermine Street.[56] The first inhumations dated to the Hadrianic-Antonine period, perhaps commencing with isolated irregular burials and a discrete area for sub-adult burials. The earliest securely dated inhumation contained a smashed Verulamium/London region whiteware jar manufactured prior to c. AD 160/165.[57]

More than 1,600 inhumations have been recovered from scientific excavations on the borders of London, most dated to the third and fourth centuries. We have estimated that London's population might have shrunk to some 10,000–15,000 people in the third century (above p. 288). If we assume an annual mortality rate of between 2.5 per cent and 3.5 per cent, as suggested by studies of analogous pre-modern communities, this would have resulted in 250–525 deaths each year.[58] If this remained constant through the third and fourth centuries, then 50,000–105,000 bodies needed burying. If we also assume, for the purposes of crude modelling, that the numbers of later Roman cremations balance out the number of earlier Roman inhumations, then the bodies recovered represents a sample of between 1.6 per cent and 3.2 per cent of the original cemetery population.

The deceased were usually buried in individual graves, marked in such a way that they were respected by later grave diggers. This required careful management sustained over generations. Burial grounds must have been owned and maintained, perhaps through collegia and guilds, with individual plots cared for by heirs and descendants. In several cases, graves were arranged in clusters suggestive of family groups. Recent work on the skeletal morphology, supported by isotopic and aDNA studies, suggests the presence of a high proportion of immigrants. The cemetery at Lant Street in Southwark included individuals of Asian and European ancestry amongst its second-century burials.[59] A disproportionate number of London's early third-century graves contained men. This was strikingly so in the Spitalfields cemetery where males outnumbered females by over five to one, with an estimated peak in adult deaths at 36–45 years old.[60] Immigration must have contributed significantly to this bias. The institutions of government were run by men, who also formed the bulk of labour employed in building the city and serving its port. Household slaves were also predominantly male. Selective burial practices may have further reinforced this gender bias, perhaps reflecting on the social marginalization of women. These trends may have been most clearly evident at times of greater inflows of migrant labour.

About one-fifth of the burials contained grave goods, chiefly items associated with funerary meals such as drinking vessels and flagons.[61] Particularly suggestive grave furniture came from a third-century burial in the eastern cemetery, where a man was buried with tweezers and a scoop-probe perhaps worn in a bag hung around the neck, leading to the suggestion that the deceased was a healer or eye doctor.[62] One unusual ritual burial in the eastern cemetery contained a dog, horse, and deer laid nose-to-tail in symbolic chase.[63] As a general rule the offerings in later Roman inhumations failed to match the wealth and quality of earlier cremations, and we have no direct evidence for post-burial ritual activities within the cemeteries.[64] It is possible that the feasts that previously occurred at the funeral pyre were relocated to private dining rooms, and burial became less important in the mourning process.

The preference for inhumation marked a significant change in how death was understood to the living. Cremation had been an important ritual choice, where the spectacular transformation of fire freed the soul from the corpse. The decision to forgo this public ceremony and bury bodies intact appears to have involved a denial of the processes of decay, as witnessed in later attempts to preserve bodies in plaster burials and sarcophagi (pp. 347 and 360). Burial promised a corporeal security. There are many different opinions as to why cadavers were treated so differently, and study is complicated by the fact that inhumation and cremation co-existed at most times.[65] Individual circumstances and choices continued to matter. But there was an inflection point, somewhere in the later second century, when majority preference changed. We should not underestimate the profound nature of this change to ritual tradition. It took place at a time when many were reassessing the relationship between human mortality and the fate of the soul. The popularity of soteriological mystery cults such as Orphism and Mithraism contributed to a re-shaping of religious practice with their doctrines of individual salvation. These belief systems drew on currents of philosophical understanding that eventually fed into the development of Hellenized Christianity. These later developments have complicated matters, since the subsequent 'ownership' of such ideas by Christian orthodoxy has hindered attempts to understand earlier belief in bodily resurrection. It is unnecessary to look for a narrowly Christian inspiration to the fashion for corporeal burial.[66] It is likely, however, that Christian ideas had reached London by the end of the second century.[67] Christian communities were certainly established at other cosmopolitan cities in the western empire, as at Lyons where bishop Irenaeus was denouncing heresies from c. AD 180, and London is unlikely to have been an exception.[68] Whenever Christianity reached Britain it is likely to have done so through London, although our earliest certain evidence for its presence here dates to the fourth century (p. 371).

London's early third-century revival probably owed much to the reforms of the Severan dynasty, and particularly to arrangements put in place after Caracalla ended campaigns in Caledonia in AD 211. During the following peace, London was established as the principal city of the new province of Britannia Superior, with its status reflected in town walls and beautified riverside temples. It remained a city of imperial bureaucrats, of officers and veterans serving the needs of empire who relied on the services of a familiar range of shippers and contractors. The events of the second century had, however, profoundly changed the city. The Antonine period was a turning point, witnessing not only urban contraction but also the arrival of new philosophies and mentalities that set the third-century city in new directions. The psychological impact of the Plague of Galen may have hastened changed attitudes to death and helped in the spread of soteriological cults. But the pandemic arrived at a time when new ideas of architectural design, perhaps influenced by the arguments of the second sophistic, had already taken root. These were important influences on an early third-century city that owed much to its role as a port, commanding a supply route that followed Rome's extended frontier from the Rhine to Hadrian's Wall by way of the east coast. London was no longer as critical as it had been in the late first century but the cumulative result of early third-century improvements meant that busy quays and wharfs extended further along London's waterfront than ever before. An influx of new people, mostly men, gave rise to a new community. This state of affairs lasted for at least a generation, but ended abruptly in the mid-third century when London's port was dismantled, reversing more than two centuries of expansion.

25

The third-century 'crisis' (*c.* AD 250–70)

The destruction of the port

One of the more perplexing discoveries made during the study of London's Roman port is that its waterfront quays were deliberately dismantled. There are several reasons why London's waterside might have been neglected, but it is distinctly curious to find that its timber revetments were systematically removed. The river embankment was a vital part of the urban topography that did far more than serve a working harbour: it defined the city boundary, articulated public buildings along the waterfront, and housed warehouses and workshops that operated independently of river traffic. Why destroy an integral, useful and expensively assembled part of the urban landscape?

The evidence itself was excellently summarized by Trevor Brigham more than 30 years ago.[1] The upper timbers of revetments along the north bank of the Thames were removed almost everywhere they were accessible, in a destruction that extended from the westernmost quays next to Queenhithe, past the site of London Bridge, all the way downstream to the Old Custom House and Sugar Quay. At most locations the retaining tiebacks were crudely axed through to release the massive horizontal timber baulks which were removed down to contemporary Mean High Water level. This left the lowermost timbers exposed to the river, which chased a tidal channel before depositing a thick band of river-lain silts and gravels. There were minor variations to this picture: in some places the baulks were removed in their entirety and in others the tier immediately above the water level also survived. But most accessible baulks were removed for a distance of 1 kilometre along the waterfront. Only the box quay at the Old Custom House, at the eastern end of the port, may have remained substantially intact.[2] The common pattern of disuse, cutting-back, erosion, and deposition suggests a single episode of destructive re-engineering.

We have a rough idea of when this happened. Several strands of evidence show that London's harbour was still busy into the 240s. The waterfront quays continued to handle imported Samian assemblages until this date (p. 314), with continued investment in London's transportation infrastructure until at least *c.* AD 241–3 (pp. 320–1). As we shall shortly see, various classes of archaeological find show that patterns of supply into London changed *c.* AD 255, perhaps following the redundancy of London's harbour. We do not know how swiftly the quays were dismantled, but finds associated with subsequent river erosion date to the middle of the third century. The revetments were certainly cut back before *c.* AD 270, since erosion preceded the construction of temporary quays that were themselves destroyed by the riverside wall *c.* AD 275 (p. 339).

It is harder to work out why it happened. It is unlikely that the old waterlogged timbers were recovered for reuse. The baulks included a significant proportion of perishable sapwood unfit for structural use, whilst grit and age would have made the remaining heartwood difficult to work.[3] In any case we know of no contemporary projects that demanded such a massive and unusual supply. Some timbers may have been used as fuel, but it is impossible to believe that fuel shortages were sufficient cause for large-scale destructive salvage. Damian Goodburn suggests that the main object of the exercise was to convert the quays into a defensive bank. This is consistent with the way in which the tie-backs behind the facing baulks were chopped back to form a slope, with the foreshore channel a defensive ditch. It seems likely that London's waterfront quays were converted into a barrier after the port's redundancy.

The atrophy of long-distance supply

This presents us with two different but related phenomena to account for: the failure of the port, and its replacement by crudely fashioned defences. There are several reasons why traffic through London might have declined in the third century. The port's role in supplying the army was eclipsed by alternative sites, such as York and South Shields, and coastal shipping meant that fewer goods were carried by road. But these changes took effect earlier in the century, at a time when London's harbour remained busy. The port's decline may instead have been provoked by tidal changes that hindered larger ships from reaching London's quays. Sediments at Queenhithe show that the Thames remained weakly saline upriver of London Bridge until the end of the second century but an accumulation of foreshore deposits at Baynard's Castle indicates that the river had ceased to be scoured by tides in the mid-third century.[4] It has been argued that the falling water levels directly caused the dismantling of the quayside between AD 250 and 270, although this seems likely to be an over simplification of a more complex situation.[5] The problems of bringing cargoes ashore without the aid of a rising tide were solved at many inland river-ports throughout the Roman world. Why not at London? It has additionally been suggested that this downward drift of the tidal head encouraged the relocation of the port facilities down-river to Shadwell where a harbour may have been established in a back channel of the Thames behind the island of Wapping.[6] Shadwell could not, however, have functioned on anything like the same scale as London. It lacked the large urban workforce needed to man the docks, and the range of storage and transportation facilities that London enjoyed. If Shadwell's docks were important, then road access to

London would have been critical. But the Shadwell road was probably blocked from direct access to the city when the town wall was built.[7] Vehicles may have deviated to enter town through Aldgate, but it is difficult to believe that serious volumes of goods were made to traffic this longer route. There is nothing to suggest that London's earlier handling capacity was replaced at Shadwell, or indeed elsewhere along the Thames before the seventh century.[8]

London's port is more likely to have failed because of a decline in long-distance trade. Until the middle of the third century, Britain received significant quantities of olive oil and wine shipped in large amphorae. This supply was directed towards areas of military demand, reaching the British Isles by transportation routes along the Rhone and Rhine. Some goods were destined for consumers in London and more passed through town *en route* to northern garrisons. Most oil was transported in large globular Dressel 20 amphorae from Baetica in southern Spain, but their supply fell away sharply *c.* AD 255/260.[9] London's later olive oil imports were more likely to arrive in North African amphorae but at massively reduced levels.[10] It also appears that fewer wooden wine barrels were imported, since these ceased to be reused to line London's wells.[11] Many types of pottery, including Samian and mortaria, similarly failed to reach London in earlier quantities. If these containers and tablewares provide a measure of the scale of long-distance supply then this had declined massively in the mid-third century.

The reasons for this decline are much debated. Studies of Dressel 20 amphorae have concentrated on three possible factors: disruptions in long-distance supply provoked by the establishment of the breakaway Gallic Empire; changed dietary preferences that reduced demand for Mediterranean imports; and a reduction in troop numbers that drove a collapse in military demand.[12] Contributory factors include the reorganization of estate production in Spain and the disappearance of a military redistributive system that subsidized transportation costs. Where large quantities of supplies were moved to military consumers, as previously, then other goods followed in their path.[13] Spare capacity came into existence in the months between campaigns and public building programmes, in the holds of vessels returning from commissioned deliveries, and in marginal spaces within larger shipments. This capacity enabled other forms of transaction, and engendered an institutional architecture that facilitated trade, carrying luxury imports to a wide range of British consumers.

We have already explored how London's fortunes may have been shaped by city's role as an entrepôt for annonary supply (p. 195). The third-century institutionalization of the *annona militaris* extended the in-kind allowances of food, fodder, clothing and equipment offered to soldiers and civil servants.[14] This accompanied a massive reduction in Rome's willingness or ability to move such provisions over long distances. As Simon Esmonde Cleary has observed, the state no longer found reason to provide its soldiers with a Mediterranean diet reliant on long-distance supply.[15] Garrisons were instead expected to support themselves through local taxation and cash purchases. The effects can be seen in a pattern of import-substitution as the army turned to locally available resources. Imported wine was replaced by beer, oil by lard and tallow, and Mediterranean fish sauce by North Sea substitutes (above p. 216). Botanical evidence shows that fewer exotic fruits were imported to London and these were replaced by locally grown produce.[16] British kilns produced fine wares to substitute for missing imports, and Roman London came to rely on pottery carried down-river from manufactories in Oxfordshire and Surrey.[17] Jerry Evans has shown how regional patterns of pottery supply were profoundly impacted by such changes. Disruptions to the bulk supply of goods within the administered *annona* and *frumentationes* had a knock-on effect on other traffic. The contraction of long-distance supply had a massive impact on London's economy and is likely to have been the main reason for the redundancy of its port.

A slump in regional productivity?

In related changes, several places involved in the large-scale extraction of raw materials around London also ceased operation in the late third century. Closures have been identified amongst ironworking sites of the Weald, including those at Bardown and Beauport Park.[18] The bathhouse at Beauport Park saw continuous use until the middle of the century and the coin assemblage included numerous issues down to Decius (AD 249–51), but an absence of later coinage suggests that the building was abandoned in the 250s.[19] It was then stripped of reusable materials and left to ruin. Although these sites in the High Weald are unlikely to have supplied London, serving the south-coast instead, a pattern of declining productivity can also be traced in areas that sent iron by road to London.[20] Places associated with the transportation infrastructure developed around the ironworking industry were closed or neglected in the late third century.[21] Malcolm Lyne has suggested that changed patterns of exploitation may have encouraged potters from iron producing areas to relocate to more accessible areas on the margins of the Weald in Hampshire and Kent.[22] Although modest levels of production continued on smaller satellite sites, the Weald witnessed a marked settlement decline. Some iron working sites around Berkhamsted in the Chilterns north-west of London were also abandoned during the third century, suggesting that similar forces were at work in other landscapes.[23]

The contraction of the iron-working industry may have followed earlier over-exploitation of fuel and ore, exacerbated by the costs of maintaining the transport infrastructure. But the timing of this decline fits within the wider patterns of failure. It may also have coincided with the ending of the involvement of the fleet in the procurement chain.[24] The *Classis Britannica* disappears from the historical and epigraphic record towards the middle of the century. The last known reference, dated AD 244–9, is found in a *curriculum vitae* inscribed on a tombstone from Arles.[25] The *Classis Germanica* is also unattested after this date, suggesting the reorganization of naval commands on both sides of the Channel. This may have involved closing the naval base at Dover, which was probably evacuated and its defences slighted in the mid- to late third century.[26] Was London's port, perhaps controlled by the fleet after its Severan restoration, closed in a similar exercise?[27] It must be acknowledged, however, that we have no direct evidence for the fleet's disbandment. Its disappearance is reconstructed from absences in the historical and archaeological record, at a time when such records were increasingly sparse. It is also possible that London's harbour remained a procuratorial responsibility, and we might instead look to a restructuring of this office to account for revised approaches to its management.[28]

Pottery export from the Thames estuary also witnesses a moderation in the scale of surplus extraction. Large storage vessels in North Kentish shelly ware, poppyhead beakers in Upchurch Ware, and black burnished ware (BB2) became scarce from the middle of the century, and were no longer exported in quantities by *c.* AD 275.[29] There was a sharp decline in the quantities of BB2 present in London assemblages dated AD 230–50/60, as amongst material recovered from Leadenhall Court when these products also stopped reaching Hadrian's Wall in significant quantities.[30] This may have followed a decline in the numbers of salterns operating in Kent and Essex, and likely that the estuary was no longer producing elevated volumes of salt and salted goods for distribution along east-coast supply routes.[31]

The stone quarries of north Kent were also less busy. London's needs were greatest during the building of the early second-century town wall, but Kentish ragstone continued to serve the needs of construction projects such as the Shadwell bathhouse and the Walbrook Mithraeum into the 240s. Many later building programmes recycled materials quarried from London's disused public buildings in a significant shift in approach to the procurement of building supplies. These changes may have been the consequence of reduced demand combined with a readier availability of materials from redundant buildings, but meant that river-barges no longer made frequent trips to bring ragstone to London from the Medway.

London's major construction projects had long drawn on timber procured from managed woodlands, but there also appears to have been a hiatus in such supply in the middle of the third century. A list of dendrochronologically dated timbers shows that London regularly imported freshly felled timbers until AD 252/253, which is the felling date of timbers used to repair roadside drains at One Poultry.[32] These were the last timbers we know to have been imported before the construction of the riverside wall some 20 years later. This interruption appears to find confirmation in the study of timbers felled for the construction of a large public building AD 293/294 (below p. 350). These timbers all started growing at dates between AD 191 and AD 254 (particularly AD 217 to AD 234) in managed woodlands where regular pollarding was practised.[33] It is striking that none started growth after AD 254. The implication is that the trees from which these later timbers were sourced had stopped being coppiced, suggesting that these woods were not used to source building timber from c. AD 254.

In sum, there is a consistent pattern of declining productivity within the London region, discernible within its managed woodlands, iron-working sites, stone quarries and salterns.[34] These extraction industries relied on the transport infrastructure established around London and its port. It is hard to decide on the extent to which the loss of transport capacity was a consequence or cause of declining regional productivity. What is clear is that the mid-third century marked a radical change, in which capacity was lost rather than enhanced.

Signs of urban stress

Changing arrangements for local supply may also have contributed to the increased frequency of coin 'forging' in third-century London. Debris from the local manufacture of copies of third-century coins has been recovered from at least three locations. We have already referred to the moulds used to forge coins from as early as c. AD 225 found in the wall turret at Warwick Square (p. 309).[35] Others were found in a ditch in Bermondsey Square in 1998.[36] The largest and best studied assemblage, consisting of fragments of more than 800 carefully made moulds, was recovered from the city ditch at 85 London Wall.[37] These moulds produced copies of silver denarii and copper-alloy dupondii and asses dated from Trajan to Trebonianus Gallus (AD 251–3), working from at least fifty-nine silver *denarii* and fourteen copper alloy coins, roughly one tenth of annual pay at the time. These coiners were working into the mid-250s if not beyond. Most of this production took place beside the city wall and was probably under military control.[38]

These copper-alloy coins were comparatively worthless, and were probably made to compensate for shortages in small change rather than for profit.[39] Low value coin facilitated small denomination payments for produce and labour, as when hauliers required cash payment on delivery (p. 199).[40] London's garrison would have included soldiers housed in the towers and gatehouses along the walled circuit who were responsible for directing traffic through city gates where shipments could be received and *portoria* taxes raised. Coin manufactured on the wall met a demand for small-change to lubricate such transactions at a time when imported supplies were inadequate.

There are signs of under-investment in some elements of London's urban infrastructure. The latest burials at Eldon Street contained grave goods of c. AD 250, but the road and cemetery were not much used afterwards.[41] It has also been suggested that roadside properties beside the main Walbrook crossing at One Poultry saw reduced use, evidenced by an unusual scarcity of coin issues of the 260s.[42] A hiatus in building activity was even more clearly evident on the extensive Lloyd's Register site, where at least five late second or early third century buildings were demolished in the mid-third century and the site left vacant for a couple of decades before redevelopment on a completely new layout c. AD 270.[43] Some city buildings were fire damaged in the mid- or late third century. Most devastatingly the forum basilica caught fire and its roof collapsed.[44] Pottery spot-dated after c. AD 250 was found beneath this collapse. The fire probably spread into adjacent areas: the road along the north side of the basilica was covered by destruction debris, charred timbers associated with late third-century material collapsed into wells opposite the entrance to the forum, and buildings to its east were reportedly damaged in a mid-third-century fire.[45] We cannot be certain that these burnt deposits traced a single event, or how widely the forum fire had spread. It is worth noting, however, that two buildings at One Poultry were also burnt. These were covered by destruction debris containing Alice Holt and Farnham pottery, which suggests that site clearance took place after c. AD 270.[46] Further-flung sites showing signs of fire destruction include a site on the banks of the Fleet, at Old Bailey, where the building provisionally identified as an octagonal temple (above p. 266) was destroyed around 270 before being replaced by a large multi-roomed building with ragstone walls and *opus signinum* floors.[47] South of the river, the roadside complex containing a shop, bakery and granary alongside the main road to London Bridge was also fire-damaged around the middle of the third century.[48] It is likely that these different observations represent separate outbreaks of accidental fire, but we cannot wholly dismiss incendiary unrest as a cause (see p. 352).

Reassessing London at a time of crisis

This chapter has summarized evidence for a series of changes that contributed to the redundancy of London's port. These took place during the period of wider disruptions known as the third-century crisis: a time of political instability, plague, barbarian invasion, and economic turbulence. The utility of the term 'crisis' has recently been questioned, given the variations of circumstance, but in many spheres the problems were acute.[49] The historical narrative tends to start with the assassination of the emperor Severus Alexander in AD 235, after which there was a rapid succession of brief reigns and damaging frontier wars. In the north-west provinces matters reached a breaking point around AD 258, when the emperor Gallienus weakened control of the Rhine frontier by transferring troops to Pannonia.[50] Franks and Alemanni from beyond the Rhine, who had been a threat throughout the 250s, used this opportunity to raid deep into Gaul. Order was restored by troops commanded by Postumus, who then rebelled from Gallienus' rule to establish a Gallic Empire (*Imperium Galliarum*) that divorced Gaul, Britain and Spain from the rest of the empire for some 15 years.[51]

As we have already noted, the establishment of the Gallic Empire may have interrupted flows of long-distance supply. There were several other contributory factors to this decline. Studies of the third-century crisis are particularly exercised by the evidence of a currency debasement, contributing to the collapse of the Augustan monetary system in the 260s.[52] This was also a turning point in architectural history: few monumental buildings were erected and the practice of setting-up of commemorative inscriptions largely ceased, witnessing a retreat from the earlier values of civic euergetism.[53] Research by Kyle Harper has drawn attention to the way in which Rome's military and economic setbacks may have been provoked by another pandemic that swept the empire in the 250s.[54] This plague, suggested by some to have been influenza or viral fever, cruelly echoed the disruptions of the Antonine plague a century earlier. It is known to historians as the plague of Cyprian, after the bishop of Carthage who described its impact in letters written *c.* AD 252, and can tentatively be traced back to an outbreak in Alexandria in Egypt *c.* AD 249 from where it reached Rome early in AD 251. The historical accounts imply recurring pestilential outbreaks, but we cannot be certain that they shared a common cause. The evidence is uncertain and contested, but Harper builds a credible case for considering this pandemic to have been critical to the disruptions of the period, adding exogenous shock to a system that was already under considerable stress.

This begs the question of how much London might have been affected by these problems.[55] There is no reason to believe that Britain was other than a peaceful part of Postumus' Gallic Empire but the evidence presented here suggests that London was more profoundly changed than is sometimes assumed.[56] The closure of the port can in part be seen as a consequence of the unsustainable nature of its earlier growth. Massive flows of *annona* goods had followed an infrastructure of military supply that was built around campaigns of advance and supported the exceptional concentrations of Roman forces found in the frontier regions. These met the strategic goals of imperial and provincial government, giving London its political and economic purpose. The disruptions of the mid-third century brought these arrangements to a rapid and decided close.

The dating of these changes is key to understanding them. The record of woodland management and timber supply suggests that London continued to expand its urban infrastructure until *c.* AD 254. A continuing concern with securing local supplies by payment in cash may have prompted officers responsible for manning the city walls to coin small-change to make good on shortages in official supply until at least AD 253. In the mid-250s, however, work ceased at several larger-scale production sites within the region, including ironworking sites in the Weald and salterns in the Thames estuary. This may reflect a diminution in the level of imperial engagement in the productive economy. This was also when the *annona* was reformed in ways that reduced the traffic of Mediterranean goods, and in the late 250s London's port ceased to handle the large-scale import of amphorae and fine-wares. We can assume that shipments of perishable goods, such as grain and leather, were similarly reduced.

In the late 250s, fewer ships travelled the seas and fewer cargoes took to roads and rivers. This may have been the combined consequence of government policy, military insecurity and economic recession, but it certainly involved a major loss of capacity. This may have been caused or compounded by labour shortages, as wars and plagues reduced manpower. Some troops were withdrawn from Britain to support Gallienus' frontier wars. In AD 255, men of Legio XX, formerly of the British garrison, set up a dedication at Mainz.[57] British legionaries were also part of Gallienus' army at Sirmium in Pannonia in the 260s, and soldiers from Britain went east with Valerian's field army in AD 258.[58] We have no measure of the scale of these troop movements, but the soldiers withdrawn from Britain didn't return and their loss may have contributed to the abandonment of vici outside forts on the northern frontier.[59] It is distinctly possible that demands placed on the forces stationed in Britain at this time resulted in the redeployment of ships from the fleet, and of official personnel managing estates within London's hinterland. Death and desertion may have compounded losses.[60] Parallels can be drawn with a depopulation of towns in Illyricum *c.* AD 260, which the historian Zosimus blamed on the combined weight of barbarian invasion and plague.[61] As we have already observed in describing London's late second-century contraction, Labour shortages are readily provoked by pandemics which not only supress military recruitment but reduce harvests and depress taxation in kind. Food insecurity is a likely outcome.

Several strands of evidence suggest that these failures of supply took place soon after AD 254, making them contemporary with the historical record of the westward spread of the plague of Cyprian. We have no evidence to show that the plague reached London, but it is difficult to believe that this cosmopolitan city would have totally escaped its effects. Whatever the immediate cause, the failures of production and supply represented a major rupture in London's history. It was no longer a vital hub in military and administered supply and its port ceased to serve government needs.

This helps us to understand the redundancy of the port, but it doesn't tell us why it became necessary to replace London's carefully engineered waterfront quays with a crude defensive bank. A speculative explanation builds from the proposition that there was a massive loss of naval capacity following the depletions of war and plague *c.* AD 254. This would not only have reduced the administration's ability to maintain *annona* supplies, but risked surrendering the waters around Britain to piracy.[62] Frankish raiders were supposedly a problem to Rome throughout the 250s, and Postumus' issue of coins carrying the legend *Neptvni*

Redvci in AD 262/263 is thought to have marked a naval victory won against such forces.[63] London's clumsily executed waterfront defences could have been an emergency response to naval threat in the late 250s or early 260s. Whatever the cause, London's defended waterfront proclaimed the continued importance of the city as a seat of power and a place worth defending.

PART 7

THE LATE ANTIQUE CITY

26

Restoration (*c.* AD 270–85)

The riverside wall

London was diminished by the changes that closed its port, but these problems were not terminal. Some 20 years later, the city was emphatically restored. This revival was announced by the construction of a monumental masonry wall along the riverfront. The quays at Billingsgate were briefly rehabilitated beforehand, using timber baulks salvaged from the earlier waterfront to re-establish a waterfront to which a new stave-built section was added.[1] Revetments at Swan Lane and New Fresh Wharf were similarly refurbished. These works might have been designed to improve transport infrastructure in the later years of the Gallic Empire, although the brevity of their use might indicate that they were built to take deliveries of building materials for the construction of the riverside wall. In either case, these quays were soon blocked from the river when the wall was built (Fig. 26.1).

The wall's existence was established by discoveries at Baynard's Castle in 1974 and has since been confirmed by numerous observations along Thames Street.[2] These trace the line of a 2.2-metre-wide tile-coursed concrete construction, faced with small ragstone blocks and incorporating a basal plinth of Reigate stone, that was set over a rammed chalk raft laid on five neat rows of squared oak piles. Although most of the riverfront was enclosed, a short length at its marshy western end was probably left open until later (p. 387). An earth bank may have been raised inside the wall, although this is not proven. The wall matched the landward wall built half-a-century earlier, but incorporated a significant amount of reused building material, witnessing an increasingly pragmatic approach to procurement.[3] Although the wall saw later alteration, the consistent design of its distinctive foundations shows it to have been planned as a single construction. Exact dating eludes us, since none of the squared-off timbers retained bark. Piles at Baynard's Castle included one with a final growth-ring of AD 255, and the heartwood-sapwood transition of others indicates that some came from trees felled no later than AD 270/275.[4] Those at New Fresh Wharf were felled after AD 268, providing a *terminus post-quem* for the wall's central section.[5] Piles beneath the eastern stretch of the wall at Sugar Quay were felled AD 279–301 and others from Three Quays are dated AD 251–87.[6] We can therefore conclude that parts of the wall were in place *c.* AD 275 but others weren't built before AD 279. The building programme probably started at the western end in the mid-270s, drawing on supplies

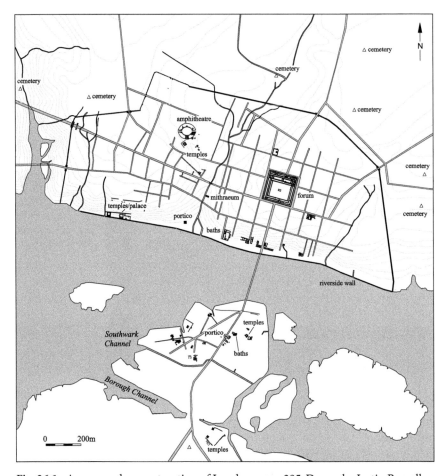

Fig. 26.1   A proposed reconstruction of London *c.* AD 295. Drawn by Justin Russell.

brought down-river, and progressed eastwards until completion around the end of the decade.

The wall severed the city from the river but was penetrated by water-gates. One marked the entrance into town over London Bridge, and others gave access to places where rivercraft beached. Billingsgate was probably the main port of entry: lead seals found on the foreshore included an example of the fourth-century emperor Constans suggesting that imported cargoes were being taxed at a nearby custom point (p. 301).[7] There is no evidence that any quays were built to receive these imports, although warehouses associated with the earlier waterfront survived.[8] In places a low bank was set in front of the wall to define the foreshore, but little other than rubbish dumping took place between wall and river. The building of the wall involved extensive reclamations of low-lying areas around the mouth of the Walbrook. Excavations at 14–16 Dowgate Hill found a 2-metre depth of rubbish dated after *c.* AD 270/275, containing large assemblages of pottery from Oxfordshire, Colchester and Nene Valley, with more than 100 leather shoes and sandals and several hundred 'barbarous radiate' coins.[9] This was a rubbish of urban wealth.

The wall's construction kicked off a period of renewal, not dissimilar to London's Severan restoration (Table 26.1). It relied on advanced engineering skills, new supplies of building materials, and a dedicated construction workforce. If the mid-third century had witnessed failures in production and supply, then part of this lost capacity was restored. The dating suggests that we should credit this to the years following the collapse of the Gallic Empire in AD 274, and Aurelian's reassertion of Roman authority offers a likely political context for this exercise.[10] At a general level, if not in details of design, inspiration may have been drawn from Rome's Aurelian wall, the building of which began in AD 271.[11] As Hendrik Dey has observed, Rome's walls witnessed the emperor's commitment to his capital city, testifying to the permanence and authority of his regime. This was a language of imperial control that was readily translated into the architecture of provincial cities.

The completion of London's defences also echoed programmes of urban fortification elsewhere in the north-west provinces, particularly Gaul and Spain. We lack sufficiently precise dating to know how these parallel initiatives influenced one another, but some are thought to have been centrally directed.[12] Several places in southern Britain also gained masonry defences at this time, most notably amongst the east-coast sites that subsequently formed the command of the Saxon Shore.[13] Richborough was part of this group, where coin evidence indicates that the masonry defences were built between AD 273 and 285.[14] Defensive circuits also encircled London's neighbouring cities: the stone walls of Canterbury are dated *c.* AD 270–90 from stratified coins and pottery, and those at Chichester, Silchester, and Verulamium were broadly contemporary.[15] This proliferation of defended sites would have placed competing claims on available resources, and their maintenance may have drawn on taxes and rents previously rendered to London. If so, some estates may have been removed from London's orbit and assigned to new commands, accounting for changes in patterns of supply within the region.

The restoration of London appears, therefore, as part of a concerted building programme involving a large-scale mobilization of resources. It also assumed a significant ongoing commitment of forces to man the 5-kilometre-long defensive circuit. James Gerrard has drawn a useful parallel with requirements described in the tenth-century Burghal Hidage, which imply that some 2,700 men would have been needed to defend Roman London properly.[16] Defensive walls both projected and protected imperial interests, and were planned at the instigation of the ruling authorities. Whether or not they were built by the state, or by cities responding to impositions and expectations, is harder to judge.[17] We should not underestimate the symbolic importance of town walls. Places where power and wealth were

Table 26.1   A suggested timeline of events affecting London in the period
AD 270–410

Date	Building activities in London	Salient events relevant to London
275–80	Riverside wall replaces earlier bank. Forum basilica restored. Houses built/refurbished. Some street repairs. New patterns of urban supply.	Gallic Empire reabsorbed within Roman Empire by Aurelian. Programmes of defensive wall-building in SE Britain and on continent.
286		Carausius appointed to organize defences against seaborne raiders, seizes power, and establishes 'British empire'. London mint established.
293–4	Work starts on building waterside temples perhaps as part of an imperial palace.	Carausius deposed and replaced by Allectus.
296	Building works abandoned incomplete.	Constantius reconquers Britain, saving London from sack by Frankish mercenaries.
306		Constantine proclaimed emperor in York on death of Constantius.
		Britain sub-divided into four provinces, with seat of *vicarius* in London. Constantine visits London.
314		Bishop Adelfius of the colony of London attends church council at Arles
310–20	Temple of Mithras altered, perhaps to house Bacchic worship. Temple icons buried.	Constantine moves headquarters from Trier.
	Forum largely demolished. Latest importation of building timber. Southwark 'mansio' demolished. Baths at Winchester Palace disused. Change of use of the 'governor's palace' complex.	
325		London mint ceases to produce new coin
342–3		Visit to London of emperor Constans.
350–3		Revolt of Magnentius in Gaul with British support.
	Final surfaces laid in arena, which is subsequently abandoned. Metalworking at sites of former public buildings. Temple precinct on southern borders subdivided.	
360		Flavius Lupicinus plans response to barbarian attacks from base in London.

367–8	Forces under Count Theodosius establish an operational base at London in response to the disorders of the 'barbarian conspiracy'.
'Bastions' added to town wall. Basilica built on Tower Hill, possibly as an episcopal church. Towers added to select domestic compounds.	
383–8	Magnus Maximus leads revolt against emperor Gratian with support of British garrison.
Stone quarried from disused public buildings and gravel from disused streets. Bridges over Walbrook and Thames cease to carry significant traffic.	
396–8	Campaigns in Britain attributed to Stilicho.
Some additions to riverside wall.	Britain no longer in receipt of significant supplies of new coin.
406–7	Sequence of British usurpers, culminating in Constantine III who withdraws troops from Britain to campaign on the Continent.
408–9	Honorius reportedly writes to British cities advising them to look to their own defences.

concentrated were made secure, and their authority and status enhanced. The walled cities formed a network of fortified strongholds at strategic points, housing the military and bureaucratic apparatus of a rejuvenated state. The completion of London's town wall also helped to control of movements of people, securing the collection of port duties on goods entering through the gates. Such taxes would have underwritten the costs of defending the city, supporting the garrison placed on its walls.

The emphasis placed on the display of strength can be seen as a reaction to earlier insecurity. Recent studies of the Saxon Shore forts have tended to downplay the importance of barbarian threat as a prompt for their construction, emphasizing their role in controlling shipments along coastal supply routes. These are, however, different sides to the same coin since Rome's investment in the logistics of supply was part of its military strategy. An increased sense of vulnerability might plausibly have contributed to the decision to set a wall along London's waterfront. Carausius' subsequent appointment to pacify the sea from Franks and Saxons (below p. 350) shows that such fears were taken seriously.[18]

The fact of London's late third-century recovery is remarkable. Despite the perils of collapse and fragmentation, Rome re-established political authority and revived its cities.[19] This restoration, perhaps instigated by Aurelian and taken to completion by Probus, may have involved a new conceptualization of London's role, setting it at the command of a network of sites that were as much a frontier as a coastal supply route (below p. 367). Following the closure of its harbour facilities London became a very different place marked by a different kind of archaeology. The abandonment of the waterfront quays deprives us of a principal source of archaeological evidence, and the late Roman city relied extensively on recycled and local resources. The story of later Roman London is therefore drawn from a slighter body of material offering fewer secure dates.

New patterns of procurement

The building of the wall coincided with a marked change in the range of pottery used in London. A new ceramic phase can be described from an influx of wares manufactured in southern Britain.[20] In particular, London started to receive significant quantities of pottery made at Alice Holt near Farnham *c.* AD 270. These kilns were located on the western margins of the Weald, in an area that benefitted from access to river transport. Alice Holt potters produced 'Romanized' products from the Flavian period onwards, but these only reached London in small quantities.[21] A suddenly increased volume of importation shows that this part of Surrey became more closely integrated with London's consumers, meeting some aspect of urban demand previously met from elsewhere. The pottery can be seen as a proxy for movements of other goods, perhaps the bulk supply of grain or timber. Since Alice Holt's ancient oak forest was an important source of wood for eighteenth- and nineteenth-century shipbuilding it may have filled a similar role in late antiquity.[22] The wood used in later Roman London was obtained from smaller faster-grown oaks than previously, and although this may have been a response to earlier deforestation it is more likely to reflect on changed supply networks involving different woodlands.[23] Some pots brought to London from Alice Holt kilns are likely to have been used as containers for local produce, such as honey and mead. Regional sources of alcohol would have been sought after when the bulk importation of continental wine ended. The value of these crops, allied to the improved transport infrastructure developed around the movement of timber or grain, might explain why London imported large quantities of Alice Holt pottery instead of stimulating the establishment of kilns closer to town.

London also started to import distinctive types of roof and flue tile made at Harrold in Bedfordshire some 87 kilometres north of London.[24] These must have been carted along Watling Street through Verulamium. There is no evident reason why London needed to procure building materials from such distant kilns, and this traffic must also have been integrated with some other aspect of supply. Few villas are known around Harrold, where production may have been geared towards more distant consumers. This too may have been dominated by grain, although several estates in the region turned to an intensive form of horticulture involving close-trench lazy bed cultivation some of which may have been planted with vines.[25]

The development of new patterns of agricultural and industrial production might have followed changes in ownership. The collapse of the Gallic Empire is likely to have provoked confiscations, interrupting and reconfiguring the relationship between London and its hinterland. The restoration of London did not result in a return to former patterns of economic exploitation, as evident in the reduced intensity of production in the Weald. Some lost capacity was never replaced, perhaps because the provincial economy had been reorganized in ways that no longer relied so heavily on London and its region, and perhaps because labour remained in short supply. It is also possible that estates that formerly sent tax and rent to the procurator in London were reassigned to other commands, such as those of the Saxon Shore. The office of procurator was itself soon to disappear and its assets, as well as its responsibilities, must have been redistributed. Although the office was still functioning in the early third century, there is no direct record of procuratorial involvement in Britain beyond the middle of the century, and the post didn't survive later reform (p. 367).[26]

Property redevelopment

There was a small-scale building boom at the close of the third century, accompanied by repairs to some city streets.[27] The extensive Lloyd's Register site, vacated in the mid-third century, was comprehensively developed with new timber and masonry buildings set out on a new layout c. AD 270 onwards.[28] The data reviewed by Peter Marsden and Barbara West (discussed above p. 282) also implies a wider demographic rebound. This is reinforced by the evidence of improved pottery supply, encouraging Robin Symonds and Roberta Tomber to describe the late third to early fourth centuries as a period of revival.[29]

The distribution of tiles imported from Harrold at this time indicates that the better-appointed town houses followed the terrace behind the riverside wall and along the Walbrook, with sparser distributions west of the Walbrook and in Southwark. Buildings were placed in areas where running water was easily obtained, and access to fresh water remained an increasingly important factor in the distribution of aristocratic housing. Several second-century masonry houses were restored and enlarged. At Plantation Place alterations c. AD 270 onwards included the addition of a small heated bathhouse, and this is the date of the renovation of heating systems in the house at Lothbury.[30] Elsewhere earlier structures were demolished and replaced, as at 25–30 Lime Street where a large apsidal-ended building was built using the close-piled foundations typical of the period.[31] Several houses included extended enclosures and colonnades, and some incorporated mosaics and stone-walled cellars.[32] This domestic architecture was rooted in the fashions of the previous century, but executed on a slightly grander scale. Earlier vernacular traditions of timber-framing and mud-brick walling continued, but chiefly in workshops and outbuildings.[33] Problems of survival make it impossible to estimate building densities, but there is no reason to believe that the city was any smaller at the end of the century than it had been at its beginning.

One of the masonry houses built at this time, at the Lloyd's Register site in Lime Street, incorporated a small coin-hoard of c. AD 275 beneath the floor, perhaps as a foundation deposit.[34] It consisted of thirty-two of the small copper issues known to numismatists as 'barbarous radiates'. This irregular coinage copying issues of the later Gallic emperors c. AD 268–73 circulated widely throughout the north-west provinces.[35] The Lime Street hoard included several coins from the same dies, suggesting that they were manufactured locally, perhaps testifying to the continued presence of authorities concerned with facilitating transactions using small change. The production of these 'radiates' expanded on earlier attempts to produce a token coinage, possibly compensating for the decreased purchasing power of the debased coin in circulation. The readier availability of currency may also have facilitated a shift towards cash taxation, encouraging the monetization of Britain's later Roman economy. Despite this, these coins remained proportionally more common on urban and military sites. Roman officials relied extensively on cash to pay for food, goods, and transport, especially when travelling on official business, and such uses are sufficient reason for London to have needed additional small change.[36]

The forum basilica was repaired following its earlier fire destruction (above p. 332), and new cement floors laid within its nave.[37] The masonry amphitheatre may also have been refurbished in the late third century. Pottery associated with a drain built reusing timbers felled AD 243 suggests that it was cleaned and repaired after c. AD 270.[38] The arena was resurfaced and seating rearranged, perhaps in rehabilitation for games in the busy late third century (below p. 350). The refurbishment of these two great public buildings shows that the city sustained public life modelled on earlier arrangements, although we have no measure of the intensity of their use (see p. 356). In any case, the monumentality that mattered was expressed by the walled circuit which was more important than the public buildings within. Attention was otherwise redirected into smaller worlds of domestic luxury, following patterns that can be traced back to Hadrianic-Antonine fashion. That earlier 'golden age' may have framed aristocratic ambition towards the end of the third century.

Later Roman cemeteries and people

The late antique city was surrounded by its dead. The main burial grounds continued to lie beyond the town gates at Aldgate, Bishopsgate, and Newgate, and in Southwark (above p. 322). These grew significantly in the late third and early fourth century, as in Southwark where cemeteries expanded to the south as well as encroaching on peripheral parts of the southern eyot.[39] These later burials outnumber earlier ones because of changed burial practices not population growth.

Only a minority of the dead was cremated. One from London's eastern cemetery at Prescot Street deserves mention for the splendid glass vessels used as grave goods.[40] These included a polychrome millefiori dish formed from hundreds of translucent petals of blue glass bordered with white, embedded in a bright red glass matrix, imported from the eastern Mediterranean. As time progressed, fewer people were buried with property. John Pearce has also described a shift in emphasis from the burial of items associated with feasting and care of the body towards those that emphasized rank and appearance.[41] This included jewellery, dress accessories and expensive clothing indicated by scraps of silk and gold thread.[42]

Most bodies were placed within oak coffins in well-ordered graves. A lack of intercutting shows that each was marked and respected. Their orientation was influenced by local topography, with graves aligned on roads and property boundaries, but with a distinct preference for laying bodies east-west with the head at the western end of the grave.[43] This cardinal arrangement, where the rising dead could face the sun, mattered in many of the belief systems of late antiquity.

London adopted a late Roman fashion of adding chalk or gypsum plaster around the corpse, following practices adopted in North Africa and the Rhineland.[44] Calcium carbonate from marine chalk was the preferred material. Some of London's earliest chalk-lined burials were set behind the second-century mausoleum within a walled enclosure alongside Watling Street, south of the city. These probably dated to the third century and may have formed a family group consisting of a young man and woman, aged 26–45, flanking a child who had suffered from rickets.[45] In the cemetery at Lant Street in Southwark the chalk burials are all likely to date after AD 270, where one in eight burials were of this type, rising to 30 per cent of all burials in an early fourth-century peak. Chalk burials were found in similar numbers in the eastern and northern cemeteries, where they made up 12.4 per cent of all burials and over 20 per cent of those dated to the late third and early fourth centuries.[46] Since the chalk was imported this was an expensive treatment, perhaps used to counter decomposition in preparation for the bodily resurrection promised by the soteriological cults of late antiquity.

In sharp contrast with the earlier predominance of male burials, which was a feature of the Severan revival of London, London's later cemeteries had a more normal male: female ratio. At Spitalfields men had outnumbered women by more than five to one in the late second and early third centuries, but from the late third century onwards this ratio had fallen to around 1.4:1.[47] At Lant Street female burials of this period slightly outnumbered male ones. In all of London's cemeteries children were under-represented, and most of those buried had died in their 20s and 30s, with few surviving beyond 50.[48] The evidence from Spitalfields also shows an earlier peak in deaths, in the 26–35 age group, than in the early third century.[49]

Although London's cemetery populations show a high level of skeletal stress compared to neighbouring towns, and pathologies indicative of dietary stress are common, Londoners were healthier than contemporary rural populations. Since London wasn't densely occupied, and enjoyed a high-protein meat diet, it didn't suffer excessively from the problems of infectious disease and inadequate sanitation associated with pre-modern cities.[50] It was a place of wealth and luxury for a ruling minority.

Recent studies by the Museum of London's Centre for Human Bioarchaeology reveal fascinating detail from a sample of London's Roman dead. Drawing on the evidence of carbon and nitrogen isotopes to study diet, oxygen isotopes to examine migration, and macromorphoscopics to assess ancestry, this research confirms London's continued demographic dependence on migration. The skeletal morphology of individuals buried in the late antique cemetery at Lant Street showed the likely African ancestry of four individuals and Asian-Chinese ancestry of two others, with oxygen isotopes suggesting that five had grown up around the Mediterranean. At least five, and probably eight, of the nineteen individuals studied in this research can be identified as migrants.[51] One was a young woman, probably about 14 years old at the time of her fourth-century death.[52] She stood about 1.6 metres tall, and her aDNA indicates that she had blue eyes and her mother's ancestry was from eastern Europe or north-east Africa. Isotope analysis shows that she grew up in a Mediterranean climate, but was eating things likely to have been produced near London by the time she was nine. Although her diet included meat, fish, vegetables, and cereals, her teeth were in poor shape and she had suffered from rickets. The cause of her early death is unknown, but she was laid to rest on a bed of chalk, with two glass vessels set beside her head and an inlaid wooden casket at her feet. The bone inlay was carved with an image of Vesta, the goddess of hearth and home. She also took with her a rare folding knife with an ivory handle carved as a leopard or panther with paws outstretched, to which a bronze key had originally been attached by a chain. This valuable object was made to an exotic design that finds closest parallel in Carthage. It seems likely that this girl was born in North Africa and had travelled to Britain as a child. Her journey from childhood malnutrition to high-status burial suggest a change in social status of the sort that might follow marriage or slavery.

Studies of the isotopic signature of tooth enamel from twenty individuals buried in London's cemeteries found that twelve had teeth consistent with a Romano-British origin, but four were unlikely to have grown up here. These immigrants included a female, probably 36–45 years old and possibly of continental origin, buried in the eastern cemetery in the mid- to late fourth century with distinctive 'Germanic' jewellery and an Alice Holt flagon at her feet. This jewellery included a composite triangular antler comb worn in her hair, and a pair of silver disc *tutuli* brooches linked by a glass-bead chain that fastened her clothes.[53] This lady went to her grave dressed in the fashion of a German of high rank. This confident expression of barbarian identity is in keeping with a rising German influence on custom and dress, perhaps accelerated by settlements in Britain late in the third century.[54] The emperor Probus is reported to have settled defeated Germans in Britain after victories of AD 278, where they are reported to have served Rome loyally. As with the earlier settlement of Sarmatians, above p. 293, it is tempting to see this as compensating for population decline. Another skeleton from this cemetery was a man of black African ancestry, with brown eyes and dark hair who was probably over 45 years old when he died and whose stable-isotope signature indicates a childhood spend in the London region.[55]

Although the sample is small, between one-fifth and two-fifths of this buried population were migrants. The establishment that ruled from London was always commanded by foreign-born elites, some only stationed in the city for a few years at a time. These individuals drew on the support of a network of clients and dependents who travelled in their wake. The transient nature of London's elite society might explain why the British were so uninvolved in the patronage networks of the wider Roman world. Unlike their Spanish and Gallic contemporaries, Britons failed to make a mark on Rome's Senatorial aristocracy or enter the social circles written about in ancient sources. Most Londoner's of account were immigrants for whom service in Britain was but a staging point in their careers. Ancient city populations were, in any case, rarely self-sustaining. Episodes of contraction encouraged corrective flows of newcomers, and London's late antique revitalization relied in part on immigration. Differences amongst cemetery populations suggest that London's late third-century restoration depended more on the settlement of entire households within which women were well represented and less on transient communities of economically active males that previously dominated.

27

City of emperors (*c.* AD 285–350)

The 'British empire'

London's revival as a seat of Roman government conferred power on those who commanded here, eventually bringing it the pretensions of an imperial capital under the usurper Carausius and his successor Allectus. London had already been the likely setting of an attempted rebellion by a provincial governor in AD 280 or 281. Anthony Birley, extrapolating from the writings of the Byzantine historian Zonaras, suggests that this ambitious governor was a Moor adding to the body of evidence for North African influence in later Roman London.[1] In AD 286, the Menapian Marcus Carausius, who had been appointed to marshal Rome's northern fleet against Frankish and Saxon piracy, seized authority over Britain and parts of Gaul.[2] The terms of his appointment imply that the fleet had needed rebuilding, and his subsequent propaganda suggested an abiding concern with coastal piracy (p. 334). His administration established new mints, including one at London, to produce coin to pay the army. The images on these coins celebrated his fleet, naval prowess, and the divine support of Neptune and Oceanus. They also emphasized his role as 'Restorer of the Romans' and argued his legitimacy as a partner in rule with the joint-emperors Diocletian and Maximian.[3] In March 293, however, these more widely recognized emperors appointed two junior colleagues to form the shared rule of the Tetrarchy. Constantius Chlorus, one of the junior emperors within this arrangement, swiftly restored Rome's authority over Gaul. Carausius was then deposed and replaced by Allectus as ruler in Britain.

It was during Allectus' reign that work started on one of later Roman London's more ambitious building projects. The foundations of a monumental architectural complex have been revealed in several excavations near the approaches to the Millennium Bridge (Fig. 27.1).[4] New terraces behind the riverside wall stretched 150 metres along the waterfront. The riverside terrace established a platform for the construction of two large buildings, probably intended as temples, over a mass of timber piles driven into the London clay that had been felled from the winter of AD 293/294 into the early summer of AD 294.[5] A chalk raft with a timber lattice set over these piles supported massive foundations of reused ashlar blocks capped by *petit appareil* masonry walls. These techniques had been deployed in Gaulish walled circuits in the 260s and 270s before use at Portchester and Pevensey. These similarities suggest that the craftsmen assigned to the

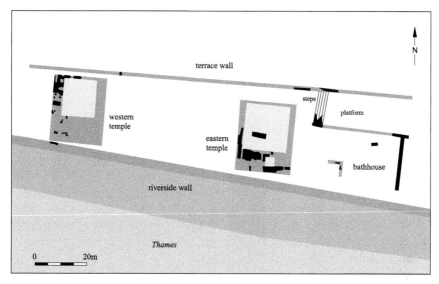

Fig. 27.1 Temples and public buildings in the south-west quarter of London after the building programmes of Allectus (PET81, QUV01: after Williams 1993 and Bradley and Butler 2008). Drawn by Justin Russell.

London project were redeployed here after completing improvements to fortifications along the Saxon Shore, indicated by the use of piles felled AD 293 in the defences at Pevensey.[6]

The two buildings erected along the Thames waterfront had exceptionally broad foundations, 8.5 metres wide, on their southern sides. The side walls were also very substantial, measuring about 3.75 metres across, with the rear formed by a narrow wall terraced into the hillside to the north. No superstructure survived over these foundations and it is fairly certain that the buildings were never finished. Tim Bradley and Jon Butler suggest that the broad southern foundation supported a rectangular podium measuring *c.* 20.5 by 8 metres, with the other walls forming the sides of an enclosed courtyard to the north. This seems improbable. The enclosed areas are more likely to have lain below the temple *cella* where deep foundations were not required, with the broader southern foundation designed to support the columns and walls of the portico and pronaos of the temple facade. If so, these were classical prostyle temples, slightly over 20 metres wide and 25 metres deep, facing south to the river. The riverside wall might have been partially dismantled to give access to the temple steps, or the structures towered above this wall on a raised terrace. In either case the new buildings were designed to be seen from the river, presenting commanding views over a waterway previously cut adrift from the city. A broad flight of steps at the east end of the terrace established a grand entrance to the precinct where a small bathhouse may have been located.

The construction of the riverside terrace involved the demolition of an earlier precinct that had probably housed a temple to Jupiter (above p. 303). It is possible that one of the new temples rehoused Jupiter since a close association between Jupiter Capitoline and Roman imperial authority made this a popular dedication under the tetrarchy.[7] It is tempting to identify the other building as a temple to Sol Invictus. A temple to the unconquered sun was built in Rome in AD 274 after Aurelius' promotion of this cult to official status. Several emperors identified closely with Sol Invictus and he featured on issues of Allectus' London coinage. Since he was the only state deity to receive such acknowledgement he is perhaps the likeliest to have been honoured with a new temple.[8] Few temples were built anywhere in the late third century, but they featured in the architecture of imperial palaces in the tetrarchic capitals.[9] The best known is Diocletian's palace at Split, which incorporated a temple to Jupiter. Allectus is particularly likely to have drawn inspiration from the palace at Trier, and the architecture of these imperial palaces suggests that he intended to arrange temples, treasuries, armouries and mints around a vast palace complex in the south-west quarter of London.[10] The northern boundary of this area was formed by the terrace walls along Knightrider Street that might have been the site of a circus.[11] Many late Roman imperial ceremonies were orchestrated in the circus, which featured prominently within the tetrarchic palaces at Milan and Thessaloniki. Allectus may have decreed himself a riverside palace to form the ceremonial centre for his imperial rule, flanked by a circus to the north and temples to the south. Whatever the master-plan, this building programme rivalled the contemporary tetrarchic capitals. It drew on engineering capacity developed around the preceding programme of urban and coastal fortification, and shows that Allectus intended to rule permanently from London.

The temples were set to dominate the Thames, proclaiming that London no longer needed cautious defending but advertising an imperial authority rooted in Roman history and sanctioned by its gods. This ambition was wholly hubristic, since in AD 296 Constantius reconquered Britain. Historical sources describe an invasion fleet that sailed in two divisions: one from the Seine under Asclepiodotus the other from Boulogne under Constantius. Asclepiodotus' ships landed in the Solent, where Allectus was engaged and killed. Constantius' crossing was delayed and he reached London just in time to halt the sack of the city by Allectus' Frankish mercenaries.[12] The event left no certain mark on the city, although some of the fire damaged buildings described above (p. 332) might possibly have been looted at this time. Constantius' rescue of London was acclaimed by panegyrists and celebrated on a commemorative gold medallion found in the suburbs of Arras in 1922.[13] This was part of a hoard buried in a vessel that contained at least twenty-five medallions, eight probably struck to commemorate the recovery of Britain, assembled by an official rewarded for his services by Constantius and his son Constantine. The most famous of these medallions, weighing 53 grams, illustrated Constantius' arrival in London in 296, proclaiming him as restorer of the eternal light (*redditor lucis aeternae*). It showed the emperor on horseback approaching the gate of a city identified as London (LON), whose female personification knelt with arms outstretched to receive him. A manned war-galley occupies the foreground.

The County Hall boat, whose discovery in 1910 caused such a stir (above p. 15), might have been involved in this campaign.[14] The hulk abandoned in a river backwater was more than 3 metres wide, with a rounded hull and a draught of around 1.8 metres. Neither end survived, but the boat is likely to have been between 19 and 26 metres long, with a capacity of between 50 and 100 tonnes. It was carvel-built, following Mediterranean rather than local shipbuilding traditions, with the oak planks fastened edge to edge by mortice-and-tenon joints. Dendrochronological analysis establishes that these timbers came from trees grown in south-east England, felled after AD 287. Four coins were found within the hulk, the latest of Allectus minted between AD 293 and 296. There was no trace of the mast-step, and the surviving evidence doesn't let us know what type of vessel it was. Peter Marsden finds evidence of a decked hull which would rule out the possibility that it was an oared ship, like the one shown on the Arras medallion, for want of headroom below deck. The absence of footrests and oarports also implies that it wasn't a warship.[15] It remains the case, however, that boats of this type of construction were rare and it is unlikely to have been a merchant vessel. It may, therefore, have been one of the ships built as part of Carausius' restoration of the fleet. According to the panegyrist, Carausius had a great many ships built in the Roman fashion (*in nostrum modum*), which fits both the style and date of the County Hall discovery.[16] This ship might alternatively have been added to the fleet after Britain was restored to the Roman Empire in AD 296, as Marsden thinks likely, although shipbuilding would have been a less pressing priority at this time.

Within the city

London changed little in the early fourth century. A panegyrist described Constantius' transfer of skilled workers (*artifices*), with whom the provinces of Britain were overflowing, to help in construction at Autun.[17] London needed fewer construction workers now that Allectus' unfinished palace was surplus to requirements, but remained sufficiently important to retain the mint established under Carausius. This continued to produce coins in silvered-bronze bearing mint marks LON or LN down to AD 325.[18] Constantius also returned to Britain in AD 305 to campaign beyond the Antonine Wall, before dying in York in AD 306

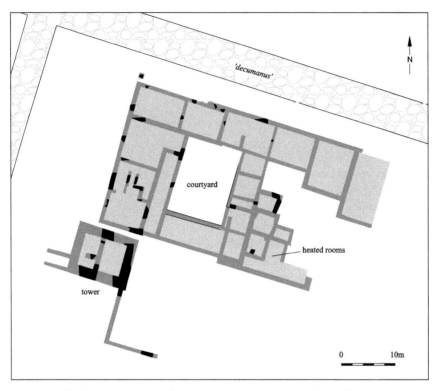

Fig. 27.2   The late Roman town house at Plantation Place, adapted from the third-century town house shown as Fig. 21.2 with the addition of heated baths and a substantial tower (FER97: after Dunwoodie *et al.* 2015). Drawn by Justin Russell.

which is where his son, Constantine, was acclaimed emperor.[19] London briefly remained an important command centre during Constantine's ascent to power, marked by coins issued to celebrate his visits in AD 312 and 314.[20]

Most of London's late third-century town houses survived into the fourth century, and a few were renovated.[21] Rear-extensions were added to roadside buildings at One Poultry, one of which contained a hypocaust, plunge bath and mosaic pavement.[22] Piles used in this construction were felled AD 302–34, making it the latest tree-ring dated Roman building known from London. A feature of the architecture of this period may have been the addition of strongly built towers within important domestic compounds, some of which were now walled (Fig. 27.2). A large early fourth-century tower was built at the end of the western wing of the town house at Plantation Place.[23] This was a massive construction, measuring some 11.5 metres by 9.25 metres, set over chalk foundations 1.7 metres wide and 3.2 metres deep. It was semi-basemented with mortar floors that included coins dated 307–10 and 330–5. Plaster from decorated niches and openings included fragments of yellow and green vegetation. This was a lordly addition, signalling a new approach to the demonstration of social status following a trend towards the creation of palatial private residences that characterized late Roman towns.[24] Another semi-basemented tower may have been attached to a property in Southwark at 4–26 St Thomas Street, where stone walls set over piles enclosed a cellar some 6.7 metres long by 4.4 metres across.[25] A curious foundation, more than 4 metres wide, built across the line of a disused road south-east of the amphitheatre temple precinct around the end of the third century may also have been associated with a large private property encroaching onto public space.[26]

The Walbrook temple remained busy: the entrance steps were worn from use and the nave floor needed relaying nine times. For 50 years it housed the mysteries of the Persian god for whom it was built. A marble slab found on a late floor surface carried a dedication that translates as 'for the welfare of our August Emperors and most noble Caesar, to the god Mithras and the Invincible Sun from the east to the west'. The details indicate that this was inscribed between May AD 307 and May AD 308.[27] Soon after, the building needed extensive repair. The columns that separated the nave from the aisles were removed, the nave floor raised and the west end rearranged. Prior to this rebuilding, dated *c.* AD 310–20 from associated finds, important cult icons were collected together and buried beneath the nave floor.[28] Others were dispatched into the waters of the Walbrook. One of the buried items was the marble head of Mithras whose discovery caused such excitement in 1954 (above p. 16). It had been broken asunder before burial by a blow to the left side of the neck, perhaps in a deliberate decapitation to exorcise the simulacrum's power before it was laid to rest. Cult images were mutilated in the destruction of other Mithraea in the Roman world, and it has been argued that militant Christians were responsible for iconoclastic attacks.[29] We have absolutely no evidence to suggest that Christians were responsible for any destructions of pagan sites in London. In some regards the dismemberment recalls the Bacchic myths of *sparagmos* and earlier rituals of corpse abuse (above p. 254), and the head of the god may have followed a similar path of dispatch to other worlds. Mithras and his companions may have been ritually sacrificed as the building was prepared for a new type of worship. New altars replaced the earlier cult image, and the open layout accommodated different liturgical and ritual activities. Martin Henig has suggested that the front of the apse was converted to form a baldacchino covering a new shrine.[30] New floors were laid and a small votive offering containing coins to AD 313–18 placed beneath timbers associated with the construction of a stone altar. Finds from in front of the apse included coins to AD 341–6 which provide a *terminus post quem* for the latest use of the temple. Objects associated with these floors suggest that the temple had been redesigned around Bacchic worship, which at this date may also have been Orphic. A small marble statuette of Bacchus and his companions was inscribed 'HOMINIBUSBAGISBITAM': you give life to wandering men. A circular silver casket and a silver bowl cut up into pieces were probably been hidden in a space in the north wall of the temple. Jocelyn Toynbee recognized that the casket was probably of late third- or fourth-century Mediterranean manufacture, decorated with hunting scenes in exotic landscapes of Bacchic inspiration. This was perhaps a *cista mystica*, to infuse and drug wine.[31] Other statues were found in the debris to the sides of the building; two marble figures found here had been hacked down to the torso in further ritual dismemberment, with their limbs perhaps removed for use as votive offerings.[32]

Redundancies

The pace of construction slowed in the early fourth century, leaving London little need to import building timber. Mosaic floors were sufficiently scarce to suggest that London is unlikely to have permanently housed skilled mosaicists.[33] London became less important to Constantine when he moved his headquarters from Trier to Serdica in AD 316/317, and as a likely consequence London's mint ceased production in AD 325.[34] No further imperial visits are known to have taken place, apart from a brief and unexplained visit by Constans in AD 343.[35] The lead seal of Constans found on the Thames foreshore near Billingsgate perhaps arrived with goods moved to London on this occasion, almost certainly the last time that a ruling emperor visited the city.[36]

London's massive forum basilica was torn down in the late third or early fourth century. Already, from the mid-third century, the portico along its eastern side had been replaced by ephemeral structures used by metalworkers.[37] The nave floor was later sealed by thick mud and roof collapse, and most of the basilica was demolished to its foundations as its building materials were quarried for use elsewhere. The cleared site was then levelled, to be covered with dark grey silts in the early fourth century. Similar deposits extended over the road to the north of the basilica showing that this too was closed for use. Several of London's other public buildings may have been made redundant. By the end of the third century parts of the building in the area of Cannon Street Station, the so-called 'governor's palace', were dilapidated.[38] In Southwark parts of the supposed *mansio* were demolished by the early fourth century, whilst the baths attached to the residential complex at Winchester Palace were demolished at the end of the third century.[39] Other parts of these buildings remained in use, with coin evidence suggesting that some occupation continued into the late fourth century.

London no longer needed all of its administrative buildings. Tetrarchic reforms may have encouraged the relocation of bureaucratic departments into the palaces of new rulers, leaving public buildings under-used. The forum was no longer a clearing point for shipments that passed through London. The shops and stores that surrounded its courtyard saw diminished use, finding fewer tenants once the flow of *annona* supplies dried and local provisioning replaced bulk importation.

Similar changes occurred in other Romano-British towns. The main hall of the basilica at Silchester was given over to metalworkers from the late third century, and Wroxeter's forum was largely abandoned after a late third-century fire.[40] Mike Fulford suggests that some public buildings were casualties of regime change, following the demotion of monuments associated with the failed *Imperium Galliarum*.[41] The changes were, however, part of a more widespread shift in the use of urban space. An important study of rubbish in Rome finds that there was a distinct change in distribution mechanisms used to support the *annona* and *frumentationes* after the mid-third century.[42] Up until this date the amphora that carried these supplies were discarded at centralized public locations, especially Rome's river port. Subsequently, however, there was a more widespread pattern of distribution that bypassed the earlier public locations. Something similar can be read from distributions of amphorae in Roman London. In earlier phases these were disproportionately concentrated around the port and forum, followed by a more dispersed pattern in later antiquity.[43] London's forum and port may have played an important role in the redistribution of *annona* and *frumentationes* until the middle of the third century, but ceased to do so after the reorganization of supply in the latter half of the century.

After building materials had been reclaimed and recycled, the sites of public buildings were converted to other uses, often housing metal workshops. Late Roman timber-framed building with hearths used for small-scale industrial production were built over the abandoned site of Allectus' temples.[44] These activities, dated *c.* AD 340, present such a contrast with earlier civic architecture that they are sometimes dismissed as a form of squatter occupation. But the settlement of metalworkers suggests urban regeneration. Their workshops generated income through rents and taxes, and secured vital industrial production. Much of the late antique economy was subordinate to military requirements which relied on the manufacture and repair of weapons and armour in both state-run and private workshops (*fabricae*).[45] Whatever the impulse, it resulted in the transformation of civic space, as marginal activities were drawn into central locations.

The buildings made redundant in the late third and early fourth centuries were those most closely associated with the earlier public administration, perhaps particularly those managed through the office of the procurator. Some places used as settings for civic ceremony may have shown greater resilience. This might account for the retention of the apse at the east end of the forum basilica after the rest of the building was demolished, perhaps saved from destruction as a setting for imperial ritual and civic memory.[46] As elsewhere, we can assume that ceremonies designed around the public demonstration of loyalty to the emperor and Rome continued.[47] London would have witnessed processions and banquets, celebrating the important feast-days that reinforced the relationship between urban communities and political authority. Coins from the latest arena surfaces date around AD 340, suggesting their continued use and repair. It is unlikely, however, that the amphitheatre hosted many gladiatorial combats at this time. From the second century these buildings were chiefly used for animal shows, particularly bear-baiting. The wider popularity of this cruel sport probably accounts for the recovery of the remains of brown bears from some sites in later Roman London.[48]

Southwark

In contrast with the city, Southwark remained unwalled. It is not certain that London Bridge survived and it has been suggested from the dates of coins found in the Thames that the crossing closed c. AD 330.[49] The evidence is, however, inconclusive and might simply witness the disuse of a bridgehead shrine from which coins were dedicated to the river. River traffic must still have been landed cargoes along Southwark's ageing waterfront, supplying the industrial district on the north island with fuel and raw materials from Hampshire and Surrey. This area continued to house metalworking and smithing, although it is not clear if these activities relied on imported or recycled iron. After a busy end to the third century, an early fourth-century contraction is implied by some sequences. This was followed by an upsurge in activity around the middle of the fourth century with metalworking and smithing attested by hearths, copper-alloy and iron objects, and slag.[50] A timber gate built across the newly resurfaced road may have controlled access to the industrial quarter, where production may have responded to official commissions involving shipbuilding or naval repairs.

Several wells of this date have been identified and Richard Hingley has drawn attention to the distinctive nature of the assemblages associated with their disuse.[51] These were probably the product of ceremonies celebrated at the moment of their closure (below p. 385). An important collection of cult items was recovered from the fills of a well beneath Southwark Cathedral, presumably derived from buildings standing here in the late third and early fourth century.[52] Most of the items had been made in the second or third century, and included a funerary chest portraying a woman reclining on a couch holding a bunch of grapes. Some might have come from a mausoleum, but others are more likely to have been found in a shrine. The reclining figure had been decapitated and burnt before being deposited in the well, offering a parallel to the cult items buried in the Mithraeum. Similar processes may have been at work, in which changing belief systems resulted in the fourth-century dispatch of items that had served outmoded third-century worship.

The temple precinct on the southern border, at Tabard Square, was divided into two separate enclosures, accommodating the different liturgies of the two temples.[53] Three plinths along the western side of the precinct supported statues, altars or columns, whose presence is indicated by fragments of stone sculptures and the left foot of a larger-than-life bronze statue. Another foundation opposite the north temple may have supported an altar or column.

The countryside

The fourth century was the great era of villa building in Roman Britain. The mosaics in these country houses show a sophisticated and cultured understanding of the philosophical arguments of the time, drawing on the literary allusions and iconography used to express *paideia*.[54] This was particularly the case in south-west Britain, where an influx of ideas, money and perhaps people, took inspiration from the imperial capital at Trier. This area is thought to have been detached from the command of London to become the separately governed province of *Britannia Prima,* perhaps in the political settlement made by the incoming regime of Constantius Chlorus.[55] Villas and their mosaics illustrate the presence of a wealthy landed gentry exercising power from country estates, in a settlement pattern inherited from the later Iron Age.[56]

Despite its political importance London failed to attract an equivalent share of spectacular grand country houses. Although several villas are known from the region, these were modestly appointed. Some may have been abandoned around the middle of the third century, probably including Ashtead in Surrey and perhaps, temporarily, the villa at Lullingstone in Kent.[57] Overall, however, villa densities in north Kent and on the Sussex coast peaked in the later third century, and declined thereafter.[58] The principal villas within London's wider orbit remained those of the Darent valley in north Kent (above p. 178), several of which prospered. Some incorporated structures likely to have been used as granaries, with unusually ample facilities at Lullingstone, Darenth, and Farningham.[59] These estates may have come to play a more important role in the collection and storage of tax in kind. Villas in Essex were also built or enlarged, notably the large courtyard villa at Chignall St James, near Chelmsford, where new enclosures may have supported ranching and stock-breeding.[60] Although these farms are likely to have fed London, their owners may have remained socially and politically attached to neighbouring cities such as Colchester and Canterbury.

A smaller group of suburban villas is more likely to have housed individuals involved in London's political life. Shadwell remained one of the most important of these.[61] Programmes of renovation to the bathhouse started c. AD 275, resulting in five different phases of remodelling over a 50-year period. Coin-finds point to peaks of activity through the 280s and 290s as the baths were enlarged and improved. Aspects of the coin supply find parallel in the Saxon Shore fort at Reculver, reinforcing the impression that Shadwell was the seat of an official mediating between the London-based government and the spreading estuary and coastal regions beyond.[62]

We can chart the distribution of the rich and powerful through the stone sarcophagi in which some were buried. These stone tombs were imported to the region at considerable expense in the late third and fourth centuries, and are usually found close to the likely locations of suburban villas. Examples include the tomb of Valerius Amandinus, designed for display within a mausoleum, from Thorney Island in Westminster.[63] Others have been found at St Martin-in-the-Fields, Lower Clapton and Ratcliffe. The early seventeenth-century discoveries at Ratcliffe included a stone sarcophagus and lead cist decorated with scallop-shells, with impressive grave-goods.[64]

Similar sarcophagi are occasional finds in London's extramural cemeteries.[65] One found at Haydon Square in 1853 was sculpted with the bust of a young man, designed to be displayed within the burial chamber of a mausoleum. A more recent example from Harper Road, on the borders of Southwark, consisted of a sarcophagus housed within a rectangular mausoleum defined by chalk foundations which contained a burial carbon-dated around AD 328. A widely publicized find was made at Spitalfields Market in March 1999, where a limestone sarcophagus, one of two from the site, contained a lead coffin that had been decorated with scallop shells symbolizing the journey to the underworld originally connected with the god Bacchus.[66] Inside the coffin was the body of a woman in her late teens or early twenties who had been buried in the mid- to late fourth century. The study of her aDNA and lead isotopes in her teeth suggests that she spent her childhood in southern Europe, possibly Rome, before coming to London. She was laid to rest on a blanket with her head on a pillow of bay leaves, and clothed in a silk damask tunic decorated with gold thread that may have incorporated purple wool. Residues show that the body had been prepared for burial with imported pine and mastic resins, and she was accompanied by goods that included a jet box and glass phial that hint at a belief system rooted in Bacchic approaches to salvation.

The settlement at Old Ford 4 kilometres north-east of London, where the road to Colchester approached the crossing of the river Lea, may have expanded at this date. Water-meadows alongside the Lea offered grazing for cattle and horse, and the roadside settlement may have managed these valuable territories and been a holding station for livestock destined for town.[67] The growth of the site, and its extensive burial grounds, dates largely after AD 270 when there was a shift towards higher cattle frequencies, meeting London's renewed demand for beef, horn and leather. Cattle was driven into town for slaughter: where butchery shows an increase in the distribution of meat taken off the bone.[68] Rebuilding took place at other roadside sites, including Enfield, Brentford and Staines, often on plots left open since the end of the second century, and involved the introduction of buildings with masonry walls and tile roofs.[69] It has been suggested that the revived fortunes of small towns and roadside sites was a consequence of their role as collection points for tax and rent drawn on for *annona* supply.[70] This might account for the development of a late third-century settlement on the south bank of the Thames at Thamesmead, where a masonry building is suggested by building debris.[71]

28

Augusta (c. AD 350–80)

Reinforcing the urban defences

For the first two centuries of London's existence, Rome's interests were written on the waterfront, where intermittent harbour improvements served the machinery of power. London's last great phase of quayside expansion ended as the city walls were built, and the history of later public architecture was largely a history of urban defences. London retained a pivotal role in Rome's network of control, but was now presented as a strong-point confronting threat and insecurity. Three main phases in the evolution of the masonry wall can be described. The massive landward circuit was built in the early third century, perhaps *c.* AD 215/225, followed by the construction of the riverside wall in the late 270s (Chapters 23 and 26). Both works can be viewed as acts of rehabilitation following periods of urban dilapidation, undertaken when high politics gave Rome reason to re-engage with affairs in southern Britain.

In this chapter we turn our attention to the third phase of defensive architecture, when new towers were added to the walled circuit (Figs 28.1 and 28.2). The period preceding the construction of these towers may also have been one of relative neglect: most fourth-century building activity is provisionally dated before *c.* AD 325 or after *c.* AD 350 and the second quarter of the century appears distinctly quieter. This hiatus in activity would be consistent with the reduced importance accorded the north-west provinces after Constantine's attention turned eastwards in the 320s (above p. 356). Soon after the middle of the century a series of D-shaped solid projecting towers, known as bastions, was built along the eastern third of the town wall.[1] Traces of fourteen have been recorded between the Walbrook and the Tower, and the locations of another seven can be conjectured from their regular 53 metre spacing. Their foundations were 5.8–7.9 metres wide, projecting forward from the wall for 4.4–5.6 metres and encroaching onto the line of the earlier V-shaped town ditch. A broad U-shaped town ditch was dug in replacement, adding defence in depth. Evidence of this ditch is scarce, since largely lost to medieval recutting, but a section north of the gateway at Ludgate was 3 metres deep and 10 metres wide.[2] The towers would have stood taller than the existing wall parapet, providing elevated platforms from which archers or small bolt-firing *ballistae* could direct enfilading fire along the wall.[3]

It is not certain that all solid towers were contemporary, but their regular spacing shows them to have been the product of a single plan. This was probably

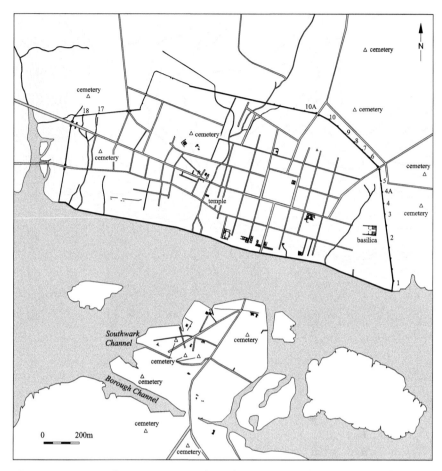

Fig. 28.1 A proposed reconstruction of London *c.* AD 370, although not all of the illustrated streets and buildings retained from earlier phases are likely to have remained in use by this date. Drawn by Justin Russell.

decided on after *c.* AD 350. At Duke's Place Peter Marsden recorded the 1-metre-high foundations of a bastion dug into deposits containing fourth-century finds, where material deposited against the structure included fourth-century pottery and coins dated AD 364–75.[4] Subsequent excavations by John Maloney recovered a coin of Constans (AD 341–4) from the V-shaped town ditch. Since the ditch was backfilled in preparation for the construction of the tower the coin provides an indirect *terminus post-quem* for its construction.

The eastern towers drew on a mix of materials, principally Kentish ragstone, set over chalk and flint foundations, and incorporating material from redundant funerary monuments. Some effigies appear to have been ritually laid to rest and Richard Hingley suggests that they had been selected for their religious potency.[5]

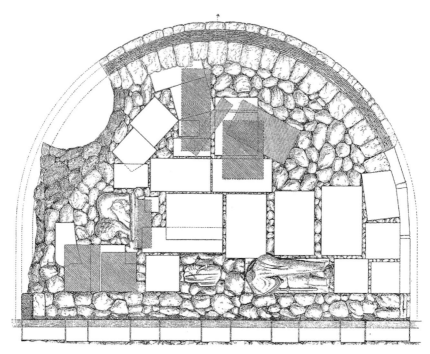

Fig. 28.2 The foundations of bastion 10 on London Wall at Camomile Street, incorporating *spolia* from earlier Roman tombs (from a drawing by Henry Hodge on behalf of the London and Middlesex Archaeological Society and first published in Price 1880).

This use of redundant tombs was also a pragmatic one. London had no local building stone, and these monuments were ready quarries.[6] The quarrying of stone from the amphitheatre also started soon after AD 355, with coins of AD 367–74 present in robber trenches and demolition debris.[7] Like other Romano-British amphitheatres the arena had ceased to host games and displays during the fourth century.[8] The supposed *mansio* in Southwark was also dismantled and stone extracted from its foundations, with mid-fourth-century pottery and a coin of AD 347–8 present in a robber trench.[9] The materials recovered from these redundant buildings could have supplied various construction projects, including the building of towers and gates along the landward wall.[10]

The series of solid towers did not continue west of the Walbrook. Although bastions were eventually built here, these were hollow structures of likely medieval date. A pair investigated at King Edward Street appear, however, to have been late Roman: one with a solid base built when the V-shaped ditch was still partly open.[11] Improvements to the town gates may also have been made, as at Aldersgate where a double gateway was built with boldly projecting D-shaped flanking towers that may have supported raised artillery platforms.[12] The decision not to build towers at most locations west of the Walbrook may have been due to the presence of an extensive marsh, Moorfields, which had formed after the second-century town wall was built.[13] Towers were also absent around the Cripplegate fort, where the closely spaced gates and corner towers were perhaps deemed sufficient.

The works of this period might have entailed closing off the *c.* 75 metres long gap at the western end of the riverside wall. Excavations at Baynard's Castle showed that this stretch lacked the piled foundations characteristic of late third-century work, and the ragstone blocks were set directly into the clay subsoil. There were no tile courses within the body of the wall, and the fact that it eventually collapsed northwards indicates that there was no earth bank behind.[14] Southwark remained largely undefended, although the protection afforded by river channels might have been enhanced by temporary earthworks around the bridgehead. A ditch measuring over 1.5 metres deep and 5 metres wide found aligned east-west at Tooley Street contained fills dated to the second half of the fourth century.[15]

London's new defences followed contemporary fashion in military architecture, designed to give defenders a tactical advantage in the event of hostile assault.[16] As in earlier times, the enhancement of the walled circuit conveyed a message of authority and stability and the serried towers signalled London's urban status to ships approaching upriver.[17] James Gerrard suggests that this symbolic statement was the essential purpose of the architecture, since gaps in coverage betray a neglect of defensive considerations. The distribution of towers may also, however, have been tactically inspired. They were placed along parts of the wall more easily approached over open ground, but missing along the stretches of wall facing Moorgate, the Fleet and Thames, where river and marsh insulated the city from attack.[18] The decision to manage without towers at these places reduced construction costs, and may have acknowledged the limited availability of soldiery to man the defences. This was, therefore, a lower-budget effort than the earlier town wall. London possessed an unusually extensive walled circuit compared to the reduced urban enceintes of late Roman Gaul, which it had inherited from an earlier and more expansive time. Its length made the circuit difficult to defend, but the decision not to retreat to a smaller area, achievable by retreating to an urban core east of the Walbrook, may have been dictated by construction costs. The building of London's towers is likely to have involved a series of pragmatic choices balancing defensive considerations against what could be achieved.[19] They offered both appearance and substance: a credible and sustainable promise of security, representing the abiding reality of revived Roman power.

The modernization of London's defences was a decided strategy implemented soon after the middle of the fourth century. Whilst it remains unfashionable to connect campaigns of wall construction with known historical events, we cannot escape the fact that programmes of investment on this scale were politically inspired.[20] It has long been thought likely that London's bastions were built in a programme of refortification that Ammianus Marcellinus attributed to Count Theodosius in AD 368.[21] This remains an attractive hypothesis, although the archaeological dating is insufficiently precise for certainty and John Casey alternatively suggested that bastions were added to Romano-British urban defences in building campaigns under Magnentius *c.* AD 350.[22] It seems unlikely, however, that Magnentius' rule generated resources for the restoration of Romano-British towns.[23] His bid for power is more likely to have entailed removing troops from the province, reducing rather than reinforcing the available manpower.

London was directly mentioned in accounts of campaigns undertaken in the 360s. In AD 360, the commander (*magister militum*) Flavius Lupicinus made directly for London to take council when he was sent to Britain to respond to attacks from Picts and Scotti in the north, showing that the city was the appropriate administrative centre for such operations. Similar considerations applied during the disorders of AD 367 that Ammianus described as a barbarian conspiracy.[24] In this account the emperor Valentinian turned to Count Theodosius to restore control. Theodosius crossed to Richborough where he waited on troop reinforcements before marching on London, intercepting bands of plunderers before relieving the imperilled town. London is where he established his operational base, from which he was credited with restoring Britain's damaged 'cities and strongholds which had been founded to secure a long period of peace, but had suffered repeated misfortunes'.

This presents a plausible context for upgrading London's defences, and Theodosius' forces would have brought manpower and resources to the exercise. A significant proportion of the Valentinian coins found around London were copies, likely to have been made in order to supplement official supplies, lubricating essential transactions and empowering officials returning to the state payroll.[25] Ammianus' account also provides the first reference to the fact that London was renamed *Augusta*, a title that can only have been awarded as an imperial mark of honour.[26] Coins minted in London down to AD 325 carry mint-marks that imply, through omission, that it had not been renamed by this date. The grant of the title was perhaps decided on by Valentinian at the time of Theodosius' restoration.[27]

London and the Roman administration

Regardless of the exact circumstances that resulted in the building of London's bastions, they declared the continued importance of the late fourth-century city. Simon Esmonde Cleary has shown that the late antique walled cities of northern

Gaul housed key institutions of the Roman administration.[28] There is a strong correlation between the possession of walls and the presence of military and state personnel, but a comparative indifference to the needs of civilian urban communities. London's defences are likely to have been similarly inspired. Some officers and departments operating out of fourth-century London are described in the lists of civil and military officials presented in the *Notitia Dignitatum*, which although amended in the fifth century reproduced elements of earlier arrangements.[29] Following third-century reform Britain was no longer ruled by a governor and procurator but divided into a series of smaller provinces, each with its own government (p. 311). Collectively these formed the Diocese of Britain that was overseen by a *vicarius* based in London who answered to the Praetorian Prefect of the Gauls. The *Notitia* lists nine department heads on the staff of the *vicarius*—managing taxes, records, correspondence and intelligence—along with assistants, secretaries and notaries. It also described London as the seat of the treasury and head of diocesan tax administration.[30] Each of these officials would have been attended by a large private household, combining to draw hundreds of notables to the fourth-century city.

Although Britain's principal military commands followed the northern frontier London may also have been the seat of operations for a mobile field army (*comitatenses*) commanded by the *Comes Britanniarum*. Although we lack any direct archaeological evidence for the presence of the *Comes* in London, and the history of the command is uncertain, this would not have been an unusual arrangement. This post wasn't allocated a fixed base in the *Notitia*, and Mark Hassall suggests that it campaigned wherever required and was billeted accordingly.[31] Roman troops were routinely stationed in strategic cities where civilian populations could be pressed into housing and feeding them.[32] London was a sensible home for the *Comes* when not on campaign and his forces would have eased the problems of finding soldiery to place on the city walls.

London might also have been the dominant site in the command infrastructure developed under the leadership of the *Comes litoris Saxonici per Britanniam*.[33] As has been noted (above p. 313) aspects of the design and supply of the suburban establishment at Shadwell showed close links with sites along the Saxon Shore, and some operations would have been best managed from the diocesan capital at London. The development of these commands, and of the coastal frontier itself, gave London much of its raison d'être.

A grave in the eastern cemetery at Mansell Street may have been the resting place of a senior figure from this community of Roman officials (Fig. 28.3). The body of a man more than 45 years old was buried in a wooden coffin with items of dress normally restricted to the upper echelons of late Roman imperial society.[34] The surviving tokens of his rank included an unworn belt set (*cingulum*) consisting of a large chip-carved buckle, strap-end, and three end-plates; and a rare crossbow brooch of the type shown on the Monza ivory diptych thought to

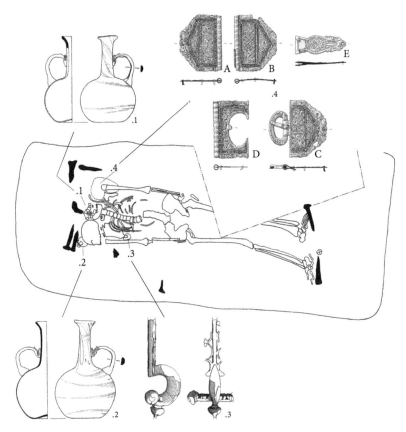

Fig. 28.3 The burial of a man dressed as a high-ranking late Roman official, with a crossbow brooch and belt set (*cingulum*), from the cemetery at Mansell Street (adapted from Barber and Bowsher 2000. Reproduced by kind permission of Museum of London Archaeology).

depict the general Stilicho.[35] The belt was designed to go around a tunic decorated with panels of silk worn over embroidered trousers, and the brooch served to fasten a heavy cloak (*chlamys*) at the shoulder. By the fifth century this had become the attire of Rome's senior military and state officials, following barbarian-influenced fashion.[36] The crossbow brooch is a type normally thought to have been introduced *c.* AD 390, but an unpublished radiocarbon date from the burial itself points to an earlier date with a high degree of probability (95.4 per cent) that the individual died within the period 237–365 cal AD.[37] Given the presence of the brooch it is likely that the burial took place in the 360s rather than earlier in this range. At such an early date these items would have been at the very cutting edge of imperial fashion, and we can assume that deceased had only recently been issued the symbols of his rank when he died. It has been suggested that this style of dress may have evoked the credentials of late Roman authority in Britain without necessarily identifying office holders, but the items buried at Mansell Street are perhaps more likely to have accompanied someone who had genuinely held high office.[38] If so, we might be looking at someone who in the mid-360s held one of the posts listed in the *Notitia*. Intriguingly the strontium and lead isotopes within his dental enamel indicate that this high-ranking individual had grown up in the London area, showing that some government officials were locally recruited. This wasn't the only person to have been buried in London with elements of the 'Germanic' style of official dress. Another relief-cast buckle in the 'chip carved' style was found in the cemetery at West Smithfield, and similar items have been found at Fulham Palace and Enfield where officials may have been placed to command satellite sites.[39]

Wealth within and beyond the walls

Although the city wasn't densely populated, with housing spread thinly across an overlarge urban footprint inherited from second-century expansion, several properties were refurbished in the late fourth century. The early Roman warehouses at Pudding Lane were still standing, and industrial slag and ash suggests that some operated as workshops. Six successive floor repairs were laid in one room, the earliest of which contained a coin of Constantius II (AD 348–51). A small bathhouse found behind this structure was refurbished with new heated rooms and a small bath late in the fourth century, with a coin of Valens (AD 367–75) found in construction levels.[40] New floors were also laid within the tower of the residential complex at Plantation Place, where the latest surfaces date after *c.* AD 370.[41] For the most part these works involved the redecoration of existing structures, but they illustrate an urban vitality sustained over several decades. These works ensured that London retained a stock of high-status housing and productive workshops, meeting the needs of the government officials stationed here.

It is possible that London had fewer skilled carpenters, following changes to the mechanisms of timber procurement earlier in the century. A well at Drapers' Gardens, coin-dated after *c.* AD 335 and associated with pottery as late as *c.* AD 350, was built using the labour-intensive 'native' styles of woodworking rather than more sophisticated Roman carpentry.[42]

A few unusually important buildings were built within the city. One of these was investigated at One Poultry where a large property with tile-faced concrete walls was built at a prime location on the south side of the main road and flanked by a large brick culvert. Coins of AD 340–6 were found in material dumped before the building's construction, and the presence of Portchester D pottery confirms that it was occupied in the second half of the century.[43] We don't know what purpose it served, but its scale hints at a public use. It stood in an area that had previously housed granaries and bakeries and it is tempting to suggest a continued association with administered food supply.

Another important property was marked by a vast mosaic floor, measuring 7.4 by 7.25 metres, found at Old Broad Street in 1854. This pavement was later displayed in the Crystal Palace at Sydenham where it was lost in the fire of 1936.[44] It incorporated red, white, yellow, and grey geometric designs, with a central panel showing Bacchus accompanied by his leopard and canthari filling the corners. The pavement belongs to a stylistic group described as the 'Corinian Saltire' school by David Smith.[45] The artisans producing these designs normally worked for West Country patrons and the London floor was almost certainly made by the same craftsmen who laid a mosaic in a villa at Halstock in Dorset coin dated after c. AD 350.[46] The scale and quality of the London pavement indicates that it adorned a grand reception room, probably a dining room or audience hall similar to those of the richest luxury villas. The West Country connection is curious. Was this the residence of an emissary or official representative of the government of Britannia Prima attending the London court of the *vicarius*? Its design shows the continued currency of Bacchic iconography. By this date Orpheus was recognized as a saviour figure within his mysteries, and several of Britain's later Roman mosaic pavements contained allegorical references to this Orphic interpretation of Bacchic cult. These ideas informed the design of the Old Broad Street pavement, without necessarily meaning that the room was a place of cult worship. This late antique Orphism, drawing also on Neoplatonist philosophy, exercised an important influence in the elaboration and evolution of Hellenized Christianity, as a consequence of which the worship of Bacchus and Christ were sometimes entwined in the fluid soteriological theologies that preceded Christian orthodoxy.[47]

Changes were also made to the temple precinct on London's southern approaches at Tabard Square.[48] In the fourth century the temenos adjacent to the north temple was redesigned, and an unusual building set along its east side. A couple of potsherds dated after c. AD 330 were recovered from the level at which its construction trenches were dug. This rectangular structure was decorated, but contained no heated rooms, and presented a façade formed by two projecting side towers or wings connected by a large corridor or portico. This reproduced the winged-corridor layout favoured in Romano-British villas. In this particular context the projecting rooms might have been suitable places to hosts cult feasts, and an abundance of pig bones, a sign of high-status dinning, were recovered from the temenos ditch.[49] Surfaces within the walled area were renewed into the middle of the fourth century, although the statues or columns set over the plinths had been removed.[50] These changes witness the continuing evolution of liturgical practice within London's pagan spaces until the middle of the fourth century. It is possible that an earlier emphasis on the architectural furniture of open areas as a stage for cult sacrifice had given way to a religious practice concerned with select gatherings around shared meals and mysteries. The increasingly private nature of cult celebration may have turned attention away from other public temples in later Roman London.

London's first Christian communities

This evidence for a diversity of pagan belief in fourth-century London contrasts with a relative scarcity of evidence for Christian worship. The cult would have found likely adherents within London's cosmopolitan communities, and some people in Britain had probably identified as Christian from as early as the second century (above p. 324). These faithful are difficult to identify. Prior to the fourth century, most Christian worship took place in undistinguished domestic spaces. The eucharistic and baptismal practices that gave structure to the faith were easily accommodated within the dining rooms and baths of late antique houses. Similarly there was no particularly Christian approach to burial, beyond a concern to preserve the corpse for bodily resurrection that was shared with other faiths.[51] A fluid and inventive syncretism of ideas and symbols, where much rested on deliberately ambiguous allegorical references, makes it difficult for the uninitiated to distinguish between the art and iconography of different communities of believers.

The most exclusively Christian symbol was the Chi-Rho monogram, combining the first two Greek letters for the name of Christ, which gained currency after its early fourth century adoption by Constantine. A Chi-Rho was engraved onto the base of a pewter bowl found at Copthall Court, perhaps marking its use in eucharistic practice, and another was scratched onto a potsherd found in Brentford. A partial Chi-Rho graffito was also scratched onto the rim of a fourth-century mortarium found at Brandon House in Southwark.[52] These fourth-century finds are the earliest archaeological evidence of Christian affiliation from London, although we cannot know how knowingly these symbols were deployed once they became associated with Constantinian authority.

Twelve oval lead alloy ingots, weighing between 0.8 and 8.5 kilos each, found in river dredging and along the foreshore near Battersea Bridge also carried Chi-Rho stamps alongside other identifiably Christian components.[53] They were executed in a style that is unlikely to be later than the fourth century and stamped as the product of Syagrius. This may have been a member of the prominent Gallic family of that name that held high political office in the late fourth century. The stamps probably marked the ingots as official consignments under Syagrius' control, dating after Theodosius made Christianity the religion of the state. Whilst they may have been lost in transit along the Thames, James Gerrard convincingly suggests that they arrived here in dumps used to reclaim marshland during the mid-nineteenth-century construction of Battersea Park, using material removed during the construction of the Shadwell basin. It is consequently possible that these ingots derived from a hoard buried near to the Shadwell estate speculatively identified as the residence of a high-ranking official (p. 313).

The written sources offer further detail on London's first Christian communities, but come with their own difficulties. A late sixth- or early seventh-century *Martyrologium* identified a martyr-bishop named Augulus or Agulus from a city in Britain identified as *civitate Augusta*.[54] The implication is that Agulus was a bishop of London killed in a persecution before Christianity was recognized as licit in the Edict of Milan of AD 313. A list of British clergymen recorded as attending a church council at Arles in AD 314 was headed by a bishop from York, followed by bishop Restitutus from London (*ciuitate Londenensi*), and bishop Adelfius of the colony of London (*ciuitate Colonia Londenensium*).[55] A literal reading might suggest that there had been two communities of London: perhaps a colonial foundation within the walled city and a separately constituted community on the south bank. Since the church hierarchy treated each community as the preserve of a single bishop, in a monepiscopate that guarded against dissenting voices, this would require us to believe that London and Southwark were now considered completely separate cities. We have no other evidence for such an unlikely arrangement and Adelfius' affiliation is therefore widely assumed to be a mistake for Lincoln, since *Lindinis* is only one vowel-shift away from *Londinis*.

British bishops participated at other fourth-century church councils, indicating a developed ecclesiastical leadership. The institutions of organized Christianity gave rise to new forms of public architecture in many late antique cities. Episcopal complexes defined the urban seats of powerful fourth-century bishops, and excavations in cities such as Geneva, Milan, and Aquileia show that these were built on a grand scale from the middle of the century.[56] These typically included a basilical church for congregational worship, a baptistery and a palace. Some communities were slower than others to follow this trend, and we cannot be certain that London housed an episcopal complex. Britain failed to match neighbouring provinces in its display of the monuments and symbols of what probably remained a minority religion. London was, however, an important administrative city that was otherwise quick to adopt architectures of Roman imperial authority. During the course of the fourth-century Christianity became the religion of the imperial household and eventually a religion of state. The patronage of emperors contributed to the monumentalization of Christian worship, and most senior appointments to London's late fourth century administration are likely to have been Christian.[57] It is therefore likely that London's bishops were sufficiently powerful and politically well-supported to have secured the resources needed to build a basilical church before the end of the fourth century.

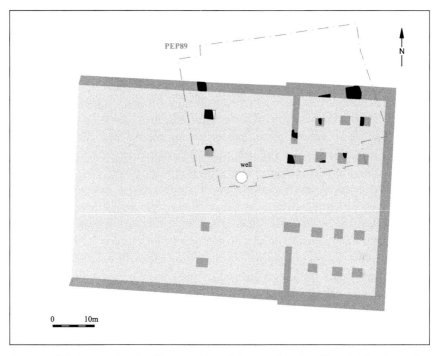

Fig. 28.4 The late antique basilica considered the possible site of London's episcopal church, as identified in excavations at Colchester House (PEP89: after Sankey 1998). Drawn by Justin Russell.

Excavations at Colchester House in Pepys Street in 1992 found the heavily robbed foundations of a fourth-century building that might just possibly have been this church (Fig. 28.4).[58] Only the north-eastern corner of the building was found, but it was clearly a substantial public building. Its massive external walls were set over 2-metre-thick foundations dug into the natural gravels and supported by timber piles. Internally a series of square pier-bases were set over timber piles capped with flint and chalk and topped with concrete. These pier-bases were arranged in two rows to form a double aisle, and a short wall marked off the eastern end of the building. The arrangement finds close parallel in the basilica of Santa Tecla in Milan. London's basilica was provided with a stone and tile floor and a well, whilst fragments of marble and window glass suggest a well-appointed interior. This debris also included limestone slates from the building's roof: these slates came into occasional use in London after *c.* AD 350 when the city ceased to import roof tile from Harrold (above p. 344).[59] A construction date after *c.* AD 350 is also suggested by the presence of significant quantities of Portchester D pottery, which marks later Roman occupation. The structure was set across the projected line of a Roman road on a prominent site on Tower Hill in the south-eastern quarter of town: a formerly suburban area that may have been absorbed within the city when it was extended to the line of the town wall. This was an appropriate location for an episcopal church, expeditiously using a vacant but prominent site on the borders of the settlement.[60]

It has alternatively been suggested that the basilica was a large granary (*horrea*) designed to hold surplus grain commanded by the *annona*. Large aisled granaries featured in late antique walled cities and frontier forts. This is not, however, a good fit for the evidence, since granaries were not normally decorated with marble interiors and Tower Hill was not ideally placed for this purpose. Other aspects of the finds assemblage also suggest that this part of Tower Hill was the focus of religious observances in the fourth century. James Gerrard has shown that the coin loss profile from Colchester House finds closest parallel with late Romano-British religious sites, whilst the pottery from beneath the basilica was marked by a concentration of an unusual type of bell-shaped bowl commonly found in votive deposits.[61] Whilst we have no proof that the building was a place of Christian worship, this is a credible proposition and is more consistent with the evidence than the alternatives.

The restoration of London in context

Little of London's earlier public landscape survived into the second half of the fourth century. Major changes to the urban topography are illustrated by the redundancy of buildings around which civic life had previously revolved: the port, forum, temples, and amphitheatre. There was a marked shift away from symbolic monumentality, and public space was more likely to have been used for industrial production than extravagant civic ceremony. These transformations followed an earlier relocation of power into the private domain, consolidated around a small number of wealthy establishments. The rites of public sacrifice that made London's temples an important part of the environment were in decline throughout the Roman world, and many expressions of belief had moved into the private sphere. Outside of the domestic arena, urban ideologies were chiefly represented by the city walls, although new places of worship may have created other focal points. Processions no longer attended the games at the amphitheatre, but ceremonial life may have been reconfigured around Christian and other cult practices.[62] It is distinctly possible that the feasts of martyrs inspired new processions and stational liturgies, uniting an episcopal basilica with other places where the remains of martyr-saints might be celebrated. As Simon Loseby has explained, we don't know how far down this route the towns of Roman Britain had progressed before the collapse of the Roman administration, but the early stages in the evolution of such topographies need not have left significant trace.[63]

Sadly we have no direct evidence for any such invention of new ideas of city living, but it is certain that the architecture of earlier forms of public life were largely redundant.

This chapter has surveyed evidence for London's mid-fourth-century revival, best explained as a centrally directed initiative to refortify the seat of diocesan institutions. This is consistent with what we know of Valentinian strategy, and of the actions taken by Count Theodosius following the barbarian conspiracy. These remain suggestions only, since we lack precise dating evidence.[64] Our purpose, however, is not to find archaeological illustration of the events of AD 367–8 but to seek explanation for one of Roman London's last major programmes of architectural renewal. Even without Ammianus' commentary it is reasonable to conclude that these works, like earlier phases of restoration, would have followed investment in the command infrastructure drawing on resources marshalled against military campaigns. History suggests that one of the most important of these campaigns was underway AD 367–8 when Theodosius over-wintered in London at the head of a field army of around 2,000 men.[65]

The new works did not embrace London's port. The earlier phase of tidal retreat appears to have reversed by the fourth century, and returning tides would have eased shipping up-river to the city.[66] It would have been possible to engineer new waterfront quays around gates through the riverside wall, but this did not happen. London was no longer needed as a supply-base. The volumes of goods being moved were massively reduced after the *annona* reforms of the previous century whilst other sites, including those of the Saxon Shore, had risen at London's expense (above p. 345).

London continued to import goods for local consumption, drawing on a range of regional sources for its pottery. From *c.* AD 350 this included Oxfordshire wares, Calcite-gritted wares likely to have been made at kilns near Harrold, and Portchester D wares from Hampshire.[67] Some reached London down the Thames, in a traffic that was also directed towards military sites.[68] Contemporary changes involved a decline in the presence of south coast Black-Burnished wares, perhaps starting from a little earlier in the century, and in grey wares from the Alice Holt kilns.[69] Malcolm Lyne observes that Alice Holt provided more than 60 per cent of the coarse pottery found in early and mid-fourth-century assemblages in London, but a much lower proportions in late fourth-century contexts. He suggests that a *negotiator* responsible for supplying London with these wares ceased operations after *c.* AD 370. Since the town was no longer importing much building timber, this may have reduced traffic from Alice Holt adding to the marginal costs of moving pottery vessels and their contents.[70] This period may also have seen a significant decline in volumes of goods travelling the east-coast routes.[71] London and coastal sites in the Thames estuary continued to receive small volumes of continental imports including pottery from the Argonne region of northern Gaul and Mayen ware (also known as *Eifelkeramik*) produced near Trier in the Rhineland.[72] Much of the pottery reaching town may have followed in the wake of the bulkier supplies of grain, beer or wine consumed by the urban population. Some aspects of London's supply may also have been driven by official requirements, sustaining links with the Rhineland and fortified coastal sites associated with the Saxon Shore.

29
Endings (*c.* A D 380–400)

Debating 'decline'

At some point London ceased to be a city. It retained little that was recognizably urban other than its walls: possessing neither the built appearance and population density, nor the dominant political and economic role. By any account it ceased to be a place of consequence. The fact of London's failure is beyond dispute, but there is much that we have yet to understand about how the once bustling city came to be hollowed-out. James Gerrard's review of the end of Roman London describes a study bedevilled by the concept of decline, echoing Edward Gibbon's famous history of the extinction of the Roman Empire in its western provinces.[1] The problem with the idea of a world in decay is that some late antique places found new vitalities, and we must be wary of assumptions that treat departures from classical form as failure. Archaeologists consequently prefer to talk in more nuanced terms of transformation and change, whilst recognizing discontinuities in the structure and representation of power.[2] Romano-British studies have become particularly uncomfortable with the idea that everything turned on an abrupt Roman departure *c.* A D 408/410. Timelines can stretch in either direction. In Richard Reece's view, many of the more important changes took place beforehand. He argues that Britain never fully adopted the social and economic institutions of urban life, leaving the late Roman town as little more than an administrative village.[3] In this model London's earlier phases of urban contraction bequeathed an economically frail entity that entered terminal decline long before the fourth century was out.[4] A contrasting, if not necessarily conflicting, narrative has formed around ideas of post- and sub-Roman continuities, where features of urban life continued after the Roman administration was gone. Ideas of sub-Roman continuity were influenced by Shepherd Frere's excavations at Verulamium, which identified a functioning piped water-supply into the middle of the fifth century.[5] This evidence seemed compatible with a description of St Germanus' visit to the shrine of St Alban to resolve church doctrinal disputes in A D 429.[6] Frere's arguments for fifth-century urban continuities build, however, on disputed evidence and an alternative reading of his sequences dates them to the late fourth century rather than the early fifth.[7] More to the point, Frere's findings have yet to be replicated in London or other Romano-British cities.

Discussion is complicated by the fact that we have so little evidence to work with. There are many reasons why evidence is elusive, themselves symptomatic of the changes we struggle to understand. Chronologies are difficult to construct because we lack timbers for dendrochronological dating.[8] Since few monumental structures were built, timber piles were no longer used in their foundations. In the absence of public procurement exercises, the large-scale import of building materials gave way to recycling. A concomitant change in architectural fashion saw a return to building in timber in place of brick and masonry, such that a late fourth-century building at Drapers' Gardens left no trace other than the lines of post-holes thought to have supported its walls.[9] We don't know how much these changes were a matter of cultural preference, as new avenues for the expression of social status and power devalued the symbolic value of classical architecture, and how much a product of a diminished capacity because materials and engineering skills were unavailable for civilian works. Whatever the explanation, the ephemeral nature of these late Roman timber buildings reduced their archaeological footprint.

The problems of dark-earth formation and bioturbation described in Chapter 22 are also particularly acute in the upper levels of the Roman archaeological sequences, which were also exposed to truncation during medieval and modern building. Although there are many phases of dark-earth formation the horizon is particularly associated with late antique change. New patterns of rubbish disposal may have seen waste piled onto surface middens, destined to be reworked into dark-earth, in place of rubbish pits. These practices witness reduced investment in urban architecture and hint at shrinking settlement densities, but limit our ability to characterize the changes underway.

Dating frameworks are further complicated by reduced supplies of new coin entering Britain following the neglect of the garrison towards the end of the fourth century. The miniscule coins minted by the House of Valentinian and Theodosius (364–402) are also easily missed during excavation, and their recovery relies on practices of metal-detecting and sieving that aren't routinely employed.[10] There was a concurrent, and related, decline in volumes of pottery produced by established Romano-British industries towards the end of the fourth century.[11] Although recent research has improved our ability to recognize fifth-century pottery, this was no longer part of widely distributed industrialized production. The pots we know to have been made in these years are few in number and difficult to date. Deprived of normal sources of evidence it becomes exceptionally difficult to establish chronologies of change.

The contrast with other parts of the Roman Empire indicates, however, that Britain suffered an unparalleled contraction as the fourth century gave way to the fifth. This relates not so much to what was going on in the countryside, but to urban uses of coin and tablewares. London was particularly vulnerable to changes in the pulse of such custom and supply. So decline remains a viable concept, but following the repeated cycles of growth and contraction rather than as a linear process of inexorable decline from second-century splendour to fifth-century failure. London's earlier phases of retreat had been followed by restoration and renewal. From the second century onwards each cycle left the city somehow diminished, as Rome developed alternative mechanisms for governing Britain and supplying its forces, but after three centuries of Roman rule London remained central to the infrastructure of government. Even as late as AD 395, it was a place where wealth and power concentrated.

Continuities and discontinuities

Distributions of late fourth-century pottery, characterized by Oxfordshire and Alice Holt wares with some Portchester D and East Midlands shell-tempered wares, have been studied by James Gerrard to show that London was inhabited to end of the fourth century. These types of pottery, along with later coin issues, are found throughout the walled area and much of Southwark. There is no evidence to suggest that the urban population retreated to a smaller enclave, although the presence of hot-spots—as around the Tabard Square temple complex and at Bermondsey Abbey—may mark areas of nucleated housing in a polyfocal settlement.[12] This late fourth century city wasn't densely populated. It had long been full of empty spaces and new demolitions further reduced the housing stock. Several third-century buildings around the site of the forum were lost, with late fourth-century pottery in demolition horizons and robbing trenches.[13] One of these, a house at Lime Street, was burnt down after the middle of the fourth century and not replaced.[14] Although the sample is small, and compromised by our uncertain ability to identify late antique architecture, there is more evidence for demolition than repair.

Streets within the walled area had long since ceased to be routinely maintained and several were no longer suitable for wheeled traffic.[15] The main road from Colchester witnessed sporadic small-scale fourth-century repair, but became heavily rutted before wind-blown detritus and rubbish accumulated along its flanks.[16] On the west side of town the gravel surfaces of the 'decumanus' were dug over by small quarry pits containing late fourth-century pottery and coins of AD 379–402 (Fig. 29.1).[17] Substantial culverts were maintained alongside this road for more than three centuries, channelling running water towards the Walbrook from springs to the north-west. These conduits ceased to function in the final third of the fourth century, presumably following the failure of water management around the springs themselves. Coins associated with the disuse of the latest culvert included issues up to AD 355–65, but nothing later. A decapitated human corpse laid out in this disused feature recalls the ditch-burials found on the outskirts of the earlier city.[18] Houses either side of this street were maintained into the middle of the fourth century, but there is no certain evidence of their occupation beyond c. AD 380. Finds associated with their final occupation

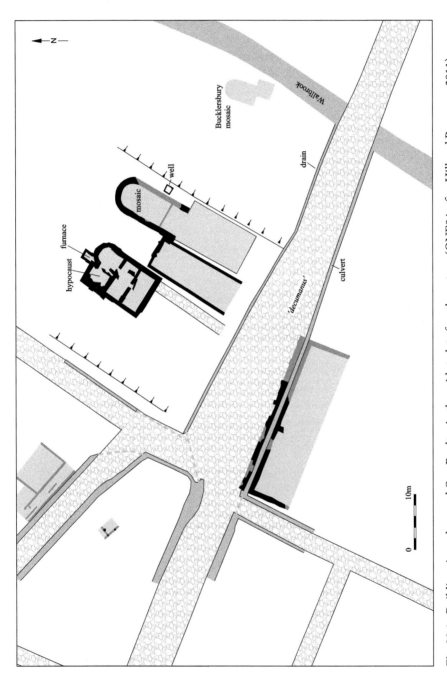

Fig. 29.1 Buildings in and around One Poultry in the mid- to late fourth century (ONE94: after Hill and Rowsome 2011). Drawn by Justin Russell.

may have formed an abandonment horizon, as marked by the disproportionate presence of items that were normally repaired or recycled. These included a large shale table-top, once the centrepiece to a formal dining room, along with high proportions of glassware and items of dress. This evidence suggests that London's principal thoroughfare had ceased to carry heavy traffic in the final quarter of the fourth century, probably in the 380s, leading to the evacuation of adjacent houses. This state of affairs may have been a consequence of damage to the bridge over the Walbrook, blocking through-traffic and leaving this as a peripheral part of the settlement.

A similar picture emerges from studies along the main road to London Bridge through Southwark, where pits containing late Roman pottery and a fourth-century coin were dug into the street surfaces. These quarries extracted gravel for building work elsewhere.[19] Whilst the road need not have become completely impassable, its functional width was greatly reduced and it no longer carried a regular traffic of ox-drawn carts. This suggests that London Bridge itself had failed. A cluster of adjacent buildings probably remained standing. Surviving elements included the colonnaded street frontage at Borough High Street and associated structure likely to have been a market building.[20] The nearby bathhouse also remained largely intact, where the presence of slag and smithing debris indicates that it had been converted into a workshop. Some high-status buildings in the area, along St Thomas Street, also remained in use until relatively late.[21]

A different sequence of late antique change can be reconstructed from the evidence of metalworking at the Courage Brewery site on the north-west side of Southwark.[22] The industry had seen a significant hiatus *c.* AD 350, with a subsequent resumption of production in the late fourth century. Earlier timber structures that housed metalworking production were demolished, but eventually replaced by slightly built timber-and-earth buildings with hearths. These generated a small volume of detritus from iron smithing and copper alloy smelting, suggesting that industrial production had resumed but failed to match levels achieved in the third century. This later production is provisionally dated *c.* AD 380, with a firm date provided by a coin of the house of Constantine dated AD 355–65. This intermittent industry might have responded to campaign needs involving ship repair and army re-equipment but wasn't sustained to the end of the fourth century when a well was closed and occupation sequences terminated.

Burial *intra urbem*

A few small late fourth-century cemeteries were established amidst the ruins of earlier high-status buildings close to the bounds of the urban site (Fig. 29.2). These were more common in Southwark, where burial clusters are found where landmark buildings had been demolished by the mid-fourth century. At least

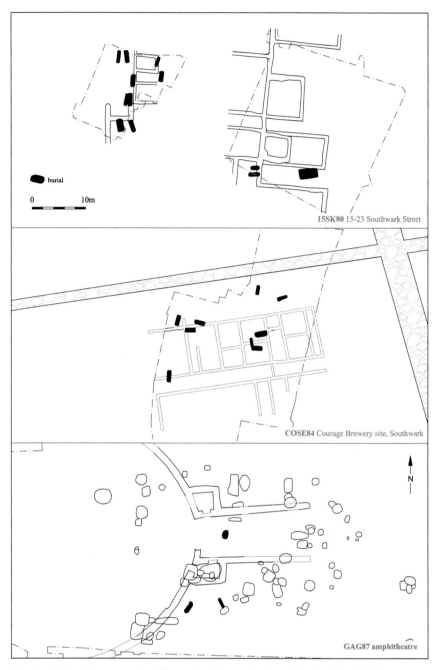

Fig. 29.2 Fourth-century burials amidst the partly demolished and robbed remains of earlier Roman masonry structures: at the site of the amphitheatre and buildings in Southwark (after Bateman *et al.* 2008, Cowan 1992, and Cowan *et al.* 2009). Drawn by Justin Russell.

thirteen graves, including adults and children, clustered around the remains of the putative *mansio* at 15–23 Southwark Street following its piecemeal robbing.[23] Wood stains and iron nails suggest that the burials were placed within coffins, and these included several 'chalk burials' and some with offerings of hobnailed boots and food. One body, of a girl about 12 years old, had been wrapped in a shroud and laid on crushed chalk in a wooden coffin accompanied by a mid-fourth-century cooking pot, bracelets, and pins. One pin was made of jet carved in the form of a cantharus, a Bacchic motif also associated with eucharistic practice. These finds are consistent with a fourth-century date, and one burial cut a robber trench that contained a coin of AD 347–8.

Excavations nearby at Courage Brewery found seven burials arranged around and respecting the robbed-out remains of a large masonry building.[24] The robber trenches contained late fourth-century pottery, and one burial was coin-dated after c. AD 340. A similar number of burials was found at The Place, although there was no evident attempt to respect earlier masonry walls and we lack dating evidence.[25] Burials also cut into earlier timber buildings at Guy's Hospital, and three inhumations have been recorded on the boundary of the Tabard Square temple precinct.[26] A smaller number of burial sites were placed within the walled city west of the Walbrook. These included three graves dated after AD 365 within the redundant amphitheatre including a wooden coffin buried beneath the floor of its eastern entrance.[27] Radiocarbon dates recovered from the other burials suggest a fourth-century date: one dated between AD 230 and 390 and the other between AD 230 and 410. Both post-dated the demolition of the amphitheatre around the middle of the fourth century, although it is tempting to suggest that the arena might still have found occasional use as an execution ground. Five late fourth-century burials were also found in a small cemetery at Paternoster Square, and contemporary single burials have been recorded at One Poultry and Baltic House.[28]

In sum there was a clear pattern of converting formerly prominent sites into small burial grounds in the late fourth century. Although none has been fully explored, even the larger ones are unlikely to have contained more than a few dozen graves. Burials had formerly been excluded from cities, but this now gave way to a closer relationship between the living and the dead.[29] Some isolated burials and small cemeteries within Italian towns date to the late fourth century, and a short-lived intramural cemetery containing about forty burials was established next to the episcopal complex in Poitiers in the second half of the century.[30] The evidence from London finds closest parallel in late antique North Africa where small urban cemeteries were established in newly peripheral areas of shrunken cities.[31] These were not randomly distributed, but exploited well-connected and prominent sites close to areas of continuing residential settlement. For instance, at Carthage the site of a bathhouse that fell into disuse between the late third and mid-fourth centuries was occupied by burials associated with mid- and late fourth-century pottery. As at London, these graveyards were not evidently associated with standing shrines or cemetery churches. The decision to bury seems to have been dictated by a desire of the living to keep the dead close by, at a time when earlier proscriptions on urban burial no longer applied. We do not know if such ideas appealed more to some communities than others, but this continuity of engagement with place would have held greater relevance for families who expected to stay living nearby.

The decision to bury within the city walls is often credited to a Christian preference to be buried *ad sanctos*, at churches that conserved the relics of martyr saints.[32] This practice derived from a comparable sense of intimacy between living and dead, in which ideas of physical resurrection and spiritual salvation created communities that hoped to transcend death. Because of the wider currency of such ideas there is no basis for identifying a specifically Christian aspect to London's new burial sites. In fifth-century Gaul, the placing of Christian burial-grounds *intra muros* was usually associated with church building, for which we have no evidence from London. London is in any case unlikely to have boasted enough saintly remains to have fuelled the creation of so many small cemeteries.

On the other hand, the changes that made it possible to negotiate and legitimize the regular placing of the dead amongst the living would have been reinforced by the rising influence of the church within the administrative bureaucracy. From *c.* AD 380, the emperor Theodosius recognized Christianity as the religion of state, decreeing orthodoxy and forbidding pagan and heretical worship. Regardless of the beliefs of the people who lived here, London was politically Christian and home to a diocesan administration bound to the outward display of catholic conformity.[33] Burials grounds on public property, such as the amphitheatre, are likely to have required formal consent and certainly needed official toleration. The change in land-use was enabled by earlier urban contraction, probably involving population decline, and saw public lands converted to more private use.

Despite the proliferation of small graveyards within town, London's suburban cemeteries continued to receive new burials until the end of the fourth century. Graves in the cemetery along the southern margins of Southwark, near Trinity Street, were dug into a horizon that included late fourth-century pottery and coins dated AD 388–402.[34] A coin of this date was also found in the fill of one of the graves in the eastern cemetery.[35] Funerals were certainly taking place in London's carefully organized extra-mural cemeteries into the 390s but we don't know for much longer this continued. There is a small body of evidence for post-Roman activity in and around these burial grounds, discussed in the next chapter, but this comes from the secondary fills of redundant enclosure ditches rather than new grave-digging.

Termination rituals

Some departures may have been celebrated in extravagant termination rituals in the course of which votive deposits were placed in disused wells and ritual shafts. Although these closure practices were of long ancestry (pp. 79 and 231), they became a particular feature of the late fourth century. A hoard recovered from a well at Drapers' Gardens was a particularly conspicuous closure deposit.[36] The well wasn't dug until the middle of the fourth century, but had already been decommissioned *c.* A D 380. Silt at its base contained two unworn coins of Gratian, the latest not minted before A D 375. These were followed into the well by two broken objects: an iron binding wrenched from a bucket and a copper-alloy bracelet bent into an 'S' shape. Deliberately 'killed' items like this are a common find on temple sites, and possibly marked the symbolic closure of the well in appeasement of the chthonic spirits within. A collection of twenty copper-alloy, lead-alloy, and iron vessels was then placed in the shaft. A large hanging basin, which carried a leonine escutcheon influenced by Bacchic iconography, was accompanied by other buckets, a cauldron, several dishes, bowls, skillets, a jug, and a trivet. These types of vessels were used in the ritual ablutions that featured in late antique dining ceremony, and in mixing wine with water in practices derived from the Greek *symposion*. They embraced the social rituals of preparing, tempering and serving alcohol that had made the cantharus such a prominent symbol of conviviality, and from which eucharistic cult practice developed. A layer of mud covered the vessels, onto which was thrown the partially articulated remains of a juvenile deer. Tooth eruption shows that the animal was 4–5 months old at death and the likely kill of an autumn hunt. This was an appropriate time of year for making offerings to the underworld.[37] Deer bones are rare in Roman faunal assemblages, but have also been found in the fills of other third-century wells in Southwark where they were almost certainly ritual deposits.[38] Deer were a symbol of the hunt, and a metaphor for the quest for understanding and the human struggle against wilderness.[39]

Another important closure assemblage was found in a well at the Bloomberg headquarters, just north of the temple of Mithras. This included four pewter vessels, a fragment of a decorated lead tank and six cattle skulls, along with late Roman military style dress accessories, in an assemblage provisionally dated to the A D 380s.[40] Several other shafts and pits containing late Roman closure deposits date to this period. These include the well found beneath Southwark Cathedral that contained an important group of stone sculptures (described above p. 358) along with the skeletons of a dog and cat, and a pit at the Courage Brewery site that contained the skeletons of six dogs, and a complete pottery vessel with the base perforated by five holes.[41] These offerings may have marked ceremonial farewells as wealthy households quit London *c.* A D 380 or soon afterwards.

The marble dedication to Mars Camulus from the Tabard Square temple had also been carefully buried in a late fourth-century pit or ritual shaft that was then sealed by new gravel surfaces, possibly drawing on materials quarried from roads nearby, showing that the walled enclosure was still used and maintained.[42] Other Romano-British temple precincts were converted into open spaces in the fourth century, as at Canterbury, after temple structures ceased to host their former ceremonies.[43] The decision to lay new pavements shows that these spaces fulfilled a new role, perhaps a ritual one that recognized some inheritance from earlier uses. Late fourth-century London must still have observed feast days and public celebrations, and these may have been relocated into other public spaces after the redundancy of the forum and amphitheatre.

Continued quarrying and re-cycling attests to sporadic demand for building materials, and the distribution of finds and burials suggests scattered occupation until the end of the century. People still lived in London, and aristocratic properties with porticoes, baths, and dining rooms housed a dwindling community of Roman officials. London remained a Roman city, but was shadowed by contraction with a degraded urban infrastructure. The situation carried echoes of London's decline in the late second and mid-third centuries, but a more fundamentally changed approach to urban living was illustrated by the failure to preserve a street system suitable for heavily laden wheeled traffic. This loss of previously essential infrastructure was clearly in evidence from as early as the 380s.

Some properties were vacated, perhaps as households departed, adding to open spaces inherited from earlier contraction. As a result, those who remained were able to establish burial grounds closer to their homes. Houses and compounds were scattered throughout the city, but the area east of the Walbrook may have been more densely inhabited than other more peripheral parts of town. Some of the changes that transformed the urban landscape can be traced back to the end of the third century, when London's port was closed. These periods of earlier neglect were followed by bursts of imperial investment, resulting in London's episodic renewal. London was now centuries old, and a necessary centre for the institutions of government. The closing decades of the late fourth century can therefore be seen as another cycle of contraction. It is only through hindsight that we see it as leading towards London's eventual demise.

Some commanders based in Britain attempted to seize imperial power in the late fourth century, bringing the province a reputation for being fertile in tyrants.[44] Magnus Maximus is perhaps the best known of these, and reportedly stripped Britain of regular soldiers to support his bid for purple in Gaul in AD 383 where he installed himself in Trier before marching on Rome and defeat in AD 388.[45] He appears to have reopened the London mint for a very small issue of gold and silver coins carrying the Augusta mint-mark.[46] These were the last Roman coins minted in Britain, and indicate that London remained the fiscal capital of the diocese and that Maximus needed bullion to secure the loyalty of some part of the British army or bureaucracy. We don't have to accept Gildas' notoriously hostile view of Maximus, whom he held responsible for depriving Britain of its soldiery, governors, and youth, to recognize that the expedition to Gaul drew vital resources away from the British garrison.[47] The depletions of London's population and infrastructure in the 380s can credibly be attributed to the period of Maximus' rule.

London's last Roman fortification

Discoveries at the Tower of London suggest that the south-east angle of the defensive circuit was the focus of unusually late attention. The riverside wall was reinforced or replaced by a masonry wall about 4 metres inside its line.[48] This neatly built structure, about 3.2 metres thick, was built from a range of reused materials presenting an external face of tile-coursed ragstone, and perhaps provided a narrow entrance onto the foreshore. Dumps laid against the wall after its construction contained several late fourth-century coins, down to an issue of Valentinian II dated AD 388–92. Further observations of this later wall found coins within its construction trench that included a coin of Arcadius dated after AD 388. These works establish a context for the nearby discovery of a late fourth or early fifth-century silver ingot weighing around one pound and stamped 'from the workshop of Honorinus' at the Tower in 1777 along with two gold coins: one of Arcadius (AD 395–408) and one of Honorius (AD 395–423).[49] The composition of this hoard suggests that it was part of a donative received on the accession of a new emperor, since this normally comprised of five gold solidi and a pound of silver.

Ralph Merrifield proposed that this last phase of defensive architecture was associated with a British campaign undertaken on Stilicho's behalf in AD 396–8.[50] He also suggested that this corner of the Roman city formed a late Roman defended citadel, following the model of late antique cities in Gaul. This remains unsubstantiated, and James Gerrard's study of the distribution of late Roman coins and pottery shows no particular concentration of finds in this area. There may, however, have been a cluster of higher-status buildings within this part of town. The massive late fourth-century basilica at Colchester House may have remained standing, and a handful of town houses along the riverside spring-line between London Bridge and the Tower were occupied at the end of the fourth century.[51] The late enhancement of riverside defences at the eastern end of town might be mirrored by repairs to the western end of the riverside wall. The collapsed section of masonry that closed the western gap at Baynard's Castle (p. 365), included a later repair executed in a different mortar and incorporating reused sculptural blocks.[52] These alterations at the close of the fourth century failed to match the scale of earlier building works, but were competently engineered. Much like earlier phases of defensive architecture, they may have been aimed at urban restoration, following earlier contraction. If so, they had negligible longer-term impact. London's problems had become terminal and many centuries passed before it witnessed engineering on a comparable scale.

PART 8

BEYOND ROME

Fifth-century landscapes

The desertion of the city

We know that some of London's houses were occupied until the very end of the fourth century, but there is no certain evidence that any were actively maintained in the early fifth century. A hoard of copper-alloy coins scattered over the latest floors of the furnace room and corridor of the domestic baths at Billingsgate was assembled after AD 395 since it included issues of Arcadius and Honorius.[1] It had probably fallen from a place of concealment in the east wing of the building, implying that the house was still standing around AD 400. This late phase of occupation was also reflected in the presence of part of a Palestinian amphorae. A few other sherds of these exotic amphorae have been recovered from sites east of the Walbrook, as at New Fresh Wharf.[2] They were rare imports, perhaps carrying wine from the Holy Land for religious liturgy. Floors associated with late Roman pottery have also been recorded at Pudding Lane and in the former Mithraeum, hinting at occupation into the early fifth century but not proving it.[3]

We cannot put a timeline to the continued use of the buildings standing at the end of the fourth century, and some slight timber constructions of this period may have escaped attention. In the previous chapter, we reviewed the difficulty faced in finding secure dating evidence after the close of the fourth century, but the little we have is consistent with the argument that most of the city was soon derelict following the trends of closure and abandonment evident in the last quarter of the fourth century. This remains the likeliest explanation for our failure to identify later phases of repair and reuse within the houses that were still occupied at the end of the fourth century. A dearth of early Saxon finds from within the walled city leaves little doubt that it was largely abandoned by AD 450. This cannot be a failure of recognition, since early Saxon material has been recovered from London's less thoroughly explored hinterland (below p. 396).[4]

London's abandonment followed the failure of the provincial government.[5] By the end of the fourth century Trier was no longer a capital city and the seat of the Praetorian Prefect transferred to Arles around AD 395.[6] This placed distance between Britain and sources of authority, leaving it increasingly isolated. Local policing by settled groups had largely replaced mobile standing armies, eliminating the need to secure long-distance supply. The garrison in Britain was no longer supplied with bronze coinage and the flow of new coin reduced to a trickle after mints were closed at Arles, Lyons, and Trier *c.* AD 395.[7] By the Theodosian period

(AD 388–402) coin-use was largely restricted to internal transactions within cities and forts. It is important to note that earlier failures in supply had provoked local episodes of copying, meeting a demand for low denomination coinage for essential transactions (above p. 331). Significantly, this did not happen after AD 395. London may have continued to use the small change already in circulation, but the failure to compensate for the decline in official supply shows that cash-based exchange mattered less.[8]

So why was there no longer an equivalent need of coin for local purchase to pay hauliers, supplement supplies, and facilitate market activity? We must conclude that London housed a different and smaller community with little need for such transactions. The people still living here were perhaps more easily fed from the immediate hinterland, where a greater degree of local self-sufficiency reduced the need to buy goods in the marketplace or pay for services. By the end of the century, London had a negligible role to play in raising taxes and rents to support the Roman administration. Few grain waggons trundled the damaged streets. It is doubtful that taxes were routinely raised at the city gates, or port duties charged on cargoes beached on the foreshore. It is unlikely that the walls were regularly manned, since the feeding of the garrison would have brought carts back onto the roads and put small change into soldiers' purses. Supplies of luxury goods diminished, and traffic shrank to the point where bridges and roads were no longer maintained.

The immediate train of events leading up to Britain's political rupture with Rome started AD 405/406 when massed barbarian forces crossed the frozen Rhine.[9] In the ensuing chaos, mutinies in Britain raised a succession of usurpers culminating in the proclamation of Constantine III in AD 407 who, following earlier example, assembled a fleet and army to cross to Gaul.[10] Constantine's doomed campaign diminished whatever was left of the professional military in south-east Britain, perhaps including the command of the *Comes Britanniarum*. According to Zosimus the British subsequently expelled the remaining Roman officials, taking up arms on their own account to free cities from barbarian threat in AD 409.[11] A complete vacuum in the Roman command structure might be implied by a letter written by Honorius, the emperor of the west, advising the cities (*poleis*) of Britain to look to their own defences, although there are some doubts as to whether this communication was not directed to Bruttium in southern Italy instead.[12] The instruction is not inconsistent, however, with the situation in Britain and might indicate that there were no Roman officials here who could be charged with this duty. Compounding the earlier redundancy of civic institutions with the abdication of Roman military authority, and for the want of any abiding social or economic function, London had no purpose. Like other Romano-British cities, it lost its role in the extraction of resources from dependent territories and as a centre of power. Desertion accompanied the withdrawal of the political and military presence.[13]

Many histories of the end of Roman Britain stress a political rupture *c.* AD 410, but it can be argued that the Roman diocesan government had struggled to recover from the break in authority under Magnus Maximus in AD 383. After that date, Britain was only intermittently governed through the Gallic prefecture, totalling only 8 years in all. London's faltering political role during this quarter-century of weakened central authority may have contributed to the loss of urban infrastructure. Urban lifestyles evaporated with the urban institutions that engendered them.

Rural continuities

Although the walled city was largely deserted in the early fifth century, the surrounding countryside fared differently (Fig. 30.1). A few late antique sites, especially in Southwark and Westminster, present compelling evidence for continuity into the fifth century, and formed focal points within the post-Roman landscape.

It is likely, however, that Shadwell shared in London's fate.[14] It is not possible to fix the precise date that the baths here were last fired up, but the destruction of associated structures seems to date from *c.* AD 375, and the nearby tower or

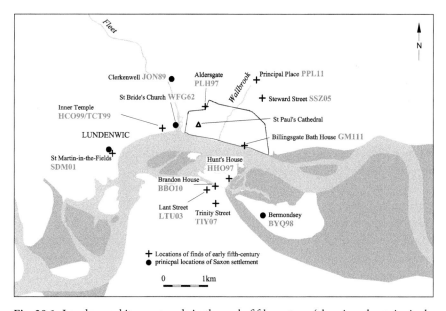

Fig. 30.1 London and its surrounds in the early fifth century (showing also principal features of the later Saxon settlement). The settlement pattern shows a striking degree of continuity with that of the late pre-Roman Iron Age, as shown on Fig. 4.3 (p. 40). Locations of pottery and finds with early fifth-century characteristics are marked + and identified by site-codes. Drawn by Fiona Griffin.

mausoleum was covered by demolition debris containing finds dated after AD 365. A crude well was dug to supply fresh water in the later stages of the settlement's life, when the piped water had presumably failed. This contained a 'closure deposit' consisting of complete and broken ceramic vessels, with a high proportion of red-slipped tablewares from around Oxfordshire, and a copper-alloy bowl. Pottery from the site included fabrics dated after AD 370 including North African and Palestinian amphorae.[15] It seems likely that the patterns of high-status social behaviour, signalled by the continued operation of the bathhouse, were not sustained until the end of the century, by which time the site was largely deserted. The fortunes of Shadwell, like those of London itself, had perhaps relied on the continued presence of the military administration. Some roadside sites around London may have followed a similar trajectory of change, although evidence is sparse. Coins found on the clay floor of a cellar at Old Ford witness its continued use beyond c. AD 383, with others of Honorius (AD 395–402) within its backfill. This late activity might follow from the continued exploitation of the Lea valley for grazing, and chart official traffic along the Colchester road, but needn't have continued long into the fifth century.[16]

Our best evidence for fifth-century continuity comes from St Martin-in-the-Fields, some 2 kilometres west of London. The presence of an important late-antique site here was suggested by the discovery of Roman brickwork and two stone sarcophagi during church building in AD 1722–5.[17] More recent discoveries included a limestone sarcophagus containing human remains carbon-dated AD 390–520 and a tile kiln.[18] The kiln had a double flue with stacked floor tiles and an outer wall of chalk blocks, and archaeomagnetic dating has placed its last firing within the period AD 400–450. Wasters derived from tile production included roofing tile and combed box-flue supplying specialist materials for building heated rooms and tiled roofs at the dawn of the fifth century.[19] These products are likely to have been used to enhance Roman-style villa architecture at a time when the necessary building materials could no longer be obtained from supplies routed through London.

The sarcophagi are likely to have been set within a mausoleum of the sort associated with other late antique suburban villas around London, in order to commemorate members of the aristocratic family seated here. This high-status Roman site became the focal point for a small early medieval cemetery, represented by a group of at least ten inhumations on the north side of the church. One of these was accompanied by a Saxon jar of a style likely to date from c. AD 430–70. We cannot know if this evidence represents a direct continuity of use of the site as a place of burial for an established community, or the reuse of a site held to be significant by later communities because of its Roman remains. Michael Garcia's PhD thesis describes how the early medieval reuse of Roman mausolea created an artificial continuity with the Roman past. Saxon churches built following St

Augustine's foundation of an English church at the end of the sixth century sometimes favoured sites of Roman tombs because these were places where the graves of martyrs were thought to be found, in an appropriation of late antique monuments that gave new Christian sites legitimacy and the illusion of continuity.[20] This may explain why several of London's medieval churches stand over important late antique buildings. Important examples include St Bride's, St Andrew Holborn, All Hallows Barking, Bermondsey Abbey, St Michael, and St Peter Cornhill, although the reuse of these sites may also have been influenced by the availability of building materials that could be quarried from Roman ruins. Most of these places probably became Christian through later re-invention, but we cannot dismiss the possibility that a few were places where saints had been venerated at the beginning of the fifth century. The graves of martyrs became places of worship on the borders of cities in Gaul and Italy in the late fourth and early fifth centuries.[21] St Germanus' visit to the tomb of St Alban suggests that the cult of saints was introduced to Britain by the end of the fourth century, and had probably developed along the same trajectory as on the continent.[22] It is therefore credible that places were found for the veneration of London's martyr saints, but since we have no archaeological evidence for their existence there is little point in speculating further.

What the evidence recovered from Al Telfer's investigations at St Martin-in-the-Fields tells us with greater certainty is that some farms and villas near London outlasted the city. Small quantities of early Saxon pottery, dated to the late fifth century, have been found on several such sites and although this is not certain evidence of continuity of settlement, it seems likely that some farmlands around London continued in cultivation through much of the fifth century. Just as the Roman conquest had a limited effect on patterns of settlement within London's more rural hinterland, so too did the failure of its Roman administration.

Two recent discoveries from just outside the walled area probably belong to this period. A coin-hoard of nineteen gold solidi and 114 silver silique, closing with issues of the house of Theodosius c. AD 402, was buried in the fills of a boundary ditch associated with the cemetery on the west side of Ermine Street about 800 metres north of the town wall.[23] This is a fifth-century treasure, and Peter Guest suggests that hoards of this type were assembled in the post-Roman period.[24] A single silver coin found within dark-earth in excavations on the southern borders of Southwark may also date to the early fifth century. This coin of Valentinian I (AD 364–7) had been clipped to remove silver from its edge so as to leave the imperial portrait intact.[25] It is thought that the fashion for clipping coins in this way began in earnest after the usurpation of Constantine III in AD 407, lasting for a few decades. It is significant that nothing similar has been found within the walled town, despite the greater intensity of archaeological research within this area. The former city seems to have been positively avoided, perhaps vacated because of its ideological redundancy in a fragmented post-Roman landscape. Roman cities had no place where Roman rule was rejected.

Early Saxon settlement

A similar pattern can be traced from distributions of late fifth-century Saxon pottery. The chaff-tempered fabrics of this period are difficult to date, but occur in small numbers immediately outside the Roman town whilst largely absent from within the walled circuit. Recently recovered material shows two principal areas of activity: one along the Fleet valley and the other on the southern shores of Borough Channel. A Saxon settlement at Clerkenwell, beyond the Roman cemetery in Smithfield and 400 metres north of the Roman town wall, is implied by a cluster of eight pits containing Germanic-type pottery dated *c.* A D 450–550 and a Saxon burial.[26] The people here may have been the source of four sherds of fifth to sixth-century pottery found in the ditch outside the city wall at Aldersgate.[27] A few sherds of similarly dated material have been found on the west side of the Fleet, at St Bride's and possibly at the Inner Temple.[28] Small-scale early Saxon activity on the other side of the Thames, next to the Borough Channel, is indicated by small assemblages of early Saxon pottery from a ditch and pit at Lant Street, which included a sherd of igneous tempered pottery with a characteristic kind of slip (schlickung) dated A D 400–600, and by material from Trinity Street.[29] Somewhat larger quantities of early Saxon pottery have been recovered from Bermondsey Abbey, where elevated numbers of later fourth-century coins have also been recovered.[30]

Most of these late fifth- or early sixth-century sites had been settled in the Roman period, and those at St Martin-in-the-Fields, Clerkenwell, and Bermondsey may have originated as late Iron Age farmsteads. These were naturally advantaged sites, occupying well-watered locations of strategic aspect near to navigable waterways. There may have been continuity of settlement in or around these places. There was no particular incentive for local farmers to abandon their fields simply because the Roman government had evacuated their London offices. The use of Saxon styles of pottery is not necessarily a marker of ethnic identity and may have been a cultural and economic choice, whilst the survival of place names with Celtic and Latin elements around London might indicate a continued British presence.[31] In sum, there is no evidence of a breakdown of order in the countryside, and those who farmed the land may have continued to do so.

Whilst evidence for a fifth-century presence beyond the city walls is thin, it exists. This contrasts with an almost complete absence of comparable evidence from within the walled area. The only stratified post-Roman artefact from the city confidently dated to the fifth century is a Germanic-style saucer brooch found among fallen roof tiles in the *frigidarium* of the ruined Roman bathhouse at

Billingsgate.[32] We do not know how the brooch reached this spot, but Billingsgate is likely to have remained a suitable point of entry into London. Finds on the foreshore suggest that official cargoes were unloaded here until the middle of the fourth century, implying the presence of a water-gate at a beaching spot for river-craft coming upriver to London (above p. 356). The brooch is identical to ones from graves in early Anglo-Saxon cemeteries established following the movement of people up the Thames and its tributaries from *c.* AD 450 onwards. The pattern of early Anglo-Saxon settlement is best explained as the result of immigration into the area after the failure of the Roman city, along with some adoption of the dominant immigrant culture by surviving rural communities. The main fifth- to sixth-century occupation sites were new settlements: villages in the river valleys housing farming communities of a few dozen people.[33] They had little or nothing to do with Roman London. This is also likely to be the case for the ring of early Anglo-Saxon settlements and cemeteries south and east of London that John Morris suggested had been placed to defend the approaches to sub-Roman London.[34] These date no earlier than the mid-fifth century, by which time the city was uninhabited. The pattern of settlement is likely to have been determined by the arrival of immigrants seeking suitable sites for settlement, where the *Adventus Saxonum* followed after the Roman government had already failed.[35]

Earthworks on the borders of the London region might mark territorial boundaries that emerged from the post-Roman fragmentation of political author-ity, but are too poorly dated for this to be established. Grim's dyke stretches west from Brockley hill to the river Pinn, and perhaps west to Manor Farm, Ruislip.[36] It survives up to 6.9 metres wide and 1.8 metres deep, alongside an earth bank and forming a substantial barrier. Excavations in Pear Wood, near Brockley Hill, found fourth-century material beneath the bank, although the south-western part of the earthwork, near Pinner, might have been thrown up in the pre-Roman Iron Age. It followed a line that might plausibly have been the boundary of a British Kingdom in the Chilterns. A bank and ditch on the east side of the Cray Valley may have similarly marked the northern boundary of a Kentish polity.

London after *Londinium*

London itself remains largely absent from the historical sources of this period. There are no reliable references between its late antique listing in the *Notitia Dignitatum* and AD 601 when Pope Gregory wrote to Augustine proposing London as the primary See.[37] The Anglo-Saxon Chronicle presents a single fifth-century entry referring to London, as a place to which Britons fled after defeat at the hands of the Jutish war-leader Hengest at Crecganford (identified as Crayford) in AD 457.[38] The entry is suspect, but even if it drew on an historical event, it tells us little of use.

A few other early medieval finds from within the walled area suggest that the city attracted sporadic interest through the sixth century. Two Frankish ceramic vessels were found at Gresham Street and Christ's Hospital and a Merovingian-style buckle loop was found in a twelfth-century context at the Guildhall.[39] London may have been uninhabited for over a century by the time these finds reached here, although it seems likely that land within the walls continued to be cultivated. Much may have been grazed. Liberated from the need to pay Rome's taxes and rents arable production may have declined, shifting emphasis from producing grain to raising livestock.[40]

The political impetus for the re-occupation of the city was provided by the foundation of a monastic community at St Paul's in AD 601 by the missionaries sent by Pope Gregory. Gregory proposed the establishment of two ecclesiastical provinces in Britain, at London and York, inspired by the former importance of these imperial cities. These expectations may have been the catalyst for the re-emergence of the walled city as a place of consequence, generating a scatter of middle Anglo-Saxon finds.[41] This was not, however, an urban site. London's seventh-century urban revival focused instead on the area of the Strand, east of the river Fleet, where new roads and houses were developed next to the site at St Martin-in-the-Fields.[42] This was *Lundenwic*, the busy *emporium* described by Bede which grew to cover an area of over 60 hectares, almost half the size of the former walled town. The reasons for the growth of this entrepôt are similar to those that encouraged the Romans to build London: it lay on the orbit of several neighbouring polities, in a geographically opportune spot with access to the sea, river, and overland travel.

The restoration of the old walled city didn't take place before the ninth century. This is generally attributed to the policies of King Alfred the Great although recent research suggests that widespread revival didn't take place until the late tenth or early eleventh century when London Bridge was probably rebuilt.[43] The surviving city walls framed and shaped the medieval city, which thrived on a fortunate location where the river was readily bridged and its tides drew the world to England. Whichever the case, this is the start of a different urban history. The medieval city was a new foundation that inherited little from the Roman city beyond the idea, still very much with us to this day, that this was a place from which Britain could be governed.

31
Afterword

Describing a city of empire

This book has drawn on a wealth of new information to trace the early history of one of the world's most consequential cities. The detail with which we can do so is a testament to the achievements of rescue archaeology. Although it presents many new conclusions, the account is in many respects a conventional one. A tightly framed historical narrative is an effective way of giving shape to the evidence and opening paths to new understandings.

We now have a substantial body of evidence to suggest that London grew on the back of the strategic choices made by emperors and their representatives. The new Roman city was brought into being to command the Thames crossing, serving as a gateway emporium to freshly conquered territories. It was then developed as the leading site for Roman rule in Britain, benefitting from significant injections of resources at times of military need and ambition. This exercise of power was political, and the city's architectural development consequently affords glimpses into the policies of particular regimes, adding important new detail to aspects of Roman history.

The view obtained from the banks of the Thames is of an imperial territory that was more directly managed than much recent scholarship has assumed. Since London was a place of Roman invention, unmoored from the interests of local land-owning aristocracies, it presents several unusual characteristics when viewed alongside the cities of the Roman Mediterranean. It was a supply-base for military campaigns, a market where the authorities turned conquest to profit, and a hive of makers and sellers serving new communities formed around provincial government. These colonial purposes made London resolutely alien, binding it to an administrative establishment drawn from the emperor's household and the governor's military forces. It was crowded with money-lenders, merchants, shippers, and tradesmen: carpet-baggers whose interests were shaped by fealty to an officer-class with roots in Gaul and Germany. The dominating presence of these agents of Rome curtailed opportunities for the development of locally based patronage networks. The political influence of the pre-conquest population in the Thames basin may have been further stunted by a preponderance of confiscated borderlands, drawn into estates owned from afar and managed through London-based agents and agencies.

The most important features of the early city were its bridge and port, the presence of which generated an attendant network of arterial roads designed for the convoys of waggons destined for the forts and cities of the interior. London's quays channelled massive flows of campaign supplies and provisions: grain, oil, leather, meat, clothing, wine, and exotic luxuries. The staples marshalled to feed the advancing army became a flow of annonary goods that fed the city and underwrote London's urban economy. After Flavian reform, this may have allowed sponsored distributions of bread baked from flour ground in technologically advanced watermills, supporting a large urban population of hauliers, builders, and makers. For the first century of its existence, London thrived on the business channelled through its docks and warehouses, and was the beneficiary of administrations seeking to advance their political cause through British conquest.

The growing city gained its shape and character through a series of planned additions. Several phases of urban expansion can be traced, each generating new capacity. The creation of new districts and topographies brought new people to London, whose presence was layered onto earlier landscapes. Once the business of supply was firmly in hand, settlement was probably encouraged by land grants in newly ordered quarters of town. It was certainly underpinned by the necessary luxuries of social bathing and lavish dinner parties, which lubricated patronage networks that ultimately relied on the emperors direct representatives in the province: the governor and procurator. Reforms under Vespasian built on London's role as a supply-base, probably involving stronger controls over regional production and taxation and incorporating new ideas about the performative display of imperial power. The amphitheatre was the quintessential symbol of this new regime and it is significant that other forms of civic architecture were slower to arrive, some perhaps delayed until Rome considered the conquest of Britain complete later in the century.

There is much to admire about the way in which the Roman engineers exploited the site. Road building and town planning chased the curve of the land and fixed new landscapes against ancient topographies. The choice of site, and the craft of its design, generated an enduring cityscape. Reuse and recycling, of places and materials, became a pragmatic choice but knowingly anchored London within its inherited landscape. This was a place where mundane supernatural forces were recognized and accommodated through constant apotropaic appeasement, whilst also yoked firmly to the divine power of Rome and its emperors.

London's engineering served various institutions of government, and the social needs of the communities who set their fortunes to this frontier city. We are offered only passing glimpses of the world of associations through which these Londoners gained social and political agency. The written record is inevitably dominated by mention of military and political office but also identifies local administrations, cult affiliations, trade associations, professions, and family relations. In the absence of any local elite society to co-opt, political control and architectural patronage depended on government officials rather than civilian association, generating an unusual urban society that gave birth to a particular urban form.

Tracing exogenous shock

London's dependency on the flows of people and goods that served Rome's colonial project made it particularly vulnerable. This can be seen in the way that two different types of exogenous shock—war and plague—find reflection in the archaeological record. One of the themes to emerge from this study is how differently these threats may have represented themselves, and how differently responses were framed. We know most about London's destruction in the Boudican revolt, which is the only one of these events for which we have incontrovertible evidence. Response to London's violent destruction was swift and decisive, and within a couple of years the city was largely restored by military engineering. A detritus of body-parts on the city borders offers a stark reminder of the brutal means by which Rome imposed its peace. The archaeology of the Hadrianic fire, and the pattern of ensuing military engineering, echoed the Boudican destruction so closely that it can also be read as evidence of revolt and response. Rome's answer to military setback was to throw overwhelming resources into the uncompromising reassertion of control. In this regard the building and rebuilding of London was both symbol and product of the Roman peace, in a landscape where urban civilization was a tool of domination and the language of the dominant. The commerce enabled by London's port and financial institutions met the needs of supply-chain management, and for those in the city's orbit the benefits of economic growth would have been offset by the attendant impositions of taxes and rents. The fact of London's repeated destruction, and the defensive character of its later architecture, signals the contested nature of the values that it represented.

Wars are difficult to identify from archaeological evidence without supporting historical testimony, but it is even harder to trace the impact of ancient plagues. We have certain epigraphic evidence, however, that the devastating pandemic of *c.* AD 165 caused alarm in London. The city suffered a pronounced urban contraction and economic dislocation at exactly the time that this plague swept through the Roman world. We cannot conclusively show that this was not some unusual coincidence, but the arrival of plague provides a coherent explanation for the exceptional changes witnessed in the middle of the second century. We cannot be certain that any Londoner died, but the impacts of plague included both short-term prophylactic measures and long-term social change. Any flight of labour, perhaps embracing the military evacuation of London's Hadrianic fort, would have had the most serious economic consequences. Full restoration appears to have taken a generation or more, eventually accomplished through the direct intervention of the state in public projects following Severan restoration. This is when London was reinvented and its town walls were built.

Just as the archaeology of the Boudican fire was echoed by that of London's Hadrianic fire, so the archaeology of London's Antonine contraction fore-shadowed the failure of London's port in the 250s. The pattern of change is con-sistent with a further loss of manpower at a time of plague and military instability. Locally it involved the collapse of long-distance supply, a retreat from organized estate production in London's hinterland, and perhaps a loss of control of the seas around Britain. Once again the city was eventually restored and re-ordered at the prompt of distant emperors, perhaps following a recessionary interval lasting one or two decades. These two episodes of urban retreat, starting *c.* AD 165 and *c.* AD 253, present a model of how pandemics might represent themselves in the archaeological record where we have no dead to count. These assumptions need further testing, but if this analysis is correct, then it adds to our understanding of how and why the world of later antiquity came to differ to that of the high empire.

The shocks of these events may have provoked systemic change, inducing the imperial administration to introduce new forms of government. The most con-spicuous consequence of change was the reduced flow of annonary goods and redundancy of London's port. We can question how sustainable the pattern of earlier supply had ever been, as frontiers became fixed and wars of conquest ceased to reward imperial advance.[1] Earlier patterns of importation, especially of goods associated with fine dining, continued—if with significant variation—into the third century. This had perhaps become a case of path dependency, where arrangements developed to support the initial conquest had persisted beyond their utility. Administrations may have been unprepared to confront the political costs of limiting the Mediterranean styles of consumption that defined and rewarded social standing.[2] These subsidies and inefficiencies could not be sus-tained in the face of the failures of the middle of the third century. External sto-chastic shock may have exposed problems and forced change. In sum, these pandemics shook the Roman world from earlier forms of path-dependency developed around the opportunities of imperial expansion, and inspired the invention of the new architectures of control that characterized late antiquity. These, in turn, contributed to the political circumstances that fuelled the later fragmentation of empire.

Resilience, persistence, and failure

Despite the sporadic problems of destruction and depopulation, London showed considerable resilience. War and plague may have provoked tectonic shifts in the way in which London functioned within the Roman world, especially with regard to the organization and role of *annona* supply, but these were not terminal shocks. Recovery was a political necessity because of London's administrative role, but the loss of manpower saw a diminished role for London's port and a concomitant decline of the subsidiary craft production that relied on seasonal labour. Whilst London's Severan revival was planned around the idea of London as both a capital city and a transportation hub, involving new administrative commands that relied on London's harbour, this was no longer the case when Roman rule was restored after the fall of the Gallic Empire *c.* AD 274. New arrangements for the supply of the provincial garrison and command of coastal regions had contributed to a significant economic rebalancing, and the port was not revived.

This allows us to describe a fundamental shift in the character of the archaeology of Roman London, following this mid-third-century turning point. The early city had been an emporium, where new programmes of waterfront construction attended the supply needs of campaigns and *annona* reform, and were accompanied by investment in roads, quays, and public porticoes. These cyclical building programmes described expansionary high-points in the history of Rome's involvement in Britain, when London was a confident staging post in imperial advance, backed by immense flows of people and resources. Following the shocks of the second and third centuries, the city was reinvented as a seat of administrative power: a wall-girt enclave of privilege and power. Sporadic imperial interest came to be expressed by additions and improvements to London's defensive architecture rather than its quays. These too responded to the political strategies of regimes that found reason to engage in British affairs, but drawing on more limited resources, using fewer people within a tighter network of control.

London's eventual failure at the dawn of the fifth century should not blind us to its impressive record of earlier recovery following catastrophic destruction, population decline, and economic contraction. Its persistent reinvention suggests a degree of urban resilience. The factors that contribute to urban resilience have been much explored in studies of how cities recover from disaster, where social capital—the networks that enable effective community action—is often seen as critically important.[3] But we have no grounds for believing that London survived because of its social capital. It was its continued utility to Rome as a place of government that ensured its revival. A parallel can be drawn with sixth-century Antioch, which survived disasters because emperors took a direct interest in its recovery, investing in large-scale reconstruction, repopulating the city after disaster, and maintaining the population through free bread doles.[4] The measures that sustained Antioch were equally determinant in shaping London's fortunes. London failed, then, when Rome ceased to find reason to support it. This exposed its lack of the social capital and economic purpose that might otherwise have underwritten urban life. London's vulnerabilities were a product of its alien identity, shrunken economic role, and dependency on flows of government investment.

During its expansion, Rome found ample resources to deal with adversity: rebuilding promptly after military setbacks and swift to re-impose authority through overwhelming force. This drew on the logistical machinery that London was built to serve. Rome not only marched on its stomach, but wined and dined its servants on unprecedented scale. The consequent traffic, and the need to raise taxes and rents to support government, stimulated economic growth. For those in command this brought many opportunities, but wealth was unevenly distributed and the benefits of city-living remained largely inaccessible to the surrounding countryside. The discoveries in London suggest that repeated shocks to the system reduced Rome's capacity to mobilize resources. These changes left the imperial systems more vulnerable to lower order threats, and as a consequence the city was reinvented in late antiquity as a defended administrative enclave within a network of such places.

London ceased to exist because Rome failed to maintain authority in Britain, and the city had no other evident reason for being. Its disappearance is unlikely to have been a matter of widespread regret. The rewards of economic growth gained from the Roman investment in productivity were unevenly distributed, offering few material benefits to the wider population.[5] The Roman administration was otherwise harsh, and the demands of tax and rent unwelcome. Whilst the achievements of Roman London were many, they failed to carry far and advantaged only the privileged few.

This account has chiefly been concerned with understanding the political and economic forces that gave structure to Roman London, building a chronology for changing patterns of investment and supply. This narrative approach, and an overriding concern with imperial strategy, makes this a top-down study concerned more with issues of political structure than those of social agency. Our understanding of how social actors, both individuals and disparate groups, responded to the exercise of Roman imperial power in London is less advanced. There is a wealth of information sitting within meaningful assemblages of rubbish that have been recovered from London's changing landscape, from which much more can be done to explore the relationship between people and power. These relationships are historically contingent. Ideas and beliefs exist of their time, and are forged in response to experience, circumstance, and opportunity. In this book I have tried to sketch out the more critical strands of change that shaped life in Roman London, in the hope that this will encourage such research, providing an architecture against which new ideas can be tested.

Excavation Sites Referred to in the Text

Table A.1 Excavation sites in the Greater London area mentioned in the text, the locations of which are shown on Figures A.1–4

Code	Address	Sources	Map
WFG1a	1–4 Hart Street, 4 Cripplegate Buildings, St Giles Cripplegate churchyard, EC2	Grimes 1968; Shepherd 2012, 47–9.	A2
WFG3	2A Windsor Court, 3–9 Castle Street, 38–40 Monkwell Street, EC2	Grimes 1968, 118–19; Shepherd 2012, 56–63.	A2
WFG5	Falcon Square, EC2	Grimes 1968, 29–32, 118–19; Shepherd 2012, 66–78.	A2
WFG7	20–8 Noble Street, EC2	Grimes 1968, 33–4; Shepherd 2012, 79–87.	A2
WFG9	31–9 Noble Street, EC2	Grimes 1968; Shepherd 2012, 88–103.	A2
WFG20	15–17 Silver Street, EC2	Grimes 1968; Shepherd 2012, 116–20.	A2
WFG22	St Alban's church, Wood Street, EC2	Grimes 1968; Shepherd 2012, 121–36.	A2
WFG44	Bucklersbury House (now Walbrook Square), Cannon Street, EC4	Grimes 1968, 92–7; Shepherd 1998.	A2
WFG62	St Bride's Church, Fleet Street, EC4	Milne 1997.	A2
GM4	Guildhall Library Extension, Aldermanbury, EC2	Marsden 1968, 4–10.	A2
GM5	Aldersgate, EC1	Schofield 1998, 31; Merrifield 1965 G8.	A2
GM25	Bush Lane (site of Governor's Palace), 152 Upper Thames Street, EC4	Marsden 1975; Marsden 1978.	A2
GM29	Dyers' Arms (site of), 78–80 Cannon Street and Cannon Street Station (site of Governor's Palace), EC4	Marsden 1975; Marsden 1978.	A2
GM31	Temple Court (formerly Temple House), 77 Cannon Street, Queen Victoria Street, 4 Budge Row, EC4	Schofield 1998, 40; Wilmott 1991.	A2

Continued

Table A.1 *Continued*

Code	Address	Sources	Map
GM37	110–16 Cheapside (Sun Life Assurance), EC2	Marsden 1976.	A2
GM44	Barber and Co's warehouse, 8–10 Cooper's Row, EC3	Marsden 1965.	A3
GM55	Duke's Place (site of Bastion 6), EC3	Marsden 1980, 172.	A3
GM60	112–14 Fenchurch Street, 17–18 Billiter Street, EC3	Marsden 1980, 24; Schofield 1998, 51.	A3
GM68	17–19 Gracechurch Street, EC3	Marsden 1987.	A3
GM70	83–7 Gracechurch Street, EC3	Marsden 1987, 119–28.	A3
GM73	All Hallows Barking church, Great Tower Street, EC3	Schofield 1998, 55–6.	A3
GM76	30 Gresham Street (formerly 26–7 King Street), EC2	Shepherd 1987, 33–4.	A2
GM82	9–12 King Street and Prudent Passage (Atlas Assurance), EC2	Shepherd 1987, 40–1.	A2
GM83	13–14 King Street, EC2	Shepherd 1987, 41–2.	A2
GM86	34–5 King Street, 6–7 Lawrence Lane, EC2	Shepherd 1987, 43–6.	A2
GM91	Salvation Army headquarters, 101 Queen Victoria Street, Lambeth Hill, EC4	Marsden 1967.	A2
GM96	41–51 Lime Street, Billiter Street (Lloyd's Site), EC3	Merrifield 1965, Site 331.	A3
GM100	54–8 Lombard Street (Barclay's Bank), EC3	Marsden 1987, 140–7.	A3
GM101	54 Lombard Street (All Hallows church), EC3	Marsden 1987, 139.	A3
GM111	Billingsgate Coal Exchange, 100 Lower Thames Street (Billingsgate bathhouse), EC3	Marsden 1968; B Richardson 1991.	A3
GM131	Central Criminal Court Extension, Old Bailey, Warwick Square, Warwick Lane, EC4	Marsden 1969b.	A2
GM136	Paternoster Square (10–14 Newgate Street, Warwick Lane, 61–70 St. Paul's Churchyard and Panyer Alley), EC4	Marsden 1969a; Marsden 1965, 137; Shepherd 1988.	A2
GM157	Bucklersbury House, 11–20 Walbrook, EC4	Wilmott 1991.	A2

GM160	Gateway House, 1 Watling Street, EC4	Shepherd 1986.	A2
GM163	St Dunstan's Hill, 84 Lower Thames Street, EC3	Marsden 1980, 155.	A3
GM182	Roman ship, Blackfriars underpass, Puddle Dock, EC4	Marsden 1994, 33–95.	A2
GM210	9–11 Bush Lane, EC4	Marsden 1975; Marsden 1978.	A2
GM213	Watling House, 12–16 Watling Street, 31–7 Cannon Street, EC4	Shepherd 1986.	A2
GM217	7–8 King Street (formerly 3–8), EC2	Schofield 1998, 103; Marsden 1980, 110.	A2
GM219	11 Ironmonger Lane, EC2	Dawe and Oswald 1952; Shepherd 1987, 34–8.	A2
GM240	Huggin Hill bathhouse, Huggin Hill, EC4	Marsden 1976.	A2
GM248	Regis House, King William Street/Fish Street Hill, EC3	Dunning 1945; Brigham and Watson in prep.	A3
GM256	Temple of Mithras, Walbrook, EC4	Shepherd 1998.	A2
GM257	Bank of England, Princes Street, EC2	Schofield 1987, 114–15.	A2
GM297	168–70 Fenchurch Street (Barclay's Bank), 22 Lime Street, EC3	Philp 1977.	A3
GM451	Guy's Hospital boat, Great Maze Pond, SE1	Marsden 1994, 97–104.	A4
BRE70	233–46 High Street, Brentford, TW8	Cowie et al. 2013.	A1
HW70	Highgate Wood, Muswell Hill Road, N6/N10	Brown and Sheldon 2018.	A1
TW70 (TW84)	Toppings Wharf, Tooley Street, SE1	Brigham 2001, 12–22; Cowan et al. 2009, Site 15.	A4
207BHS72	201–11 Borough High Street, SE1	Ferretti and Graham 1978; Cowan et al. 2009, Site 72.	A4
CASS72	20–30 Aldgate, EC3	Chapman and Johnson 1973.	A3
FNS72	110–14 Fenchurch Street, EC3	Schofield 1998, 128.	A3
106BHS73	106–14 Borough High Street, SE1; Cowan et al. 2009, Site 62.	Schwab 1978.	A4
BLH73	Bush Lane House, 80 Cannon Street, EC4	Chapman and Johnson 1973; Marsden 1975; Brigham 2001a.	A2

Continued

Table A.1 *Continued*

Code	Address	Sources	Map
CUS73	Old Custom House, Wool Quay, Lower Thames Street, EC3	Brigham 1990b, 118–25; Tatton-Brown 1974.	A3
MC73	84–94 Queen Victoria Street (formerly St Mildred's Church, Bread Street), EC4	Marsden et al. 1975.	A2
1STS74	1–7 St Thomas Street, SE1	Dennis 1978; Cowan et al. 2009, Site 28.	A4
64BHS74	64–70 Borough High Street, SE1	AH Graham 1998a; Cowan et al. 2009, Site 55.	A4
8US74	8 Union Street, SE1	Cowan et al. 2009, Site 58.	A4
88BHS74	88 Borough High Street, SE1	Yule 1988; Cowan et al. 2009, Site 60.	A4
ACW74	1–8 Angel Court, 30–5 Throgmorton Street, EC2	Blurton 1977.	A3
BC74 (BC75)	Baynard House (site of Baynard's Castle), Upper Thames Street, Queen Victoria Street, EC4	C Hill et al. 1980.	A2
BRE74	231–2 High Street, Brentford, TW8	Cowie et al. 2013.	A1
HL74	Harp Lane, St Dunstan's Hill, Cross Lane, EC3	Hobley and Schofield 1977, 56.	A3
LD74 (HIG74, LD76)	172–6 The Highway, Shadwell, E1	Lakin 2002.	A1
LH74	44–6 Ludgate Hill/1–6 Old Bailey, EC4	Schofield 1998, 134.	A2
MM74	Upper Thames Street, east of the Mermaid Theatre, EC4	C Hill et al. 1980.	A2
NFW74 (FRE78)	St Magnus House, New Fresh Wharf, 2–6 Lower Thames Street, EC3	Miller et al. 1986.	A3
SH74 (SH76)	Seal House, 106–8 Lower Thames Street, EC4	Brigham 1990b, 107–11.	A3
TR74	Billingsgate Buildings, 101–10 Lower Thames Street, EC3	DM Jones 1980.	A3
84BHS75	84–6 Borough High Street, SE1	AH Graham 1988b, 67–70; Cowan et al. 2009 Site 57.	A4

Code	Site	Reference	Grade
CAS75	3–4 Jewry Street, EC3	Hobley and Schofield 1977, 57.	A3
CS75	48–50 Cannon Street, EC4	Boddington 1979.	A2
DHS75	District Heating Scheme, Montague Close/Tooley Street, SE1	AH Graham 1988c; Cowan et al. 2009, Site 7.	A4
GPO75	General Post Office, 76–80 Newgate Street, EC1	Perring and Roskams 1991.	A2
175BHS76	175–7 Borough High Street, SE1	Schaaf 1976; Cowan et al. 2009, Site 66.	A4
CHR76	Christchurch, Newgate Street, EC1	Schofield 1998, 146.	A2
FSE76	160–2 Fenchurch Street, 22–3 Lime Street, EC3	Boddington and Marsden 1987.	A3
LC76	2–3 Lombard Court, 39–40 Lombard Street, EC2	Schofield 1998, 147.	A3
MLK76 (MIL72)	1–6 Milk Street, 5–6 Russia Row, EC2	Perring and Roskams 1991.	A2
11STS77	11–15 St Thomas Street, SE1	Cowan et al. 2009, Site 28.	A4
124BHS77	124–6 Borough High Street, SE1	Cowan et al. 2009, Site 63.	A4
213BHS77	213 Borough High Street, SE1	Cowan et al. 2009, Site 74.	A4
BRE77	9–14 New Spring Gardens, High Street, Brentford, TW8	Cowie et al. 2013.	A1
DUK77	St James Passage, subway, 2–7 Duke's Place, EC3	J Maloney 1979.	A3
GST77	GPO Tunnel, Gracechurch Street, EC3	Marsden 1987.	A3
SCC77	Southwark Cathedral crypt, SE1	Hammerson 1978b; Cowan et al. 2009, Site 11.	A4
AB78	Arcadia Buildings, Silvester Street, Great Dover Street, SE1	Dean 1980; Dean and Hammerson 1980; Cowan et al. 2009, Site 83.	A4
CUT78	The PLA Warehouses, Cutler Street, E1	Schofield 1998, 152.	A3
GP78	Greenwich Park, Maze Hill, SE10	Sheldon and Yule 1979.	A1
THL78b	Tower Hill, EC3	Whipp 1980.	A3
WAT78	Watling Court, 41–53 Cannon Street, 11–14 Bow Lane, 19–28 Watling Street, EC4	Perring and Roskams 1991.	A2

Continued

Table A.1 *Continued*

Code	Address	Sources	Map
BAR79	Medical School, St Bartholomew's Hospital, EC1	Bentley and Pritchard 1982.	A2
HEN79	6–10 Heneage Lane, EC3	Schofield 1998, 158.	A3
HIB79	Hibernia Wharf, Montague Close, SE1	Cowan *et al.* 2009, Site 4; Seeley and Wardle 2009.	A4
HR79 (HR77)	Harper Road, 19 Merrick Square, 18–19 Dickens Square, SE1	Dean and Hammerson 1980; Cotton 2008; Cowan *et al.* 2009, Site 91; Redfern *et al.* 2017.	A4
ILA79	Miles Lane, 132–7 Upper Thames Street, EC4	Miller 1982; Hillam 1986.	A3
PEN79	Peninsular House, 112–16 Lower Thames Street, EC3	Milne 1985.	A3
TOL79–84	Tower of London, EC3	Parnell 1985.	A3
WEL79	Well Court, 44–8 Bow Lane, EC4	Perring and Roskams 1991, 51–7.	A2
WOW79	128–33 Cheapside, 1 Gutter Lane, 130 Wood Street (formerly Woolworths), EC2	Schofield 1998, 161–2.	A2
XWL79	8–10 Crosswall, EC3	J Maloney 1980.	A3
15SK80	Calvert's Buildings, 15–23 Southwark Street, SE1	Cowan 1992.	A4
FEC80	47–9 Fenchurch Street, EC3	Schofield 1998, 164.	A3
FSP80	60 Fenchurch Street, EC3	Schofield 1998, 164.	A3
IRO80	24–5 Ironmonger Lane, 9–12 King Street, EC2	Perring and Roskams 1991, 57–63.	A2
PUB80	86 Fenchurch Street, EC3	Schofield 1998, 166.	A3
107BHS81	107–15 Borough High Street, SE1	Yule 1982; Cowan *et al.* 2009, Site 56.	A4
223BHS81	223–37 Borough High Street, SE1	Cowan *et al.* 2009, Site 80.	A4
CLE81	29–32 Clements Lane, EC3	Schofield 1998, 168–9; Evans and James 1983.	A3
CNI81	66–73 Cornhill, EC3	Evans and James 1983; P James 1987.	A3
OPT81	2–3 Cross Keys Court, Copthall Avenue, EC2	C Maloney 1990.	A2

Code	Address	Reference	
PDN81	Namura House, 11–11A Pudding Lane, 121–7 Lower Thames Street, EC3	Milne 1985.	A3
PET81	Peter's Hill, 223–5 Upper Thames Street (now City of London Boy's School), EC4	Williams 1993.	A2
PHI81	5–7 Philpot Lane, EC3	Schofield 1998, 175.	A3
SWA81	Swan Lane Car Park, 95–103 Upper Thames Street, EC4	Brigham 1990b, 111–17.	A2
4STS82	4–26 St Thomas Street, SE1	Cowan et al. 2009, Site 33.	A4
BIG82 (BWB83)	Billingsgate Market Lorry Park, Lower Thames Street, EC3	Brigham 1990b, 100–7.	A3
BIS82	76–86 Bishopsgate, EC3	Schofield 1998, 180.	A3
BOP82	28–32 Bishopsgate, 2–3 Crosby Square, 2–3 Great St Helen's, EC2	Schofield 1998, 181–2; Evans and James 1983.	A3
GHR82	Guy's Hospital Development (Area 7), St Thomas Street, SE1	Cowan et al. 2009, Site 38.	A4
LIB82	119–21 Cannon Street, 1–3 Abchurch Yard, 14 Sherbourne Lane, EC4	Schofield 1998, 183.	A2
LUD82	42–6 Ludgate Hill and 1–6 Old Bailey, EC4	Rowsome 2014a; Rowsome 2014b.	A2
OST82	7–10 Foster Lane, 5–6 Rose and Crown Court, EC2	Blair 1983; Schofield 1998, 185.	A2
POT82	9–10 Philpot Lane, EC3	Schofield 1998, 186.	A3
RAG82	1–12 Rangoon Street, 61–5 Crutched Friars, 2–4 Carlisle Avenue, 11–13 Northumberland Alley, EC3	Bowler 1983.	A3
SLO82	Beaver House, Sugar Loaf Court, 1 Queen Victoria Street, Little Trinity Lane, Great Trinity Lane, 14 Garlic Hill, EC4	Davies et al. 1994, 232.	A2
BOA83	Bank of Argentina, 11 Ironmonger Lane, EC2	Schofield 1998, 190.	A2
CHWH83	Chamberlain's Wharf, Tooley Street, SE1	Cowan et al. 2009, Site 17.	A4
CW83	Cotton's Wharf, Tooley Street, SE1	Cowan et al. 2009, Site 17.	A4
EST83	23–9 Eastcheap, 14–15 Philpott Lane, EC3	Henig 1984; Schofield 1998, 192–3.	A3
FEN83	5–12 Fenchurch Street, 1 Philpott Lane, EC3	Hammer 1985; Hammer 1987; Schofield 1998, 193–4.	A3

Continued

Table A.1 *Continued*

Code	Address	Sources	Map
HOP83	3–5 Bishopsgate, EC3	Milne *et al.* 1984.	A3
IME83	27–30 Lime Street, EC3	Williams 1985.	A3
KEY83	15–35 Copthall Avenue, 45–9 London Wall, Cross Keys House, 2–3 Cross Key Court, EC2	C Maloney 1990.	A3
LIM83	25–6 Lime Street, EC3	Williams 1984; Williams 1985.	A3
SCS83	9 St. Clare Street, EC3	Barber and Bowsher 2000, 51–2, Site I; Ellis 1985, 117.	A3
TEL83	8 Telegraph Street, EC2	C Maloney 1990.	A2
WIT83	18–23 St Swithin's Lane, 113–14 Cannon Street, EC4	Schofield 1998, 198.	A2
WP83	Winchester Palace, Cathedral Street, Clink Street, SE1	Yule 2005.	A4
28PS84	28 Park Street, SE1	Cowan 2003, Site Q.	A4
ALG84	7–12 Aldersgate Street, EC1	Schofield 1998, 199.	A2
BA84 (TOB95)	Bermondsey Abbey, Long Walk/Abbey Street, SE1	Cowan 2009, Site 92.	A4
CHL84	4–6 Copthall Avenue, EC2	C Maloney 1990.	A3
COSE84	Courage Brewery (south east), Park Street, SE1	Cowan *et al.* 2009, Site 1.	A4
ENG84	8–13 Clerkenwell Close, 33–6 Clerkenwell Green, EC1	Sloane 2012, Site B.	A2
HIL84	7–8 Philpot Lane, EC3	Schofield 1998, 202.	A3
LCT84	Lloyd's Building, 1 Lime Street (formerly Leadenhall Court, 91–100 Gracechurch Street, 1–6 Leadenhall Street, 2–12 Whittington Avenue), EC3	Milne 1992; Milne and Wardle 1993; Brigham 1990a.	A3
LWA84	43 London Wall, EC2	C Maloney 1990.	A2
WTN84	West Tenter Street, E1	Barber and Bowsher 2000, Site L; Whytehead 1986.	A3

Code	Address	Reference	Category
FMO85	37–40 Fish Street Hill, 16–20 Monument Street, EC3	Bateman 1986.	A3
FST85	94–7 Fenchurch Street, EC3	Rivière and Thomas 1987.	A3
KNG85	36–7 King Street, EC2	Rowsome 1987; Hill and Rowsome 2011, Site F; Shepherd 1987.	A2
PCH85	1–3 St Paul's Churchyard, 1–9 Ludgate Hill, EC4	Schofield 2011, Site 55.	A2
QUN85	61 Queen Street, EC4	Burch 1987.	A2
TRT85	41–2 Trinity Square, EC3	B Richardson 1986a, 164; Howell *et al.* 2015.	A3
TTL85	The Three Lords Public House, 27 Minories, EC3	Barber and Bowsher 2000, Site J.	A3
WHY85	White Hart Yard, rear of 53–61 Borough High Street, SE1	Swain 1988; Cowan *et al.* 2009, Site 37.	A4
ABS86	St Alban's House, 124 Wood Street, EC2	Chitwood and Hill 1987.	A2
CAP86	Capel House, 54–62 New Broad Street, EC2	Schofield 1998, 224.	A3
CIL86	62–4 Cornhill, EC3	Schofield 1998, 225.	A2
CLK86	42–6 Clerkenwell Close, EC1	Sloane 2012, Site C.	A2
COA86	16 Coleman Street, EC2	Wardle 2015.	A2
CON86	76 Cannon Street, EC4	Schofield 1998, 225.	A2
DGH86	Dowgate Hill House, 14–16 Dowgate Hill, EC4	Brigham 1990b, 99–183.	A2
DOW86	3–7 Dowgate Hill, EC4	Schofield 1998, 228.	A2
HAY86	13 Haydon Street, EC3	Barber and Bowsher 2000, Site C.	A3
MOG86	49–53 Moorgate, 72–3 Coleman Street, EC2	Schofield 1998, 231.	A2
NHA86	9 Northumberland Avenue, EC3	Rivière and Thomas 1987.	A3
ORG86	St Martin Orgar Churchyard, 24–32 King William Street, EC4	Schofield 1998, 232–3.	A3
STO86	Stothard Place, 284–94 Bishopsgate, EC2	Schofield 1998, 234.	A3
SUN86	Sunlight Wharf, Upper Thames Street, EC3	Williams 1993.	A2

Continued

Table A.1 *Continued*

Code	Address	Sources	Map
TRM86	19 Throgmorton Avenue, 21 Austin Friars (The Garden House), EC2	Hunting 1987; Tomlin 1996.	A3
ABC87	Abacus House, 33–9 Gutter Lane, EC2	Schofield 1998, 237.	A2
ASQ87	12–16 America Square, 15–17 Crosswall, 15 Cooper's Row, EC3	Schofield 1998, 239; Sankey and Stephenson 1991, 122.	A3
AST87	22–5 Austin Friars, EC2	Spence and Grew 1990, 14–15.	A3
BAA87	Barnard's Inn, Holborn, 78–81 Fetter Lane, 7–13 Norwich Street, EC1	Schofield 1998, 240–1; Spence 1989, 26–7.	A2
BBH87	Billingsgate bathhouse, 100 Lower Thames Street, EC3	Rowsome 1996.	A3
BLM87	Blomfield House, 85–6 London Wall and 53 New Broad Street, EC2	Schofield 1998, 242–3; Hall 2014.	A3
BRL87	19–25 Birchin Lane, EC3	Schofield 1998, 244.	A3
BUC87	Dockland Light Railway (DLR) shaft, Bucklersbury, EC4	Hill and Rowsome 2011, 124, Site C.	A2
COV87	10–12 Copthall Avenue, EC2	Schofield 1998, 246.	A3
GAG87	Guildhall Art Gallery, Guildhall Yard, EC2	Bateman *et al.* 2008.	A2
LFE87	65–8 Leadenhall Street, 98 Fenchurch Street, EC3	Schofield 1998, 250.	A3
MFI87	4–12 Monument Street, 17 Fish Street, EC4	Schofield 1998, 252.	A3
MGT87	55–61 Moorgate, 75–9 Coleman Street, EC2	Schofield 1998, 252–3; Spence 1989, 14.	A2
MSL87	49–55 Mansell Street, E1	Barber and Bowsher 2000, Site F.	A3
MST87	31–43 Mansell Street, 2–8 Alie Street, 29–31 West Tenter Street, E1	Barber and Bowsher 2000, Site G.	A3
NEW87	6 Newcastle Row, EC1	Sloane 2012, Site A.	A2
PPO87	2–3 Philpot Lane, EC3	Schofield 1998, 256.	A3
RIV87	River Plate House, 7–11 Finsbury Circus, EC2	Harward *et al.* 2015, Site A.	A3
SCT87	36–41 Scotswood Street, EC1	Sloane 2012, Site E.	A2
SNS87	8–13 Sans Walk, EC1	Sloane 2012, Site F.	A2

UTA87	Cannon Street Station (South), Upper Thames Street, EC4	Schofield 1998, 259–60; Spence and Grew 1990, 22–3.	A2
22BHS88	22 Borough High Street, SE1	Cowan 2009, Site 22.	A4
ANT88	9–10 Angel Court, EC2	Schofield 1998, 261.	A3
BAS88	55 Basinghall Street, EC2	Schofield 1998, 261.	A2
BRD88 (DOC87, LOM88)	Lombard Street, opposite No 80, EC3	Hill and Rowsome 2011, Site E.	A2
CO88 (CO87)	Courage Brewery bottling plant, 38–40 Southwark Street, Park Street, SE1	Brigham et al. 1995; Cowan 2003 Sites D and E; Hammer 2003 Sites D-F	A4
COT88	Cotts House, 27–9 Camomile Street, EC3	Schofield 1998, 265.	A3
DMT88	Dominant House, 85 Queen Victoria Street, 205 Upper Thames Street (Huggin Hill), EC4	Rowsome 1999.	A2
ELD88	Liverpool House, 15–17 Eldon Street, EC2	Harward et al. 2015, Site B.	A3
ETN88	East Tenter Street, E1	Barber and Bowsher 2000, Site A.	A3
FIB88	12–15 Finsbury Circus, EC2	Harward et al. 2015, Site C.	A3
FNC88	88–93 Fenchurch Street, EC3	Schofield 1998, 268.	A3
GAM88	52 Gresham Street, 14 Ironmonger Lane, EC2	Schofield 1998, 269.	A2
HOO88	Hooper Street, E1	Barber and Bowsher 2000, Site D.	A3
LAH88	80–4 Leadenhall Street, EC3	Schofield 1998, 271.	A3
LDL88	Albion House, 34–5 Leadenhall Street, 4 Billiter Street, Street, EC3	Schofield 1998, 272.	A3
LHY88	DLR ventilation shaft opposite 5 Lothbury, EC2	Hill and Rowsome 2011, Site B.	A2
LOW88	60 London Wall (formerly 52–63 London Wall, 20–56 Copthall Avenue), EC2	Lees et al. 1989.	A3
LSO88	Leith House, 47–57 Gresham Street, 22–6 Wood Street, EC2	Schofield 1998, 274.	A2
LYD88	Cannon Street Station (North), Upper Thames Street, Dowgate Hill, EC4	Schofield 1998, 274–5; Spence and Grew 1990, 20–1.	A2

Continued

Table A.1 *Continued*

Code	Address	Sources	Map
MNL88	65–73 Mansell Street, E1	Barber and Bowsher 2000, Site E.	A1
OBA88	18–25 Old Bailey, 10–18 Bishop's Court, 29–37 Fleet Lane, EC4	Schofield 1998, 277.	A2
SXE88	Cayzer House, 2–4 St Mary Axe, EC3	Schofield 1998, 281–2.	A3
TEX88	Thames Exchange, 78 Upper Thames Street, EC4	Parry 1994; Schofield 1998, 282.	A2
USA88	10–18 Union Street, SE1	Heard 1989; Cowan et al. 2009, Site 58.	A4
VAL88	Fleet Valley between Blackfriars and Holborn Viaduct Stations, EC4	McCann and Orton 1989; McCann 1993; Schofield 1998, 283–4.	A2
WIV88	1–7 Whittington Avenue, EC3	Brown and Pye 1992.	A3
179BHS89	179–91 Borough High Street, SE1	Cowan et al. 2009, Site 66.	A4
52SOS89	52–4 Southwark Street, SE1	Cowan 2003, Site M.	A4
AW89	Alaska Works, Grange Road, SE1	Cowan et al. 2009, Site 96.	A4
BTB89	British Telecom shaft, Bishopsgate and Wormwood Street, EC2	Schofield 1998, 289.	A3
CED89	64–6 Cheapside, EC4	Schofield 1998, 290.	A2
CRT89	8–11 Crescent, EC3	Schofield 1998, 291.	A3
ETA89	7–11 Bishopsgate, EC2	Sankey 2002.	A3
GHI89 (GHD90)	Guy's Hospital, St Thomas Street, SE1	Cowan et al. 2009, Site 39.	A4
GRA89	170–6 Grange Road, SE1	Cowan et al. 2009, Site 93.	A4
GWS89	Pinners Hall, Great Winchester Street, 8 Austin Friar's Square, 105–8 Old Broad Street, EC2	Schofield 1998, 293; Rosborough 1990.	A3
HSD89	58–60 Houndsditch, EC3	Schofield 1998, 293.	A3
JON89	42–7 St John's Square, Clerkenwell, EC1	Sloane and Malcolm 2004.	A2

LEN89	145–6 Leadenhall Street, EC3	Schofield 1998, 294.	A3
PEP89	Colchester House, Woodruffe House, Savage Gardens, Pepys Street, 9 Cooper's Row, EC3	Sankey 1998; Gerrard 2011; Schofield 1998, 295.	A3
PRE89	63–6 Prescot Street, E1	Barber and Bowsher 2000, Site H.	A3
STS89	21–7 St Thomas Street, SE1	Cowan et al. 2009, Site 34.	A4
TWR89	1–4 Great Tower Street, EC3	Spence and Grew 1990, 18.	A3
VRY89	Vintry House (Vintners' Place), 68–9 Upper Thames Street, EC4	Schofield 1998, 298.	A2
WES89	24–30 West Smithfield, EC1	Schofield 1998, 299.	A2
CCT90	20–6 Cutler Street, E1	Schofield 1998, 302.	A3
CID90	72–5 Cheapside, 83–93 Queen Street, 9–12 Pancras Lane, EC2 and EC4	Hill and Woodger 1999; Hill and Rowsome 2011, Site D.	A2
PRK90	18 Park Street, SE1	Cowan 2003, Site S.	A4
RAC90	55–8 Gracechurch Street, St Benet's Place, EC3	Schofield 1998, 307–8; Museum of London 1990.	A3
SOB90	British Telecom tunnels under Old Broad Street and Threadneedle Street, EC2	Barber and Bowsher 2000, 51–2.	A3
UPT90	Bull Wharf Lane, 66–7 Upper Thames Street, EC4	Schofield 1998, 310; Esmonde Cleary 1996, 424.	A2
BSP91	14 Eldon Street, 6 Broad Street Place, EC2	Harward et al. 2015, Site D.	A3
BTBHS91	BT Tunnel, Borough High Street, SE1	Wallace 2014, Site 105.	A4
GRW91	41–5 Grange Walk, SE1	Cowan et al. 2009, Site 93.	A4
JSS92	Borough High Street, Battle Bridge sewer diversion, SE1	Drummond-Murray and Thompson 2002.	A4
MSA92	Mayor Sworder's Arches, Joiner Street, Jubilee Line Main Ticket Hall, SE1	Drummond-Murray and Thompson 2002.	A4
BTJ93	Borough High Street, British Telecom junction box (JLE), SE1	Drummond-Murray and Thompson 2002.	A4
PSW93	Gas main diversion, Parliament Square, Parliament Street, SW1	C Thomas 2008.	A1
BSE94	Borough High Street ticket Hall utility diversion, SE1	Drummond-Murray and Thompson 2002.	A4
KWS94	Regis House, 41–6 King William Street, 18–20 Fish Street Hill, EC3	Brigham 1998; Brigham and Watson in prep.	A3

Continued

Table A.1 *Continued*

Code	Address	Sources	Map
LEG94	Lambeth Palace Gardens, SE1	Sloane *et al.* 1995.	A1
NST94	Shelly House, 3 Noble Street, EC2	Howe and Lakin 2008, Site B.	A2
ONE94	One Poultry, 1–19 Poultry, 2–38 Queen Victoria Street, 3–9, 35–40 Bucklersbury, Pancras Lane, Sise Lane, EC2/EC4	Hill and Rowsome 2011.	A2
RWG94	Grouting Shaft, Redcross Way, SE1	Drummond-Murray and Thompson 2002; Cowan *et al.* 2009, Site 44.	A4
SQU94	Spital Square, Lamb Street/Nantes Passage/Folgate Street, E1	Thomas *et al.* 1997.	A3
SUF94	Governor's House (formerly Suffolk House), 5 Laurence Pountney Hill, 154–6 Upper Thames Street, EC4	Brigham 2001.	A2
BAX95	Baltic House ('the Gherkin'), Baltic Exchange (Swiss Re Tower), 14–32 St Mary Axe, 19–28 Bury Street, EC3	Howe 2002.	A3
BGH95	Borough High Street Ticket Hall extension, SE1	Drummond-Murray and Thompson 2002.	A4
BPL95	Monument House, 30–5 Botolph Lane, EC3	Blair and Sankey 2007.	A3
FCC95	Lloyd's Register, 71 Fenchurch Street, EC3	Bluer and Brigham 2006.	A3
FEH95	168 Fenchurch Street, EC3	Dunwoodie 2004.	A3
GAH95	31–45 Gresham Street, EC2	Howe and Lakin 2004, Site C.	A2
IRL95	11 Ironmonger Lane, EC2	Grainger 1995.	A2
LBE95	London Bridge Station, MEPC car park, ticket hall/escalator shaft, SE1	Drummond-Murray and Thompson 2002.	A4
LEK95	Lefevre Walk Estate, Old Ford, E3	G Brown 2008.	A1
MRG95	Northgate House, 20–8 Moorgate, EC2	Seeley and Drummond-Murray 2005.	A2
PLQ95	Parliament Square (south-east corner), SW1	C Thomas 2008.	A1
SH195	19 St Mary at Hill, EC3	Greenwood and Maloney 1996, 8.	A3

CAO96	25 Cannon Street, EC4	Elsden 2002.	A2
FSS96	51–3 Southwark Street, SE1	Killock 2005.	A4
GDV96	165 Great Dover Street, SE1	Mackinder 2000.	A4
MGE96	12–18 Moorgate, EC2	Bruce et al. 2009.	A2
ATC97	Atlantic House, 45–60 Holborn Viaduct, EC1	S Watson 2003.	A2
ESC97	13–21 Eastcheap, EC3	Blair and Sankey 2007.	A3
FER97	Plantation Place (formerly Plantation House), 26–38 Fenchurch Street, 1–16 Mincing Lane, 23 Rood Street, 53 Great Tower Street, EC3	Dunwoodie et al. 2015.	A3
GSM197	10 Gresham Street (formerly the Post Office Engineers' building, 2–12 Gresham Street), EC2	Casson et al. 2014.	A2
HHO97	Hunt's House, Guy's Hospital, SE1	Taylor-Wilson 2002.	A4
LVL97	Barrington House, 59–67 Gresham Street, 27–34 Wood Street and 1–6 Love Lane, EC2	Howe and Lakin 2004, Site E.	A2
OBL97	16–17 Old Bailey, EC4	Pitt 2006b.	A2
PLH97	Alder, Castle and Falcon House, 1–6 Aldersgate Street, EC1	Butler 2001.	A2
SHN97	Christchurch Court (formerly Sudbury House), 10–15 Newgate Street, EC4	Askew 2007.	A2
SWY97 (SNY97)	Summerton Way, Thamesmead, SE28	Lakin 1999.	A1
WOO97	90–2 and 100 Wood Street and St Albans Court, EC2	Howe and Lakin 2008, Site D.	A2
BGB98	201 Bishopsgate, EC2	Swift 2003.	A3
BWL98	40–3 Bow Lane and 67–71 Watling Street, EC4	Hill and Rowsome 2011, 273–4.	A2
BYQ98	Igloo Bermondsey Square Regeneration Project, Bermondsey Square, SE1	Maloney and Holroyd 2007, 77.	A1
KEW98	King Edward Buildings (former GPO Headquarters), Merrill Lynch Financial Centre, 2 King Edward Street, EC1	Lyon 2007.	A2
MRL98	Moor House, 120 London Wall, EC2	Butler 2006.	A2

Continued

Table A.1 *Continued*

Code	Address	Sources	Map
NEG98	Svenska House, Craythorne House, 3–9 Newgate Street, EC1	Pitt 2006b.	A2
NHG98	25 Gresham Street (formerly 19–29 Gresham Street, 1 Noble Street), EC2	Lyon 2004; Howe and Lakin 2008.	A2
OJW98	8–10 Old Jewry, EC2	S Watson 2004.	A2
SRP98	Spitalfields Market, E1	McKenzie and Thomas 2020; Barber and Hall 2000; C Thomas 2004.	A3
SWN98	Old Sorting Office, Swan Street, SE1	Beasley 2006.	A4
TEA98	Lion Plaza, 1–18 Old Broad Street and 41–53 Threadneedle Street, EC2	McKenzie 2011.	A3
TYT98	London Bridge City, Tooley Street, SE1	Cowan *et al.* 2009, Site 21.	A4
CDV99	Premier Place, 2½ Devonshire Square, London EC2	Sankey and Connell 2007.	A3
CPW99 (CPQ03) (CRZ06)	Grange City Hotel, 8–14 Cooper's Row, EC3	G Hunt 2010.	A3
GMA99	Greenwich Park, SE10	Wallower 2002a; Wallower 2002b.	A1
HCO99 (TCT99)	Hare Court, Church Court, Inner Temple, EC4	Butler 2005.	A2
LDH99	11 Leadenhall Street, EC3	Hart and Melkian 2007.	A3
LGK99	5–27 Long Lane, SE1	Douglas 2007.	A4
MTA99	Southwark Cathedral, SE1	Divers *et al.* 2009.	A4
GHT00	Blossom's Inn, 20–30 Gresham Street, 20–3 Lawrence Lane, 3–6 Trump Street, 1–10 Milk Street and Mumford Court, EC2	Blair *et al.* 2006.	A2
HUD01	St Andrews, Holborn, EC2	Featherby 2002.	A2
NGT00	Newgate Triangle, Paternoster Square, EC4	S Watson 2006, Site B.	A2
SLY00	Juxon House, Paternoster Square, EC4	S Watson 2006, Site A.	A2

TLT00	285–91 Tooley Street, SE1	Leary 2004.	A1
AMA01	1 America Street, SE1	Cowan et al. 2009, 164.	A4
AUT01	Minster House, 12 Arthur Street, EC4	Swift 2008.	A2
CPN01	Crispin Street, Artillery Lane and Gun Street, E1.	Sudds and Douglas 2014.	A3
EAE01	41 Eastcheap, EC3	Pitt 2014.	A3
FOT01	2–4 Carey Lane, 11–12 Foster Lane, EC2	Lyon 2003.	A2
FNE01	60–3 Fenchurch Street, EC3	Birbeck and Schuster 2009.	A3
PNS01	Paternoster Row, Paternoster Square, EC4	S Watson 2006, Site C.	A2
QUV01	Salvation Army International Headquarters, 99–101 Queen Victoria Street, EC4	Bradley and Butler 2008.	A2
SMD01	St Martin-in-the-Fields Church, 12 Adelaide Street, WC2	Telfer 2007; Telfer 2010.	A1
THY01	6–8 Tokenhouse Yard, EC2	Leary and Butler 2012.	A3
LLS02	Tabard Square, 34–70 Long Lane, 31–47 Tabard Square Street, SE1	Killock et al. 2015.	A4
TOC02	Tobacco Dock, bounded by The Highway, Chigwell Hill, Wapping Lane and Pennington Street, E1	Douglas et al. 2011, Site A.	A1
BDC03	6 Broad Street Place, EC2	Harward et al. 2015, Site E.	A3
ENS03	16–18 Finsbury Circus, 18–31 Eldon Street, EC2	Harward et al. 2015, Site F.	A3
LTU03	52–6 Lant Street, SE1	Ridgeway et al. 2013.	A4
SBK03	56 Southwark Bridge Road, SE1	Ridgeway et al. 2013.	A4
USS03	33 Union Street, SE1	Gerrard 2009.	A4
BEU04	Beaumont Road Estate, Leyton, E10	G Brown 2016.	A1
CDP04	120–2 Cheapside and 4–9 Wood Street, EC2	S Watson 2015, Site A.	A2
OCU04	82–96 Old Kent Road, SE1	Thrale 2008.	A4
BAZ05	35 Basinghall Street, EC2	Wardle 2015.	A2

Continued

Table A.1 *Continued*

Code	Address	Sources	Map
BBH05	Bow Bells House, 1 Bread Street, EC4	Howell 2013.	A2
CYQ05	The Pinnacle, 4 Crosby Square, EC2	Maloney and Holroyd 2009, 51.	A3
GHM05	25 Milk Street and 14–18 Gresham Street, EC2	S Watson 2015, Site B.	A2
NSS05	11–23 New Fetter Lane, 25 New Street Square, 11 Bartlett Court, 1 and 8–9 East Harding Street, London, EC4	Telfer and Blackmore 2017.	A2
POU05	36–9 Poultry, EC2	Pitt 2006a.	A2
SGY05	St George the Martyr Church, Borough High Street, SE1	B Watson 2014, 50.	A4
SSZ05	Steward Street, Tower Hamlets, E1	Cass and Preston 2010.	A3
DGT06	Drapers' Gardens, Throgmorton Avenue, EC2	Ridgeway 2009; N Hawkins forthcoming.	A3
GHB06	6–12 Basinghall Street and 93–5 Gresham Street (Princes House, Bartlett House), EC2	S Watson 2014.	A2
GSJ06	54–66 Gresham Street, EC2	Booth 2008, 317; Booth 2007, 287; Bateman *et al.* 2008.	A2
HLW06	Holywell Lane, Shoreditch, Hackney, EC2	Bull *et al.* 2011, Site A.	A3
LMZ06	8–13 Lime Street, EC3	Betts and Telfer 2018.	A3
PCO06	41–63 Prescot Street, E1	Hunt and Shepherd 2009; https://www.lparchaeology.com/prescot/	A3
RKH06	Riverbank House, 2 Swan Lane, EC4	Mackinder 2015.	A2
WAO06	The Walbrook, St Swithin House, Walbrook House and Granite House (30–7 Walbrook and 97–101 Cannon Street), EC4	Booth 2007, 291; Booth 2008, 319–20; Blair 2010.	A2
NCZ07	1 New Change, EC4	Maloney and Holroyd 2008, 9.	A2
SDX07	196–200 Shoreditch High Street, E1	Bull *et al*, Site D.	A3
TIY07	28–31 Trinity Street, SE1	Killock *et al.* forthcoming.	A4

Code	Location	Reference	
CNV08 (CCP04)	Cannon Street Station, Cannon Place, EC4	Maloney and Holroyd 2009, 50.	A2
ECO08	Embassy Court, Welling High Street, DA16	Maloney and Holroyd 2009, 46.	A1
FEU08	20 Fenchurch Street (the 'walkie talkie'), EC3	Wroe-Brown 2014.	A3
LBN08	The Place, 25 London Bridge Street, SE1	Mackinder and Whittingham 2013.	A4
TRH08	38–40 Trinity Square, London, EC3	Howell et al. 2015.	A3
BVQ09	Thameslink: Park Street, Southwark Street and Redcross Way, SE1	Ridgeway et al. 2019.	A4
BVT09	Thameslink: Stoney Street, SE1	Ridgeway et al. 2019.	A4
BVX09	Thameslink: 7 Bedale Street, 1–5 Green Dragon Court and 16–26 Borough High Street, SE1	Ridgeway et al. 2019.	A4
BBO10	Brandon House, 170–94 Borough High Street, SE1	Booth 2016, 341.	A4
BOJ10	St Bartholomew's Hospital, EC1	Wroe-Brown 2016, Site B.	A2
BVB10	Thameslink: Park Street, SE1	Ridgeway et al. 2019.	A4
BVF10	Thameslink: Borough Market, SE1	Ridgeway et al. 2019.	A4
BZY10 (BBU05)	Bloomberg London, Walbrook Square (formerly Bucklersbury House: bounded by Queen Street, Cannon Street, Queen Victoria Street, Bucklersbury, and Walbrook), EC4	Tomlin 2016; MOLA 2017; S. Watson 2013.	A2
GHY10	Guy's Hospital College, Great Maze Pond, SE1	B Watson 2012.	A4
KXU10	King's Cross Central: Pancras Road, Goods Way, Milk Dock and The Boulevard, N1	Booth 2012, 333–4.	A1
TEQ10 (LTS95) (TQH02)	Three Quays House, Lower Thames Street, EC3	Booth 2012, 332.	A3
XSM10	Broadgate ticket hall, Liverpool Street, EC2	Ranieri and Telfer 2017.	A3
BVK11	Thameslink: 11–15 Borough High Street, 2 London Bridge Street, SE1	Ridgeway et al. 2019.	A4

Continued

Table A.1 *Continued*

Code	Address	Sources	Map
DKN11	Baitul Aziz Mosque, 1 Dickens Square, SE1	N Hawkins 2009.	A4
PPL11	Principal Place, Plough Yard, Shoreditch High Street, E1/EC2	Daykin 2017.	A3
BVM12	London Bridge Station Improvement works, SE1	Ridgeway et al. 2019.	A4
CSD12	Cannon Street (dropshaft adjacent to junction with Dowgate Hill), EC4	Booth 2013, 325.	A2
IMG12	The Rectory, 9 Ironmonger Lane, EC2	C Maloney 2014, 9.	A2
MNR12	24–6 Minories, EC3	Lerz et al. 2017.	A3
SGA12	Sugar Quay (now Landmark Place), 16 Lower Thames Street, EC3	S Watson 2016; S Watson 2017, 393–5.	A3
BMC13	Bartholomew Close, Smithfield, EC1	S Watson 2018, 380.	A2
FEN14	116–20 Fenchurch Street, EC3	Grew and Watson 2016.	A3
BAH15	St Bartholomew's Hospital, Maggie's Centre (north wing), West Smithfield, EC1	S Watson 2017.	A2
MLW15	56–62 Moorgate and 41–2 London Wall, EC2	Nesbitt and Watson 2019, 97.	A2
HRE16	25–9 Harper Road, SE1	Grew 2018, 74; Grosso 2017.	A4
LIE17	Asia House, 31–3 Lime Street, EC3	Hartle 2017.	A3

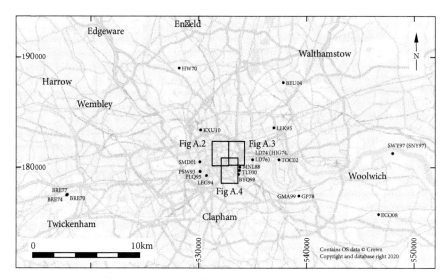

Fig. A.1 Location of excavation sites in the Greater London area as mentioned in the text and listed in Table A.1. Drawn by Justin Russell.

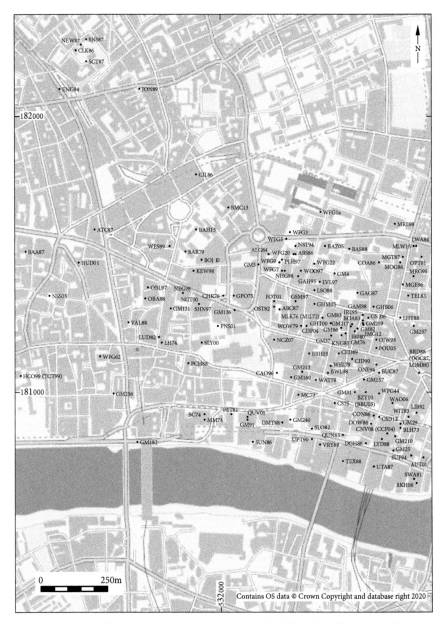

Fig. A.2 Location of excavation sites on the western side of the City of London and adjacent areas as mentioned in the text and listed in Table A.1. Drawn by Justin Russell.

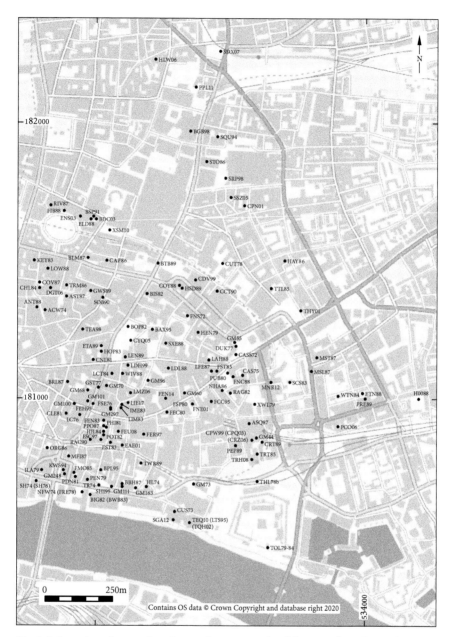

Fig. A.3 Location of excavation sites on the eastern side of the City of London and adjacent areas as mentioned in the text and listed in Table A.1. Drawn by Justin Russell.

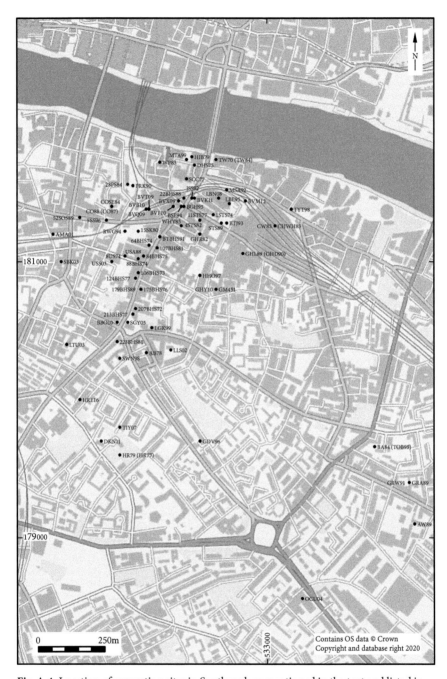

Fig. A.4 Location of excavation sites in Southwark as mentioned in the text and listed in Table A.1. Drawn by Justin Russell.

Notes

Chapter 1

1. Book-length treatments include RCHME 1928; Merrifield 1965; Marsden 1980; Merrifield 1983; Perring 1991; Milne 1995; Hingley 2018.
2. E.g. Richard Reece as quoted in Johnston 1977, 1.
3. Scheidel 2007.
4. Swain and Williams 2008.
5. E.g. Horden and Purcell 2000, 90–7.
6. Flohr and Wilson 2017, 1.
7. Finley 1985; Perring 1991, vii–viii.
8. Wallace 2016, 131.
9. A distinction can be drawn between the *annona*, the yearly import of grain and produce that fed cities, and free monthly distributions of grain and supplies known as *frumentationes*. The term *annona* leaves open the issue of how the goods were distributed.

Chapter 2

1. RCHME 1928, 1–7; Milne 1995, 15–19.
2. Stow 1603, 3.
3. Schnapp 1996, 140–1.
4. Stow 1603, 168–70.
5. S. Pearce 1990; Hepple 2003; Arnold 2006.
6. Bacon 1876.
7. Hingley 2008, 179–80; Hingley 2016.
8. Woodward 1713; Seymour 1735.
9. J. Clark 2008.
10. Stow 1842, 3.
11. Schofield 1998, 1–5.
12. Tite 1848.
13. C. Smith 1883, 114; Kidd 1977, 113.
14. Marsden 1996, 14; S. Scott 2017; Orton *et al.* 1993, 9; C. Smith 1854; C. Smith 1859 iii.
15. D. Wilson 2002, 133.
16. J. Price 1870; S. Wardle 2020.
17. Lane-Fox 1867; J. Price 1880.
18. Marsden 1987, 5–6.
19. Hingley 2000; Gardner 2016, 482.
20. Haverfield 1915.

21. VCH 1909.
22. Marsden 1994, 109.
23. Schofield 1998, 1–5.
24. Quoted by Hawkes 1982, 105.
25. RCHME 1928; R. Wheeler 1930, 17.
26. Marsden 1980, 194–5.
27. Fulford 2007, 360; Schofield 1998, 1–5.
28. Grimes 1968; Shepherd 1998, 13–15; Merrifield 1965, 13–21.
29. Millett 2016b, 27.
30. Marsden 1980, 205.
31. B. Jones 1984.
32. Biddle *et al.* 1973.
33. Milne 2005, 72.
34. Museum of London 1990, 47–8; J. Maloney 2020, 27.
35. Carver 1993, 9; J. Maloney 2020, 28–9: DMT88.
36. DoE 1990.
37. Perring 2015, 20.

Chapter 3

1. Collingwood 1939.
2. Popper 1959.
3. Medawar 1996.
4. Bradley 1997, following Shanks and McGuire 1996.
5. Barker 1977, 145; Lucas 2001, 56–8; Spence 1990; Roskams 2001.
6. R. Thomas 2019.
7. Perring 2016.
8. E.g. Woolf 2004; Millett 2016b, 31 taking issue with Barker 1977, 12; Hamilton and Barrett 2018.
9. Hingley 2008, 329–32.
10. Chapman and Wylie 2016.
11. Bell 1994.
12. Frere 1999, xvi–xvii.
13. Storey 1999; Gardner 2016, 490.
14. I. Morris 2000, 3–36.
15. Brien 2013.
16. I. Tyers 2008a.
17. D. Goodburn 1995; D. Goodburn 2008.
18. Orton *et al.* 1993; Marshall and Seeley 2018.
19. Davies *et al.* 1994; Symonds and Tomber 1991.
20. Verboven 2015, 51.
21. Pitts 2018. For objectscapes see Pitts and Verlsuys 2021.
22. Laurence 2012, 65–6; Gardner 2016, 489–99.
23. Laurence 2011; Newsome 2011a.
24. Carl *et al.* 2000, 346.

25. Noreña 2011, 9.
26. Creighton 2006, 93–107.
27. Laurence 2012, 62; Finley 1985. See p. 191.
28. Millett 1990, 60–1; Millett 2007, 137.
29. See Pitts and Versluys 2015, 6; Laurence 2012; Gardner 2016.
30. Mattingly 2011.
31. Perring and Pitts 2013.
32. R. Moore 2016, 2.

Chapter 4

1. E.g. Ackroyd 2000, 11.
2. Kent 1978, 53.
3. Baker and Brookes 2013, 269.
4. Lewis 2000a; Sidell *et al. 2002*; Lewis 2000c, 54.
5. Bradley 1990, Bradley 2000; Lewis 2000b, 74; Hingley 2018, 13–24.
6. Myers 2016; Sidell 2008.
7. Brown and Cotton 2000, 92; Powell 2017.
8. Holder and Jamieson 2003.
9. Milne 1985, 79–86; Sidell 2008, 67: PDN81.
10. Marsden 1994, 23–4.
11. Museum of London Archaeology 2011.
12. Bentley 1984.
13. Myers 2016, 327–8; T. Taylor 2020; Ranieri and Telfer 2017, 47–9; Shepherd 1998, 216; Ridgeway 2009, 42; Hill and Rowsome 2011, 18, 255; Wallace 2014, 34; Scaife 2011, 535; Sidell 2008, 68; Bull *et al.* 2011: HLW06; SDX07.
14. Cowan *et al.* 2009, 14.
15. Dark 2017, 17.
16. T. Moore 2016, 263; Champion 2016, 158–67; Pitts 2018.
17. Evans 2016, 511–12.
18. Caes. *BGall.* 1.3–18.
19. Champion 2016, 159; Haselgrove 2006.
20. Caes. *BGall.* 5.12; Hawkes and Dunning 1931; Birchall 1965.
21. T. Moore 2016, 263–70; Pitts 2017, 55; Gosden 2004, 109.
22. Caes. *BGall.* 4.20–36; 5.8–23.
23. Fitzpatrick 2018.
24. Champion 2016, 163; Strabo *Geog.* 4.5.3.
25. Laurence 2001, 68; Tac. *Ann.* 2.24.
26. T. Moore 2011.
27. Nash 1987.
28. Creighton 2000, 80–125.
29. Pitts 2018, 66, 104–6.
30. Suet. *Calig.* 44.2; Mattingly 2011, 88.
31. Perring and Pitts 2013, 88; Atkinson and Preston 2015.
32. Fulford and Timby 2000, 545–64.

33. Fulford and Timby 2000, fig. 238.
34. F. Morris 2013, 43.
35. Kent 1978, 53–8; Cotton 2018, 64.
36. Wait and Cotton 2000; P. Tyers 1996a.
37. Cotton 2018, 64.
38. I. Thompson 1982.
39. P. Tyers 1996a, 139; Rayner 2017, 348.
40. I. Thompson 2015, 123.
41. Bowlt 2008.
42. P. Tyers 1996a; Rayner 2017, 348.
43. Cowan *et al.* 2009, 14: GRA89; GRW91; AW89.
44. Rayner 2009, 38–40.
45. TLT00.
46. Cowan *et al.* 2009, 38–40.
47. Killock *et al.* 2015, 140.
48. Cowan 1992, 11: 15SK80.
49. Hammerson 1996, 154.
50. Cowan 1992, 183–4.
51. Creighton 2006, 49. The evidence finds parallel at Fishbourne: Manley and Rudkin 2005.
52. Hingley 2018.
53. S. Watson 2015, 8: GHM05; Dunwoodie *et al.* 2015, 13: FER97.
54. WAO06.
55. Harward *et al.* 2015, 14: RIV87; MRL98.
56. Field 1985: TOL79-84.
57. B. Davies 1990: GWS89.
58. Sloane 2012, 10–14: ENG84; CLK86; NEW87; SCT87; SNS87.
59. Cowan *et al.* 2009, 39.
60. Telfer 2010, 50: SMD01.
61. P. Tyers 1996a.
62. Tac. *Ann.* 14.33; Tomlin 2016, 70–1<WT45>.
63. Jackson 1953; Coates 1998, 204–5.
64. Bynon 2016.
65. Ptol. *Geog.* 2.3, 12; Rivet and Smith 1979, 115, 144.
66. Rivet and Smith 1979, 398.
67. Millett 1996, 35.
68. Hassall 2017, 118.
69. Marsh 1979a.
70. Braund 1988; Mattingly 2011, 75, 84–5; Dio Cass. 60.19.1–2.

Chapter 5

1. Tac. *Ann.* 14.33.
2. Home 1948; Merrifield 1965, 34–5.
3. Dio Cass. 60.20.5–60.21.30.

4. Hind 1989; Frere and Fulford 2001; Manley 2002, 52; Grainge 2005, 111; Kaye 2015.

5. G. Webster 1966.

6. E.g. Chapman and Johnson 1973, 71.

7. E.g. Merrifield and Sheldon 1974.

8. Marsden 1980, 17–26.

9. Hammerson 1978a.

10. Haverfield 1911, 149.

11. Finley 1985.

12. Millett 1990; Grahame 1998; Wallace 2014, 12.

13. Millett 1994, 433.

14. Millett 1996, 34.

15. J. Morris 1982, 78; Fuentes 1985.

16. WAO06.

17. Merrifield and Sheldon 1974, 189; Sheldon 2014, fig. 1.

18. Wallace 2013; Wallace 2016.

19. Thorp 2010.

20. Sankey 2002, 3: ETA89.

21. R. Wilson 2006, 28.

22. Fulford *et al.* 2018, 15–17.

23. Wallace 2013, 70, 286.

24. R. Wilson 2006, 26–7.

25. Bushe-Fox 1932, 3; Cunliffe 1968, 232–4. Research by Philip Smither suggests a later Claudian date.

26. Frere and St Joseph 1974, 10.

27. E.g. P. Crummy 1988, 29.

28. KWS94.

29. E. Hartley 2012, fig. 7.

30. R. Wilson 2006, 25; von Schnurbein 2003.

31. See p. 41 for isolated late Iron Age or early Roman pottery assemblages.

32. R. Jones 2014.

33. Wallace 2014, 112; Davies *et al.* 1994, 166.

34. Milne and Wardle 1993, 28: LCT84.

35. P. Crummy 1997, 35.

36. Manley 2002, 109, drawing on Hyginus. R. Jones 2014 reviews problems in assessing occupation densities in temporary camps but illustrates how figures of 480–620 men per hectare might be proposed.

37. Mason 2003, 78; B. Hoffmann 2013, 56.

38. P. Tyers 1996a, 143: PRK90.

39. Yule 2005, 23–5: WP83.

40. Dio Cass. 60.20.5.

41. Thornhill 1976, 119–28.

42. Baker and Brookes 2013, 279; Phillips 1981, 69.

43. VCH 1909, 29–30; Margary 1967, 54.

44. Haverfield 1911. For a recent instance see Rowsome 2018, 91.

45. C. Thomas 2008.

46. Sloane *et al.* 1995, 369: LEG94.

47. Van der Meer 2007. For a description of how the army built such bridges see Dio Cass. 71.3.
48. Merrifield 1983, 25. Brigham 2001b, 33: GM248.
49. Dio Cass. 60.21.3.
50. B. Hoffmann 2013, 66.
51. Grainge 2005, 133–4.

Chapter 6

1. Cowan *et al.* 2009, 43: 15SK80.
2. Reece 1995, 191; Hammerson 1996, 153.
3. Hammer 1985, 7–8: FEN83; Dunwoodie *et al.* 2015, 13: FER97.
4. Wallace 2014, 104.
5. ONE94.
6. Wallace 2014, 22; Hill and Rowsome 2011, 23–4.
7. Keily 2011, 553.
8. Graham and Hinton 1988; Cowan *et al.* 2009, 55–61; Drummond-Murray and Thompson 2002, 25: BGH95.
9. P. Tyers 1996a.
10. Margary 1967, 53.
11. Kaiser 2011, 25.
12. Dunwoodie *et al.* 2015, 20: FER97.
13. Houston 1988; Roth 1999, 175, 216–17.
14. Marsden 1987, 18–21: GM297; GST77.
15. Wallace 2014, 60.
16. Amiens was laid out around a similar central space: Bayard and Massy 1983, 74–7.
17. Philp 1977, 8–9: GM297; Marsden 1987, 18–19.
18. Marsden 1987, 140–2: GM100.
19. Frere 1983, 193–4.
20. Dunwoodie *et al.* 2015, 18: FER97.
21. WAO06.
22. Lennon 2014, 44–5.
23. Hill and Rowsome 2011, 26; Birbeck and Schuster 2009, 13–16; Graham and Hinton 1988; Westman 2009, 52–60.
24. Wallace 2014, 43, 56.
25. Laurence 2008; Laurence 2012, 90; S. Stevens 2017, 69–71.
26. Newsome 2011a.
27. Wallace 2014, 38: CASS72; FST85; LFE87; CID90; BBH05; NEG98. In similar arrangements at *Verulamium* the widely spaced flanking ditches were only deployed to define carriageways outside town: Niblett 2001, 69–70; Niblett and Thomson 2005, 66.
28. S. Watson 2006, 17–20: NGT00.
29. Holbrook 2015, 97.
30. NHA86.

31. Dean and Hammerson 1980; R. Goodburn 1978, 453; Rayner 2009, 38; Connell 2009, 254: 124BHS77.
32. Cowan *et al.* 2009, 14.
33. Parnell 1985, 5–7; Bayley 1985; Chapman 1985, 63–5: TOL79-84.
34. Birley 2005, 25–9; Mattingly 2006a, 102–3; Tac. *Agr.* 14.1; Tac. *Ann.* 12.31–2.
35. Frere 1983, 5.
36. Cunliffe 1968, 234–43; Perring 1991, 18; Wallace 2014, 18.
37. Ptol. *Geog.* 2.3, 12.
38. E.g. Caes. *BGall.* 6.32; Roth 1999, 169–76.
39. Wallace 2014, 112, 127: BTBHS91; Philp 1977, 9: GM297.
40. Woolf 2012, 76.
41. Caes. *BGall.* 7.3.1; Roth 1999, 230, 251, 275.
42. E.g. Hingley 2018, 34–5.
43. Millett 1990, 88–91; Millett 1996; Millett 2016b.
44. Fulford 2015a, 196.
45. Woolf 2012, 35–6.
46. Strabo *Geog.* 4.3, 2; Desbat 2007, 179–80.
47. Tchernia 2016, 256.
48. Ottaway 1993, 20.
49. Purcell 2013.

Chapter 7

1. Dunwoodie *et al.* 2015, 20: FER97.
2. FEU 08; Philp 1977, 9–16: GM297.
3. Wallace 2014, 95–100.
4. Buildings flanking a 5-metre-wide road at Whittington Avenue were destroyed in a fire likely to date AD 60/61: WIV88. Wallace 2014, 56 fn 77 questions this dating, but it seems supported by spot-date records (e.g. context 1923). Other components of the street grid include a street-side ditch at LIM83 and an east-west gravel surface at BRL87. A small cremation cemetery at LCT84 marks its northern limits.
5. ONE94.
6. Milne 1985, 25: PDN81.
7. Waterfront 1: Brigham and Watson 1996; Brigham 1998, 23; D. Goodburn in prep.: KWS94. Some piles were prepared by small round-bladed axes rather than the larger straighter-edged axes typical of Roman woodworking.
8. D. Swift 2008, 16–17: AUT01; Brigham 2001a, 17: SUF94; Hillam 1986, 99: ILA79.
9. I. Tyers 2008a, fig. 2.2.1.
10. Birley 2005, 31–7; Gambash 2016, 260–1; Tac. *Ann.* 12.40.1–5.
11. Suet. *Ner.* 18.
12. Tomlin 2016, <WT30>.
13. Tomlin 2016, <WT44>.
14. GM297; FSE76; FEH95.
15. P. Crummy 1984, 22, 37; Desbat 1981, 55–8; Perring 2002, 99–101.

16. Similar in plan to a pre-Flavian courtyard building beneath the Silchester forum. Fulford and Timby 2000, 565–6.

17. Straker 1987; A. Davis 2004.

18. C. Stevens 2009: FNE01; A. Davis 2014: FEU08.

19. Dunwoodie 2004, 20: FEH95.

20. D. Smith 2012, 51–4.

21. Hill and Rowsome 2011, 21, 264–72: ONE94.

22. Smith and Davis 2011; Smith and Kenward 2011, 253.

23. Dunwoodie 2004, 19: FEH95.

24. Neal and Cosh 2009, 398–9: Mosaic 370.54: LCT84.

25. Monteil 2008, 178; A. Wardle 2016, 163–6.

26. Dunwoodie et al. 2015, 36: FER97.

27. Hammer 1985, 9: FEN83; Wallace 2014, 113–14: KWS94.

28. Henig 1984a, 11–15: EST83.

29. Laurence et al. 2011, 213; Revell 2016, 781.

30. Bidwell 2009, 55; Ottaway 1993, 31.

31. Pringle 2007; Betts 2017a, 99; Betts 2016, 171–6: FER97.

32. Hingley 2018, 32 is unconvinced, but the materials were made to build a bathhouse somewhere in London.

33. Wilmott 1982; Philp 1977, 15: GM297. Roman London's water-pipes were formed from lengths of squared oak bored through the centre and clamped together by iron collars.

34. Grew and Watson 2016: FEN14.

35. RCHME 1928, 118–19.

36. D. Swift 2008, 16–17: AUT01.

37. ONE94 Road 2.

38. Blair et al. 2006, 5: GHT00.

39. Niblett 1999, 319, 415; Creighton 2006, 126–7.

40. King 1990; A. Smith 2018b, 141; Serv. Aen. 7.42.

41. Derks 1998, 137–8; A. Smith 2001; Laurence et al. 2011, 135–7; Vitr. De arch. 1.6.7, 4.5.

42. Frankfurter 2006, 547–8; McInerney 2006.

43. Yule 2005, 17; Brigham 2001b, 12–27: WP83; TW70.

44. Divers et al. 2009, 12: MTA99. Some reconstructions show this road continuing towards Westminster, but the topography makes this highly unlikely.

45. Drummond-Murray and Thompson 2002, 31, 50: BGH95.

46. 15SK80.

47. Ridgeway et al. 2019, 149–50: BVF10; BVT09; BVB10.

48. Hammerson 1978a, 587–600; Hammerson 1988; Hammerson 1992, 143; Hammerson 2011, 518; Walton and Moorhead 2016, 839.

49. Marsden 1980, 26; Lawrence 1940.

50. Yule 2005, 25, 47; Pringle 2007: WP83.

51. Mattingly 2006a, 274.

52. Hayward 2015: LLS02.

53. LGK99.

54. SWN98.

55. Ghey 2007, 25; Fulford 2001; Gerrard 2011e, 558; A. Smith 2016, 641. Douglas 2007, 34. This may account for lamb skulls in a pre-Flavian roadside ditch at 201–211 Borough High Street: Ferretti and Graham 1978, 63: 207BHS72.

56. Drummond-Murray and Thompson 2002, 31: BGH95.

57. Niblett 1985, 24–5.

58. Hill and Rowsome 2011, 97, 291–305, 471; D. Goodburn et al. 2011, 419–24.

59. Mainly mustard and dill, with fennel, celery, coriander, and black cumin.

60. A. Wardle 2016, 162; S. Watson 2013: BZY10.

61. WAO06.

62. Perring and Roskams 1991, 5–6: GPO75. See also CID90 and CDP04.

63. S. Watson 2006, 70–1: NGT00.

64. Birbeck and Schuster 2009, 15: FNE01. See also FST85.

65. BOP82.

66. Perring and Roskams 1991, 3–6: GPO75.

67. Hill and Woodger 1999, 10; Hill and Rowsome 2011, 271–4: CID90.

68. Casson et al. 2014: GSM97; Bluer and Brigham 2006, 15–16: FCC95; Brigham 2001b: TW70.

69. Wallace 2014, 110; Hingley 2018, 40.

70. A. Rogers 2016, 759.

71. E.g. Neal et al. 1990, Buildings 7 and 18.

72. Wallace 2014, 138.

73. J. Webster 2005; Perring 2011, 255.

74. Rayner 2009, 40: AB78.

75. Brigham 2001b: TW70. This and the 'native' carpentry of an early second-century wattle and pale wall at Tokenhouse Yard are more likely to be the product of later immigration rather than witnessing a continuing local tradition: D. Goodburn 2012, 54–5: THY01.

76. Davies et al. 1994, 29; Symonds 2003; Rayner 2017: SLO82.

77. Rayner 2017, 359: FNE01.

78. S. Watson 2006, 75–6.

79. BAH15. Nothing has yet been published to suggest a date for this feature.

80. Shepherd and Chettle 2012, 148: BAR79; WES89; BMC13.

81. Hill and Rowsome 2011, 308–10; Elsden 2002, 55.

82. Bryan et al. 2016, 34: BZY10.

83. McCann and Orton 1989, 105: VAL88.

84. Perring and Roskams 1991, 29, 115: WAT 78; Hill and Rowsome 2011, 273–4: BWL98; Shepherd 1987.

85. Elsden 2002, 8–12: CAO96.

86. Hill and Rowsome 2011, 70–2: KNG85; Perring and Roskams 1991, 112: MLK76 Roads 5 and 3.

87. Blair 1983, 23; Shepherd 2012, 150; Wallace 2014, 77: OST82; ABC87. The interim dating is questioned by Wallace but her grounds for doing so are not clear: the data itself is unpublished.

88. Hill and Rowsome 2011, 440, 264–72; Hillam 1986.

89. KWS94.

90. Birley 2005, 43–50; Mattingly 2006a, 104–5.

91. E.g. Monteil 2004; N Crummy 2008; Wallace 2014, 138–43.
92. LCT84.

Chapter 8

1. Wallace 2014, 100; Swain and Williams 2008, 37.
2. Pitts 2014; Pitts 2018.
3. Perring and Pitts 2013, 244; Hill and Rowsome 2011, 264–72.
4. Wallace 2014, 24.
5. Tac. *Ann.* 14.29; B. Hoffmann 2013, 93–100.
6. Birley 2005, 45, 302; below p. 92.
7. Tac. *Ann.* 14.33.
8. Drummond-Murray and Thompson 2002, 46–8: BGH95; Ridgeway *et al.* 2109: BVQ09; Hingley 2018, 54.
9. Fuentes 1983, 316–17.
10. E.g. Birley 2005, 43–52; K. Carroll 1979.
11. Tac. *Ann.* 14.38.2.
12. Hill and Rowsome 2011, 75: ONE94; Ridgeway 2009: DGT06. See p. 99.
13. Gambash 2015, 67.
14. Tomlin 2016, 55 <WT 45>, below p. 199.
15. Zuiderhoek 2016, 9.
16. E.g. Wacher 1995.
17. Tac. *Ann.* 14, 32–3.
18. Birley 2005, 45; Roth 1999, 156.
19. Suet. *Ner.* 39.1; Dio Cass. 62.1, 62.7.1.
20. B. Hoffmann 2013, 78.
21. Millett 1996, 34.
22. de la Bédoyère 2003, 41.
23. Fuhrmann 2012, 240–1.
24. Mattingly 2006a, 16–20.
25. Tac. *Agr.* 15.2.
26. Plin. *Ep.* 10.17b, 10.23, 10.37, 10.70, 10.80, 10.90; Laurence *et al.* 2011, 82.
27. Birley 2005, 298; Reece 2015; Roth 1999, 175.
28. Tac. *Ann.* 14.32.2–3.
29. Fuhrmann 2012, 196; Dondin-Payre and Loriot 2008.
30. P. Crummy 1997, 70–2; Birley 2005, 12.
31. Below pp. 105–7; Hassall 1996.
32. Marsden 1975; Brigham 2001, 45–6; but see pp. 138–9.
33. E.g. Dondin-Payre and Loriot 2008.
34. E.g. Hingley 2018, 34–5, 74.
35. Mann 1998.
36. RCHME 1928, 170.
37. RIB 2436.9: Collingwood and Wright 1991b, 92; Hingley 2018, 7: BWB83.
38. Dondin-Payre and Loriot 2008.
39. Haverfield 1911, followed by Wilkes 1996, 28–9.

40. R. Wilson 2006, 30.
41. Sheldon 2014, 12–13 drawing on Selkirk 1995.
42. Birley 2005, 14; Hassall 2017, 120.
43. Tomlin 2018a, 170–1 <WT51>.
44. Fuhrmann 2012, 198.

Chapter 9

1. FER97.
2. Tac. *Ann.* 14.38.1; Tomlin 2016, 56, 200: <WT55> <WT48> <WT33> <WT62> <WT61>; Millett 2016a questions the Vangiones identification.
3. Tomlin 2016: <WT33>.
4. A. Wardle 2016, 159; Marshall 2017.
5. DGT06; TRM86.
6. Hill and Rowsome 2011, 306–9: ONE94; Bryan *et al.* 2016, 42: BYZ10.
7. Marsden 1987, 22: GM100.
8. Brigham 1998: Waterfront 2; Brigham 2001b, 43: KWS94.
9. Hassall and Tomlin 1996, 449.
10. Milne 2000, 129.
11. van Driel-Murray in prep.
12. Marsden 1994, 178–9.
13. Milne 2005, 72.
14. Brigham 1998, 27; Brigham and Watson 1996; Shepherd 2008: KWS94.
15. Bateman 1986, 233–8: FMO85; Hillam 1986; Miller 1982: ILA79.
16. Brigham 2001b: GM248. Brigham 1990b 142; Marsden 1994, 70.
17. Blair *et al.* 2006; A. Wilson 2009a, 352–3: GHT00.
18. Howell 2013, 17: BBH05; Marsden 1976: GM37.
19. S. Watson 2015, 30: CDP04.
20. Rowsome 1999, 274; Laurence *et al.* 2011, 222; Ghey 2007, 26.
21. Booth 2014, 371; S. Watson 2013; Bryan *et al.* 2016, 37–42: BZY10.
22. Hill and Rowsome 2011, 306–9: ONE94.
23. WIV88.
24. Cowan and Rowsome 2009, 170; Fulford 2008b, 10; Milne 1985, 143.
25. NCZ07.
26. Millett 1994, 430; Rayner 2009, 46; Davies *et al.* 1994, 186.
27. Casson *et al.* 2014; A. Wardle 2015, 184: GSM97.
28. B. Hoffmann 2013, 110–1.
29. *Twelve Tablets* 10.1; Cic. *Leg.* 2.58; Lennon 2014, 137; Favro and Johanson 2010.
30. Birbeck and Schuster 2009, 11–12: FNE01.
31. Marsden 1980, 24: GM60.
32. Milne and Wardle 1993, 28–32: LCT84.
33. LIM83.
34. Shepherd 1988, 10–11.
35. Tylor 1884; RCHME 1928, 154.
36. Perna 2015, 126–31.

37. Toller 1977, 3.
38. Blyth 1997, 187–90; Pl. *Phdr.*
39. H. Hoffmann 1963.
40. Birley 2005, 28.
41. Marsden 1969a; Marsden 1980, 76–7: GM131.
42. RIB 12: Collingwood and Wright 1965; Cottrill 1936; Grasby and Tomlin 2002, 71; Coombe *et al.* 2015, no. 82; Hope 2016, 293.
43. Tac. *Ann.* 14.38.3; Birley 2005, 303.
44. Dean and Hammerson 1980; Redfern *et al.* 2017; Cotton 2008: HR79.
45. Joy 2012.
46. N. Crummy 2005.
47. S. Watson 2006, 19–21: NGT00.
48. Birbeck and Schuster 2009, 11–12: FNE01.
49. Conheeney in prep.; Brigham and Watson in prep.; Rowsome 2018, 92: GM248; KWS94.
50. S. Watson 2013, 242; Booth 2014, 373: BZY10.
51. GHT00. I am grateful to David Bowsher for providing information in advance of publication.
52. SWN98.
53. Cotton 1996, 89; Perring 2017, 67–8: Hingley 2018, 20–2: BHS72; WAT78; WAO06; LIB82.
54. Milella *et al.* 2010; Crerar 2016; A. Smith 2018a, 226–30.
55. Toynbee 1971, 43; A. Taylor 2008; Hor. *Carm.* 1.28; M. Carroll 2018, 239–40; Rebillard 2009, 62.
56. Hingley 2018, 16–20.
57. Armit 2012; Carr 2007; Craig *et al.* 2005; Cotton 1996; Bradley and Gordon 1988, 503–9; Knüsel and Carr 1995; West 1996; Schulting and Bradley 2013.
58. *Dig.* 48.24.1; Kyle 1998, 147, fn 45; Hope 2007; A. Taylor 2008; Perring 2017.
59. Euseb. *Hist. eccl.* 5.1.63.
60. E.g. Dio Cass. 61.35.4; Luc. *Pharsalia* 2.210–220; App. *B Civ.* 1.90–93; Cic. *Sest.* 77. Hope 2000; Kyle 1998; Lennon 2014.
61. Mattison 2016; A. Reynolds 2009, 178.
62. Barley 1995, 82–3.
63. Diod. Sic. 5.29.4–5; Strabo *Geog.* 4.4.5; Livy 10.26.11; Voisin 1984; Fields 2005; Isserlin 1997, 95; J. Pearce 2013, 100–1; P. Crummy 1984, 94–7; Benfield and Garrod 1992, 37; Mays and Steele 1996; Curle 1911, 113–14; W. S. Hanson 2012, 70; Ross and Feachem 1976; Loe 2003; Creighton 2016, 371–3.
64. Tucker 2016. Cut marks associated with three decapitated individuals in London's late antique northern cemetery probably evidence execution: McKenzie and Thomas 2020, 68: PPL11.
65. Armit 2012, 197, 223; Cotton 1996, 89; Wait 1985, 51–82, 117; M. Green 2001, 104; L. Walker 1984.
66. Holst *et al.* 2018; Roymans 2018; Fitzpatrick 2018.
67. Campbell 2000, 44–5; 69–70; Laurence *et al.* 2011, 147.
68. Ridgeway 2009, 12: DGT06.

69. M. Carroll 2018, 180.

70. Varner 2005, 67–88; Russell and Manley 2015, 166.

71. Coombe *et al.* 2015, 216; Shotter 2004, 4; Bayley *et al.* 2009: GHT00.

72. Coombe *et al.* 2015, no. 20.

73. Frere 1983, 8; P. Crummy 2003, 50–1.

74. Fulford 2008b, 9–11.

75. K. Carroll 1979.

76. D. Walker 1988, 281–6.

77. Perring and Pitts 2013, 245–6; Evans 2016, 512; Pitts 2018, 209.

Chapter 10

1. Juv. 10.80.

2. Bateman *et al.* 2008: GAG87.

3. Wilmott 2008, 55.

4. Laurence *et al.* 2011, 260.

5. S. Price 1984, 74; Fishwick 2002.

6. Allason-Jones 2011, 223; Wilmott 2008, 18.

7. Latham 2016, 161–80; Hingley 2018, 80–1; G. Rogers 1991.

8. Revell 2016, 779; A. Wardle 2011, 330. We don't know if London also had a purpose-built theatre.

9. Welch 2007; Fuhrmann 2012, 187.

10. Ridgeway 2009, 12: DGT06.

11. Cowan *et al.* 2009, 67; Cowan 2003, 16–18: 52SOS89; Killock 2005, 31: FSS96.

12. 15SK80.

13. Hingley 2018, 99, following Neal and Cosh 2009, 457. Another possibility is that it housed a guild or corporation.

14. Drury 1988.

15. Leveau 2016.

16. G. Rogers 1991, 13.

17. Hammer 2003.

18. Brigham 1998, 2.

19. Milne 1985, 27: PDN81.

20. Hillam 1986, refined through reference to Millard 2002.

21. TEQ10; SGA12.

22. Hassall and Tomlin 1996, 446–7: KWS94.

23. ETA89; WAO06.

24. Barber and Bowsher 2000, 51–2: FST85; LAH88; SOB90; SCS83.

25. S. Watson 2004; Hill and Rowsome 2011, 310: OJW98 Road 8; Perring and Roskams 1991, 57: IRO80.

26. Blair *et al.* 2006: GHT00 Road 4; Casson *et al.* 2014, 10–12: GSM97 Structure 2; S. Watson 2015, 16–17: CDP04 Road 1.

27. ALG84.

28. McCann 1993, 25–31: VAL88.

29. Hill and Rowsome 2011, 310–11, fig. 82: ONE94 Roads 3 and 4.

30. Hill and Rowsome 2011, 124, Site C: BUC87 Building 4.

31. Killock *et al.* 2015, 13, 238–9: LLS02 and LGK99.

32. G. Rogers 1991, 24–7.

33. Lodwick 2017, 68.

34. E.g. Hill and Woodger 1990, 17: CID90; Wallace 2014, 118; C. Green 2017, 173; J. Hill *et al.* 2011, 347–8: ONE94.

35. Merrifield 1965, 240–1.

36. Hill and Rowsome 2011, 350: BUC87; A. Davis 2011, 304; J. Price 1873, 66.

37. Hill and Rowsome 2011, 316–17: ONE94 Building 18/48.

38. Philp 1977, 22–3: GM297; BRL87.

39. Marsden 1980, 72; Wilmott 1991, 177; S. Watson 2013; A. Wilson 2009a and 2009b, 355–7: BZY10. I am grateful to Sadie Watson for providing details in advance of publication.

40. GWS89.

41. Myers 2016, 320.

42. McCann 1993, 25–31: VAL88.

43. Rickman 1980, 187.

44. R. Wilson 2006, 15–17: BAX95.

45. G. Hunt 2010, 50: CPW99.

46. The '1955' ditch: Niblett and Thompson 2005, 66–9; Niblett 2001, 72.

47. Creighton 2016, 322–7.

48. R. Wilson 2006, 1–15.

49. GSM97.

50. OST82; ABC87; Howe and Lakin 2004, 37, Site E, Road 2: LVL 97.

51. Howe and Lakin 2004, 18–20: LVL97 Structure 7. A large flat-bottomed ditch found at Aldersgate Street also anticipated the fort's orientation: ALG84.

52. Occasional remains of Flavian timber buildings have been found beneath the Cripplegate fort, but may derive from sporadic later phases of use. Howe and Lakin 2004, 15–24, 23, 48: NST94, WOO97; Lyon 2004: NHG98; Shepherd 2012, 70, 148–54: WFG3, WFG5.

53. S. Watson 2017, 392: BAH15.

54. Dunwoodie *et al.* 2015, 62–6: FER97.

55. Joseph. *BJ* 82f.

56. Discarded timbers associated with rebuilding at the site of the Neronian wells were felled in the winter AD 70/71, suggesting that repairs were in hand around the time that Cerialis reached the province.

57. Gambash 2016.

58. Grant 2007, 92.

59. W. H. Hanson 1988, 62.

60. Tac. *Hist.* 2. 67, 2.

61. Tac. *Agr.* 17. 1–2; Grant 2007, 72; Birley 2005, 67.

62. Gambash 2016, 264; Birley 2005, 67.

63. Birley 2005, 70.

64. D. Walker 1988.

Chapter 11

1. Zuiderhoek 2009.
2. Tomlin 2016 <WT37>. For an important alternative reading of this text see Costabile 2017.
3. W. H. Hanson 1988, 63–4.
4. Tomlin 2016 <WT51>.
5. Marsden 1987.
6. Revell 2016, 769.
7. The area behind the basilica may have been defined by an enclosure ditch: CNL81.
8. Marsden 1987, 73, 119: GM70; Philp 1977, 48 no. 51: GM297.
9. Frere 1983, 55, 69; Birley 2005, 82; Fulford and Timby 2000, 569.
10. Tac. *Agr.* 21.
11. E.g. Marsden 1987, 73; Dondin-Payre and Loriot 2008, 151.
12. Millett 1994, 432–3; see Wilkes 1996, 29 on why a later date might be preferred.
13. Niblett 2001, 75–6.
14. Marsden 1980, 40.
15. Wacher 1995, 90.
16. Marsden 1987, 106–14: GM68.
17. Marsden 1987: walls 32–5 at 17–19 Gracechurch Street: GM68; wall E at All Hallows, Lombard Street; early stone foundations at 54–58 Lombard Street: GM100.
18. Laurence *et al.* 2011, 180.
19. Frankfurter 2006, 547–8.
20. NVMC PROV BRITA. RIB 5: Collingwood and Wright 1965; C. Smith 1859, 29; Fishwick 1969, 83–4.
21. Zuiderhoek 2016, 165; Ando 2000; Noreña 2011, 7–8.
22. B. Hoffmann 2013, 90; Boatwright 2000, 96.
23. Esmonde Cleary 2005, 3.
24. Dunwoodie *et al.* 2015, 79–81: FER97.
25. PEP89.
26. Hammer 1987, 6–12: FEN83.
27. Wallace 2014, 91–3, followed by Hingley 2018, 32. Since the foundations were associated with Flavian material, this remains the preferred dating.
28. RAC90.
29. Marsden 1975; Marsden 1978; Marsden 1980, 92: GM25, GM29, GM 210.
30. J. Price 1870.
31. CNV08.
32. DOW86.
33. Milne 1996; Spence and Grew 1990, 20–1: LYD88.
34. Brigham 2001a, 45–7: SUF94.
35. Milne 1996.
36. Perring 1991, 33; Betts 2017b, 370.
37. Laurence *et al.* 2011, 216–21.
38. LIB82.
39. WAO06; CNV08.
40. GM257.

41. Leary and Butler 2012, 12: THY01.
42. Dunwoodie *et al.* 2015, 81: FER97.
43. Brigham 2001a, 31–3: SUF94 Building 1.
44. Bryan *et al.* 2016, 49: BZY10.
45. KWS94.
46. Brigham 2001a, 46.
47. Betts 1995; Betts 2015; Betts 2017b; P P BRI LON and variants.
48. S. Watson 2015, 11–13: GHM05.
49. Betts 1995, 221: GPO75.
50. Birley 2005, 92–4; Tac. *Agr.* 38.
51. Hingley 2018, 73.
52. E.g. DeLaine 1999, 72.
53. J. Reynolds 1988, 38; Plin. *Ep.* 10-23-24.
54. Merrifield 1983, 87–9.
55. Bushe-Fox 1949, 38; Birley 2005, 93.
56. Betts 2003; Betts 1995, 217.
57. Marsden 1976: GM240; DMT88.
58. Perring and Roskams 1991, 30: Perring 2002, 62; Hurst 1999: WAT78.
59. RIB 2401.5: Collingwood and Wright 1990; Roxan 1983; Haynes 2013, 339–42.
60. Hassall 2012, 160; *Tab. Vindol.* II.154; Bowman and Thomas 1991, 72, below pp. 220–2.
61. Goldsworthy 2003, 73; Gilliam 1957.
62. S. Watson 2015, 63–4: GHM05.
63. ABC87.
64. Neal and Cosh 2009; Pritchard 1988, 177; Merrifield 1965, Site 106; CS75; MC73; NCZ07.
65. BOP82; ETA89.
66. Dunwoodie *et al.* 2015, 82–86, 107: FER97.
67. Yule 2005, 33–41: WP83.
68. Goffin 2005, 105–13.
69. Rielly 2015, 220.
70. Cowan 1992, 35; 15SK80.
71. Crowley 1992, 155.
72. Cowan 1992, 101.
73. Gerrard 2009a, 132: USS03.
74. Drummond-Murray and Thompson 2002, 59–60: BGH95; BSE94; JSS92.
75. Wacher 1995, 64.
76. Richard 2014.
77. Drummond-Murray and Thompson 2002, 55: BGH95 Buildings 10 and 31.
78. Killock *et al.* 2015, 13, 19: LLS02.
79. TIY07.

Chapter 12

1. Hill and Woodger 1999, 7, 13, 21: CID 90. Two street repairs within the same time-frame were identified at One Poultry and three at Well Court between *c.* AD 85/90 and

c. A D 120. Hill and Rowsome 2011, 131–3: ONE94; Perring and Roskams 1991, 54–5: WEL79.

2. Mattingly 2006a, 151; Grant 2007, 112; B. Hoffmann 2013, 137.

3. D. Walker 1988, 286–7.

4. de la Bédoyère 2003, 125.

5. Hill and Rowsome 2011, 83, 127–8: ONE94; S. Watson 2015, 9: GHM05; Schofield 1998, 164: FSP80. See also Shepherd 2012, 149 on burnt Flavian pottery from near Cripplegate.

6. Milne and Wardle 1993, 34–5: LCT84.

7. Cowan *et al.* 2009, 46–7: 22BHS88.

8. Marsh 1981; Monteil 2005, fig. 19.

9. Hingley 2018, 147; Howell 2013, 19–28: BBH05.

10. Marsden 1987: GM297.

11. Bateman *et al.* 2008, 34–8: GAG87.

12. Milne 1985, 44–54; Hillam 1986: PDN81.

13. A revised approach to estimations of sapwood allowance suggests that these timbers were probably felled no later than A D 104, see Millard 2002.

14. KWS94.

15. Brigham 1990b, Waterfront 3.

16. Milne 1985, 36–9; Hillam 1986: PDN81; PEN79.

17. Bryan *et al.* 2016, 49–51: BZY10.

18. Brigham 1990b; Devoy 1979.

19. McCann 1993: VAL88. Identifications by Alan Pipe summarized in Brigham and Watson in. prep.

20. *Colonia Nervia Glevensium*: CIL 6.3346.

21. Wacher 1995, 150.

22. Shotter 2013.

23. C. Smith 1842, 150; Rhodes 1991, 184.

24. Elkins 2017, 58–64.

25. CIL 6.8681.

26. Brigham 1990b Waterfront 3; KWS94.

27. Keay 2012, 36, 55; A. Wilson 2008, 187.

28. Willis 2005, chart 12; Mees 2018.

29. Rhodes 1987b: FEN83.

30. Verboven 2016, 174–88; Verboven 2009; C. Hawkins 2016, 70.

31. RIB 91: Collingwood and Wright 1965.

32. Blair *et al.* 2006: GHT00.

33. As at Gresham Street. S. Watson 2015, 63–4: GHM05.

34. DMT88.

35. Shepherd 1987, 22–3; Bateman 2009, 159.

36. E.g. Niblett and Thompson 2005, 91–2.

37. Bateman *et al.* 2008, 120. Shepherd 1987, 40–1: GM82.

38. Bateman *et al.* 2008, 116; Killock *et al.* 2015, 251: GHT00; Shepherd 1987, 33–4: GM76.

39. T. Moore 2016, 270; Derks 1998, 243; Revell 2016, 777.

40. BVK11.

41. Sudds 2019, 192.

42. Ridgeway *et al.* 2019, 157: LBN08.
43. Tomlin 2012, 395.
44. Dorcey 1992.
45. RIB 2503.127: Collingwood and Wright 1995; Hall and Shepherd 2008, 31.
46. Takacs 2015.
47. Bakker 1994.
48. Laurence *et al.* 2011, 229.
49. BAX95.
50. The argument, however, that the presence of this boundary deflected the line of the west road is unsubstantiated: Hill and Rowsome 2011, 438; Perring 1991, 14–15.
51. Bentley 1987; Askew 2007, 259: SHN97; VAL88.
52. Norman and Reader 1912, 274–84; Lyon 2007, 11–12, 17: KEW98.
53. Marsden 1965, 137: GM136.
54. BOJ10.
55. Hall 1996, 58–64.
56. Barber and Bowsher 2000, 51.
57. RCHME 1928, 165.
58. Milne and Reynolds 1997, 20.
59. Philpott 1991, 112.
60. J. Pearce 2016, 346; Barber and Bowsher 2000, 60–3: MST87; Mackinder 2000, 11–12: GDV96.
61. J. Pearce 2015, 147.
62. Barber and Bowsher 2000, 75–6.
63. Barber and Bowsher 2000, 69–70; Roth 1999, 25; Plut. *Vit. Crass.* 19.5.
64. Barber and Bowsher 2000, 80.
65. J. Pearce 2015, 150; C. Hawkins 2016, 70.
66. Lerz *et al.* 2017.
67. Barber and Bowsher 2000, 110–16.
68. J. Price 1880; Burkitt 1852, 240; C. Smith 1859; Coombe *et al.* 2015, no. 80.
69. Coombe *et al.* 2015, no. 68: DGT06.
70. Grimes 1968, 30; Shepherd 1998, 38; Howe and Lakin 2004, 28: WFG5.
71. Coombe *et al.* 2015 17 no. 65.
72. J. Pearce 2016, 354; I. Morris 1992; Hope 2016, 297.

Chapter 13

1. Graafstal 2018; SHA *Hadr.* Millar 1992, 35–6; Birley 2005, 119–224; Birley 1997, 125–8.
2. RIB 3006: Tomlin *et al.* 2009; Tomlin 2006. See also Wilkes 1996.
3. Marsden 1987; Milne 1992; Brigham 1990a; Revell 2016, 769: LCT84.
4. CNL81; WIV88.
5. Fulford and Timby 2000, 569.
6. WIV88.
7. Vitr. *De arch.* 5.1.8. Hingley 2018, 126; Revell 2016, 138.
8. Fulford and Timby 2000, 574.

9. Brigham 1990a; Marsden 1987, 53–60: Room 13: GST77. Revell 2007, 138; Revell 2016, 772.
10. Vitr. *De arch.* 5.2.1; Lawrence *et al.* 2011, 170, 182.
11. Wacher 1995, 42.
12. Brigham 1990a, 67.
13. Newsome 2011b.
14. Hmood 2017, 264.
15. Vitr. *De arch.* 5.1.2; Tomlin 2016: <WT30>.
16. Ulpian, preserved in *Frag. Vat.* 134.
17. Temin 2013, 105.
18. SHA *Comm.* 2.1.
19. Ando 2000, 228–32; Noreña 2011, 271.
20. cited by Noreña 2011, 201.
21. Philp 1977: GM297; Marsden 1987, 63: GM101; Dunwoodie 2004, 32: FEH95.
22. Coombe *et al.* 2015.
23. Ando 2000, 207–8.
24. Marsden 2019; Marsden 1987, fig. 55.
25. Marsden 1987, 64–6: GST77.
26. Marsden 1987, 76; Brigham 1990a, 81.
27. Milne 1992, 68.
28. Betts 2015: types 2A and 3.
29. Packer 2001, 4.
30. SHA *Hadr.* 12; Boatwright 2000. Birley 1997, 101–4; Graafstal 2018, 89; Elsner 1998, 68–9.
31. Laurence *et al.* 2011, 58.
32. Fulford and Timby 2000, 573; Brewer 1993, 65; Wacher 1995, 345.
33. Blagg 1984, 254.
34. Boatwright 2000, 32, 117.
35. Brigham 1998, 29–30: KWS94; GM248.
36. This phase of riverside reclamation is not separately identified in Brigham's 1990 survey of London's Roman port, intervening between the Nervan/Trajanic waterfront 3 and the post-fire waterfront 4.
37. Hillam 1986, 10–11: ILA79.
38. Brigham 1990a, 143–7.
39. CLE81; GSM97.
40. WAT78.
41. West and Milne 1993: LCT84.

Chapter 14

1. Kolb 2002, 68.
2. Roman *Vagniacae.* P. Andrews *et al.* 2011, 212; A. Smith 2016, 651.
3. Sheldon and Schaaf 1978, 68.
4. Philp and Garrod 1992; ECO08.

5. Sheldon and Yule 1979: GP78; Tomlin and Hassall 2000, 433; Henig 2007, 47; Wallower 2002a; Wallower 2002b: GMA99.

6. Rivet 1970; Fuentes 1986a; Sheldon and Schaaf 1978, 73. Another roadside site is posited at Ilford.

7. G. Brown 2008: LEK95.

8. G. Brown 2016: BEU04.

9. Sheldon 1996, 240; I. Thompson 2008.

10. Niblett 2001, 69–70.

11. Cowie *et al.* 2013, 46: BRE70, BRE74, BRE77.

12. D. Swift 2003: BGB98.

13. Perring 2000, 157; Dearne 2017, 321.

14. Dearne 2017, 11.

15. D. Bird 2002; D. Bird 2004, 60.

16. Sheldon and Schaaf 1978, 73.

17. HRE16.

18. J. Graham 1936.

19. Philp 1980; Perring 2000, 150; possibly *Noviomago* mentioned in the Antonine Itinerary.

20. Davies *et al.* 1994, 40.

21. MGT87. RCHME 1928 pl. 52; Coombe *et al.* 2015, 36.

22. Hall and Shepherd 2008, 35; Merrifield 1996, 111; Coombe *et al.* 2015, 36.

23. Caes. *BGall.* 6.17; Derks 1998, 115.

24. Sheldon and Schaaf 1978, 63; Laurence 2001, 81.

25. Rickman 1980, 120; Nelson and Drummond 2015, 92.

26. Kolb 2002, 71.

27. Hdn.7.8.11; Chevalier 1976, 34, 186–7.

28. de Ligt 1993, 128, 142–3, 204.

29. Fuhrmann 2012, 216–22.

30. Perring 2000, 151; Fuentes and Greenwood 1993; Elliston Erwood 1916; Lakin 1999: SWY97/SNY97.

31. Cowan *et al.* 2009, 228: BA84; AW89; GRA89; GRW91; Sloane 2012, 14: ENG84; Telfer 2010: SMD01.

32. Barber and Bowsher 2000, 51–2; Ellis 1985, 117: SCS83.

33. Douglas *et al.* 2011, 9–13: TOC02.

34. Cuming 1858, 356; RCHME 1928, 163–4.

35. McCann 1993, 25–31: VAL88.

36. Grimes 1968, 182–5; Groves 1997, 53: WFG62.

37. NSS05.

38. C. Thomas 2008, 105: PSW93; PLQ95.

39. Adams 2012, 227.

40. Mills 1980, 77.

41. Hodder and Millet 1980.

42. Green *et al.* 1997; Sheldon *et al.* 1993; Smith *et al.* 2016, 79.

43. Sheldon and Schaaf 1978, 76.

44. F. Clark 1985; Potter and Shepherd 2009: WKN07; F. Clark 1998; Brooks 1977.

45. Meates 1979; Black 1987.

46. Philp *et al.* 1991.
47. Ptol. *Geog.* 2.3.12.
48. Tomlin 1996; Tomlin 2018a, 258; Du Plessis 2015: TRM86.
49. Dondin-Payre and Loriot 2008, 148 responding to Mann 1998.
50. D. Bird 1996, 223; Black 1987, 57–8.
51. P. Andrews *et al.* 2011; Smith *et al.* 2016, 116.
52. von Reden 2012, 271.

Chapter 15

1. Allen 2018, 80–1, 91.
2. Elliott 2014; Elliott 2018, 84–90; Pearson 2002, 82.
3. E.g. Dawkes 2015, 111–13.
4. Russell 2013; Russell 2017, 246.
5. Marsden 1994, 16–17.
6. Liddle *et al.* 2009.
7. Albarella *et al.* 2008, 1831.
8. Biddulph *et al.* 2012, 171–4.
9. Milne 1985, 87–95: PEN79.
10. Tsigarida 2015.
11. Gerrard 2008, 121.
12. Hathaway 2013, 466; Biddulph 2017; A. Smith 2017, 214.
13. Gerrard 2008; Allen and Fulford 1996.
14. Monaghan 1987, 202; Biddulph 2017, 227–9; Davies *et al.* 1994, 102. See Chapter 19.
15. Perring and Pitts 2013, 34–5.
16. Schofield 1991, 11.
17. Harris 2017, 212.
18. Leach 2017, 167–72; Humphreys 2021.
19. D. Goodburn 1991; D. Goodburn 1995, 33–43; D. Goodburn 2001; D. Goodburn 2005; D. Goodburn in prep.
20. D. Goodburn 1995: CO88.
21. Harris 2017, 228; Nelson and Drummond 2015, 117.
22. Rayner 2017.
23. Marsh and Tyers 1978, 533–82.
24. Perring 1991, 50; Marsh and Tyers 1978, 534.
25. Evans 2013.
26. Symonds 2003; P. Tyers 1998.
27. Brown and Sheldon 2018; Davies *et al.* 1994, 74; Rayner 2017, 351: HW70.
28. Davies *et al.* 1994, 203.
29. Rayner 2017, 349–50; Lyne and Jefferies 1979, 54.
30. Leach 2017, 176.
31. Crowley and Betts 1992, 221.
32. Betts 2017a, 104–5; Betts 2017b, 371–2; D. Bird 1996, 226, 229 fn. 25.
33. Margary 1965, 124; D. Bird 2017, 46.
34. Millum and Wallace 2017, 8.

35. Cleere and Crossley 1995, 57–60; Hodgkinson 2008, 30–4; Dungworth 2016, 544–9; Hodgkinson 2017, 286.
36. Mason 2003, 12.
37. A. Smith 2017, 181; Hammer 2003; below pp. 212–3.
38. Bray 2010, 180–1.
39. RIB 3036: Tomlin *et al.* 2009; Brodribb 1969; Brodribb and Cleere 1988, 261; Hirt 2010, 288; Elliott 2018, 104. Millett 2007 notes that this reading is uncertain.
40. Cleere 1974; Cleere and Crossley 1995, 66–9.
41. See Hirt 2010, 192 on our uncertain knowledge of the fleet's role.
42. CIL 11. 5632; Birley 2005, 307.
43. Hodgkinson 2012.
44. Cleere 1974, 176.
45. Hodgkinson 2017, 291–3.
46. Mattingly 2006a, 507.
47. A. Wilson 2008, 176.
48. RIB 2409.26: Collingwood and Wright 1990; Birley 2005, 300.
49. Cleere 1974; Cleere 1977, 18.
50. Millett 1990, 120–1; Millett 2007, 178–9; A. Smith 2017, 181.
51. Hirt 2010; Lo Cascio 2015, 63–8.
52. Hirt 2015.
53. Drury and Rodwell 1980, 64; Jackson and Potter 1996, J. Taylor 2000.
54. Millar 1992, 621; Kehoe 2006, 298–9; *Cod. Theod.* 11.28.
55. Salway 1981, 104.
56. Tac. *Ann.* 14.31.
57. Fulford and Timby 2000, 569. The emphasis is my own.
58. Hirt 2010, 357–9.
59. Lo Cascio 2007b, 641.
60. Kehoe 1988.
61. Tsigarida 2015.
62. Brindle 2017, 278–9.
63. Plin. *Ep.* 7.18, 9.37; Kehoe 2007, 80–1.
64. Cleere 1970; Lucy and Evans 2106, 433.
65. Rickman 1980, 85.
66. Tac. *Agr.* 31.2.
67. Tac. *Agr.* 19.4; Birley 2005, 80; B. Hoffmann 2013, 74.
68. A. Jones 1964, 457; Gerrard 2016, 853.
69. Duncan-Jones 1990, 187–93; Kehoe 2007, 165; Elton 2006, 202; Mattingly 2006a, 496.
70. Pitts and Versluys 2015, 9.
71. Evers Grønlund 2011, 29; *P. Dura-Europos* 64.A; Hopkins 1983.
72. Erdkamp 2002, 60; de Ligt 2002, 57; Hopkins 2002, 215; Bang 2009, 114.
73. Laurence 2012, 63.
74. As attested in late antique Egypt: Kehoe 2006, 299; N. Pollard 2000, 103 drawing on the Abinnaeus archive.
75. Erdkamp 2002, 55.
76. Plin. *Ep.* 10.27–28.

77. Rathbone 2009, 308–9.
78. P. Brown 2012, 13.

Chapter 16

1. E.g. Rostovtzeff 1957, 177, 192–3; Finley 1985, 33–4, 105–6; Temin 2001; Cartledge 2002, 13–15; Flohr and Wilson 2016.
2. Finley 1985; Whittaker 1995; Erdkamp 2001, 340; Bang 2008, 27–9.
3. Scheidel and von Reden 2002; Andreau 2002; Mattingly 2006b, 283; Zuiderhoek 2015, 5.
4. North 1991; Scheidel *et al.* 2007; Bang 2012, 197; Verboven and Laes 2016.
5. Bowman and Wilson 2009; Scheidel and Friesen 2009; Hobson 2014, drawing on Hopkins 1978.
6. Fulford 2004.
7. E.g. Lo Cascio 2007a.
8. Roth 1999, above p. 90.
9. A. Jones 1964 111, 191–2; Kehne 2007, 324–5; Tchernia 2016, 99.
10. Whittaker 2004, 94.
11. Tchernia 2016, 99.
12. Irby-Massie 1999, 15–17; *Tab. Vindol.* II.190.
13. Bowman and Thomas 1984; Bowman 1994; Evers Grønlund 2011.
14. *Tab. Vindol.* II.343.
15. *Tab. Vindol.* III.645.
16. J. Jones 2004.
17. Mattingly and Aldrete 2000, 151.
18. Whittaker 2004, 91; *Tab. Vindol.* II.180.
19. Tchernia 2016, 94.
20. Verboven 2007, 297–303.
21. Whittaker 2002, 207–13; Carreras Monfort 2002, 70–7; S. James 2001.
22. Rathbone 2009, 310.
23. CIL 2.1180; Carreras Monfort 1998, 162; Blázquez 1992, 177; Patterson 1998, 160.
24. Middleton 1979; Erdkamp 2002; Rice 2016; Tchernia 2016, 103.
25. Swain and Williams 2008.
26. Rickman 1980; Palomera 2010, 15; P. S. Johnson 2012, 22.
27. Scapini 2016.
28. A. Wilson 2012, 289; Tchernia 2016, 97.
29. Rickman 1980, 80; Broekart 2011; Plin. *Pan.* 29. 4–5.
30. A. Wilson 2008, 187; Suet. *Claud.* 17,2–19,1.
31. Mattingly and Aldrete 2000, 146; Kehoe 2015a, 189–96; Zuiderhoek 2016.
32. Fulford 1987.
33. Davies *et al.* 1994, 9; Rayner 2011, 281.
34. Remesal Rodriguez 1986 and 2002; Carreras Monfort 1998, 160–2.
35. Notably Wierschowski 1982, 38–9; Ehmig 2003; Tchernia 2016, 255–6; Mees 2018.
36. Tomlin 2016, 9; Wilmott 1982; below p. 219.

37. D. Goodburn 2011, 394–6: ONE94.
38. Livarda and Orengo 2015.
39. Hayward 2009; Coombe *et al.* 2015.
40. Pitts 2018.
41. Willis 2005.
42. Roymans 2011, 150.
43. Fulford 2017, 317–18.
44. Mees 2018.
45. Pitts 2018.
46. Verboven 2015, 53.
47. Reece 1987; Millett 1990, 58–9; Brindle 2017, 240.
48. Verboven 2007, 309; von Reden 2012, 266.
49. Reece 2002, 115.
50. Abdy 2002, 14; see also Walton 2015; Walton and Moorhead 2016.
51. Tomlin 2016, 158–9 <WT45>; BZY10.
52. Zuiderhoek 2016, 142.
53. Bowman 2017, 38–9.
54. S. Graham 2005, 110.
55. Henig 2008, 226.
56. Bang 2008, 216–26; de Laet 1949, 427–35.
57. Whittaker 1994, 111–12.
58. Milne 1985, 149.
59. Bowman and Wilson 2017, 7.
60. Tchernia 2016, 259–60.
61. Kolb 2002.
62. Mattingly 2006b, 295–6.
63. Cunliffe 1968, 234–43.
64. Pitts 2018.
65. Ogilvie 2007.

Chapter 17

1. Tomlin 2016, <WT7>.
2. Sirks 2017, 79–80; Eckardt 2018, 23–4; Tomlin 2016, <WT31>; R. Wheeler 1930, 54–5.
3. Tomlin 2016, <WT50>.
4. RIB 2443.7: Collingwood and Wright 1992; Richmond 1953, 206–8; Tomlin 2016, 287;.
5. Tomlin 2016, <WT29>.
6. Mattingly and Aldrete 2000, 148; Erdkamp 2012, 250.
7. For comparative figures on Mediterranean ports see Wilson *et al.* 2012. With a capacity approaching *c.* 100 vessels London was comparable in scale with the port at Lepcis Magna.
8. Brigham 1990b, 101: BIG82.
9. Swain and Williams 2008; Erdkamp 2012; Mattingly and Aldrete 2000, 155.
10. C. Hawkins 2016, 28.
11. Vegetius 4–39; Beresford 2013.

12. Roth 1999, 177–9; Tac. *Agr.* 18.1–2.
13. Bernard 2016, 64; C. Hawkins 2016, 29.
14. DeLaine 2000, 135–6; Kehoe 2012, 123.
15. Perring 2002, 87–98.
16. D. Goodburn 2001, 83; D. Goodburn *et al.* 2011; D. Goodburn 1995, 43.
17. Perring 2002, 98–106.
18. Kehoe 2015a, 195; Erdkamp 2015, 27–9.
19. Scheidel 2012, 99.
20. Evers Grønlund 2011, 26; *Tab. Vindol.* II.155.
21. Verboven and Laes 2016, 12.
22. Turner and Skutsch 1960; Marsden 1980, 42: GM31.
23. Betts 2017a, 106.
24. Biddulph *et al.* 2012, 171.
25. Lodwick 2017, 45.
26. *Tab. Vindol.* II.310; Tomlin 2016, 56: <WT56>; above p. 93.
27. C. Hawkins 2016, 29, 48.
28. Birley 1979, 131.
29. Flohr and Wilson 2016, 37.
30. Smither 2017.
31. Booth 2016, 341; Ridgeway 2009, 33.
32. Perring and Roskams 1991, 18: GPO75.
33. Zuiderhoek 2016, 136.
34. Flohr 2016, 149.
35. MacMahon 2003.
36. Perring and Roskams 1991: GPO75.
37. Hill and Rowsome 2011, 194–220: ONE94.
38. Hill and Rowsome 2011, 441.
39. Evans 2005.
40. Bowman and Thomas 2003, 40–2: *Tab. Vindol.* III.588.
41. Perring and Pitts 2013, 249.
42. Milne 1992, 77; Milne and Wardle 1993: LCT84.
43. Perring and Roskams 1991: GPO75.
44. Mattingly 2011, 114.
45. Mason 2003, 20; Tac. *Ann.* 2.6.
46. Marsden 1994, 97: GM451; GM182; Grainge 2005, 67, 75.
47. Mason 2003, 48; Cunliffe 2013; Caes. *BGall.* 4.21.
48. Wild 2002; Lambrick and Robinson 2009, 254.
49. RIB 2443.16: Collingwood and Wright 1992; R. Wheeler 1930, 54–5.
50. The area of St Katherine Docks, downriver of the Tower, might also have been suitable for shipyards, but the construction of the docks in 1827 leaves a gap in our knowledge.
51. Hammer 2003, 33, 310, 166–7; Cowan 2003, 45; Cowan *et al.* 2009, 106: CO88/CO87; PRK90.
52. Yorkshire coal was sometimes used in later periods.
53. *Tab. Vindol* II. 310.
54. Hall 2005, 130–1; Dungworth 2016, 549; Perring and Roskams 1991: 106BHS73; 207BHS72; GP075.

55. See p. 76 on London's gem-cutters whose works would have been set within rings made in local workshops.

56. Drummond-Murray and Thompson 2002, 40–1; Hingley 2018, 43: JSS92.

57. E.g. LEN89; ALG84. Perhaps also TW70.

58. Drummond-Murray and Thompson 2002, 28–9, 61–2, 96–9, 83: BGH95.

59. Dungworth 2016, 543–8.

60. Hingley 2018, 105.

61. Cowan and Wardle 2009, 107: 1STS74.

62. Wilmott 1991, 18–33: GM157.

63. Merrifield 1995; Merrifield and Hall 2008; Manning 1985.

64. Humphreys 2021.

65. RIB 2428.5–8: Collingwood and Wright 1991a; Hall 2005, 132; I. Scott 2017, 316;.

66. C. E. Jones 1983, 49–59; Dungworth 2016, 532.

67. Jones and Sherlock 1996, 165.

68. Hall 2005, 132: DMT88, LYD88.

69. Marsden 1975, 9–12: BLH73; Dennis and Ward 2001, 116–20: SUF94.

70. Hall 2005, 133; Sheldon 1978, 31: 1STS74; C. Maloney 1990, 84: KEY83; Dungworth 2016, 549: CIL86.

71. Nelson and Drummond 2015, 78–81.

72. van Driel-Murray 2016, 137; Keily and Mould 2017, 237.

73. E.g. Grimes 1968, 97; RCHME 1928, 145–7; Lees *et al.* 1989, 119; Wilmott 1991; Sheldon 1978, 31; Shepherd 1998: WFG44.

74. Rhodes 1986, 89, 211–16: NFW74/FRE78; Rhodes 1987a; Keily and Mould 2017, 244–5; van Driel-Murray 2016.

75. Manning 1985, 39–42; Keily and Mould 2017, 247–9; Humphreys 2021.

76. Keily and Mould 2017, 246; LOW88, DGT06.

77. Cool 2016, 408.

78. Groves 1990, 82; Hall 2005, 136: OPT81; Humphreys 2021; E. Swift 2017, 92.

79. Wild 2002, 29.

80. Tomlin 2016, <WT12>, <WT14>.

81. Tomlin and Hassall 2006, 478: GHT00.

82. Humphreys 2021.

83. D. Goodburn 2016, 8–13: PDN82.

84. Milne 1985, 91–5: PDN81; KWS94.

85. Milne 1985, 87: PEN79.

86. Ridgeway *et al.* 2019, 230; Liddle 2008: GAG87; Rielly in prep: DGT06.

87. N. Crummy 2017, 262.

88. Lees *et al.* 1989, 32: LOW88; Ewens and Pipe 2017, 175: XSM10.

89. Shepherd 1986, 141–3: GM160; Howell 2013: BBH05.

90. FER97; PEP89.

91. Bayley and Shepherd 1985, 72–3: TOL79-84.

92. Keily and Shepherd 2005, 147–9: MGT87; MRG95; Perez-Sala and Shepherd 2008: GAG87. See also KEY83 and OPT81.

93. A. Wardle 2015: BAZ05; COA86.

94. OBA88.

95. Marsden 1969b: GM136.

96. Seeley and Drummond Murray 2005; Hall 2005, 137; Rayner 2017, 361: MRG95; Nesbitt and Watson 2019: MLW15.
97. Swan 1984, 107; Amicone and Quinn 2015.
98. Humphreys 2021, 138; Lodwick 2017, 74; Davies *et al.* 1994, 37.
99. WIV88; TRM86; RAG82; BOP82; THY01.

Chapter 18

1. Blagg 1990; Hope 2016, 287–90; Hurst 2016, 107; J. Pearce 2016, 351.
2. N. Holder 2007, 29.
3. Tomlin 2016, 58.
4. Harris 1991.
5. Monteil 2008; Eckardt 2018, 55–6.
6. See p. 76 on the post-Boudican assemblage from Plantation Place.
7. Derks 1998; C. Andrews 2012.
8. Henig 2008, 234.
9. Coombe *et al.* 2015; Bishop 1983, 31–48; Tomlin 2016, 56.
10. Fuhrmann 2012, 204–5; Rankov 1999, 24–5.
11. N. Pollard 2006, 224.
12. RIB 19: Collingwood and Wright 1965; Coombe *et al.* 2015, 46; Fuhrmann 2012, 193.
13. Speidel 1978, 26–8; Hassall 2017, 106.
14. Haynes 2016.
15. Bowman and Thomas 1991, 72: *Tab. Vindol.* II.154 and 310.
16. Tomlin 2016 <WT56>.
17. Tomlin 2016 <WT20>.
18. Hassall 2012.
19. Birley 2005, 298.
20. Cool 2016, 416; Bishop and Coulston 2006, 254–9.
21. Dunwoodie *et al.* 2015, fig. 60.
22. Lo Cascio 2007b, 636; Roth 1999.
23. Allason-Jones 2016, 473–4.
24. Rosenstein 2009, 36; G. Rogers 1991, 13.
25. Temin 2013, 129.
26. RIB 2443.2: Collingwood and Wright 1992.
27. Tomlin 2003; Hill and Rowsome 2011, 128, 515: ONE94.
28. RIB 21: Collingwood and Wright 1965; Coombe *et al.* 2015, no. 83.
29. Blagg 1990.
30. Boatwright 2000, 15; *Cod. Iust.* 10.40.7.
31. RIB 9: Collingwood and Wright 1965; RCHME 1928, 170–1; Coombe *et al.* 2015, no. 81.
32. Hingley 2018, 122.
33. Kolbeck 2018.
34. Tomlin 2016, 54.
35. Nixon *et al. 2002*, 30.
36. Hall 2005, 125.
37. Marsden 1980, 25.
38. Eckardt 2010; Verboven 2009.

39. Redfern *et al.* 2016; Redfern *et al.* 2017; Redfern *et al.* 2018; Millard 2013; Montgomery *et al.* 2010, 217–19.
40. Verboven 2007, 303–4.
41. Tomlin 2016, 54.
42. Scheidel 2012, 91.
43. Gowland and Redfern 2010.
44. Harper 2017, 80–3; Rohnbogner 2018, 342; Pitts and Griffin 2012.
45. Eckardt and Müldner 2016, 214.
46. Morley 2011.
47. Cool 2016, 410; A. Wardle 2011.
48. A. Wardle 2011; Cool and Baxter 2016.
49. Eckardt and Crummy 2008, 24; N. Crummy 2008, 218.
50. Monteil 2005.
51. RIB 2492.24: Collingwood and Wright 1994; Yule 2005, 22: WP83.
52. K. Hartley 1996.
53. Symonds 2012.
54. Above p. 80; van der Veen *et al.* 2007.
55. Cowan *et al.* 2009, 113–14; A. Davis 2011.
56. C. Stevens 2009; A. Davis 2014.
57. Liddle *et al.* 2009; Rielly 2015; Pipe 2011.
58. Locker 2007.
59. Henig 1984b, 25–35.
60. RIB 2443.11: Collingwood and Wright 1992.
61. A. Rogers 2013, 16.
62. Creighton 2006, 95.
63. GDV96: Blagg 2000, 61–2; Coombe *et al.* 2015 no. 37.
64. Coombe *et al.* 2015.
65. Durham 2016, 75; Fittock 2015, 168.
66. Carl *et al.* 2000.
67. J. Reynolds 1988, 48–9.
68. Esmonde Cleary 2013, 355.
69. A. Smith 2001.
70. Drummond-Murray and Thompson 2002, 87: BGH95; Merrifield 1995, 37–8; Wilmott 1991, 178.
71. Howell *et al.* 2015, 147: TRT85.
72. Frankfurter 2006, 557–8.
73. E.g. Hingley 2018, 108; Davies *et al.* 1994, 229: MFI87.
74. Serv. *Aen.* 1.446.
75. A. Smith 2016, 642.
76. Merrifield 1995; Merrifield and Hall 2008; also Leary and Butler 2012, 85–6.
77. Zoll 2016, 635; Frankfurter 2006, 554; A. Smith 2016, 642.
78. Hurst 2016, 109.
79. Hill and Rowsome 2011, 186. For other examples see Birley 1979, 124; Cowan *et al.* 2009, 148, and p. 244.
80. E.g. Perring and Roskams 1991, 69–70: GPO75; Ridgeway *et al.* 2019, 42: BVQ09.
81. E.g. Hart and Melikian 2007, 305: LDH99 and other examples.

82. S. Watson 2013.
83. G. Davis 2018, 76 drawing on unpublished reports by Michael Marshall.
84. Bowsher and Marshall 2013: BZY10.
85. A. Smith 2016, 654. For examples see pp. 79 and 385.
86. Fulford 2001.
87. Ridgeway *et al.* 2013, 54: LTU03.

Chapter 19

1. Dunning 1945, 60; Roskams and Watson 1981; Perring 2017.
2. KWS94; AUT01; PDN81.
3. CSD12.
4. Rowsome 1999, 269–700; Bateman 1998, 48: DMT88.
5. PCH85; KEW98; NEG98.
6. Bateman *et al.* 2008, 61, 116 and Fig 114: GSJ06; KIG95; IRO80; GHT00.
7. ETA89; TEA98; BIS82.
8. E.g. LC76; BRL87; FEC80; FSP80; IME83; LIM83.
9. Brigham 1990a, 70; Milne 1992, 70: LCT84.
10. Dunwoodie *et al.* 2015, 118: FER97; Dunning 1945, 57; Roskams and Watson 1981, site 250; Parnell 1985, 9.
11. Bluer and Brigham 2006, 18: FCC95; Hobley and Schofield 1977, 57; Roskams and Watson 1981, site 242: CAS75.
12. FST85, LFE87 and LAH 88; PUB80; Bluer and Brigham 2006, 27: FCC95.
13. Howe and Lakin 2004, 21.
14. E.g. S. Watson 2015, 30: CDP04.
15. Cowan *et al.* 2009, 46.
16. Yule 2005, 39: WP83.
17. Marsh 1981; Symonds 1998, 340.
18. Hill and Rowsome 2011, 162.
19. Brigham 1998, 29; Brigham 2001, 27, 41: Building 4; Blair *et al.* 2006, 18–20: GHT00; Hillam 1986, 14.
20. Brigham and Watson 1996: KWS94.
21. Brigham 1998, 29; Brigham 1990b, Waterfront 4; Brigham 2001a, 27, 41: SUF94, Building 4.
22. Parnell 1985, 8: TOL79-84.
23. Milne 1992, 68.
24. Casson *et al.* 2014, 37, 61–2, 86–92: GSM97.
25. E.g. Dunning 1945, 60; Merrifield 1965, 46; Perring 1991, 73.
26. Gibbon 1776, 95–6.
27. Fronto *Ep. de bello Parthico* 2.
28. Dio Cass. 69.14.1.
29. SHA *Hadr.* 5.2.
30. Jarrett 1976; Birley 1997, 123; Birley 2007b.
31. CIL 11.5632; CIL 10.5829; R. Davies 1977; Frere 2000; Breeze *et al.* 2012, 27; B. Hoffman 2013, 140–3; Hodgson 2021 makes a case for a slightly earlier date.

32. Graafstal 2018, 98–100; P. Holder 2003; Birley 1998; P. Hill 2006, 144; Breeze 2003, 13–16.
33. Casey 1987, although the identification is uncertain.
34. The Alexandrian calendar year ran from September.
35. Cowie *et al.* 2013, 18, 20; Parnum and Cotton 1983, 320; Sheldon and Schaaf 1978, 66; P. Jones 2010, 16, 20.
36. Allen and Lodwick 2017, 157 173.
37. Sealey 1995.
38. 'BB2': Davies *et al.* 1994, 107, 205–9.
39. Gerrard 2008; Allen and Fulford 1999, 178; Bidwell 2017, 292–8.
40. Monaghan 1987; R. Pollard 1988, 173–7; Allen and Lodwick 2017, 157; Millett 2007, 167.
41. Biddulph 2012.
42. Allen and Fulford 1999, 178; Boatwright 2000, 204.
43. Tac. *Ann.* 14.31.
44. Birley 1997, 2.
45. Grimes 1968, 17–40; Shepherd 2012; Howe and Lakin 2004.
46. Butler 2001, 237: PLH97.
47. Marsden 1968a, 8: GM4.
48. Shepherd 2012: WFG1a, WFG7, WFG9; Lyon 2004: NHG98.
49. Grimes 1968: WFG5.
50. Shepherd 2012.
51. M. Lavan 2019b, 189. This is a lower settlement density than suggested for earlier temporary camps crowded with tents.
52. Hassall 2012; Howe and Lakin 2004, 55–8: WFG20, WFG22, NST94, WOO97, NHG98.
53. Shepherd 2012, 50, 154; Howe and Lakin 2004, 37–9, table 7.
54. Fuhrman 2012, 45, 157, 194; Plin. *Ep.* 10.77.
55. Wacher 1995, 94; Shepherd 2012, 155.
56. Hassall 2017, 91–7; above pp. 220–2.
57. Hassall 2012, 166–8; Yule and Rankov 1998.
58. Philp 1981, 91–7; Breeze 1983.
59. A. Wardle 2015, 101.
60. Bateman *et al.* 2008: 101: GAG87.
61. Bateman *et al.* 2008, 58, 196.
62. Bateman 2009.
63. Brown and Pye 1992: WIV88.
64. Brigham 2001a, 21–30: SUF94; D. Swift 2008, 34–6: AUT01; Brigham 1990b Waterfront 4: Seal House I: SH74/SH76, Swan Lane I: SWA81; table 10.
65. Brigham 1990b: NFW74 I, CUS73 I, BC75.
66. Milne 1985, 54; Brigham 2001b, 44.
67. Hassall and Tomlin 1987, 360–3.
68. Rhodes 1991. See p. 271.
69. Bateman 1986: FMO85; KWS94.
70. Drummond-Murray and Thompson 2002, 96–107.
71. R. Burns 2017.
72. MacDonald 1986; Laurence *et al.* 2011, 116.

73. Boatwright 2000, 172–4; Birley 1997, 74; J. Reynolds 1988, 43.
74. Birbeck and Schuster 2009, 24–5: FNE01.
75. E.g. Lime Street: IME83.
76. Perring and Roskams 1991, 41: WAT78.
77. E.g. Hill and Rowsome 2011, 418: ONE94; Dunwoodie *et al.* 2015, 118; FER97.
78. KWS94.
79. C. Maloney 1990, 85–88, 89–112, 114–15; Leary and Butler 2012, 78–83; Harward *et al.* 2015, 15; DGT06.
80. Schofield 1998, 246, 253; I. Tyers 2008a, table 2.2.1: MGT87; COV87.
81. Seeley and Drummond-Murray 2005, 142: MRG95.
82. C. Maloney 1990, 26–39: OPT81, KEY83, TEL83, CHL84; MGE96; TEA98; COV87; ACW74; Shepherd 1987.
83. Ridgeway 2009, 22: DGT06; A. Wardle 2015, 9.
84. Leary and Butler 2012, 80.
85. Perring 2000, 141: Lees *et al.* 1989, 118; LOW88; Perez-Sala and Shepherd 2008; A. Wardle 2015, 97: MGT87; Shepherd 2012, 156.
86. Hingley 2018, 163; Bruce *et al.* 2009, 77: MGE96.
87. Reddaway 1940, 26.

Chapter 20

1. Harward *et al.* 2015, 24–5, 83–5; Ranieri and Telfer 2017: RIV87; ELD88; FIB88; BSP91; BDC03; ENS03; XSM10.
2. Hyland 1990, 259; Dixon and Southern 1992, 229–31; Roth 1999, 203; N. Crummy 2006, 24.
3. Denyer 1935, 13; Booth 2012, 333: KXU10. RIB 18: Collingwood and Wright 1965, which referes to a soldier of Legio XX.
4. RCHME 1928, 56. These have alternatively been used to hypothesize a road bypassing London along the line of Old Street.
5. Ranieri and Telfer 2017, 12, 86.
6. Harward *et al.* 2015, 21.
7. Ranieri and Telfer 2017, 24.
8. Tac. *Hist.* 2.45, 70.
9. Harward *et al.* 2015, 92–107: RIV87; ELD88; FIB88; BDC03; ENS03.
10. Ranieri and Telfer 2017, 22, 89–92: XSM10.
11. Tucker 2016, 103.
12. Geoffrey of Monmouth HRB, 5, 4; Lane Fox 1867; Norman and Reader 1906.
13. Perring 2017, table 1; Ranieri and Telfer 2017, fig. 104; Schulting and Bradley 2013; Edwards *et al.* 2009; Marsh and West 1981.
14. Schulting and Bradley 2013, 54; Marsh and West 1981, 97.
15. Hall 1996, 83; J. Pearce 2015, table 1.
16. Reader 1903; RCHME 1928, 15; Powers 2015, 127–34; Haglund 1993.
17. E.g. Cipin 2015, 10.
18. E.g. Daykin 2017: PPL11; BGB98.
19. Butler 2006, 40: MRL98.

20. Marsh and West 1981; Ross 1967; Cotton 1996.

21. Ranieri and Telfer 2017, 25–28, 115–17: XSM10.

22. Ranieri and Telfer 2017, 58–61, 109–10; Harward *et al.* 2015, 21.

23. Ranieri and Telfer 2017, 112.

24. E.g. Brittany, the Central Massif in France, the Rhine Graben, the Alps and the Bohemian Massif.

25. P. Brown 2012, 297; Haynes 2013, 364; Shaw 1993: 335–6. It was not possible to consult Elliott 2021 on theories that connect a massacre in London with the supposed disappearance of the Ninth legion, for which see also Hodgson 2021.

26. Lees *et al.* 1989, 116; Redfern and Bonney 2014; Shaw *et al.* 2016, 65; LOW88.

27. Shaw *et al.* 2016.

28. Redfern and Bonney 2014: LOW88.

29. Hope 2000; Ash 1997; Bauman 1996, 151; Varner 2005, 69; Kyle 1998, 53.

30. Above p. 220. RIB 19: Collingwood and Wright 1965; Furhman 2012, 171–4.

31. Hinard 1987, 119; Kyle 1998, 217–20.

32. Luc. *Pharsalia* 2.103; Livy 24.20.6, 24.30.6; Val. Max. 9.2.1; *BHisp.* 32; App. *B Civ.* 1.71, 4.2.5–4.20; Plut. *Vit. Ant.* 20, Plut. *Vit. Cic.* 48–9; Lennon 2014, 157; Kyle 1998, 132–3, 220–4.

33. Scenes 71, 24 and 113. Fields 2005; Goldsworthy 1998.

34. RIB 522: Collingwood and Wright 1965; RIB 3185: Tomlin *et al.* 2009; Bull 2007. See also Birley 2002, 34.

35. CIL 6. 1523. Birley 2005, 152.

36. Campbell 2000, 44–5; 69–70; Fields 2005.

37. Howe 2002: BAX95.

38. J. Maloney 1979: DUK77; Morgan 1980, 114: TR74.

39. S. Watson 2006, 48: SLY00.

40. Pitt 2006b, 27–31: OBL97.

41. Hingley 2018, 164; LLS02; SWN98; TIY07; LTU03.

42. Armit 2012, 91; M. Green 2001, 151.

43. Hingley 2018, 110–14.

44. Braithwaite 2007, 255, 348, 323–403 Casson *et al.* 2014, 59–60; Ranieri and Telfer 2017, 32; Wilmott 1991, 28–30, 177–8.

45. Noreńa 2011, 202; Russell and Manley 2015, 166; Varner 2005, 67–88.

Chapter 21

1. Betts 1995, 222. Later building supplies were occasionally marked as the products of civilian tileries. Betts 2017b, 370: RIB 2489.13–15: Collingwood and Wright 1993.

2. Hill and Rowsome 2011, 445; Pritchard 1988, 186.

3. E.g. LBN08; WHY85; DHS75 Building 4; 11STS77 Building 3; LBE95 Building 1; BGH95 Buildings 30–2; Bird and Graham 1978, site 10; BOP82; FCC95, Buildings 16 and 32; TEA98; BRD88 Building 1; LFE87, FNC88; WIV88; S. Butcher 1982; TEL83; SUF94, Buildings 3 and 4; BAX95, Building 1; KNG85; FNE01 Building 16; WAO06; LIE14; LIM83 and IME83; IMG12; AUT01 Building 12; LSO88; FER97 Building 31;

WAT78. Possibly also: BBH87; GM160 and GM213; GM37; GM73; HOP83 Building 5; GM136 Building 1; ESC97; BBH05 Building 15; OJW98 Building 3; LDH99; BZY10.

4. Hill and Rowsome 2011, 187: LHY88.

5. Neal and Cosh 2009, 399–400: Camomile Street 370.22, Finch Lane 370.43, Birchin Lane 370.7; Crosby Hall 370.36; Cullum Street 370.40; Founders Court 370. 65; Mansion House 370.71.

6. Milne 1985, 138–40: PDN81 Building 6; Maloney and Holroyd 2009, 51: CYQ05. Rowsome 1999, 273.

7. Ridgeway 2009, 22–5: DGT06. Water pipes feeding the building incorporated timbers felled A D 155–87 and a writing tablet internally dated to A D 158 was found in a drain alongside the building.

8. Neal and Cosh 2009: Mosaic 370.72.

9. Niblett and Thompson 2005, 114–5, 155.

10. Frere 1983, 16; Millett 1990, 107.

11. Perring 2005.

12. E. Thomas 2017.

13. Schmitz 2011, 306–10.

14. Teçusan 1990; Perring 2015.

15. Described by Jas Elsner as the apogee of Second Sophistic monuments: Elsner 1998, 174.

16. Yule 2005: WP83.

17. Goffin 2005, 120–5.

18. Crowley 2005, 92–4.

19. RIB 3016: Tomlin *et al.* 2009: Yule and Rankov 1998; Hassall 2017, 107; Hingley 2018, 139.

20. Mattingly 2006a, 274; above p. 79.

21. Above p. 185; Birley 2005, 307.

22. Cowan 1992, 49; Neal and Cosh 2009, 456: 15SK80.

23. Cowan *et al.* 2009 Site 44: RWG94.

24. C. Thomas 2008, 105: PSW93; PLQ95.

25. Howell 2005; Philp *et al.* 1991.

26. E.g. Walton-on-the-Hill, Titsey, Darenth, Farningham (Franks), Ash and Cobham: Black 1987, 34–5.

27. Perring and Pitts 2013, 247.

28. S. Watson 2016; S. Watson 2017, 394: SGA12; Booth 2012, 332; Symonds 1995: LTS95; Monteil 2005, 70, 115–119, 141 and pers. comm.: TEQ10; Rhodes 1986, 91: NFW74.

29. Following Nieto 1997 the port might be seen to have ceased serving as a principal emporia for redistribution, adopting a secondary role within the more extended lines of supply. See also Wilson *et. al.* 2012.

30. G. Brown 2008.

31. Brigham 1990a, 73; Tyers and Vince 1983, 303–4.

32. Brigham *et al.* 1995: CO88.

33. Ridgeway *et al.* 2019, 30–31, Fig 4.32: BVM12; Cowan *et al.* 2009, 73–6: GHL89; Taylor Wilson 2002: HHO97.

34. Bateman *et al.* 2008, 62–72: GAG87.

35. de la Bédoyère 2003, 125.

36. Frere 1999, 139.
37. Horne and King 1980.
38. Williams 1993, 120: PET81; Pritchard 1988, 187.
39. Bradley and Butler 2008, 65–9: QUV01; Marsden 1967: GM91.
40. D. Goodburn 2008, 45.
41. Bateman 1998, 49.
42. Zoll 2016, 629; Whittaker 1997, 151–2.
43. Williams 1993, 77–87; RCHME 1928, 141; Humphrey 1986, 431; Fuentes 1986b, 144–7. Smithfield Market, north of town, is an alternative location.
44. P. Crummy 2008.
45. Perring 1991, 81–2; Schofield 1998, 277 and 283–4; McCann 1993, 39: OBA88.
46. Merrifield 1996, 110–1.
47. Bateman *et al.* 2008, 118; Booth 2007, 287; Booth 2008, 317: GSJ06 and GAM88.
48. Dawe and Oswald 1952, 15–107: GM219; re-investigated as BOA83 and IRL95.
49. Grainger 1995: IRL95.
50. Neal and Cosh 2009: Mosaic 370.51.
51. Shepherd 1987, 41–2: GM83.
52. Blair 2005: KIG95.
53. Bayley *et al.* 2009, 155: GHT00.
54. RCHME 1928, 120; Merrifield 1996, 106, 112.
55. Killock *et al.* 2015: LLS02.
56. Beasely 2006: SWN98.
57. A. Smith 2016, 648.
58. Evershed *et al.* 2004.
59. RIB 3014: Tomlin *et al.* 2009; Grew 2008; Tomlin 2015.
60. Bynon 2016.
61. RIB 678: Collingwood and Wright 1965; Birley 1979, 126; CIL 13.8164a; RCHME 1962.
62. Tomlin 2018a, 304; Dondin-Payre and Loriot 2008.
63. Adams 2017, 200.
64. Tomlin 2018a, 304–6; Hassall 2017, 177.
65. Lis 2009, 61–2; C. Hawkins 2016, 70; Verboven 2016, 196.
66. Millett 2016a.
67. Millett 1990, 107.
68. Vitr. *De arch.* 1.6.7.
69. P. Andrews 2008; A. Smith 2016, 651.
70. A. Smith 2001.
71. Creighton 2006, 129–45.
72. G. Rogers 1991.
73. Irby-Massie 1999, 15–17.
74. Henig 1984b, 41.
75. Biddulph *et al.* 2019, 208–10: BVX09; Marsh 1979b, 265.
76. The adjacent bathhouse may have been restored, and rubbish indicates that an adjacent masonry building hosted banquets. Ridgeway *et al.* 2019, 91, 190, 205–6: BVK11.
77. Hill and Rowsome 2011, 174, 377: ONE94, Building 69.
78. Mackinder 2000: GDV96.

79. J. Pearce 2016, 354; J. Pearce 2015, 143.
80. Thrale 2008: OCU04.
81. Blagg 2000; Hingley 2018, 166; Hayward 2015, 190.
82. Barber and Bowsher 2000, 111–16: MSL87, with others at ETN88 and WTN84.
83. Hunt and Shepherd 2009, 136: PCO06.
84. Pitt 2006b, 50–3: NEG98.
85. Rowsome 2014b, 38: LUD82.
86. S. Stevens 2017, 92.
87. Norman and Reader 1912, 294; Marsden 1980, 124.
88. Schofield 1998, 289: BTB89. Hingley 2018, 177.
89. J. Maloney 1979: DUK77; Butler 2001, 45–6: PLH97; Sankey and Stephenson 1991, 117–18; BLM 87; CAP86.
90. Howe 2002, 12: BAX95.
91. RCHME 1928, pl 55.
92. Frere 1983, 35–6; Niblett and Thompson 2005, 155.
93. Swain and Williams 2008, 39.

Chapter 22

1. Marsden 1980, 110: GM217.
2. Waddington 1930, 68–9.
3. Sheldon 1975, 278–84.
4. J. Morris 1975, 343–4; Symonds and Tomber 1991, 59.
5. E.g. Roskams and Schofield 1978, 227–8; Marsden 1980, 110–17; Merrifield 1983, 140; Perring and Roskams 1991, 120.
6. Yule 1990.
7. Hill and Rowsome 2011, 166: ONE94; Bluer and Brigham 2006, 44: FCC95.
8. E.g. Howe and Lakin 2004, Rowsome 2006; 51; Rowsome 2008, 30; Cowan and Rowsome 2009; Rowsome 2018, 94.
9. S. Watson 2006, 56–7.
10. Hingley 2018, 155–92.
11. B. Watson 1998, 103–5; Macphail 2003; Macphail 2005; Lyon 2007, 36; Cowan and Seeley 2009; Ridgeway et al. 2019, 173.
12. Sankey 2002, 13–17.
13. Hingley 2018, 147: GPO75.
14. E.g. Shepherd 1987, 36, 48–50: GM 129 and KNG85; Hill and Rowsome 2011, 237–9: BRD88/DOC87, KNG85.
15. Perring and Roskams 1991, 19 and 67: GPO75 Group 8.8–13.
16. OST82; ABS86.
17. Yule 1988, 79: 88BHS74.
18. Howe and Lakin 2004, 42: NST94.
19. Crabtree 2018, 23–5.
20. Rielly 2006, 117: PNS01 and 1STS74.
21. Perring and Roskams 1991, 26, 57: GPO75; WEL79.
22. Rielly et al. 2006.

23. Marsden and West 1992, 138.
24. Vince 1987, fig. 102; Monteil 2005, 67; Symonds 2006, fig 80.
25. Marshman 2015, 218–20.
26. 66 sites present evidence of contraction or abandonment: GM217; TW70, 207BHS72, FNS72, 106BHS73, 64BHS74, 88BHS74, CAS75, GPO75, CHR76, MLK76, 213BHS77, WAT78, BAR79, HEN79, WOW79, IRO80, PUB80, 107BHS81, 223BHS81, CLE81, BOP82, EST83, HOP83, HIL84, KNG85, PCH85, ABS86, MOG86, ORG86, BLM87, COV87, LFE87, MGT87, LOW88, VAL88, WIV88, CED89, TWR89, NST94, BGH95, MRG95, GSM97, WOO97, KEW98, MRL98, NEG98, OJW98, MTA99, SLY00, EAE01, FOT01, PNS01,CDP04, BAZ05, BBH05, CYQ05, GHM05, POU05, SGY05, GHB06, LMZ06, FEU08, BBO10, BVF10 and IMG12. By contrast 50 sites present evidence of continued occupation: 1STS74, 175BHS76, AB78, WEL79, OPT81, PDN81, PHI81, BIS82, OST82, POT82, FEN83, KEY83, TEL83, WIT83, LWA84, CON86, NHA86, ABC87, AST87, BUC87, CO88, PPO87, BRD88, LHY88, LSO88, SXE88, USA88, 179BHS89, ETA89, PEP89, CID90, KWS94, ONE94, SUF94, BAX95, BPL95, FCC95, SHI95, CAO96, ESC97, FER97, TEA98, LGK99, NGT00, USS03, AUT01, FNE01, THY01, DGT06 and FEN14. This sample excludes public works, sites where appropriate levels were truncated, and those with inadequate dating frameworks. The data can be compared with Hingley 2018 fig 7.13 which addresses a smaller sample using a more liberal definition of late antique continuity, but none-the less shows reduced building density on a third of sites.
27. Hill and Rowsome 2011, 187: LHY88.
28. Birbeck and Schuster 2009, 29–30: FNE01 Building 14.
29. Bluer and Brigham 2006: FCC95 Period 4.
30. An archaeomagnetic date recovered from one of the hearths is dated A D 180–220 at a 95 per cent confidence level.
31. Keily 2006, 146.
32. Dunwoodie et al. 2015, 119–24: FER97.
33. RCHME 1928, 189.
34. Hill and Rowsome 2011, 358–9, 450: ONE94.
35. Shepherd 2012, 156; Howe and Lakin 2004, 41–7: NST94; GAH95.
36. BAS88.
37. Lyon 2004, 160: NHG98.
38. Harward et al. 2015, 32: ELD88, BDC03.
39. S. Watson 2015, 34–9: GHM05; Casson et al. 2014, 101: GSM 97; Shepherd 1987, 45: GM86.
40. Pitt 2006a, 35: POU05.
41. McCann 1993, 34: VAL88.
42. Merrifield 1962, 38–52; Wilmott 1991; Shepherd 1998, 219. It is not certain, however, that this mill survived the Hadrianic fire.
43. Blair et al. 2006: GHT00; Wilmott 1982.
44. RAG82.
45. Mackinder 2000, 7: GDV96; Drummond-Murray and Thompson 2002, fig. 93: BGH95.
46. Cowan et al. 2009: STS88 and GHL89; Taylor Wilson 2002, fig. 36: HHO97.
47. Ridgeway et al. 2019, 101–6: BVK11.

48. Killock *et al.* 2015, 39: LLS02.
49. Marsh and Tyers 1978, 533–82; Seeley and Drummond-Murray 2005; Rayner 2017; Brown and Sheldon 2018.
50. Betts 2017a, 107; Betts 2017b, 376; Pringle 2002, 161.
51. A. Wardle 2015, 21, 107: BAZ05.
52. Hammer 2003, 58–67, 171: CO88/CO87.
53. I. Tyers 2008a: SHI95; Hill and Rowsome 2011, 181–2: ONE94 Structure 53.
54. Dearne 2017, 316; Pemberton 1973, 84–6; Cowie *et al.* 2013; Bickleman 2016, 243; P. Jones 2010, 29–30; Crouch and Shanks 1984, 3.
55. Fulford and Allen 2017, 8–9; Smith *et al.* 2016, 81, 416–17; Margetts 2018, 124–7.
56. Hathaway 2013, 467; Lucy and Evans 2016; Biddulph 2012; Biddulph *et al.* 2012, 158; Perring 2000, 155.
57. Cunliffe 1968, 243; Perring 2003, 211–12; Esmonde Cleary 2013, 107–9. This might have contributed to Verulamium's slow recovery after fire destruction *c.* AD 155: Niblett 2001, 112–13.
58. Millett 1990, 123.
59. See Roymans 2019, 455 on the impact of war on rural populations. For frontier wars in Britain see SHA *Ant. Pius* 5.4 and SHA *Marc.* 8.7.
60. Dio Cassius 74; SHA *Marc*; Birley 1987.
61. Harper 2017, 98–114; Flemming 2019; Gal. *Ind.* 1–7, 31–5; Gal. *Libr. Propr.* 3.3; Aristid. *Or.* 48.38–45; Amm. Marc. 23.6.24; SHA *Verus* 8.1.1–2; SHA *Marc.* 13, 17; Dio Cass.71.2.4; Lucian *Hist. conscr.* 15; Oros. 7.15.5, 27.7; Eutr. 8.12. Jerome *Chron.* (Helm 287); Dio Cass.73.14.3; Hdn. 1.12.1–2.
62. Harper 2017; Littman and Littman 1973, 254–5; Zelner 2012. We lack proof, however, that *variola* was present in the Roman world: Flemming 2019 and Haldon *et al.* 2018.
63. Salient contributions to this debate include Duncan-Jones 1996; Rathbone 1997; Scheidel 2002; Bagnall 2002; Greenberg 2003; Bruun 2007; Bruun 2012; Duncan-Jones 2018.
64. Sheldon 1981, followed by Merrifield 1983, 147–8 and Perring 2011.
65. Tomlin 2014; C. P. Jones 2016, 30; Tomlin 2018a, 358 <12.67>. This was one of five tablets found at VRY89, another of which referred to recurrent fever: Tomlin 2018b, 446.
66. Harper 2017, 98–101.
67. RIB 1579: Collingwood and Wright 1965; C. P. Jones 2005.
68. Merrifield 1996, 112.
69. RCHME 1928, 120.
70. SHA *Marc.* 21. Liebeschuetz 1979, 209.
71. Disease may have caused the death of a youth and two children buried together *c.* AD 170–200 at Lant Street in Southwark. Ridgeway *et al.* 2013, 76: LTU03. A second-century mass burial at Gloucester is argued to have been a product of the Antonine plague: Simmonds *et al.*, 2008, 140; Chenery *et al.* 2010; J. Pearce 2015, 154.
72. M. Lavan 2019a, 34–5.
73. RIB 2404 19–20: Collingwood and Wright 1990; Duncan-Jones 1996, 121, fn. 118; Swan and Philpott 2000.
74. Dio Cass.71.16.2.
75. Defoe 2010.

76. Ottaway 1993, 73, 89.
77. E.g. Meier 2016, 282.
78. Cool 2016, 414; van Driel-Murray 2016.

Chapter 23

1. B. Hoffmann 2013, 158; Birley 2005, 172–3; Dio Cass. 72.9.22, 80; SHA *Pert.* 3.5–3.9; SHA *Comm.* 6.2, 8.4.
2. Birbeck and Schuster 2009, 35: FNE01; D. Swift 2008, 41: AUT01; Rowsome 1987: KNG85; Sankey 2002, 10–11: ETA89; Drummond-Murray and Thompson 2002, 123–4: BGH95.
3. Gwladys Monteil pers. comm.
4. M. Walsh 2017.
5. Richardson and Tyers 1984, 133–41; Hassall 1978, 43.
6. Coombe *et al.* 2015 xii, xxiv; Henig 2007; de Kind 2005.
7. SHA *Clod*; Dio Cass. 76.14.3.
8. Hdn. 3.8.1.
9. Hodgson 2014; Mennen 2011, 208; Birley 2005, 161; Dio Cass. 77.13.1; Hdn. 3.15.6.
10. Brigham 1990b: Seal House II, Swan Lane II: SH74; SWA81. Possibly also Tatton-Brown 1974; Brigham 1990b: CUS73 I.
11. Timbers missing sapwood cannot be ascribed a precise felling date but a range can be estimated where the heartwood-sapwood transition survives. Most studies assume a 10–55-year sapwood allowance, but recent research proposes a shorter allowance of 9–36 years to a 95 per cent degree of certainty. Hillam 1990; Millard 2002.
12. ANT88.
13. A piecemeal approach to redevelopment at Swan Lane might indicate that these preparations devolved to a variety of contractors.
14. Brigham 1990b waterfront 6; Brigham 1998, 30.
15. Esmonde Cleary 1996, 424: UPT90; Brigham 1990b, 138; I. Tyers 2008a, 72: VRY89.
16. Mennen 2011, 133; B. Hoffmann 2013, 163; Dio Cass. 75.5.4.
17. Marsden 1976: GM240; Schofield 1998, 265; Rowsome 1999: DMT88.
18. Schofield 1998, 259; I. Tyers 2008a, 72; Spence and Grew 1990: UTA87; **Schofield 1998**, 274–5 LYD88. For plan see Brigham 2001a, fig 48.
19. Brigham 1990b, 129–30: DGH86.
20. Brigham 1990b, 118–19; Tatton-Brown 1974, Custom House II: CUS73; Booth 2012, 332: TEQ10; S. Watson 2017, 394: SGA12.
21. Brigham 1990b, 128; Miller *et al.* 1986, 8: Billingsgate Lorry Park, New Fresh Wharf III; Seal House III; Swan Lane III: BIG82; NFW74; SH74; SWA81.
22. Parry 1994; Schofield 1998, 282: TEX88; Brigham 1990b, 119, Custom House III: CUS73.
23. Hillam 1990; Brigham 1990b 165: BIG82; Hillam and Morgan 1986, 78–84: NFW74.
24. D. Goodburn 2008, 48: PET81.
25. RIB 2411.18–19, 29, 33, 39, 91–92, 303: Collingwood and Wright 1990.
26. Brigham 1990b, 156–7: BIG82, see p. 203.
27. Tomlin 2018a, 309 <11.40>. For other examples see Marsden 1994, 195.

28. Marsden 1994, 33–80.
29. Marsden 1994, 97–104; B. Watson 2012: GYH10.
30. Bradley and Butler 2008, 18–22, 67–9: QUV01. The dating combines evidence from Phase 6b timber structure and piles reported by I. Tyers 2008b. Hingley 2018, 136 points out that the foundations may alternatively have been those of a palatial house although this seems unlikely.
31. Blagg 1980, 125–93; C. Hill *et al.* 1980; Coombe *et al.* 2015 xii: BC75.
32. Coombe *et al.* 2015, 81.
33. RIB 3001–3002: Tomlin *et al.* 2009; Hassall 1980, 195–8; Birley 2005, 361. BC75.
34. Coombe *et al.* 2015 no. 77; Garman 2008; Zoll 2016, 630. An inscription found in Budge Row apparently records the restoration of a temple or shrine dedicated to the Mother Goddesses, RIB 2: Collingwood and Wright 1965.
35. Burch 1987, 9–12; Schofield 1998, 218: QUN85.
36. Marsden 1975: GM210.
37. Blair and Sankey 2007, 9–14: BPL 95.
38. Lusnia 2014, 119.
39. Marsden 1980: GM163.
40. Birley 2005, 206: RIB 8: Collingwood and Wright 1965.
41. Coombe *et al.* 2015, Nos. 23–4.
42. RCHME 1928, 29–32, 153–63; Merrifield 1965, 298–325; J. Maloney 1983. More recently DUK77; ASQ87, KEW98, CPW99, TRH08.
43. ASQ87; CPW99. The presence of an inter-vallum road might be implied by interim reports on a road found at 56–62 Moorgate but more information is needed: MLW15.
44. Myers 2016, 292; C. Smith 1842, 152.
45. Merrifield 1965: W3, W5 and W10; Marsden 1980, 121–6: GM131; Butler 2001, 49: PLH97; G. Hunt 2010: CPW99, GM44; Whipp 1980, 47–67: THL78b.
46. Norman and Reader 1912, 294–5. For more recent observations of fragmentary foundations of the town gates see Schofield 1998, 289: BTB89; Rowsome 2014a, Rowsome 2014b: LUD82.
47. Shepherd 2012, 78.
48. Schofield 1998, 283–4. McCann 1993, 37: VAL88.
49. Sheldon 2010 prefers a later third-century date, but lacks evidence in support.
50. Sankey and Stephenson 1991, 122: ASQ87.
51. Grimes 1968, 51: WFG5.
52. Marsden 1970, 2–6; Marsden 1980, 126–7: GM131.
53. Hall 2014b: BLM87.
54. Marsden 1994, 80–3; Milne 2017; Elliott 2018, 81–100.
55. The implications of this are illustrated in an inscription from Rome showing that command of the Rhine and Danube fleets had been combined with that of the *Classis Britannica*, presumably pooling resources to support the British campaign. Birley 2005, 320: CIL 6. 1643.
56. E.g. South Shields, Corbridge and Vindolanda: Hodgson 2014, 36–8; Roach 2013, 107–8. See also Hekster and Zair 2008, 36.
57. Ottaway 1993, 58–61. See also Esmonde Cleary 1987, 166; Esmonde Cleary 2003.
58. S. Stevens 2017, 62.
59. Palmer 1980.

60. Bowden 2008, 286; S. Stevens 2017, 88–9; R. Wilson 2006.

61. Hdn. 3, 8, 2.

62. Birley 2005, 333–6; Birley 2007a, 46; Mennen 2011, 213; A. J. Graham 1966, 97–107; Hassall 1996, 23.

63. Wacher 1995, 167; Birley 2007a; Dondin-Payre and Loriot 2008, 156; Aur. Vict. *Caes.* 2027; Courteault 1921.

64. Dio Cass.78.9.5; *Dig.* 1.5.17.

65. Millar 1992, 171; Kehoe 2015a, 191; Broekart 2011; Lo Cascio 2015, 66–7; SHA *Sev.* 18, 3; Kehoe 2015b, 102–3; Verboven 2016, 188.

66. E.g. an enclosure where the London-Lewes road exits the Weald, see Millum and Wallace 2017, and salt-working and fish-processing enclosures at Stanford Wharf, see Biddulph *et al.* 2012, 158.

Chapter 24

1. Douglas *et al.* 2011: TOC02.

2. T. Johnson 1975, 278–80; Lakin 2002; D. Bird 2013; Gerrard 2011b: LD74.

3. RCHME 1928, 163; Cuming 1858, 37.

4. J. Bird 2011.

5. Gerrard 2011b, 168–70.

6. Pearson 2003, 105–7; Mason 2003, 140–3; B. Hoffmann 2013, 168; Philp 2005, 216.

7. Allen and Fulford 1999, 181.

8. Monteil 2005, 119; B. Richardson 1986b, 98; Swan and McBride 2002; Swan 2009, 85–91: NFW74. The mid-third-century pottery at New Fresh Wharf was mixed with earlier material, but a discrete assemblage *c.* AD 235 can be reassembled from the evidence.

9. Neal and Cosh 2009, 460: Mosaic 372.1.

10. Harward *et al.* 2015 137; D. Swift 2003, 8; Thomas *et al.* 1997, 11–13: SQU94.

11. Featherby 2002: HUD01.

12. Telfer 2010: SMD01.

13. Coombe *et al.* 2015, no. 17.

14. E.g. Pitt 2014, 167: EAE01.

15. E.g. Rhodes 1986, 95; for third-century tile manufacture see Betts 2017a, 108; Betts and Foot 1994.

16. Neal and Cosh 2009, 436; P. Johnson 1993, 159.

17. Hill and Rowsome 2011, 194: ONE94.

18. Neal and Cosh 2009, 422: Mosaics 370.56–60.

19. Marsden 1968b; Marsden 1980, 151–5: GM111. Adjacent town houses, probably built *c.* AD 200–230, have been recorded at Harp Lane and Pudding Lane. Hobley and Schofield 1977, 56: HL74; Milne 1985, 140: PDN81 Building 6.

20. E.g. BIS82. C. Maloney 1990, 60: LWA84.

21. Cowan *et al.* 2009, 25: 1STS74; 4STS82; 22BHS88; CW83; COSE84; BTJ93; 28PS84; 52SOS89; USA88.

22. Cowan *et al.* 2009, 76: CHWH83, TYT98.b.

23. Grimes 1968, 98–118; Shepherd 1998; MOLA 2017: GM256; BZY10.

24. Shepherd 1998, 47.
25. See Porph. *De Antr. Nymph.* 6.
26. RIB 3: Collingwood and Wright 1965.
27. Toynbee 1986, 55–6; Shepherd 1998, 109; Coombe *et al.* 2015.
28. Other third-century sculptures, in limestone from the Costwolds and Lincolnshire, included a depiction of rider gods, a relief of one of the torchbearer companions of Mithras identified as Cautopates, and one of the Dioscuri.
29. Liebeschuetz 1979, 233.
30. Francis 1926; Henig 1984b, 110–11.
31. Hall and Shepherd 2008, 37; Coombe *et al.* 2015 Nos. 66, 69 and 87; Hall and Wardle 2005; J. Bird 1996; J. Bird 2008; Arthur 1977, 367.
32. Hall and Shepherd 2008, 35.
33. Neal and Cosh 2009 lists various pavements with peacocks and canthari, and two showing Bacchus himself.
34. GHT00.
35. Jones and Sherlock 1996.
36. Bispham 2008, 226–9.
37. Athanassiadi and Frede 1999.
38. Brigham 1990a, 73–4: LCT84.
39. Brigham 1990a, 82: LCT84; Schofield 1998, 287–8: WIV88.
40. These timbers were re-used in a construction otherwise dated *c.* A D 270. Bateman *et al.* 2008: GAG87. Coincidentally this refurbishment was contemporary with a restoration of the Colosseum indicated by coins of Gordian III.
41. Harward *et al.* 2015, 66–8.
42. Ranieri and Telfer 2017, 38, 65–73: XSM10.
43. In medieval folklore the shrub was believed to offer protection from evil forces on the journey to the otherworld: S. Hunt 2016; Cole 1656; Zohary and Hopf 2000.
44. Cowan *et al.* 2009, 76; L. Wheeler 2009, 76: GHL89.
45. SHA *Gord.* 28.2; Mennen 2011, 138–9.
46. Ranieri and Telfer 2017, 84.
47. RIB 17: Collingwood and Wright 1965; Coombe *et al.* 2015, no. 79.
48. RIB 11: Collingwood and Wright 1965.
49. See also RIB 3003: Tomlin *et al.* 2009.
50. J. Pearce 2011.
51. Hall 1996, 58–64; BAR79; ATC97; BAA87; WES89.
52. Barber and Bowsher 2000; Ellis 1985: SCS83; WTN84; TTL85; HAY86; MSL87; MST87; ETN88; HOO88; MNL88; PRE89; PCO06.
53. McKenzie and Thomas 2020; Barber and Hall 2000; Sankey and Connell 2007; Sudds and Douglas 2014, 3; D. Swift 2003; Daykin 2017; Stow 1603, 152–3; Schofield 1998, 234, 299: CUT78; STO86; COT88; HSD89; CCT90; BGB98; SRP98; CPN01; SSZ05; HLW06; PPL11.
54. Hall 1996, 75–83; Cowan *et al.* 2009, 164; Ridgeway *et al.* 2013, 106: AMA01; SBK03; GDV96; LTU03; TIY07; HRE16.
55. I. Morris 1992, 31; Philpott 1991, 53–7; J. Pearce 2013, 146–7; E. Graham 2015.
56. McKenzie and Thomas 2020.
57. Burial 69.

58. J. Pearce 2013, 24; Redfern *et al.* 2017, 175.
59. Redfern *et al.* 2016, Table 3: LTU03.
60. McKenzie and Thomas 2020, 87. The eastern cemetery had a male: female ratio of 1.7:1 including later burials when the gender imbalance may have been less pronounced: Barber and Bowsher 2000, 311–13.
61. Ridgeway *et al.* 2013, 110–12; Philpott 1991, 231; McKenzie and Thomas 2020, 118.
62. Whytehead 1986, 33, 62–4; Eckardt and Crummy 2008, 82–3: WTN84.
63. Barber and Bowsher 2000, 319–20: MSL87.
64. McKenzie and Thomas 2020, 72.
65. E. Graham 2015, 41.
66. R. Jones 1987, 816.
67. Tert. *Adv. Iudaeos 7.4*; Origen *Hom. Ez.* 4.1.
68. Irenaeus *Adv. Haereses.*

Chapter 25

1. Brigham 1990b, 139; 158–60; Miller *et al.* 1986, 30–2; Tatton-Brown 1974; Parry 1994: NFW74; SH74; SWA81; BIG82; DGH86; TEX88; UPT90; SGA12.
2. Brigham 1990b, 140: CUS73.
3. I am grateful to Damian Goodburn for pointing this out.
4. Brigham 1990b, 132, 144: BC75; Wilkinson 1998: UPT90.
5. Rowsome 2008, 31.
6. Douglas *et al.* 2011, 4; Cowan *et al.* 2009, 32.
7. Barber and Bowsher 2000, 51–2.
8. D. Bird 2013.
9. Carreras Monfort 1998, 166.
10. Evans 2013, 520–1.
11. Wilmott 1982.
12. Carreras Monfort and Williams 2003, 68; Bourne 2000, 299.
13. Lewit 2013; Middleton 1979, 81; Middleton 1983, 80.
14. Hebblewhite 2017, 90; Bowman 2017, 37; Strobel 2007, 280.
15. Esmonde Cleary 2013, 310–11.
16. van der Veen *et al.* 2007.
17. Evans 2013; Mattingly 2006a, 500–17.
18. Mattingly 2006a, 386; Brodribb and Cleere 1988, 242–4; Cleere 1977, 18–19; A. Smith 2017, 180–3; Fulford and Allen 2017.
19. A nearby coin hoard included issues down to AD 268. Stuart-Hutcheson 2012.
20. E.g. Great Cansiron. Rudling 1986.
21. See Cunliffe 1988, 86 on the loss of maritime infrastructure around Romney Marsh, and Millum and Wallace 2017 on the dismantling of an enclosure commanding the London-Lewes road at Bridge Farm.
22. Lyne 2016, 84.
23. Niblett 2001, 126.
24. Cleere and Crossley 1995, 81; Hodgkinson 2008, 34.

25. Cleere 1977, 19; CIL 13.686.

26. Philp 1981, 115.

27. Argued by Milne 2017.

28. See Houston 1980 on arrangements for the command of the port and *annona* at Ostia, where authority resided with a procurator rather than fleet command.

29. Monaghan 1987, 221; Biddulph *et al.* 2012, 171–4.

30. Symonds and Tomber 1991, 71: LCT84. Evans 2013.

31. Gerrard 2011d.

32. I. Tyers 2008a; Hill and Rowsome 2011, 204: ONE94. A near contemporary well at Drapers' Gardens was lined with timber felled in the winter of AD 250: DGT06.

33. Williams 1993, 101; Hillam 1993, 97: PET81.

34. A military retreat from managing industrial production is implied by the mid-third-century cessation of legionary tile production: Warry 2010, 144.

35. Marsden 1970, 2–6: GM131.

36. Hall 2014b, 180: BYQ98.

37. Hall 2014b: BLM87.

38. For turrets housing military metalworking see Allason-Jones and Dungworth 1997.

39. Reece 2002, 45–6.

40. Tomlin 2016: <WT 45>.

41. Harward *et al.* 2015, 33–4.

42. Hammerson 2011, 518: ONE94.

43. Bluer and Brigham 2006, 49–56: FCC95 Period 5 Phases 1–2.

44. Brigham 1990a, 75, 81: LCT84.

45. FEN83; IME83/LIM83.

46. Hill and Rowsome 2011, 211: ONE94.

47. Schofield 1998, 277, 283–4: VAL88.

48. Drummond-Murray and Thompson 2002, 123–4: BGH95.

49. Hekster and Zair 2008, 84; de Blois 2002, 210; Liebeschuetz 2007, 17–18; Woolf 2012, 191.

50. de Blois 2018; de Blois 1976, 6–7.

51. Bourne 2000, 12; Birley 2007a, 49.

52. K. Butcher 2015, 183.

53. Liebeschuetz 1979, 306; Bourne 2000, 69.

54. Harper 2015, 224; Harper 2017, 138; de Blois *et al. 2002*, xvi; Euseb. *Hist. eccl.* 7; SHA *Gall.* 5.5.

55. Esmonde Cleary 2013, 18 explores the problems involved in attempting to answer this question.

56. Birley 2007a, 48.

57. Frere 1999, 179–80: CIL 13.6780.

58. Birley 2007a, 48–9.

59. Bidwell and Hodgson 2009, 33–4.

60. Depopulation perhaps influenced the decision to settle Burgundians and Vandals in Britain in AD 278, in much the way that Sarmatians were settled here AD 175. Birley 2007a, 48; Zos. 1.68.3.

61. Zos. 1.37.3.

62. S. Johnson 1976, 6–7.
63. Eutr. 9.9; de Blois 2018; Birley 2007a, 50; Mairat 2014; Pearson 2005.

Chapter 26

1. Brigham 1990b, 105–6: BIG82; SWA81 IV and V.
2. C. Hill *et al.* 1980, 57–64; Barker *et al.* 2018: MM74; PET81; RKH06; CUS73; NFW74; SGA12; TEQ10; TOL79–84.
3. Blocks of carved Hassock and ragstone with rebates and Lewis holes reused in the wall at Sugar Quay had been stripped from a large Antonine building.
4. Brigham 1990b, 106; Sheldon and Tyers 1983, 358–60; Hillam and Morgan 1986, 83–4. These incorporate a long sapwood allowance. It is possible that the Baynard's Castle stretch was built before the rest of the wall.
5. Hillam 1990, 166: FRE78.
6. I am grateful to Sadie Watson for providing information in advance of publication.
7. RIB 2411.23: Collingwood and Wright 1990.
8. Milne 1985, 133–8: PDN82 Building 2.
9. Brigham 1990b, 130; Schofield 1998, 227; Williams 1991, 134: DGH86.
10. We cannot discount the possibility that works started before the fall of the Gallic Empire, although this seems improbable. It is likely that they were completed under Probus' administration.
11. Dey 2011, 110–16.
12. S. Johnson 1983, 74; Rambaldi 2009; Dey 2011, 125–30.
13. S. Johnson 1976; Pearson 2002; 56–66, 125–38. As in London, these defences can be separated into two main phases, one early in the third century and another towards the end of that century.
14. J. Johnson 1970.
15. Frere *et al.* 1982, 17; Magilton 2003, 162–5; Fulford 2015b, 59–60; Niblett and Thompson 2005, 73.
16. Gerrard 2013, 48.
17. S. Johnson 1983, 69; Esmonde Cleary 2013, 75.
18. Mason 2003, 164.
19. Omissi 2018, 72.
20. Symonds and Tomber 1991.
21. Lyne and Jefferies 1979; Davies *et al.* 1994, 97–8.
22. Nail 2008, 27.
23. Ridgeway 2009, 43.
24. Betts 2017a, 108; Unger 2009.
25. A. Brown *et al.* 2001; Smith *et al.* 2016, 183. A policy of increasing wine production in late third century Britain is implied by Probus' grant of permission to the Gauls, Spaniards and Britons to cultivate vineyards: SHA Probus, 18.8.
26. E.g. RIB 179 and 2066: Collingwood and Wright 1965; Birley 2005, 337.
27. Late third-century road repairs have been identified at LCT84 and SCS83. Few major street repairs took place after this date.

28. Bluer and Brigham 2006, 49–56: FCC95 Period 5 Phases 1- 2. Something similar might have taken place on the western side of the Southwark eyot, where CO87/CO88 Buildings 41–43 were built in the late third century: Hammer 2003, 84.
29. Marsden and West 1992; Symonds and Tomber 1991, 83.
30. Dunwoodie *et al.* 2015, 124: FER97; Hill and Rowsome 2011: LHY88.
31. LIM83.
32. McKenzie 2011, 17: TEA98; Pitt 2006a: POU05; Pitt 2014: EAE01.
33. E.g. C. Maloney 1990, 68–9: CHL84; Rowsome 1987: KNG85.
34. Merrifield 1965, 54: Site 331; Merrifield 1955: GM96.
35. Hammerson 1996, 155; Walton and Moorhead 2016, 841–2; D. Walker 1988, 306; Bourne 2000, 257, 266.
36. de Blois 2002, 217.
37. Brigham 1990a, 75–82; Brigham 1992, 93–5: LCT 84.
38. Bateman *et al.* 2008, 86: GAG87.
39. Ridgeway *et al.* 2013, 79: LTU03; SBK03; DKN11.
40. Hunt and Shepherd 2009: PCO06.
41. J. Pearce 2013; J. Pearce 2016, 351.
42. E.g. WES89; Swain and Roberts 2001.
43. Barber and Bowsher 2000, 5–7; McKenzie and Thomas 2020.
44. Ramm 1971, 188–91; Philpott 1991, 90–1; J. Pearce 2013; J. Pearce 2015, 148; Barber and Bowsher 2000, 9.
45. Mackinder 2000, 27: Burial 26.
46. Ridgeway *et al.* 2013; Barber and Bowsher 2000, 101–3; McKenzie and Thomas 2020, 64.
47. McKenzie and Thomas 2020.
48. Ridgeway *et al.* 2013, 110.
49. McKenzie and Thomas 2020.
50. J. Pearce 2015, 156; Gowland and Redfern 2010; Pitts 2016, 726–34; Pitts and Griffin 2012.
51. Redfern *et al.* 2016.
52. Ridgeway *et al.* 2013; Redfern *et al.* 2017.
53. Shaw *et al.* 2016; Barber and Bowsher 2000, Burial 374: MSL87.
54. Birley 2007, 48; Zos. 1.68.3.
55. Redfern *et al.* 2017, 12–14; Barber and Bowsher 2000, Burial 604: MNL88.

Chapter 27

1. Birley 2007a, 51; Birley 2005, 367; Zonaras 12.2.
2. Davenport 2019; Birley 2005, 371–93; B. Hoffmann 2013, 177; Aur. Vict. *Caes.* 39.20; *Pan. Lat.* 8.5; Eutr. 9.21.
3. Casey 1994, 59; Walton and Moorhead 2016.
4. Williams 1991; Williams 1993; Bradley and Butler 2008: PET81; SUN86; QUV01.
5. A third temple might have occupied the space between the two.
6. Grainge 2005, 154; Fulford and Tyers 1995, 1013.
7. Leone 2013, 34.

8. Hijmans 2009; Casey 1994, 68.
9. L. Lavan 2011, xliii.
10. Williams 1993, 37.
11. Above p. 266. Williams 1993, 86–7.
12. B. Hoffmann 2013, 179; *Pan. Lat.* 8.11–19; Eutr. 9.22.2; Aur. Vict. *Caes.* 39.22.
13. Casey 2010.
14. Riley and Gomme 1912, 17–22; Marsden 1994, 125–8; Mason 2003, 53–5.
15. Marsden 1994, 126, 176–7.
16. Omissi 2018, 97; *Pan. Lat.* 8.12.1.
17. *Pan. Lat.* 8.5; B. Hoffmann 2013, 180.
18. Reece 2002, 55–6.
19. Birley 2005, 406; Omissi 2018, 104–5; B. Hoffmann 2013, 187; *Pan. Lat.* 7.6.
20. Cloke and Toone 2015; Casey 1978; Birley 2005, 411.
21. E.g. Schofield 1998, 272: LDL88; Milne 1985, 139–41: PDN81 Building 6; Merrifield 1965, Site 331: GM96; Sheldon 1978, 39–40; Hingley 2018, 227–8; Cowan *et al.* 2009, 25, 86–7: CW83, Building 2, AB78, Building 17; Hammer 2003, 87–8: CO88/CO87, Building 45; Heard 1989: USA88/USB88: Drummond Murray and Thompson 2002, 146: MSA92; Neal and Cosh 2009: Mosaic 371.4.
22. Hill and Rowsome 2011, 214–17; Neal and Cosh 2009: Mosaic 370.80.
23. Dunwoodie *et al.* 2015, 128: FER97.
24. E.g. Bowden 2008, 276.
25. Cowan *et al.* 2009: 4STS82. A fourth-century basement at 20 Fenchurch Street may have been beneath another tower: FEU08 Building 48.
26. POU06 Building 11. These foundations might alternatively have supported a monumental gateway into the temple precinct around the amphitheatre.
27. RIB 4: Collingwood and Wright 1965; Shepherd 1998, 174–5.
28. Shepherd 1998, 84–7; Grimes 1968; Toynbee 1986.
29. Sauer 2003; Merrifield 1983, 211.
30. Henig 1998, 230.
31. Toynbee 1986, 42–52.
32. Merrifield 1977.
33. Neal and Cosh 2009, 400.
34. B. Hoffmann 2013, 188.
35. Birley 2005, 414; Lib. *Or.* 59.137–41. It is worth noting that London may have seen as many imperial visits in the first half of the fourth century as Rome itself: at four apiece.
36. RIB 2411.23: Collingwood and Wright 1990; Tomlin 2018a, 425–6.
37. A. Rogers 2011, 78–9: WIV88.
38. Marsden 1975, 73–9: GM25 Areas 5 and 6.
39. Cowan 1992, 53: 15SK80; Yule 2005, 85: WP83.
40. Fulford and Timby 2000, 577; White and Barker 1998, 73–74, 86; A. Rogers 2011, 78–9, 141; Mackreth 1987, 139.
41. Fulford 2008a.
42. P. S. Johnson 2012, 162.
43. Tyers and Vince 1983, 303–4.
44. Williams 1993, 52: PET81.
45. Swiętoń 2007; Esmonde Cleary 2013, 88.

46. Brigham 1990a, 79; M. Scott 2013, 44.

47. P. Brown 2012, 103.

48. Rossiter 2016. Ridgeway 2009, 54; Rielly 2008, 31: CO88; LLS02; DGT06.

49. Rhodes 1991.

50. Hammer 2003, 79–112: CO88/CO87.

51. Hingley 2018, 204–5: USA88; 8US74; 107BHS81; HIB79.

52. Hammerson 1978b; Gerrard 2011e, 558: SCC77.

53. Killock *et al.* 2015, 43, 195, 259; Hayward 2015, 185: LLS02.

54. Esmonde Cleary 2016, 142; Bowes 2010, 90–3.

55. Hassall 1996, 24; White 2007. The province of *Britannia Prima* was first mentioned in the Verona list compiled *c.* AD 312. Its location is uncertain.

56. Perring 2002, fig. 71 maps how distributions of wealthy late Roman villas, marked by 'schools' of mosaics, reproduce areas of political affiliation implied by distributions of late Iron Age coins. See Brindle 2017, 278 on different patterns of fourth-century coin loss between the south-east and south-west.

57. Black 1987, 35, Sites 84, 104 and 183; Meates 1979.

58. Smith *et al.* 2016, 18, 92.

59. Black 1987, 126–9.

60. Biddulph *et al.* 2012, 174; Germany 2003.

61. Douglas *et al.* 2011, 27.

62. D. Bird 2013.

63. Henig 2015; Coombe *et al.* 2015, no. 85.

64. Weever 1631, xxxi. We can provisionally identify nine early fourth-century suburban villas north of the river: St Martin-in-the-Fields, Thorney Island, St Bride's, St Andrew Holborn, Artillery Ground, Spital Square, Shadwell, Ratcliffe, and Lower Clapton.

65. C. Thomas 2004: SRP98; Coombe *et al.* 2015, No 86; RCHME 1928, 157; S. Watson 2018, 384: HRE16.

66. Montgomery *et al.* 2010, 217–19; Eckardt and Müldner 2016, 213; Cool 2016, 419; Brettell *et al.* 2015, 643; McKenzie and Thomas 2020, 39: Burial 90.

67. G. Brown 2011; Sheldon 1971, 42–7; Allen 2017, 90–1.

68. Ridgeway 2009, 39: DGT06.

69. Ivens and Deal 1977, 64; Laws 1976, 182; Crouch and Shanks 1984, 3.

70. Allen and Lodwick 2017, 174–5; Millett 1990, 143–51.

71. Lakin 1999, 337: SWY97/SNY97.

Chapter 28

1. RCHME 1928, 99–106; J. Maloney 1983, 105–11; J. Maloney 1980, 70–4; Marsden 1980, 170–3; Merrifield 1965, 320–5; Merrifield 1983, 228–35; Hingley 2018, 218–19; J. Maloney 1979, 297; Sankey and Stephenson 1991, 122: XWL79; CRT89; BLM87. The surviving bastions were numbered sequentially, east to west, by the Royal Commission survey of Roman London. Subsequent discoveries are inserted into the series, such that Bastion 2A is between Bastions 2 and 3.

2. Marsden 1980, 172–3; J. Maloney 1983, 111: GM55; LH74; Butler 2001, 51: MRL98; Rowsome 2014a, 5: LUD82.

3. Elton 1996.

4. RCHME 1928: Bastion 6. Marsden 1980, 172: GM55; J. Maloney 1979, 295–7, J. Maloney 1983, 105–8: DUK77.

5. Frey 2016; Blagg 1983; Hingley 2018, 205, 232–4.

6. Barker *et al.* 2018.

7. Bateman *et al.* 2008, 92: GAG87.

8. Wilmott 2008, 55.

9. Cowan 1992, 54–8: 15SK80.

10. As in sixth-century Catania where city notables sought the government's authority to remove stones from their ruined amphitheatre to repair the town walls: see Christie 2020, 335 drawing on Cassiod. *Var.* 3.49.

11. Merrifield 1965, 72; Lyon 2007, 47–52: KEW98.

12. Merrifield 1965, G8: GM5.

13. Harward *et al.* 2015, 66–8; Myers 2016, 292.

14. C. Hill *et al.* 1980, 57–64; Coombe *et al.* 2015, 74: BC75.

15. DHS75 Area E.

16. Sarantis 2013, 256; Intagliata *et al.* 2020; Rambaldi 2009; Crickmore 1984, 74–95.

17. Gerrard 2013, 47–9.

18. William Fitzstephen writing *c.* AD 1173 described towers along the riverside wall. The Lanthorn, Wakefield and Bell towers on the inner curtain wall of the Tower of London could stand over Roman bastions: Parnell 1985, 29.

19. Loseby 2000, 326.

20. Gerrard 2013, 47–8 summarizes the arguments.

21. Amm. Marc. 20.1.1. Corder 1955; Merrifield 1983, 235; Birley 2005, 425; Sarantis 2013, 265.

22. Casey 1983.

23. Birley 2005, 418; Frere 1999, 343.

24. B. Hoffmann 2013, 192; Amm. Marc. 27.8.1–6, 28.3.3.

25. Hammerson 1996, 156.

26. Amm. Marc. 28.3.1 'Augusta…quam veteres apellavere Lundinium'.

27. Kalafikis 2014; Collins and Weber 2015, 2–3; B. Hoffmann 2013, 198.

28. Esmonde Cleary 2020.

29. Rivet and Smith 1979, 216–25; Seeck 1876; Elton 2006, 201; Kulikowski 2000.

30. *Not. Dign. occ.* 11.37.

31. Hassall 2017, 220; Collins and Breeze 2014, 64; Bland *et al.* 2018, 125.

32. *Cod. Theod.* 7.8.5.

33. I am grateful to Andy Gardner for reminding me of London's importance to Britain's coastal frontier.

34. Barber and Bowsher 2000, 183–4, 305: MSL87 Burial 538; Collins 2017, 39–42; Shaw *et al.* 2016; J. Pearce 2013, 142; Cool 2016, 416.

35. Keller Type 6, drawing on dating by Pröttel 1988, cited by Collins 2017.

36. Parani 2007; P. Brown 2012, 27.

37. SUERC-67611. I am grateful to Rebecca Redfern for providing information ahead of publication and to Jim Stevenson and Lucy Allott for re-running results through Ox Cal 4.4 in 2020. This assemblage is the subject of ongoing research by Michael

Marshall. The accepted date-range for the style of Crossbow brooch may need review and the scientific dating further scrutinized.

38. E. Swift 2000, 211. Michael Marshall advises that whilst the Mansell Street burial wore the trappings of power, the most powerful had dress items in gold and silver.

39. Cowie and Blackmore 2008, 128; Hawkes and Dunning 1961, 62.

40. Milne 1985, 33, 133–41: PDN82 Buildings 5 and 6.

41. Dunwoodie *et al.* 2015, 129: FER97. For broadly contemporary occupation elsewhere in the walled area see Williams 1993, 56: PET 81; S. Butcher 1982, 105; Hill and Rowsome 2011, 217–20: ONE94, Building 64.

42. Gerrard 2009b: DGT06.

43. Hill and Rowsome 2011, 221–4; 383, 447: ONE94, Building 72.

44. Neal and Cosh 2009: Mosaic 370.76.

45. D.J. Smith 1969; Cosh 1992.

46. Neal and Cosh 2009, 437.

47. K. Burns forthcoming; Friedman 2000; Stoyanov 2000, 30; Athanassiadi and Frede 1999; Bowersock 1990; SHA *Sev. Alex.* 39.3; Guthrie 1966, 253–5; Perring 2003.

48. Killock *et al.* 2015, 263: LLS02.

49. Rielly 2015, 223.

50. Killock *et al.* 2015, 57.

51. Rebillard 2009, 57.

52. R. Wheeler 1930, 25; Merrifield 1965, 61–2; Hall and Shepherd 2008, 36; Tomlin 2019, 510: BBO10. The unpublished Brentford Chi-Rho grafitto was identified in 2016 by volunteers at the Museum of London Archaeological Archive when processing pottery excavated in 1970.

53. RIB 2406.1–10: Collingwood and Wright 1990; Hall 2014a; Petts 2003, 109; Douglas *et al.* 2011, 164.

54. Inconsistent spelling leaves the identification with Augusta uncertain. Birley 1979, 152; Thacker 2004.

55. Munier 1963, 15 cited by A. Rogers 2011, 33; Petts 2016, 66.

56. Cantino Wataghin *et al.* 1996, 29; Esmonde Cleary 2013, 152–153, 175; Esmonde Cleary 2016, 143.

57. The certain example is Chrysanthus who was *vicarius* of Britain at the close of the fourth century before becoming the Novatianist Bishop of Constantinople, a post previously held by his father, where he was responsible for establishing and enlarging the churches of this Christian sect. Socrates *Hist. eccl.* 7.12.1; Salway 1981, 407–8.

58. Sankey 1998; Gerrard 2011a; Schofield 1998, 295; Petts 2016, 62–5: PEP89.

59. Betts 2017b, 381; Unger 2009, 113.

60. Cantino Wataghin 1999, 156.

61. Bowls of type CAM306. Gerrard 2011a. Also Haynes 2008; G. Hunt 2010, 57.

62. P. Brown 2012, 242; Esmonde Cleary 2013, 180.

63. Loseby 2000, 327.

64. See Reece 1982 for a critique of attempts to explain archaeological evidence through reference to the barbarian conspiracy.

65. Mattingly 2006a, 236.

66. Brigham 1990b, 148–9.

67. Symonds and Tomber 1991; Rayner and Seeley 2008; P. Tyers 1996b, 192–5; Evans 2013.
68. Fulford and Hodder 1974.
69. Gerrard 2011d; Lyne 2016, 89.
70. There is no evidence for supplies of new building timber reaching London after *c.* AD 302–34, see p. 354.
71. Evans 2013.
72. Esmonde Cleary 2013, 321; Esmonde Cleary 2016, 139–40; Fulford and Bird 1975.

Chapter 29

1. Gerrard 2011c; A. Rogers 2011, 14–26; Gibbon 1776.
2. Carneiro *et al.* 2020.
3. Reece 1980; Reece 1992.
4. Esmonde Cleary 1989, 82–3; Perring 1991, 128.
5. Frere 1983, 223–6: House 27.2.
6. Higham 2014; Constantius *Vita Sancti Germani* 12–18, 25–7.
7. Neal 2003; Faulkner and Neal 2009; Frere and Witts 2011.
8. I. Tyers 2008a.
9. Gerrard 2011c: DGT06. For a wider trend towards timber architecture in late antiquity, see Esmonde Cleary 2016, 143.
10. Hammerson 1996, 164.
11. Gardner 2016, 495; Going 1992, 102–3; Millett 1990, 224–7.
12. Gerrard 2011c.
13. E.g. HL74; EAE01; BIS82.
14. Marsden 1980, 169: GM96.
15. Some may have been built over by the fourth century, as Hill and Rowsome 2011, 238, 447: KNG85 Roads 2 and 6.
16. G. Brown 2008, 87: LEK95.
17. Hill and Rowsome 2011, 365: ONE94, Road 1.
18. Hill and Rowsome 2011, 386–7.
19. Cowan *et al.* 2009, 33: 84BHS75, AB78; Ridgeway *et al.* 2019, 133–134, fig. 5.18: BVX09.
20. Drummond-Murray and Thompson 2002, 59: BGH95; Ridgeway *et al.* 2019, 174: BVK11.
21. Dennis 1978; Killock *et al.* 2015, 265: 1STS74; 4TST82.
22. Hammer 2003, 102–3: CO88/CO87.
23. Cowan 1992, 53–9: 15SK80.
24. Cowan 2003, 70–3: COSE84.
25. LBN08.
26. Cowan *et al.* 2009, 250–4: GHR82; Killock *et al.* 2015, 69–70: LLS02.
27. Bateman *et al.* 2008, 91–3: GAG87.
28. S. Watson 2006, 64–5: PNS01; Hill and Rowsome 2011, 248: ONE94; Howe 2002, 23: BAX95.
29. Galinié and Zadora-Rio 1996.

30. Cantino Wataghin *et al.* 1996, 33; Cantino Wataghin 1999, 152–8; Le Masne de Chermont 1987.

31. Leone 2007, 168–89.

32. Frankfurter 2006, 550; Esmonde Cleary 2013, 160–4; J. Pearce 2015, 145.

33. *Cod. Theod.* 16.10.4, 16.10.24.

34. TIY07. See also Ridgeway *et al.* 2013, 26–7, 115: LTU03.

35. Barber and Bowsher 2000, 305: Burial 557.

36. Gerrard 2009b; Gerrard 2011e, 552; Ridgeway 2009, 52–3: DGT06.

37. By way of example Rome's ritual underground shaft, the Mundus, was opened for offerings to the underworld on 24 August, 5 October, and 8 November: Warde Fowler 1912, 25; Rykwert 1976, 59; Woodward and Woodward 2004, 69–70. See also Fulford 2001.

38. Seeley and Wardle 2009; Hingley 2018: USA88 and 8US74.

39. Allen 2015, 181–2.

40. MoLA 2017: BZY10.

41. Hingley 2018, 231; Hammerson 1978b: SCC77; Hammer 2003, 113–15: CO87.

42. Killock *et al.* 2015, 66: LLS02.

43. D. Walsh 2020, 291.

44. Jerome *Ep.* 133.9; Birley 2005, 455; B. Hoffmann 2013, 198; Esmonde Cleary 2016, 135; Collins and Breeze 2014, 65–6.

45. Zos. 4.35; Sozom. *Hist. eccl.* 7.13; Birley 2005, 447–9; Halsall 2007, 196–8; Wijnendaele 2020.

46. RCHM 1928, 188. Coins carrying the mint-mark AVGOB and AVGPS are thought to refer to Augusta, although this is not universally accepted, see Tomlin 2006, 58–9 and Fuentes 1991, 333.

47. Gildas *De Excidio* 13.

48. Parnell 1985: TOL79-84.

49. RIB 2402.4: Collingwood and Wright 1990: Milles 1779; Painter 1981; Merrifield 1983, 241; Bland *et al.* 2018, 124.

50. Merrifield 1983, 226, 246.

51. PDN82, Building 6; GM111; S. Butcher 1982, see above p. 369.

52. C. Hill *et al.* 1980, 57–64: BC75.

Chapter 30

1. Marsden 1980, 180–1; Merrifield 1983, 247–55; Rowsome 1996; Symonds and Tomber 1991, no. 119: GM111.

2. B. Richardson 1986b, 129: NFW74.

3. Milne 1985, 33: PDN82; Shepherd 1998, 103: GM256.

4. Gerrard 2011c.

5. Faulkner 2004.

6. Esmonde Cleary 2016, 135.

7. Walton and Moorhead 2016, 844.

8. Gardner 2016, 495; Reece 2002, 62; Esmonde Cleary 2013, 348.

9. Esmonde Cleary 2013, 339.

10. Drinkwater 1998; Procop. *Vand.* 3.2.31, 37–8; Birley 2005, 463.
11. Zos. 6.5.2–6.1, 6.10.2; Gerrard 2016, 860–1.
12. E. Thompson 1983; Bartholemew 1982.
13. Esmonde Cleary 2016, 138–43; Loseby 2000, 336.
14. Douglas *et al.* 2011, 57–9; Lakin 2002, 24; Gerrard 2011b, 172: TOC02.
15. Gerrard 2011d, 68.
16. Sheldon 1971, 52.
17. RCHME 1928, 147.
18. Telfer 2010: SMD01. The intercept of the radiocarbon age with the calibrated result is AD 410.
19. Betts 2017a, 108.
20. Garcia 2010, 152–3; 210–12.
21. Esmonde Cleary 2013, 152–3.
22. Garcia 2010, 207.
23. Booth 2015, 336: PPL11.
24. Guest 2014.
25. Gerrard *et al.* 2019: BBO10.
26. Cowie 2008, 52; Sloane and Malcolm 2004, 20–3: JON89.
27. PLH97.
28. Cowie and Blackmore 2008, 19–21: WFG62; Butler 2005: HCO99/TCT99.
29. Ridgeway *et al.* 2013, 115: LTU03; TIY07.
30. Hammerson 1996, 164; Ridgeway *et al.* 2013, 50: BYQ98.
31. Cowie 2000, 177–8.
32. Gerrard 2011c, 190; Cowie 2008, 50; Cook 1969; Inker 2006, Type Bix: GM111.
33. Cowie 2008; Cowie and Blackmore 2008.
34. J. Morris 1973, 108.
35. Loseby 2000, 327–8.
36. Bowlt 2008; Castle 1975, 274; R. Wheeler 1935.
37. Bede *Ecclesiastical History* 1.29.
38. ASC *sub anno* 457.
39. Evison 1978, 270–1, fig. 2a; Bowsher *et al.* 2007, 300–1.
40. Gerrard 2016, 860–1.
41. A. Reynolds forthcoming.
42. Loseby 2000, 356; Naismith 2019, 14.
43. Haslam 2010.

Chapter 31

1. Following Tainter 1988, 148–52.
2. Ogilvie 2007; Zuiderhoek 2015, 10.
3. E.g. McAnany and Yoffee 2010, 10–11; Lindell 2013; Norris *et al.* 2008.
4. Summarized in Izdebski *et al.* 2018.
5. Hobson 2014, 19.

Bibliography

Ancient and medieval sources

Aelius Aristides, *Orations, Vol. 1*, ed. and trans. M. Trapp, Loeb Classical Library, Cambridge MA: Harvard University Press (2017).

Ammianus Marcellinus, *History, Vol. 1: Books 14–19*, trans. J.C. Rolfe, Loeb Classical Library, Cambridge MA: Harvard University Press (1950).

Appian, *Roman History, Vol. 4: The Civil Wars*, trans. H. White, Loeb Classical Library, Cambridge MA: Harvard University Press (1913).

ASC: *The Anglo-Saxon Chronicles*, trans. M. Swanton, London: Phoenix Press (2000).

Aurelius Victor, *Caesares*, trans. H.W. Bird, Liverpool: Liverpool University Press (1994).

Bede, Colgrave, B and Mynors, R.A.B., 1969, *Bede's Ecclesiastical History of the English people*, Oxford: Clarendon.

Caesar, *Alexandrian War. African War. Spanish War*, trans. A.G. Way, Loeb Classical Library, Cambridge MA: Harvard University Press (1955).

Caesar, *The Gallic War*, trans. C. Hammond, Oxford: Oxford University Press (1996).

Cassiodorus, *Variae*, trans. S.J.B. Barnish, Translated Texts for Historians 12, Liverpool: Liverpool University Press (1992).

Cicero, *'On the Republic' and 'On the Laws'*, trans. D. Fott, Ithaca NY: Cornell University Press (2014).

Cicero, 'Pro Sestio. In Vatinium', trans. R. Gardner. Loeb Classical Library. Cambridge MA: Harvard University Press (1958).

Codex Justinianus, *The Codex of Justinian: A New Annotated Translation*, trans. F.H. Blume, Cambridge: Cambridge University Press (2016).

Codex Theodosianus, *The Theodosian Code and Novels and Sirmondian Constitution*, trans. C. Pharr, New York: Greenwood (1952).

Constantius of Lyon: 'The Life of St Germanus of Auxerre', ed. and trans. T. Noble and T. Head, in *Soldiers of Christ: Saints Lives from Late Antiquity and the Early Middle Ages*, Philadelphia PA: Pennsylvania State University Press (1994), 75–106.

Digest, *The Digest of Justinian*, eds T. Mommsen with P. Krueger, trans. A. Watson, Philadelphia PA: University of Pennsylvania Press (1985).

Dio Cassius, *Roman Histories*, trans. E. Cary and H.B. Foster, Loeb Classical Library, Cambridge MA: Harvard University Press (1960–70).

Diodorus Siculus, *The Library of History, Vol. 3: Books 4.59–8*, trans. C.H. Oldfather, Loeb Classical Library: Cambridge MA: Harvard University Press (1939).

Eusebius, *Ecclesiastical History: Complete and Unabridged*, trans. C.F. Crusé, Peabody MA: Hendrickson (1998).

Eutropius, *Breviarium*, trans. H.W. Bird, Translated Texts for Historians 14, 128 Krakow Karmelicka 3, Liverpool: Liverpool University Press (1993).

Frag. Vat.: 'Fragmenta quae dicuntur Vaticana', in T. Mommsen (ed.), *Collectio librorum iuris anteiustiniani*, Vol III, Weidmann: Berlin (1890).

Fronto: *Correspondence, Vol. 1*, trans. C.R. Haines, Loeb Classical Library, Cambridge MA: Harvard University Press (1919).

Galen 'Avoiding Distress', trans. V. Nutton, in P.N. Singer. (ed.), *Galen. Psychological Writings: Avoiding Distress, Character Traits, The Diagnosis and Treatment of the*

Affections and Errors Peculiar to Each Person's Soul, The Capacities of the Soul Depend on the Mixtures of the Body, Cambridge Galen Translations, Cambridge: Cambridge University Press (2013), 43–106.

Galen 'My Own Books', ed. and trans. P.N. Singer, *Galen: Selected Works, translation with an introduction and notes*, Oxford: Oxford University Press (1997).

Geoffrey of Monmouth, *The History of the Kings of Britain: An Edition and Translation of De gestis Britonum (Historia regum Britanniae)*, translated by N. Wright (2007), Woodbridge: Boydell Press.

Gildas, 'The Ruins of Britain', *De Excidio*, ed. and trans. M. Winterbottom, Chichester: Phillimore (1978).

Herodian, *Roman History*, trans. C.R. Whittaker, Loeb Classical Library, Cambridge MA: Harvard University Press (1969).

Horace, 'Carmen Saeculare', *Odes and Epodes*, trans. N. Rudd, Loeb Classical Library, Cambridge MA: Harvard University Press (2004).

Irenaeus, 'Against Heresies', *Five Books of S. Irenaeus, Against the Heresies*, trans. J. Keble, London: J Parker (1872).

Jerome, *A Translation of Jerome's Chronicon with Historical Commentary*, ed. and trans. M.D. Donalson, Lewiston: Mellen University Press (1996).

Jerome, *Letters and Select Works*, ed. P. Schaaf and H. Wace, trans. W.H. Freemantle, A Select Library of Nicene and Post-Nicene Fathers of the Christian Church, Grand Rapids MI: Eerdmans (1892).

Josephus, *The Jewish War*, trans. H. St. J. Thackeray, Loeb Classical Library: Cambridge MA: Harvard University Press (1927–1928).

Juvenal, Persius. *Juvenal and Persius*, ed. and trans. S.M. Braund. Loeb Classical Library, Cambridge, MA: Harvard University Press (2004).

Libanius, 'Oratio LIX', trans. M.H. Dodgeon in S. Lieu and D. Montserrat (eds), *From Constantine to Julian: Pagan and Byzantine Views: a source history*, London: Routledge (1996), 164–209.

Livy, *The History of Rome*, Vols 2 and 3, trans. W.M. Roberts, London: Everyman's Library (1905).

Lucan, *The Civil Wars (Pharsalia)*, trans. J.D. Duff, Loeb Classical Library, Cambridge MA: Harvard University Press (1928).

Lucian, *How to Write History. The Dipsads. Saturnalia. Herodotus or Aetion. Zeuxis or Antiochus. A Slip of the Tongue in Greeting. Apology for the 'Salaried Posts in Great Houses.' Harmonides. A Conversation with Hesiod. The Scythian or The Consul. Hermotimus or Concerning the Sects. To One Who Said 'You're a Prometheus in Words.' The Ship or The Wishes*, trans. K. Kilburn, Loeb Classical Library 430, Cambridge MA: Harvard University Press (1959).

Notitia Dignitatum, ed. O. Seek, Berlin: Weidmann (1876).

Origen, *Origen of Alexandria: Exegetical Works on Ezekiel. The Fourteen Homilies and the Greek fragments of the Homilies, Commentaries and Scholia*, ed. R. Pearse, trans. M. Hooker, Ancient Texts in Translation, 2, Ipswich: Chieftain Publishing (2014).

Orosius, *Seven Books of History against the Pagans*, ed. and trans. A.T. Fear, Translated Texts for Historians, Liverpool: Liverpool University Press (2010).

P. Dura-Europos, *The Excavations at Dura-Europos, Final Report V. Part 1: The Parchments and Papyri* by C.B. Welles. R.O. Fink, J.F. Gilliam, and W.B. Henning, New Haven: Yale University Press (1959).

Panegyrici Latini, C.E.V. Nixon, Barbara Saylor Rodgers, R.A.B. Mynors, *In Praise of Later Roman Emperors: The Panegyrici Latini: Introduction, Translation, and Historical commentary, with the Latin text of R.A.B. Mynors*, The Transformation of the Classical Heritage 21, Berkeley: University of California Press (1994).

Plato, *Euthyphro. Apology. Crito. Phaedo*, ed. and trans. C. Emlyn-Jones and W.Preddy, Loeb Classical Library, Cambridge, MA: Harvard University Press (2017).

Pliny: *Letters*, trans. B. Radice, Loeb Classical Library, Cambridge MA: Harvard University Press (1989).

Plutarch, 'Crassus, Cicero and Antony', *Lives*, Vols 7 and 9, trans. B. Perrin, Loeb Cambridge MA: Harvard University Press (1919–20).

Porphyry, *De Antro Nympharum: On the Cave of the Nymphs in the Thirteenth Book of the Odyssey from the Greek of Porphyry*, trans. T. Taylor, London: J.M. Watkins (1917).

Procopius. *History of the Wars, Vol. 2: Books 3–4. (Vandalic War)*, trans. H.B. Dewing. Loeb Classical Library 81. Cambridge MA: Harvard University Press (1916).

Ptolemy, *Geographia*, trans. E.L. Stevenson. Mineola NY: Dover (1991).

Servius, Ad Aen. *Commentary on the Aeneid of Virgil*, http://www.perseus.tufts.edu/hopper/text?doc=Perseus%3atext%3a1999.02.0053.

Scriptores Historiae Augustae: *Historia Augusta, Vol.1: Hadrian. Aelius. Antoninus Pius. Marcus Aurelius. L. Verus. Avidius Cassius. Commodus. Pertinax. Didius Julianus. Septimius Severus. Pescennius Niger. Clodius Albinus*, trans. D. Magie, Loeb Classical Library, Cambridge MA: Harvard University Press (1921).

Scriptores Historiae Augustae: *Historia Augusta, Vol. 2: Caracalla. Geta. Opellius Macrinus. Diadumenianus. Elagabalus. Severus Alexander. The Two Maximini. The Three Gordians. Maximus and Balbinus*, trans. D. Magie, Loeb Classical Library, Cambridge MA: Harvard University Press (1924).

Scriptores Historiae Augustae: *Historia Augusta, Vol. 3: The Two Valerians. The Two Gallieni. The Thirty Pretenders. The Deified Claudius. The Deified Aurelian. Tacitus. Probus. Firmus, Saturninus, Proculus and Bonosus. Carus, Carinus and Numerian*, trans. D. Magie, Loeb Classical Library, Cambridge MA: Harvard University Press (1932).

Socrates, *The Ecclesiastical History of Socrates Scholasticus*, trans. A.C. Zenos, London: Aeterna Press (2016).

Sozomenus, *The Ecclesiastical History of Sozomen: Comprising a History of the Church from A.D. 324 to A.D. 440*, trans. E. Walford, London: H.G. Bohn (1855).

Strabo, *Geography, Vol. 2: Books 3–5*, trans. H.L. Jones, Loeb Classical Library, London: Heinemann (1923).

Suetonius, *The Lives of the Twelve Caesars*, trans. J.C. Rolfe, Loeb Classical Library, Cambridge MA: Heinemann (1914).

Tab. Vindol: *The Vindolanda Writing-Tablets (Tabulae Vindolandenses II)*, A.K. Bowman and J.D. Thomas (eds), London: British Museum Press (1994).

Tacitus, *Agricola and the Germania*, trans. H. Mattingly, rev. S. Handford, London: Penguin (2003).

Tacitus, *Annals*, ed. and trans. J. Jackson. Loeb Classical Library, Cambridge MA: Harvard University Press (1979–86).

Tacitus, *The Histories*, trans. W.H. Fyfe, rev. D.S. Lenen, Oxford: Oxford University Press (1997).

Tertullian, *Ante-Nicene Christian Library: Vol XVIII. The Writings of Tertullian, Vol III: with the extant works of Victorinus and Commodianus*, trans. S. Thelwall, Edinburgh: T & T Clark (1870).

Twelve Tablets: *The Library of Original Sources. Vol. 3: The Roman World*, trans. O.J. Thatcher, Milwaukee: University Research Extension Co. (1901).

Valerius Maximus: *Memorable Doings and Sayings, Vol. 2: Books 6–9*, trans. D.R. Shackleton Bailey, Loeb Classical Library, Cambridge MA: Harvard University Press (2000).

Vegetius: *Epitome of Military Science*, trans. N.P. Milner, Liverpool: University of Liverpool Press (1996).

Vitruvius: *De Architectura*, trans. F. Granger, Loeb Classical Library, Cambridge MA: Harvard University Press (1931).

Zonaras: *The History of Zonaras: from Alexander Severus to the death of Theodosius the Great*, trans. T.M. Banchich and E.N. Lane, London: Routledge (2009).

Zosimus, *A New History*, trans. R.T. Ridley, Byzantina Australiensia 2, Sydney: University of Sydney (1982).

Modern Sources

Abdy, R., 2002, *Romano-British Coin Hoards*, Princes Risborough: Shire.

Ackroyd, P., 2000, *London: The Biography*, London: Chatto & Windus.

Adams, C., 2012, 'Transport', in W. Scheidel (ed.), *The Cambridge Companion to the Roman Economy*, Cambridge: Cambridge University Press, 218–40.

Adams, C., 2017, 'Nile River Transport under the Romans', in A. Bowman and A. Wilson (eds), *Trade, Commerce and the State in the Roman World*, Oxford: Oxford University Press, 175–210.

Albarella, U., Johnstone, C. and Vickers, K., 2008, 'The Development of Animal Husbandry from the Late Iron Age to the End of the Roman Period: A Case Study from South-east Britain', *Journal of Archaeological Science* 35.7, 1828–48.

Allason-Jones, L., 2011, 'Recreation', in L. Allason-Jones (ed.), *Artefacts in Roman Britain: Their Purpose and Use*, Cambridge: Cambridge University Press, 219–42.

Allason-Jones, L., 2016, 'Roman Military Culture', in M. Millett, L. Revell, and A. Moore (eds), *The Oxford Handbook of Roman Britain*, Oxford: Oxford University Press, 464–78.

Allason-Jones, L. and Dungworth, D., 1997, 'Metalworking on Hadrian's Wall', in W. Groenman-van Waateringe, B.L. van Beek, W.J.H. Willems, and S.L. Wynia (eds), *Roman Frontier Studies 1995: Proceedings of the XVIth International Congress of Roman Frontier Studies*, Oxford: Oxbow Books, 317–21.

Allen, J.R.L. and Fulford, M., 1996, 'The Distribution of South-East Dorset Black Burnished Category 1 Pottery in South-West Britain', *Britannia* 27, 223–81.

Allen, J.R.L. and Fulford, M., 1999, 'Fort Building and Military Supply along Britain's Eastern Channel and North Sea Coasts: The Later Second and Third Centuries', *Britannia* 30, 163–84.

Allen, M., 2015, 'Chasing Sylvia's Stag: Placing Deer in the Countryside of Roman Britain', in K. Baker, R. Carden, and R. Madgwick (eds), *Deer and People*, Oxford: Windgather, 174–86.

Allen, M., 2017, 'Pastoral Farming', in M. Allen, L. Lodwick, T. Brindle, M. Fulford, and A. Smith (eds), *New Visions of the Countryside of Roman Britain Vol. 2: The Rural Economy of Roman Britain*, Britannia Monograph 30, London: Society for the Promotion of Roman Studies, 85–141.

Allen, M., 2018, 'The Social Context of Animals and Exploitation of Wild Resources', in A. Smith, M. Allen, T. Brindle, M. Fulford, L. Lodwick, and A. Rohnburger, *New Visions of the Countryside of Roman Britain Vol. 3: Life and Death in the Countryside of Roman Britain*, Britannia Monograph 31, London: Society for the Promotion of Roman Studies, 78–119.

Allen, M. and Lodwick, L., 2017, 'Agricultural Strategies in Roman Britain', in M. Allen, L. Lodwick, T. Brindle, M. Fulford, and A. Smith (eds), *New Visions of the Countryside of*

Roman Britain, Vol. 2: The Rural Economy of Roman Britain, Britannia Monograph 30, London: Society for the Promotion of Roman Studies, 142–77.

Amicone, S. and Quinn, P.S., 2015, 'Verulamium Region White Ware Production at the Roman Kiln Site of Brockley Hill, Middlesex: A Compositional and Technological Reassessment', *Journal of Roman Pottery Studies* 16, 1–22.

Ando, C., 2000, *Imperial Ideology and Provincial Loyalty in the Roman Empire*, Berkeley CA: University of California Press.

Andreau, J., 2002, 'Twenty Years after Moses I. Finley's *The Ancient Economy*', in W. Scheidel and S. von Reden (eds), *The Ancient Economy*, Edinburgh: Edinburgh University Press, 33–49.

Andrews, C., 2012, *Roman Seal-Boxes in Britain*, BAR British Series 567, Oxford: Archaeopress.

Andrews, P., 2008, 'Springhead, Kent—Old Temples and New Discoveries', in D. Rudling (ed.), *Ritual Landscapes of Roman South-East Britain*, Oxford and Great Dunham: Heritage Marketing and Publications, 45–62.

Andrews, P., Biddulph, E., Hardy, A., and Brown, R., 2011, *Settling the Ebbsfleet Valley: High Speed 1 Excavations at Springhead and Northfleet, Kent, Vol. 1: The Sites*, Salisbury: Oxford and Wessex Archaeology.

Armit, I., 2012, *Headhunting and the Body in Iron Age Europe*, Cambridge: Cambridge University Press.

Arnold, B., 2012, 'Gender, Temporalities, and Periodization in Early Iron Age West Central Europe', *Social Science History* 36.1, 85–112.

Arnold, K., 2006, *Cabinets for the Curious: Looking Back at Early English Museums*, Aldershot: Ashgate.

Arthur, P., 1977, 'Eggs and Pomegranates as an Example of Symbolism in Roman Britain', in J.M.C. Toynbee, J. Munby, and M. Henig (eds), *Roman Life and Art in Britain*, BAR British Series 41, Oxford: Archaeopress, 367–72.

Ash, R., 1997, 'Severed Heads: Individual Portraits and Irrational Forces in Plutarch's Galba and Otho', in J.M. Mossman (ed.), *Plutarch and His Intellectual World: Essays on Plutarch*, London: Duckworth, 189–214.

Atkinson, M. and Preston, S., 2015, *Heybridge, a Late Iron Age and Roman Settlement: Excavations at Elms Farm 1993–5 Vol. 1*, East Anglian Archaeology 154, Chelmsford: Essex County Council.

Askew, P., 2007, 'Streams in the City', *London Archaeologist* 11.10, 255–59.

Athanassiadi, P. and Frede, M., 1999, *Pagan Monotheism in Late Antiquity*, Oxford: Clarendon Press.

Bacon, F., 1876, *The Advancement of Learning*, Oxford: Clarendon Press.

Bagnall, R.S., 2002, 'The Effects of Plague: Model and Evidence', *Journal of Roman Archaeology* 15, 114–20.

Baker, J. and Brookes, S., 2013, *Beyond the Burghal Hidage: Anglo-Saxon Civil Defence in the Viking Age*, Leiden: Brill.

Bakker, J.T., 1994, *Living and Working with the Gods: Studies of Evidence for Private Religion and Its Material Environment in the City of Ostia (100–500 AD)*, Amsterdam: J.C. Gieben.

Bang, P.F., 2008, *The Roman Bazaar: A Comparative Study of Trade and Markets in a Tributary Empire*, Cambridge: Cambridge University Press.

Bang, P.F., 2009, 'Commanding and Consuming the World: Empire, Tribute and Trade in Roman and Chinese History', in W. Scheidel (ed.), *Rome and China: Comparative Perspectives on Ancient World Empires*, Oxford: Oxford University Press, 100–20.

Bang, P.F., 2012, 'Predation', in W. Scheidel (ed.), *The Cambridge Companion to the Roman Economy*, Cambridge: Cambridge University Press, 197–217.

Barber, B. and Bowsher, D., 2000, *The Eastern Cemetery of Roman London*, MoLAS Monograph 4, London: Museum of London Archaeology Service.

Barber, B. and Hall, J., 2000, 'Digging Up the People of Roman London: Interpreting Evidence from Roman London's Cemeteries', in I. Haynes, H. Sheldon, and L. Hannigan (eds), *London Underground: The Archaeology of a City*, Oxford: Oxbow Books, 102–20.

Barker, P., 1977, *Techniques of Archaeological Excavation*, New York NY: Universe Books.

Barker, S.J., Coombe, P., and Perna, S., 2018, 'Re-use of Roman Stone in London City-walls', in C. Coquelet, G. Creemers, R. Dreesen, and E. Goemaere (eds), *Roman Ornamental Stones in North-Western Europe. Natural resources, Manufacturing, Supply, Life and After-life*, Études et Documents, Archeologie 38, Namur: Agence Wallonne du Patrimoine, 327–48.

Barley, N., 1995, *Dancing on the Grave: Encounters with Death*, London: John Murray.

Bartholemew, P., 1982, 'Fifth-century Facts', *Britannia* 13, 261–70.

Bateman, N., 1986, 'Bridgehead Revisited', *London Archaeologist* 5.9, 233–41.

Bateman, N., 1998, 'Public Buildings in Roman London: Some Contrasts', in B. Watson (ed.), *Roman London: Recent Archaeological Work*, JRA Supplementary Series 24, Portsmouth RI: Journal of Roman Archaeology, 47–57.

Bateman, N., 2009, 'What's the Point of London's Amphitheatre?—A Clue from Diana', in T. Wilmott (ed.), *Roman Amphitheatres and Spectacula: A 21st -century Perspective: Papers from an International Conference Held at Chester 16th–18th February 2007*, BAR International Series 1946, Oxford: Archaeopress, 157–63.

Bateman, N., Cowan, C., and Wroe-Brown, R., 2008, *London's Roman Amphitheatre: Guildhall Yard, City of London*, MoLAS Monograph 35, London: Museum of London Archaeology Service.

Bauman, R.A., 1996, *Crime and Punishment in Ancient Rome*, London & New York: Routledge.

Bayard, D. and Massy, J-L., 1983, *Amiens romain: Samarobriva Ambianorum*, Revue archéologique de Picardie, Amiens: Heilly.

Bayley, J., 1985, 'Human Bone', in G. Parnell, 'The Roman and Medieval Defences and the Later Development of the Inmost Ward, Tower of London: Excavations 1955–77', *Transactions of the London and Middlesex Archaeological Society* 36, 51.

Bayley, J., Croxford, B., Henig, M., and Watson, B., 2009, 'A Gilt-bronze Arm from London', *Britannia* 40, 151–62.

Bayley, J. and Shepherd, J., 1985, 'The Glass-working Waste', in G. Parnell, 'The Roman and Medieval Defences and the Later Development of The Inmost Ward, Tower of London: Excavations 1955–77', *Transactions of the London and Middlesex Archaeological Society* 36, 72–3.

Beasley, M., 2006, 'Roman Boundaries, Roads and Ritual. Excavations at the Old Sorting Office, Swan Street, Southwark', *Transactions of the London and Middlesex Archaeological Society* 57, 23–68.

Bell, J.A., 1994, *Reconstructing Prehistory. Scientific Method in Archaeology*, Philadelphia PA: Temple University Press.

Benfield, S. and Garrod, S., 1992, 'Two Recently-discovered Roman Buildings at Colchester', *Essex Archaeology and History* 14, 25–38.

Bentley, D., 1984, 'A Recently Identified Valley in the City', *London Archaeologist* 5.1, 13–16.

Bentley, D., 1987, 'The Western Stream Reconsidered: An Enigma in the Landscape', *London Archaeologist* 5.12, 328–34.

Bentley, D. and Pritchard, F.A., 1982, 'The Roman Cemetery at St. Bartholomew's Hospital', *Transactions of the London and Middlesex Archaeological Society* 33, 134–72.

Beresford, J., 2013, *The Ancient Sailing Season*, Leiden: Brill.

Bernard, S.G., 2016, 'Workers in the Roman Imperial Building Industry', in K. Verboven and C. Laes (eds), *Work, Labour and Professions in the Roman World*, Leiden: Brill, 62–86.

Betts, I.M., 1995, 'Procuratorial Tile Stamps from London', *Britannia* 26, 207–29.

Betts, I.M., 2003, 'Stone and Ceramic Building Materials', in C. Cowan, *Urban Development in north-west Roman Southwark: Excavations 1974–90*, MoLAS Monograph 16, London: Museum of London Archaeology, 105–19.

Betts, I.M., 2015, 'Building Materials', in S. Watson, *Urban Development in the North-west of Londinium: Excavations at 120–122 Cheapside to 14–18 Gresham Street, City of London, 2005–7*, MoLAS Study Series 32, London: Museum of London Archaeology, 67–70.

Betts, I.M., 2016, 'Building Materials', in L. Dunwoodie, C. Harward, and K. Pitt, *An Early Roman Fort and Urban Development on Londinium's Eastern Hill. Excavations at Plantation Place, City of London, 1997–2003*, MoLAS Monograph 65, London: Museum of London Archaeology, 170–81.

Betts, I.M., 2017a, 'Ceramic Building Material: Production, Supply and Use in Roman London', in J. DeLaine, S. Camporeale, and A. Pizzo (eds), *Arqueologia de la Construccion V: Man-made Materials, Engineering and Infrastructure*, Mérida: Consejo Superior de Investigaciones Cientificas, 99–110.

Betts, I.M., 2017b, 'The Supply of Tile to Roman London', in D. Bird (ed.), *Agriculture and Industry in South-Eastern Roman Britain*, Oxford: Oxbow Books, 368–83.

Betts, I.M. and Foot, R., 1994, 'A Newly Identified Late Roman Tile Group from Southern England', *Britannia* 25, 21–34.

Betts, I.M. and Telfer, A., 2018, 'Finches, Flowers and Fruit: Painted Wall Plaster from 2nd-century Buildings at 8–13 Lime Street, London, EC3', *Transactions of the London and Middlesex Archaeological Society* 69, 27–48.

Bickleman, S., 2016, 'Brentford's Roman Roadside Settlement: Excavations at Lion Gate, Syon Park', *London Archaeologist* 14.9, 241–44.

Biddle, M., Hudson, D. and Heighway, C., 1973, *The Future of London's Past: A Survey of the Archaeological Implications of Planning and Development in the Nation's Capital*, Rescue publication 4, London: Rescue.

Biddulph, E., 2012, 'Made in Dagenham: Burial and Pottery Production in the Iron Age and Roman Periods', *London Archaeologist* 13.6, 143–48.

Biddulph, E., 2017, 'The Roman Salt Industry in South-Eastern Britain', in D. Bird (ed.), *Agriculture and Industry in South-Eastern Roman Britain*, Oxford: Oxbow Books, 210–35.

Biddulph, E., Rielly, K., and Ridgeway, V., 2019, 'Evidence for Ritual Activity and Structured Deposition', in V. Ridgeway, J. Taylor, and E. Biddulph, *A Bath House, Settlement and Industry on Roman Southwark's North Island: Excavations along the route of Thameslink Borough Viaduct and at London Bridge Station*, Thameslink Monograph Series 1, London: Oxford Archaeology and Pre-Construct Archaeology, 207–14.

Biddulph, E., Stafford, E., Foreman, S., Stansbie, D., and Nicholson, R.A., 2012, *London Gateway: Iron Age and Roman Salt Making in the Thames Estuary, Excavation at Stanford Wharf Nature Reserve, Essex*, OA Monograph 18, Oxford: Oxford Archaeology.

Bidwell, P., 2009, 'The Earliest Occurrences of Baths at Auxiliary Forts', in W.S. Hanson (ed.), *The Army and Frontiers of Rome: Papers Offered to David J. Breeze on the Occasion of his Sixty-fifth Birthday and Retirement from Historic Scotland*, JRA Supplementary Series 74, Portsmouth RI: Journal of Roman Archaeology, 55–62.

Bidwell, P., 2017, 'Rural Settlement and the Roman Army in the North: External Supply and Regional Self-sufficiency', in M. Allen, L. Lodwick, T. Brindle, M. Fulford, and

A. Smith (eds), *New Visions of the Countryside of Roman Britain Vol. 2: The rural economy of Roman Britain*, Britannia Monograph 30, London: Society for the Promotion of Roman Studies, 290–305.

Bidwell, P. and Hodgson, N., 2009, *The Roman Army in Northern England*, South Shields: Arbeia Society.

Birbeck, V. and Schuster, J., 2009, *Living and Working in Roman and Later London: Excavations at 60–63 Fenchurch Street*, Wessex Archaeology Report 25, Salisbury: Wessex Archaeology.

Birchall, A., 1965, 'The Aylesford-Swarling Culture: The Problem of the Belgae Reconsidered', *Proceedings of the Prehistoric Society* 31, 241–367.

Bird, D., 1996, 'The London Region in the Roman Period', in J. Bird, M. Hassall, and H. Sheldon (eds), *Interpreting Roman London. Papers in Memory of Hugh Chapman*, Oxbow Monograph 58, Oxford: Oxbow Books, 217–32.

Bird, D., 2002, 'Roads and Temples: Stane Street at Ewell', *London Archaeologist* 10.2, 41–5.

Bird, D., 2004, *Roman Surrey*, Tempus: Stroud.

Bird, D., 2013, 'New Tales of Old London: The Lost Roman Port, Shadwell, and Other Stories', *London Archaeologist* 13.10, 271–5.

Bird, D., 2017, 'The Countryside of the South-east in the Roman Period', in D. Bird (ed.), *Agriculture and Industry in South-Eastern Roman Britain*, Oxford: Oxbow Books, 35–54.

Bird, J., 1996, 'Frogs from the Walbrook: A Cult Pot and its Attribution', in J. Bird, M. Hassall, and H. Sheldon (eds), *Interpreting Roman London. Papers in Memory of Hugh Chapman*, Oxbow Monograph 58, Oxford: Oxbow Books, 119–27.

Bird, J., 2008, 'A Samian Bowl by Crucuro and the Cult of Hercules in London', in J. Clark, J. Cotton, J. Hall, R. Sherris, and H. Swain (eds), *Londinium and Beyond: Essays on Roman London and its Hinterland for Harvey Sheldon*, CBA Research Report 156, London: Council for British Archaeology, 134–41.

Bird, J., 2011, 'The Samian', in A. Douglas, J. Gerrard, and B. Sudds, *A Roman Settlement and Bath House at Shadwell: Excavations at Tobacco Dock and Babe Ruth's Restaurant, The Highway, London*, London: PCA Monograph 12, 71–4.

Bird, J. and Graham, A.H., 1978, 'Gazetteer of Roman Sites in Southwark', in J. Bird, A.H. Graham, H. Sheldon, and P. Townsend (eds), *Southwark Excavations 1972–74*, LAMAS and SAS Joint Publication 1, London: London and Middlesex Archaeological Society and Surrey Archaeological Society, 517–26.

Birley, A.R., 1979, *The People of Roman Britain*, London: Batsford.

Birley, A.R., 1987, *Marcus Aurelius: a Biography*, London: Batsford.

Birley, A.R., 1997, *Hadrian: The Restless Emperor*, London: Routledge.

Birley, A.R., 1998, 'A New Tombstone from Vindolanda', *Britannia* 29, 299–306.

Birley, A.R., 2002, *Garrison Life at Vindolanda: A Band of Brothers*, Stroud: Tempus.

Birley, A.R., 2005, *The Roman Government of Britain*, Oxford: Oxford University Press.

Birley, A.R., 2007a, 'Britain during the Third Century Crisis', in O. Hekster, G. de Kleijn, and D. Slootjes (eds), *Crisis and the Roman Empire. Proceedings of the Seventh Workshop of the International Network Impact of Empire (Nijmegen, June 20–24, 2006)*, Leiden: Brill, 45–56.

Birley, A.R., 2007b, 'The Frontier Zone in Britain: Hadrian to Caracalla', in L. de Blois and E. Lo Cascio (eds), *The Impact of the Roman Army (200 BC–AD 476): Economic, Social, Political, Religious and Cultural Aspects*, Leiden: Brill, 355–70.

Bishop, M.C., 1983, 'The Camomile Street Soldier Reconsidered', *Transactions of the London and Middlesex Archaeological Society* 34, 31–48.

Bishop, M.C, and Coulston, J.C.N., 2006, *Roman Military Equipment: From the Punic Wars to the Fall of Rome* (2nd edn.), Oxford: Oxbow Books.

Bispham, E., 2008, 'Religions', in E. Bispham (ed.), *Roman Europe: The Short Oxford History of Europe*, Oxford: Oxford University Press, 203–33.

Black, E.W., 1987, *The Roman Villas of South East England*, BAR British Series 171, Oxford: Archaeopress.

Blagg, T.F.C., 1980, 'The Sculptured Stones', in C. Hill, M. Millet, and T.F.C. Blagg (eds), *The Roman Riverside Wall and Monumental Archway in London. Excavations at Baynards Castle, Upper Thames Street, London, 1974–76*, LAMAS Special Paper 3, London: London and Middlesex Archaeological Society, 124–93.

Blagg, T.F.C., 1983, 'The Reuse of Monumental Masonry in Late Roman Defensive Walls', in J. Maloney and B. Hobley (eds), *Roman Urban Defences in the West*, CBA Research Report 51, London: Council for British Archaeology, 130–35.

Blagg, T.F.C., 1984, 'An Examination of the Connexions between Military and Civilian Architecture', in T.F.C. Blagg and A.C. King (eds), *Military and Civilian in Roman Britain: Cultural Relationships in a Frontier Province*, BAR British Series 136, Oxford: Archaeopress, 249–64.

Blagg, T.F.C., 1990, 'Architectural Munificence in Roman Britain: The Evidence of the Inscriptions', *Britannia*, 21, 13–31.

Blagg, T.F.C., 2000, 'Sculptures and Architectural Fragments', in A. Mackinder (ed.), *A Romano-British Cemetery on Watling Street: Excavations at 165 Great Dover* Street, *Southwark, London*, MoLAS Archaeology Studies Series 4, London: Museum of London Archaeology Service, 61–3.

Blair, I., 1983, 'Foster Lane—the Finding of the Foster Lane Glass', *Popular Archaeology* 5.4, 23–7.

Blair, I., 2005, 'Roman and Medieval Buildings, an Assemblage of Rare 18th-century Glass, and Other Finds from 15–17 King Street, London EC2', *London Archaeologist* 10.12, 313–22.

Blair, I., 2010, 'The Walbrook. St Swithin's House, Walbrook House and Granite House, London EC4, City of London', unpub. MoLAS Post-excavation Assessment.

Blair, I. and Sankey, D., 2007, *A Roman Drainage Culvert, Great Fire Destruction Debris and Other Evidence from Hillside Sites North-east of London Bridge: Excavations at Monument House and 13–21 Eastcheap, City of London*, MoLAS Archaeology Study 17, London: Museum of London Archaeology.

Blair, I., Spain, R., Swift, D., Taylor, T., and Goodburn, D., 2006, 'Wells and Bucket-chains: Unforeseen Elements of Water Supply in Early Roman London', *Britannia* 37, 1–52.

Bland, R., Chadwick, A., Ghey, E., Haselgrove, C., and Mattingly, D., 2018, *Iron Age and Roman Coin Hoards in Britain*, Oxford: Oxbow.

Blázquez, J.M., 1992, 'The Latest Work on the Export of Baetican Olive Oil to Rome and the Army', in *Greece & Rome* 39.2, 173–88.

Bluer, R. and Brigham, T., 2006, *Roman and Later Development East of the Forum and Cornhill: Excavations at Lloyd's Register, 71 Fenchurch Street, City of London*, MoLAS Monograph 30, London: Museum of London Archaeology.

Blurton, T.R., 1977, 'Excavations at Angel Court, Walbrook, 1974', *Transactions of the London and Middlesex Archaeological Society* 28, 14–100.

Blyth, D., 1997, 'The Ever-moving Soul in Plato's "Phaedrus"', *American Journal of Philology* 118.2, 185–217.

Boatwright, M.T., 2000, *Hadrian and the Cities of the Roman Empire*, Princeton: Princeton University Press.

Boddington, A., 1979, 'Excavations at 48–50 Cannon Street, City of London, 1975', *Transactions of the London and Middlesex Archaeological Society* 30, 1–38.

Boddington, A. and Marsden, P., 1987, '160–162 Fenchurch Street, 1976', in P. Marsden (ed.), *The Roman Forum in London: Discoveries before 1985*, London: HMSO, 92–100.

Booth, P., 2007, 'Roman Britain in 2006: Greater London', *Britannia* 38, 286–94.

Booth, P., 2008, 'Roman Britain in 2007: Greater London', *Britannia* 39, 315–24.

Booth, P., 2012, 'Roman Britain in 2011: Greater London', *Britannia* 43, 328–37.

Booth, P., 2013, 'Roman Britain in 2012: Greater London', *Britannia* 44, 324–33.

Booth, P., 2014, 'Roman Britain in 2013: Greater London', *Britannia* 45, 370–79.

Booth, P., 2015, 'Roman Britain in 2014: Greater London', *Britannia* 46, 333–38.

Booth, P., 2016, 'Roman Britain in 2015: Greater London', *Britannia* 47, 333–48.

Bourne, R.J., 2000, 'Aspects of the Relationship between the Central and Gallic Empires in the Mid to Late Third Century AD with Special Reference to Coinage Studies', PhD thesis, Durham University.

Bowden, W., 2008, 'The Fourth Century', in E. Bispham (ed.), *Roman Europe: The Short Oxford History of Europe*, Oxford: Oxford University Press, 265–98.

Bowersock, G.W., 1990, *Hellenism in Late Antiquity*, Cambridge: Cambridge University Press.

Bowes, K., 2010, *Houses and Society in the Later Roman Empire*, London: Duckworth.

Bowlt, C., 2008, 'A Possible Extension to Grim's Dyke', in J. Clark, J. Cotton, J. Hall, R. Sherris, and H. Swain (eds), *Londinium and Beyond: Essays on Roman London and its Hinterland for Harvey Sheldon*, CBA Research Report 156, London: Council for British Archaeology, 107–11.

Bowler, D., 1983, 'Rangoon Street', *Popular Archaeology* 5.6, 13–18.

Bowman, A.K., 1994, *Life and Letters on the Roman Frontier*, London: British Museum Press.

Bowman, A.K., 2017, 'The State and the Economy: Fiscality and Taxation', in A.K. Bowman and A. Wilson (eds), *Trade, Commerce and the State in the Roman World*, Oxford: Oxford University Press, 27–52.

Bowman, A.K. and Thomas, J.D., 1984, *Vindolanda: The Latin Writing-tablets*, Britannia Monograph 4, London: Society for the Promotion of Roman Studies.

Bowman, A.K. and Thomas, J.D., 1991, 'A Military Strength Report from Vindolanda', *Journal of Roman Studies* 81, 62–73.

Bowman, A.K. and Thomas, J.D., 2003, *The Vindolanda Writing Tablets (Tabulae Vindolandenses 3)*, London: British Museum Publications.

Bowman, A.K. and Wilson, A., 2009, 'Quantifying the Roman Economy: Integration, Growth, Decline?', in A.K. Bowman and A. Wilson (eds), *Quantifying the Roman Economy: Problems and Methods*, Oxford: Oxford University Press, 3–84.

Bowman, A.K. and Wilson, A., 2017, 'Introduction: Trade, Commerce, and the State', in A.K. Bowman and A. Wilson (eds), *Trade, Commerce and the State in the Roman World*, Oxford: Oxford University Press, 1–26.

Bowsher, D., Dyson, T., Holder, N., and Howell, I., 2007, *The London Guildhall: An Archaeological History of a Neighbourhood from Early Medieval to Modern Times*, MoLAS Monograph 36, London: Museum of London Archaeology Service.

Bowsher, J. and Marshall, M., 2013, 'A First Glance at Two Prehistoric Objects from Roman London', *Lucerna* 45, 14–16.

Bradley, R., 1990, *The Passage of Arms: An Archaeological Analysis of Prehistoric Hoards and Votive Deposits*, Cambridge: Cambridge University Press.

Bradley, R., 1997, '"To See is to Have Seen": Craft Traditions in British Field Archaeology', in B.L. Molyneaux (ed.), *The Cultural Life of Images*, London: Routledge, 62–72.

Bradley, R., 2000, *An Archaeology of Natural Places*, London: Routledge.

Bradley, R. and Gordon, K., 1988, 'Human Skulls from the River Thames, Their Dating and Significance', *Antiquity* 62.236, 503–9.

Bradley, T. and Butler, J., 2008, *From Temples to Thames Street—2000 years of Riverside Development; Archaeological Excavations at the Salvation Army International Headquarters*, PCA Monograph 7, London: Pre-Construct Archaeology.

Braithwaite, G., 2007, *Faces from the Past: A Study of Roman Face Pots from Italy and the Western Provinces of the Roman Empire*, BAR International Series 1651, Oxford: Archaeopress.

Braund, D.C., 1988, 'Client Kings', in D.C. Braund (ed.), *The Administration of the Roman Empire 241 BC–AD 193*, Studies in History 18, Exeter: University of Exeter, 69–96.

Bray, L., 2010, '"Horrible, Speculative, Nasty, Dangerous": Assessing the Value of Roman Iron', *Britannia* 41, 175–85.

Breeze, D.J., 1983, review of B. Philp (1981), 'The Excavation of the Roman Forts of the Classis Britannica at Dover, 1970–1977', *Britannia* 14, 372–75.

Breeze, D.J., 2003, 'Warfare in Britain and the Building of Hadrian's Wall', *Archaeologia Aeliana* 32, 13–16.

Breeze, D.J., Dobson, B., and Maxfield, V., 2012, 'Maenius Agrippa, a Chronological Conundrum', *Acta Classica* 55, 17–30.

Brettell, R.C., Schotsmans, E.M.J, Walton Rogers, P., Reifarth, N, Redfern, R.C., Stern, B., and Heron, C.P., 2015, '"*Choicest unguents*": molecular evidence for the use of resinous plant exudates in late Roman mortuary rites in Britain', *Journal of Archaeological Science* 53, 639–48.

Brewer, R.J., 1993, 'Venta Silurum: A Civitas Capital', in S.J. Greep (ed.), *Roman Towns: the Wheeler Inheritance*, CBA Research Report 93, York: Council for British Archaeology, 56–65.

Brien, J., 2013, 'The Role of Causation in History', *History in the Making* 2.2, 72–81.

Brigham, T., 1990a, 'A Reassessment of the Second Basilica in London A.D. 100–400: Excavations at Leadenhall Court, 1984–86', *Britannia* 21, 53–98.

Brigham, T., 1990b, 'The Late Roman Waterfront in London', *Britannia* 21, 99–184.

Brigham, T., 1992, 'Civic Centre Redevelopment: Forum and Basilica Reassessed', in G. Milne (ed.), *From Roman Basilica to Medieval Market: Archaeology in Action in the City of London*, London: HMSO, 81–95.

Brigham, T., 1998, 'The Port of Roman London', in B. Watson (ed.), *Roman London: Recent Archaeological Research*, JRA Supplementary Series 24, Portsmouth RI: Journal of Roman Archaeology, 23–34.

Brigham, T., 2001a, *Roman and Medieval Townhouses on the London Waterfront: Excavations at Governor's House, City of London*, MoLAS Monograph 9, London: Museum of London Archaeology.

Brigham, T., 2001b, 'The Thames and the Southwark Waterfront in the Roman Period' and 'Roman London Bridge', in B. Watson, T. Brigham, and T.Dyson (eds), *London Bridge, 2000 Years of a River Crossing*, MOLAS Monograph 8, London: Museum of London Archaeology, 12–51.

Brigham, T, Goodburn, D., and Tyers, I., 1995, 'A Roman Timber Building on the Southwark Waterfront, London', *Archaeological Journal* 152, 1–72.

Brigham, T. and Watson, B., 1996, 'Current Archaeological Work at Regis House in the City of London (Part 2)', *London Archaeologist* 8.3, 63–9.

Brigham, T. and Watson, B., in prep., *Early Roman Waterfront Development: Excavations at Regis House, City of London, 1994–96*, London: Museum of London Archaeology.

Brindle, T., 2017, 'Coins and Markets in the Countryside', in M. Allen, L. Lodwick, T. Brindle, M. Fulford, and A. Smith (eds), *New Visions of the Countryside of Roman*

Britain, Vol. 2: The Rural Economy of Roman Britain, Britannia Monograph 30, London: Society for the Promotion of Roman Studies, 237–80.

Brodribb, G., 1969, 'Stamped Tiles of the Classis Britannica', *Sussex Archaeological Collections* 107, 102–25.

Brodribb, G. and Cleere, H., 1988, 'The Classis Britannica Bath-house at Beauport Park, East Sussex', *Britannia* 19, 217–74.

Broekaert, W., 2011, 'Oil for Rome during the Second and Third Century AD: A Confrontation of Archaeological Records and the "Historia Augusta"', *Mnemosyne* 64.4, 591–623.

Brooks, R.T., 1977, 'The Roman Villa at Hill Farm, Abridge', *Essex Journal* 12, 51–61.

Brown, A.E. and Sheldon, H.L., 2018, *The Roman Pottery Manufacturing Site in Highgate Wood: Excavations 1966–78*, Roman Archaeology 43, Oxford: Archaeopress.

Brown, A.G., Meadows, I., Turner, S.D., and Mattingly, D.J., 2001, 'Roman Vineyards in Britain: Stratigraphic and Palynological Date from Wollaston in the Nene Valley', *Antiquity* 75, 745–57.

Brown, G., 2008, 'Archaeological Evidence for the Roman London to Colchester Road between Aldgate and Harold Hill', in J. Clark, J. Cotton, J. Hall, R. Sherris, and H. Swain (eds), *Londinium and Beyond: Essays on Roman London and its Hinterland for Harvey Sheldon*, CBA Research Report 156, London: Council for British Archaeology, 82–95.

Brown, G., 2011, '"The Graveyard Draws the Living Still, But Never Anymore the Dead": 150 Years of Roman Funerary Archaeology in Old Ford, Tower Hamlets', *Transactions of the London and Middlesex Archaeological Society* 65, 31–68.

Brown, G., 2016, 'A Road to Where?', *London Archaeologist* 14.8, 217–21.

Brown, G. and Pye, B., 1992, 'Whittington Avenue Excavations: A Summary', in G. Milne, *From Roman Basilica to Medieval Market: Archaeology in Action in the City of London*, London: HMSO, 135–38.

Brown, N. and Cotton, J., 2000, 'The Bronze Age', in Museum of London, *The Archaeology of Greater London*, MoLAS Monograph, London: Museum of London Archaeology, 81–100.

Brown, P., 2012, *Through the Eye of a Needle: Wealth, The Fall of Rome, and the Making of Christianity in the West, 350–550 AD*, Princeton: Princeton University Press.

Bruce, G., Perring, D., Stevens, T., and Melikian, M., 2009, 'Roman and Medieval Activity in the Upper Walbrook Valley: Excavations at 12–18 Moorgate, City of London, EC2, 1997', *Transactions of the London and Middlesex Archaeological Society* 60, 73–89.

Bruun, C., 2007, 'The Antonine Plague and the "Third-Century Crisis"', in O. Hekster, G. de Kleijn, and D. Slootjes (ed.), *Crises and the Roman Empire: Proceedings of the Seventh Workshop of the International Network Impact of Empire, Nijmegen, June 20–24, 2006.* Leiden: Brill, 201–18.

Bruun, C., 2012, 'La mancanza di prove di un effetto catastrofico della "peste antonina" (dal 166 d.C. in poi)', in E. Lo Cascio (ed.), *L'Impato della 'Peste Antonina'*, Bari: Edipuglia, 123–65.

Bryan, J., Hill, J., and Watson, S., 2016, 'The Archaeological Context', in R.S.O.Tomlin, *Roman London's First Voices: Writing Tablets from the Bloomberg Excavations, 2010–14*, MOLA Monograph 72, London: Museum of London Archaeology, 31–51.

Bull, S., 2007, *Triumphant Rider: The Lancaster Roman Cavalry Tombstone*, Lancaster: Lancashire Museums.

Bull, R., Davis, D., Lewis, H., and Phillpotts, C., 2011, *Holywell Priory and the Development of Shoreditch to c. 1600. Archaeology from the London Overground East London Line*, MOLA Monograph 53, London: Museum of London Archaeology.

Burch, M., 1987, 'Roman and Medieval Occupation in Queen Street', *Archaeology Today* 8.11, 9–12.

Burkitt, A.H., 1852, 'On Excavations Near the Roman Wall on Tower Hill, London, August 1852', *Journal of British Archaeological Association* 8.3, 240–42.

Burns, K.K., forthcoming, *The Iconography of Mystery: The Relationship between Orpheus and Bacchus on the Orpheus Mosaics of Southwest Britain*, Summertown: Archaeopress.

Burns, R., 2017, *Origins of the Colonnaded Streets in the Cities of the Roman East*, Oxford: Oxford University Press.

Bushe-Fox, J.P., 1932, *Third Report on the Excavations of the Roman Fort at Richborough*, Oxford: Oxford University Press.

Bushe-Fox, J.P., 1949, *Fourth Report on the Excavations of the Roman Fort at Richborough*, Oxford: Oxford University Press.

Butcher, S.A, 1982, 'Excavation of a Roman Building on the East Side of the White Tower 1956–7', in G. Parnell, 'The Roman and Medieval Defences and the Later Development of the Inmost Ward, Tower of London: Excavations 1955–77', *Transactions of the London and Middlesex Archaeological Society* 36, 101–14.

Butcher, K., 2015, 'Debasement and the Decline of Rome', in R. Bland and D. Calomino (eds), *Studies in Ancient Coinage in Honor of Andrew Burnett*, London: Spink, 181–205.

Butler, J., 2001, 'The City Defences at Aldersgate', *Transactions of the London and Middlesex Archaeological Society* 52, 41–112.

Butler, J., 2005, *Saxons, Templars and Lawyers in the Inner Temple: Archaeological Investigations in Church Court and Hare Court*, PCA Monograph 4, London: Pre-Construct Archaeology.

Butler, J., 2006, *Reclaiming the Marsh: Archaeological Excavations at Moor House, City of London*, PCA Monograph 6, London: Pre-Construct Archaeology.

Bynon, T., 2016, 'London's Name', *Transactions of the Philological Society* 114.3, 281–97.

Campbell, B., 2000, *The Writings of the Roman Land Surveyors: Introduction, Text, Translation and Commentary*, Journal of Roman Studies Monograph 9, London: Society for the Promotion of Roman Archaeology.

Cantino Wataghin, G., 1999, 'The Ideology of Urban Burials', in G.P. Brogiolo and B. Ward-Perkins, *The Idea and Ideal of the Town between Late Antiquity and the Early Middle Ages*, Leiden: Brill, 147–63.

Cantino Wataghin, G., Gurt Esparraguera, J.M., and Guyon, J., 1996, 'Topografia della Civitas Christiana tra IV e VI sec', in G.P. Brogiolo (ed.), *Early Medieval Town in the Western Mediterranean*, Mantova: Società Archeologica Padana, 17–41.

Carl, P., Kemp, B., Laurence, R., Coningham, R., Higham, C., and Cowgill, G.L., 2000, 'Were Cities Built as Images?', *Cambridge Archaeological Journal* 10, 327–65.

Carneiro, A., Christie, N., and Diarte-Blasco, P., 2020, *Urban Transformations in the late Antique West: Materials, Agents, and Models*, Humanitas Supplementum 63, Evora: Coimbra University Press.

Carr, G.C., 2007, 'Excarnation to Cremation: Continuity or Change?', in C. Haselgrove and T. Moore (eds), *The Later Iron Age in Britain and Beyond*, Oxford: Oxbow Books, 444–53.

Carreras Monfort, C., 1998, '*Britannia* and the Imports of Baetican and Lusitanian Amphorae', *Journal of Iberian Archaeology* 1, 159–70.

Carreras Monfort, C., 2002, 'The Roman Military Supply during the Principate: Transportation and Staples', in P Erdkamp (ed.), *The Roman Army and Economy*, Amsterdam: J.C. Gieben, 70–89.

Carreras Monfort, C. and Williams, D.F., 2003, 'Spanish Olive Oil Trade in Late Roman Britain: Dressel 23 Amphorae from Winchester', *Journal of Roman Pottery Studies* 10, 64.

Carroll, K.K., 1979, 'The Date of Boudica's Revolt', *Britannia* 10, 197–202.

Carroll, M., 2018, *Infancy and Earliest Childhood in the Roman World: 'A Fragment of Time'*, Oxford: Oxford University Press.

Cartledge, P., 2002, 'The Economy (Economies) of Ancient Greece', in W. Scheidel and S. von Reden (eds), *The Ancient Economy*, Edinburgh: Edinburgh University Press, 11–32.

Carver, M.O.H., 1993, *Arguments in Stone: Archaeological Research and the European Town in the First Millenium*, Oxbow Monograph 29, Oxford: Oxbow Press.

Casey, P.J., 1978, 'Constantine the Great in Britain, the Evidence of the Coinage of the London Mint, A.D. 312–314', in J. Bird, H. Chapman, and J. Clark (eds), *Collectanea Londiniensia. Studies in London Archaeology and History Presented to Ralph Merrifield*, LAMAS Special Paper 2, London: London and Middlesex Archaeological Society, 180–93.

Casey, P.J., 1983, 'Imperial Campaigns and 4th Century Defences in Britain', in J. Maloney and B. Hobley (eds), *Roman Urban Defences in the West*, CBA Research Report 51, London: Council for British Archaeology, 121–24.

Casey, P.J., 1987, 'The Coinage of Alexandria and the Chronology of Hadrian', in H. Huvelin, M. Christol, and G. Gautier (eds), *Mélanges de numismatique offerts a Pierre Bastien à l'occasion de son 75e anniversaire*, Cultura Press: Wetteren, 65–72.

Casey, P.J., 1994, *Carausius and Allectus: The British Usurpers*, London: Batsford.

Casey, P.J., 2010, 'Liberalitas Augusti: Imperial Military Donatives and the Arras Hoard', in G. Alföldy, B. Dobson, and W. Eck (eds), *Kaiser, Heer und Gesellschaft in der Römischen Kaiserzeit: Gedenkschrift für Eric Birley*, Stuttgart: Franz Steiner Verlag, 445–58.

Cass, S. and Preston, S., 2010, 'Roman and Saxon Burials at Steward Street, Tower Hamlets', *Transactions of the London and Middlesex Archaeological Society* 60, 53–72.

Casson, L., Drummond-Murray, J., and Francis, A., 2014, *Romano-British Round Houses to Medieval Parish. Excavations at 10 Gresham Street, City of London, 1999–2002*, MoLA Monograph 67, London: Museum of London Archaeology.

Castle, S.A., 1975, 'Excavations in Pear Wood, Brockley Hill, Middlesex, 1948–1973', *Transactions of the London and Middlesex Archaeological Society* 26, 267–77.

Champion, T., 2016, 'Britain before the Romans', in M. Millett, L. Revell, and A. Moore (eds), *The Oxford Handbook of Roman Britain*, Oxford: Oxford University Press, 150–78.

Chapman, H., 1985, 'Small Finds', in G. Parnell, 'The Roman and Medieval Defences and the Later Development of the Inmost Ward, Tower of London: Excavations 1955–77', *Transactions of the London and Middlesex Archaeological Society* 36, 60–7.

Chapman, H. and Johnson, T., 1973, 'Excavations at Aldgate and Bush Lane House in the City of London 1972', *Transactions of the London and Middlesex Archaeological Society* 24, 1–73.

Chapman, R. and Wylie, A., 2016, *Evidential Reasoning in Archaeology*, London: Bloomsbury.

Chenery, C., Müldner, G., Evans, J., Eckardt, H., and Lewis, M., 2010, 'Strontium and Stable Isotope Evidence for Diet and Mobility in Roman Gloucester', *Journal of Archaeological Science* 37, 150–63.

Chevalier, R., 1976, *Roman Roads*, London: Batsford.

Chitwood, P. and Hill, J., 1987, 'Excavations at St Alban's House Wood Street', *Archaeology Today* 8, 13–16.

Christie, N., 2020, 'From Royalty to Refugees: Looking for the People in Reconstructing Urban Change in Late Antique Italy', in A. Carneiro, N. Christie, and P. Diarte-Blasco, *Urban Transformations in the Late Antique West: Materials, Agents, and Models*, Humanitas Supplementum 63, Evora: Coimbra University Press, 323–50.

CIL: *Corpus Inscriptorum Latinorum*. Consilio et Ductoritate Academie Litterarum Regiae Borussical Edition, Berlin: Academieder Wissenschaften, 1862–to date.

Cipin, I., 2015, '8–10 Paul Street, Shoreditch, London, EC2A 4JH: Assessment of an Archaeological Watching Brief', unpublished Pre-Construct Archaeology Report R12029.

Clark, F.R., 1985, 'The Lost Roman Villa at Wanstead', *West Essex Archaeological Group Newsletter* 10, 1–2.

Clark, F.R., 1998, *The Romano-British Settlement at Little London, Chigwell*, Woodford Green: West Essex Archaeological Group.

Clark, J., 2008, '"Fanciful Iconography": William Stukeley's Maps of (?) Roman London', in J. Clark, J. Cotton, J. Hall, R. Sherris, and H. Swain (eds), *Londinium and Beyond: Essays on Roman London and its Hinterland for Harvey Sheldon*, CBA Research Report 156, London: Council for British Archaeology, 4–10.

Cleere, H., 1970, *The Romano-British Industrial Site at Bardown*, Lewes: Sussex Archaeological Society.

Cleere, H., 1974, 'The Roman Iron Industry of the Weald and its Connexions with the Classis Britannica', *Archaeological Journal* 131, 171–99.

Cleere, H., 1977, 'The Classis Britannica', in S. Johnson (ed.), *The Saxon Shore*, CBA Research Report 18, London: Council for British Archaeology, 16–19.

Cleere, H. and Crossley, D., 1995, *The Iron Industry of the Weald* (2nd edition), Cardiff: Merton Priory Press.

Cloke, H.J. and Toone, E., 2015, *The London Mint of Constantius and Constantine*, London: Spink.

Coates, R., 1998, 'A New Explanation of the Name of London', *Transactions of the Philological Society* 96.2, 203–29.

Cole, W., 1656, *Art of Simpling, or an Introduction to the Knowledge and Gathering of Plants*, London: JG for Nath' Brook.

Collingwood, R.G., 1939, *An Autobiography*, London: Oxford University Press.

Collingwood, R.G. and Wright, R.P., 1965, *The Roman Inscriptions of Britain 1. Inscriptions on Stone*, Oxford: Clarendon Press.

Collingwood, R.G. and Wright, R.P., 1990, *The Roman Inscriptions of Britain 2. Instrumentum Domesticum (Personal Belongings and the Like), Fascicule 1*, ed. S.S. Frere, M. Roxan and R.S.O. Tomlin, Stroud: Sutton.

Collingwood, R.G. and Wright, R.P., 1991a, *The Roman Inscriptions of Britain 2. Instrumentum Domesticum (Personal Belongings and the Like), Fascicule 2*, ed. S.S. Frere and R.S.O. Tomlin, Stroud: Sutton.

Collingwood, R.G. and Wright, R.P., 1991b, *The Roman Inscriptions of Britain 2. Instrumentum Domesticum (Personal Belongings and the Like), Fascicule 3*, ed. S.S. Frere and R.S.O. Tomlin, Stroud: Sutton.

Collingwood, R.G. and Wright, R.P., 1992, *The Roman Inscriptions of Britain: Instrumentum domesticum (Personal Belongings and the Like). Fascicule 4*, ed. S.S. Frere and R.S.O. Tomlin, Stroud: Sutton.

Collingwood, R.G. and Wright, R.P., 1993, *The Roman Inscriptions of Britain: Instrumentum domesticum (Personal Belongings and the Like). Fascicule 5*, ed. S.S. Frere and R.S.O. Tomlin, Stroud: Sutton.

Collingwood, R.G. and Wright, R.P., 1994, *The Roman Inscriptions of Britain: Instrumentum domesticum (Personal Belongings and the Like). Fascicule 6*, ed. S.S. Frere and R.S.O. Tomlin, Stroud: Sutton.

Collingwood, R.G. and Wright, R.P., 1995, *The Roman Inscriptions of Britain: Instrumentum domesticum (Personal Belongings and the Like). Fascicule 8*, ed. S.S. Frere and R.S.O. Tomlin, Stroud: Sutton.

Collins, R., 2017, 'Soldiers in Life and Death. Material Culture, the Military, and Mortality', in A. Van Oyen and M. Pitts (eds), *Materialising Roman Histories*, Oxford: Oxbow Books, 31–46.

Collins, R. and Breeze, D., 2014, 'Limitanei and Comitatenses: Military Failure at the End of Roman Britain?', in F.K. Haarer (ed.), *AD 410: The History and Archaeology of Late Roman and Post-Roman Britain*, London: Society for the Promotion of Roman Studies, 61–72.

Collins, R. and Weber, M., 2015, 'Late Roman Military Architecture: An Introduction', in R. Collins, M. Weber, and M. Symonds (eds), *Roman Military Architecture on the Frontiers: Armies and Their Architecture in Late Antiquity*, Oxford: Oxbow Books, 1–5.

Conheeney, J., in prep., 'Human Bone', in T. Brigham and B. Watson, *Early Roman Waterfront Development: Excavations at Regis House, City of London, 1994–96*, London: Museum of London Archaeology.

Connell, B., 2009, 'Human Bone', in C. Cowan, F. Seeley, A. Wardle, A. Westman, and L Wheeler, *Roman Southwark Settlement and Economy: Excavations in Southwark 1973–91*, MoLAS Monograph 42, London: Museum of London Archaeology, 248–57.

Cook, N., 1969, 'An Anglo-Saxon Saucer Brooch from Lower Thames Street, London', *Antiquaries Journal* 49, 395.

Cool, H.E.M., 2016, 'Clothing and Identity', in M. Millett, L. Revell, and A. Moore (eds), *The Oxford Handbook of Roman Britain*, Oxford: Oxford University Press, 406–24.

Cool, H.E.M. and Baxter, M., 2016, 'Brooches and Britannia', *Britannia* 47, 71–98.

Coombe, P., Grew, F., Hayward, K., and Henig, M., 2015, *Roman Sculpture from London and the South-East*, Corpus Signorum Imperii Romani, Great Britain 1.10, Oxford: Oxford University Press.

Corder, P., 1955, 'The Re-organisation of the Defences of Romano-British Towns in the 4th Century', *Archaeological Journal* 112, 20–42.

Cosh, S.P., 1992, 'A New Look at the Corinian Saltire School', *Mosaic* 19, 7–10.

Costabile, F., 2017, '"De cautione damni accipere" nella Nuova Tabella Cerata Londinese di "Atigniomarus"', *Zeitschrift für Papyrologie und Epigraphik* 204, 303–310.

Cotton, J., 1996, 'A Miniature Chalk Head from the Thames at Battersea and the "Cult of the Head" in Roman London', in J. Bird, M. Hassall, and H. Sheldon (eds), *Interpreting Roman London: Papers in Memory of Hugh Chapman*, Oxford: Oxbow Monograph 58, 85–96.

Cotton, J., 2008, 'Harper Road, Southwark: An Early Roman Burial Revisited', in J. Clark, J. Cotton, J. Hall, R. Sherris, and H. Swain (eds), *Londinium and Beyond: Essays on Roman London and its Hinterland for Harvey Sheldon*, CBA Research Report 156, London: Council for British Archaeology, 151–61.

Cotton, J., 2018, 'Prehistoric London: Retrospect and Prospect', *London Archaeologist* 15.3, 59–66.

Cottrill, F., 1936, 'A Bastion of the Town Wall of London, and the Sepulchral Monument of the Procurator, Julius Classicianus', *Antiquaries Journal* 16, 1–7.

Cowan, C., 1992, 'A Possible Mansio in Roman Southwark: Excavations at 15–23 Southwark Street 1980–6', *Transactions of the London and Middlesex Archaeological Society* 43, 2–192.

Cowan, C., 2003, *Urban Development in North-west Roman Southwark: Excavations 1974–90*, MoLAS Monograph 16, London: Museum of London Archaeology.

Cowan, C. and Rowsome, P., 2009, 'Roman London, its Districts and Comparable Urban Centres', in C. Cowan, F. Seeley, A. Wardle, A. Westman, and L. Wheeler, *Roman Southwark Settlement and Economy: Excavations in Southwark 1973–91*, MoLAS Monograph 42, London: Museum of London Archaeology, 169–71.

Cowan, C. and Seeley, F., 2009, 'Contraction and Decline of the Settlement', in C. Cowan, F. Seeley, A. Wardle, A. Westman, and L. Wheeler, *Roman Southwark Settlement and Economy: Excavations in Southwark 1973–91*, MoLA Monograph 42, London: Museum of London Archaeology, 157–66.

Cowan, C. and Wardle, A., 2009, 'Economy', in C. Cowan, F. Seeley, A. Wardle, A. Westman, and L. Wheeler, *Roman Southwark Settlement and Economy: Excavations in Southwark 1973–91*, MoLA Monograph 42, London: Museum of London Archaeology, 91–118.

Cowan, C. Seeley, F. Wardle, A. Westman, A., and Wheeler, L., 2009, *Roman Southwark Settlement and Economy: Excavations in Southwark 1973–91*, MoLA Monograph 42, London: Museum of London Archaeology.

Cowie, R., 2000, 'Saxon Settlement and Economy from the Dark Ages to Domesday', in Museum of London, *The Archaeology of Greater London*, MoLAS Monograph, London, 171–206.

Cowie, R., 2008, 'Descent into Darkness: London in the 5th and 6th Centuries', in J. Clark, J. Cotton, J. Hall, R. Sherris, and H. Swain (eds), *Londinium and Beyond: Essays on Roman London and its Hinterland for Harvey Sheldon*, CBA Research Report 156, London: Council for British Archaeology, 49–53.

Cowie, R. and Blackmore, L., 2008, *Early and Middle Saxon Rural Settlement in the London Region*, MoLAS Monograph 41, London: Museum of London Archaeology.

Cowie, R., Thorp, A., and Wardle, A., 2013, *Roman Roadside Settlement and Rural Landscape at Brentford: Archaeological Investigations at Hilton London Syon Park Hotel, 2004–10*, MoLAS Archaeology Studies 29, London: Museum of London Archaeology.

Crabtree, P.J., 2018, *Early Medieval Britain. The Rebirth of Towns in the Post-Roman West*, Case Studies in Early Societies, Cambridge: Cambridge University Press.

Craig, R., Knüsel, C.J., and Carr, G.C., 2005, 'Fragmentation, Mutilation and Dismemberment: An Interpretation of Human Remains in Iron Age Sites', in M. Parker Pearson and N. Thorpe (eds), *Violence, Warfare, and Slavery*, BAR International Series, Oxford: Archaeopress, 165–80.

Creighton, J., 2000, *Coins and Power in Late Iron Age Britain*, Cambridge: Cambridge University Press.

Creighton, J., 2006, *Britannia. The Creation of a Roman Province*, Abingdon: Routledge.

Creighton, J., 2016, *Silchester: Changing Visions of a Roman Town. Integrating Geophysics and Archaeology—the Results of the Silchester Mapping Project 2005–10*. Britannia Monograph 28, London: Society for the Promotion of Roman Studies.

Crerar, B., 2016, 'Deviancy in Late Romano-British Burial', in M. Millett, L. Revell, and A. Moore (eds), *The Oxford Handbook of Roman Britain*, Oxford: Oxford University Press, 381–405.

Crickmore, J., 1984, *Romano-British Urban Defences*, BAR British Series126, Oxford: Archaeopress.

Crouch, K.R. and Shanks, S.A., 1984, *Excavations in Staines 1975–6. The Friends' Burial Ground site*, LAMAS and SAS Joint Publication 2, London: London and Middlesex Archaeological Society and Surrey Archaeological Society.

Crowley, N., 1992, 'Building Materials', in C. Cowan, 'A Possible Mansio in Roman Southwark: Excavations at 15–23 Southwark Street 1980–6', *Transactions of the London and Middlesex Archaeological Society* 43, 144–57.

Crowley, N., 2005, Building Materials', in B. Yule, *A Prestigious Roman Building Complex on the Southwark Waterfront: Excavations at Winchester Palace, London, 1983–90*, MoLAS Archaeology Studies Series 23, London: Museum of London Archaeology, 90–100.

Crowley, N. and Betts, I.M., 1992, 'Three Classis Britannica Stamps from London', *Britannia* 23, 218–22.

Crummy, N., 2005, 'From Bracelets to Battle-honours: Military Armillae from the Roman Conquest of Britain', in N. Crummy (ed.), *Image, Craft and the Classical World. Essays in Honour of Donald Bailey and Catherine Johns*, Monographies Instrumentum 29, Montagnac: Éditions Monique Mergoil, 93–105.

Crummy, N., 2006, 'Travel and Transport', in L. Allason-Jones (ed.), *Artefacts in Roman Britain: Their Purpose and Use*, Cambridge: Cambridge University Press, 46–67.

Crummy, N., 2008, 'Small Toilet Instruments from London: A Review of the Evidence', in J. Clark, J. Cotton, J. Hall, R. Sherris, and H. Swain (eds), *Londinium and Beyond: Essays on Roman London and its Hinterland for Harvey Sheldon*, CBA Research Report 156, London: Council for British Archaeology, 212–25.

Crummy, N., 2017, 'Working Skeletal Materials in South-Eastern Roman Britain', in D. Bird (ed.), *Agriculture and Industry in South-Eastern Roman Britain*, Oxford: Oxbow Books, 255–81.

Crummy, P., 1984, *Excavations at Lion Walk, Balkerne Lane and Middleborough, Colchester*, Colchester Archaeological Report 3, Colchester: Colchester Archaeological Trust.

Crummy, P., 1988, 'Colchester (Camulodunum/Colonia Victricensis)', in G. Webster (ed.), *Fortress into City: The Consolidation of Roman Britain, First Century A D*, London: Batsford, 24–47.

Crummy, P., 1997, *City of Victory: The Story of Colchester—Britain's First Roman Town*, Colchester: Colchester Archaeological Trust.

Crummy, P., 2003, 'Colchester's Roman Town Wall', in P. Wilson (ed.), *The Archaeology of Roman Towns: Studies in Honour of J.S. Wacher*, Oxford: Oxbow Books, 44–52.

Crummy, P., 2008, 'The Roman Circus at Colchester', *Britannia* 39, 15–32.

Cuming, H.S., 1858, 'Roman Coffin from Shadwell', *Journal of the British Archaeological Association* 14, 355–57.

Cunliffe, B.W., 1968, *Richborough: Fifth Report of the Excavations of the Roman Fort at Richborough, Kent*, Society of Antiquaries Research Report 23, Oxford: Society of Antiquaries of London.

Cunliffe, B.W., 1988, 'Romney Marsh in the Roman Period', in J. Edison and C. Green (eds), *Romney Marsh: Evolution, Occupation, Reclamation*, Oxford University Committee for Archaeology, Oxford: Oxford University Press, 83–87.

Cunliffe, B.W., 2013, *Britain Begins*, Oxford: Oxford University Press.

Curle, J., 1911, *A Roman Frontier Post and its People: The Fort of Newstead in the Parish of Melrose*, Glasgow: James MacLehose.

Dark, P., 2017, 'The Environment of Southern Roman Britain', in D. Bird (ed.), *Agriculture and Industry in South-Eastern Roman Britain*, Oxford: Oxbow, 15–34.

Davenport, C., 2019, 'Carausius and His Brothers: The Construction and Deconstruction of an Imperial Image in the Late Third Century A D', *Antichthon: Journal of the Australian Society for Classical Studies* 53, 108–33.

Davies, B., 1990, 'Roman Pottery Appraisal Report, Great Winchester Street (GWS89)', unpublished Museum of London Archaeology Report.

Davies, B., Richardson, B., and Tomber, R., 1994, *A Dated Corpus of Early Roman pottery from the City of London; The Archaeology of Roman London 5*, CBA Research Report 98, York: Council for British Archaeology.

Davies, R.W., 1977, 'Cohors I Hispanorum and the Garrisons of Maryport', *Transactions of the Cumberland and Westmorland Antiquarian Archaeological Society* 77, 7–16.

Davis, A., 2004, 'The Plant Remains', in L. Dunwoodie, *Pre-Boudican and Later Activity on the Site of the Forum: Excavations at 168 Fenchurch Street, City of London*, MoLAS Archaeology Study 13, London: Museum of London Archaeology, 54–7.

Davis, A., 2011, 'Grain Processing/Storage', in J. Hill and P. Rowsome, *Roman London and the Walbrook Stream Crossing: Excavations at 1 Poultry and Vicinity 1985–96*, MoLA Monograph 37, London: Museum of London Archaeology, 304.

Davis, A., 2014, 'The Plant Remains', in R. Wroe-Brown, *Roman Occupation South-East of the Forum: Excavations at 20 Fenchurch Street, City of London, 2008–9*, MoLA Archaeology Studies Series 31, London: Museum of London Archaeology, 94–7.

Davis, G., 2018, 'Rubbing and Rolling, Burning and Burying: The Magical Use of Amber in Roman London', in A. Parker and S. McKie, *Material Approaches to Roman Magic: Occult Objects and Supernatural Substances*, Oxford: Oxbow books, 69–81.

Dawe, D. and Oswald, A., 1952, *11 Ironmonger Lane, London*, London: Hutchinson.

Dawkes, G., 2015, *Flavian and Later Buildings at Roman Villa Snodland: Excavations at Cantium Way, Snodland, Kent*, Spoilheap Monograph 9, Portslade: Spoilheap.

Daykin, A., 2017, 'Principal Place (Residential) Plough Yard, Shoreditch High Street, London, EC2, London Borough of Hackney: Post-excavation Assessment and Updated Project Design', unpublished Museum of London Archaeology report.

de Blois, L., 1976, *The Policy of the Emperor Gallienus*, Leiden: Brill.

de Blois, L., 2002, 'The Crisis of the Third Century A.D. in the Roman Empire: A Modern Myth?', in L. de Blois and J. Rich (eds), *The Transformation of Economic Life under the Roman Empire. Proceedings of the Second Workshop of the International Network Impact of Empire (Roman Empire c. 200 BC–AD 476), Nottingham, July 4–7, 2001*, Amsterdam: J.C. Gieben, 204–17.

de Blois, L., 2018, *Image and Reality of Roman Imperial Power in the Third Century*, Routledge Studies in Ancient History, London: Routledge.

de Blois, L., Pleket, H., and Rich, J., 2002, 'Introduction', in L. de Blois and J. Rich (eds), *The Transformation of Economic Life under the Roman Empire. Proceedings of the Second Workshop of the International Network Impact of Empire (Roman Empire c. 200 BC–AD 476), Nottingham, July 4–7, 2001*, Amsterdam: J.C. Gieben, ix–xx.

de Kind, R., 2005, 'The Roman Portraits from the Villa of Lullingstone: Pertinax and His Father P. Helvius Sucessus', in T. Ganschow and M. Steinhart, *Otium: Festschrift für Volker Michael Strocka*, Remshalden: Greiner, 47–53.

de la Bédoyère, G., 2003, *Roman Towns in Britain*, Stroud: The History Press.

de Laet, S.J., 1949, *Portorium. Étude sur l'organisation douanière chez les Romains surtout à l'époque du Haut-Empire*, Bruges: Faculté des Lettres de Gand.

de Ligt, L., 1993, *Fairs and Markets in the Roman Empire: Economic and Social Aspects of Periodic Trade in a Pre-industrial Society*, Dutch Monographs on Ancient History and Archaeology 11, Amsterdam: Gieben.

de Ligt, L., 2002, 'Tax transfers in the Roman Empire', in L. Blois and J. Rich (eds), *The transformation of economic life under the Roman empire. Proceedings of the Second Workshop of the International Network Impact of Empire (Roman Empire, c. 200 BC–AD 476), Nottingham, July 4–7, 2001*, Leiden: Brill, 48–66.

Dean, M., 1980, 'Excavations at Arcadia Buildings, Southwark', *London Archaeologist* 3.14, 367–73.

Dean, M. and Hammerson, M., 1980, 'Three Inhumation Burials from Southwark', *London Archaeologist* 4.1, 17–22.

Dearne, M., 2017, *First Stop North of Londinium: the Archaeology of Roman Enfield and its Roadline Settlement*, London: Enfield Archaeological Society.

Defoe, D., 2010, *A Journal of the Plague Year* (eds. L. Landa and D. Roberts), Oxford World's Classics, Oxford: Oxford University Press.

DeLaine, J., 1999, 'Benefactions and Urban Renewal: Bath Buildings in Italy', in J. Delaine and D.E. Johnston (eds), *Roman Baths and Bathing: Proceedings of the 1st International Conference on Roman Baths Held at Bath, England, 30 March–4 April 1992*, JRA Supplementary Series 37, Portsmouth RI: Journal of Roman Archaeology, 67–74.

DeLaine, J., 2000, 'Building the Eternal City: The Construction Industry in Imperial Rome', in J. Coulston and H. Dodge (eds), *Ancient Rome: The Archaeology of the Eternal City*, Oxford University School of Archaeology Monograph 54, Oxford: Oxford University, 119–41.

Dennis, G., 1978, '1–7 St Thomas Street', in J. Bird, A.H. Graham, H. Sheldon, and P. Townsend (eds), *Southwark Excavations 1972–74*, LAMAS and SAS Joint Publication 1, London: London and Middlesex Archaeological Society and Surrey Archaeological Society, 291–422.

Dennis, M. and Ward, M., 2001, 'The Roman Goldworking Evidence', in T. Brigham, *Roman and Medieval Townhouses on the London Waterfront: Excavations at Governor's House, City of London*, MoLAS Monograph 9, London: Museum of London Archaeology, 116–20.

Denyer, C.H., 1935, *St. Pancras through the Centuries*, London: Le Play House Press.

Derks, T., 1998, *Gods, Temples and Ritual Practices: The Transformation of Religious Ideas and Values in Roman Gaul*. Amsterdam: Amsterdam University Press.

Desbat, A, 1981, 'L'architecture de terre à Lyon à l'époque romaine', in S. Walker (ed.), *Récentes recherches en archéologie gallo-romaine et palaeochrétienne sur Lyon et sa région*, BAR International Series 108, Oxford: Archaeopress, 55–81.

Desbat, A., 2007, 'La topographie historique de Lugdunum', in A-C. Le Mer and C. Chomer (eds), *Lyon, Carte archéologique de la Gaule 69/2*, Paris: Acédemie des Insriptions et Belles-Lettres, 179–91.

Devoy, R.J.N., 1979, 'Flandrian Sea-level Changes and Vegetational History of the Lower Thames Estuary', *Philosophical Transactions of the Royal Society, London*, B. 285, 355–407.

Dey, H.W., 2011, *The Aurelian Wall and the Refashioning of Imperial Rome, AD 271–855*, Cambridge: Cambridge University Press.

Divers, D., Mayo, C., Cohen, N., and Jarrett, C., 2009, *A New Millennium at Southwark Cathedral: Investigations into the First Two Thousand Years*, PCA Monograph 8, London: Pre-Construct Archaeology.

Dixon, K.R. and Southern, P., 1992, *The Roman Cavalry: From the First to the Third Centuries AD*, London: Batsford.

DoE, 1990, *Planning Policy Guidance Note 16: Archaeology and Planning*, London: HMSO.

Dondin-Payre, M. and Loriot, X., 2008, 'Tiberinius Celerianus à Londres: Bellovaque et moritix', *L'Antiquité Classique* 77, 127–69.

Dorcey, P.F., 1992, *The Cult of Silvanus: A Study in Roman Folk Religion*, Columbia Studies in the Classical Tradition 20, Leiden: Brill.

Douglas, A., 2007, 'An Excavation at 5–27 Long Lane, London Borough of Southwark London SE1', *Transactions of the London and Middlesex Archaeological Society* 58, 15–51.

Douglas, A., Gerrard, J., and Sudds, B., 2011, *A Roman Settlement and Bath House at Shadwell: Excavations at Tobacco Dock and Babe Ruth's Restaurant, The Highway, London*, PCA Monograph 12, London: Pre-Construct Archaeology.

Drinkwater, J.F., 1998, 'The Usurpers Constantine III (407–411) and Jovinus (411–413)', *Britannia* 29, 269–98.

Drummond-Murray, J. and Thompson, P., 2002, *Settlement in Roman Southwark: Archaeological Excavations (1991–8) for the London Underground Limited Jubilee Line Extension Project*, MoLAS Monograph 12, London: Museum of London Archaeology.

Drury, P.J., 1988, *The Mansio and Other Sites in the South-Eastern Sector of Caesaromagus*, Chelmsford Archaeological Trust Report 3 and CBA Research Report 66, Chelmsford: Council for British Archaeology.

Drury, P.J. and Rodwell, W.J., 1980, 'Settlement in the Later Iron Age and Roman Periods', in D.G. Buckley (ed.), *Archaeology in Essex to AD 1500*, CBA Research Report 34, London: Council for British Archaeology, 59–75.

Du Plessis, P.J., 2015, 'Return to the Wood in Roman Kent', in E. Jakab (ed.), *Sale and Community Documents from the Ancient World. Individuals' Autonomy and State Interference in the Ancient World. Proceedings of a Colloquium supported by the University of Szeged. Budapest 5-8.10.2012*, Trieste: EUT Edizioni Università di Trieste, 171–180.

Duncan Jones, R.P., 1982, *The Economy of the Roman Empire. Quantitative Studies* (2nd edn.), Cambridge: Cambridge University Press.

Duncan-Jones, R.P., 1990, *Structure and Scale in the Roman Economy*, Cambridge: Cambridge University Press.

Duncan Jones, R.P., 1996, 'The Impact of the Antonine Plague', *Journal of Roman Archaeology* 9, 108–36.

Duncan Jones, R.P., 2018, 'The Antonine Plague Revisited', *Arctos* 52, 41–72.

Dungworth, D., 2016, 'Metals and Metalworking', in M. Millett, L. Revell, and A. Moore (eds), *The Oxford Handbook of Roman Britain*, Oxford: Oxford University Press, 532–54.

Dunning, G.C., 1945, 'Two Fires of Roman London', *Antiquaries Journal* 25, 48–77.

Dunwoodie, L., 2004, *Pre-Boudican and Later Activity on the Site of the Forum: Excavations at 168 Fenchurch Street, City of London*, MoLAS Archaeology Study 13, London: Museum of London Archaeology.

Dunwoodie, L., Harward, C., and Pitt, K., 2015, *An Early Roman Fort and Urban Development on Londinium's Eastern Hill: Excavations at Plantation Place, City of London, 1997–2003*, MOLA Monograph 65, London: Museum of London Archaeology.

Durham, E., 2016, 'Metropolitan Styling: Metal Figurines from London and Colchester', in S. Hoss and A. Whitmore (eds), *Small Finds and Ancient Social Practices in the Northwest Provinces of the Roman Empire*, Oxford: Oxbow Books, 75–97.

Eckardt, H. (ed.), 2010, *Roman Diasporas: Archaeological Approaches to Mobility and Diversity in the Roman Empire*, JRA Supplementary Series 78, Portsmouth RI: Journal of Roman Archaeology.

Eckardt, H., 2018, *Writing and Power in the Roman World: Literacies and Material Culture*, Cambridge: Cambridge University Press.

Eckardt, H. and Crummy, N., 2008, *Styling the Body in Late Iron Age and Roman Britain: A Contextual Approach to Toilet Instruments*, Monographies Instrumentum 36, Montagnac: Éditions Monique Mergoil.

Eckardt, H. and Müldner, G., 2016, 'Mobility, Migration, and Diasporas in Roman Britain', in M. Millett, L. Revell, and A. Moore (eds), *The Oxford Handbook of Roman Britain*, Oxford: Oxford University Press, 203–23.

Edwards, Y.H., Weisskopf, A., and Hamilton, D., 2009, 'Age, Taphonomic History and Mode of Deposition of Human Skulls in the River Thames', *Transactions of the London and Middlesex Archaeological Society* 60, 35–51.

Ehmig, U., 2003, 'Die römischen Amphoren aus Mainz', *Frankfurter Archäologische Schriften* 4, 1–243.

Elkins, N.T., 2017, *The Image of Political Power in the Reign of Nerva, AD 96–98*, Oxford: Oxford University Press.

Elliott, S., 2014, 'The Medway Formula: A Search for Evidence that the Roman Authorities Improved the River's Navigability to Facilitate Their Extensive Ragstone Quarrying Industry', *Archaeologia Cantiana* 135, 251–60.

Elliott, S., 2018, *Ragstone to Riches: Imperial Estates, Metalla and the Roman Military in the South East of Britain during the Occupation*, BAR British Series 638, Oxford: Archaeopress.

Elliott, S., 2021, *Roman Britain's Missing Legion—What Really Happened to IX Hispana?*, Barnsley: Pen & Sword.

Ellis, R., 1985, 'Excavations at 9 St. Clare Street', *London Archaeologist* 5.5, 115–20.

Elliston Erwood, F.C., 1916, 'The Earthworks at Charlton, London, SE', *Journal of the British Archaeological Association* NS 22, 123–91.

Elsden, N.J., 2002, *Excavations at 25 Cannon Street, City of London: From the Middle Bronze Age to the Great Fire*, MOLAS Archaeological Studies Series 5, London: Museum of London.

Elsner, J., 1998, *Imperial Rome and Christian Triumph: the Art of the Roman Empire AD 100–450*, Oxford History of Art, Oxford: Oxford University Press.

Elton, H., 1996, *Warfare in Roman Europe, 350–425*, Oxford Classical Monographs, Oxford: Oxford University Press.

Elton, H., 2006, 'The Transformation of Government under Diocletian and Constantine', in D.S. Potter (ed.), *A Companion to the Roman Empire*, Princeton: Blackwell, 193–205.

Erdkamp, P.M., 2001, 'Beyond the Limits of the Consumer City: A Model of the Urban and Rural Economy in the Roman World', *Historia: Zeitschrift für Alte Geschichte* 50.3, Wiesbaden, 332–56.

Erdkamp, P.M., 2002, 'The Corn Supply of the Roman Armies during the Principate (27 BC–235 AD)', in P.M. Erdkamp (ed.), *The Roman Army and the Economy*, Amsterdam: J.C. Gieben, 47–69.

Erdkamp, P.M., 2012, 'Urbanism', in W. Scheidel (ed.), *The Cambridge Companion to the Roman Economy*, Cambridge: Cambridge University Press, 241–65.

Erdkamp, P.M., 2015, 'Structural Determinants of Economic Performance in the Roman World and Early Modern Europe. A Comparative Approach', in P. Erdkamp and K. Verboven (eds), *Structure and Performance in the Roman Economy: Models, Methods and Case Studies*, Latomus 350: Brussels: Éditions Latomus, 17–31.

Esmonde Cleary, A.S., 1987, *Extra-Mural Areas of Romano-British Towns*. BAR British Series 169, Oxford: Archaeopress.

Esmonde Cleary, A.S., 1989, *The Ending of Roman Britain*, London: Batsford.

Esmonde Cleary, A.S., 1996, 'Roman Britain in 1995', *Britannia* 27, 405–38.

Esmonde Cleary, A.S., 2003, 'Civil Defences in the West under the High Empire', in P. Wilson (ed.), *The Archaeology of Roman Towns: Studies in Honour of J.S. Wacher*, Oxford: Oxbow Books, 72–85.

Esmonde Cleary, A.S., 2005, 'Beating the Bounds: Ritual and the Articulation of Urban Space in Roman Britain', in A. MacMahon and J. Price (eds), *Roman Working Lives and Urban Living*, Oxford: Oxbow Books, 1–17.

Esmonde Cleary, A.S., 2013, *The Roman West AD 200–500. An Archaeological Study*, Cambridge: Cambridge University Press.

Esmonde Cleary, A.S., 2016, 'Britain at the End of Empire', in M. Millett, L. Revell, and A. Moore (eds), *The Oxford Handbook of Roman Britain*, Oxford: Oxford University Press, 134–49.

Esmonde Cleary, A.S., 2020, 'Urban Defences in Late Roman Gaul: Civic Monuments or State Installations', in E. Intagliata, S.J. Barker, and C. Courault (eds), *City Walls in Late Antiquity: An Empire-wide Perspective*, Oxford: Oxbow Books, 27–50.

Evans, C. and James, P., 1983, 'The Roman Cornhill', *Popular Archaeology* 5, 19–26.

Evans, J., 2005, 'Pottery in Urban Romano-British Life', in A. MacMahon and J. Price (eds), *Roman Working Lives and Urban Living*, Oxford: Oxbow Books, 145–66.

Evans, J., 2013, 'Balancing the Scales: Romano-British Pottery in Early Late Antiquity', in L. Lavan (ed.), *Local Economies? Production and Exchange of Inland Regions in Late Antiquity*, Leiden: Brill, 425–50.

Evans, J., 2016, 'Forms of Knowledge: Changing Technologies of Romano-British Pottery', in M. Millett, L. Revell, and A. Moore (eds), *The Oxford Handbook of Roman Britain*, Oxford: Oxford University Press, 511–31.

Evers Grønlund, K., 2011, *The Vindolanda Tablets and the Ancient Economy*, BAR British Series 544, Oxford: Archaeopress.

Evershed, R.P., Berstan, R., Grew, F., Copley, M.S., Charmant, A.J.H., Barham, E., Mottram, H.R., and Brown, G., 2004, 'Formulation of a Roman Cosmetic', *Nature* 432, 35–6.

Evison, V., 1978, 'Early Anglo-Saxon Applied Disc Brooches: Part II: in England', *Antiquaries Journal* 58.2, 260–78.

Ewens, V. and Pipe, A., 2017, 'Roman Animal Bone', in S. Ranieri and A. Telfer, *Outside Roman London: Roadside Burials by the Walbrook Stream*, MOLA Crossrail Archaeology Series 9, London: Museum of London Archaeology, 165–77.

Faulkner, N., 2004, *The Decline and Fall of Roman Britain*, Stroud: Tempus.

Faulkner, N. and Neal, D., 2009, 'The End of Roman Verulamium', *Current Archaeology* 237, 29–35.

Favro, D. and Johanson, C., 2010, 'Death in Motion: Funeral Processions in the Roman Forum', *Journal of the Society of Architectural Historians* 69.1, 12–37.

Featherby, R., 2002, 'The Roman Pottery. St Andrews, Holborn EC2', unpublished Museum of London Archaeology report.

Ferretti, E. and Graham, A.H., 1978, '201–211 Borough High Street', in J. Bird, A. Graham, H. Sheldon, and P. Townend (eds), *Southwark Excavations 1972–1974*, LAMAS and SAS Joint Publication 1, London: London and Middlesex Archaeological Society and Surrey Archaeological Society, 53–176.

Field, D.J., 1985, 'The Prehistoric Pottery', in G. Parnell, 'The Roman and Medieval Defences and the Later Development of the Inmost Ward, Tower of London: Excavations 1955–77', *Transactions of the London and Middlesex Archaeological Society* 36, 51.

Fields, N., 2005, 'Headhunters of the Roman Army', in A. Hopkins and M. Wyke (eds), *Roman Bodies. Antiquity to the 18th century*, Rome: The British School at Rome, 55–66.

Finley, M.I., 1985, *The Ancient Economy* (2nd edn.), London: Hogarth Press.

Fishwick, D., 1969, 'The Imperial Numen in Roman Britain', *Journal of Roman Studies* 59, 76–91.

Fishwick, D., 2002, *The Imperial Cult in the Latin West: Studies in the Ruler Cult of the Western Provinces of the Roman Empire: Vol. 3: Provincial Cult: Part 1, Institutions and Evolution*, Religions in the Graeco-Roman world, Leiden: Brill.

Fittock, M.G., 2015, 'Broken Deities: The Pipe-clay Figurines from Roman London', *Britannia* 46, 111–34.

Fitzpatrick, A.P., 2018, 'Ebbsfleet, 54 BC: Searching for the Launch Site of Caesar's British Invasions', *Current Archaeology* 337, 26–32.

Fleming, R., 2019, 'Galen's Treatise Περὶ Ἀλυπίας (De indolentia) in Context: A Tale of Resilience', *Studies in Ancient Medicine* 52, Leiden: Brill.

Flohr, M., 2016, 'Work, Labour, and Professions in the Roman World', in K. Verboven and C. Laes (eds), *Work, Labour and Professions in the Roman World*, Leiden: Brill, 147–72.

Flohr, M. and Wilson, A., 2016, 'Roman Craftsmen and Traders: Towards an Intellectual History', in A. Wilson and M. Flohr (eds), *Urban Craftsmen and Traders in the Roman World*, Oxford: Oxford University Press, 23–54.

Flohr, M. and Wilson, A. (eds), 2017, *The Economy of Pompeii. Oxford Studies on the Roman Economy*, Oxford: Oxford University Press.

Francis, A.G., 1926, 'On a Romano-British Castration Clamp Used in the Rites of Cybele', *Proceedings of the Royal Society of Medicine* 19, 95–110.

Frankfurter, D., 2006, 'Traditional Cult', in D.S. Potter (ed.), *A Companion to the Roman Empire*, Princeton: Blackwell, 543–64.

Frere, S.S., 1983, *Verulamium Excavations 2*, Society of Antiquaries Research Report 41, Oxford: Society of Antiquaries.

Frere, S.S., 1999, *Britannia: A History of Roman Britain* (4th edn.), London: Folio Society.

Frere, S.S., 2000, 'M. Maenius Agrippa, the "Expeditio Britannica" and Maryport', *Britannia* 31, 23–8.

Frere, S.S. and Fulford, M., 2001, 'The Roman Invasion of A.D. 43', *Britannia* 32, 45–56.

Frere, S.S. and St Joseph, J.K., 1974, 'The Roman Fortress at Longthorpe', *Britannia* 5, 1–129.

Frere, S.S. and Witts, P., 2011, 'The Saga of Verulamium Building XXVII 2', *Britannia* 42, 263–74.

Frere, S.S., Stow, S., and Bennett, P., 1982, *Excavations on the Roman and Medieval Defences of Canterbury*, The Archaeology of Canterbury 2, Maidstone: Canterbury Archaeological Trust.

Frey, J.M., 2016, *Spolia in Fortifications and the Common Builder in Late Antiquity*, Mnemosyne Supplements, 389, Leiden: Brill.

Friedman, J.B., 2000, *Orpheus in the Middle Ages* (2nd edn.), New York: Harvard University Press.

Fuentes, N., 1983, 'Boudicca Re-visited', *London Archaeologist* 4.12, 311–17.

Fuentes, N., 1985, 'Of Castles and Elephants', *London Archaeologist* 5.4, 90–4.

Fuentes, N., 1986a, 'Durolitum Found? At Romford, on Spur above Market Place?', *Essex Journal* 21.1, 18–21.

Fuentes, N., 1986b, 'Some Entertainment in Londinium', *London Archaeologist* 5.6, 144–47.

Fuentes, N., 1991, 'London/Augusta: A Rejoinder', *London Archaeologist* 6.12, 333–38.

Fuentes, N. and Greenwood, P., 1993, *Roman Putney*, London: Wandsworth Historical Society.

Fuhrmann, C.J., 2012, *Policing the Roman Empire: Soldiers, Administration and Public Order*, Oxford: Oxford University Press.

Fulford, M., 1987, 'Economic Interdependence among Urban Communities of the Roman Mediterranean', *World Archaeology* 19.1, 58–75.

Fulford, M., 2001, 'Links with the Past: Pervasive "Ritual" Behaviour in Roman Britain', *Britannia* 32, 199–218.

Fulford, M., 2004, 'Economic Structures', in M. Todd (ed.), *A Companion to Roman Britain*, Oxford: Blackwell, 309–26.

Fulford, M., 2007, 'The Grand Excavation Projects of the Twentieth Century', in S. Pearce (ed.), *Visions of Antiquity: The Society of Antiquaries of London, 1707-2007*, London: Society of Antiquaries of London, 353–82.

Fulford, M., 2008a, 'Imperium Galliarum, Imperium Britanniarum. Developing New Ideologies and Settling Old Scores: Abandonments, Demolitions and New Building in

South-east Britain, c A D 250–300', in J. Clark, J. Cotton, J. Hall, R. Sherris, and H. Swain (eds), *Londinium and Beyond: Essays on Roman London and its Hinterland for Harvey Sheldon*, CBA Research Report 156, London: Council for British Archaeology, 41–5.

Fulford, M., 2008b, 'Nero and Britain: The Palace of the Client King at Calleva and Imperial Policy towards the Province after Boudicca', *Britannia* 39, 1–14.

Fulford, M., 2015a 'Retrospect and Prospect: Advancement of Knowledge, Methodologies and Publication', in M. Fulford and N. Holbrook (eds), *The Towns of Roman Britain: The Contribution of Commercial Archaeology since 1990*, Britannia Monograph 27, London: Society for the Promotion of Roman Studies, 194–211.

Fulford, M., 2015b, 'The Towns of South-east England', in M. Fulford and N. Holbrook (eds), *The Towns of Roman Britain: The Contribution of Commercial Archaeology since 1990*, Britannia Monograph 27, London: Society for the Promotion of Roman Studies, 59–89.

Fulford, M., 2017, 'Procurators' Business? Gallo-Roman Sigillata in Britain in the Second and Third Centuries A D ', in A. Bowman and A. Wilson (eds), *Trade, Commerce and the State in the Roman World*, Oxford: Oxford University Press, 301–26.

Fulford, M. and Allen, M., 2017, 'Introduction: Population and the Dynamics of Change in Roman South-Eastern England', in D. Bird (ed.), *Agriculture and Industry in South-Eastern Roman Britain*, Oxford: Oxbow, 1–14.

Fulford, M. and Bird, J., 1975, 'Imported Pottery from Germany in Late Roman Britain', *Britannia* 6, 171–81.

Fulford, M. and Hodder, I., 1974, 'A Regression Analysis of Some Late Romano-British Pottery: A Case Study', *Oxoniensia* 39, 26–33.

Fulford, M. and Timby, J.R., 2000, *Late Iron Age and Roman Silchester: Excavations on the Site of the Forum-Basilica 1977, 1980–86*, Britannia Monograph 15, London: Society for the Promotion of Roman Studies.

Fulford, M. and Tyres, I., 1995, 'The Date of Pevensey and the Defence of an "Imperium Britanniarum"', *Antiquity* 69.266, 10,009–14.

Fulford, M., Clarke, A., Durham, E., and Pankhurst, N., 2018, *Late Iron Age Calleva: The Pre-conquest Occupation at Silchester Insula IX*, Britannia Monograph 32, London: Society for the Promotion of Roman Studies.

Galinie, H. and Zadora-Rio, E. (eds), 1996, *Archéologie du cimetière chrétien*, Revue Archéologique du Centre de la France Supplementary Series 11, Tours: Fédération pour l'édition de la Revue archéologique du Centre de la France.

Gambash, G., 2015, *Rome and Provincial Resistance*, London: Routledge.

Gambash, G., 2016, 'Flavian Britain', in A. Zissos (ed.), *A Companion to the Flavian Age of Imperial Rome*, Chichester: John Wiley & Sons, 255–73.

Garcia, M.M., 2010, 'Saint Alban and the Cult of Saints in Late Antique Britain', PhD thesis, University of Leeds.

Gardner, A., 2016, 'Changing Materialities', in M. Millett, L. Revell, and A. Moore (eds), *The Oxford Handbook of Roman Britain*, Oxford: Oxford University Press, 481–508.

Garman, A.G., 2008, *The Cult of the Matronae in the Roman Rhineland: An Historical Evaluation of the Archaeological Evidence*, Lewiston NY: Edwin Mellen Press.

Germany, M., 2003, *Excavations at Great Holts Farm, Boreham, Essex*, East Anglian Archaeology 105, Chelmsford: Essex County Council.

Gerrard, J., 2008, 'Feeding the Army from Dorset: Pottery, Salt and the Roman State', in S. Stallibrass and R. Thomas (eds), *Feeding the Roman Army: The Archaeology of Production and Supply in NW Europe*, Oxford: Oxbow Books, 116–27.

Gerrard, J., 2009a, 'Dumps and Tesserae: High-Status Building Materials from 33 Union Street, Southwark', *London Archaeologist* 12.5, 130–34.

Gerrard, J., 2009b, 'The Drapers' Gardens Hoard: A Preliminary Account', *Britannia* 40, 163–83.

Gerrard, J., 2011a, 'Cathedral or Granary? The Roman Coins from Colchester House (PEP89)', *Transactions of the London Middlesex Archaeological Society* 62, 81–8.

Gerrard, J., 2011b, 'Discussion and Conclusions', in A. Douglas, J. Gerrard, and B. Sudds, *A Roman Settlement and Bath House at Shadwell: Excavations at Tobacco Dock and Babe Ruth's Restaurant, The Highway, London*, PCA Monograph 12, London: Pre-Construct Archaeology, 165–72.

Gerrard, J., 2011c, 'New Light on the End of Roman London', *Archaeological Journal* 168, 181–94.

Gerrard, J., 2011d, 'Roman Pottery', in A. Douglas, J. Gerrard, and B. Sudds, *A Roman Settlement and Bath House at Shadwell: Excavations at Tobacco Dock and Babe Ruth's Restaurant, The Highway, London*, PCA Monograph 12, London: Pre-Construct Archaeology, 61–86.

Gerrard, J., 2011e, 'Wells and Belief Systems at the End of Roman Britain: A Case Study from Roman London', in L. Lavan and M. Mulryan (eds), *The Archaeology of Late Antique Paganism*, Late Antique Archaeology 7, Leiden: Brill, 551–72.

Gerrard, J., 2013, *The Ruin of Roman Britain*, Cambridge: Cambridge University Press.

Gerrard, J., 2016, 'Economy and Power in Late Roman Britain', in M. Millett, L. Revell, and A. Moore (eds), *The Oxford Handbook of Roman Britain*, Oxford: Oxford University Press, 850–68.

Gerrard, J., Gerrard, S., and Haslam, R., 2019, 'The First Clipped Siliqua from Southwark', *London Archaeologist* 15.7, 215.

Ghey, E., 2007, 'Empty Spaces or Meaningful Places? A Broader Perspective on Continuity', in R. Haeussler and A. King (eds), *Continuity and Innovation in Religion in the Roman West: Vol. 1*, JRA Supplementary Series 67, Portsmouth, RI: Journal of Roman Archaeology, 19–30.

Gibbon, E., 1776, *The History of the Decline and Fall of the Roman Empire, Vol. 1*, New York: Fred De Fau and Company.

Gilliam, J.F., 1957, 'The Appointment of Auxiliary Centurions', *Transactions and Proceedings of the American Philological Association* 88, 155–68.

Goffin, R., 2005, 'Painted Wall Plaster', in B. Yule, *A Prestigious Roman Building Complex on the Southwark Waterfront: Excavations at Winchester Palace, London, 1983–90*, MoLAS Studies 23, London: Museum of London Archaeology, 103–45.

Going, C.J., 1992, 'Economic "Long Waves" in the Roman Period? A Reconnaissance of the Romano-British Ceramic Evidence', *Oxford Journal of Archaeology* 11.1, 93–117.

Goldsworthy, A.K., 1998, *The Roman Army at War 100 BC–AD 200*, Oxford classical monographs, Oxford: Clarendon Press.

Goldsworthy, A.K., 2003, *The Complete Roman Army*, London: Thames & Hudson.

Goodburn, D., 1991, 'A Roman Timber-framed Building Tradition', *Archaeological Journal* 148, 182–204.

Goodburn, D., 1995, 'From Tree to Town', *Archaeological Journal* 152, 33–47.

Goodburn, D., 2001, 'The Roman and Post-Roman Timber Technology', in T. Brigham, *Roman and Medieval Townhouses on the London Waterfront: Excavations at Governor's House, City of London*, MoLAS Monograph 9, London: Museum of London Archaeology, 78–84.

Goodburn, D., 2005, 'The Wood', in F. Seeley and J. Drummond-Murray, *Roman Pottery Production in the Walbrook Valley. Excavations at 20–28 Moorgate, City of London, 1998–2000*, MoLAS Monograph 24, London: Museum of London Archaeology, 191–97.

Goodburn, D., 2008, 'Timber', in T. Bradley and J. Butler, *From Temples to Thames Street—2000 years of Riverside Development; Archaeological Excavations at the Salvation Army International Headquarters, London*, PCA Monograph 7, London: Pre-Construct Archaeology, 41–51.

Goodburn, D., 2011, 'Woodworking', in J. Hill and P. Rowsome, *Roman London and the Walbrook Stream Crossing: Excavations at 1 Poultry and Vicinity 1985–96*, MoLA Monograph 37, London: Museum of London Archaeology, 393–96.

Goodburn, D., 2012, 'Worked Wood', in J. Leary and J. Butler, *Roman Archaeology in the Upper Reaches of the Walbrook Valley. Excavations at 6–8 Tokenhouse Yard, London EC2*, PCA Monograph 14, London: Pre-Construct Archaeology, 48–55.

Goodburn, D., 2016, 'The Manufacture of Waxed Stylus Writing Tablets in Roman London', in R.S.O. Tomlin, *Roman London's First Voices: Writing Tablets from the Bloomberg Excavations, 2010–14*, MoLA Monograph 72, London: Museum of London Archaeology, 8–13.

Goodburn, D., Goffin, R., Hill, J., and Rowsome, P., 2011, 'Domestic Buildings and Other Structures of Timber', in J. Hill and P. Rowsome, *Roman London and the Walbrook Stream Crossing: Excavations at 1 Poultry and Vicinity 1985–96*, MoLA Monograph 37, London: Museum of London Archaeology, 414–37.

Goodburn, D., in prep., 'Timber Technology', in T. Brigham and B. Watson, *Early Roman Waterfront Development: Excavations at Regis House, City of London, 1994–96*, London: Museum of London Archaeology.

Goodburn, R., 1978, 'Roman Britain in 1977. I: Sites Explored', *Britannia* 9, 404–72.

Gosden, C., 2004, *Archaeology and Colonialism*, Cambridge: Cambridge University Press.

Gowland, R. and Redfern, R., 2010, 'Childhood Health in the Roman World: Perspectives from the Centre and Margin of the Empire', *Childhood in the Past* 3, 15–42.

Graafstal, E., 2018, 'What Happened in the Summer of A.D. 122? Hadrian on the British Frontier—Archaeology, Epigraphy and Historical Agency', *Britannia* 49, 79–111.

Graham, A.H., 1988a, '64–70 Borough High Street', in P. Hinton (ed.), *Excavations in Southwark 1973–6, Lambeth 1973–9*, LAMAS and SAS Joint Publication 3, London: London and Middlesex Archaeological Society and Surrey Archaeological Society, 55–66.

Graham, A.H., 1988b, '84–86 Borough High Street', in P. Hinton (ed.), *Excavations in Southwark 1973–6, Lambeth 1973–9*, LAMAS and SAS Joint Publication 3, London: London and Middlesex Archaeological Society and Surrey Archaeological Society, 67–70.

Graham, A.H., 1988c, 'District Heating Scheme', in P. Hinton (ed.), *Excavations in Southwark 1973–6, Lambeth 1973–9*, LAMAS and SAS Joint Publication 3, London: London and Middlesex Archaeological Society and Surrey Archaeological Society, 27–54.

Graham, A.H. and Hinton, P., 1988, 'The Roman Roads in Southwark', in P. Hinton (ed.), *Excavations in Southwark 1973–6, Lambeth 1973–9*, LAMAS and SAS Joint Publication 3, London: London and Middlesex Archaeological Society and Surrey Archaeological Society, 19–26.

Graham, A.J., 1966, 'The Division of Britain', *Journal of Roman Studies* 56, 92–107.

Graham, E-J., 2015, 'Corporeal Concerns: The Role of the Body in the Transformation of Roman Mortuary Practices', in Z.L. Devlin and E-J. Graham (eds), *Death Embodied: Archaeological Approaches to the Study of the Corpse*, Studies in Funerary Archaeology 9, Oxford: Oxbow Books, 41–61.

Graham, J.G., 1936, 'A Romano-Celtic Temple at Titsey, and the Roman Road', *Surrey Archaeological Collections* 44, 84–101.

Graham, S., 2005, 'Of Lumberjacks and Brick Stamps: Working with the Tiber as Infrastructure', in A. MacMahon and J. Price (eds), *Roman Working Lives and Urban Living*, Oxford: Oxbow Books, 106–24.

Grahame, M., 1998, 'Redefining Romanization: Material Culture and the Question of Social Continuity in Roman Britain', in C. Forcey, J. Hawthorne, and R. Witcher (eds), *TRAC 97. Proceedings of the Seventh Annual Theoretical Roman Archaeology Conference, Nottingham 1997*, Oxford: Oxbow Books, 1–10.

Grainge, G., 2005, *The Roman Invasions of Britain*, Stroud: Tempus.

Grainger, I., 1995, '11 Ironmonger Lane, London EC4: An Archaeological Excavation and Watching Brief', unpublished Museum of London Archaeology report.

Grant, A.E., 2007, *Roman Military Objectives in Britain under the Flavian Emperors*, BAR British Series 440, Oxford: Archaeopress.

Grasby, R.D. and Tomlin, R.S.O., 2002, 'The Sepulchral Monument of the Procurator C. Julius Classicianus', *Britannia* 33, 43–75.

Green, C., 2017, 'Querns and Millstones in Late Iron Age and Roman London', in D. Bird (ed.), *Agriculture and Industry in South-Eastern Roman Britain*, Oxford: Oxbow, 156–79.

Green, D., Sheldon, H., Hacker, M., Woon, C., and Rowlinson, H., 1997, 'The Distribution of Villas in Some South-Eastern Counties: Some Preliminary Findings from a Survey', *London Archaeologist* 8.7, 187–95.

Green, M., 2001, *Dying for the Gods: Human Sacrifice in Iron Age and Roman Europe*, Stroud: Tempus.

Greenberg, J., 2003, 'Plagued by Doubt: Reconsidering the Impact of a Mortality Crisis in the 2nd c. A.D.', *Journal of Roman Archaeology* 16, 413–25.

Greenwood, P. and Maloney, C., 1996, 'London Fieldwork and Publication Round-up 1996', *London Archaeolog*ist 8, suppl.1.

Grew, F., 2008, 'Who was Mars Camulus', in J. Clark, J. Cotton, J. Hall, R. Sherris, and H. Swain (eds), *Londinium and Beyond; Essays on Roman London and its hinterland for Harvey Sheldon*. York, Council for British Archaeology, 142–50.

Grew, F., 2018, 'London Fieldwork and Publication Round-up 2017', *London Archaeologist* 15, suppl. 2.

Grew, F. and Watson, S., 2016, 'London Fieldwork and Publication Round-up 2015', *London Archaeologist* 14, suppl. 3.

Grimes, W., 1968, *The Excavation of Roman and Medieval London*, London: Routledge and Kegan Paul.

Grosso, I., 2017, 'A Sarcophagus and a Roman Road in Southwark: Excavation at 25–29 Harper Road', *Transactions of the London and Middlesex Archaeological Society* 68, 260–61.

Groves, J., 1990, 'Summary Finds Report', in C. Maloney, *The Upper Walbrook Valley*, The Archaeology of Roman London 1, CBA Research Report 69, London: Council for British Archaeology, 82–4.

Groves, J., 1997, 'Unstratified Roman Pottery', in G. Milne, *St Bride's Church London: Archaeological Research 1952–60 and 1992–5*, EH Archaeological Report 11, London: English Heritage, 53.

Guest, P., 2014, 'The Hoarding of Roman Metal Objects in Fifth-Century Britain', in F.K. Haarer (ed.), *AD 410: The History and Archaeology of Late and Post-Roman Britain*, London: Society for the Promotion of Roman Studies, 117–29.

Guthrie, W.K.C., 1966, *Orpheus and Greek Religion: a Study of the Orphic Movement*, New York: Princeton University Press.

Haglund, W.D., 1993, 'Disappearance of Soft Tissue and the Disarticulation of Human Remains from Aqueous Environments', *Journal of Forensic Science* 38.4, 806–15.

Haldon, J., Elton, H., Huebner, S.R., Izdebski, A., Mordechai, L., and Newfield, T.P., 2018, 'Plagues, Climate Change, and the End of an Empire: A Response to Kyle Harper's The Fate of Rome (2): Plagues and a Crisis of Empire', *History Compass* 16.12, DOI: 10.1111/hic3.12506.

Hall, J., 1996, 'The Cemeteries of Roman London', in J. Bird, M. Hassall, and H. Sheldon (eds), *Interpreting Roman London: Papers in Memory of Hugh Chapman*, Oxford: Oxbow Monograph 58, 57–84.

Hall, J., 2005, 'The Shopkeepers and Craft-workers of Roman London', in A. MacMahon and J. Price (eds), *Roman Working Lives and Urban Living*, Oxford: Oxbow Books, 125–44.

Hall, J., 2014a, 'Public, Personal or Private—Roman Lead-alloy Ingots from Battersea', in J. Cotton, J. Hall, J. Keily, R. Sherris, and R. Stephenson (eds), *Hidden Histories and Records of Antiquity: Essays on Saxon and Medieval London for John Clark, Curator Emeritus, Museum of London*, LAMAS Special Paper 17, London: London and Middlesex Archaeology Society, 116–21.

Hall, J., 2014b, 'With Criminal Intent? Forgers at Work in Roman London', *Britannia* 45, 165–94.

Hall, J. and Shepherd, J., 2008, 'Places of Worship in Roman London and Beyond', in D. Rudling (ed.), *Ritual Landscapes of Roman South-East Britain*, Oxford and Great Dunham: Heritage Marketing and Publications, 27–43.

Hall, J. and Wardle, A., 2005, 'Dedicated Followers of Fashion?—Decorative Bone Hairpins from Roman London', in N. Crummy (ed.), *Image, Craft and the Classical World*, Monographies Instrumentum 29, Montagnac: Éditions Monique Mergoil, 173–79.

Halsall, G., 2007, *Barbarian Migrations and the Late Roman West 376–568*, Library of European Civilisation, Cambridge: Cambridge University Press.

Hamilton, S. and Barrett, J., 2018, 'Theory in the Field', in A. Gardner, M. Lake, and U. Sommer (eds), *The Oxford Handbook of Archaeological Theory*, Oxford: Oxford University Press.

Hammer, F., 1985, 'Early Roman Buildings in Fenchurch Street', *Popular Archaeology* 6.12, 7–13.

Hammer, F., 1987, 'A Roman Basilica Hall and Associated Buildings at Fenchurch Street', *Archaeology Today* 8.9, 6–12.

Hammer, F., 2003, *Industry in North-west Roman Southwark: Excavations 1984–8*, MoLAS Monograph 17, London: Museum of London Archaeology.

Hammerson, M., 1978a, 'Coins', in J. Bird, A. Graham, H. Sheldon, and P. Townend (eds), *Southwark Excavations 1972–1974*, LAMAS and SAS Joint Publication 1, London: London and Middlesex Archaeological Society and Surrey Archaeological Society, 587–600.

Hammerson, M., 1978b, 'Excavations under Southwark Cathedral', *London Archaeologist* 3.8, 206–12.

Hammerson, M., 1988, 'Roman Coins from Southwark', in P. Hinton (ed.), *Excavations in Southwark 1973–6, Lambeth 1973–9*, LAMAS and SAS Joint Publication 3, London: London and Middlesex Archaeological Society and Surrey Archaeological Society, 417–26.

Hammerson, M., 1992, 'Coins', in C. Cowan, 'A Possible Mansio in Roman Southwark: Excavations at 15–23 Southwark Street 1980–6', *Transactions of the London and Middlesex Archaeological Society* 43, 137–44.

Hammerson, M., 1996, 'Problems of Roman Coin Interpretation in Greater London', in J. Bird, M. Hassall, and H. Sheldon (eds), *Interpreting Roman London: Papers in Memory of Hugh Chapman*, Oxbow Monograph 58, Oxford: Oxbow Books, 153–64.

Hammerson, M., 2011, 'The Claudian Coins', in J. Hill and P. Rowsome, *Roman London and the Walbrook Stream Crossing: Excavations at 1 Poultry and Vicinity 1985-96*, MoLA Monograph 37, London: Museum of London Archaeology, 261-62.

Hanson, W.H., 1988, 'Administration, Urbanisation and Acculturation', in D. Braund (ed.), *The Administration of the Roman Empire 241 BC-AD 193*, Exeter Studies in History 8, Exeter: University of Exeter, 53-68.

Hanson, W.S., 2012, 'Newstead and Roman Scotland: The Flavian to Antonine Periods', in F. Hunter and L.J.F. Keppie (eds), *A Roman Frontier Post and its People a Hundred Years on: Newstead 1911-2011*, Edinburgh: National Museums of Scotland, 62-75.

Harper, K., 2015, 'Pandemics and Passages to Late Antiquity: Rethinking the Plague of c.249-70 Described by Cyprian', *Journal of Roman Archaeology* 28, 223-60.

Harper, K., 2017, *The Fate of Rome: Climate, Disease, and the End of an Empire*, Princeton and Oxford: Princeton University Press.

Harris, W.V., 1991, *Ancient Literacy*, Cambridge, MA: Harvard University Press.

Harris, W.V., 2017, 'The Indispensable Commodity: Notes on the Economy of Wood in the Roman Mediterranean', in A. Bowman and A. Wilson, A. (eds), *Trade, Commerce and the State in the Roman World*, Oxford: Oxford University Press, 211-36.

Hart, D. and Melikian, M., 2007, 'Ritual Deposit on a Roman Site in the City', *London Archaeologist* 11.11, 300-5.

Hartle, R., 2017, 'Further Evidence for Development East of the Roman Forum-basilica: Excavations at Asia House, 31-33 Lime Street, EC3', *London Archaeologist* 15.2, 37-40.

Hartley, E., 2012, 'Excavation of an Early Roman Fort and Watling Street at Wigston Parva, 1969 to 1970', *Transactions of the Leicestershire Archaeology and History Society* 86, 117-33.

Hartley, K.F., 1996, 'Procuratorial Mortarium Stamps', in J. Bird, M. Hassall, and H. Sheldon (eds), *Interpreting Roman London. Papers in Memory of Hugh Chapman*, Oxbow Monograph 58, Oxford: Oxbow Books, 147-52.

Harward, C., Powers, N., and Watson, S., 2015, *The Upper Walbrook Cemetery of Roman London: Excavations at Finsbury Circus, City of London, 1987-2014*, MoLAS Archaeology Studies 32, London: Museum of London Archaeology.

Haselgrove, C., 2006, 'Early Potin Coinage in Britain: An Update', in P. de Jersey (ed.), *Celtic Coinage: New Discoveries, New Discussion*. BAR International Series 1532. Oxford: Archaeopress, 17-28.

Haslam, J., 2010, 'King Alfred and the Development of London', *London Archaeologist* 12.8, 208-12.

Hassall, M.W.C., 1978, 'Britain and the Rhine Provinces: Epigraphic Evidence for Roman Trade', in H. Cleere and J du Plat Taylor (eds), *Roman Shipping and Trade: Britain and the Rhine Provinces*, CBA Research Report 24, London: Council for British Archaeology, 41-8.

Hassall, M.W.C., 1980, 'The Inscribed Altars', in C. Hill, M. Millett, and T. Blagg (eds), *The Roman Riverside Wall and Monumental Arch in London: Excavations at Baynard's Castle, Upper Thames Street, London 1974-76*, LAMAS Special Paper 11, London: London Middlesex Archaeological Society, 195-97.

Hassall, M.W.C., 1996, 'London as a Provincial Capital', in J. Bird, M. Hassall, and H. Sheldon (eds), *Interpreting Roman London. Papers in Memory of Hugh Chapman*, Oxbow Monograph 58, Oxford: Oxbow Books, 19-26.

Hassall, M.W.C., 2012, 'The 2nd-century AD Garrison of Londinium', in J. Shepherd, *The Discovery of the Roman Fort at Cripplegate, City of London. Excavations by W.F. Grimes 1947-68*, MOLA Monograph, London: Museum of London Archaeology, 158-63.

Hassall, M.W.C., 2017, *Roman Britain: The Frontier Province*, Hobnob Press: Warminster.

Hassall, M.W.C. and Tomlin, R.S.O., 1987, 'Roman Britain in 1986: II Inscriptions', *Britannia* 18, 360–77.

Hassall, M.W.C. and Tomlin, R.S.O., 1996, 'Roman Britain in 1995: II Inscriptions', *Britannia* 27, 439–57.

Hathaway, S-J. E., 2013, 'Making the Invisible, Visible. Iron Age and Roman Salt-production in Southern Britain', PhD thesis, Bournemouth University.

Haverfield, F., 1911, 'Roman London', *Journal of Roman Studies* 1, 141–72.

Haverfield, F., 1915, *The Romanization of Britain* (3rd edn), Oxford: Clarendon Press.

Hawkes, C.F.C. and Dunning, G.C., 1931, 'The Belgae of Gaul and Britain', *Archaeological Journal* 87, 150–335.

Hawkes, J., 1982, *Mortimer Wheeler: Adventurer in Archaeology*, London: Weidenfeld & Nicolson.

Hawkins, C., 2016, *Roman Artisans and the Urban Economy*, Cambridge: Cambridge University Press.

Hawkins, N., 2019, 'A Roman Cemetery at Dickens Square, Southwark', *London Archaeologist* 15.10, 275–82.

Hawkins, N., forthcoming, *Excavations at Drapers' Gardens, City of London*, PCA monograph, London: Pre-Construct Archaeology.

Haynes, I., 2008, 'Sharing Secrets? The Material Culture of Mystery Cults from Londinium, Apulum and Beyond', in J. Clark, J. Cotton, J. Hall, R. Sherris, and H. Swain (eds), *Londinium and Beyond: Essays on Roman London and its Hinterland for Harvey Sheldon*, CBA Research Report 156, London: Council for British Archaeology, 128–33.

Haynes, I., 2013, *Blood of the Provinces: The Roman Auxilia and the Making of Provincial Society from Augustus to the Severans*, Oxford: Oxford University Press.

Haynes, I., 2016, 'Identity and the Military Community in Roman Britain', in M. Millett, L. Revell, and A. Moore (eds), *The Oxford Handbook of Roman Britain*, Oxford: Oxford University Press, 448–63.

Hayward, K.M.J., 2009, *Roman Quarrying and Stone Supply on the Periphery. Southern England: A Geological Study of First-Century Funerary Monuments and Monumental Architecture*, BAR British Series 500, Oxford: Archaeopress.

Hayward, K.M.J., 2015, 'Building Materials', in D. Killock, J. Shepherd, J. Gerrard, K. Hayward, K. Rielly, and V. Ridgeway, *Temples and Suburbs; Excavations at Tabard Square, Southwark*, London: Pre-Construct Archaeology Monograph 18, 172–86.

Heard, K., 1989, 'Excavations at 10–18 Union Street, Southwark', *London Archaeologist* 6.5, 126–31.

Hebblewhite, M., 2017, *The Emperor and the Army in the Later Roman Empire, AD 235–39 6*, London: Routledge.

Hekster, O and Zair, N., 2008, *Rome and Its Empire, AD 193–284*, Edinburgh: Edinburgh University Press.

Henig, M., 1984a, 'A Cache of Roman Intaglios from Eastcheap, City of London', *Transactions of the London and Middlesex Archaeological Society* 35, 11–15.

Henig, M., 1984b, *Religion in Roman Britain*, London: Batsford.

Henig, M., 1998, 'Appendix 1. The Temple as a Bacchium or Sacrarium in the Fourth Century', in J. Shepherd, *The Temple of Mithras London: Excavations by W F Grimes and A Williams at the Walbrook*, London: English Heritage, 230–31.

Henig, M., 2007, 'The Victory-Gem from Lullingstone Roman Villa', *Journal of the British Archaeological Association* 160, 1–7.

Henig, M., 2008, 'Intaglios from Roman London', in J. Clark, J. Cotton, J. Hall, R. Sherris, and H. Swain (eds), *Londinium and Beyond: Essays on Roman London and its Hinterland for Harvey Sheldon*, CBA Research Report 156, London: Council for British Archaeology, 226–38.

Henig, M., 2015, '"A Fine and Private Place": The Sarcophagus of Valerius Amandinus and the Origins of Roman Westminster', in W. Rodwell and T Tatton-Brown (eds), *Westminster I: The Art, Architecture and Archaeology of the Royal Abbey*, British Archaeological Association Transactions 39.1, London: Routledge.

Hepple, L.W., 2003, 'William Camden and Early Collections of Roman Antiquities in Britain', *Journal of the History of Collections* 15.2., 159–74.

Higham, N., 2014, 'Constantius, St Germanus and Fifth-century Britain', *Early Medieval Europe* 22.2, 113–37.

Hijmans, S.E., 2009, 'Sol: The Sun in the Art and Religions of Rome', PhD thesis, University of Groningen.

Hill, C., Millett, M., and Blagg, T., 1980, *The Roman Riverside Wall and Monumental Arch in London: Excavations at Baynard's Castle, Upper Thames Street, London 1974–76*, LAMAS Special Paper 11, London: London Middlesex Archaeological Society.

Hill, J., Peacock, D., and Williams, D., 2011, 'Evidence for grain processing and storage', in J. Hill and P. Rowsome, *Roman London and the Walbrook Stream Crossing: Excavations at 1 Poultry and Vicinity, City of London*, MoLA Monograph 37, London: Museum of London Archaeology, 349–52.

Hill, J. and Rowsome, P., 2011, *Roman London and the Walbrook Stream Crossing: Excavations at 1 Poultry and Vicinity, City of London*, MoLA Monograph 37, London: Museum of London Archaeology.

Hill, J. and Woodger, A., 1999, *Excavations at 72–75 Cheapside/83–93 Queen Street City of London*, MoLAS Archaeological Studies 2, London: Museum of London Archaeology.

Hill, P.R., 2006, *The Construction of Hadrian's Wall*, Stroud: Tempus.

Hillam, J., 1986, 'Tree-Ring Dating in the City of London: The Bridgehead Sites and the Dating of the Roman Harbour', English Heritage AML Report 4794.

Hillam, J., 1990, 'The Dendrochonology of the Late Roman Waterfront at Billingsgate Lorry Park and Other Sites in the City of London', *Britannia* 21, 164–70.

Hillam, J., 1993, 'Appendix 1: Tree-ring Dating of Oak Timbers from Peter's Hill and Sunlight Wharf', in T.D. Williams, *Public Buildings in the South West Quarter of Roman London*, The Archaeology of Roman London 3, CBA Research Report 88, London: Council for British Archaeology, 95–9.

Hillam, J. and Morgan, R.A., 1986, 'Tree-ring Analysis of the Roman Timbers', in L. Miller, J. Schofield, and M. Rhodes, *The Roman Quay at St Magnus House, London: Excavations at New Fresh Wharf, Lower Thames Street, London 1974–78*, LAMAS Special Paper 8, London: London Middlesex Archaeological Society, 75–86.

Hinard, F., 1987, 'Spectacle des executions et espace urbain', in CNRS, *L'Urbs: espace urbain et histoire (Ier siècle av. J.-C.- IIIe siècle ap. J.-C.): Acte du colloque international organise par le Centre national de la recherche scientifique a l'Ecole française de Rome (Rome, 8–12 mai 1985)*, EFR 98, Rome: Ecole Française de Rome, 111–25.

Hind, J.G.F., 1989, 'The Invasion of Britain in AD 43: An Alternative Strategy for Aulus Plautius', *Britannia* 20, 1–21.

Hingley, R., 2000, *Roman Officers and English Gentlemen: The Imperial Origins of Roman Archaeology*, London: Routledge.

Hingley, R., 2008, *The Recovery of Roman Britain 1586–1906: Colony So Fertile*, Oxford Studies in the History of Archaeology, Oxford: Oxford University Press.

Hingley, R., 2016, 'Early Studies in Roman Britain: 1610 to 1906', in M. Millett, L. Revell, and A. Moore (eds), *The Oxford Handbook of Roman Britain*, Oxford: Oxford University Press, 3–21.

Hingley, R., 2018, *Londinium: A Biography. Roman London from its Origins to the Fifth Century*, Bloomsbury: London.

Hirt, A.M., 2010, *Imperial Mines and Quarries in the Roman World*, Oxford: Oxford University Press.

Hirt, A.M., 2015, 'Centurions, Quarries, and the Emperor', in P. Erdkamp, K. Verboven, and A. Zuiderhoek (eds), *Ownership and Exploitation of Land and Natural Resources in the Roman World*, Oxford University Press, 289–413.

Hmood, K.F., 2017, 'Traditional Markets in Islamic Architecture: Successful Past Experiences', *Transactions on The Built Environment* 171, 263–73.

Hobley, B. and Schofield, J.A., 1977, 'Excavations in the City of London. First Interim Report, 1974–1975', *Antiquaries Journal* 57, 31–66.

Hobson, M.S., 2014, 'A Historiography of the Study of the Roman Economy: Economic Growth, Development and Neoliberism', in H. Platts, J. Pearce, C. Barron, J. Lundock, and J. Yoo (eds), *TRAC 2013: Proceedings of the 23rd Theoretical Roman Archaeology Conference*, Oxford: Oxbow Books, 11–26.

Hodder, I. and Millett, M., 1980, 'Romano-British Villas and Towns: A Systematic Analysis', *World Archaeology* 121, 69–76.

Hodgkinson, J., 2008, *The Wealden Iron Industry*, Stroud: History Press.

Hodgkinson, J., 2012, Wealden Iron Research Group Newletter 55, htttp://www.wealdeniron.ork.uk/Newsletters/Mar%202,012%20col.pdf.

Hodgkinson, J., 2017, 'The Development of Iron Production in the Roman Weald', in D. Bird (ed.), *Agriculture and Industry in South-Eastern Roman Britain*, Oxford: Oxbow Books, 282–300.

Hodgson, N., 2014, 'The British Expedition of Septimius Severus', *Britannia* 45, 31–51.

Hodgson, N., 2021, 'The End of the Ninth Legion, War in Britain and the Building of Hadrian's Wall', *Britannia* 52.

Hoffmann, B., 2013, *The Roman Invasion of Britain: Archaeology v History*, Barnsley: Pen & Sword Books.

Hoffmann, H., 1963, 'Helios', *Journal of the American Research Center in Egypt* 2, 117–24.

Holbrook, N., 2015, 'The Towns of South-west England', in M. Fulford and N. Holbrook (eds), *The Towns of Roman Britain: The Contribution of Commercial Archaeology since 1990*, Britannia Monograph 27, London: Society for the Promotion of Roman Studies, 90–116.

Holder, N., 2007, 'Mapping the Roman Inscriptions of London', *Britannia* 38, 13–34.

Holder, N. and Jamieson, D., 2003, 'The Prehistory of the City of London: Myths and Mythologies', *Archaeological Journal* 160, 23–43.

Holder, P., 2003, 'Auxiliary Deployment in the Reign of Hadrian', *Bulletin of the Institute of Classical Studies* 46. S81, 101–14.

Holst, M.K., Heinemeier, J., Hertz, E., Jensen, P., Løvschal, M., Mollerup, L., Odgaard, B.V., Olsen, J., Søe, N.E., and Kristiansen, S.M., 2018, 'Direct Evidence of a Large Northern European Roman Period Martial Event and Post-battle Corpse Manipulation', *Proceedings of the National Academy of Sciences of the United States of America* 21, 5920–25.

Home, G., 1948, *Roman London, AD 43–457*, London: Eyre and Spottiswoode.

Hope, V.M., 2000, 'Contempt and Respect: The Treatment of the Corpse in Ancient Rome', in V.M. Hope and E. Marshall (eds), *Death and Disease in the Ancient City*, London: Routledge, 104–27.

Hope, V.M., 2007, *Death in Ancient Rome: A Sourcebook*, London: Routledge.

Hope, V.M., 2016, 'Inscriptions and Identity', in M. Millett, L. Revell, and A. Moore (eds), *The Oxford Handbook of Roman Britain*, Oxford: Oxford University Press, 285–302.

Hopkins, K., 1978, 'Economic Growth and Towns in Classical Antiquity', in P. Abrams and E.A. Wrigley (eds), *Towns in Societies. Essays in Economic History and Historical Sociology*, Cambridge: Cambridge University Press, 35–77.

Hopkins, K., 1983, 'Models, Ships and Staples', in P. Garnsey and C.R. Whittaker (eds), *Trade and Famine in Classical Antiquity*, Cambridge Philological Society 8, Cambridge: Cambridge Philological Society, 84–110.

Hopkins, K., 2002, 'Rome, Taxes, Rents and Trade', in W. Scheidel and S. von Reden (eds), *The Ancient Economy*, Edinburgh: Edinburgh University Press, 190–230.

Horden, P. and Purcell, N., 2000, *The Corrupting Sea: A Study of Mediterranean History*, Oxford: Blackwell.

Horne, P.D. and King, A.C., 1980, 'Romano-Celtic Temples in Continental Europe: a Gazetteer of Those with Known Plans', in W. Rodwell (ed.), *Temples, Churches and Religion in Roman Britain*, BAR British Series 77, British Archaeological Reports: Archaeopress, 369–556.

Houston, G.W., 1980, 'The Administration of Italian Seaports during the First Three Centuries of the Roman Empire', *The Seaborne Commerce of Ancient Rome: Studies in Archaeology and History*, Memoirs of the American Academy in Rome 36, Rome: University of Michigan Press, 157–71.

Houston, G.W., 1988, 'Ports in Perspective: Some Comparative Materials on Roman Merchant Ships and Ports', *American Journal of Archaeology* 92, 553–64.

Howe, E., 2002, *Roman Defences and Medieval Industry: Excavations at Baltic House, City of London*, MoLAS Monograph 7, London: Museum of London Archaeology.

Howe, E. and Lakin, D., 2004, *Roman and Medieval Cripplegate, City of London: Excavations 1992–8*, MoLAS Monograph 21, London: Museum of London Archaeology.

Howell, I., 2005, *Prehistoric Landscape to Roman Villa: Excavations at Beddington, Surrey, 1981–7*, MoLAS Monograph 21, London: Museum of London Archaeology.

Howell, I., 2013, *Roman and Medieval Development South of Cheapside: Excavations at Bow Bells House, City of London, 2005–6*, MoLA Studies 26, London: Museum of London Archaeology.

Howell, I., Wroe-Brown, R., and Thorp, A., 2015, 'New Evidence for the Development of the Roman City Wall: Excavations at 38–40 Trinity Square, London EC3', *London Archaeologist* 14.6, 143–49.

Humphrey, J.H., 1986, *Roman Circuses: Arenas for Chariot Racing*, London: Batsford.

Humphreys, O.J., 2021, *London's Roman Tools: Craft, Agriculture and Experience in an Ancient City*, BAR British Series 663, Oxford: Archaeopress.

Hunt, G., 2010, 'Along the Eastern Defences: Excavations at 8–14 Cooper's Row and 1 America Square, City of London', *Transactions of the London and Middlesex Archaeological Society* 61, 41–80.

Hunt, G. and Shepherd, J., 2009, 'Glorious Glass from Prescott Street', *London Archaeologist* 12.5, 136–7.

Hunt, S., 2016, *Reviving Roman Religion: Sacred Trees in the Roman World*, Cambridge: Cambridge University Press.

Hunting. P., 1987, *The Garden House*, London: MEPC.

Hurst, H., 1999, 'Civic Space at Glevum', in H. Hurst (ed.), *The Coloniae of Roman Britain: New Studies and a Review. Papers of the Conference held at Gloucester on 5–6 July 1997*, JRA Supplementary Series 36, Portsmouth RI: Journal of Roman Archaeology, 152–60.

Hurst, H., 2016, 'The Textual and Archaeological Evidence', in M. Millett, L. Revell, and A. Moore (eds), *The Oxford Handbook of Roman Britain*, Oxford: Oxford University Press, 95–116.

Hyland, A.H., 1990, *Equus: The Horse in the Roman World*, New Haven and London: Yale University Press.

Inker, P., 2006, *The Anglo-Saxon Relief Style*, BAR British Series 410, Oxford: Archaeopress.

Intagliata, E., Barker, S.J., and Courault, C., 2020, 'Approaching Late Antique City Walls with an Empire-wide Perspective', in E Intagliata, S.J. Barker, and C. Courault (eds), *City Walls in Late Antiquity: An Empire-wide Perspective*, Oxford: Oxbow Books, 1–7.

Irby-Massie, G.L., 1999, *Military Religion in Roman Britain*, Leiden: Brill.

Isserlin, R.M.J., 1997, 'Thinking the Unthinkable: Human Sacrifice in Roman Britain?', in K. Meadows, C. Lemke, and J. Heron (eds), *TRAC 96. Proceedings of the Sixth Annual Theoretical Roman Archaeology Conference*, Oxford: Oxbow Books, 91, 100.

Ivens, J. and Deal, G., 1977, 'Finds and Excavations in Roman Enfield', *London Archaeologist* 3.3, 59–65.

Izdebski, A., Mordechai, L., and White, S., 2018, 'The Social Burden of Resilience: A Historical Perspective', *Human Ecology* 46, 291–303.

Jackson, R.P.J. and Potter, T.W., 1996, *Excavations at Stonea, Cambridgeshire, 1980–85*, London: British Museum Press.

Jackson, K., 1953, *Language and History in Early Britain*, Edinburgh: Edinburgh University Press.

James, P., 1987, '68 Cornhill, 1981–2', in P. Marsden, *The Roman Forum Site in London*, London: HMSO, 87–9.

James, S., 2001, 'Soldiers and Civilians: Identity and Interaction in Roman Britain', in S. James and M. Millett (eds), *Britons and Romans: Advancing an Archaeological Agenda*, CBA Research Report 125, London: Council for British Archaeology, 77–89.

Jarrett, M.G., 1976, 'An Unnecessary War', *Britannia* 7, 145–51.

Johnson, J.S., 1970, 'The Date of the Construction of the Saxon Shore Fort at Richborough', *Britannia* 1, 240–248.

Johnson, P., 1993, 'Town Mosaics and Urban Officinae', in S.J. Greep (ed.), *Roman Towns: The Wheeler Inheritance*, CBA Research Report 93, London: Council for British Archaeology, 147–65.

Johnson, P.S., 2012, *Economic Evidence and the Changing Nature of Urban Space in Late Antique Rome*, Collecció Instrumenta 42, Barcelona: Universitat de Barcelona.

Johnson, S., 1976, *The Roman Forts of the Saxon Shore*, London: St. Martin's Press.

Johnson, S., 1983, 'Late Roman Urban Defences in Europe', in J. Maloney and B. Hobley (eds), *Roman Urban Defences in the West*, CBA Research Report 51, London: Council for British Archaeology, 68–76.

Johnson, T., 1975, 'A Roman Signal Station at Shadwell, E.1', *Transactions of the London and Middlesex Archaeological Society* 26, 278–80.

Johnston, D.E., 1977, 'Editor's Forward', in D.E. Johnston (ed.), *The Saxon Shore*, CBA Research Report 18. London: Council for British Archaeology, v.

Jones, A.H.M., 1964, *The Later Roman Empire 284–602: A Social, Economic and Administrative Survey*, Baltimore: Johns Hopkins University Press.

Jones, B., 1984, *Past Imperfect: The Story of Rescue Archaeology*, Henemann: London.

Jones, C.E.E., 1983, 'A Review of Roman Lead-alloy Material Recovered from the Walbrook Valley in the City of London', *Transactions of the London and Middlesex Archaeological Society* 34, 49–59.

Jones, C.E.E. and Sherlock, D., 1996, 'Early Decorated Roman Spoons from London', in J. Bird, M. Hassall, and H. Sheldon (eds), *Interpreting Roman London. Papers in Memory of Hugh Chapman*, Oxbow Monograph 58, Oxford: Oxbow Books, 165–76.

Jones, C.P., 2005, 'Ten Dedications "To the Gods and Goddesses" and the Antonine Plague', *Journal of Roman Archaeology* 18, 293–301.

Jones, C.P., 2016, 'An Amulet from London and Events Surrounding the Antonine Plague', *Journal of Roman Archaeology* 29, 469–72.

Jones, D.M., 1980, *Excavations at Billingsgate Buildings 'Triangle', Lower Thames Street 1974*, LAMAS Special Paper 4, London: London and Middlesex Archaeological Society.

Jones, J.E., 2004, 'Water Transport in the Bristol Channel, Wales and the Marches during the Romano British Period', PhD thesis, University of Bristol.

Jones, P., 2010, *Roman and Medieval Staines: The Development of the Town*, SpoilHeap Monograph 2, Woking: SpoilHeap Publications.

Jones, R., 2014, 'Known Unknowns: "Invisible" People in Temporary Camps', in R. Collins and F. McIntosh (eds), *Life in the Limes: Studies of the People and Objects of the Roman Frontiers*, Oxford: Oxbow Books, 172–82.

Jones, R.F.J., 1987, 'Burial Customs of Rome and the Provinces', in J. Wacher (ed.), *The Roman World*. London: Routledge, 812–38.

Joy, J., 2012, 'Exploring Status and Identity in Later Iron Age Britain: Reinterpreting Mirror Burials', in T. Moore and X-L. Armada (eds), *Atlantic Europe in the First Millennium BC: Crossing the Divide*, Oxford: Oxford University Press, 468–84.

Kaiser, A., 2011, *Roman Urban Street Networks*, Abingdon & New York: Routledge.

Kalafikis, G., 2014, 'Ammianus Marcellinus on the Military Strategy of the Emperor Valentinian I (364–375 AD): General Principles and Implementation', *Byzantiaka* 31, 15–50.

Kaye, S., 2015, 'The Roman Invasion of Britain, AD 43: Riverine, Wading and Tidal Studies Place Limits on the Possible Locations of the Two-day River Battle and Beachhead', *Archaeologia Cantiana* 136, 227–40.

Keay, S., 2012, 'The Port System of Imperial Rome', in S. Keay (ed.), *Rome, Portus and the Mediterranean*, BSR Monograph 21, London: British School at Rome, 33–67.

Kehne, P., 2007, 'War- and Peacetime Logistics: Supplying Imperial Armies in East and West', in P. Erdkamp (ed.), *A Companion to the Roman Army*, Oxford: Blackwell, 323–38.

Kehoe, D.P., 1988, *The Economics of Agriculture on Roman Imperial Estates in North Africa*, Hypnomnemata 89, Göttingen: Vandenhoeck & Ruprecht.

Kehoe, D.P., 2006, 'Landlords and Tenants', in D.S. Potter (ed.), *A Companion to the Roman Empire*, Blackwell: Princeton, 298–311.

Kehoe, D.P., 2007, *Law and Rural Economy in the Roman Empire*, Ann Arbor: University of Michigan Press.

Kehoe, D.P., 2012, 'Contract Labour', in W. Scheidel (ed.), *The Cambridge Companion to the Roman Economy*, Cambridge: Cambridge University Press, 114–30.

Kehoe, D.P., 2015a, 'Poverty, Distribution of Wealth, and Economic Growth in the Roman Empire', in P. Erdkamp and K. Verboven (eds), *Structure and Performance in the Roman Economy: Models, Methods and Case Studies*, Latomus 350: Brussels: Éditions Latomus, 183–96.

Kehoe, D.P., 2015b, 'Property Rights over Land and Economic Growth in the Roman Empire', in P. Erdkamp, K. Verboven, and A. Zuiderhoek (eds), *Ownership and Exploitation of Land and Natural Resources in the Roman World*, Oxford: Oxford University Press, 88–106.

Keily, J., 2006, 'The Accessioned Finds', in R. Bluer and T. Brigham, *Roman and Later Development East of the Forum and Cornhill*, MoLAS Monograph 30, London: Museum of London Archaeology, 142–59.

Keily, J., 2011, 'Leather', in J. Hill and P. Rowsome, *Roman London and the Walbrook Stream Crossing: Excavations at 1 Poultry and Vicinity, City of London*, MoLA Monograph 37, London: Museum of London Archaeology, 540–57.

Keily, J. and Mould, Q., 2017, 'Leatherworking in South-eastern Britain in the Roman Period', in D. Bird (ed.), *Agriculture and Industry in South-Eastern Roman Britain*, Oxford: Oxbow, 236–54.

Keily, J. and Shepherd, J., 2005, 'Glass Working in the Upper Walbrook Valley', in F. Seeley and J. Drummond-Murray, *Roman Pottery Production in the Walbrook Valley: Excavations at 20–28 Moorgate, City of London, 1998–2000*, MoLAS Monograph 25, London: Museum of London Archaeology, 146–55.

Kent, J., 1978, 'The London Area in the Late Iron Age: and Interpretation of the Earliest Coins', in J. Bird, H. Chapman, and J. Clark (eds), *Collectanea Londiniensia. Studies in London Archaeology and History Presented to Ralph Merrifield*, LAMAS Special Paper 2, London: London and Middlesex Archaeological Society, 53–8.

Kidd, D., 1977, 'Charles Roach Smith and the Museum of London Antiquities', *Collectors and Collections, The British Museum Year Book 2*, London: British Museum, 105–35.

Killock, D., 2005, 'Roman River Bank Use and Changing Water Levels at 51–53 Southwark Street, Southwark, London', *Transactions of the London and Middlesex Archaeological Society* 56, 27–44.

Killock, D., Gerrard, J., and Langthorne, J., forthcoming, *Excavations at 28–30 Trinity Street*, London: Pre-Construct Archaeology Monograph.

Killock, D., Shepherd, J., Gerrard, J., Hayward, K., Rielly, K., and Ridgeway, V., 2015, *Temples and Suburbs; Excavations at Tabard Square, Southwark*, PCA Monograph 18. London: Pre-Construct Archaeology.

King, A.C., 1990, 'The Emergence of Romano-Celtic Religion', in T. Blagg and M. Millett (eds), *The Early Roman Empire in the West*, Oxford: Oxbow Books, 220–41.

Knüsel, C.J. and Carr, G.C., 1995, 'On the Significance of the Crania from the River Thames and Its Tributaries', *Antiquity* 69, 162–69.

Kolb, A., 2002, 'The Impact and Interaction of State Transport in the Roman Empire', in L. Blois and J. Rich (eds), *The Transformation of Economic Life under the Roman Empire. Proceedings of the Second Workshop of the International Network Impact of Empire (Roman Empire c. 200 BC–AD 476), Nottingham*, Amsterdam: Gieben, 67–76.

Kolbeck, B., 2018, 'A Foot in Both Camps: The Civilian Suppliers of the Army in Roman Britain', *Theoretical Roman Archaeology Journal* 1.1, 1–19, DOI: 10.16995/traj.355.

Kulikowski, M., 2000, 'The "Notitia Dignitatum" as a Historical Source', *Historia* 49.3, 358–77.

Kyle, D.G., 1998, *Spectacles of Death in Ancient Rome*, London: Routledge.

Lakin, D., 1999, 'A Romano-British site at Summerton Way, Thamesmead, London Borough of Bexley', *Archaeologia Cantiana* 119, 311–41.

Lakin, D., 2002, *The Roman Tower at Shadwell London: A Reappraisal*, MoLA Archaeology Studies 8, London: Museum of London Archaeology.

Lambrick, G. and Robinson, M., 2009, *The Thames Through Time: the Archaeology of the Gravel Terraces of the Upper and Middle Thames: the Thames Valley in Late Prehistory, 1500 BC–AD 50*, Oxford: Oxford University School of Archaeology.

Lane Fox, A.H., 1867, 'A Description of Certain Piles Found Near London Wall and Southwark, Possibly the Remains of Pile Buildings', *Anthropological Review* 5, 71–80.

Latham, J.A., 2016, *Performance, Memory and Processions in Ancient Rome: The Pompa Circensis from the Late Republic to Late Antiquity*, Cambridge: Cambridge University Press.

Laurence, R., 2001, 'The Creation of Geography: An Interpretation from Roman Britain', in C. Adams and R. Laurence (eds), *Travel and Geography in the Roman World*, London: Routledge, 67–94.

Laurence, R., 2008, 'City Traffic and the Archaeology of Roman Streets from Pompeii to Rome. The Nature of Traffic in the Ancient City', in D. Mertens (ed.), *Palilia 18, Stadtverkehr in der antiken Welt: Internationales Kolloquium zur 175-Jahrfeier des Deutschen Archäologischen Instituts Rom*, Palilia 18, Rome: Ludwig Reichert, 87–106.

Laurence, R., 2011, 'Endpiece: From Movement to Mobility: Future Directions', in R. Laurence and D.J. Newsome (eds), *Rome, Ostia and Pompeii: Movement and Space*, New York: Oxford University Press, 386–401.

Laurence, R., 2012, *Roman Archaeology for Historians*, London: Routledge.

Laurence, R., Esmonde Cleary, A.S., and Sears, G., 2011, *The City in the Roman West c. 250 BC–c. AD 250*, Cambridge: Cambridge University Press.

Lavan, L., 2011, 'The End of Temples: Towards a New Narrative?', in L. Lavan and M. Mulryan (eds), *The Archaeology of Late Antique Paganism*, Late Antique Archaeology 7, Leiden: Brill, xv–lxv.

Lavan, M., 2019a, 'The Army and the Spread of Roman Citizenship', *Journal of Roman Studies* 109, 27–69.

Lavan, M., 2019b, 'The Manpower of the Roman Fleets', *Journal of Roman Archaeology* 23, 183–200.

Lawrence, L.A., 1940, 'A Hoard of Plated Roman Denarii', *Numismatic Chronical* 5.20, 185–9.

Laws, A., 1976, 'Excavations at Northumberland Wharf, Brentford', *Transactions of the London and Middlesex Archaeological Society* 27, 179–205.

Le Masne De Chermont, N., 1987, 'Les fouilles de l'ancien évêché de Poitiers (Vienne)', *Aquitania* 5, 149–75.

Leach, D.S., 2017, 'Carpenters in Medieval London c. 1240 – c. 1540', PhD thesis, University of London.

Leary, J., 2004, '285–291 Tooley Street: Further Evidence for Late Iron Age/Early Roman Settlement in Bermondsey', *London Archaeologist* 10.11, 283–88.

Leary, J. and Butler, J., 2012, *Roman Archaeology in the Upper Reaches of the Walbrook Valley. Excavations at 6–8 Tokenhouse Yard, London EC2*, PCA Monograph 14, London: Pre-Construct Archaeology.

Lees, D., Woodger, A., and Orton, C., 1989, 'Excavations in the Walbrook Valley', *London Archaeologist* 6.5, 115–19.

Lennon, J.J., 2014, *Pollution and Religion in Ancient Rome*, Cambridge: Cambridge University Press.

Leone, A., 2007, 'Changing Urban Landscapes: Burials in North African Cities from the Late Antique to Byzantine Periods', in L. Stirling and D. Stone (eds), *Mortuary Landscapes of North Africa*, Toronto: University of Toronto Press, 164–203.

Leone, A., 2013, *End of the Pagan City: Religion, Economy, and Urbanism in Late Antique North Africa*, Oxford: Oxford University Press.

Lerz, A., Henig, M., and Hayward, K., 2017, 'The Minories Eagle: A New Sculpture from London's Eastern Roman Cemetery', *Britannia* 48, 359–63.

Leveau, P., 2016, 'Praetoria et tabernae en Gaule: Contribution à l'identification des établissements de bord de route', in F. Colleoni (ed.), *Stations, routières en Gaule Romaine. Architecture, équipements et fonctions*, Gallia 73.1, Paris: CNRS, 29–38.

Lewis, J., 2000a, 'The Lower Palaeolithic Period', in Museum of London, *The Archaeology of Greater London*, MoLAS Monograph: London: Museum of London Archaeology, 29–43.

Lewis, J., 2000b, 'The Neolithic Period', in Museum of London, *The Archaeology of Greater London*, MoLAS Monograph, London: Museum of London Archaeology, 63–80.

Lewis, J., 2000c, 'The Upper Palaeolithic and Mesolithic Periods', in Museum of London, *The Archaeology of Greater London*, MoLAS Monograph, London: Museum of London Archaeology, 45–62.

Lewit, T., 2013, 'The Lessons of Gaulish Sigillata and Other Finewares', in L. Lavan (ed.), *Local Economies? Production and Exchange of Inland Regions*, Late Antique Archaeology 10, Leiden: Brill, 227–57.

Liddle, J., 2008, 'The Animal Bones', in N. Bateman, C. Cowan, and R. Wroe-Brown, *London's Roman Amphitheatre: Guildhall Yard, City of London*, MoLAS Monograph Series 35, London: Museum of London Archaeology, 213–17.

Liddle, J., Ainsley, C., and Rielly, K., 2009, 'Animal Bone', in C. Cowan, F. Seeley, A. Wardle, A. Westman, and L Wheeler, *Roman Southwark Settlement and Economy: Excavations in Southwark 1973–91*, MoLA Monograph 42, London: Museum of London Archaeology, 244–48.

Liebeschuetz, J.H.W.G., 1979, *Continuity and Change in Roman Religion*, Oxford: Oxford University Press.

Liebeschuetz, J.H.W.G., 2007, 'Was There a Crisis of the Third Century?', in O. Hekster, G. de Kleijn and D. Slootjes (eds), *Crisis and the Roman Empire. Proceedings of the Seventh Workshop of the International Network Impact of Empire (Nijmegen, June 20–24, 2006)*, Leiden: Brill, 11–22.

Lindell, M.K., 2013, 'Disaster Studies', *Current Sociology* 61, 797–825.

Lis, C., 2009, 'Perceptions of Work in Classical Antiquity: A Polyphonic Heritage', in J. Ehmer and C. Lis (eds), *The Idea of Work in Europe from Antiquity to Modern Times*, Farnham: Ashgate, 33–70.

Littman, R.J. and Littman, M.L., 1973, 'Galen and the Antonine Plague', *American Journal of Philology* 94, 243–55.

Livarda, A. and Orengo, A., 2015, 'Reconstructing Roman London Flavourscape: New Insights into the Exotic Food Plant Trade Using Network and Spatial Analyses', *Journal of Archaeological Science* 55, 244–52.

Lo Cascio, E., 2007a, 'L'approvvigionamento dell'esercito Romano: mercato libero o 'commercio amministrato?', in L. De Blois and E. Lo Cascio (eds), *The Impact of the Roman Army (200 BC–AD 476): Economic, Social, Political, Religious and Cultural Aspects*, Leiden: Brill, 195–206.

Lo Cascio, E., 2007b, 'The Early Roman Empire: The State and the Economy', in W. Scheidel, I. Morris, and R.P. Saller (eds), *The Cambridge Economic History of the Graeco-Roman World*, Cambridge: Cambridge University Press, 619–47.

Lo Cascio, E., 2015, 'The Imperial Property and its Development', in P. Erdkamp, K. Verboven, and A. Zuiderhoek (eds), *Ownership and Exploitation of Land and Natural Resources in the Roman World*, Oxford: Oxford University Press, 62–70.

Locker, A., 2007, 'In Piscibus Diversis: The Bone Evidence for Fish Consumption in Roman Britain', *Britannia* 38, 141–80.

Lodwick, L., 2017, 'Arable Farming, Plant Foods and Resources', in M. Allen, L. Lodwick, T. Brindle, M. Fulford, and A. Smith (eds), *New Visions of the Countryside of Roman Britain, Vol. 2: The Rural Economy of Roman Britain*, Britannia Monograph 30, London: Society for the Promotion of Roman Studies, 11–84.

Loe, L., 2003, 'Specialist Report on the Human Skull (8658) from Vindolanda, Northumberland', in A. Birley (ed.), *Vindolanda Report 2003 Vol. 1: The Excavation of 2001–2002: Civilian Settlement, Severan and Second Century Forts and the Pre-Hadrianic Occupation, with a Report on the Trial Excavations at Carvoran*, Hexham: Vindolanda Trust, 213–49.

Loseby, S.T., 2000, 'Power and Towns in Late Roman Britain and Early Anglo-Saxon England', in G. Ripoll and J.M. Gurt (eds), *Sedes Regiae (ann. 400–800)*, Barcelona: Reial Acadèmia de Bones Lletres, 319–70.

Lucas, G., 2001, *Critical Approaches to Fieldwork: Contemporary and Historical Archaeological Practice*, London: Routledge.

Lucy, S. and Evans, J., 2016, *Romano-British Settlement and Cemeteries at Mucking: Excavations by Margaret and Tom Jones, 1965–1978*, Cambridge Archaeological Unit Landscape Archives 3, Oxford: Oxbow Books.

Lusnia, S.S., 2014, *Creating Severan Rome. The Architecture and Self-Image of L. Septimius Severus (A.D. 193–211)*, Latomus 345, Brussels: Latomus.

Lyne, M., 2016, *Late Roman Handmade Grog-tempered Ware Producing Industries in South East Britain*, Archaeopress Roman Archaeology 12, Oxford: Archaeopress.

Lyne, M. and Jefferies, R.S., 1979, *The Alice Holt/Farnham Roman Pottery Industry*, CBA Research Report 30, London: Council for British Archaeology.

Lyon, H., 2003, 'New Evidence for Early Roman Road Alignments and Medieval Activity South of Cripplegate; Excavations at 1 and 2–4 Carey Lane and 11–12 Foster Lane', *London Archaeologist* 10.7, 187–93.

Lyon, J., 2004, 'New Work on the Cripplegate Fort: Excavations at 25 Gresham Street', *Transactions of the London and Middlesex Archaeological Society* 55, 153–82.

Lyon, J., 2007, *Within These Walls: Roman and Medieval Defences North of Newgate at the Merrill Lynch Financial Centre, City of London*, MoLAS Monograph 33, London: Museum of London Archaeology.

MacDonald, W., 1986, *The Architecture of the Roman Empire*. New Haven: Yale University Press.

Mackinder, A., 2000, *A Romano-British Cemetery on Watling Street Excavations at 165 Great Dover Street, Southwark*. MoLAS Studies 4, London: Museum of London Archaeology.

Mackinder, A., 2015, *Roman and Medieval Revetments on the Thames Waterfront. Excavations at Riverbank House, City of London, 2006–9*, MOLAS Studies 33: London: Museum of London Archaeology.

Mackinder, A. and Whittingham, L, 2013, 'The Place, Formerly New London Bridge House, 25 London Bridge Street, London SE1, London Borough of Southwark, Post-excavation Assessment', unpublished Museum of London Archaeology report.

Mackreth, D.F., 1987, 'Roman Public Buildings', in J.A. Schofield and R. Leech (eds), *Urban Archaeology in Britain*, CBA Research Report 61, London: Council for British Archaeology, 133–46.

MacMahon, A., 2003, *The Taberna Structures of Roman Britain*, BAR British Series 356, Oxford: Archaeopress.

Macphail, R.I,. 2003, 'Soil Microstratigraphy: A Micromorphological and Chemical Approach', in C. Cowan, *Urban Development in North-west Roman Southwark: Excavations 1974–90*, MoLAS Monograph 16, London: Museum of London Archaeology, 89–105.

Macphail, R.I., 2005, 'Soil Micromorphology', in B. Yule, *A Prestigious Roman Building Complex on the Southwark Waterfront: Excavations at Winchester Palace, London, 1983–90*, MoLAS Archaeology Studies 23, London: Museum of London Archaeology, 88–90.

Magilton, J., 2003, 'The Defences of Roman Chichester', in P. Wilson (ed.), *The Archaeology of Roman Towns. Studies in Honour of John S Wacher*, Oxford: Oxbow Books, 156–67.

Mairat, J., 2014, 'The Coinage of the Gallic Empire', PhD thesis, University of Oxford.

Maloney, C., 1990, *The Upper Walbrook Valley*, The Archaeology of Roman London 1, CBA Research Report 69, London: Council for British Archaeology.

Maloney, C., 2014, 'Fieldwork Round-up 2013', *London Archaeologist* 14, Supplement 1, 1–44.

Maloney, C. and Holroyd, I., 2007, 'London Fieldwork and Publication Round-up 2006', *London Archaeologist* 11, Supplement 3, 56–87.

Maloney, C. and Holroyd, I., 2008, 'London Fieldwork and Publication Round-up 2007', *London Archaeologist* 12, Supplement 1, 1–43.

Maloney, C. and Holroyd, I., 2009, 'London Fieldwork and Publication Round-up 2008', *London Archaeologist* 12, Supplement 2, 45–84.

Maloney, J., 1979, 'The Excavations at Dukes Place: The Roman Defences', *London Archaeologist* 3.11, 292–97.

Maloney, J., 1980, 'The Discovery of Bastion 4A in the City of London and Its Implications', *Transactions of the London and Middlesex Archaeological Society* 31, 68–76.

Maloney, J., 1983, 'Recent Work on London's Urban Defences', in J. Maloney and B. Hobley (eds), *Roman Urban Defences in the West*, CBA Research Report 51, London: Council for British Archaeology, 96–117.

Maloney, J., 2020, 'The DUA (Department of Urban Archaeology): Managing Archaeological Investigations in the City of London 1973–1991', in V. Ridgeway, D. Briscoe, J. Hall, and B. Wallower (eds), *London Archaeologist: 50 years of London's Archaeology: Papers from the 50th Anniversary Conference*, London: London Archaeologist, 23–34.

Manley, J., 2002, *AD 43: The Roman Invasion of Britain*, Stroud: Tempus.

Manley, J. and Rudkin, D., 2005, 'A Pre-AD 43 Ditch at Fishbourne Roman Palace, Chichester', *Britannia* 36, 55–99.

Mann, J.C., 1998, 'London as a Provincial Capital', *Britannia* 29, 336–39.

Manning, W.H., 1985, *Catalogue of the Romano-British Iron Tools, Fittings and Weapons in the British Museum*, London: British Museum.

Margary, I.D., 1965, *Roman Ways in the Weald*, London: Phoenix House.

Margary, I.D., 1967, *Roman Roads in Britain* (2nd edn), London: John Baker.

Margetts, A., 2018, *Wealdbǣra: Excavations at Wickhurst Green, Broadbridge Heath and the landscape of the West Central Weald*, SpoilHeap Monograph 9, Portslade: SpoilHeap.

Marsden, P., 1965, 'Archaeological Finds in the City of London 1961', *Transactions of the London and Middlesex Archaeological Society* 21.2, 135–39.

Marsden, P., 1967, 'The River-side Defensive Wall of Roman London', *Transactions of the London and Middlesex Archaeological Society* 21.3, 149–56.

Marsden, P., 1968a, 'Archaeological finds in the City of London, 1965–6', *Transactions of the London and Middlesex Archaeological Society* 22.1, 1–17.

Marsden, P., 1968b, 'Roman House and Bath at Billingsgate', *London Archaeologist* 1.1, 3–5.

Marsden, P., 1969a, 'Archaeological Finds in the City of London, 1966–8', *Transactions of the London and Middlesex Archaeological Society* 22.2, 1–26.

Marsden, P., 1969b, 'The Roman Pottery Industry of London', *Transactions of the London and Middlesex Archaeological Society* 22.2, 39–44.

Marsden, P., 1970, 'Archaeological Finds in the City of London, 1966–1969', *Transactions of the London and Middlesex Archaeological Society* 22.3, 1–9.

Marsden, P., 1975, 'Excavation of a Roman Palace Site in London, 1961–1972', *Transactions of the London and Middlesex Archaeological Society* 26, 1–102.

Marsden, P., 1976, 'Two Roman Public Baths in London', *Transactions of the London and Middlesex Archaeological Society* 27, 2–70.

Marsden, P., 1978, 'The Excavation of a Roman Palace Site in London: Additional Details', *Transactions of the London and Middlesex Archaeological Society* 29, 99–103.

Marsden, P., 1980, *Roman London*, London: Batsford.

Marsden, P., 1987, *The Roman Forum in London: Discoveries before 1985*, London: HMSO.

Marsden, P., 1994, *Ships of the Port of London: First to Eleventh Centuries AD*, London: English Heritage.

Marsden, P., 1996, 'The Beginnings of Archaeology in the City of London', in J. Bird, M. Hassall, and H. Sheldon (eds), *Interpreting Roman London. Papers in Memory of Hugh Chapman*, Oxford: Oxbow Monograph 58, 11–18.

Marsden, P., 2019, 'Reconstructing the Forum and Basilica of Roman London', *London Archaeologist* 15.8, 219–21.

Marsden, P., Dyson, T., and Rhodes, M., 1975, 'Excavations on the Site of St Mildred's Church, Bread Street, London, 1973–1974', *Transactions of the London and Middlesex Archaeological Society* 26, 171–208.

Marsden, P. and West, B., 1992, 'Population Change in Roman London', *Britannia* 23, 133–40.

Marsh, G., 1979a, 'Nineteenth and Twentieth Century Antiquities Dealers and Arretine Ware from London', *Transactions of the London and Middlesex Archaeological Society* 30, 125–29.

Marsh, G., 1979b, 'Three "Theatre" Masks from London', *Britannia* 10, 263–65.

Marsh, G., 1981, 'London's Samian Supply and its Relationship to the Development of the Gallic Samian Industry', in A.C. and A.S. Anderson (eds), *Roman Pottery Research in Britain and North-West Europe. Papers Presented to Graham Webster*, BAR International Series 13, Oxford: Archaeopress, 173–238.

Marsh, G. and Tyers, P., 1978, 'The Roman Pottery from Southwark', in J. Bird, A. Graham, H. Sheldon, and P. Townend (eds), *Southwark Excavations 1972–1974*, LAMAS and SAS Joint Publication 1, London: London and Middlesex Archaeological Society and Surrey Archaeological Society, 533–82.

Marsh, G. and West, B., 1981, 'Skullduggery in Roman London', *Transactions of the London and Middlesex Archaeological Society* 32, 86–102.

Marshall, M., 2017, 'Where There's Walbrook Muck, There's Roman Brass: the Early Roman Artefacts from Bloomberg', *Transactions of the London and Middlesex Archaeological Society* 68, 261–2.

Marshall, M. and Seeley, F., 2018, 'From the Spreadsheet to the Table? Using "Spot-dating" Level Pottery Records from Roman London to Explore Functional Trends among Open Vessel Forms', *Internet Archaeology* 50, DOI: 10.11141/ia.50.9.

Marshman, I.J., 2015, 'Making Your Mark in Britannia: An Investigation into the Use of Signet Rings and Intaglios in Roman Britain', PhD thesis, University of Leicester.

Mason, D.J.P., 2003, *Roman Britain and the Roman Navy*, Stroud: Tempus.

Mattingly, D.J, 2006a, *An Imperial Possession: Britain in the Roman Empire 55 BC–AD 409*, London: Penguin.

Mattingly, D.J., 2006b, 'The Imperial Economy', in D.S. Potter (ed.), *A Companion to the Roman Empire*, Blackwell: Princeton, 283–97.

Mattingly, D.J., 2011, *Imperialism, Power and Identity: Experiencing the Roman Empire*, Oxford: Princetown University Press.

Mattingly, D.J. and Aldrete, G.S., 2000, 'The Feeding of Rome: the Mechanics of the Food Supply System', in J. Coulston and H. Dodge, *Ancient Rome: the Archaeology of the Eternal City*, Oxford University School of Archaeology Monograph 54, Oxford: Oxford University, 142–65.

Mattison, A., 2016, 'The Execution and Burial of Criminals in Early Medieval England, c. 850–1150: An Examination of Changes in Judicial Punishment across the Norman Conquest', PhD thesis, University of Sheffield.

Mays, S. and Steele, J., 1996, 'A Mutilated Human Skull from Roman St Albans, Hertfordshire, England', *Antiquity* 70, 155–61.

McAnany, A. and Yoffee, N., 2010, 'Why We Question Collapse and Study Human Resilience, Ecological Vulnerability, and the Aftermath of Empire', in A. McAnany and N.Yoffee (eds), *Questioning Collapse: Human Resilience, Ecological Vulnerability and the Aftermath of Empire*, Cambridge: Cambridge University Press, 1–17.

McCann, B., 1993, 'Fleet Valley Project, Interim Report', unpublished Museum of London Archaeology report.

McCann, B. and Orton, C., 1989, 'The Fleet Valley Project', *London Archaeologist* 6.4, 102–7.

McInerney, J., 2006, 'On the Border: Sacred Land and the Margins of the Community', in R.M. Rosen and I. Sluiter (eds), *City, Countryside, and the Spatial Organisation of Value in Classical Antiquity*, Leiden: Brill, 33–59.

McKenzie, M., 2011, 'Roman, Medieval and Later Occupation at Lion Plaza, 1–18 Old Broad Street and 41–53 Threadneedle Street, London, EC2', *Transactions of the London and Middlesex Archaeological Society* 62, 1–30.

McKenzie, M. and Thomas, C., 2020, *In the Northern Cemetery of Roman London: Excavations at Spitalfields Market, London E1, 1991–2007*, MOLA monograph, 58 London: Museum of London Archaeology.

Meates, G.W., 1979, *The Lullingstone Roman Villa. 1: The Site*, Kent Archaeological Society Monograph 1, Maidstone: Kent Archaeological Society.

Medawar, P., 1996, 'Is the Scientific Paper a Fraud?' in P. Medawar, *The Strange Case of the Spotted Mice and Other Classic Essays on Science*, Oxford: Oxford University Press.

Mees, A., 2018, 'Was There a Difference between Roman "Civil" and "Military" Samian (*terra sigillata*) Market Supply? Finding Answers with Statistical Distribution Analysis Methods', *Internet Archaeology* 50, DOI: 10.11141/ia.50.16.

Meier, M., 2016, 'The "Justinianic Plague": The Economic Consequences of the Pandemic in the Eastern Roman Empire and Its Cultural and Religious Effects', *Early Medieval Europe* 24.3, 267–92.

Mennen, I., 2011, *Power and Status in the Roman Empire, AD 193–284*, Leiden: Brill.

Merrifield, R., 1955, 'The Lime Street (1952) Hoard of Barbarous Radiates', *Numismatic Chronicle* 6.15, 113–24.

Merrifield, R., 1962, 'Coins from the Bed of the Walbrook, and Their Significance', *Antiquaries Journal* 62, 38–52.

Merrifield, R., 1965, *The Roman City of London*, London: Ernest Benn.

Merrifield, R., 1977, 'Art and Religion in Roman London: An Inquest on the Sculptures of Londinium', in J. Munby and M. Henig (eds), *Roman Life and Art in Britain*, BAR British Series 41, Oxford: Archaeopress, 375–406.

Merrifield, R., 1983, *London: City of the Romans*, London: Batsford.

Merrifield, R., 1995, 'Roman Metalwork from the Walbrook—Rubbish, Ritual or Redundancy?', *Transactions of the London and Middlesex Archaeological Society* 46, 27–44.

Merrifield, R., 1996, 'The London Hunter-God and His Significance in the History of Londinium', in J. Bird, M. Hassall, and H. Sheldon (eds), *Interpreting Roman London. Papers in Memory of Hugh Chapman*, Oxbow Monograph 58, Oxford: Oxbow Books, 105–13.

Merrifield, R. and Hall, J., 2008, 'In its Depths, What Treasures—the Nature of the Walbrook Stream Valley and the Roman metalwork Found Therein', in J. Clark, J. Cotton, J. Hall, R. Sherris, and H. Swain (eds), *Londinium and Beyond: Essays on Roman London and its Hinterland for Harvey Sheldon*, CBA Research Report 156, London: Council for British Archaeology, 121–27.

Merrifield, R. and Sheldon, H., 1974, 'Roman London Bridge: A View from Both Banks', *London Archaeologist* 2.8, 183–91.

Middleton, P., 1979, 'Army Supply in Roman Gaul: An Hypothesis for Roman Britain', in B.C. Burnham and H.B. Johnson (eds), *Invasion and Response: the Case of Roman Britain*, BAR British Series 73, Oxford: Archaeopress, 81–97.

Middleton, P., 1983, 'The Roman Army and Long Distance Trade', in P. Garnsey and C.R. Whittaker (eds), *Trade and Famine in Classical Antiquity*, Cambridge: Cambridge Philological Society, 75–83.

Milella, M., Mariotti, V., Maria Giovanna Belcastro, M.G., and Knüsel, C.J., 2015, 'Patterns of Irregular Burials in Western Europe (1st–5th Century A.D.)', PLoS ONE 10.6: e0130616, DOI: 10.1371/journal.pone.0130616.

Millar, F., 1992, *The Emperor in the Roman World (31 BC–AD 337)* (2nd edn), London: Duckworth.

Millard, A., 2002, 'Bayesian Approach to Sapwood Estimates and Felling Dates in Dendrochronology', *Archaeometery* 44.1, 137–43.

Millard, A., 2013, 'Isotopic Investigation of Diet and Mobility', in V. Ridgeway, K. Leary, and B. Sudds, *Roman Burials in Southwark. Excavations at 52–56 Lant Street and 56 Southwark Bridge Road, London SE1*, PCA Monograph 17, London: Pre-Construct Archaeology, 65–70.

Miller, L., 1982, 'Miles Lane: The Early Roman Waterfront', *London Archaeologist* 4.6, 143–47.

Miller, L., Schofield, J., and Rhodes, M., 1986, *The Roman Quay at St Magnus House, London*, LAMAS Special Paper 8, London: London and Middlesex Archaeological Society.

Milles, J., 1779, 'Observations on Some Antiquities Found in the Tower of London in the Year 1777', *Archaeologia* 5, 291–305.

Millett, M.J., 1990, *The Romanization of Britain: An Essay in Archaeological Interpretation*, Cambridge: Cambridge University Press.

Millett, M.J., 1994, 'Evaluating Roman London', *Archaeological Journal* 151, 427–35.

Millett, M.J., 1996, 'Characterizing Roman London', in J. Bird, M. Hassall, and H. Sheldon (eds). *Interpreting Roman London. Papers in Memory of Hugh Chapman*, Oxbow Monograph 58, Oxford: Oxbow Books, 33–8.

Millett, M.J., 2007, 'Roman Kent', in J.H. Williams (ed.), *The Archaeology of Kent to AD 800*, Kent History Project 8, Woodbridge: Boydell, 135–84.

Millett, M.J., 2016a, 'Improving our Understanding of Londinium', *Antiquity* 90, 1692–99.

Millett, M.J., 2016b, 'Roman Britain since Haverfield', in M. Millett, L. Revell, and A. Moore (eds), *The Oxford Handbook of Roman Britain*, Oxford: Oxford University Press, 22–42.

Mills, P., 1980, 'A Roman Well on Welbeck Street, W1', *Transactions of the London and Middlesex Archaeological Society* 31, 77.

Millum, D. and Wallace, R., 2017, 'The 2013 Excavations of the Romano-British Settlement at Bridge Farm, Wellingham: An Interim Summary', *Surrey Archaeological Collections* 155, 81–96.

Milne, G., 1985, *The Port of Roman London*, London: Batsford.

Milne, G., 1992, *From Roman Basilica to Medieval Market: Archaeology in Action in the City of London*, London: HMSO.

Milne, G., 1995, *Roman London*, London: Batsford.

Milne, G., 1996, 'A Palace Disproved: Reassessing the Provincial Governor's Presence in 1st-century London', in J. Bird, M. Hassall, and H. Sheldon (eds), *Interpreting Roman London. Papers in Memory of Hugh Chapman*, Oxbow Monograph 58, Oxford: Oxbow Books, 49–55.

Milne, G., 2000, 'A Roman Provincial Fleet: The Classis Britannica reconsidered', in G. Oliver, R. Brock, T. Cornell, and S Hodgkinson (eds), *The Sea in Antiquity*, BAR International Series 899, Oxford: Archaeopress, 127–31.

Milne, G., 2005, 'Port of Roman London', in M. Urteaga Artigas and M.J. Noain Maura (eds), *Mar Exterior. El Occidente atlántico in época romana*, Rome: Escuela Española de Historia y Arqueología, 71–6.

Milne, G., 2017, 'Discovering the Port of Roman London', Gresham College lecture, http://content.gresham.ac.uk.s3.amazonaws.com/data/binary/2524/2017-09-27_GustavMilne_RomanPort.pdf.

Milne, C., Milne, G., and Bateman, N., 1984, 'Bank Deposits with Interest', *London Archaeologist* 4.15, 395–400.

Milne, G. and Reynolds, A., 1997, 'Archaeology of St Bride's Church', in G. Milne, *St Bride's Church London: Archaeological Research 1952-60 and 1992-5*, English Heritage Archaeological Report 11, London: English Heritage, 19–49.

Milne, G. and Wardle, A., 1993, 'Early Roman Development at Leadenhall Court, London and Related Research', *Transactions of the London and Middlesex Archaeological Society* 44, 23–169.

MOLA 2017, *Archaeology at Bloomberg*, https://data.bloomberglp.com/company/sites/30/2017/11/BLA-web.pdf.

Monaghan, J., 1987, *Upchurch and Thameside Roman Pottery. A Ceramic Typology for Northern Kent, First to Third Centuries A.D.*, BAR British Series 173, Oxford: Archaeopress.

Monteil, G., 2004, 'Samian and Consumer Choice in Roman London', in B. Croxford, H. Eckardt, J. Meade, and J. Weekes (eds), *TRAC 2003: Proceedings of the Thirteenth Annual Theoretical Roman Archaeology Conference, Leicester 2003*, Oxford: Oxbow Books, 1–15.

Monteil, G., 2005, 'Samian in Roman London', PhD thesis, University of London.

Monteil, G., 2008, 'The Distribution and Use of Samian Inkwells in Londinium', in J. Clark, J. Cotton, J. Hall, R. Sherris, and H. Swain (eds), *Londinium and Beyond: Essays on Roman London and its Hinterland for Harvey Sheldon*, CBA Research Report 156, London: Council for British Archaeology, 177–83.

Mongomery, J., Evans, J., Chenery, S., Pashley, V., and Killgrove, K., 2010, ' "Gleaming with and Deadly": Using Lead to Track Human Exposure and Geographic Origins in the Roman Period in Britain', in H. Eckardt (ed.), *Roman Diasporas: Archaeological Approaches to Mobility and Diversity in the Roman Empire*, JRA Supplementary Series 78, Portsmouth RI: Journal of Roman Archaeology, 199–226.

Moore, R., 2016, *Slow Burn City: London in the Twenty-first Century*, London: Picador.

Moore, T., 2011, 'Detribalizing the Later Prehistoric Past: Concepts of Tribes in Iron Age and Roman Studies', *Journal of Social Archaeology* 11.3, 334–60.

Moore, T., 2016, 'Britain, Gaul, and Germany: Cultural Interactions', in M. Millett, L. Revell, and A. Moore (eds), *The Oxford Handbook of Roman Britain*, Oxford: Oxford University Press, 262–82.

Morgan, R.A., 1980, 'The Carbon 14 and Dendrochronology', in D.M. Jones, *Excavations at Billingsgate Buildings 'Triangle', Lower Thames Street 1974*, LAMAS Special Paper 4, London: London and Middlesex Archaeological Society 4, 88–94.

Morley, N., 2011, 'Cities and Economic Development in the Roman Empire', in A. Bowman and A. Wilson (eds), *Settlement, Urbanization and Population*, Oxford Studies in the Roman Economy 2, Oxford: Oxford University Press, 143–60.

Morris, F.M., 2013, 'Cunobelinus' Bronze Coinage', *Britannia* 44, 27–83.

Morris, I., 1992, *Death-ritual and Social Structure in Classical Antiquity*, Key Themes in Ancient History, Cambridge: Cambridge University Press.

Morris, I., 2000, *Archaeology as Cultural History: Words and Things in Iron Age Greece*, Oxford: Blackwell.

Morris, J., 1973, *The Age of Arthur: A History of the British Isles from 350–360*, London: Weidenfeld & Nicolson.

Morris, J., 1975, 'London's Decline AD 150–250', *London Archaeologist* 2.13, 343–44.

Morris, J., 1982, *Londinium: London in the Roman Empire*, London: Weidenfeld & Nicolson.

Munier, C., 1963, *Concilia Galliae A.314–A.506*, Corpus Christianorum 148, Turnholti: Typographi Brepols editores Pontificii.

Museum of London, Department of Urban Archaeology, 1990, *The Annual Review 1989*, London: Museum of London.

Museum of London Archaeology, 2011, *Ordnance Survey Map of Roman London*, London: Museum of London.

Myers, S.D., 2016, 'The River Walbrook and Roman London', PhD thesis, University of Reading.

Nail, S., 2008, *Forest Policies and Social Change in England*, Berlin: Springer.

Naismith, R., 2019, *Citadel of the Saxons: The Rise of Early London*, London: Tauris & Co.

Nash, D., 1987, *Coinage in the Celtic World*, London: Spink.

Neal, D.S., 2003, 'Building 2, Insula XXVII from Verulamium: A Reinterpretation of the Evidence', in P. Wilson (ed.), *The Archaeology of Roman Towns. Studies in Honour of John S Wacher*, Oxford: Oxbow Books, 195–202.

Neal, D.S. and Cosh, S.R., 2009, *Roman Mosaics of Britain III: South East Britain Part 2*, London: The Society of Antiquaries of London.

Neal, D.S., Wardle, A., and Hunn, J.R., 1990, *Excavation of the Iron Age, Roman and Medieval Settlement at Gorhambury, St Albans*, English Heritage Archaeology Reports 14, Historic Buildings & Monuments Commission for England: London.

Nelson, L.H. and Drummond, S.K., 2015, *The Western Frontiers of Imperial Rome*, M.E. Sharpe: London.

Nesbitt, D. and Watson, B., 2019, 'London Fieldwork and Publication Round-up 2018', *London Archaeologist* 15, Suppl. 3.

Newsome, D.J., 2011a, 'Introduction: Making Movement Meaningful', in R. Laurence and D.J. Newsome (eds), *Rome, Ostia and Pompeii: Movement and Space*, New York: Oxford University Press, 1–54.

Newsome, D.J., 2011b, 'Movement and Fora in Rome (the Late Republic to the First Century CE)', in R. Laurence and D.J. Newsome (eds), *Rome, Ostia and Pompeii: Movement and Space*, New York: Oxford University Press, 290–311.

Niblett, R., 1985, *Sheepen: An Early Roman Industrial Site at Camulodunum*. CBA Research Report 57, London: Council for British Archaeology.

Niblett, R., 1999, *The Excavation of a Ceremonial Site at Folly Lane, Verulamium*, London: Society for the Promotion of Roman Studies.

Niblett, R., 2001, *Verulamium: The Roman City of St Albans*, Stroud: Tempus.

Niblett, R. and Thompson, I., 2005, *Alban's Buried Town: An Assessment of St Alban's Archaeology up to AD 1600*, Oxford: Oxbow Books.

Nieto, X., 1997, 'Le commerce de cabotage et de redistribution', in P. Pomey (ed.), *La navigation dans l'Antiquité*, Aix-en-Provence, Édisud, 146–59.

Nixon, T., McAdam, E., Tomber, R., and Swain, H., 2002, *A Research Framework for London Archaeology 2002*, London: Museum of London Archaeology.

Noreña, C.F., 2011, *Imperial Ideals in the Roman West*, Cambridge: Cambridge University Press.

Norman, P. and Reader, F.W., 1906, 'Recent Discoveries in Connexion with Roman London', *Archaeologia* 60, 169–250.

Norman, P. and Reader, F.W., 1912, 'Further Discoveries Relating to Roman London, 1906–12', *Archaeologia* 63, 257–344.

Norris, F.H., Stevens, S.P., and Pfefferbaum, B., 2008, 'Community Resilience as a Metaphor, Theory, Set of Capacities and Strategy for Disaster Readiness', *American Journal of Community Psychology* 41, 127–50.

North, D., 1991, 'Institutions', *Journal of Economic Perspectives* 5.1, 97–112.

Ogilvie, S., 2007, '"Whatever Is, Is Right"? Economic Institutions in Pre-industrial Europe', in *Economic History Review* 60, 649–84.

Omissi, A., 2018, *Emperors and Usurpers in the Later Roman Empire: Civil War, Panegyric, and the Construction of Legitimacy*, Oxford Studies in Byzantium, Oxford: Oxford University Press.

Orton, C., Tyers, P., and Vince, A., 1993, *Pottery in Archaeology*, Cambridge: Cambridge University Press.

Ottaway, P., 1993, *Roman York*, London: Batsford.

Packer, J.E., 2001, *The Forum of Trajan in Rome: A Study of the Monuments in Brief*, London: University of California Press.

Painter, K.S., 1981, '"A Roman Silver Ingot"', Department of Greek and Roman Antiquities, Acquisitions 1976', *B.M. Occasional Paper* 35. London: British Museum.

Palmer, R.E.A., 1980, 'Customs on Market Goods Imported into the City of Rome', in J.H. D'Arms and E.C. Kopff (eds), *The Seaborne Commerce of Ancient Rome*, Studies in Archaeology and History, Memoires of the American Academy in Rome 36, Rome: University of Michigan Press, 217–33.

Palomera, G., 2010, *La Annona y la política agraria durante el Alto Imperio romano*, BAR International Series 2112, Oxford: Archaeopress.

Parani, M., 2007, 'Defining Personal Space: Dress and Accessories in Late Antiquity', in L. Lavan, E. Swift, and T. Putzeys (eds), *Objects in Context, Object in Use: Material Spatiality in Late Antiquity*, Leiden: Brill, 500–1.

Parnell, G., 1985, 'The Roman and Medieval Defences and the Later Development of the Inmost Ward, Tower of London: Excavations 1955–77', *Transactions of the London and Middlesex Archaeological Society* 36, 1–80.

Parnum, A. and Cotton, J., 1983, 'Recent Work in Brentford: Excavations and Observations 1974–82', *London Archaeologist* 4.12, 318–25.

Patterson, J., 1998, 'Trade and Traders in the Roman World: Scale, Structure, and Organisation', in H. Parkins and C. Smith (eds), *Trade and Traders in the Ancient City*, London: Taylor & Francis, 149–67.

Parry, J., 1994, 'The Roman Quay at Thames Exchange', *London Archaeologist* 7.10, 263–67.

Pearce, J., 2011, 'Marking the Dead: Tombs and Topography in the Roman Provinces', in M. Carroll and J. Rempel (eds), *Living Through the Dead: Burial and Commemoration in the Classical World*, Oxford: Oxbow Books, 134–58.

Pearce, J., 2013, *Contextual Archaeology of Burial Practice. Case Studies from Roman Britain*, BAR British Series 508, Oxford: Archaeopress.

Pearce, J., 2015, 'Urban Exits: Commercial Archaeology and the Study of Death Rituals and the Dead in the Towns of Roman Britain', in M. Fulford and N. Holbrook (eds), *The Towns of Roman Britain: The Contribution of Commercial Archaeology since 1990*, Britannia Monograph 27, London: Society for the Promotion of Roman Studies, 138–66.

Pearce, J., 2016, 'Status and Burial', in M. Millett, L. Revell, and A. Moore (eds), *The Oxford Handbook of Roman Britain*, Oxford: Oxford University Press, 342–62.

Pearce, S., 1990, *Archaeological Curatorship*, London: Leicester University Press.

Pearson, A.F., 2002, *The Roman Shore Forts: Coastal Defences of Southern Britain*, Stroud: Tempus.

Pearson, A.F., 2003, *The Construction of the Saxon Shore Forts*, BAR British Series 349, Oxford: Archaeopress.

Pearson, A.F., 2005, 'Barbarian Piracy and the Saxon Shore: A Reappraisal', *Oxford Journal of Archaeology* 24.1, 73–88.

Pemberton, F., 1973, 'A Romano-British Settlement on Stane Street, Ewell, Surrey', *Surrey Archaeological Collections* 69, 1–26.

Perez-Sala, M. and Shepherd, J., 2008, 'The Cullet Dump and Evidence of Glass Working', in N. Bateman, C. Cowan, and R. Wroe-Brown, *London's Roman Amphitheatre: Guildhall Yard, City of London*, MoLAS Monograph 35, London: Museum of London Archaeology, 142–46.

Perna, S., 2015, 'Cinerary Urns in Coloured Egyptian Stone', in P. Coombe, F. Grew, K. Hayward, and M. Henig, *Roman Sculpture from London and the South-East, Corpus Signorum Imperii Romani, Great Britain 1.10*, Oxford: Oxford University Press, 126–31.

Perring, D., 1991, *Roman London*, London: Seaby.

Perring, D., 2000, 'London and Its Hinterland: The Roman Period', in Museum of London, *The Archaeology of Greater London*, MoLAS Monograph, London: Museum of London Archaeology, 119–70.

Perring, D., 2002, *The Roman House in Britain*, London: Routledge.

Perring, D., 2003, 'Gnosticism in Fourth Century Britain: The Frampton Mosaics Reconsidered', *Britannia* 34, 97–127.

Perring, D., 2005, 'Domestic Architecture and Social Discourse in Roman towns', in A. MacMahon and J. Price (eds), *Roman Working Lives and Urban Living*, Oxford: Oxbow Books, 18–28.

Perring, D., 2011, 'Two Studies on Roman London: A. London's Military Origins – B. Population Decline and Ritual Landscapes in Antonine London', *Journal of Roman Archaeology* 24.1, 249–82.

Perring, D., 2015, 'Recent Advances in the Understanding of Roman London', in M. Fulford and N. Holbrook (eds), *The Towns of Roman Britain: The Contribution of Commercial Archaeology since 1990*, Britannia Monograph 27, London: Society for the Promotion of Roman Studies, 20–43.

Perring, D., 2016, 'Working for Commercial Clients: The Practice of Development-led Archaeology in the UK', in P. Florjanowicz (ed.), *When Valletta Meets Faro: The Reality of European Archaeology in the 21st Century*, EAC Occasional Paper 11, Namur: Europae Archaeologica Consilium, 95–104.

Perring, D., 2017, 'London's Hadrianic War?', *Britannia* 48, 37–76.

Perring, D. and Pitts, M., 2013, *Alien Cities: Consumption and the Origins of Urbanism in Roman Britain*, SpoilHeap Monograph 7, Portslade: SpoilHeap.

Perring, D. and Roskams, S.P., 1991, *The Early Development of Roman London to the West of the Walbrook*, CBA Research Report 70, London: Council for British Archaeology.

Petts, D., 2003, *Christianity in Roman Britain*, Stroud: Tempus.

Petts, D., 2016, 'Christianity in Roman Britain', in M. Millett, L. Revell, and A. Moore (eds), *The Oxford Handbook of Roman Britain*, Oxford: Oxford University Press, 660–80.

Phillips, G., 1981, *Thames Crossings: Bridges, Tunnels and Ferries*, Newton Abbott: David & Charles.

Philp, B.J., 1977, 'The Forum of Roman London Excavations of 1968–9', *Britannia* 8, 1–64.

Philp, B.J., 1980, 'A New Roman Site at West Wickham', *Kent Archaeological Review* 61, 12–18.

Philp, B.J., 1981, *The Excavation of the Roman Forts of the Classis Britannica at Dover, 1970–1977*, Kent Monograph Series Research Report 3, Dover: Kent Archaeological Rescue Unit.

Philp, B.J., 2005, *The Excavation of the Roman Fort at Reculver, Kent*, Dover: Kent Archaeological Rescue Unit.

Philp, B.J. and Garrod, D., 1992, *The Roman Settlement at Welling*, Dover: Kent Archaeological Rescue Unit,

Philp, B.J., Parfitt, K., Wilson, J., Dutto, M., and Williams, W., 1991, *The Roman Villa Site at Keston, Kent, First Report (Excavations 1968–78)*, Dover: Kent Archaeological Rescue Unit.

Philpott, R., 1991, *Burial Practices in Roman Britain. A Survey of Grave Treatment and Furnishing A.D. 43–410*, BAR British Series 219, Oxford: Archaeopress.

Pipe, A., 2011, 'Animal Bones', in J. Hill and P. Rowsome, *Roman London and the Walbrook Stream Crossing: Excavations at 1 Poultry and Vicinity 1985–96*, MoLA Monograph 37, London: Museum of London Archaeology, 538–39.

Pitt, K., 2006a, 'Excavations at 36–39 Poultry, London EC2', *Transactions of the London and Middlesex Archaeological Society* 64, 13–56.

Pitt, K., 2006b, *Roman and Medieval Development South of Newgate: Excavations at 3–9 Newgate Street and 16–17 Old Bailey, City of London*, MoLAS Archaeology Studies Series 14, London: Museum of London Archaeology.

Pitt, K., 2014, 'Excavations at 41 Eastcheap, London EC3', *Transactions of the London and Middlesex Archaeological Society* 65, 149–83.

Pitts, M., 2014, 'Reconsidering Britain's First Urban Communities', *Journal of Roman Archaeology* 27, 133–73.

Pitts, M., 2016, 'Rural Transformation in the Urbanized Landscape', in M. Millett, L. Revell, and A. Moore (eds), *The Oxford Handbook of Roman Britain*, Oxford: Oxford University Press, 720–40.

Pitts, M., 2017, 'Gallo-Belgic Wares. Objects in Motion in the Early Roman Northwest', in A. Van Oyen and M. Pitts (eds), *Materialising Roman Histories*, Oxford: Oxbow Books, 47–64.

Pitts, M., 2018, *The Roman Object Revolution: Objectscapes and Intra-cultural Connectivity in Northwest Europe*, Amsterdam Archaeological Studies 27: Amsterdam: Amsterdam University Press.

Pitts, M. and Griffin, R., 2012, 'Exploring Health and Social Well-being in Late Roman Britain: An Inter-cemetery Approach', *American Journal of Archaeology* 116.2, 253–76.

Pitts, M. and Versluys, M., 2015, 'Globalisation and the Roman World: Perspectives and Opportunities', in M. Pitts and M.J. Versluys (eds), *Globalisation and the Roman World: World History, Connectivity and Material Culture*, Cambridge: Cambridge University Press, 3–31.

Pitts, M. and Versluys, M., 2021, 'Objectscapes: A Manifesto for Investigating the Impacts of Object Flows on Past Societies', *Antiquity*, 1–15. DOI: 10.15184/aqy.2020.148

Pollard, N., 2000, *Soldiers, Cities and Civilians in Roman Syria*, Ann Arbor: University of Michigan Press.

Pollard, N., 2006, 'The Roman Army', in D.S. Potter (ed.), *A Companion to the Roman Empire*, Princeton: Blackwell, 206–27.

Pollard, R.J., 1988, *The Roman Pottery of Kent*, Maidstone: Kent Archaeological Society.

Popper, K., 1959, *The Logic of Scientific Discovery*, New York: The Free Press.

Potter, R. and Shepherd, J., 2009, 'Wanstead Park: Epping Forest London Borough of Redbridge Archaeological Evaluation', unpublished West Essex Archaeological Group report.

Powell, A.B., 2017, *Queen Mary's Hospital Carshalton: An Iron Age and Early Romano-British Settlement*, WA Archaeology Occasional Papers, Salisbury: Wessex Archaeology.

Powers, N., 2015, 'The Effect of Fluvial Erosion on the Burials', in C. Harward, N. Powers, and S. Watson, *The Upper Walbrook Cemetery of Roman London: Excavations at Finsbury Circus, City of London, 1987–2014*, MoLAS Archaeology Studies 32, London: Museum of London Archaeology, 127–32.

Price, J.E., 1870, *A Description of the Roman Tesellated Pavement Found in Bucklersbury: with Observations on Analogous Discoveries*, London: Nichols and Sons.

Price, J.E., 1873, *Roman Antiquities Illustrated by Remains Recently Discovered on the Site of the National Safe Deposit Company's Premises, Mansion House, London*, London: Nichols and Sons.

Price, J.E., 1880, *On a Bastion of London Wall, or Excavations in Camomile Street, Bishopsgate*, London: J.B. Nichols and Sons.

Price, S.R.F., 1984, *Rituals and Power: The Roman Imperial Cult in Asia Minor*, Cambridge: Cambridge University Press.

Pringle, S., 2002, 'The Building Materials', in J. Drummond-Murray and P. Thompson, *Settlement in Roman Southwark: Archaeological Excavations (1991–8) for the London Underground Limited Jubilee Line Extension Project*, MOLAS Monograph 12, London: Museum of London Archaeological Service, 151–61.

Pringle, S., 2007, 'London's Earliest Roman Bath-houses?', *London Archaeologist* 11.8, 205–9.

Pritchard, F.A., 1988, 'Ornamental Stonework from Roman London', *Britannia* 19, 169–89.

Pröttel, P., 1988, 'Zur Chronologie der Zwiebelknopffibeln', *Jahrbuch des Römisch-Germanischen Zentralmuseum Mainz* 35, 347–72.

Purcell, N., 2013, 'Rivers and the Geography of Power', *Pallas* 90, 373–87.

Rambaldi, S., 2009, *L'edilizia pubblica nell'impero romano all'epoca dell'anarchia militare (235–284 D.C.)*, Studi e scavi 22, Bologna: Ante Quem.

Ramm, H.G., 1971, 'The End of Roman York', in R.M. Butler (ed.), *Soldier and Civilian in Roman Yorkshire*, Leicester: Leicester University Press, 187–99.

Ranieri, S. and Telfer, A., 2017, *Outside Roman London: Roadside Burials by the Walbrook Stream*, MOLA Crossrail Archaeology Series 9, London: Museum of London Archaeology.

Rankov, B., 1999, 'The Governor's Men: The Officium Consularis in Provincial Administration', in A. Goldsworthy and I. Haynes (eds), *The Roman Army as a Community*, JRA Supplementary Series 34, Portsmouth RI: Journal of Roman Archaeology, 15–34.

Rathbone, D., 1997, 'Prices and Price Formation in Roman Egypt', in *Economie antique: Prix et formation des prix dans les economies antiques*, Saint- Bertrand-de-Comminges: Musée archéologique départmental, 183–244.

Rathbone, D., 2009, 'Earnings and Costs: Living Standards and the Roman Economy (First to Third Centuries AD)', in A. Bowman and A. Wilson (eds), *Quantifying the Roman Economy: Problems and Methods*, Oxford: Oxford University Press, 299–326.

Rayner, L., 2009, 'Origins and Earliest Development of the Settlement', in C. Cowan, F. Seeley, A. Wardle, A. Westman, and L Wheeler, *Roman Southwark Settlement and Economy: Excavations in Southwark 1973–91*, MoLA Monograph 42, London: Museum of London Archaeology, 38–52.

Rayner, L., 2011, 'The General Character of the Suburb in *c* AD 60: Pottery', in J. Hill and P. Rowsome, *Roman London and the Walbrook Stream Crossing: Excavations at 1 Poultry and Vicinity 1985–96*, MoLA Monograph 37, London: Museum of London Archaeology, 78–82.

Rayner, L. and Seeley, F., 2008, 'The Southwark Pottery Type Series: 30 Years On', in J. Clark, J. Cotton, J. Hall, R. Sherris, and H. Swain (eds), *Londinium and Beyond: Essays on Roman London and its Hinterland for Harvey Sheldon*, CBA Research Report 156, London: Council for British Archaeology, 184–93.

Rayner, L., 2017, 'Clay, Water, Fuel: An Overview of Pottery Production In and Around Early Roman London', in D. Bird (ed.), *Agriculture and Industry in South-Eastern Roman Britain*, Oxford: Oxbow, 346–67.

RCHME, 1928, *An Inventory of the Historical Monuments in London 3, Roman London* (R.E.M. Wheeler ed.), London: Royal Commission on Historical Monuments of England.

RCHME, 1962, *An Inventory of the Historical Monuments in City of York*, Vol. 1 *Eburacum, Roman York*, London: Royal Commission on Historical Monuments of England.

Reader, F.W., 1903, 'Pile Structures in the Walbrook Near London Wall', *Archaeological Journal* 60, 137–212.

Rebillard, E., 2009, *The Care of the Dead in Late Antiquity*, Ithaca and London: Cornell University Press.

Reddaway, T.F., 1940, *Rebuilding London after the Great Fire*, London: Jonathan Cape.

Redfern, R. and Bonney, H., 2014, 'Headhunting and Amphitheatre Combat in Roman London, England: New Evidence from the Walbrook Valley', *Journal of Archaeological Science* 43, 214–26.

Redfern, R., Gowland, R., Millard, A., Powell, L., and Gröcke, D., 2018, ' "From the Mouths of Babes": A Subadult Dietary Stable Isotope Perspective on Roman London (Londinium)', *Journal of Archaeological Science: Reports* 19, 1030–40.

Redfern, R.C., Gröcke, D.R., Millard, A.R., Ridgeway, V., Johnson, L., and Hefner, J.T., 2016, 'Going South of the River: A Multidisciplinary Analysis of Ancestry, Mobility and Diet in a Population from Roman Southwark, London', *Journal of Archaeological Science* 74, 11–22.

Redfern, R.C., Marshall, M., Eaton, K., and Poinar, H.N., 2017, ' "Written in Bone": New Discoveries about the Lives and Burials of Four Roman Londoners', *Britannia* 48, 253–77.

Reece, R., 1980, 'Town and Country: The End of Roman Britain', *World Archaeology* 12, 77–92.

Reece, R., 1982, 'Roman Britain by P. Salway', *Archaeological Journal* 139, 453–56.

Reece, R., 1987, *Roman Coinage in Britain*, London: Seaby.

Reece, R., 1992, 'The End of the City in Roman Britain', in J. Rich (ed.), *The City in Late Antiquity*, London: Routledge, 136–44.

Reece, R., 1995, 'Site-finds in Roman Britain', *Britannia* 26, 179–206.

Reece, R., 2002, *The Coinage of Roman Britain*, Stroud: Tempus.

Reece, R., 2015, 'Money for the Roman Army', *Journal of Roman Archaeology* 28, 717–32.

Remesal Rodríguez, J., 1986, *La annona militaris y la exportación de aceite bético a Germania*, Madrid: Universidad Complutense de Madrid.

Remesal Rodriquez, J., 2002, 'Military Supply during Wartime', in L. Blois and J. Rich (eds), *The Transformation of Economic Life under the Roman Empire. Proceedings of the Second Workshop of the International Network Impact of Empire (Roman Empire c. 200 BC–AD 476), Nottingham*, Leiden: Brill, 77–92.

Revell, L., 2007, 'Architecture, Power and Politics: The Forum-basilica in Roman Britain', in J. Sofaer (ed.), *Material Identities*, Oxford: Blackwell, 127–51.

Revell, L., 2016, 'Urban Monumentality in Roman Britain', in M. Millett, L. Revell, and A. Moore (eds), *The Oxford Handbook of Roman Britain*, Oxford: Oxford University Press, 767–90.

Reynolds, A., 2009, *Anglo-Saxon Deviant Burial Customs*, Oxford: Oxford University Press.

Reynolds, A., forthcoming, 'London into the Age of Cnut: An Archaeological Perspective', in R. North, E. Goeres, and A. Finlay (eds), *Anglo-Danish Empire: A Companion to the Reign of King Cnut the Great*, Medieval Institute Publications, Berlin: Walter de Gruyter.

Reynolds, J., 1988, 'Cities', in D. Braund (ed.), *The Administration of the Roman Empire 241 BC–AD 193*, Exeter Studies in History 8, Exeter: University of Exeter, 15–51.

Rhodes, M., 1986, 'The Finds: Discussion', in L. Miller, J. Schofield, and M. Rhodes, *The Roman Quay at St Magnus House, London: Excavations at New Fresh Wharf, Lower Thames Street, London 1974–78*, LAMAS Special Paper 8, London: London Middlesex Archaeological Society, 88–95.

Rhodes, M., 1987a, 'Inscriptions on Leather Waste from Roman London', *Britannia* 18, 173–81.

Rhodes, M., 1987b, 'Wall-paintings from Fenchurch Street, City of London', *Britannia* 18, 169–72.

Rhodes, M., 1991, 'The Roman Coinage from Roman London Bridge and the Development of the City and Southwark', *Britannia* 22, 179–90.

Rice, C., 2016, 'Mercantile Specialization and Trading Communities: Economic Strategies in Roman Maritime Trade', in A. Wilson and M. Flohr (eds), *Urban Craftsmen and Traders in the Roman World*, Oxford: Oxford University Press, 97–114.

Richard, J., 2014, 'Macellum/μάκελλον: "Roman" Food Markets in Asia Minor and the Levant', *Journal of Roman Archaeology* 27, 255–74.

Richardson, B., 1986a, 'Excavation Round-up', *London Archaeologist* 5.6, 157–64.

Richardson, B., 1986b, 'Pottery', in L. Miller, J. Schofield, and M. Rhodes, *The Roman Quay at St Magnus House, London: Excavations at New Fresh Wharf, Lower Thames Street, London 1974–78*, LAMAS Special Paper 8, London: London Middlesex Archaeological Society, 96–139.

Richardson, B., 1991, 'Billingsgate Bath House (GM111/ER), 100 Lower Thames St [Coal Exchange], EC3', *Transactions of the London and Middlesex Archaeological Society* 42, 61–2.

Richardson, B. and Tyers, P., 1984, 'North Gaulish Pottery in Britain', *Britannia* 15, 133–41.

Richmond, I.A., 1953, 'Three Roman Writing-tablets from London', *Antiquaries Journal* 33, 206–8.

Rickman, G., 1980, *The Corn Supply of Ancient Rome*, Oxford: Clarendon Press.

Ridgeway, V. (ed.), 2009, *Secrets of the Gardens: Archaeologists Unearth the Lives of Roman Londoners at Drapers' Gardens, London*, London: Pre-Construct Archaeology.

Ridgeway, V., Leary, K., and Sudds, B., 2013, *Roman Burials in Southwark: Excavations at 52–56 Lant Street and 56 Southwark Bridge Road*, PCA Monograph 17, London: Pre-Construct Archaeology.

Ridgeway, V., Taylor, J., and Biddulph, E., 2019, *A Bath House, Settlement and Industry on Roman Southwark's North Island: Excavations along the route of Thameslink Borough*

Viaduct and at London Bridge Station, Thameslink Monograph 1, London: Pre-Construct Archaeology.

Rielly, K., 2006, 'Animal Bone', in S. Watson and K. Heard, *Development on Roman London's Western Hill: Excavations at Paternoster Square, City of London*, MoLAS Monograph 32, London: Museum of London Archaeology, 113–17.

Rielly, K., 2008, 'The Drapers Gardens Bear', *London Archaeologist* 11.12, 318.

Rielly, K., 2015, 'Animal Bone', in D. Killock, J. Shepherd, J. Gerrard, K. Hayward, K. Rielly, and V. Ridgeway, *Temples and Suburbs; Excavations at Tabard Square, Southwark*, PCA Monograph 18, London: Pre-Construct Archaeology, 206–24.

Rielly, K., in prep. 'The Animal Bones', in N. Hawkins, *Excavations at Drapers' Gardens, City of London*, London: Pre-Construct Archaeology.

Riley, W. and Gomme, L., 1912, *Ship of the Roman Period Discovered on the Site of the New County Hall*, London: London County Council.

Rivet, A.L.F., 1970, 'The British Section of the Antonine Itinerary', *Britannia* 1, 34–82.

Rivet, A.L.F. and Smith, C., 1979, *Place Names of Roman Britain*. London: Batsford.

Rivière, S. and Thomas, A.B., 1987, 'Excavations at 94–97 Fenchurch Street and 9 Northumberland Alley', *Archaeology Today* 8.9, 13–17.

Roach, L., 2013, 'From the Severans to Constantius Chlorus: The Lost Century', in R. Collins and M. Symonds (eds), *Breaking Down Boundaries: Hadrian's Wall in the 21st Century*, JRA Supplementary Series 93, Portsmouth RI: Journal of Roman Archaeology, 105–22.

Rogers, A., 2011, *Late Roman Towns in Britain: Rethinking Change and Decline*, Cambridge: Cambridge University Press.

Rogers, A., 2013, *Water and Roman Urbanism; Towns, Waterscapes, Land Transformation and Experience in Roman Britain*, Leiden: Brill.

Rogers, A., 2016, 'The Development of Towns', in M. Millett, L. Revell, and A. Moore (eds), *The Oxford Handbook of Roman Britain*, Oxford: Oxford University Press, 741–66.

Rogers, G., 1991, *The Sacred Identity of Ephesos: Foundation Myths of a Roman City*, London and New York: Routledge.

Rohnbogner, A., 2018, 'The Rural Population', in A. Smith, M. Allen, T. Brindle, M. Fulford, L. Lodwick, and A. Rohnburger, *New Visions of the Countryside of Roman Britain. Vol 3: Life and Death in the Countryside of Roman Britain*, Britannia Monograph 31, London: Society for the Promotion of Roman Studies, 281–345.

Rosborough, C., 1990, 'Excavations at Pinners' Hall (GWS89), Interim Report', unpublished Museum of London report.

Rosenstein, N., 2009, 'War, State Formation and the Evolution of Military Institutions in Ancient China and Rome', in W. Scheidel (ed.), *Rome and China: Comparative Perspectives on Ancient World Empires*, Oxford: Oxford University Press, 24–51.

Roskams, S.P., 2001, *Excavation*, Cambridge: Cambridge University Press.

Roskams, S.P. and Schofield, J.A., 1978, 'The Milk Street Excavations: Part 2', *London Archaeologist* 3.9, 227–34.

Roskams, S.P. and Watson, L., 1981, 'The Hadrianic Fire of London', *London Archaeologist* 4.3, 62–6.

Ross, A., 1967, *Pagan Celtic Britain; Studies in Iconography and Tradition*, London: Routledge and Kegan Paul.

Ross, A. and Feachem, R., 1976, 'Ritual Rubbish? The Newstead Pits', in J.V.S. Megaw (ed.), *To Illustrate the Monuments: Essays on Archaeology Presented to Stuart Piggott*, London: Thames and Hudson.

Rossiter, J., 2016, 'In ampitζatru Carthaginis: The Carthage Amphitheatre and Its Uses', *Journal of Roman Archaeology* 29, 239–58.

Rostovtzeff, M.I., 1957, *The Social and Economic History of the Roman Empire* (2nd edn), revised by P Fraser, Oxford: Clarendon Press.

Roth, J.P., 1999, *The Logistics of the Roman Army at War (264 BC–AD 235)*, Leiden: Brill.

Rowsome, P, 1987, '36–37 King Street', in J. Shepherd, 'The Pre-urban and Roman Topography in the King Street and Cheapside Areas of the City of London', *Transactions of the London and Middlesex Archaeological Society* 38, 46–50.

Rowsome, P., 1996, 'The Billingsgate Roman House and Bath—Conservation and Assessment', *London Archaeologist* 7.16, 415–23.

Rowsome, P., 1999, 'The Huggin Hill Baths and Bathing in London: Barometer of the Town's Changing Circumstances?', in J. DeLaine and D.E. Johnston (eds), *Roman Baths and Bathing: Proceedings of the 1st International Conference on Roman Baths held at Bath, England, 30 March–4 April 1992*, JRA Supplementary Series 37, Portsmouth RI: Journal of Roman Archaeology, 262–77.

Rowsome, P., 2006, 'Conclusions', in R. Bluer and T. Brigham, *Roman and Later Development East of the Forum and Cornhill*, MoLAS Monograph 30, London: Museum of London Archaeology, 96–9.

Rowsome, P., 2008, 'Mapping Roman London: Identifying Its Urban Patterns and Interpreting Their Meaning', in J. Clark, J. Cotton, J. Hall, R. Sherris, and H. Swain (eds), *Londinium and Beyond: Essays on Roman London and its Hinterland for Harvey Sheldon*, CBA Research Report 156, London: Council for British Archaeology, 25–32.

Rowsome, P., 2014a, 'Roman and Medieval Defences North of Ludgate: Excavations at 42–6|Ludgate Hill and 1–6 Old Bailey, London EC4', *London Archaeologist* 14.1, 3–10.

Rowsome, P., 2014b, 'Searching for King Lud's Gate', in J. Cotton, J. Hall, J. Keily, R. Sherris, and R. Stephenson (eds), *Hidden Histories and Records of Antiquity: Essays on Saxon and Medieval London for John Clark, Curator Emeritus, Museum of London*, London and Middlesex Arch. Soc. Special Paper 17, 35–40.

Rowsome, P., 2018, 'Roman London: Researching Its Rise and Fall', *London Archaeologist* 15.4, 91–8.

Roxan, M., 1983, 'A Roman Military Diploma from London', *Transactions of the London and Middlesex Archaeological Society* 34, 67–72.

Roymans, N., 2011, 'Ethnic Recruitment, Returning Veterans and the Diffusion of Roman Culture among Rural Populations in the Rhineland Frontier Zone', in N. Roymans and T. Derks (eds), *Villa Landscapes in the Roman North. Economy, Culture and Lifestyles*, Amsterdam Archaeological Studies 17, Amsterdam: Amsterdam University Press, 139–60.

Roymans, N., 2018, 'A Roman Massacre in the Far North: Caesar's Annihilation of the Tencteri and Usipetes in the Dutch River Area', in M. Fernández-Götz and N. Roymans (eds,), *Conflict Archaeology. Materialities of Collective Violence from Prehistory to Late Antiquity*, London: Routledge, 167–82.

Roymans, N., 2019, 'Conquest, Mass Violence and Ethnic Stereotyping: Caesar's Actions', *Journal of Roman Archaeology* 32, 437–58.

Rudling, D., 1986, 'The Excavation of a Roman Tilery on Great Cansiron Farm, Hartfield, East Sussex', *Britannia* 17, 191–230.

Russel, B., 2013, *The Economics of the Roman Stone Trade*, Oxford Studies on the Roman Economy, Oxford: Oxford University Press.

Russell, B., 2017, 'Stone Use and the Economy: Demand, Distribution, and the State', in A. Bowman and A. Wilson (eds), *Trade, Commerce and the State in the Roman World*, Oxford: Oxford University Press, 237–63.

Russell, M. and Manley, H., 2015, 'Trajan Places: Establishing Identity and Context for the Bosham and Hawkshaw Heads', *Britannia* 46, 151–69.

Rykwert, J., 1976, *The Idea of a Town: The Anthropology of Urban Form in Rome, Italy and the Ancient World*, Princeton: Princeton University Press.

Salway, P., 1981, *Roman Britain*, Oxford: Clarendon Press.

Sankey, D., 1998, 'Cathedrals, Granaries and Urban Vitality in Late Roman London', in B. Watson (ed.), *Roman London: Recent Archaeological Research*, JRA Supplementary Series 24, Portsmouth RI: Journal of Roman Archaeology, 78–82.

Sankey, D., 2002, 'Roman, Medieval and Later Development at 7 Bishopsgate, London EC2: from a 1st Century Cellared Building to the 17th Century Properties of the Merchant Taylors' Company', *Transactions of the London and Middlesex Archaeological Society* 53, 1–24.

Sankey, D. and Connell, B., 2007, 'Late Roman Burials and Extramural Medieval and Later Development at Premier Place, Devonshire Square, Houndsditch, London EC2', *Transactions of the London and Middlesex Archaeological Society* 58, 53–77.

Sankey, D. and Stephenson, A., 1991, 'Recent Work on London's Defences', in V.A. Maxfield and M.J. Dobson (eds), *Roman Frontier Studies 1989: Proceedings of the XVth International Congress of Roman Frontier Studies*, Exeter: University of Exeter Press, 117–24.

Sarantis, A., 2013, 'Fortifications in the West: A Bibliographic Essay', in A. Sarantis and N. Christie (eds), *War and Warfare in Late Antiquity: Current Perspectives*, Late Antique Archaeology 8.1–8.2, Leiden: Brill, 255–96.

Sauer, E., 2003, *The Archaeology of Religious Hatred in the Roman and Early Medieval World*, Stroud: Tempus.

Scaife, R., 2011, 'Pollen Analysis of Sediments', in J. Hill and P. Rowsome, *Roman London and the Walbrook Stream Crossing: Excavations at 1 Poultry and Vicinity 1985-96*, MoLA Monograph 37, London: Museum of London Archaeology, 533–8.

Scapini, M., 2016, 'Studying Roman Economy and Imperial Food Supply. Conceptual and Historical Premises of the Study of the Economic Initiatives of the Emperors in the 1st and 2nd Century A D', *Gerión* 34, 217–48.

Schaaf, L., 1976, 'Excavations at 175-7 Borough High Street, Southwark', *London Archaeologist* 3.1, 3–7.

Scheidel, W., 2002, 'A Model of Demographic and Economic Change in Roman Egypt after the Antonine Plague', *Journal of Roman Archaeology* 15, 97–114.

Scheidel, W., 2007, 'Demography', in W. Scheidel, I. Morris, and R.P. Saller (eds), *The Cambridge Economic History of the Graeco-Roman World*, Cambridge: Cambridge University Press, 38–86.

Scheidel, W., 2012, 'Slavery', in W. Scheidel (ed.), *The Cambridge Companion to the Roman Economy*, Cambridge: Cambridge University Press, 89–113.

Scheidel, W. and Friesen, S.J., 2009, 'The Size of the Economy and the Distribution of Income in the Roman Empire', *Journal of Roman Studies* 99, 61–91.

Scheidel, W., Morris, I., and Saller, R. (eds), 2007, *The Cambridge Economic History of the Greco-Roman World*, Cambridge: Cambridge University Press.

Scheidel, W. and von Reden, S. (eds), 2002, *The Ancient Economy*, Edinburgh: Edinburgh University Press.

Schmitz, T.A., 2011, 'The Second Sophistic', in M. Peachin (ed.), *The Oxford Handbook of Social Relations in the Roman World*, Oxford: Oxford University Press, 304–16.

Schnapp, A., 1996, *The Discovery of the Past*, London: British Museum Press.

Schofield, J.A., 1991, 'The Construction of Medieval and Tudor Houses in London', *Construction History* 7, 3–28.

Schofield, J.A., 1998, *Archaeology in the City of London, 1907-1991: A Guide to Records of Excavations by the Museum of London and its Predecessors*, The Archaeological Gazetteer Series 1, London: Museum of London.

Schofield, J.A., 2011, *St Paul's Cathedral Before Wren*, Swindon: English Heritage.

Schulting, R.J. and Bradley, R., 2013, 'Of Human Remains and Weapons in the Neighbourhood of London: New AMS 14C Dates on Thames "River Skulls" and Their European Context', *Archaeological Journal* 170, 30–77.

Schwab, I., 1978, '106-114 Borough High Street', in J. Bird, A. Graham, H. Sheldon, and P. Townend (eds), *Southwark Excavations 1972-1974*, LAMAS and SAS Joint Publication 1, London: London and Middlesex Archaeological Society and Surrey Archaeological Society, 177–220.

Scott, I., 2017, 'Ironwork and its Production', in D. Bird (ed.), *Agriculture and Industry in South-Eastern Roman Britain*, Oxford: Oxbow Books, 301–29.

Scott, M., 2013, *Space and Society in the Greek and Roman Worlds*, Cambridge: Cambridge University Press.

Scott, S., 2017, '"Gratefully Dedicated to the Subscribers": The Archaeological Publishing Projects and Achievements of Charles Roach Smith', *Internet Archaeology* 45, DOI: 10.11141/ia.45.6.

Seeck, O., 1876, *Notitia Dignitatum: Accedunt Notitia Urbis Constantinopolitanae et Laterculi Provincarium*, Berlin: Weidman.

Seeley, F. and Drummond-Murray, J., 2005, *Roman Pottery Production in the Walbrook Valley: Excavations at 20-28 Moorgate, City of London, 1998-2000*, MoLAS Monograph 25, London: Museum of London Archaeology.

Seeley, F. and Wardle, A., 2009, 'Religion and Cult', in C. Cowan, F. Seeley, A. Wardle, A. Westman, and L. Wheeler, *Roman Southwark Settlement and Economy: Excavations in Southwark 1973-91*, MoLA Monograph 42, London: Museum of London Archaeology, 143–56.

Selkirk, A., 1995, 'What Was the Status of Roman London?', *London Archaeologist* 7.12, 328–31.

Seymour, R., 1735, *A Survey of the Cities of London and Westminster, Borough of Southwark and Parts Adjacent*, London: J. Read.

Shanks, M. and McGuire, R.H., 1996, 'The Craft of Archaeology', *American Antiquity* 61.1, 75–88.

Shaw, B., 1993, 'The Bandit', in A. Giardina (ed.), *The Romans*, Chicago: University of Chicago Press, 300–41.

Shaw, H., Montgomery, J., Redfern, R., Gowland, R., and Evans, J., 2016, 'Identifying Migrants in London Using Lead and Strontium Stable Isotopes', *Journal of Archaeological Science* 66, 57–68.

Sheldon, H.L., 1971, 'Excavations at Lefevre Road, Old Ford, E3, Sept 1969–June 1970' *Transactions of the London and Middlesex Archaeological Society* 23.1, 42–77.

Sheldon, H.L., 1975, 'A Decline in the London Settlement, A.D. 150-250', *London Archaeologist* 2.11, 278–84.

Sheldon, H.L., 1978, 'The 1972-74 Excavations: Their Contribution to Southwark's History', in J. Bird, A. Graham, H. Sheldon, and P. Townend (eds), *Southwark Excavations 1972-1974*, LAMAS and SAS Joint Publication 1, London: London and Middlesex Archaeological Society and Surrey Archaeological Society, 11–49.

Sheldon, H.L., 1981, 'London and South-East Britain', in A. King and M. Henig (eds), *The Roman West in the Third Century*, BAR International Series 109, Oxford: Archaeopress, 363–82.

Sheldon, H.L., 1996, 'In search of Sulloniacis', in J. Bird, M. Hassall, and H. Sheldon (eds), *Interpreting Roman London. Papers in Memory of Hugh Chapman*, Oxbow Monograph 58, Oxford: Oxbow Books, 233–41.

Sheldon, H.L., 2010, 'Enclosing Londinium: The Roman Landward and Riverside Walls', *Transactions of the London and Middlesex Archaeological Society* 61, 227–35.

Sheldon, H.L., 2014, 'Roman London: Early Myths and Modern Realities', in J. Cotton, J. Hall, J. Keily, R. Sherris, and R. Stephenson (eds), *Hidden Histories and Records of Antiquity: Essays on Saxon and Medieval London for John Clark, Curator Emeritus, Museum of London*, LAMAS Special Paper 17, London: London and Middlesex Archaeological Society 6–13.

Sheldon, H.L, Corti, G., Green, D., and Tyers, P., 1993, 'The Distribution of Villas in Kent, Surrey and Sussex: Some Preliminary Findings from a Survey', *London Archaeologist* 7.2, 40–6.

Sheldon, H.L. and Schaaf, L., 1978, 'A Survey of Roman Sites in Greater London', in J. Bird, H. Chapman, and J. Clark (eds), *Collectanea Londiniensia. Studies in London Archaeology and History Presented to Ralph Merrifield*, London and Middlesex Archaeological Society Special Paper 2, London, 59–88.

Sheldon, H.L. and Tyers, I., 1983, 'Recent Dendrochronological Work in Southwark and Its Implications', *London Archaeologist* 4.13, 355–61.

Sheldon, H.L. and Yule, B., 1979, 'Excavations in Greenwich Park 1978-9', *London Archaeologist* 12, 311–317.

Shepherd, J.D., 1986, 'The Roman Features at Gateway House and Watling House, Watling Street, City of London (1954)', *Transactions of the London and Middlesex Archaeological Society* 37, 125–44.

Shepherd, J.D., 1987, 'The Pre-urban and Roman Topography in the King Street and Cheapside Areas of the City of London', *Transactions of the London and Middlesex Archaeological Society* 38, 11–60.

Shepherd, J.D., 1998, *The Temple of Mithras, London: Excavations by W. F. Grimes and A. Williams at the Walbrook, London*, EH Archaeological Report 12, London: English Heritage.

Shepherd, J.D., 2008, 'Luxury Colourless Glass Vessels in Flavian London', in J. Clark, J. Cotton, J. Hall, R. Sherris, and H. Swain (eds), *Londinium and Beyond: Essays on Roman London and its Hinterland for Harvey Sheldon*, CBA Research Report 156, London: Council for British Archaeology, 239–50.

Shepherd, J.D., 2012, *The Discovery of the Roman Fort at Cripplegate, City of London. Excavations by W F Grimes 1947-68*, London; Museum of London Archaeology.

Shepherd, J.D. and Chettle, S., 2012, 'The Cripplegate Fort and Londinium', in J. Shepherd, *The Discovery of the Roman Fort at Cripplegate, City of London. Excavations by W F Grimes 1947-68*, London; Museum of London Archaeology, 142–63.

Shotter, D., 2004, 'Vespasian, Auctoritas and Britain', *Britannia* 35, 1–8.

Shotter, D., 2013, 'A Rare Find: A Neptune As of the Roman Emperor, Nerva', *Numismatic Chronicle* 173, 85–97.

Sidell, J., 2008, 'Londinium's Landscape', in J. Clark, J. Cotton, J. Hall, R. Sherris, and H. Swain (eds), *Londinium and Beyond: Essays on Roman London and Its Hinterland for Harvey Sheldon*, CBA Research Report 156, London: Council for British Archaeology, 62–8.

Sidell, J., Cotton, J., Rayner, L. and Wheeler, L., 2002, *The Prehistory and Topography of Southwark and Lambeth*, MoLAS Monograph Series 14, London: Museum of London Archaeology.

Simmonds, A., Márquez-Grant, N., and Loe, L., 2008, *Life and Death in a Roman City: Excavation of a Roman Cemetery with a Mass Grave at 120–122 London Road, Gloucester*, OA Monograph 6, Oxford: Oxford Archaeological Unit.

Sirks, B., 2017, 'Law, Commerce, and Finance in the Roman Empire', in A. Bowman and A. Wilson, A. (eds), *Trade, Commerce and the State in the Roman World*, Oxford: Oxford University Press, 53–116.

Sloane, B., 2012, *The Augustinian Nunnery of St Mary Clerkenwell, London*, MOLA Monography 57, London; Museum of London Archaeology.

Sloane, B., Swain, H., and Thomas, C., 1995, 'The Roman Road and the River Regime; Archaeological Investigations in Westminster and Lambeth', *London Archaeologist* 7.14, 359–70.

Smith, A.T., 2001, *The Differential Use of Constructed Sacred Space in Southern Britain from the Late Iron Age to the 4th Century AD*, BAR British Series 318, Oxford: Archaeopress.

Smith, A.T., 2016, 'Ritual Deposition', in M. Millett, L. Revell, and A. Moore (eds), *The Oxford Handbook of Roman Britain*, Oxford: Oxford University Press, 641–59.

Smith, A.T, 2017, 'Rural Crafts and Industry', in M. Allen, L. Lodwick, T. Brindle, M. Fulford, and A. Smith (eds), *New Visions of the Countryside of Roman Britain, Vol. 2: The Rural Economy of Roman Britain*, Britannia Monograph 30, London: Society for the Promotion of Roman Studies, 178–236.

Smith, A.T., 2018a, 'Death in the Countryside: Rural Burial Practices', in A. Smith, M. Allen, T. Brindle, M. Fulford, L. Lodwick, and A. Rohnburger, *New Visions of the Countryside of Roman Britain. Vol 3: Life and Death in the Countryside of Roman Britain*, Britannia Monograph 31, London: Society for the Promotion of Roman Studies, 205–80.

Smith, A.T, 2018b, 'Religion and the Rural Population', in A. Smith, M. Allen, T. Brindle, M. Fulford, L. Lodwick, and A. Rohnburger, *New Visions of the Countryside of Roman Britain. Vol 3: Life and Death in the Countryside of Roman Britain*, Britannia Monograph 31, London: Society for the Promotion of Roman Studies, 120–204.

Smith, A.T., Allen, M., Brindle, T., and Fulford, M., 2016, *New Visions of the Countryside of Roman Britain. Vol 1: The Rural Settlement of Roman Britain*, Britannia Monograph 29, London: Society for the Promotion of Roman Studies.

Smith, A.T., Allen, M., Brindle, T., Fulford, M., Lodwick, L., and Rohnburger, A., 2018, *New Visions of the Countryside of Roman Britain. Vol 3: Life and Death in the Countryside of Roman Britain*, Britannia Monograph 31, London: Society for the Promotion of Roman Studies.

Smith, C.R., 1842, 'Observations on Roman Remains Recently Found in London', *Archaeologia* 29, 145–66.

Smith, C.R., 1854, *Catalogue of the Museum of London Antiquities. Collected by and the Property of Charles Roach Smith*, London: Printed by subscription.

Smith, C.R., 1859, *Illustrations of Roman London*, London: Printed by subscription.

Smith, C.R., 1883, *Retrospections*, London: Printed by subscription.

Smith, D., 2012, *Insects in the City: An Archaeoentological Perspective on London's Past*, BAR British Series 561, Archaeopress: Oxford.

Smith, D. and Davis, A., 2011, 'Cereal Processing and the Pests of Stored Products', in J. Hill and P. Rowsome, *Roman London and the Walbrook Stream Crossing: Excavations at 1 Poultry and Vicinity 1985–96*, MoLA Monograph 37, London, 353–4.

Smith, D. and Kenward, H., 2011, 'Roman Grain Pests in Britain: Implications for Grain Supply and Agricultural Production', *Britannia* 42, 243–62.

Smith, D.J., 1969, 'The Mosaic Pavements', in A.L.F. Rivet (ed.), *The Roman Villa in Britain*, London: Routledge & Kegan Paul, 71–125.

Smither, P., 2017, 'Weighing Up the Economy of Roman London', *Transactions of the London and Middlesex Archaeological Society* 68, 41–58.

Speidel, M., 1978, *Guards of the Roman Armies*, Antiquitas 1.28, Bonn: Habelt.

Spence, C., 1989, *Digging in the City: The Annual Review 1988*, London: Museum of London, Department of Urban Archaeology.

Spence, C. (ed.), 1990, *Archaeological Site Manual* (2nd edn.), London: Museum of London, Department of Urban Archaeology.

Spence, C. and Grew, F., 1990, *Museum of London, Department of Urban Archaeology, The Annual Review 1989*, Museum of London.

Stevens, C., 2009, 'Charred Plant Remains', in V. Birbeck and J. Schuster, *Living and Working in Roman and Later London: Excavations at 60–63 Fenchurch Street*, WA Report 25, Salisbury: Wessex Archaeology, 103–10.

Stevens, S., 2017, *City Boundaries and Urban Development in Roman Italy*, Leuven: Peeters.

Storey, G.R., 1999, 'Archaeology and Roman Society: Integrating Textual and Archaeological Data', *Journal of Archaeological Research* 7.3, 203–48.

Stow, J., 1603, *A Survey of London. Reprinted From the Text of 1603*, ed. C L Kingsford, Oxford: Clarendon Press (1908).

Stow, J., 1842, *Survey of London, Written in the Year 1598: A New Edition* (W.J. Thomas, ed.), London: Whittaker & Co.

Stoyanov, Y., 2000, *The Other God: Dualist Religions from Antiquity to the Cathar Heresy*, New Haven: Yale University Press.

Straker, V., 1987, 'Carbonised Cereal Grain from First Century London: A Summary of the Evidence for Importation and Crop Processing', in P. Marsden, *The Roman Forum site in London*, London: HMSO, 151–3.

Strobel, K., 2007, 'Strategy and Army Structure between Septimius Severus and Constantine the Great', in P. Erdkamp (ed.), *A Companion to the Roman Army*, Malden MA: Blackwell, 267–85.

Stuart-Hutcheson, A., 2012, 'The High Weald Roman Coin Hoard', http://brightonmuseums.org.uk/discover/2012/07/13/the-high-weald-roman-coin-hoard/.

Stukeley, W., 1776, *Itinerarium Curiosum: Or, an Account of the Antiquities and Remarkable Curiosities in Nature or Art…* (2nd edn.), London: Baker & Leigh.

Sudds, B., 2008, 'Ceramic and Stone Building Material and Structural Remains', in T. Bradley and J. Butler, *From Temples to Thames Street—2000 Years of Riverside Development; Archaeological Excavations at the Salvation Army International Headquarters*, PCA Monograph 7, London: Pre-Construct Archaeology, 34–40.

Sudds, B., 2019, 'The Bath House', in V. Ridgeway, J. Taylor, and E. Biddulph, *A Bath House, Settlement and Industry on Roman Southwark's North Island: Excavations along the route of Thameslink Borough Viaduct and at London Bridge Station*, Thameslink Monograph 1, London: Pre-Construct Archaeology, 192–203.

Sudds, B. and Douglas, A., 2014, 'Excavations at Crispin Street, Spitalfields: From Roman Cemetery to Post-Medieval Artillery Ground', *Transactions of the London and Middlesex Archaeological Society* 65, 1–50.

Swain, H., 1988, 'Gazetteer of Sites', in P. Hinton (ed.), *Excavations in Southwark 1973–6, Lambeth 1973–9*, LAMAS and SAS Joint Publication 3, London: London and Middlesex Archaeological Society and Surrey Archaeological Society, 479–88.

Swain, H. and Roberts, M., 1999, *The Spitalfields Roman*, London: Museum of London.

Swain, H. and Williams, T., 2008, 'The Population of Roman London', in J. Clark, J. Cotton, J. Hall, R. Sherris, and H. Swain (eds), *Londinium and Beyond: Essays on Roman London and Its Hinterland for Harvey Sheldon*, CBA Research Report 156, London: Council for British Archaeology, 33–9.

Swan, V.G., 1984, *The Pottery Kilns of Roman Britain*, RCHM Supplementary Series 5, London: Royal Commission on Historical Monuments.

Swan, V.G., 2009, *Ethnicity, Conquest and Recruitment: Two Cases from the Northern Military Provinces*, JRA Supplementary Series 72, Portsmouth RI: Journal of Roman Archaeology.

Swan, V.G. and McBride, R.M., 2002, 'A Rhineland Potter at the Legionary Fortress of York', in M. Aldhouse-Green and P. Webster (eds), *Artefacts and Archaeology: Aspects of the Celtic and Roman World*, Cardiff: University of Wales, 190–234.

Swan, V.G. and Philpott, R.A., 2000, 'Legio XX VV and Tile Production at Tarbock, Merseyside', *Britannia* 31, 55–67.

Swiętoń, A., 2007, 'Some Elements of Centrally Planned Economy in the Late Antiquity? Searching for Parallels in the Theodosian Code', *Revue Internationale des droits de l'Antiquité* 54, 503–17.

Swift, D., 2003, *Roman Burials, Medieval Tenements and Suburban Growth: 201 Bishopsgate, City of London* MoLA Archaeology Studies Series 10, London: Museum of London Archaeology.

Swift, D., 2008, *Roman Waterfront Development at 12 Arthur Street, City of London*, MoLAS Archaeology Studies 19, London: Museum of London Archaeology.

Swift, E., 2000, *The End of the Western Roman Empire: An Archaeological Investigation*, Stroud: Tempus.

Swift, E., 2017, *Roman Artefacts and Society*, Oxford: Oxford University Press.

Symonds, R.P., 1995, 'Pottery Assessment for Three Quays House (LTS95)', Museum of London Archaeology Service, unpublished report.

Symonds, R.P., 1998, 'Quelques apercus sur le port romain de Londres provoques par les traveaux du project Cesar', in SFECAG, *Actes du Congres d'Istres*, Marseilles: Société Française d'Etude de la Céramique Antique en Gaule, 339–48.

Symonds, R.P., 2003, 'Romano-British Amphorae', *Journal of Roman Pottery Studies* 10, 50–9.

Symonds, R.P., 2006, 'The Pottery', in S. Watson and K. Heard, *Development on Roman London's Western Hill: Excavations at Paternoster Square, City of London*, MoLAS Monograph 32, London: Museum of London Archaeology, 81–6.

Symonds, R.P., 2012, 'A Brief History of the Ceramic Mortarium in Antiquity', *Journal of Roman Pottery Studies* 15, 169–214.

Symonds, R.P. and Tomber, R.S., 1991, 'Late Roman London: An Assessment of the Ceramic Evidence from the City of London', *Transactions of the London and Middlesex Archaeological Society* 42, 59–99.

Tainter, J.A., 1988, *The Collapse of Complex Societies*, Cambridge: Cambridge University Press.

Takacs, S.A., 2015, *Isis and Sarapis in the Roman World*, Leiden: Brill.

Tatton-Brown, T., 1974, 'Excavations at the Custom House site, City of London, 1973', *Transactions of the London and Middlesex Archaeological Society* 25, 117–219.

Taylor, A., 2008, 'Aspects of Deviant Burial in Roman Britain', in E.M. Murphy (eds), *Deviant Burial in the Archaeological Record*, Oxford: Oxbow Books, 91–114.

Taylor, J., 2000, 'Stonea in its Fenland Context: Moving Beyond an Imperial Estate', *Journal of Roman Archaeology* 13, 647–58.

Taylor, T., 2020, 'The Pre-Roman Walbrook Landscape and Roman London', *London Archaeologist* 16.1, 3–9.

Taylor-Wilson, R., 2002, *Excavations at Hunt's House, Guy's Hospital, London Borough of Southwark*, PCA Monograph 1, London: Pre-Construct Archaeology.

Tchernia, A., 2016, *The Romans and Trade*, Oxford: Oxford University Press.

Teçusan, N., 1990, 'Logos Sympotikos: Patterns of the Irrational in Philosophical Drinking: Plato Outside the Symposium', in 0. Murray (ed.), *Sympotica. A Symposium on the Symposion*, Oxford: Clarendon Press, 238–60.

Telfer, A., 2010, 'New Evidence for the Transition from the Late Roman to the Saxon Period at St Martin-in-the-Fields, London', in M. Henig and N. Ramsay (eds), *Intersections: the Archaeology and History of Christianity in England, 400–1200: Papers in Honour of Martin Biddle and Birthe Kjolbye-Biddle*, BAR British Series 505, Oxford: Archaeopress, 49–58.

Telfer, A. and Blackmore, L., 2017, 'In the Path of the Flames: Evidence for Daily Life Before and After the Great Fire, from Excavations at 11–23 New Fetter Lane, 25 New Street Square, 11 Bartlett Court, 1 and 8–9 East Harding Street, London, EC4', *Transactions of the London and Middlesex Archaeological Society* 68, 151–89.

Temin, P., 2001, 'A Market Economy in the early Roman Empire', *Journal of Roman Studies* 91, 169–81.

Temin, P., 2013, *The Roman Market Economy*, Princeton: Princeton University Press.

Thacker, A., 2004, 'The Cult of Saints and the Liturgy in the Middle Ages', in D. Keene, A. Burns and A. Saint (eds), *St Paul's: The Cathedral Church of London, 604–2004*, New Haven and London: Yale University Press, 113–22.

Thomas, C., 2004, *Life and Death in London's East End: 2000 Years at Spitalfields*, London: Museum of London Archaeology.

Thomas, C., 2008, 'Roman Westminster: Fact or Fiction', in J. Clark, J. Cotton, J. Hall, R. Sherris, and H. Swain (eds), *Londinium and Beyond: Essays on Roman London and Its Hinterland for Harvey Sheldon*, CBA Research Report 156, London: Council for British Archaeology, 102–6.

Thomas, C., Sloane, B., and Phillpotts, C., 1997, *Excavations at the Priory and Hospital of St Mary Spital, London*, MoLAS Monograph 1, London: Museum of London Archaeology.

Thomas, E.V., 2017, 'Performance Space', in D.S. Richter and W.A. Johnson (eds), *The Oxford Handbook of the Second Sophistic*, Oxford: Oxford University Press, 181–201.

Thomas, R., 2019, 'It's Not Mitigation! Policy and Practice in Development-led Archaeology in England', *The Historic Environment: Policy and Practice*, 10:3–4, 328–44.

Thompson, E.A., 1982, 'Zosimus 6.10.2 and the Letters of Honorious', *Classical Quarterly* 32, 445–62.

Thompson, I.M., 1982, *Grog-tempered 'Belgic' Pottery of South-Eastern England*, BAR British Series 108, Oxford: Archaeopress.

Thompson, I.M., 2008, 'Harrow in the Roman Period', *Transactions of the London and Middlesex Archaeological Society* 59, 61–80.

Thompson, I.M., 2015, 'When Was the Roman Conquest of Hertfordshire?', in K. Lockyear (ed.), *Archaeology in Hertfordshire: Recent Research, A Festschrift for Tony Rook*, Hatfield: Welwyn Archaeological Society, 117–34.

Thornhill, P., 1976, 'A Lower Thames Ford and the Campaigns of 54 BC and AD 43', *Archaeologia Cantiana* 92, 119–28.

Thorp, A., 2010, 'The Roman Pottery', in I. Blair, 'The Walbrook. St Swithin's House, Walbrook House and Granite House, London EC4, City of London', post-excavation assessment, unpublished Museum of London report, 48–59.

Thrale, P., 2008, 'Roman Stone Buildings, Ditches and Burials along Watling Street', *London Archaeologist* 12.1, 19–22.

Tite, W., 1848, *A Descriptive Catalogue of the Antiquities Found in the Excavations for the New Royal Exchange and Preserved in the Museum of the Corporation of London*, London: Corporation of London.

Toller, H., 1977, *Roman Lead Coffins and Ossuaria in Britain*, BAR British Series 38, Oxford: Archaeopress.

Tomlin, R.S.O., 1996, 'A Five-acre Wood in Roman Kent', in J. Bird, M. Hassall, and H. Sheldon (eds), *Interpreting Roman London. Papers in memory of Hugh Chapman*, Oxbow Monograph 58, Oxford: Oxbow Books, 209–16.

Tomlin, R.S.O., 2003, '"The Girl in Question": A New Text from Roman London', *Britannia* 34, 41–51.

Tomlin, R.S.O., 2006, 'Was Roman London Ever a Colonia? The Written Evidence', in R.J.A. Wilson (ed.), *Romanitas: Essays on Roman Archaeology in Honour of Sheppard Frere on the Occasion of his Ninetieth Birthday*, Oxbow Books: Oxford, 49–64.

Tomlin, R.S.O., 2012, 'Roman Britain in 2011. Inscriptions', *Britannia* 43, 395–421.

Tomlin, R.S.O., 2014, 'Drive Away the Cloud of Plague: A Greek Amulet from Roman London', in R. Collins and F. McIntosh (eds), *Life in the Limes: Studies of the People and Objects of the Roman Frontiers*, Oxford: Oxbow Books, 197–205.

Tomlin, R.S.O., 2015, 'Inscriptions', in D. Killock, J. Shepherd, J. Gerrard, K. Hayward, K. Rielly, and V. Ridgeway, *Temples and Suburbs; Excavations at Tabard Square, Southwark*, PCA Monograph 18, London: Pre-Construct Archaeology, 192–4.

Tomlin, R.S.O., 2016, *Roman London's First Voices: Writing Tablets from the Bloomberg Excavations, 2010–14*, MoLA Monograph 72, London: Museum of London Archaeology.

Tomlin, R.S.O., 2018a, *Britannia Romana: Roman Inscriptions and Roman Britain*, Oxford: Oxbow Books.

Tomlin, R.S.O., 2018b, 'Roman Britain in 2017: III. Inscriptions', *Britannia* 49, 427–60.

Tomlin, R.S.O., 2019, 'Roman Britain in 2018: III. Inscriptions', *Britannia* 50, 495–524.

Tomlin, R.S.O. and Hassall, M.W.C., 2000, 'Roman Britain in 1999: II. Inscriptions', *Britannia* 31, 439–46.

Tomlin, R.S.O. and Hassall, M.W.C., 2006, 'Roman Britain in 2005: II. Inscriptions', *Britannia* 37, 467–88.

Tomlin, R.S.O., Wright, R.P., and Hassall, M.W.C. (eds), 2009, *Roman Inscriptions of Britain 3. Inscriptions on Stone, Found or Notified between 1 January 1955 and 31 December 2006*, Oxford: Oxbow Books.

Toynbee, J.M.C., 1971, *Death and Burial in the Roman World*, Baltimore: John Hopkins University Press.

Toynbee, J.M.C., 1986, *The Roman Art Treasures from the Temple of Mithras*, LAMAS Special Paper 7, London: London and Middlesex Archaeological Society.

Tsigarida, I., 2015, 'Salt in Asia Minor: An Outline of Roman Authority Interest in the Resource', in P. Erdkamp, K. Verboven, and A. Zuiderhoek (eds), *Ownership and Exploitation of Land and Natural Resources in the Roman World*, Oxford: Oxford University Press, 277–88.

Tucker, K., 2016, *An Archaeological Study of Human Decapitation Burials*, Barnsley: Pen and Sword Books.

Turner, E.G. and Skutsch, O., 1960, 'A Roman Writing-tablet from London', *Journal of Roman Studies* 50, 108–11.

Tyers, I., 2008a, 'A Gazetteer of Tree-ring Dates from Roman London', in J. Clark, J. Cotton, J. Hall, R. Sherris, and H. Swain (eds), *Londinium and Beyond: Essays on Roman London and Its Hinterland for Harvey Sheldon*, CBA Research Report 156, London: Council for British Archaeology, 69–74.

Tyers, I., 2008b, 'Dendrochronology', in T. Bradley and J. Butler, *From Temples to Thames Street—2000 Years of Riverside Development*, PCA Monograph 7, London: Pre-Construct Archaeology, 52–4.

Tyers, P.A., 1996a, 'Late Iron Age and Early Roman Pottery Traditions of the London Region', in J. Bird, M. Hassall, and H. Sheldon (eds), *Interpreting Roman London. Papers in Memory of Hugh Chapman*, Oxbow Monograph 58, Oxford: Oxbow Books, 139–46.

Tyers, P.A., 1996b, *Roman Pottery in Britain*, London: Batsford.

Tyers, P.A., 1998, 'Amphoras and the Origins of the Brockley Hill Roman Pottery Industry', *London Archaeologist* 8.11, 292–97.

Tyers, P. and Vince, A., 1983, 'Computing the DUA Pottery', *London Archaeologist* 4.11, 299–304.

Tylor, A., 1884, 'New Points in the History of Roman Britain, as Illustrated by Discoveries at Warwick Square in the City of London', *Archaeologia* 48, 221–47.

Unger, S., 2009, 'Red or Yellow? The Changing Colour of Roman London's Roof Line', *London Archaeologist* 107–15.

van der Meer, M.N., 2007, 'Bridge over Troubled Waters? The Γέφυρα in the Old Greek of Isaiah 37:25 and Contemporary Greek Sources', *XIII Congress of the International Organization for Septuagint and Cognate Studies*, Ljubljana: IOSCS, 305–24.

van der Veen, M., Livarda, A., and Hill, A., 2007, 'The Archaeobotany of Roman Britain: Current State and Identification of Research Priorities', *Britannia* 38, 181–210.

van Driel-Murray, C., 2016, 'Fashionable Footwear: Craftsmen and Consumers in the North-West Provinces of the Roman Empire', in A. Wilson and M. Flohr (eds), *Urban Craftsmen and Traders in the Roman World*, Oxford: Oxford University Press, 132–52.

van Driel-Murray, C. in prep., 'Leather', in T. Brigham and B. Watson, *Early Roman Waterfront Development: Excavations at Regis House, City of London, 1994–96*, London: Museum of London Archaeology.

Varner, E.R., 2005, 'Execution in Effigy: Severed Heads and Decapitated Statues in Imperial Rome', in A. Hopkins and M. Wyke (eds), *Roman Bodies. Antiquity to the 18th Century*, Rome: The British School at Rome, 67–82.

VCH, 1909, *A History of the County of London: Vol. 1, London Within the Bars, Westminster and Southwark*, W. Page (ed.), London: Victoria County Histories.

Verboven, K.S., 2007, 'Good for Business. The Roman Army and the Emergence of a "Business Class" in the Northwest Provinces of the Roman Empire (1st Century BCE–3rd Century CE)', in L. de Blois and E. Lo Cascio (eds), *The Impact of the Roman Army (200 BC–AD 476): Economic, Social, Political, Religious, and Cultural Aspects*, Leiden: Brill.

Verboven, K.S., 2009, 'Resident Aliens and Translocal Merchant *Collegia* in the Roman Empire', in O. Hekster and T. Kaizer (eds), *Frontiers in the Roman World. Proceedings of the Ninth Workshop of the International Network Impact of Empire (Durham, 16–19 April 2009)*, Leiden & Boston: Brill, 335–48.

Verboven, K.S., 2015, 'The Knights Who Say NIE. Can Neo-Institutional Economics Live up to Its Expectations in Ancient History Research?', in P. Erdkamp and K. Verboven (eds), *Structure and Performance in the Roman Economy: Models, Methods and Case Studies*, Latomus 350: Brussels: Éditions Latomus, 33–57.

Verboven, K.S., 2016, 'Guilds and the Organisation of Urban Populations During the Principate', in K. Verboven and C. Laes (eds), *Work, Labour and Professions in the Roman World*, Leiden: Brill, 173–202.

Verboven, K.S. and Laes, C., 2016, 'Work, Labour, Professions. What's in a Name?', in K. Verboven and C. Laes (eds), *Work, Labour and Professions in the Roman World*, Leiden: Brill, 1–19.

Vince, A., 1987, 'The Study of Pottery from Urban Excavations', in J. Schofield and R. Leech (eds), *Urban Archaeology in Britain*, CBA Research Report 61, London: Council for British Archaeology, 201–13.

Voisins, J.L., 1984, 'Les Romains, chasseurs des têtes', in *Du châtiment dans la cite: supplices corporels et peine do mort dans le monde antique*, Collection de l'École Française de Rome 79, Rome: École Française de Rome, 241–93.

von Reden, S., 2012, 'Money and Finance', in W. Scheidel (ed.), *The Cambridge Companion to the Roman Economy*, Cambridge: Cambridge University Press, 266–86.

von Schnurbein, S., 2003, 'Augustus in Germania and his New "Town" at Waldgirmes East of the Rhine', *Journal of Roman Archaeology* 16, 93–108.

Wacher, J.S., 1995, *The Towns of Roman Britain*, London: Batsford.

Waddington, Q., 1930, 'Recent Light on London's Past: A Few Remarks on the Results of Excavations in the City in the Years 1924 to 1929', *Journal of the British Archaeological Association New Series* 36, 59–80.

Wait, G.A., 1985, *Ritual and Religion in Iron Age Britain*, BAR British Series 149, Oxford: Archaeopress.

Wait, G.A. and Cotton, J., 2000, 'The Iron Age', in Museum of London, *The Archaeology of Greater London*, MoLAS Monograph, London: Museum of London Archaeology, 101–17.

Walker, D., 1988, 'The Roman Coins', in B. Cunliffe, *The Temple of Sulis Minerva at Bath, Vol. 2, The Finds from the Sacred Spring*, OUCA Monograph 16, Oxford: Oxford University Committee for Archaeology, 281–358.

Walker, L., 1984, 'The Deposition of the Human Remains', in B. Cunliffe, *Danebury. An Iron Age Hillfort in Hampshire*, CBA Research Report 52, York: Council for British Archaeology, 442–63.

Wallace, L.M., 2013, 'The Foundation of Roman London: Examining the Claudian Fort Hypothesis', *Oxford Journal of Archaeology* 32.3, 275–91.

Wallace, L.M., 2014, *The Origin of Roman London*, Cambridge: Cambridge University Press.

Wallace, L.M., 2016, 'The Early Roman Horizon', in M. Millett, L. Revell, and A. Moore (eds), *The Oxford Handbook of Roman Britain*, Oxford: Oxford University Press, 117–33.

Wallower, B., 2002a, 'Roman Temple Complex in Greenwich Park? Part 1', *London Archaeologist* 10.2, 46–54.

Wallower, B., 2002b, 'Roman Temple Complex in Greenwich Park? Part 2', *London Archaeologist* 10.3, 76–81.

Walsh, D., 2020, 'Military Communities and Temple Patronage: A Case Study of Britain and Pannonia', *American Journal of Archaeology* 124.2, 275–99.

Walsh, M., 2017, *Pudding Pan: A Roman Shipwreck and its Cargo in Context*, London: British Museum Press.

Walton, P., 2015, 'From Barbarism to Civilisation? Rethinking the Monetisation of Roman Britain', *Revue Belge de Numismatique et de Sigillographie* 161, 105–20.

Walton, P. and Moorhead, S., 2016, 'Coinage and the Economy', in M. Millett, L. Revell, and A. Moore (eds), *The Oxford Handbook of Roman Britain*, Oxford: Oxford University Press, 834–49.

Warde Fowler, W., 1912, 'Mundus Patet', *Journal of Roman Studies* 2, 25–33.

Wardle, A., 2011, 'Finds from the Walbrook Deposits', in J. Hill and P. Rowsome, *Roman London and the Walbrook Stream Crossing: Excavations at 1 Poultry and Vicinity 1985–96*, MoLA Monograph 37, London, 329–48.

Wardle, A., 2015, *Glass Working on the Margins of Roman London. Excavations at 35 Basinghall Street, City of London, 2005*, MoLA Monograph 70, London: Museum of London Archaeology.

Wardle, A., 2016, 'Military Aspects of the Accessioned Finds Assemblage', in L. Dunwoodie, C. Harward, and K. Pitt, *An Early Roman Fort and Urban Development on Londinium's Eastern Hill. Excavations at Plantation Place, City of London, 1997–2003*, MOLA Monograph 65, London: Museum of London, 159–66.

Wardle, S., 2020, 'Discovering the Bucklersbury Mosaic', *London Archaeologist* 16.2, 31–36.

Warry, P., 2010, 'Legionary Tile Production in Britain', *Britannia* 41, 127–47.

Watson, B., 1998, 'Dark Earth and Urban Decline in Late Roman London', in B. Watson (ed.), *Roman London: Recent Archaeological Research*, JRA Supplementary Series 24, Portsmouth RI: Journal of Roman Archaeology, 100–12.

Watson, B., 2012, 'The Guy's Hospital Roman Boat Fifty Years On', *London Archaeologist* 13.5, 119–25.

Watson, B., 2014, 'Recent Archaeological Work at St George's Church, Borough High Street, Southwark', *Surrey Archaeological Collections* 98, 29–72.

Watson, S., 2003, *An Excavation in the Western Cemetery of Roman London: Atlantic House, City of London*, MoLAS Archaeological Studies 7, London: Museum of London Archaeology.

Watson, S., 2004, 'Roman and Medieval Occupation at 8–10 Old Jewry, City of London', *London Archaeologist* 10.10, 264–70.

Watson, S., 2006, *Development on Roman London's Western Hill: Excavations at Paternoster Square, City of London*, MoLAS Monograph 32, London: Museum of London Archaeology.

Watson, S., 2013, 'The Bloomberg Bonanza', *London Archaeologist* 13.9, 242–43.

Watson, S., 2014, 'Excavations at 6–12 Basinghall Street and 93–95 Gresham Street, City of London EC2', *Transactions of the London and Middlesex Archaeological Society* 65, 185–219.

Watson, S., 2015, *Urban Development in the North-west of Londinium: Excavations at 120–122 Cheapside and 14–18 Gresham Street, City of London, 2005–7*, MOLA Archaeology Study Series 32, London: Museum of London Archaeology.

Watson, S., 2016, 'Timber and Taxes: Excavations at the Old Custom House, Sugar Quay, City of London', *Transactions of the London and Middlesex Archaeological Society* 67, 309–10.

Watson, S., 2017, 'Roman Britain in 2016: Greater London', *Britannia* 48, 391–97.

Watson, S., 2018, 'Roman Britain in 2017: Greater London', *Britannia* 49, 380–88.

Webster, G., 1966, 'Fort and Town in Early Roman Britain', in J.S. Wacher (ed.), *The Civitas Capitals of Roman Britain: Papers Given at a Conference Held at the University of Leicester, 13–15 December 1963*, Leicester: Leicester University Press, 31–45.

Webster, J., 2005, 'Archaeology of Slavery and Servitude', *Journal of Roman Archaeology* 18, 161–79.

Weekes, J., 2016, 'Cemeteries and Funerary Practice', in M. Millett, L. Revell, and A. Moore (eds), *The Oxford Handbook of Roman Britain*, Oxford: Oxford University Press, 425–47.

Weever, 1631, *Ancient Funerall Monuments*, London: Thomas Harper.

Welch, K., 2007, *The Roman Amphitheatre from its Origins to the Colosseum*, Cambridge: Cambridge University Press.

West, B., 1996, 'Ritual or fluvial? A Further Comment on the Thames Skulls', *Antiquity* 70, 190–91.

West, B. and Milne, G., 1993, 'Owls in the Basilica', *London Archaeologist* 7.2, 31–5.

Westman, A., 2009, 'Infrastructure: Roads and Layout of the Settlement', in C. Cowan, F. Seeley, A. Wardle, A. Westman, and L Wheeler, *Roman Southwark Settlement and Economy: Excavations in Southwark 1973–91*, MoLA Monograph 42, London: Museum of London Archaeology, 52–66.

Wheeler, L., 2009, 'Infrastructure: Waterfronts, Land Reclamation, Drainage and Water Supply', in C. Cowan, F. Seeley, A. Wardle, A. Westman, and L Wheeler, *Roman Southwark Settlement and Economy: Excavations in Southwark 1973–91*, MoLA Monograph 42, London: Museum of London Archaeology, 66–77.

Wheeler, R.E.M., 1930, *London in Roman Times*, London Museum Catalogue 3, London: London Museum.

Wheeler, R.E.M., 1935, *London and the Saxons*, London Museum Catalogue 6, London: London Museum.

Whipp, D., 1980, 'Excavations at Tower Hill 1978', *Transactions of the London and Middlesex Archaeological Society* 31, 47–67.

White, R.H., 2007, *Britannia Prima*, Stroud: Tempus.

White, R.H. and Barker, P., 1998, *Wroxeter: Life and Death of a Roman City*. Stroud: Tempus.

Whittaker, C.R., 1994, *Frontiers of the Roman Empire. A Social and Economic Study*, Baltimore: Johns Hopkins University Press.

Whittaker, C.R., 1995, 'Do Theories of the Ancient City Matter?', in T.J. Cornell and K. Lomas (eds), *Urban Society in Roman Italy*, London: UCL Press, 9–26.

Whittaker, C.R., 1997, 'Imperialism and Culture: The Roman Initiative', in D.J. Mattingly and S.E. Alcock (eds), *Dialogues in Roman Imperialism: Power, Discourse, and Discrepant Experience in the Roman Empire*, JRA Supplementary Series 23, Portsmouth RI: Journal of Roman Archaeology, 143–63.

Whittaker, C.R., 2002, 'Supplying the Army: Evidence from Vindolanda', in P. Erdkamp (ed.), *The Roman Army and the Economy*, Amsterdam: J.C. Gieben, 204–34.

Whittaker, C.R., 2004, *Rome and Its Frontiers: The Dynamics of Empire*, London: Routledge.

Whytehead, R., 1986, 'The Excavation of an Area within a Roman Cemetery at West Tenter Street, London E1', *Transactions of the London and Middlesex Archaeological Society* 37, 23–124.

Wierschowski, L., 1982, 'Soldaten und Veteranen der Prinzipatszeit im Handel und Transportgewerbe', *Münstersche Beiträge zur Antiken Handelgeschichte* 1.2, 31–48.

Wijnendaele, J.W.P., 2020, 'Ammianus, Magnus Maximus and the Gothic Uprising', *Britannia* 51, 330–335.

Wild, J.P., 2002, 'The Textile Industries of Roman Britain', *Britannia* 33, 1–42.

Wilkes, J., 1996, 'The Status of Londinium', in J. Bird, M. Hassall, and H. Sheldon (eds), *Interpreting Roman London. Papers in Memory of Hugh Chapman*, Oxbow Monograph 58, Oxford: Oxbow Books, 27–32.

Wilkinson, K.N., 1998, 'An Investigation into the Geoarchaeology of Foreshore Deposits at Bull Wharf', unpublished King Alfred's College report.

Williams, T.D., 1984, 'Excavations at 25–26 Lime Street', *London Archaeologist* 4.16, 426–29.

Williams, T.D., 1985, 'Redevelopment in the City: What is New?' *Popular Archaeology* 6.14, 31–6.

Williams, T.D., 1991, 'Allectus's Building Campaign in London: Implications for the Development of the Saxon Shore', in V.A. Maxfield and M.J. Dobson (eds), *Roman Frontier Studies 1989: Proceedings of the XVth International Congress of Roman Frontier Studies*, Exeter: University of Exeter Press, 132–41.

Williams, T.D., 1993, *Public Buildings in the South West Quarter of Roman London*, The Archaeology of Roman London 3, CBA Research Report 88, London: Council for British Archaeology.

Willis, S., 2005, 'Samian Pottery, a Resource for the Study of Roman Britain and Beyond: The Results of the English Heritage Funded Samian Project. An e-Monograph', *Internet Archaeology* 17, DOI: 10.11141/ia.17.1.

Wilmott, T.D., 1982, 'Excavations at Queen Street, City of London, 1953 and 1960, and Roman Timber-lined Wells in London', *Transactions of the London and Middlesex Archaeological Society* 33, 1–78.

Wilmott, T.D., 1991, *Excavations in the Middle Walbrook Valley, City of London, 1927–1960*, LAMAS Special Papers 13, London: London and Middlesex Archaeological Society.

Wilmott, T.D., 2008, *The Roman Amphitheatre in Britain*, Stroud: Tempus.

Wilson, A.I., 2008, 'Economy and Trade', in E. Bispham (ed.), *Roman Europe: the Short Oxford History of Europe*, Oxford: Oxford University Press, 170–202.

Wilson, A.I., 2009a, 'Hydraulic Engineering and Water Supply', in J.P. Oleson (ed.), *The Oxford Handbook of Engineering and Technology in the Classical World*, Oxford: Oxford University Press, 285–317.

Wilson, A.I., 2009b, 'Machines in Greek and Roman Technology', in J.P. Oleson (ed.), *The Oxford Handbook of Engineering and Technology in the Classical World*, Oxford: Oxford University Press, 337–68.

Wilson, A.I., 2012, 'A Forum on Trade', in W. Scheidel (ed.), *The Cambridge Companion to the Roman Economy*, Cambridge: Cambridge University Press, 287–318.

Wilson, A., Schörle, K., and Rice, C., 2012, 'Roman Ports and Mediterranean Connectivity', in S. Keay (ed.), *Rome, Portus and the Mediterranean*, Archaeological Monographs of the British School at Rome 21, London: British School at Rome, 367–92.

Wilson, D.M., 2002, *The British Museum: A History*, London: British Museum Press.

Wilson, R.J.A., 2006, 'Urban Defences and Civic Status in Early Roman Britain', in R.J.A. Wilson (ed.), *Romanitas: Essays on Roman Archaeology in Honour of Sheppard Frere on the Occasion of his Ninetieth Birthday*, Oxford: Oxbow Books, 1–47.

Woodward, J., 1713, *An Account of some Roman Urns and Other Antiquitues Lately Digg'd Up Near Bishops-Gate, London*, London: printed for E. Curll.

Woodward, P. and Woodword, A., 2004, 'Dedicating the Town: Urban Foundation Deposits in Roman Britain', *World Archaeology* 36.1, 68–86.

Woolf, G., 2004, 'The Present State and Future Scope of Roman Archaeology: A Comment', *American Journal of Archaeology* 108, 417–28.

Woolf, G., 2012, *Rome: An Empire's Story*, Oxford and New York: Oxford University Press.

Wroe-Brown, R., 2014, *Roman Occupation South-east of the Forum: Excavations at 20 Fenchurch Street, City of London, 2008–9*, MOLAS Monograph 23, London: Museum of London Archaeology.

Wroe-Brown, R., 2016, 'A Possible Early Roman Settlement Boundary and the Medieval City Ditch: Excavations at St Bartholomew's Hospital, London EC3', *Transactions of the London and Middlesex Archaeological Society* 67, 37–98.

Yule, B., 1982, 'A Third Century Well Group and the Later Roman Settlement in Southwark', *London Archaeologist* 4.9, 243–49.

Yule, B., 1988, ''88 Borough High Street', in P. Hinton (ed.), *Excavations in Southwark 1973–6, Lambeth 1973–9*, LAMAS and SAS Joint Publication 3, London: London and Middlesex Archaeological Society and Surrey Archaeological Society, 71–81.

Yule, B., 1990, 'The "Dark Earth" and Late Roman London', *Antiquity* 64, 620–28.

Yule, B., 2005, *A Prestigious Roman Building Complex on the Southwark Waterfront: Excavations at Winchester Palace, London, 1983–90*, MoLAS Archaeology Studies 23, London: Museum of London Archaeology.

Yule, B. and Rankov, B., 1998, 'Legionary Soldiers in 3rd-c. Southwark', in B. Watson (ed.), *Roman London: Recent Archaeological Research*, JRA Supplementary Series 24, Portsmouth RI: Journal of Roman Archaeology, 67–77.

Zelener, Y., 2012, 'Genetic Evidence, Density Dependence and Epidemiological Models of the "Antonine Plague"', in E. Lo Cascio (ed.), *L'Impato della 'Peste Antonina'*, Bari: Edipuglia, 167–77.

Zohary, D. and Hopf, M., 2000, *Domestication of Plants in the Old World. The Origin and Spread of Cultivated Plants in West Asia, Europe, and the Nile Valley* (3rd ed.), Oxford: Clarendon Press.

Zoll, A., 2016, 'Names of Gods', in M. Millett, L. Revell, and A. Moore (eds), *The Oxford Handbook of Roman Britain*, Oxford: Oxford University Press, 619–40.

Zuiderhoek, A., 2009, *The Politics of Munificence in the Roman Empire: Citizens, Elites and Benefactors in Asia Minor*, Cambridge: Cambridge University Press.

Zuiderhoek, A., 2015, 'Introduction', in P. Erdkamp, K. Verboven, and A. Zuiderhoek (eds), *Ownership and Exploitation of Land and Natural Resources in the Roman World*, Oxford: Oxford University Press, 1–17.

Zuiderhoek, A., 2016, *The Ancient City*, Cambridge: Cambridge University Press.

Index of Sites

General Index

militaris 193, 328, 374
    provisioning Britain 9, 151, 166, 189–90,
        193–201, 207, 228, 289, 293, 321, 333,
        345, 361, 376, 400, 403
Antiola (daughter of Domitius) 231
antiquarian study 11
antiquities dealers 44
Antonine Itinerary 171–2, 448
Antoninus Pius (emperor) 159, 247, 261, 289
apiculture 215
Aquilinus (imperial freedman) 303
Archaeology South-East v
archaeomagnetic dating 237, 394, 464
arches, ceremonial 44, 85, 273–4, 302–4, 474
    Richborough 140
army, Roman
    archers 362
    auxiliaries 43, 82, 87, 92, 104, 113, 222, 256,
        270, 292, 314, 321
        cavalry 69, 88, 180, 241–2, 248, 254, 255
        Celts 59
        centurions 142
        Lingones 97
        Nervians 97
        Sarmatians 293
        singulares 220–2, 242
        Thracians 99
        Tungrians 220
        Vangiones 97
    beneficiarii 220, 261
    centurions 92, 94, 142, 242, 322
    comitatenses 367
    deserters 253
    emperor's bodyguard 222
    legions 62, 220, 260–2
        Legio II Augusta 220, 312, 319, 322
        Legio VI 322
        Legio XX 69, 334, 459
        pay 74, 185
    Praetorian Guard 62, 159
    speculators 220, 254, 311
    veterans 41, 57, 69, 88, 91, 124, 150, 187, 194,
        200, 319, 321, 324
army engineering 6, 8, 50, 54, 65, 69–70, 92, 99,
        101, 112, 120, 130, 139, 184, 194, 201,
        246, 312, 401
army supply 7, 69, 70, 76, 82, 88, 92, 99, 113,
        182, 183, 190, 192, 195–6, 200–1, 220,
        264, 288, 293, 328, 333, 399
    see also annona
artillery platforms 364
Asclepiodotus, Julius (praetorian prefect) 352
Atia 315
Atigniomarus 132

Atrebates 37–8, 44
Audax (temple patron) 303
Augulus (bishop) 372
Augusta 366, 372, 386
Augustus (emperor) 71, 155
Aulus Plautius (governor) 49, 54, 57, 58, 59, 61
Aurelian (emperor) 341–2, 344, 352
Aurelius Saturninus 231
Aylesford-Swarling culture 35, 36, 39

Bacchic iconography 214, 257, 259, 270, 319,
        360, 370, 383, 385
    see also canthari, peacocks
Bacon, Francis 11
Baker, John 32
bakeries 118, 125, 127
    Birchin Lane 125
    Borough High Street 80, 147, 155, 332
    Fenchurch Street 125
    Poultry 125
balsamarium 320
baptism 319, 371
barbarian invasions 332, 334, 343, 392
    barbarian conspiracy, the 343, 366, 375
Barker, Philip 23
barrels 196, 203, 215, 264, 301, 328
Basilius (cutler) 214
Bassus/Bassianus (vilicus) 185
Batavian revolt 97, 130
baths 77, 145, 182, 216, 265, 371, 386
    Beauport Park, Sussex 185, 329
    Caerleon (legionary) 79
    Carthage 383
    Exeter (legionary) 79
    Folly Lane (Verulamium) 77
    Pompeii 155
    Silchester 79, 141
    Vindolanda 206
baths, London 8, 73, 77, 113, 132, 139, 155, 166
    15–23 Southwark Street 121, 263
    Arthur Street 77
    Billingsgate 316, 391, 396
    Borough High Street 147, 154, 286, 381, 462
    caldaria (hot rooms) 77, 102, 141, 152, 260
    Cannon Street ('governor's palace') 118,
        140, 306
    changing rooms 138
    Cheapside 102, 152, 154
    Crosby Square 257
    frigidaria (cold rooms) 102, 316, 396
    Huggin Hill 19, 118, 141–2, 152, 159, 164,
        235, 299
    London Bridge Street 155
    near Plantation Place 77, 79, 138

Neal, David 315
Neolithic 32
Neoplatonism 320, 370
Nero (emperor) 57, 74, 112, 113
Nerva (emperor) 150, 201
Nesbitt, Dan v
New Institutional Economics 191
Norman, Philip 15
Notitia Dignitatum 367, 397
nymphaea 306

olive oil 192, 193, 195–6, 198, 216, 228, 312, 328,
    329, 400
Olussa, A. Alfidius 223
oppida 37, 39, 44
Optatus (businessman) 203
opus sectile 77, 143
opus signinum 83, 142, 144, 260, 266, 286,
    320, 332
oracle of Claros 291
Ostorius Scapula, P. (governor) 57, 68, 70,
    74, 90, 105
ostraka 192
Oswald, Adrian 16, 266
ovens 40, 80, 125, 147, 267, 281

paideia 259, 359
painted wall plaster 77, 282, 306, 315, 318,
    319, 354
palaces
    of Allectus (imperial) 350, 352
    of governor 93, 136, 137, 138
    of procurator 79, 92, 145
    tetrarchic 352
Palaeolithic 32
palisades 68, 138
    with hastate pales 55, 120
panegyrists 352–3
Parisi 71
Parthians 290
path dependency 201, 402
patronage 349
    civic 28–9, 132, 140, 152, 191, 333, 399
    imperial 30, 94, 130, 133, 135, 140, 150, 198,
        229, 245, 289, 306, 312, 372
    mercantile 208, 269
    military 193, 198
    of government officials 6, 28, 49, 91, 97, 139,
        200, 226, 305, 400
peacocks 108, 469
Pearce, John 347
peoples of London 219
    Africans 255, 348–9, 350
    Asians 323

Britons 82, 109, 226, 229, 397
    Chinese 348
    Europeans 323, 360
    Gauls 97, 107, 223, 227
    Germans 97, 227, 349
    Greeks 223
    highlanders 253
    immigrants 6, 7, 10, 31, 87, 208, 219, 223,
        225–6, 230, 232, 289, 312, 322, 349, 400
    Italians 223
    Mediterraneans 253, 348
    Roman citizens 94
Perna, Simona 105
Pertinax, Publius Helvius (emperor) 294, 297
Petillius Cerialis (governor) 118, 130
Petronius Turpilianus (governor) 89
pewter 214, 291–2, 371, 385
Philip 'the Arab' (emperor) 322
Philp, Brian 17
phytoliths 281
pine resin 302
piracy 334, 342, 350
Pitt-Rivers, Augustus (Lane Fox) 14
Pitts, Martin v, 87, 196, 198
place-name evidence 43, 396
plagues 10, 292, 332, 334, 402
    Black Death, the 293
    of Cyprian 9, 333, 334
    of Galen 9, 290–4, 325, 333, 401
Plancus (governor of Gaul) 71
Planning Policy Guidance note 16 20
plant remains
    almonds 80, 271
    anise 210
    apple/pear 228
    bay leaves 360
    bitter vetch 76
    black pepper 196
    cabbages 228
    caraway 210
    carrots 228
    cherries 228
    crop-processing waste 76, 127, 280
    cucumbers 196, 228
    dates 271
    figs 196, 228, 271
    fruit 196, 231, 329
    grain 76, 80, 147
        barley 125
        spelt wheat 76, 124–5, 127, 239
    grapes 80, 196, 228
    hazelnuts 228
    herbs 196
    lentils 157